"This book provides the reader with an extensive and analytic overview of the complex issue of human rights in tourism. It does so through the authors' unique combination of expert knowledge in tourism, political science and law, bringing together theoretical and empirical perspectives in a clear and rewarding way. The book should be mandatory reading for researchers and students interested in understanding the notion of sustainability in tourism and its many connections to human rights issues."

Dr. Kristina Nilsson Lindström, *University of Gothenburg, Sweden*

"This is a very timely and welcome volume, written by experts in the field. Not only does the book deliver authoritative chapters on the concepts and contemporary thinking on tourism and human rights but then goes on to provide a range of cutting-edge, sometimes challenging and unsettling, examples and cases. The book fills a much-needed gap in the tourism literature and will become a classic in the field."

Professor Chris Cooper, *Leeds Beckett University, UK*

"The important relationship between human rights and tourism is an under researched field in tourism studies. Most tourists and tourism scholars do not let human rights get in the way of their international travel. The book provides a welcome addition to this neglected field and will hopefully serve to promote this important area of study to academics, students and policy makers alike."

Professor C. Michael Hall, *University of Canterbury, New Zealand*

HUMAN RIGHTS ISSUES IN TOURISM

This book uniquely focuses on human rights issues associated with tourism development and tourism businesses. Tourism is a manifestation of globalization and it intersects with human rights on so many levels. These implications are increasingly relevant in light of the COVID-19 pandemic and subsequent global economic hardship.

Split into two main sections, the first section establishes a background to human rights issues with reference to tourism, and the second section provides a multi-disciplinary analysis of a range of selected human rights issues in tourism; these include displacement, security, privacy, discrimination, freedom of movement, the rights of Indigenous people, sex tourism and labour conditions. All chapters include case studies to showcase specific issues such as legal rulings or tourism policies/regulations. This book is written by a highly regarded team of authors specializing in tourism studies and human rights law.

This significant volume on the interaction between tourism development and the safeguarding of human rights will be of interest to a variety of disciplines, in the fields of tourism, political science and tourism/human rights.

Atsuko Hashimoto is Associate Professor in the Department of Geography and Tourism Studies at Brock University, Canada. Her research focuses on socio-cultural, cross-cultural and human aspects of tourism, human rights and equity issues in tourism development, and issues in sustainable tourism development in rural areas. She holds a BA in Psychology from the University of British Columbia, Canada, and an MSc and PhD in Tourism Development and Management from the University of Surrey, UK. She has also worked for Tourism Canada (now Destination Canada) at the Canadian Embassy in Tokyo, Japan. She taught at the University of Luton (now University of Bedfordshire, UK) in the Department of Tourism and Leisure Studies before immigrating to Canada to take up a position at Brock University.

Elif Härkönen, PhD, is an Associate Professor at the Department of Business Law at Linkoping University in Sweden. She has a background in international and comparative law with an LL.M. in International and Comparative Law from Tulane University in the United States, as well as a doctorate degree in private law from Gothenburg University, Sweden. She is licensed to practice law in Sweden and the state of New York. She also holds a National Committee on Accreditation Certificate of Qualification in Canadian Law. Dr. Härkönen has published articles in tourism and legal journals in subjects ranging from child sex tourism to human rights, supply chain management and corporate social responsibility/corporate criminal liability. She has been responsible for a course in Tourism and Hospitality Law at the post-graduate level and was a member of the advisory board of the MSc of Tourism and Hospitality Management Program at Gothenburg University. She contributed as a Global Study Partner to the 2016 ECPAT Global Study on Sexual Exploitation of Children in Travel and Tourism.

Edward Nkyi is a Director at The Salvation Army Northumberland (Cobourg and Port Hope) Community and Family Services in Ontario, Canada. Edward has research interests in tourism, human rights, human security, international development and political economy. He holds an MA in Political Science from Brock University, Canada, and a Master of Laws Degree in Human Rights and Criminology from the University of Hull, UK. In addition, he has a BA in Political Science from the University of Ghana.

Tourism, Environment and Development Series

Edited by **Richard Sharpley**, *School of Sport, Tourism & The Outdoors, University of Central Lancashire, UK*

Editorial Board: **Chris Cooper**, *Leeds Beckett University, UK*; **Andrew Holden**, *University of Bedfordshire, UK*; **Bob McKercher**, *Hong Kong Polytechnic University*; **Chris Ryan**, *University of Waikato, New Zealand*; **David Telfer**, *Brock University, Canada*

Tourism, Development and the Environment: Beyond Sustainability?
Richard Sharpley

Tourism and Poverty Reduction: Pathways to Prosperity
Jonathan Mitchell and Caroline Ashley

Slow Travel and Tourism
Janet Dickinson and Les Lumsdon

Sustainable Tourism in Island Destinations
Sonya Graci and Rachel Dodds

Climate Change and Tourism
Susanne Becken and John Hay

Justice and Ethics in Tourism
Tazim Jamal

Human Rights Issues in Tourism
Atsuko Hashimoto, Elif Härkönen and Edwawrd Nkyi

For more information about this series, please visit: www.routledge.com/Tourism-Environment-and-Development/book-series/ECTED

HUMAN RIGHTS ISSUES IN TOURISM

Atsuko Hashimoto, Elif Härkönen and Edward Nkyi

First published 2021
by Routledge
2 Park Square, Milton Park, Abingdon, Oxon OX14 4RN

and by Routledge
52 Vanderbilt Avenue, New York, NY 10017

Routledge is an imprint of the Taylor & Francis Group, an informa business

© 2021 Atsuko Hashimoto, Elif Härkönen and Edward Nkyi

The right of Atsuko Hashimoto, Elif Härkönen and Edward Nkyi to be identified as authors of this work has been asserted by them in accordance with sections 77 and 78 of the Copyright, Designs and Patents Act 1988.

All rights reserved. No part of this book may be reprinted or reproduced or utilised in any form or by any electronic, mechanical, or other means, now known or hereafter invented, including photocopying and recording, or in any information storage or retrieval system, without permission in writing from the publishers.

Trademark notice: Product or corporate names may be trademarks or registered trademarks, and are used only for identification and explanation without intent to infringe.

British Library Cataloguing-in-Publication Data
A catalogue record for this book is available from the British Library

Library of Congress Cataloging-in-Publication Data
A catalog record has been requested for this book

ISBN: 978-1-138-49103-8 (hbk)
ISBN: 978-1-138-49106-9 (pbk)
ISBN: 978-1-351-03386-2 (ebk)

Typeset in Bembo
by Newgen Publishing UK

To Kyoko and Sakura. And to people who are trying to make the world a better place to live with dignity – A.H.

To Davod and Alyssa. For being the light of my life – E.H.

To my late father, Mr. John Kwaku Agyim, I hope this would be a lasting memory for all the love, care and support he provided to me throughout my educational life – E.N.

CONTENTS

List of boxes *xiii*
Preface *xv*
Acknowledgements *xx*
List of acronyms *xxi*

SECTION 1
Background of human rights in tourism   1

1 Introduction to human rights and civil rights in tourism and hospitality   3

2 Tourism enterprises and human rights   40

3 Human rights, development, and the Sustainable Development Goals   60

4 Politics, human rights, and tourism   83

SECTION 2
Human rights issues in tourism   107

5 Human security, human rights, and tourism   109

6 Right to privacy and tourism   137

7   Displacement in tourism   159

8   Discrimination of patrons in tourism establishments   185

9   Rights to freedom of movement and tourism   208

10 Human rights and labour conditions in tourism establishments   236

11 Human rights, the environment, and tourism   265

12 Indigenous people's rights and tourism   296

13 Sex tourism   326

SECTION 3
Conclusion   **349**

14 Human rights in tourism: concluding remarks   351

Appendices   **365**

A Universal Declaration of Human Rights (1948)   367
International Covenant on Civil and Political Rights   374
International Covenant on Economic, Social and Cultural Rights   393

Index   *404*

BOXES

1.1	Core International Human Rights Instruments	11
1.2	Hierarchy of International Human Rights Law	22
1.3	Human Rights Bodies	29
2.1	Protect, Respect and Remedy Framework	45
2.2	The Ten Principles of the United Nations Global Compact	46
3.1	Women's Rights, Development and Tourism	63
3.2	Poverty Reduction, Pro-poor Tourism, and a Human Rights Approach	73
4.1	Political Instability, Human Rights and Tourism in Somalia and Ethiopia	93
4.2	Tourism Boycotts: Human Rights and Politics	95
5.1	Intersection of Human Security, Human Rights and Tourism	114
7.1	Hosting Mega Events and Displacement of Local People – Brazil	162
7.2	The Padaung Long Neck Women – Thailand/Myanmar	174
8.1	Case Study: South Africa	188
9.1	The Convention on the Rights of Persons with Disabilities 2006 – Articles 9 and 18	217
10.1	Agenda 2030 Sustainable Development Goals	237
10.2	Fundamental ILO Conventions	239
10.3	Case Study: The Myanmar Tourism Business	242
10.4	Examples of Reasonable Accommodations	252
11.1	European Convention Article 8: Two Contrasting Cases	271
11.2	Polluter's Responsibility: The Case of India	283
12.1	The Jarawa People of Andaman Island – India	306
12.2	Indigenous Tourism Development in Northern Canada and Alaska	312

13.1 Global Code of Ethics for Tourism, art 2(3)/Framework
     Convention on Tourism Ethics, art. 5(3) 330
13.2 Optional Protocol to the Convention on the Rights of the
     Child on the Sale of Children, Child Prostitution and Child
     Pornography 334
13.3 Council of Europe Convention on the Protection of Children
     Against Sexual Exploitation and Sexual Abuse 341
13.4 The Code of Conduct for the Protection of Children From
     Sexual Exploitation in Travel and Tourism 342

PREFACE

At the end of the 20th century and into the first two decades of the 21st century, the world has witnessed so many disquieting, and at times, violent events. Intra- and interstate conflicts, terrorism activities, religious conflicts, both natural and man-made environmental disasters, rising numbers of asylum seekers, religious and ethnic persecutions, an increase in discrimination, and the COVID-19 global pandemic have all had serious implications for human rights. With globalisation and round-the-clock media and social media presence, the distribution of information has brought these incidents to the world's attention at far greater speeds than ever before. As will be explored in this book, tourism is a manifestation of globalisation and it intersects with human rights on many levels. An activity in which people engage in for leisure, also reveals the realities of human rights violations within the industry for many others. Non-Governmental Organizations and Non-Profit Organizations have been tirelessly investigating, reporting and campaigning against human rights violations around the world. Towards the end of 2019 and into 2020 has been a particularly tumultuous time. Amid the COVID-19 pandemic and the resulting global economic downturn and rapid decline in travel, natural disasters and climate change continued to impact many countries. Both climate change and COVID-19 have been referred to as threat multipliers making the most vulnerable even at more risk. Anti-racism demonstrations and the Black Lives Matter movement which began in the USA quickly spread within the country and around the world reflecting the anger at continued racial discrimination. Elsewhere pro-democracy demonstrations in Hong Kong were suppressed after changes were made to Hong Kong security laws. While people are more and more aware about these incidents and about human rights violations, how much do we know about the protection of human rights?

There is a need for a book that provides an introductory understanding of human rights issues, and a broad picture of the relationship between tourism and human rights. While this book often discusses laws and regulations, it was not written primarily for students of the Law. Rather this book was written for interested citizens, practitioners, and students and academics in various disciplines, with a focus on people in the fields of tourism, political science, social justice and tourism and human rights. The aim of this introductory book is to contribute to both academic and non-academic discussions in the field of tourism, with a focus on the interaction between tourism development and the safeguarding of human rights. For this reason, court cases are often used as examples to make a point or to illustrate the concepts examined in the text. While this book attempts to focus on human rights issues from several angles, the subject covers such a broad range of topics that one book alone cannot cover every issue. Multiple volumes would be required to encompass all avenues of inquiry about human rights equally. The topics in the book are also very subjectively categorised – the human rights issues the authors of this book have selected could be approached from completely different perspectives and other authors may give higher importance to certain topics than what is presented here. The three authors come from very different backgrounds and academic disciplines. Each chapter has a leading author whose strengths are reflected in the chapter structure and the emphases placed on the content. Consequently, the author's approaches to human rights issues and tourism also vary considerably. We hope the variety of approaches taken adds to the discussion on human rights and tourism and will lead to further debate. The authors are keenly aware that this book does not include independent chapters on children's and women's rights, nor on the right to freedom of speech, economic rights, rights to specific natural resources (e.g. water) and so on, albeit the authors have endeavoured to include these issues within the chapters of this book. This book addresses human rights and civil rights issues and concerns in general, and in relation to the tourism industry, with legal responses wherever possible. It is the authors' hope that this book will raise questions and provide readers with opportunities for further discussion on these topics.

This book is divided into three main sections. The first section establishes the background to human rights issues, with particular reference to tourism. Chapter 1 contains an introduction to Human Rights and Civil Rights as the two concepts are often used interchangeably. The chapter highlights some of the historical changes in these concepts and sets the foundation for exploring these rights in the context of tourism throughout the book. Chapter 2 then discusses the development of human rights principles applicable to tourism corporations. This includes an examination of various international, transnational and national instruments by focusing on the responsibility of tourism enterprises and human rights. The chapter raises the question – if there is a moral or legal responsibility for tourism enterprises to improve conditions where they operate. Jurisdictional issues are raised as many tourism enterprises have operations in multiple countries. Chapter 3 examines issues of human rights explored in the context of more global movements such as the United Nations Sustainable Development Goals. The evolution of development paradigms over the years is examined with sustainable development presented as a framework to achieve human rights standards. A consequential shift in tourism development to a rights-based development paradigm is evident, yet implementation has not been realised. Chapter 4 focuses broadly on politics as it intersects with human rights, and the operations of the tourism industry by focusing on issues of power and control. It examines the political environment, laws and principles of good governance, national human rights records along with the political economy of tourism. Political instability is often a detriment for human rights which have led to tourism boycotts. These four introductory chapters lay the foundation for the human rights topics in Section 2.

In Section 2, selected human rights issues in tourism are examined. Chapter 5 examines current human security issues (real and perceived threats) facing tourists, host communities and other stakeholders in the tourism industry. As human security is a relatively recent concept, the evolution of human security is examined in comparison to the concept of human rights. Human security issues that affect tourism, i.e. personal safety, health and human needs are then explored. Like the right to human security, the right to privacy is a fundamental human right which is explored in Chapter 6. The applicability of the right to privacy in the tourism sector raises the question of the proper balance between individual rights and national security. The chapter explores the right to privacy in international and domestic laws as individual countries often have different privacy laws. The advancement of technology has allowed for the collection of personal data, e.g., in accommodation establishments, screening at airports and how this data is stored and used has significant privacy implications. Possible remedies in tort and criminal law when an invasion of privacy has been committed are also examined. Chapter 7 reviews various displacement issues in tourism from three different approaches: physical and geographical displacement, economic displacement, and cultural displacement. Displacement issues in tourism involve the deprivation of rights to life and rights to natural resources. However, even if people are not physically displaced, discrimination can also threaten the right to life. Prohibition of discrimination is one of the most widely embraced and universally accepted parts of the Human Rights agenda. Chapter 8 explores the right to live a life free from discrimination and discusses discrimination of patrons in tourism establishments. It explores themes of discrimination based on race, nationality or ethnic origin, sex/gender, sexual orientation and gender identity, religious orientation and disability. Discrimination also applies to the issue of freedom of movement of people, which is explored in Chapter 9. The right to the freedom of mobility is considered a fundamental human right and needed in the context of tourism to travel – often discussed in relation to social justice. Tourism is a global activity – and while globalisation influences the mobility of people – the political and economic motivations of corporations operating in a neoliberal context can lead to human rights abuses. Businesses, for example, can benefit from the mobile pool of cheaper labour of migrant workers. To further elaborate on business and human rights issues, Chapter 10 investigates human rights and labour conditions in tourism establishments, especially in conditions that have been equated with sweatshop work and modern slavery. The Chapter examines labour standards, and the freedom of association and collective bargaining in tourism. It also explores the themes of child labour, right to decent work, discrimination of employees and the rights of migrant workers. In Chapter 11, the recognition that a healthy and sustainable environment enables people to enjoy many human rights, and the world's inability to secure "human rights to environment" is addressed – including tourism's contribution to climate change. Chapter 12 examines the United Nation's Declaration of Rights of Indigenous People, and discusses Indigenous Peoples' rights in the context of tourism. The chapter traces the evolution of conflict between Indigenous Peoples and non-Indigenous Peoples along with decolonisation. Both the challenges and opportunities for Indigenous tourism are explored. The final chapter in Section 2 (Chapter 13) focuses on the subject of sex tourism. The overall objective of the chapter is to explore existing legal and soft law instruments, while addressing sex tourism, with a special focus on corporate responsibility. The topics of exploitation of children, human trafficking, modern slavery and forced exploitation of adults in the tourism industry are explored. The socio-cultural, economic and political contexts are also considered as to why the existing legal frameworks do not eradicate sexual exploitation or sex tourism. Possible corporate measures against commercial sexual exploitation in tourism are presented. The book concludes with Chapter 14 (Section 3), highlighting key relationships between tourism and human rights. After reviewing the contribution of each chapter, discussion questions are presented as a way to stimulate further research and debate on the future discourse of human rights issues in tourism. Finally, the evolving situation of the COVID-19 pandemic on tourism and human rights will be addressed.

A holistic approach to human rights issues will be used, in order that each chapter can be read on its own or as part of the larger collection. It is important to note that many human rights issues are intertwined and overlap, and therefore issues may recur in various chapters. However, the issues are discussed from different perspectives and in different contexts, helping to provide further understanding and also illustrating the complexity of human rights issues.

Each chapter raises questions by providing unsettling facts and information, as well as positive examples on what supranational, international and state organisations and tourism enterprises are doing to address issues of human rights and to rectify them. By exploring some unpleasant facts, the authors hope to raise questions for the readers as to why situations are the way they are, and why they cannot be changed for the better. Many of these questions may be referred back to the first four chapters (Section 1) that establish the background on human rights in regard to laws, businesses development paradigms and politics. The authors wish to invoke a conversation about human rights, the responsibilities and provisions of human rights standards; and a further discourse on how these human rights challenges may be improved for the success of tourism and hospitality as a business and as a social phenomenon.

Towards the completion of this book, in May 2020 the COVID-19 pandemic was in its initial stages. The World Health Organization (WHO) indicated it had already spread to 213 countries, areas or territories, and worldwide, over 6.1 million cases and over 376,000 deaths had been confirmed by early June. Tourism had come to halt as travel restrictions spread. Airlines significantly cut flights, cruise ships were docked and tourism businesses were shuttered as borders closed. By the end of June 2020, the number of cases had risen above 9.2 million and over 479,000 deaths had occurred according to the WHO. Some locations were gradually easing restrictions while other countries saw an increase in cases and future waves of COVID-19 have been predicted. Spain which was severely impacted early in the pandemic is hoping to attract tourists for the summer while there are rising numbers of cases in places such as the USA and in South America. The magnitude of this unprecedented event is still unknown at this time, and it has not only caused an unimaginable human toll, it has also resulted in substantial economic and social impacts leading to dramatic unemployment and daily life being significantly altered. As the globe struggles to face this pandemic, new concerns are being raised over mobility, security, privacy and human rights.

Atsuko Hashimoto, Elif Härkönen and Edward Nkyi

ACKNOWLEDGEMENTS

We would like to acknowledge Dr. Richard Sharpley (Series Editor) for the opportunity to write this book; and Editors Lydia Kessell, Megan Smith, and Carlotta Fanton and their editorial and production team at Routledge. Without your encouragement, reminders, suggestions and seemingly endless patience, we could not have finished this book. We would also like to acknowledge the anonymous reviewer(s) of the book proposal, whose insightful comments and suggestions helped shaped the final format of the book.

Our book is owed to people working in organisations around the world, who tirelessly produce valuable reports, statistics and information on human rights, human rights violations and court proceedings; and to the legal teams who are fighting for the most vulnerable people facing deportation, prosecution, discrimination and gross human rights abuses that are happening every day. Their efforts inspire us and some of their reports have been cited in this book. Many thanks are due to their dedication and for being "guardians of human rights."

We would like to express our gratitude to our research assistants. Rebekah Kraulis (Brock University) was very helpful in researching necessary materials at the earlier stages of the book production (2018–2019). Thanks to Kyoko Telfer (Huron University College at Western University) at the later stages of production (2019–2020) for keeping all the documents in good shape, and for careful proofreading and editing our multiple drafts and providing insightful comments.

Edward would like to thank his mum, Sophia Asamoah, for her support and encouragement during the writing of this book.

Last but not the least, we would like to thank our partners, David Telfer, Hamid Jalali and Harriet Amoah-Nkyi for their patience and support during the writing of this book. They deserve more than just our gratitude. And our children, you just being our children gave us courage, energy and motivation to complete this book. Thank you for being there when we needed you.

ACRONYMS

ACI	Airports Council International
ADA	Americans with Disabilities Act of 1990 (USA)
AfCHPR	African Convention/Charter on Human and Peoples' Rights
AIDS	Acquired Immunodeficiency Syndrome
AmCHR	American Convention on Human Rights
APIS	Advance Passenger Information Systems
APTA	Asia Pacific Trade Agreement
ASEAN	Association of Southeast Asian Nations
AU	African Union
BBC	British Broadcasting Corporation
BDPA	Beijing Declaration and Platform for Action
CACM	Central American Common Market
CARICOM	Caribbean Community
CAT	Committee Against Torture (UN)
CBC	Canadian Broadcasting Corporation
CE	Council of Europe
CED	Committee on Enforced Disappearances (UN)
CEDAW	Committee on the Elimination of Discrimination Against Women (UN)
CEFTA	ECOWAS and the Central European Free Trade Agreement
CERD	Committee on the Elimination of Racial Discrimination (UN)
CESCR	Committee on Economic, Social and Cultural Rights (UN)
CFR	Code of Federal Regulations (USA)
CIS	Commonwealth of Independent States
CMW	Committee on Migrant Workers (UN)
CNN	Cable News Network (USA)
COMESA	Common Market for Eastern and Southern Africa

COVID-19	CO: corona, VI: virus, and D: disease; '2019 novel coronavirus' disease
CRC	Convention on the Rights of the Child (UN)
CRPD	Convention on the Rights of Persons with Disabilities (UN)
CSR	Corporate Social Responsibility
CSW	Commission on the Status of Women (UN)
CTV	Canadian Television Network
DAW	Division for the Advancement of Women (UN)
DELC	Division of Environmental Law and Conventions (UN)
DESA	Department of Economic and Social Affairs (UN)
DEVAW	Declaration on the Elimination of Violence Against Women
ECHR	European Convention for the Protection of Human Rights and Fundamental Freedoms
ECOWAS	Economic Community of West African States
ECPAT	End Child Prostitution and Trafficking
ECtHR	European Court of Human Rights
ECTWT	Ecumenical Coalition on Third World Tourism
EED	Education and Economic Development
EEOC	United States Equal Employment Opportunity Commission
EFTA	EU/European Free Trade Association
ESTA	Electronic System for Travel Authorization (USA)
ETA	Electronic Travel Authorizations (Australia)
eTA	Electronic Travel Authorizations (Canada)
ETIAS	European Travel Information and Authorisation System (EU)
FAO	Food and Agriculture Organization (UN)
FASB	Financial Accounting Standards Board
GATS	General Agreement on Trade in Services
GCC	Gulf Cooperation Council
GCET	Global Code of Ethics for Tourism
GDP	gross domestic product
GDPR	General Data Protection Regulation (EU)
GNP	gross national product
GRI	Global Reporting Initiative
H1N1	A type of Influenza A; aka Swine Flu
HIV	Human Immunodeficiency Virus
HRC	Human Rights Committee (UN)
IASB	International Accounting Standards Board
IASC	Inter-Agency Standing Committee (UN)
IAS	International Accounting Standards (Regulation)
IATA	International Air Transport Association
ICAO	International Civil Aviation Organization (UN)
ICC	International Criminal Court
ICCPR	International Covenant on Civil and Political Rights (UN)

ICESCR	International Covenant on Economic, Social and Cultural Rights (UN)
ICF	International Classification of Functioning, Disability and Health (UN/WHO)
ICO	Information Commissioner's Office (UK)
ICRPD	Convention on the Rights of Persons with Disabilities (UN)
IDD	Inter-Agency Internal Displacement Division (UN)
ILO	International Labour Organization
IOG	Institute of Governance
IRA	Irish Republican Army
LDC	less developed countries
LEDS	Less Economically Developed Countries
LGTQ+	Lesbian, Gay, Transgender and Queer/Questioning
LGBTQ QIP2SAA	Lesbian, gay, bisexual, transgender, questioning, queer, intersex, pansexual, two-spirit (2S), androgynous and asexual
MENA	Middle East and North Africa region
MEDS	More Economically Developed Countries
MERCOSUR	Southern Common Market (MERCOSUR for its Spanish initials)
MNE	multi-national enterprise
NAACP	National Association for the Advancement of Colored People (USA)
NAFTA	North American Free Trade Agreement
NATO	North Atlantic Treaty Organizations
NGO	non-governmental organization
NLD	National League for Democracy (Myanmar/Burma)
OCHA	Office for the Coordination of Humanitarian Affairs (UN)
OECD	Organisation for Economic Co-operation and Development
OHCHR	Office of the High Commissioner for Human Rights (UN)
OPA	Office of the Privacy Commissioner of Canada
OSAGI	Office of the Special Adviser on Gender Issues and the Advancement of Women (UN)
PAFTA	Pan-Arab Free Trade Area
PCIJ	Permanent Court of International Justice (UN)
PPCG	Convention on the Prevention and Punishment of the Crime of Genocide (UN)
RBC	The National Action Plan on Responsible Business Conduct
RDA	Racial Discrimination Act (Australia)
SACU	Southern African Customs Union
SADC	South African Development Community
SAFTA	South Asian Free Trade Agreement
SARS	Severe Acute Respiratory Syndrome
SDG	Sustainable Development Goals
SEC	Securities and Exchange Commission

TEN	Third World Tourism Ecumenical European Net
TIDE	The Terrorist Identities Datamart Environment (USA)
TPP	Trans-Pacific Partnership
UDHR	Universal Declaration of Human Rights (UN)
UN-HABITAT	United Nations Human Settlements Programme (UN)
UN-Women	United Nations Entity for Gender Equality and the Empowerment of Women (UN)
UNAIDS	Joint United Nations Programme on HIV/AIDS (UN)
UNCED	United Nations Conference on Environment and Development (UN)
UNCRC	United Nations Convention on the Rights of the Child (UN)
UNDP	United Nations Development Programme (UN)
UNDRIP	United Nations Declaration on the Rights of Indigenous Peoples (UN)
UNESCO	United Nations Educational, Scientific and Cultural Organization (UN)
UNFCCC	United Nations Framework Convention on Climate Change (UN)
UNFPA	United Nations Population Fund (UN)
UNGP	Guiding Principles on Business and Human Rights (UN)
UNGPRF	Guiding Principles Reporting Framework (UN)
UNHCR	United Nations High Commissioner for Refugees (UN)
UNHRC	United Nations Human Rights Council (UN)
UNICEF	United Nations Children's Fund (UN)
UNMAS	United Nations Mine Action Service (UN)
UNODC	United Nations Office on Drugs and Crime (UN)
UNSOM	United Nations Assistance Mission in Somalia (UN)
UNUDHR	United Nations Universal Declaration of Human Rights (UN)
UNWTO	World Tourism Organization (UN)
US GAAP	US Generally Accepted Accounting Principles
WFP	World Food Programme (UN)
WHO	World Health Organization
WTO	World Tourism Organization (prior to Dec. 2005)
WTO	World Trade Organization
WTTC	World Travel and Tourism Council

SECTION 1
Background of human rights in tourism

1
INTRODUCTION TO HUMAN RIGHTS AND CIVIL RIGHTS IN TOURISM AND HOSPITALITY

1.1 Introduction: human rights and tourism

Human rights issues have long been the subject of debate, and numerous attempts have been made to protect and record human rights from ancient times. The United Nations (UN) Universal Declaration of Human Rights (UDHR) was adopted in 1948 and since that time, a diversity of other human rights covenants, treaties, and publications have been added, establishing the framework for improving human rights. In addition to forming the basis of law in many countries, human rights have been advocated for by a variety of organisations including governments, businesses, civil society, and non-governmental organisations (NGOs). Despite progress, there continue to be many individuals and groups of people around the world who do not enjoy the benefits of human rights protections. In looking towards twenty-first century challenges in human rights, Brysk (2019) notes that while the "scope conditions" for the effectiveness of human rights have improved, there has not been a commensurate enhancement of human rights. Interstate war has been replaced by protracted internecine conflicts with horrendous war crimes and sexual violence, while the rise of democracy has been "blunted by overlapping combinations of stalled transitions, regressions, illiberal democracies, populism, and rising authoritarianism that undermine civil liberties and treatment of minorities" (Brysk, 2019, p. 7). Collective human rights are also under threat in the context of climate change, and governments have been pressured to implement stronger regulation to protect the environment. While there is a duty for the state to protect human rights, there is also a growing concern over exploitation in the work environment under globalisation (Venkatesan, 2019). Globalisation has facilitated the rapid growth of tourism, and not surprisingly, there have been violations of human rights caused by a variety of organisations and individuals, including states, the tourism industry, and tourists. Vulnerable individuals and communities face issues of displacement, loss of livelihoods, loss of access to natural resources, exploitation, and poor pay as a result of tourism development (Tourism Concern, 2019). Still others face discrimination and barriers to travel. Ruggie (2009) argues that all rights need to be considered within the context of protection, empowerment, accountability, and remedy. In 2011, the UN Office of the High Commissioner of Human Rights (OHCHR) released the "Guiding Principles on Business and Human Rights: Implementing the United Nations 'Protect, Respect and Remedy' Framework". The document affirms that states and businesses have distinct yet complementary responsibilities and focuses on three areas: (1) the state duty to protect against human rights abuses by all actors, (2) corporate responsibility to respect human rights, and (3) access to a remedy when a right is violated. With an evolving framework on human rights, and differing levels of commitment to human rights in destinations around the world, the purpose of this book is to explore a range of human rights issues in tourism.

With tourism and hospitality gaining in popularity since the mid-1950s, there has been increased competition amongst a growing number of destinations. Unfortunately, the growth in tourism has also led to an increasing number of human rights abuses and violations. In 2019 international tourist arrivals (overnight visitors) reached 1.5 billion, with all regions enjoying an increase in arrivals (UNWTO, 2020a). Tourism continues to be viewed as an economic engine for development. While international arrival numbers have in recent years continued to grow, others are prevented from travelling. Overtourism has become a significant challenge in many destinations, resulting in the displacement of local residents, forcing governments to regulate the tourism industry, including those employed in the sharing economy. Greater numbers of tourists have been reaching into ever more remote locations, raising the possibilities of human rights violations and requiring an evaluation of the role of tourism in the development process. The COVID-19 pandemic (the disease was declared a pandemic in March 2020 by the World Health Organization (WHO)) will change tourism and travel patterns for many years to come. It is still too early to predict the lasting impact of the pandemic on tourism development, but the United Nations World Tourism Organization (UNWTO) (2020b) estimated in May 2020 that tourism arrivals could decline by 60–80 percent in 2020. This would lead to a loss of US$910 billion to US$1.2 trillion in export revenues, as well as put 100 to 120 million direct tourism jobs at risk. Poor and marginalised people have suffered disproportionately from the worldwide lockdowns of non-essential businesses and services. According to the World Bank, low- and middle-income countries will suffer the greatest consequences in terms of extreme poverty, with estimates suggesting that COVID-19 will push an additional 71 million people into extreme poverty (Mahler, et al., 2020). Extreme poverty is both a cause and consequence of human rights violations (OHCHR, 2012). It is therefore plausible that human rights violations will become more common in the tourism sector as a result of the pandemic, making the topic of this book even more important when the tourism sector starts to recover in 2021 and beyond.

Since the 1990s, development studies have been focusing on human development and global development. At the heart of the development agenda has been the UN Millennium Development Goals, which were replaced by the 2030 UN Sustainable Development Goals. The year 2016 was the 30th Anniversary of the Declaration on the Right to Development (OHCHR, 2016), while 2017 was declared the International Year of Sustainable Tourism for Development by the UNWTO. In support of this and in association with the UN Sustainable Development Goals, the Berlin Declaration on "Transforming Tourism" was signed in March 2017 by a diverse group of participants from civil society. One of the fundamental concepts of the Declaration is that "[h]uman rights and self-determination of communities must be at the core of every tourism development" (Transforming Tourism, 2017).

Various organisations including international NGOs, such as Amnesty International and Human Rights Watch, raise awareness and generate campaigns for human rights. Amnesty International is present in over 150 countries and characterises itself as a global movement of more than 7 million people who campaign to end human rights violations. The organisation also raises climate change as a human rights issue (Amnesty International, 2019). Human Rights Watch investigates and reports on human rights abuses and publishes an annual review of human rights practices in specific countries around the world. As a reflection of the scope of issues related to human rights, Human Rights Watch also engages in specific work on "children's rights; women's rights; arms and military issues; business and human rights; health and human rights; disability rights; the environment and human rights; international justice; terrorism and counterterrorism; refugees and displaced people; and lesbian, gay, bisexual and transgendered people" (Human Rights Watch, 2019). In addition to the aforementioned NGOs, non-profit organisations such as Tourism Concern, ECPAT, and World Vision have been advocating a human rights approach to tourism. The study of human rights issues in the context of tourism began to appear in academic literature in the form of case study-based journal articles, while some tourism textbooks have started to incorporate sections on human rights: yet, there is no book in Tourism and Hospitality that focuses exclusively on human rights issues associated with tourism development and tourism businesses.

The UNWTO and other tourism-related organisations are aware that there has been a clear shift in the tourism market. While high-income countries, predominantly developed nations, continue to participate in international tourism activities at a slightly slower rate, middle-income countries such as China and India had been increasingly sending larger numbers of international tourists abroad. Prior to COVID-19, in 2019, China had the highest international tourism expenditure in the world. Several other Asian countries/territories, Hong Kong (China), Korea, Singapore, India, and Japan, were included in the top 15 countries (UNWTO, 2020b). Several factors have contributed to the increase in outbound travel in Asian countries. Many South-East Asian countries liberalised their aviation industries in the late 1990s and 2000s, allowing low-cost carriers to operate in their countries, benefiting tourism in the region. China, however, has been conservative in its liberalisation of the aviation industry and low-cost carriers have a low penetration rate in the country (Lai et al., 2019). Chinese outbound travel has instead mainly benefited from the easing of visa-issuing procedures for Chinese citizens, high economic growth, increased disposable income at home, and more liberalised policies towards tourism in the first decade of 2000s (Xie and Tveterås, 2020). As noted in the Travel and Tourism Competitive Index for 2019, the Asia-Pacific region has continued to grow in importance, being the second largest destination for international travellers, receiving the second largest volume of international tourism receipts, and being the biggest source of global outbound spending, with the majority spent on intraregional travel (based on 2017 data) (World Economic Forum, 2019). The dynamics of international tourism will continue to change in the near future as a result of COVID-19, yet it is clear that there has, in recent decades, been a shift from Western dominance in tourism to more Asia-Pacific dominance. Many new tourist destinations will continue to open up as travel restrictions are reduced, and tourists will face challenges in destinations in which human rights are viewed differently and where laws are different. For example, an increasing number of openly Lesbian, Gay, Bisexual, Transgender, Queer/Questioning (LGBTQ+) persons are travelling. However, there are many destinations where laws do not protect the human rights of LGBTQ+ persons. In 2019, being homosexual was a punishable offense in 70 countries (Mendos, 2019). Members of the LGBTQ+ community have faced protests when travelling, and cruise ships focusing on this market have been turned away from ports, highlighting the fact that sender and destination countries of tourists sometimes view human rights differently.

In order for human rights in the UDHR to be effective, these rights must be enshrined and protected at the national level. There are examples throughout this book that demonstrate how human rights can be in conflict with each other and as a result, human rights of individuals or groups of people can be restricted. What is worse, some laws or policies of nation-states, regions, or provinces have been recently revised to restrict the freedom of religion or discriminate against certain groups of people based on sexual orientation. For example, during the decade from 2007 to 2017, the number of countries imposing "high" to "very high" levels of restrictions on religion increased from 40 to 52 governments (Lipka and Majumdar, 2019). Also, anti-homosexual laws existed in 33 African countries in 2019 (Mendos, 2019) and 30 states in the USA introduced 129 anti-LGBTQ+ laws in 2017 (Moreau, 2018). Another example addressed in this book is when existing laws and regulations hinder the protection of human rights. One such case is the right to a healthy environment (see Chapter 11). For example, many transportation laws were made when non-petroleum-based micro-mobility vehicles (e.g. e-automobiles, e-scooters, e-skateboards, Segways, self-balancing unicycles, and e-motorised bicycles) did not exist. Legislation needs to be updated to adapt to new forms of personal vehicles, which can help cut CO_2 emissions, as long as the safety of pedestrians and other vehicles is not compromised. The use of e-vehicles is becoming increasingly more popular among tourists, and strong demands for the right to clean air from locals and tourists are forcing governments to take action.

The updating of laws is not always easy; however, it is necessary. Germany, France, Austria, and Switzerland have already made accommodations for these types of e-vehicles on public roads (Adam, 2018). Other countries are slowly following. Micro-mobility vehicles that were illegal on public roads in 2019 in the UK will likely soon be legal (BBC Click, 2019; Department for Transport, 2020). The updating of laws to more clearly align with human rights can benefit both locals and tourists.

The main purpose of this chapter is to provide readers with an introduction to the key concepts in human rights and civil rights, which along with Chapters 2–4 serve as a foundation for exploring these rights in the context of tourism throughout the book. Section 1.2 in this chapter gives a brief history of human rights, followed by an outline of core international human rights instruments in Section 1.3. This will be followed by Section 1.4, which focuses on modern definitions and concepts of human rights, including a discussion on universalism versus cultural relativism and Section 1.5, where the similarities and differences between human rights, civil rights, and civil liberties are explored. Section 1.6 then focuses on the relationship between international human rights laws and national implementation, along with access to justice and remedies in Section 1.7. Finally, Section 1.8 concludes this chapter by briefly reviewing the interface between tourism and human rights as an underpinning for the other chapters in this book.

1.2 Brief historical account of the evolution of human rights concepts

The idea of "human rights" has existed for quite a long time, albeit not in the same way that various modern judiciary systems and the people of today discuss this issue. As reviewed briefly in this section, the idea of rights as espoused in the modern concept of human rights can be traced back to the ancient world. For instance, in ancient Babylon, circa 1780 BCE, Hammurabi's code recognised the need to protect human freedom and dignity (Clapham, 2007) and the Cyrus Cylinder by Cyrus the Great of Persia incorporated a declaration of the right to religion and racial equality in 539 BCE (Kuhrt, 1983; United for Human Rights, 2019). The UN in 1971 acknowledged the Cyrus Cylinder as the first declaration of concern for rights (Srikanth and Chowdhury, 2018), although there are sceptical views (e.g. Schultz, 2008). Other civilisations, such as the Inca, Aztec, Hindu, and the First Nations of North America, also established systems to protect people's health, welfare, and property rights through a written or oral "code of conduct" (Flowers, 1999).

Many scholars agree that the foundation of contemporary human rights is relatively modern (e.g., Goodhart, 2016; Davidson, 1993). Lamb (2019) citing James Griffin, points out that the notion of human rights of today emerged by the end of the Enlightenment, though has not theoretically developed since then. The emergence of the concept of human rights in medieval Europe has foundations in divine/natural law theory; proponents of this theory were mostly Western medieval theologians. Medieval theologians believed one God created all human beings, and therefore, they are all made equal (Shestack, 2000). Humans are, however, obliged to keep harmony with others in the pursuit of their freedoms. In medieval cosmology, all natural (human) "rights" and "duties" come from the Golden Rule of the Bible, namely "in everything, do to others as you would have them do to you" (Holy Bible, Matthew 7:12).

Since medieval times in Europe, there have been notable attempts to protect individual rights: The *Magna Charta Libertatum* (or simply '*Magna Carta*') in Britain in 1215, limited the powers of the British monarchy, and secured protection for the noble class and other citizens of England (Ishay, 2004; Tremblay, et al., 2008). Similar documents attempting to secure protection for the rights and liberties of citizens at national and regional levels in Europe and America include: legal texts from the Kingdom of Leon, Spain in 1188, (Shelton, 2003); 'the Golden Bull (*Aranybulla*)' of Hungary in 1222, which is often compared to the *Magna Carta* (Péter and Lojkó, 2012); the Danish King Erik Klipping's *Håndfæstning* ("handbinding" document also known as '*King Valdemar's Laws*') of 1282 (Andersen, 2011); the *Joyeuse Entrée* (charter of liberties, also known as '*the Code of Dutch Freedom*') of 1356 in Brabant (Duke, 2017); the *Grand Privilège* of 1477 by Mary of Burgundy, which guaranteed certain civic rights (van Gelderen, 2002); the Union of Utrecht Treaty of 1579 (The Netherlands), declaring religious freedom (Spirer, 1990); the English Bill of Rights of 1689 that translated natural laws into positive laws (Cranston, 1983), and inspired Virginia: Declaration of Rights (1776), the 1776 American Declaration of Independence, and the 1789 French Declaration of the Rights of Man and of the Citizen (Shelton, 2003).

During Mediaeval times in Europe, the protection of human rights only applied to a group of people who were thought to be in possession of rational judgement, i.e., free male citizens. However, there were attempts by women to present challenges on the principles of "equality" in the 18th and 19th centuries: Olympe de Gouge's "Declaration of the Rights of Women" in 1791 is one example, and Mary Wollstonecraft's "Vindication of the Rights of Woman" in 1792 is another. Although John Stuart Mills' effort to replace the term "man" with "person" in the Reform Bill of 1867 was unsuccessful, this Bill can be seen as a first step towards acknowledging wealthy female property owners' rights to vote in British jurisdictions. (The gendered language, i.e. describing a person as he/his/him, was used later in the 1948 UDHR and in other UN documents and this gender equality issue is yet to be resolved (see Chapters 3 and 8).) Thomas Spence (Spence, 1797) championed children's rights in Britain in 1797/8, yet it was not until in the 20th century that children's rights and legal status were seriously reviewed (Medina, n.d.).

During the Enlightenment era (17th–18th century), secular scholars like John Locke attempted to transform natural law theory into natural rights theory by giving the former a "rationalistic identity" (Davidson, 1993; Shestack, 2000). Locke argued that nature gave every individual a right to life, liberty, and property (Morgan, 2005; van der Vyver, 1979). Kant's writing declaring that "a single, innate 'right belonging to every man by virtue of his humanity'" (1797, cited in Macklem, 2015, p. 76) became the foundation for contemporary human rights. Locke advocated for individuals "in the state of nature" to devise a social contract together, to form a political community and establish a government. Locke's idea was to limit government or to separate powers (Morgan, 2005) and make the government obliged to protect the natural rights of individuals in the political community (van der Vyver, 1979). The French Revolution (1789) and the American Declaration of Independence (1776) were later inspired by Locke's natural rights theory.

Contrarily, a school of thought called "positivism" impugned natural law theory and natural rights theory as "cognitively meaningless" (Davidson, 1993). Positivism, championed by scholars like David Hume and Jeremy Bentham, sought to deny any "a priori moral" sources of rights, and asserted that all rights derived their sources from state (positive) laws (Davidson, 1993). The current international human rights regime, which provides legal systems and mechanisms to protect human rights, owes its success to positivism thinking (Davidson, 1993; Shestack, 2000). Nevertheless, one criticism to positivism is that positivism could urge citizens to obey bad laws regardless of their moral consequences (Shestack, 2000): for example, torturing criminals may be considered "right" regardless of its ethical implications (Davidson, 1993). A "cultural critique" by Amartya Sen cautions that some human rights issues are unknown or are foreign concepts in some cultures, and that human rights are not the same as "legislated legal rights" (Clapham, 2007; Sen, 1999) (see Section 1.5 for further discussions on the topic).

In spite of the shortcomings of various human rights theories, Davidson (1993) focuses on each theory's contribution to the emergence of contemporary ideas of human rights. Davidson (1993) also elucidates that the moral and ethical invocation of resistance against the infringement of basic human rights may be explained by natural law and natural rights law; however, positive laws must systematically define the actual rights everyone possesses.

1.3 Core international human rights instruments

The 1919 Covenant of the League of Nations can be seen as an early international effort to secure protection for human rights. According to article 23 (a), (b), and (c) of the Covenant, state parties of the League agreed to:

> (a) … endeavour to secure and maintain fair and humane conditions of labour for men, women, and children, both in their own countries and in all countries to which their commercial and industrial relations extend, …;
> (b) undertake to secure just treatment of the native inhabitants of territories under their control; (c) … entrust the League with the general supervision over the execution of agreements with regards to the traffic in women and children
>
> *(League of Nations, 1919)*

The atrocities of World War II, and the devastation of European nations, led to the creation of the United Nations. After the war, the Charter of the United Nations was signed in June 1945 in San Francisco and came into force in October 1945. The founders of the UN incorporated in the preamble to the Charter of the UN a significant reference to human rights, which reads:

> We the peoples of the United Nations [are] determined ... to *reaffirm* faith in fundamental human rights, in the dignity and worth of the human person, in the equal rights of men and women and of nations large and small.
>
> *(UN, n.d.; Bailey, 2019)*

Article 1.3 of the Charter also reads:

> The Purposes of the United Nations are: To achieve international co-operation in solving international problems of an economic, social, cultural, or humanitarian *character*, and in promoting and encouraging respect for human rights and for fundamental freedoms for all without distinction as to race, sex, language, or religion.
>
> *(UN, n.d.)*

According to the UN Charter's operative provisions addressing human rights, article 68 requires the Economic and Social Council to set up commissions in the human rights, and economic and social fields. By June 1946, under the chairpersonship of Eleanor Roosevelt, the interim body had suggested that the new Commission should develop an international bill of human rights as its first task. Subsequently a Commission on Human Rights was established (UN, n.d.; Bailey, 2019). Eleanor Roosevelt also chaired the new Commission of Human Rights of 18 members that included, China's P. C. Chang, Rene Cassin from France, and Dr Charles Malik of Lebanon. Two noteworthy points are: first, the Commission chose to include both "civil and political" and "economic and social" rights in the declaration; second, the Commission decided to separate the initial declaration from a formally legally binding covenant (Bailey, 2019). Over 50 out of the 58 member states participated in the final drafting of the UDHR, and in December 1948, the declaration was endorsed as A/RES/3/217A by 48 in favour, zero against, eight abstention and two non-votes (UN, n.d.). Every year on December 10th, Human Rights Day is observed, commemorating the day the UDHR was adopted in 1948. By 2018, over 90 countries had embedded the principles of the UDHR in their constitutions and other laws (Stand up for Human Rights, 2018). Article 1 of the UDHR states:

> All human beings are born free and equal in dignity and rights. They are endowed with reason and conscience and should act towards one another in the spirit of brotherhood.

The entire 30 articles of the UDHR can be found at the end of this book. The core principles within the UDHR include universality, interdependence and indivisibility, equality and non-discrimination, as well as holding human rights to comprise both rights and obligations from duty bearers and rights owners (UN, n.d.).

As Ignatieff (2001, 2000) noted, the UDHR reflects Eurocentric notions of moral progress, where moral intuition influences the conduct of individuals and nation-states. Global diffusion of the concepts of human rights is viewed as establishing reciprocal good treatment of each other, i.e., treat others as you wish to be treated (c.f. the Golden Rule of the Bible), and the subsequent reduction of "unmerited cruelty and suffering of the world" (Ignatieff, 2000). The UDHR has achieved many things, but most notably it realised the rights of individuals to earn international legal recognition (Ignatieff, 2000). This recognition allows individuals to contest unjust laws or repressive customs in the case of gross violations of human rights. Goodhart (2016) argues that this assertion of human rights of individuals is a political claim because (1) it is a demand to rearrange society politically, economically, and culturally so that everyone receives inalienable respect and dignity; and (2) the protection of human rights can be used politically, for example, launching attacks on unfriendly nation-states that abuse human rights.

The UDHR is not the only declaration responsible for human rights protection: it works collaboratively with a series of major treaties and declarations (see Box 1.1). A number of other treaties and optional protocols advancing human rights have been agreed on since 1948 (Stand up for Human Rights, 2018).

BOX 1.1 CORE INTERNATIONAL HUMAN RIGHTS INSTRUMENTS

The three core texts of human rights are: the Universal Declaration of Human Rights (UDHR), the International Covenant on Civil and Political Rights (ICCPR) and the International Covenant on Economic, Social and Cultural Rights (ICESCR). Collectively, these three core texts are known as the **International Bill of Human Rights**. The ICCPR and ICESCR come with optional protocols. For the ICCPR, the optional protocols 1) allow individuals claiming to be victims of violations of any of the rights set forth in the Covenant to bring complaints to the Human Rights Committee (ICCPR-OP1); and 2) aim at the abolition of the death penalty (ICCPR-OP2). The one optional protocol to the ICESCR (ICESCR-OP1) allows individuals claiming to be victims of violations of any of the rights set forth in the Covenant to bring complaints to the UN Committee of Economic, Social and Cultural Rights (OHCHR, 2020c). The significance of ICCPR-OP1 and ICESCR-OP1 is that both clarify the individual complaints mechanism at the international level.

The OHCHR has listed nine international human rights instruments as core instruments in the protection of human rights (Table 1.1).

TABLE 1.1 International Human Rights Instruments

	THE 9 CORE INTERNATIONAL HUMAN RIGHTS INSTRUMENTS	Date
ICERD	International Convention on the Elimination of All Forms of Racial Discrimination	21 Dec 1965
ICCPR	International Covenant on Civil and Political Rights	16 Dec 1966
ICESCR	International Covenant on Economic, Social and Cultural Rights	16 Dec 1966
CAT	Convention Against Torture and Other Cruel, Inhuman or Degrading Treatment or Punishment	10 Dec 1984
CRC	Convention on the Rights of the Child	20 Nov 1989
ICMW	International Convention on the Protection of the Rights of All Migrant Workers and Members of Their Families	18 Dec 1990
CPED	International Convention for the Protection of All Persons from Enforced Disappearance	20 Dec 2006
CRPD	Convention on the Rights of Persons with Disabilities	13 Dec 2006
	OPTIONAL PROTOCOLS TO THE 9 CORE INTERNATIONAL HUMAN RIGHTS INSTRUMENTS	
ICESR-OP	Optional Protocol to the Covenant on Economic, Social, and Cultural Rights	10 Dec 2008
ICCPR-OP1	Optional Protocol to the International Covenant on Civil and Political Rights	16 Dec 1966
ICCPR-OP2	Second Optional Protocol to the International Covenant on Civil and Political Rights, aiming at the abolition of the death penalty	15 Dec 1989
OP-CEDAW	Optional Protocol to the Convention on the Elimination of Discrimination against Women	10 Dec 1999
OP-CRC-AC	Optional Protocol to the Convention on the Rights of the Child on the involvement of children in armed conflict	25 May 2000
OP-SRC-SC	Optional Protocol to the Convention on the Rights of the Child on the sale of children, child prostitution and child pornography	25 May 2000
OP-CRC-IC	Optional Protocol to the Convention on the Rights of the Child on a communication procedure	14 April 2014
OP-CAT	Optional Protocol to the Convention against Torture and Other Cruel, Inhuman of Degrading Treatment or Punishment	18 Dec 2002
OP-CRPD	Optional Protocol to the Convention on the Rights of Persons with Disabilities	12 Dec 2006

Source: (OHCHR, 2018).[1]

Below are some examples of other important human rights instruments:

WORLD CONFERENCE ON HUMAN RIGHTS AND MILLENNIUM ASSEMBLY

- Vienna Declaration and Programme of Action
- United Nations Millennium Declaration

FREEDOM OF ASSOCIATION

- Freedom of Association and Protection of the Right to Organise Convention, 1948 (No. 87)
- Right to Organise and Collective Bargaining Convention, 1949 (No. 98)

RIGHTS OF THE CHILD

- Minimum Age Convention, 1973 (No. 138)
- Worst Forms of Child Labour Convention, 1999 (No. 182)

WAR CRIMES AND CRIMES AGAINST HUMANITY, INCLUDING GENOCIDE

- Convention on the Prevention and Punishment of the Crime of Genocide
- Convention on the Non-Applicability of Statutory Limitations to War Crimes and Crimes against Humanity
- Principles of international co-operation in the detection, arrest, extradition and punishment of persons guilty of war crimes and crimes against humanity
- Statute of the International Tribunal for the Former Yugoslavia
- Statute of the International Tribunal for Rwanda
- Rome Statute of the International Criminal Court

RIGHTS OF PERSONS WITH DISABILITIES

- Declaration on the Rights of Mentally Retarded Persons
- Declaration on the Rights of Disabled Persons
- Principles for the protection of persons with mental illness and the improvement of mental health care
- Standard Rules on the Equalization of Opportunities for Persons with Disabilities

PREVENTION OF DISCRIMINATION

- Equal Remuneration Convention, 1951 (No. 100)
- Discrimination (Employment and Occupation) Convention, 1958 (No. 111)
- Declaration on Race and Racial Prejudice
- Convention against Discrimination in Education
- Protocol Instituting a Conciliation and Good Offices Commission to be responsible for seeking a settlement of any disputes which may arise between States Parties to the Convention against Discrimination in Education
- Declaration on the Elimination of All Forms of Intolerance and of Discrimination Based on Religion or Belief
- World Conference against Racism, 2001 (Durban Declaration and Programme of Action)

RIGHTS OF INDIGENOUS PEOPLES AND MINORITIES

- Declaration on the Rights of Indigenous Peoples
- Indigenous and Tribal Peoples Convention, 1989 (No. 169)
- Declaration on the Rights of Persons Belonging to National or Ethnic, Religious and Linguistic Minorities

RIGHTS OF MIGRANTS

- Protocol against the Smuggling of Migrants by Land, Sea and Air, supplementing the United Nations Convention against Transnational Organized Crime

NATIONALITY, STATELESSNESS, ASYLUM AND REFUGEES

- Convention on the Reduction of Statelessness
- Convention relating to the Status of Stateless Persons
- Convention relating to the Status of Refugees
- Protocol relating to the Status of Refugees
- Declaration on the Human Rights of Individuals who are not nationals of the country in which they live

RIGHTS OF OLDER PERSONS

- United Nations Principles for Older Persons

PROMOTION AND PROTECTION OF HUMAN RIGHTS

- Principles relating to the status of national institutions (The Paris Principles)
- Declaration on the Right and Responsibility of Individuals, Groups and Organs of Society to Promote and Protect Universally Recognized Human Rights and Fundamental Freedoms
- United Nations Declaration on Human Rights Education and Training

THE RIGHT OF SELF-DETERMINATION

- United Nations Declaration on the Granting of Independence to Colonial Countries and Peoples
- General Assembly resolution 1803 (XVII) of 14 December 1962, "Permanent sovereignty over natural resources"
- International Convention against the Recruitment, Use, Financing, and Training of Mercenaries

SLAVERY, SLAVERY-LIKE PRACTICES AND FORCED LABOUR

- Slavery Convention
- Protocol amending the Slavery Convention signed at Geneva on 25 September 1926
- Supplementary Convention on the Abolition of Slavery, the Slave Trade, and Institutions and Practices Similar to Slavery
- Forced Labour Convention, 1930 (No. 29)
- Protocol of 2014 to the Forced Labour Convention, 1930
- Abolition of Forced Labour Convention, 1957 (No. 105)
- Convention for the Suppression of the Traffic in Persons and of the Exploitation of the Prostitution of Others
- Protocol to Prevent, Suppress and Punish Trafficking in Persons, Especially Women and Children, supplementing the United Nations Convention against Transnational Organized Crime

SOCIAL WELFARE, PROGRESS AND DEVELOPMENT

- Declaration on Social Progress and Development
- Universal Declaration on the Eradication of Hunger and Malnutrition
- Declaration on the Use of Scientific and Technological Progress in the Interests of Peace and for the Benefit of Mankind
- Declaration on the Right of Peoples to Peace
- Declaration on the Right to Development

- Universal Declaration on the Human Genome and Human Rights
- Universal Declaration on Cultural Diversity

RIGHTS OF WOMEN

- Declaration on the Protection of Women and Children in Emergency and Armed Conflict
- Declaration on the Elimination of Violence against Women

RIGHT TO WORK AND TO FAIR CONDITIONS OF EMPLOYMENT

- Employment Policy Convention, 1964 (No. 122)

Source: (OHCHR, 2018).

In January of 2020, the UN High Commissioner for Human Rights identified five key 'frontier' areas that are having an accelerating impact on fundamental human rights, and where the UN will focus its work on. These five areas include climate change, the expanding digital space, inequalities, corruption, and people on the move, i.e., international migrants facing discrimination, exploitation and violence (OHCHR, 2020a). The fact that more conventions, declarations, charters, and other instruments in relation to human rights are still emerging, being adopted, and generating further discourse on human rights demonstrates the complexity of the issue.

1.4 Universalism vs. cultural relativism discourse on human rights

Human rights as declared in the UDHR are based on the assumption that human beings are bestowed these rights by the virtue of being human. These human rights are necessary for humans to achieve a dignified and respectful life. Yet, there is no standard definition of human rights around the world, and some state and non-state actors do not recognise the UDHR (Nkyi and Hashimoto, 2014). A criticism against universal human rights, as expressed in the UDHR, is that they are a reflection of Western values. The UDHR clearly has roots in Eurocentric traditions. Scholars argue that the basis of the declaration is the protection of individuals' rights from oppressive states or authorities (e.g., Humphreys, 2018; Schmidt-Leukel, 2006). Cultural relativism critics advocate that often the UDHR's concepts of individualism and individual rights do not align with religious teachings and traditions within the cultural environment in the non-Western world. For instance, Asian societies and African societies perceive communities or societies as preceding individuals in importance (Tharoor, 1999). Individualism in Western nations has a tendency to overlook the individual responsibilities that complements human rights (Nkyi and Hashimoto, 2014). McGregor (2010) analysed the use of the English language in supranational and national documents and argues that the use of the word "responsibility" appeals to one's inner ethic, rather than external laws. That is, moral pressure is often not as strong as legally binding laws. The word "duties" on the other hand was dismissed by supranational agencies because legal responsibilities tend to weaken rights. In contrast to individualistic societies, socialist nations or collective societies – particularly in Asia – have an understanding of human rights that places more emphasis on the collective good, rather than on individual rights. Individual responsibilities to the social good, safety and order precede individual rights. For example, this ideology is reflected in a Singaporean politician's comment: "to save people from dire poverty or other devastating circumstances, a right must be temporarily compromised" (Nkyi and Hashimoto, 2014). Traditional African societies place community before individuals; traditional laws are based on moral principles and animistic reverence, and are based on principles of community (Kawamura, 2013). African communities have a complex structure of community entitlement and obligations: respect, restraint, responsibility and reciprocity; these four "r's", or community rights, precede individual rights (Tharoor, 1999). In most traditional African societies, democracy is also called *la démocratie de l'arbre à palabre* in which individual rights exist within the community without absolute authoritarianism or opposing stance of individual rights and rights of state (Kawamura, 2013).

Another perceived or real conflict exists between religion and human rights. There are examples of religious scholars and practitioners in all major world religions, who have held that universal human rights conflict with values and teachings of the religion in question. In Asia, Buddhism, Confucian and Vedic traditions value duties and obligations as coming before individual rights (Humphreys, 2018; Desai, 2014; Schmidt-Leukel, 2006; Tharoor, 1999). One of the Hindu texts *Manusmriti* explains "the nature of social order ... the four classes of people, the four stages of life, and the duties of each according to class, age, gender ..." (Desai, 2014, p. 33). This demonstrates that in the Hindu interpretation, humans are born unequal, and duties and obligations keep social order. Buddhism aims to eradicate worldly sufferings such as war, social discord, crime, poverty, and legal insecurity; to achieve this aim, the ruling monarch must follow the moral principle of Dharma, and the monarch needs citizens who fulfil individual duties and obligations (Schmidt-Leukel, 2006).

Christian nationalism has been linked to the ideological underpinnings of the apartheid system in South Africa (see Chapter 8). The white Afrikaners perceived themselves as a superior people, justifying racial inequality and the oppression of the black majority population (Dubow, 1992). Similarly, Israel was in 2020 criticised by the UN Committee on the basis of Elimination of Racial Discrimination because of the discriminatory effects of the Basic Law: Israel – The Nation-State of the Jewish People (2018), which stipulates that the right to exercise self-determination in Israel is "unique to the Jewish people", discriminating against the Arab Israeli population (CERD/C/ISR/CO/17–19). In 1981, the Islamic Council of Europe adopted the Universal Islamic Declaration of Human Rights (Azzam, 1998) in an effort to complement universal human rights with an Islamic view on the topic. Similarly, in 1990, the Organisation of Islamic Cooperation adopted the Cairo Declaration of Human Rights in Islam with a similar intention (UN, 1990). The Cairo Declaration does not include the freedom of conscience, and the right to choose one's religion (Ahmad, 2019). Some traditional Islamic scholars regard the UDHR as a reflection of primarily Western values that is not agreeable with the Muslim worldview (George and Varghese, 2007). More progressive Islamic scholars argue instead that Islam, as a set of ethical and religious values, should be interpreted in its context and is fully compatible with universal human rights (Juul Petersen, 2018; Bielefeldt, 1995).

All religions contain a multitude of practitioners and voices, dependent on the cultural, social, and political context. Therefore, we do not intend to classify the Christian, Muslim, or Jewish (or any other religious) position on human rights in this book. However, we do explore the tension and interaction between religion and human rights in various settings (c.f. Chapter 8).

1.5 Human rights, civil rights, and civil liberties – similarities and differences in terminology

In 1977, Karel Vašák provided three classifications of human rights, also known as the three generations of human rights. The first generation of human rights focused on "negative" rights, in which the state does not do anything to deprive or interfere with individual rights. This generation corresponds to civil and political liberties (Macklem, 2015). The second generation on the other hand concerns "positive" action of the state to protect social, economic, and cultural rights of individuals (Vašák, 1977). These first two generations of rights came into realisation in 1966, when the International Covenant on Civil and Political Rights (ICCPR) was signed, representing the first generation of human rights; and the International Covenant on Economic, Social, and Cultural Rights (ICESCR) representing the second generation of human rights (Domaradzki, Khvostova and Pupovac, 2019). The third generation of human rights is called "rights of solidarity" which include: the right to development, the right to a healthy environment, the right to peace, the right to ownership of the common heritage of human kind (Vašák, 1977, p. 29), the right of self-determination, and minority rights (Macklem, 2015). However, researchers argue that Vašák's categorisation by "generation" is inaccurate if it is treated as a "chronological" approach, and the generation categories are too ambiguous to be useful (see Pocar, 2015; Domaradzki, Khvostova and Pupovac, 2019; Macklem, 2015, and others for further discussions). Nevertheless, this approach to human rights discourse has shifted its focus towards collectives rather than individuals, therefore highlighting the "rights of solidarity" (Domaradzki, Khvostova and Pupovac, 2019). In the case of tourism, the state not interfering with a citizen who wishes to travel abroad is an example of a first-generation right. A state taking action to protect an individual's right to open a tourism-related business is an example of a second-generation right. Finally, the displacement of an entire village from a beachfront area for a new hotel development could be examined under the concept of the collective rights of the village.

Often human rights are confused with civil rights. While human rights and civil rights may overlap in many areas, it is important to clearly point out the similarities and differences between the two concepts. It is essential to examine how these two concepts (though alike, yet distinct) should be promoted and advanced in tourism development. In international human rights law, the concept of civil rights has often been used to illustrate certain core rights, such as the right to live free from discrimination, and be treated equally in society, as opposed to economic, social, and cultural rights, such as the right to enjoy just and favourable conditions of work. For example, the ICCPR contains a codification of the most important civil and political rights, while the ICESCR contains a codification of the most important economic and social rights. The exact classification of each particular right can cause difficulties, but in general, the expression "civil rights" in international human rights law is, through ICCPR and other similar conventions, relatively clearly established.

In the human rights discourse, the phrase "civil rights" is however also often used in an effort to illustrate something different, diverging from the phrase "human rights", which in this context includes both ICCPR and ICESCR rights. From a philosophical perspective, a distinction is often made between *moral rights* and *legal rights*. Human rights are considered moral rights belonging to every human (Cranston, 1983). There exists a universal right, independent of any codification or enforcement in a treaty or convention. Just by virtue of being human everyone is covered, without discrimination. Legal rights, or civil rights, on the other hand, are dependent on the enforcement of laws in a particular country. The distinction between moral/human and legal/civil rights can however be blurred. Martin (1980) argues that a right, here a human right, needs appropriate practices of recognition and maintenance with it. Otherwise there is just a moral claim to a right. Since human rights are asserted against governments, governmental recognition and promotion are necessarily included in the very existence of such a right. Without such recognition, it can still be a morally valid claim, but it cannot be described as a right. Furthermore, a human right needs to be relativised to particular societies. A law introducing a human right as a legal right, having a universal or near universal scope within the particular society, can, according to Martin, be called a civil right. Civil rights are claimed against and enforced by particular governments. Human rights are dependent on civil rights. If a particular civil right does not exist in a country, it cannot be argued that a human right exists in that particular time and place, there is only a moral claim to introduce a civil right. A human right would therefore have to have the legal form of a civil right.

Martin's (1980) argument that human rights and civil rights are interconnected but still distinct, is reflected in the categorisation of both rights in legal jurisprudence. From a legal perspective, human rights can be categorised according to the parties that codify and enforce the rights in question. Although it can be argued that human rights exist independently, human rights law, a body of law articulating the general inalienable human rights principles, is an expression of such rights. Human rights law is articulated in an interrelated and overlapping system at the international level, with the exact wording and coverage of human rights law negotiated between nation-states. International human rights law, which can be categorised as international public law, obligates the signatories, who are nation-states, to act in a certain manner, protecting those rights in a national context. However, international human rights laws seldom contain any enforcement mechanisms. Even in cases where enforcement mechanisms exist, in the form of a court or complaints procedure, such courts can only exercise their jurisdiction if a state party has acknowledged and accepted the jurisdiction of the court. For example, the International Criminal Court (ICC) (see Section 1.6) can only prosecute crimes which are committed by a national or on the territory of a state party to the Rome statute establishing the ICC (A/CONF.183/9), unless the Security Council of the United Nations refers a matter to the court, according to Chapter VII of the United Nations Charter. Similarly, the European Court of Human Rights only hears complaints allegedly committed by a state party to the European Convention on Human Rights. Even when international organs can claim jurisdiction over a violation of a human right, they often have weak remedial powers. Civil rights, on the other hand, are applicable in a national context, covering citizens of a nation state and categorised as domestic public law. Sometimes civil rights are also extended to permanent residents or persons who are inside the territorial boundaries of a nation state, but civil rights are never universal. Instead they are attached to either citizenship, residency, or location, thus applicable in a specific setting, covering some, but not all humans. In contrast to international human rights enforcement mechanisms, the nation state can most often, if it chooses to do so, provide for effective enforcement through a police force, courts, and a prison system.

A distinction, which is seen as critical in the United States, but often ignored in other countries, is the distinction between civil rights and civil liberties. Civil rights in this context is understood as the right to equal treatment without any form of discrimination, while civil liberties consist of liberties from the state and its oppressive authority, for example the right to free speech. The distinction was created during the Cold War, when liberal anti-Communists wanted to restrict the right to free speech and due process in the interest of national security. In an effort to separate the "race issue" from the "Communist issue," liberal anti-Communists created the distinct definitions of civil rights and civil liberties (Schmidt, 2016). In this book, we are exploring subjects, which can be characterised as civil rights (discrimination in Chapter 8), as well as concepts which can be characterised as civil liberties (the right to privacy in Chapter 6). The distinction between civil rights and liberties has survived until present day in the United States human rights discourse. However, the two terms are often used interchangeably in other countries.

Rights can sometimes be in conflict with each other or be competing rights. For example, according to the First Amendment to the United States of America (U.S.) Constitution, everyone has the right to practice their religion, but this right can be in conflict with the right to equal treatment, as recently illustrated in the "wedding cake battles", where Christian bakers in the U.S. refused to bake wedding cakes for homosexual couples (see Chapter 8 for further discussion). In the human rights discourse, the definitions "absolute" and "qualified" human rights are often used to illustrate the fact that some human rights are more important than others, or to reconcile two competing human rights. For example, the ICCPR (art. 4) allows states to take measures derogating from their obligations in times of public emergency. However, no derogation may be made from certain absolute rights, such as the right to life, the right to not be subjected to torture, the right to live free from slavery, and the right to be recognised as a person before the law. Most human rights are, however, qualified human rights, meaning that they can be restricted. In fact, some courts have argued that all human rights are qualified rights. According to the Canadian Supreme Court, all human rights are inherently limited by the rights and freedoms of other persons (P. (D.) v. S. (C.), [1993] 4 S.C.R. 141). The COVID-19 pandemic serves as a practical example of a situation where many states restricted the human rights enumerated in the ICCPR. The OHCHR (2020b) issued a guidance document in connection with the pandemic, where it stated that some rights, such as the freedom of movement, freedom of expression, or right to peaceful assembly, may be restricted for public health reasons, even without a state of emergency, if the restrictions meet the following requirements: legality (restrictions are contained in a law), necessity (restrictions are necessary for the protection of public health), proportionality, and non-discrimination. During a state of emergency, more human rights can be restricted. However, some rights, such as the right to life and prohibition from torture, can never be derogated from. In conclusion, in many ways human rights and civil rights are similar in their content. The same right can be both a human right and a civil right. Yet the two sets of rights can also be distinguished from each other, in several different ways, depending on if it can be classified as a distinction within international human rights law (civil and political rights – economic and social rights), a philosophical distinction (moral and legal rights) or a distinction between different levels of regulation (international human rights law – national civil rights law).

1.6 The relationship between international human rights law and domestic law

Human rights declared under the UDHR cannot be protected if there are no legally binding international agreements (for example conventions and treaties) or domestic laws to implement these protections. For example, the UDHR guarantees the freedom of religion (art. 18), but if a state has not incorporated that right in a national setting (either through national law, or by making international legally binding conventions directly applicable in the country) a person who cannot exercise his/her religion has no possibility to force the state to acknowledge the right through legal means.

In order for human rights to be protected within a territory, they must be incorporated into its governing institutions. When they are incorporated, the state is responsible for protecting and enforcing human rights by guaranteeing the protection and monitoring of governments, non-government agents, corporations and individuals, so that they do not violate other people's rights. It is stated in the preamble to the UDHR that "human rights should be protected by the rule of law". "This means that in order to enable the human person fully to enjoy his or her rights, *these rights must be effectively protected by domestic legal systems* [original emphasis]" (OHCHR, 2003, p. 6). It is therefore of uttermost importance that human rights are implemented at the national level. An independent and accredited body, such as a national human rights institution, can also promote human rights among citizens and professionals, and act as an intermediary between the state and society (Cardenas, 2016). There are several different sources of international human rights law, from international legal agreements to customary law and case law from regional human rights courts (see Box 1.2).

BOX 1.2 HIERARCHY OF INTERNATIONAL HUMAN RIGHTS LAW

The Statute of the International Court of Justice (ICJ) (art. 38) lists the following sources of international law:

a. international conventions, whether general or particular, establishing rules expressly recognized by the contesting states;
b. international custom, as evidence of a general practice accepted as law;
c. the general principles of law recognized by civilized nations;
d. subject to the provisions of Article 59 [*article 59 states that the decision of the Court has no binding force except in that particular case, author's note*], judicial decisions and the teachings of the most highly qualified publicist of the various nations, as subsidiary means for the determinations of law.

The sources mentioned in the Statute of the ICJ are further elaborated on in the OHCHR Manual on Human Rights for Judges, Prosecutors and Lawyers (2003).

1. International treaties, conventions, covenants, and pacts

A treaty, convention, covenant or a pact is a legally binding, written agreement concluded between states. Once ratified, accepted or approved, a treaty which has entered into force is binding upon the contracting states, i.e., the contracting parties are legally bound to perform their obligations and cannot avoid them under international law. The mere signing of a treaty, convention, covenant or a pact does not usually create any legal obligations. Such obligations are only created by the ratification, acceptance or approval of a written agreement. According to international human rights law, states have strict responsibility for the fulfilment of obligations of the agreement. International human rights law presupposes a teleological and holistic interpretative approach for interpretation, meaning that a state must not only follow the exact wording of the text, but try to achieve the objective of the international agreement, i.e., the protection of the human rights in question.

2. International customary law

States can also be bound by international customary law, even without any active ratification/acceptance/approval of a written agreement, if there is a general practice of adhering to a legal principle and a belief among states that the general practice is binding. The practice should be extensive and show that states believe that there is a legal obligation involved. The prohibition of racial discrimination, slavery, arbitrary detention and crimes of genocide are generally considered as obligations owed by states to the international community as a whole, and form part of customary international law.

3. General principles of law recognised by the community of nations

A general principle of law is a legal proposition on human rights which is to be found in all major legal systems in the world. The foundations of international human rights law incorporate legally binding principles so that when judges and lawyers need, they can look at human rights laws in different countries to determine if a particular human rights law is widely accepted enough to become an international norm.

4. Subsidiary means for the determination of rules of law

Subsidiary means for the determination of rules of law are defined as "judicial decisions and the teachings of the most highly qualified publicists" (Article

38 of Statute of the International Court of Justice). In human rights laws, judicial decisions are of great importance for a full understanding of international human rights law and are regarded as authoritative evidence of the state of law. However, international human rights courts are not obligated to follow previous legal decisions, as is the custom in common law countries, but rather, need to be flexible to adjust to dynamic social needs. Also, the reference to the "teachings of the most highly qualified publicists" was included at a time when legal jurisprudence was scarce. Today, it is advisable not to rely on written material by private bodies outside the framework of the officially established treaty organs, as they may not correctly represent the current status of the law.

Source: (OHCHR 2003).

Within a territory, the state institution plays an invaluable role. If a domestic government operates on the principles of democratic governance, human rights are more likely to be protected, unlike in non-democratic regimes, such as in military regimes or in countries under a one-party rule (Cardenas, 2016). Democratic governance allows individuals whose rights are violated to have access to various levels of institutions, including support from civil society organisations, and can ultimately approach the state for accountability. As the OHCHR (2019) outlined, democracy is the core value of the United Nations, and a key attribute of good governance, i.e., transparency, responsibility, accountability, participation, responsiveness (to the needs of the people), which is to be linked to democratic institutions (see Chapter 4 for discussions on good governance).

However, it is also known that democratic institutions do not always respect all human rights (Cardenas, 2016). Human Rights Watch (2019b) reported that the USA has "continued to move backward on human rights at home and abroad" (p. 619) since 2017, by allowing government administrators to "pass laws, implement regulations, and carry out policies that violate or undermine human rights" (p. 619). In her research on torture in democratic nations, Conrad (2013; Conrad and Moore, 2010) found that while violent dissent or threat occurred within/to the nation, democratic institutions had little effect on the state to terminate the use of torture. Divided authorities in democratic institutions are, according to Conrad, one cause of the inability to stop democratic governments preventing the violation of human rights of others, i.e., when others are declared "enemies of the state". As Frankenberg (2014) argues, perceived violent threats have permitted states to justify their repressive practices.

The UDHR is a non-binding declaration, and the UN does not have coercive power on member states to incorporate it into national (or sub-national) law; though some argue that over the decades since the invocation of the UDHR, it has become binding as part of customary international law (Australian Human Rights Commission, 2008). Once a state ratifies and implements international law, such as different human rights treaties, the state is bound by them and therefore it would be difficult to justify its "non-respect" of international law (Council of Europe, 2014). The implementation of international human rights laws has profound impacts on a state's domestic (national and sub-national levels) laws. Almost all states participate in some form of human rights treaties through the United Nations and the International Labour Organization, as well as regional organisations such as the Organization of American States, the African Union, and the Council of Europe. However, how each state implements human rights standards into its domestic laws is not uniform. While it is beyond the scope of this chapter to get into the details of the mechanisms of such processes, it will outline some of the major reasons why many states do not fully implement international human rights laws.

Different states have different legal cultures, attitudes towards laws, and political orientation. Democratic attitudes tend to embrace human rights as a core value. Countries that have revised or adopted their fundamental laws recently have a higher tendency to "explicitly regulate the legal status of international human rights treaties" (Council of Europe, 2014). Two legal theories, the monistic approach (monism) and the dualist approach (dualism), focus on the relationship between international law and domestic laws. The pure monist approach considers international laws and domestic laws as parts of the same legal system; and thus, once an international agreement is ratified and has entered into force, it will be considered as part of the national legal system. In the pure dualist approach, international law and domestic law are two separate legal systems, and as such, international law or treaties do not have any effect at the national level. According to the dualist view, an international legal agreement must be implemented at the national level in a law or other national regulation, to become part of national law. In a mixed approach some international agreements become directly applicable at the national level, while other agreements need to be implemented at the national level to become effective. Each state decides at the national level, if the state wants to follow a monistic, dualist or a mixed approach. Even if a state is more inclined to one of the approaches, each state's level of incorporating international law varies. For instance, there are varying degrees of how extensively incorporation clauses refer to international human rights law or other sources, how extensively jurisdictions rely on case law, or if the constitution clearly states that international law prevails over domestic law, etc.

For international human rights treaties to be successfully implemented, domestic law plays a significant role. However, not all states that ratify human rights treaties have shown successful results. The case of the U.S. has been researched by many scholars and human rights organisations (e.g., Kalb, 2011; Human Rights Watch, 2019b; The Advocates for Human Rights, 2020). The U.S. has 50 states (sub-national level or localities) and the state and localities have taken "fewer legislative and administrative actions to implement the commitments of the binding human rights instruments" (Kalb, 2011, p. 73). Although the U.S. played a prominent role in founding the universal human rights systems, it withdrew from the human rights systems in the 1950s during the Cold War period; only in 1988 did the U.S. ratify the Convention on the Prevention and Punishment of the Crime of Genocide. The U.S. has a strong tradition of federalism, which makes the federal government solely responsible for international law and foreign affairs. Although the U.S. federal government has approved and ratified several international human rights treaties, it has failed to raise significant interest at the sub-national level, in addition to changing sub-national level ignorance of, and resistance against, international human rights law (Kalb, 2011). Moreover, the federalism tradition and the dualist approach of the legal system limits sub-national jurisdictional authorities, as human rights treaty projects are in the hands of the federal government (Kalb, 2011). Implementation of international human rights treaties is at different stages at the federal level of the U.S. government. The U.S. has signed some human rights treaties that have yet to be approved by the Senate; there are human rights treaties signed, approved by the Senate and ratified by the President, but not implemented through federal legislation; and there are treaties signed, approved, ratified, and implemented through federal legislation (see The Advocate for Human Rights, 2020 for a list of major international treaties the U.S. has not ratified). The U.S. usually ratifies treaties with reservations. For example, many agreements are ratified with the understanding that "nothing in the Convention requires or authorizes legislation or other action by the United States of America prohibited by the Constitution of the United States as interpreted by the United States" (Convention on the Prevention and Punishment of the Crime of Genocide; see also ICCPR; ICERD; CAT). Also, the U.S. regularly declares that a treaty, convention or covenant is not self-executing, but has to be implemented by the federal, state or local governments who exercise jurisdiction over the matter (e.g., ICCPR; ICERD; CAT). These reservations and declarations reveal that the U.S. has limited the scope of international human rights law, which has implications for the domestic protection of human rights, especially when there is a case of perceived threats to the state.

1.7 Access to justice and remedies for human rights violations

An important part of the international human rights system is the right to access to justice and an effective remedy.

> People may not agree why we have rights, but they can agree that they need them. Such grounding as modern human rights requires, ... that human beings are at risk of their lives if they lack agency; that agency itself requires protection in internationally agreed standards; that these standards should entitle individuals to oppose and resist unjust laws and orders within their own states; and finally, that when all other remedies have been exhausted, these individuals have the right to appeal to other peoples, nations, and international organizations for assistance in defending their rights.
>
> *(Ignatieff, 2000, p. 321).*

Without access to justice and effective remedies, the core human rights have little value. Persons whose rights have been violated would not have any way of making their complaints known, violators of human rights would not be punished and there would not be any reparations to the victims. Access to justice for victims of human rights violations can be provided through state-based domestic judicial and non-judicial grievance mechanisms, non-state-based domestic grievance mechanisms as well as through regional and international judicial and non-judicial grievance mechanisms.

Domestic state-based judicial grievance mechanisms are of importance in democratic countries where the courts follow the rule of law and apply the laws fairly and impartially. According to the UDHR (art.8), "[e]veryone has the right to an effective remedy by the competent national tribunals for acts violating the fundamental rights granted him by the constitution or by law". Similarly, according to the ICCPR (art. 2), state parties to the covenant undertake to "ensure that any person whose rights or freedoms ... are violated shall have an effective remedy, notwithstanding that the violation has been committed by persons acting in an official capacity". Many other international human rights conventions also require states to provide for access to justice and effective remedies at the national level. For example, the CRPD requires state parties to ensure "effective access to justice for persons with disabilities on an equal basis with others" (art. 13). Throughout the book, there are several examples of domestic court decisions, where violations of international human rights, implemented at the national level, have formed a cause of action in national court proceedings. As mentioned above, national court decisions, especially if rendered by the supreme court of the country, can form part of international law, if they amount to general principles of law recognised by the community of nations.

In addition to national remedies, there are regional complaints procedures available in the form of the courts and advisory councils in several parts of the world. The African Court of Human and Peoples' Rights, which started its operations in 2006, is authorised to hear cases brought by NGOs and individuals regarding the interpretation of the African Charter on Human and Peoples' Rights. Currently only nine African states recognise the competence of the court. The Inter-American Court of Human Rights, established in 1979, interprets and applies the American Convention on Human Rights. It can resolve complaints brought by individuals as well as give advisory opinions. Currently twenty South and Central American countries have accepted the court's jurisdiction. The European Court of Human Rights is the oldest regional court, established in 1959. It resolves contentious cases and can give advisory opinions about the interpretation of the European Convention on Human Rights. All 47 European member states of the convention acknowledge the court's jurisdiction.

At the international level, after over a century of discussions, the International Criminal Court (ICC) came into existence through the Rome Statute of the International Criminal Court ("the Rome Statute") and was adopted by the UN ICC-ASP/2/Res.3 in 1998, coming into effect in 2002. Since then, the ICC has been independent from the UN Secretariat as an intergovernmental organisation (UN, 2003). It is located in The Hague. The ICC tries individuals accused of committing the crime of genocide, crimes against humanity, war crimes, and the crime of aggression (ICC, n.d.). It is permanently an autonomous court (ICC, n.d.), however, the conception and formation of the organisation through the UN and its working relationship with the UN Security Council is often criticised (Holmes Armstead Jr., 1998). The ICC exists beyond the national legal systems to deal with violations by individuals and states.

When the UDHR was proclaimed in 1948 and ratified, it set the foundation for international human rights law (UN, n.d.); however, many laws were "domesticated", requiring implementation of the rights at the national level, so that each country's sovereignty was not undermined (Chandler, 2016). For this reason, UN bodies restrained in their criticism or intervention on human rights violations of member states until the 1960s (Ignatieff, 2000). However, today, the international human rights framework contains a multitude of bodies and agencies within the UN system (see Box 1.3).

Many international human rights conventions contain articles on the establishment of a committee for the monitoring of the state's adherence to the convention. The committees are usually consisting of experts on the subject and serve in their personal capacity. Each state party to a convention shall submit to the committee comprehensive reports on measures taken to give effect to the convention in question. Thereafter, states are required to submit periodic reports on the progress and implementation of the convention. The reports are considered by the committee, which makes suggestions and recommendations to the state party concerned. The reports and recommendations are published and form part of the informal guidance documents for the convention in question.

Several human rights conventions have more recently been complemented with optional protocols, where states can ratify the optional protocol recognising the competence of the committee to hear and consider communications from individuals or groups of individuals claiming to be victims of a violation of the convention in question (see Box 1.1). Such optional protocols have been adopted for the ICESCR, ICCPR, CRC, CEDAW, and CRPD. The optional protocols establish an international grievance procedure, which resembles to a certain extent an international court of human rights. The procedure of a committee hearing as well as the remedies available are however not fully comparable with courts. The meetings of the committee are closed meetings, and all communications in relation to a complaint are handled confidentially. The committees are only obligated to provide a summary of their activities in a report at certain prescribed intervals. Also, the Committee can only give a recommendation to the parties as to the outcome. In addition to the optional protocols on communication procedures, the CAT contains an optional protocol to CAT and establishes a system of regular visits by independent international and national bodies to places where people are deprived of their liberty, in order to prevent torture and other cruel, inhuman or degrading punishment (art. 1, OP-CAT). It is important to note that the committee can only hear grievances submitted by individuals or conduct visits at prisons and other similar places if the state in question has ratified the optional protocol. A state may thus be a party to a convention, but not party to an optional protocol. In such cases, the committee is only allowed to receive reports and make recommendations as to general issues, as stated in the convention.

BOX 1.3 HUMAN RIGHTS BODIES

The Office of the High Commissioner for Human Rights (OHCHR) works to offer expertise and support to different human rights monitoring mechanisms in the United Nations system under the following two major collaborative entities:

A. UN Charter-based bodies, including the Human Rights Council;
B. Bodies created under international human rights treaties, comprised of independent experts mandated to monitor State parties' compliance with their treaty obligations.

Charter-based bodies within the system:

- Human Rights Council
- Universal Periodic Review
- Commission on Human Rights (replaced by the Human Rights Council)
- Special Procedures of the Human Rights Council
- Human Rights Council Complaint Procedure

Special Procedures bodies also fall under the UN's Charter-based bodies and are independent human rights experts with mandates to report and advise on human rights, from a thematic or country-specific perspective.

The Human Rights Council Complaints Procedure addresses communications submitted by individuals, by groups, or by non-governmental organisations. Two working groups (the Working Group on Communications and the Working Group on Situations) are responsible for examining written communications and bringing consistent patterns of gross and reliably attested violations of human rights and fundamental freedoms to the attention of the Council.

The UN has ten treaty bodies, made up of independent experts, that monitor the implementation of core international human rights treaties:

- Committee on the Elimination of Racial Discrimination (CERD)
- Committee on Economic, Social, and Cultural Rights (CESCR)
- Human Rights Committee (CCPR)
- Committee on the Elimination of Discrimination against Women (CEDAW)
- Committee against Torture (CAT)
- Committee on the Rights of the Child (CRC)
- Committee on Migrant Workers (CMW)

- Subcommittee on the Prevention of Torture (SPT)
- Committee on the Rights of Persons with Disabilities (CRPD)
- Committee on Enforced Disappearances (CED)

Other United Nations agencies and partners that are involved in the promotion and protection of human rights and interact with the main human rights bodies include:

- United Nations High Commissioner for Refugees (UNHCR)
- Office for the Coordination of Humanitarian Affairs (OCHA)
- Inter-Agency Internal Displacement Division
- International Labour Organization (ILO)
- World Health Organization (WHO)
- United Nations Educational, Scientific and Cultural Organization (UNESCO)
- Joint United Nations Programme on HIV/AIDS (UNAIDS)
- Inter-Agency Standing Committee (IASC)
- Department of Economic and Social Affairs (DESA)
- Commission on the Status of Women (CSW)
- Office of the Special Adviser on Gender Issues and the Advancement of Women (OSAGI)
- Division for the Advancement of Women (DAW)
- United Nations Population Fund (UNFPA)
- United Nations Children's Fund (UNICEF)
- United Nations Entity for Gender Equality and the Empowerment of Women (UN-Women)
- United Nations Development Programme (UNDP)
- Food and Agriculture Organization of the United Nations (FAO)
- United Nations Human Settlements Programme (HABITAT)
- United Nations Mine Action

Source: (OHCHR, n.d., 2019a, 2019b).[2]

As discussed in this section, there exist a multitude of different mechanisms to provide access to justice and effective remedies for persons who have experienced human rights violations. Yet, human rights violations do not seem to be disappearing – some states are re-introducing laws that clearly violate the human rights of certain groups of people. Recent trends in the rise of nationalism and military intervention also pose concerns for human rights. Researchers are finding that there is a shift towards collective human rights, which Vašák called the third generation of human rights. States are practicing such human rights at home, and in their foreign policy. However, the use of "nationalism" as a human right on behalf of its people can create two national groups: victorious groups, and victims' groups, whose human rights situation deteriorates (Ignatieff, 2000). Furthermore, military intervention to protect citizens of another country or waging a war, imposing sanctions, and other types of intervention are contentious actions. The question is, who decides which country deserves such actions? What is required is an international mechanism for a global consensus on human rights, the rule of law and good governance (Chandler, 2016).

1.8 Conclusion: the interface between tourism and human rights

This chapter has explored the concepts of human rights as a foundation to exploring the relationship between these rights and tourism in the remainder of the book. Although the contemporary concept of human rights has been heavily influenced by European philosophies and cosmologies, ancient civilisations' codes, laws, religions, and moral and ethical teachings have often touched on individual and collective rights from different perspectives. It has often been the case that devastating wars have led to the formation of treaties and organisations, which have resulted in stepping stones towards the notion of human rights, i.e., the Thirty Years War led to the Peace of Westphalia; the League of Nations formed after World War I; and World War II led to the formation of the United Nations. The history of human rights attests to the fact that the concept of human rights is of significance to all human communities; unfortunately however, equality, justice, and human rights are still not afforded to all.

The UDHR stresses that every human being deserves rights to dignity and life, just by virtue of being human. However, this fundamental right may not be honoured, if national or domestic laws do not legally protect citizen's human rights. While human rights and civil rights are closely connected, civil rights are applicable in a national context and govern citizens. While the UDHR is not a binding document, it along with various treaties and covenants (also known as instruments), fall to each nation state as the primary agency responsible for the protection of human rights.

International human rights laws have typically focused on gross human rights violations of states, but individuals have been held to account through agencies such as the ICC. In an era of globalisation, the challenges of protecting human rights are becoming increasingly complex, especially when the crime is committed abroad, or outside a nation state's jurisdiction, leaving limited recourse against such actions. The UDHR is not without criticism. There has been much discourse surrounding the UDHR, and many additions and adjustments have been made through more recent human rights instruments. These discourses, dissenting views, and the latest developments on universal human rights will be introduced and examined throughout the book.

32 Background of human rights in tourism

Tourism intersects with human rights in compounded ways over a wide range of areas explored in the different chapters of this book. On a positive note, tourism has the potential to promote empowerment, provide meaningful employment, and protect the environment. Laws, policies, and strategies developed from a human rights perspective based on the principles of sustainability have the ability to enhance the contributions of tourism towards human rights. On one hand, there is increasing pressure on tourism businesses to create a positive work environment with just pay, and for governments to ensure appropriate regulations on labour conditions. On the other hand, the tourism industry is about making a profit and this can lead to exploitation on a number of different levels, leading to violations of human rights. Tourism has, for example, been criticised for low pay, displacing communities, and exploiting Indigenous Peoples and their culture. Exploitation and discrimination have been the result of not only the actions of the tourism industry, but also of tourists themselves.

The relationship between tourism and human rights goes far beyond just the positive and negative aspects associated with tourism. It is an intricate relationship that covers important topics such as security, privacy, the freedom of movement, and the right to development and the environment. Changing trends in travel patterns and tourist types will undoubtedly impact various human rights issues in destination countries and in the tourism industry. For example, the LGBTQ+ tourist market has made significant gains in recent years, but there remain destinations where homosexuality is illegal. Furthermore, prior to COVID-19, there was a shift in the balance of tourism towards Asian countries beginning to dominate the industry, which in the past was led by Western countries. Tourists and the tourism industry reach across borders where different policies of human rights operate. As noted above, there are major challenges in incorporating international human rights laws and treaties into domestic laws so that all human rights are protected. As the industry continues to evolve, it is of even greater importance for the industry to adopt a human rights approach.

Tourism is also a contributor to climate change which continues to impact those most vulnerable, including tourist destinations in developing countries. It raises the question as to whether the consumption of tourism by those that can afford it, is contributing to climate change and thereby impacting the human rights of those in the destinations. When tourism begins to recover after COVID-19 pandemic, there are opportunities for the industry to further embrace sustainability and human rights but whether that occurs, only time will tell.

The first four chapters of this book establish the foundation for examining human rights in the context of tourism studies, focusing on key concepts of human rights, the operation of tourism enterprises, sustainable development, and the political dynamics of tourism and human rights. Chapters 5 to 13 then provide a narrower focus on specific human rights challenges in tourism and hospitality. Chapter 14 highlights the key contributions of each chapter and poses discussion questions to further the discourse on the relationship between tourism and human rights. It also reflects on the recent COVID-19 pandemic which has not only had unprecedented health and economic impacts but has also introduced a wide range of travel restrictions.

Permissions

1 Box 1.1 is composed of material from The Core International Human Rights Instruments and their monitoring bodies, by Office of the High Commissioner of Human Rights (OHCHR), ©1996–2020, UnitedNations and Universal Human Rights Instruments, by Office of the High Commissioner of Human Rights (OHCHR), ©1996–2020, UnitedNations. Reprinted with the permission of the United Nations.
2 Box 1.3 is composed of material from Human Rights Bodies by Office of the High Commissioner of Human Rights (OHCHR), ©1996-2020 United Nations; Special Procedures of the Human Rights Council by Office of the High Commissioner of Human Rights (OHCHR), ©1996-2020 United Nations; United Nations Human Rights Council , by Office of the High Commissioner of Human Rights (OHCHR), ©1996–2020 United Nations. Reprinted with the permission of the United Nations.

References

Adam, 2018. Is it Legal to Ride an Electric Scooter in the UK. *Honeycomb Lifestyle*. [online] 27 January. Available at: <www.honeycomblifestyle.com/ev/legal-electric-scooter/#europe> [Accessed 19 August 2019].

Ahmad, R., 2019. Islam, Universal Human Rights, and Cairo Declaration. *Al Islam*. [online]. Available at: <www.alislam.org/updates/islam-universal-human-rights-and-cairo-declaration/> [Accessed 2 September 2019].

Amnesty International, 2019. Home. *Amnesty International*. [online]. Available at: <www.amnesty.org/en/> [Accessed 15 December 2019].

Andersen, P., 2011. *Legal Procedure and Practice in Medieval Denmark*. Translated from Danish by Frederik and Sarah Pedersen. Leiden: Brill.

Anjum, F., 2013. Human Rights, Cultural Relativism and Islam, *Journal of Research Society of Pakistan*, 50(2), pp. 160–189.

Azzam, S., 1998. Universal Islamic Declaration of Human Rights. *The International Journal of Human Rights*, 2(3) (Autumn), pp.102–112.

Bailey, P., 2019. The Creation of The Universal Declaration of Human Rights. *Universal Rights Network*. [online]. Available at: <www.universalrights.net/main/creation.htm> [Accessed 9 December 2019].

BBC Click, 2019. E-Scooters: Should they be legal on public roads? *BBC Click*. [video] 19 August 2019. Available at: <www.bbc.com/news/av/technology-49322216/e-scooters-should-they-be-legal-on-public-roads> [Accessed 19 August 2019].

Bielefeldt, H., 1995. Muslim Voices in the Human Rights Debate. *Human Rights Quarterly*, 17(4), pp. 587–617.

Brysk, A., 2019. Introduction: contesting human rights – pathways of change. In: A. Brysk and M. Stohl, (eds.), *Contesting Human Rights Norms, Institutions and Practice*. Cheltenham: Edward Elgar Publishing Limited, pp. 1–11.

Chandler, D., 2016. 7 Contemporary critiques of human rights. In: M. Goodhart, (ed.), *Human Rights: Politics and Practice*, 3rd Edition. Oxford: Oxford University Press, pp. 110–126.

Clapham, A., 2007. *Human Rights: A Very Short Introduction*. Oxford: Oxford University Press.

Conrad, C. and Moore, W., 2010. What Stops the Torture? *American Journal of Political Science*, [online] 54 (2), pp. 459–476. Available at: <www.jstor.org/stable/25652217> [Accessed 8 April 2020].

Conrad, C.R., 2013. Why democracy doesn't always improve human rights. *LSE European Politics and Policy (EUROPP)* [Blog]. 18 October 2013. Available at: <https://scholars.org/contribution/why-democracy-does-not-always-improve-human-rights> [Accessed 8 April 2020].

Convention against Torture and Other Cruel, Inhuman or Degrading Treatment or Punishment, December 10, 1984, 1465 U.N.T.S. 85.

Convention on the Elimination of All Forms of Discrimination against Women, Dec. 18, 1979, 1249 U.N.T.S 13.

Convention on the Rights of Persons with Disabilities, December 13, 2006, 2515 U.N.T.S. 3.

Convention on the Rights of the Child, November 20, 1989, 1577 U.N.T.S. 3.

Council of Europe, 2014. *Report on the Implementation of International Human Rights Treaties in Domestic Law and the Role of Courts.* CDL-A(2014)036. Study No. 690/2012. Available at: <www.venice.coe.int/webforms/documents/default.aspx?pdffile=CDL-AD(2014)036-e>

Cranston, M., 1983. Are There Any Human Rights? *Daedalus: Human Rights (Fall)*, 112(4), pp.1–17. Available at: <www.jstor.org/stable/20024883> [Accessed 18 February 2020].

Davidson, L., 2018/19. Religion, Human Rights and the Problem of Organizational Structure. *The Journal of Human Rights Semi-Annual*, 13(2), Fall 2018–Winter 2019 Issue 26, pp. 49–64. DOI: 10.22096/HR.2019.105272.1098.

Davidson, S., 1993. *Human Rights*. Buckingham: Open University Press.

Department for Transport, 2020. *Future of Transport Regulatory Review: Call for Evidence. Moving Britain Ahead* [pdf] Department for Transport, UK. Available at: <https://assets.publishing.service.gov.uk/government/uploads/system/uploads/attachment_data/file/886686/future-of-transport-regulatory-review-call-for-evidence.pdf> [Accessed 15 June 2020].

Desai, P., 2014. The Language of Rights is Alien to Hindu Religion. *Studia Bioethica*, 7(1), pp. 33–38.

Domaradzki, S., Khvostova, M. and Pupovac, D., 2019. Karel Vasak's Generations of Rights and the Contemporary Human Rights Discourse. *Human Rights Review*, 20(4), pp. 423–443.

Donnelly, J., 2003. *Universal Human Rights in Theory and Practice*, 2nd Edition. New York: Cornell University Press.

Dubow, S., 1992. Afrikaner Nationalism, Apartheid and Conceptualization "Race". *The Journal of African History*, 33(2), pp. 209–237.

Duke, A., 2017. The Use of 'Privileges' in Political Discourse in the Early Modern Low Countries. *Parliaments, Estates and Representation* [e-journal] 37(1), pp.17–31. DOI: 10.1080/02606755.2016.1256130.

Flowers, N., 1999. A Short History of Human Rights. *Human Rights Here and Now: Celebrating the Universal Declaration of Human Rights*. Minneapolis: Human Rights Resource Center.

George, B. and Varghese, V., 2007. Human Rights in Tourism: Conceptualization and Stakeholder Perspectives. *Electronic Journal of Business Ethics and Organization Studies* [e-journal] 12(2), pp. 40–48. Available at: <ejbo.jyu.fi/pdf/ejbo_vol12_no2_pages_40-48.pdf> [Accessed 10 June 2013].

Goodhart, M., 2016. Introduction. In: M. Goodhart, (ed.), *Human Rights: Politics and Practice*, 3rd Edition. Oxford: Oxford University Press, pp. 1–8.

Holmes Armstead Jr., J., 1998. The International Criminal Court: History, Development and Status. *Santa Clara Law Review*, 38(3), pp. 745–835. Available at: <http://digitalcommons.law.scu.edu/lawreview/vol38/iss3/3> [Accessed 2 October 2019].

Holy Bible: The New International Version, 2011. Colorado Spring: Biblica Inc.

Human Rights Watch, 2019. *World Report 2019*. [online]. Available at: <www.hrw.org/sites/default/files/world_report_download/hrw_world_report_2019.pdf> [Accessed 15 December 2019].

Humphreys, S., 2018/19. Human Rights as the Negation of Religious Ethics. *The Journal of Human Rights Semi-Annual*, 13(2), Fall 2018–Winter 2019 Issue 26, pp. 193–204. DOI: 10.22096/HR.2019.105285.1104.

ICC, n.d. Understanding the International Criminal Court [pdf] Available at: <www.icc-cpi.int/iccdocs/PIDS/publications/UICCEng.pdf> [Accessed 1 October 2019].

Ignatieff, M., 2000. I. Human Rights as Politics, II. Human Rights as Idolatry. *The Tanner Lectures on Human Values*. Delivered at Princeton University April 4–7. [online]. Available at: <www.pgil.pk/wp-content/uploads/2014/11/Human-Rights-politics1.pdf> [Accessed 1 October 2019].

Ignatieff, M., 2001. *Human Rights as Politics and Idolatry*. Princeton, NJ: Princeton University Press.

Inter-American Court of Human Rights, 1987. *Habeas Corpus in Emergency Situations* (arts. 27(2), 25(1) and 7(6), Advisory Opinion OC-8/87 of January 30, 1987, Series A, No. 8, para. 18.

International Convention on the Elimination of All Forms of Racial Discrimination, Mar. 7, 1966, 660 U.N.T.S. 195.

International Convention for the Protection of All Persons from Enforced Disappearance, Dec. 20, 2006, 2716 U.N.T.S. 3.

International Convention on the Protection of the Rights of All Migrant Workers and Members of Their Families, Dec. 18, 1990, 2220 U.N.T.S. 3.

International Covenant on Civil and Political Rights, Dec. 16, 1966, 999 U.N.T.S. 171.

International Covenant on Economic, Social and Cultural Rights, Dec. 16, 1966, 993 U.N.T.S. 3.

Ishay, M.R., 2004. *The History of Human Rights: From Ancient Times to the Globalization Era*. Berkeley, CA: University of California Press.

Juul Petersen, M., 2018. Islam and Human Rights: Clash or Compatibility? [blog]. Available at: <https://blogs.lse.ac.uk/religionglobalsociety/2018/06/islam-and-human-rights-clash-or-compatibility/> [Accessed 15 June 2020].

Kalb, J., 2011. The Persistence of Dualism in Human Rights Treaty Implementation. *Yale Law & Policy Review*, 30(1), pp. 71–121. www.jstor.org/stable/23340059.

Kano, K., 2015. Shūkyōteki Jinken no Genzai: Sono Rekishiteki Kei'i to Jirei [Religious Human Rights Today: The History and Case Studies] *Kwansei Gakuin University Journal of Human Rights Studies*, 19, pp. 19–31. [online]. 31 March. Available at: <http://hdl.handle.net/10236/13052> [Accessed 30 September 2019].

Kawamura, S., 2013. Gendai Kokusai Shakai ni Okeru Jinken Kihan no Huhenka ni Kansuru Shakaigaku Riron kara no Kento. *Toyo Hogak* [e-journal] 57(1), pp. 217–236. Available at: <http://id.nii.ac.jp/1060/00006020/> [Accessed 21 September 2019].

Kuhrt, A., 1983. The Cyrus Cylinder and Achaemenid Imperial Policy. *Journal of the Study of the Old Testament*, 8(25), pp. 83–97. DOI: https://journals.sagepub.com/doi/pdf/10.1177/030908928300802507.

Lai P., Jang H., Xu, C. and Xin, S., 2019. The Impact of Low-Cost Carriers on Inbound Tourism of Thailand. *International Journal of Supply Chain Management*, 8(3), pp.

846–853. [online]. Available at: <https://ojs.excelingtech.co.uk/index.php/IJSCM/article/view/2787> [Accessed 14 June 2020].

Lamb, R., 2019. Historicising the Idea of Human Rights. *Political Studies*, 67(1), pp. 100-115. https://doi.org/10.1177/0032321717752516.

League of Nations, 1919. Covenant of the League of Nations, 28 April. *UNHCR RefWorld*. [online]. Available at: <www.refworld.org/docid/3dd8b9854.html> [Accessed 9 December 2019].

Lipka, M. and Majumdar, S., 2019. A Closer Look at How religious Restrictions Have Risen Around the World. *Pew Research Center*. [pdf] 15 July. Available at: <www.pewforum.org/2019/07/15/a-closer-look-at-how-religious-restrictions-have-risen-around-the-world/> [Accessed 17 August 2019].

Macklem, P., 2015. Human Rights in International Law: Three Generations or One? *London Review of International Law*, 3(1), pp. 61–92. https://doi.org/10.1093/lril/lrv001.

Mahler, D. G., Lakner, C., Castaneda Aguilar, A. and Wu, H., 2020. *Updated estimates of the impact of COVID-19 on global poverty The World Bank* [blog] 8 June. Available at: <https://blogs.worldbank.org/opendata/updated-estimates-impact-covid-19-global-poverty> [Accessed 11 June 2020].

Martin, R., 1980. Human Rights and Civil Rights. *Philosophical Studies: An International Journal for Philosophy in the Analytic Tradition*, 37(4), pp. 391–403. www.jstor.org/stable/4319386.

McGregor, S., 2010. The Human Responsibility Movement. *2010 International Cultural Research Network Conference*. Halifax, Nova Scotia, Canada. 2–6 May. [online]. Available at: <www.consultmcgregor.com/documents/research/The_Human_Responsibility_Movement_ppt.pptx.> [Accessed 10 June 2013].

Medina, R., n.d. Introduction by Dr. Rubens Medina. Children's Rights: International and National Laws and Practices. *The Library of Congress*. [online]. Available at: <www.loc.gov/law/help/child-rights/> [Accessed May 2013].

Mendos, L.R., 2019. *State-Sponsored Homophobia 2019 Global Legislation Overview Update. ILGA World*. [pdf] December 2019. Available at: <https://ilga.org/downloads/ILGA_World_State_Sponsored_Homophobia_report_global_legislation_overview_update_December_2019.pdf> [Accessed 12 June 2020].

Moreau, J., 2018. 129 anti-LGBTQ State Bills were Introduced in 2017, New Report Says. *NBC News*. [online] 12 January. Available at: <www.nbcnews.com/feature/nbc-out/129-anti-lgbtq-state-bills-were-introduced-2017-new-report-n837076> [Accessed 17 August 201W9].

Morgan, M.L., (ed.) 2005. *Classics of Moral and Political Theory*, 4th Edition. Indianapolis: Hackett Publishing Company.

Nkyi, E. and Hashimoto, A., 2014. Human rights issues in tourism development. In: R. Sharpley and D.J. Telfer, (eds.), *Tourism and Development: Concepts and Issues*. Bristol: Channel View Publications. Chapter 13.

OHCHR, 2003. *Professional Training Series No. 9. Human Rights in the Administration of Justice: A Manual on Human Rights for Judges, Prosecutors and Lawyers*. New York and Geneva: United Nations.

OHCHR, 2011. *Guiding Principles on Business and Human Rights: Implementing the United Nations 'Protect, Respect and Remedy'*. [online]. Available at: <www.ohchr.org/documents/publications/guidingprinciplesbusinesshr_en.pdf> [Accessed 15 December 2019].

OHCHR, 2012. *Guiding Principles on Extreme Poverty and Human Rights*. [pdf] Geneva: OHCHR. Available at: <www.ohchr.org/Documents/Events/EmergencyMeasures_COVID19.pdf> [Accessed 12 June 2020].

OHCHR, 2016. 30th anniversary of the adoption of the Declaration on the Right to Development by the UN General Assembly on 4 December 1986. *News and Events*. [online] 2 December 2016. Available at: <www.ohchr.org/EN/NewsEvents/Pages/DisplayNews.aspx?NewsID=20973&LangID=E%23sthash.mEAPJbGp.dpuf>

OHCHR, 2018. Universal Human Rights Instruments. [online] 31 December. Available at: <www.ohchr.org/en/professionalinterest/pages/universalhumanrightsinstruments.aspx> [Accessed 7 January 2019].

OHCHR, 2019a. *Special Procedures of the Human Rights Council*. [online] 5 June. Available at <www.ohchr.org/en/HRBodies/SP/Pages/Welcomepage.aspx> [Accessed 9 June 2019].

OHCHR, 2019b. *United Nations Human Rights Council*. [online] 25 May. Available at: <www.ohchr.org/EN/HRBodies/HRC/Pages/Home.aspx> [Accessed 9 June 2019].

OHCHR, 2020a. *Presentation of the Annual Appeal: Statement by Michelle Bachelet, UN High Commissioner for Human Rights*. Available at: <www.ohchr.org/EN/NewsEvents/Pages/DisplayNews.aspx?NewsID=25463&LangID=> [Accessed 20 January 2020].

OHCHR, 2020b. *Emergency Measures and COVID-19: Guidance*. [pdf] Available at: <www.ohchr.org/Documents/Publications/OHCHR_ExtremePovertyandHumanRights_EN.pdf> [Accessed 12 June 2020].

OHCHR, 2020c. *Optional Protocol to the International Covenant on Economic, Social and Cultural Rights*. [online] Available at <www.ohchr.org/EN/ProfessionalInterest/Pages/OPCESCR.aspx>.

OHCHR, n.d. Human Rights Bodies. Available at: <www.ohchr.org/en/hrbodies/Pages/HumanRightsBodies.aspx> [Accessed 9 June 2019].

Optional Protocol to the Convention against Torture and Other Cruel, Inhuman of Degrading Treatment or Punishment, Dec. 18, 2002, 2375 U.N.T.S. 237.

Optional Protocol to the Convention on the Elimination of Discrimination against Women, Oct. 6, 1999, 2131 U.N.T.S. 83.

Optional Protocol to the Convention on the Rights of Persons with Disabilities, Dec. 13, 2006, 2518 U.N.T.S. 283.

Optional Protocol to the Convention on the Rights of the Child on a communication procedure, Dec. 19, 2011, A/RES/66/138.

Optional Protocol to the Convention on the Rights of the Child on the involvement of children in armed conflict, May 25, 2000, 2173 U.N.T.S. 222.

Optional Protocol to the Convention on the Rights of the Child on the sale of children, child prostitution and child pornography, May 25, 2000, 2171 U.N.T.S. 227.

Optional Protocol to the Covenant on Economic, Social, and Cultural Rights, Dec. 10, 2008, C.N.869.2009.

Optional Protocol to the International Covenant on Civil and Political Rights, Dec. 16, 1966, 999 U.N.T.S. 171.

P. (D.) v. S. (C.), [1993] 4 S.C.R. 141.

Péter, L. and Lojkó, M., 2012. The Holy Crown of Hungary, visible and invisible. In: *Hungary's Long Nineteenth Century*. Leiden: Brill, pp. 15–112.

Pocar, F., 2015. Some Thoughts on the Universal Declaration of Human Rights and the "Generations" of Human rights. *Intercultural Human Rights Law Review*, 10(3), pp. 43–53.

Polisi, C.E., 2004. Universal Rights and Cultural Relativisinduism and Islam Deconstructed, *World Affairs* [e-journal] 167(1) (Summer), pp. 41–46. Available at: <www.jstor.org/stable/20672704> [Accessed 30 September 2019].

Ruggie, J.G., 2009. Protect, Respect and Remedy: A United Nations Policy Framework for Business and Human Rights. *Proceedings of the Annual Meeting (American Society of*

International Law) [e-journal] 103, pp. 282–287. Available at: <www.jstor.org/stable/10.5305/procannmeetasil.103.1.0282> [Accessed 30 September 2019].

Schmidt, C.W., 2016. The Civil Rights-Civil Liberties Divide. *Stanford Journal of Civil Rights and Civil Liberties*, 12(1), pp. 1–41.

Schmidt-Leukel, P., 2006. Buddhism and the Idea of Human Rights: Resonances and Dissonances. *Buddhist-Christian Studies*, 26, pp. 33–49. [online]. Available at: <www.jstor.org/stable/4139179> [Accessed 11 October 2019].

Schultz, M., 2008. Falling for Ancient Propaganda: UN Treasure Honors Persian Despot. *Spiegel International*. [online] 15 July. Available at: <www.spiegel.de/international/world/falling-for-ancient-propaganda-un-treasure-honors-persian-despot-a-566027.html> [Accessed 12 July 2020].

Second Optional Protocol to the International Covenant on Civil and Political Rights, aiming at the abolition of the death penalty, Dec. 15, 1989, 1462 U.N.T.S. 414.

Sen, A., 1999. *Development as Freedom*. New York: Anchor.

Shelton, D. L., 2003. An Introduction to the History of International Human Rights Law (2007). *GW Law Faculty Publications & Other Works. Paper 1052*. [online]. Available at: <http://scholarship.law.gwu.edu/faculty_publications/1052> [Accessed 18 February 2020].

Shestack, J.J., 2000. The philosophical foundations of Human Rights. In: J. Symonides (ed.), *Human Rights: Concepts and Standards*. Aldershot: Dartmouth Publishing Company Ltd., pp. 31–66.

Spence, T., 1797. *The rights of infants; or, the imprescriptible right of mothers to such a share of the elements as is sufficient to enable them to suckle and bring up their young in a dialogue between the aristocracy and a mother of children. To which are added, by way of preface and appendix, strictures on Paine's Agrarian justice*. [online]. Early English Books Online Text Creation Partnership, 2011. Available at: <https://quod.lib.umich.edu/e/ecco/004843040.0001.000> [Accessed May 2013].

Spirer, H.F., 1990. Violations of human rights—how many? The statistical problems of measuring such infractions are tough, but statistical science is equal to it. *American Journal of Economics and Sociology*, 49(2), pp. 199–210. [online]. Available at: <www.jstor.org/stable/3487435> [Accessed 18 February 2020].

Srikanth, R. and Chowdhury, E., 2018. Introduction. In: R. Srikanth and E. Chowdhury, (eds.), *Interdisciplinary Approaches to Human Rights: History, Politics, Practice*. New York: Routledge.

Stand up for Human Rights, 2018. *The Universal Declaration of Human Rights 70th Anniversary* [pdf]. Available at: <www.standup4humanrights.org/layout/files/proposals/UDHR70-MediaFactSheet.pdf> [Accessed 9 December 2019].

Tharoor, S., 1999/2000. Are Human Rights Universal? *World Policy Journal*, 16(4), Winter, pp. 1–6. Available at: <www.jstor.org/stable/40209657> [Accessed 30 September 2019].

Tourism Concern, 2019. *Human Rights and Tourism*. [online]. Available at: <www.tourismconcern.org.uk/campaign/human-rights/> [Accessed 17 December 2019].

Transforming Tourism, 2017. Berlin Declaration on "*Transforming Tourism*". [online]. 26 April. Available at: <www.transforming-tourism.org/berlin-declaration-on-transforming-tourism.html> [Accessed 30 April 2017].

Tremblay, R., Kelly, J., Lipson, M. and Mayer, J.F., 2008. *Understanding Human Rights: Origins, Currents, and Critiques*. Toronto: Thomson Nelson.

UN, 1990. *Cairo Declaration on Human Rights in Islam, Aug. 5, 1990, U.N. GAOR, World Conf. on Hum. Rts., 4th Sess., Agenda Item 5, U.N. Doc. A/CONF.157/PC/62/Add.18 (1993)* [English translation]. [online]. Available at: <http://hrlibrary.umn.edu/instree/cairodeclaration.html> [Accessed 2 September 2019].

UN, 2003. Rome Statute of International Criminal Code. *Codification Division, Office of Legal Affairs*. [online]. Available at: <https://legal.un.org/icc/index.html> [Accessed 9 December 2019].

UN, n.d. *Shaping our Future Together*. [online]. Available at: <www.un.org/en/sections/universal-declaration/human-rights-law/index.html> [Accessed 12 December 2019].

United for Human Rights, 2019. *A Brief History of Human Rights: The Cyrus Cylinder (539 BC)*. [online]. Available at: <www.humanrights.com/what-are-human-rights/brief-history/>

Universal Declaration of Human Rights, G.A. Res. 217 (III) A, U.N. Doc. A/RES/217(III) (Dec. 10, 1948).

UNWTO, 2020a. *UNWTO World Tourism Barometer and Statistical Annex, January 2020*. [online]. Available at: <https://doi.org/10.18111/wtobarometereng> [Accessed 11 June 2020].

UNWTO, 2020b. *UNWTO World Tourism Barometer and Statistical Annex May 2020. Special focus on the Impact of COVID-19*. [online]. Available at: <https://doi.org/10.18111/wtobarometereng> [Accessed 11 June 2020].

van der Vyver, J.D., 1979. The Concept of Human Rights: Its History, Contents and Meaning. In: C.F. Forsyth and J.E. Schiller, (eds.), *Human Rights: The Cape Town Conference: Proceedings of the First International Human Rights Conference on Human Rights in South Africa*, 22–26, January 1979. Cape Town: Juta & Company Ltd., pp. 10–32.

Van Gelderen, M., 2002. *The Political Thought of the Dutch Revolt 1555–1590 (Vol. 23)*. Cambridge: Cambridge University Press.

Vašák, K., 1977. Human Rights: A Thirty-Year Struggle: The Sustained Efforts to give Force of law to the Universal Declaration of Human Rights. *UNESCO Courier*, 11, pp. 29–32. [pdf] Available at: <https://unesdoc.unesco.org/ark:/48223/pf0000074816> [Accessed 1 December 2019].

Venkatesan. R., 2019. The UN Framework on Business and Human Rights: A Workers' Rights Critique. *Journal of Business Ethics*, 157, pp. 635–652. DOI: https://doi.org/10.1007/s10551-017-3664-6.

World Economic Forum, 2019. *Asia-Pacific Travel and Tourism Competitiveness Index 2019*. Available at: <http://reports.weforum.org/travel-and-tourism-competitiveness-report-2019/regional-profiles/asia/?doing_wp_cron=1576098763.0799560546875000000000> [Accessed 11 December 2019].

Xie, J. and Tveterås, S., 2020. Economic Drivers for the Chinese Tourists. *Scandinavian Journal of Hospitality and Tourism*, 20(2), pp. 110–125. DOI: https://doi.org/10.1080/15022250.2020.1734076.

2
TOURISM ENTERPRISES AND HUMAN RIGHTS

2.1 Tourism enterprises and human rights – an introduction

The travel and tourism sector has been a major economic force in the world economy. Tourism enterprises contribute directly and indirectly to the economy by hiring workers, paying taxes, investing in infrastructure and purchasing goods and services from a multitude of suppliers, who in their turn buy goods and services from other suppliers further up the supply chain. The induced impact of the travel and tourism sector to domestic expenditure, sales, cumulative employment and local taxes is even more substantial and affects almost every sector in the economy. In 2019, the direct economic impact of the sector was estimated at 3.2% of global GDP. The total contribution of the travel and tourism sector, including indirect (investments, purchases from suppliers) and induced effects (household spending of income earned by direct and indirect employees), was estimated at 10.3% of GDP (World Travel and Tourism Council, 2020). The rapid decline of the industry due to COVID-19 in 2020 has illustrated how important the tourism industry is for the economy in many destinations (see Chapter 14 for further discussion on the impacts of COVID-19). In addition to generating a profit for their owners and having a considerable economic impact on the global economy, tourism enterprises can have positive social and environmental effects through their activities.

> The International Labour Organization (ILO) has noted that "[t]ourism is an important driving force of inclusive socio-economic development, with significant potential to stimulate enterprise and job creation, and facilitate the development of infrastructure and public services. Tourism directly and indirectly contributes to job creation, particularly for women and young people, while fuelling growth through micro-, small and medium enterprises…".
>
> *(2017, p. 1)*

However, there is also concern that tourism enterprises contribute to human rights violation through active participation or through aiding and abetting violations.

> Telfer and Sharpley have drawn attention to the existence of a "tourism development dilemma" in developing countries; "tourism undoubtedly represents a potentially attractive (and frequently the only viable) means of stimulating social and economic development in destination areas and nations, yet frequently that development fails to materialize, benefits only local elites or is achieved at significant economic, social or environmental cost to local communities. The dilemma for many developing countries, therefore, lies in the challenge of accepting or managing such negative consequences for the potential longer-term benefits offered by tourism development".
>
> *(Telfer and Sharpley, 2016, p. 4)*

In this chapter, the aim is to give a foundation for discussing the involvement of tourism enterprises in the global human rights agenda. It is important to note that out of the 330 million direct and indirect jobs worldwide in the tourism and hospitality industry (pre-COVID-19), a majority of the jobs were in tourism enterprises classified as micro, small and medium sized enterprises, with less than 50 employees (ILO, 2020; World Travel and Tourism Council, 2020). A fundamental question raised in Section 2.2 is if there is a moral or legal responsibility for tourism businesses to improve conditions in the countries where they operate. The section contains an overview of the history and current debate on the purposes of business enterprises. In the two following sections, the evolution of voluntary human rights guidelines for business enterprises is discussed in Section 2.3, while legally enforceable human rights rules affecting tourism businesses are discussed in Section 2.4. The chapter continues with an introduction to jurisdictional issues in Section 2.5. The section gives an overview of the principles in international public law determining *when* a country is allowed to regulate an activity and *where* it can enforce its laws. Questions relating to jurisdiction are of particular importance for tourism businesses, which often operate in several different jurisdictions. Finally, some concluding remarks on tourism enterprises and responsibility for human rights violations are included in Section 2.6.

2.2 Should tourism enterprises be held responsible for human rights violations?

Apart from the smallest micro enterprises, a tourism business is often organized in a legal entity, separate from its owners. This legal entity can take different forms, from close, private, public or publicly listed corporations, to limited companies, limited liability companies and similar legal forms, depending on the country of origin. Regardless of the business form, there is usually one common trait; that the legal entity is separate from the physical persons who are in charge of the entity. Multi-national tourism enterprises are almost always organized as corporations.

Corporations are artificial persons, with powers conferred to them by national legislatures. The granting of powers and capabilities to a corporation has throughout history been accompanied by certain responsibilities. In the 1850s, the North Carolina Supreme Court stated that "[t]he purpose in making all corporations is the accomplishment of some public good … unless the public are to be benefited, it is no more lawful to confer "exclusive rights and privileges" upon an artificial body than upon a private citizen" (Mills v. Williams, p. 561). Davis (1897, p. 290) noted early on that corporations find justification for their existence in the society's notion that public welfare is materially promoted by the pursuit of private interest in the corporate form. In modern times, the creation of corporations has been linked to lower production costs, technological innovation, economic growth as well as higher living standards (Wright, 2010; Pepelasis and Emmanouilidi, 2013). Corporations have thus been credited not only with providing the founders with prosperity, but also with contributing to the development and prosperity of the society as a whole.

A difficulty in the use of the corporate form and the granting of powers and capabilities to corporations has throughout history been the reconciliation of the private motive and the public purpose of the activity exercised within the corporation (Davis, 1897, p. 290). The debate has often been framed as a struggle between shareholder primacy, where the purpose of the corporation is to produce a profit for the shareholders, and stakeholder primacy, where the corporation shall be operated for the benefit of shareholders, but also for the benefit of other stakeholders, such as employees, customers, local residents or other actors affected by the activities of the corporation.

> The reconciliation of the private motive and the public purpose of corporations was famously litigated at the turn of the 20th century in the United States case *Dodge v. Ford Motor Co.* After several successful years of assembling and manufacturing cars, the president and majority owner of the Ford Motor Co., Henry Ford, declared that it was the new policy of the company to not pay any future special dividends to shareholders, but to put back the money into the corporation. The company continued to pay its regular dividends of 60 per cent yearly upon the capital stock of the company. The declaration of the future policy was published in the press throughout the United States, where Mr. Ford declared that: [m]y ambition … is to employ still more men; to spread the benefits of this industrial system to the greatest possible number, to help them build up their lives and their homes" (p. 468). Two minority shareholders objected to the policy and pointed out that the company had more than 100 million in surplus capital. The Michigan Supreme Court ruled for the minority shareholders, and stated that: "[t]he difference between an incidental humanitarian expenditure of corporate funds for the benefit of the employés, like the building of a hospital for their use and the employment of agencies for the betterment of their condition, and a general purpose and plan to benefit mankind at the expense

of others, is obvious. There should be no confusion (of which there is evidence) of the duties which Mr. Ford conceives that he and the stockholders owe to the general public and the duties which in law he and his codirectors owe to protesting minority stockholders. A business corporation is organized and carried on primarily for the profit of the stockholders. The powers of the directors are to be employed for that end. The discretion of directors is to be exercised in the choice of means to attain that end, and does not extend to a change in the end itself, to the reduction of profits, or to the nondistribution of profits among stockholders in order to devote them to other purposes".

(Dodge v. Ford Motor Co., pp. 506–507)

Proponents of free market reforms have argued that reliance on market forces within an open economy is fundamental for economic growth and social progress (Balcerowicz and Fischer, 2006; Shleifer, 2009). The idea of free markets is connected to the principle of shareholder primacy, where the primary responsibility of managers of the corporation is to the shareholders of the corporation. One of the most influential economists of the 20th century, Milton Friedman, famously argued that "there is one and only one social responsibility of business- to use its resources and engage in activities designed to increase its profits so long as it stays within the rules of the game, which is to say, engages in open and free competition without deception or fraud" (Friedman, 1970, p. 124). Corporate social responsibility (CSR) is acceptable according to the free-market approach only to achieve economic objectives and ultimately wealth creation within the corporation (Garriga and Melé, 2004, p. 53).

The free-market, liberal approach has not gone unchallenged. It has been argued that the purpose of the management of corporations, and particularly of large corporations, is not only to increase the profits as much as possible but also to contribute to society with their business. Bowen, who is considered as one of the seminal authors on CSR, has defined *social responsibilities of businessmen* as the obligations of businessmen "to pursue those policies, to make those decisions, or to follow those lines of action which are desirable in terms of the objectives and values of our society" (1953, p. 6). The *doctrine of social responsibility* rests on the idea that a voluntary assumption of social responsibility by businesses could aid us in reaching the goal of ameliorating economic problems and attaining the societal goals we seek as a society (Bowen, 1953, pp. 6–8).

At the European Union (EU) level, CSR was promoted in the 2001 Green Paper on Corporate Social Responsibility as a voluntary initiative which will help companies to save costs, contribute to higher levels of occupational safety and health leading to increased competitiveness and profitability (Commission of the European Communities, 2001). Ten years later, the European Commission (2011) published an updated EU Corporate Social Responsibility strategy promoting a "modern understanding of corporate social responsibility". In the new strategy document the Commission focuses on both the public as well as private interests of companies. The European Commission states for example that "[h]elping to mitigate the social effects of the current economic crisis, including job losses, is part of the social responsibility of enterprises" (2011, p. 3). To meet their CSR, companies should "integrate social, environmental, ethical, human rights and consumer concerns into their business operations" (2011, p. 6).

In 2014, the United States committed to developing a similar national action plan on CSR as in the EU. The National Action Plan on Responsible Business Conduct (RBC) was published two years later in 2016 (The Secretary of State, 2016). The role of governments according to the RBC is to provide guidance and encouragement to businesses through several different initiatives, consisting of laws, policies, programmes and other initiatives to promote the responsible operation and respect of human rights. The RBC does not contain any legal requirements on corporations to engage in CSR activities. Instead, India became in 2014 the first country in the world to include mandatory CSR requirements in its company law. Large companies with a certain net worth, turnover or net profit shall according to the Indian Companies Act (2013) constitute a CSR Committee of the Board, which shall formulate a CSR policy with activities to be undertaken by the company. In addition, the board shall ensure that the company spends at least 2 percent of the average net profits (on a comply or explain basis) in pursuance of its CSR policy. Preference shall be given to local area and areas where the company operates (§ 135).

In addition to national initiatives, there are several internationally recognized frameworks and principles guiding the corporate social responsibility approaches of companies. One of the most notable initiatives is the OECD Guidelines for Multinational Enterprises, first adopted in 1976 (OECD, 1976). The guidelines consist of recommendations from governments on how multinational corporations should conduct their business in a responsible way in a global context. In 2011, the OECD included a new human rights chapter to the guidelines, thus further putting an emphasis on the role enterprises have in preventing and mitigating human rights violations (OECD, 2011).

2.3 The evolvement of voluntary human rights guidelines for corporations

International human rights have traditionally been developed and enforced by states. According to international law, states must protect against human rights abuses on their territory. The globalization of the world economy is however making it difficult for nation-states to enforce their laws in all circumstances. International undertakings, with increasingly complicated organizational structures and turnovers rivalling the GDP of many countries, are becoming important economic, political, environmental and social actors. This has in its turn led to a movement towards involving businesses in the fight against human rights violations (Härkönen, 2018). The involvement of private actors in the development of human rights is especially important in the tourism sector. Businesses in the tourism sector have the potential to provide and spread wealth to different parts of the population through job opportunities and direct foreign investment in destination countries. However, tourism development can also exacerbate poverty in destination countries and tourism businesses can contribute to the violation of human rights.

In the 1990s, the issue of involving corporations on a more direct basis in the struggle to end human rights abuses became prominent, mainly as a result of the activities of businesses in the oil, gas and mining sector. In 2005, the UN Secretary-General decided to appoint John Ruggie as a Special Representative, with the task to clarify "the roles and responsibilities of states, companies and other social actors in the business and human rights sphere" (Ruggie, 2010). Three years later, the Special Representative presented the "Protect, Respect and Remedy" Framework to the UN Human Rights Council. The Framework rests on three pillars, all focused on the relationship between corporations and victims of human rights violations (see Box 2.1).

BOX 2.1 PROTECT, RESPECT AND REMEDY FRAMEWORK

1) The state duty to protect against human rights abuses by third parties, including businesses, through appropriate policies, regulation and adjudication,
2) The corporate responsibility to respect human rights and
3) Greater access by victims to an effective remedy.

Source: (Human Rights Council, 2008).[1]

The UN Human Rights Council unanimously approved the framework in 2008, at the same time as it extended the Special Representative's mandate until 2011, with the task to operationalize and promote the framework (Human Rights Council, 2008; United Nations General Assembly, 2010). In March 2011, the Special Representative published the United Nations Guiding Principles on Business and Human Rights (UNGP) (Human Rights Council, 2011; United Nations, 2011), implementing the three pillars from the framework. The UN Human Rights Council endorsed the UNGP in June 2011, making the UNGP the first universally accepted principles addressing human rights abuses by corporations (Office of the High Commissioner for Human Rights, 2011). The principles are applicable to all enterprises, regardless of their size or location. However, the actions required can vary according to size, sector, operational context, ownership and structure (principle no.14). The principles do not create any new international human rights law obligations, or limit or undermine any legal obligations under international law. They can thus be classified as non-binding soft law. However, both the "Protect, Respect and Remedy" framework and the UNGP have been endorsed at the regional and national levels by various intergovernmental organizations and countries (Ruggie, 2011). For example, the European Commission has stated that it expects all European businesses to respect human rights, as defined in the UNGP (European Commission, 2011, p. 14).

The first chapter of the UNGP addresses foundational and operational principles, focusing on the state duty to protect affected individuals and communities against human rights abuses by business enterprises (principles no. 1–10). The second chapter addresses the duty of businesses to respect human rights (principles no. 11–24), while the third and final chapter consists of principles enumerating state and business duties to provide access to a remedy for victims of human right abuses (principles no. 25–31). Businesses should according to the second chapter avoid causing or contributing to adverse human rights impacts, address such impacts when they occur and seek to prevent and mitigate adverse human rights impacts directly linked to their operations (principle no. 13). Businesses should also have in place appropriate policies and due diligence processes to identify, prevent, mitigate and account for human rights impacts as well as processes to enable remediation (principle no. 15). In addition, businesses should express their commitment to respect human rights in a publicly available statement of policy, which is embedded in the business enterprise and approved at the most senior level of the business (principle no. 16). In order to verify whether adverse human rights impacts are being addressed, businesses should track the effectiveness of the implementation of their policies as well as their response to reported human rights impacts (principle no. 20). Business enterprises should also be prepared to communicate externally how they address their human rights impacts. Such communication can according to the principles take various forms, with an expectation of formal reporting "where risks of severe human rights impacts exist, whether this is due to the nature of the business operations or the operating contexts" (principle no. 21).

In addition to the UNGP, there are several other international human rights instruments addressing businesses and the impact they have in the countries where they operate. In particular, the UN Global Compact, which was launched in 2000, has evolved into the world's largest initiative on corporate policy in the field of human rights. The ten principles of UN Global Compact are derived from fundamental human rights documents, such as the Universal Declaration of Human Rights (1948), the Declaration on Fundamental Principles and Rights at Work (1998), the Rio Declaration on Environment and Development (1992) and the United Nations Convention against Corruption (2003). The focus is on four key areas; human rights, labour conditions, environment and anti-corruption.

BOX 2.2 THE TEN PRINCIPLES OF THE UNITED NATIONS GLOBAL COMPACT

Human Rights

- *Principle 1*: Businesses should support and respect the protection of internationally proclaimed human rights; and
- *Principle 2*: make sure that they are not complicit in human rights abuses.

Labour

- *Principle 3*: Businesses should uphold the freedom of association and the effective recognition of the right to collective bargaining;
- *Principle 4*: the elimination of all forms of forced and compulsory labour;
- *Principle 5*: the effective abolition of child labour; and
- *Principle 6*: the elimination of discrimination in respect of employment and occupation.

Environment

- *Principle 7*: Businesses should support a precautionary approach to environmental challenges;
- *Principle 8*: undertake initiatives to promote greater environmental responsibility; and
- *Principle 9*: encourage the development and diffusion of environmentally friendly technologies.

Anti-corruption

- *Principle 10*: Businesses should work against corruption in all its forms, including extortion and bribery.

Source: (United Nations Global Compact Progress Report, 2018).[2]

In 2019, the ten principles of the UN Global Compact had been adopted by more than 10 000 companies in 159 countries. More than 68 million people were working in the private sector for a UN Global Compact participant. In addition, the UN Global Compact had more than 3000 non-business signatories (United Nations Global Compact, 2019, pp. 114–115). Among the signatories, there is a wide variety of tourism enterprises, from accommodation enterprises (such as Hilton Worldwide, InterContinental Hotels Group and AccorHotels) transportation enterprises (such as Air Canada, Air France-KLM, Air New Zealand, Finnair, Iberia, Japan Airlines, SAS and United Airlines) to other travel and leisure enterprises (such as Carlson, TUI AG and American Express Global Business Travel). In total, 280 companies in the travel and leisure sector are participants of the UN Global Compact (United Nations Global Compact, 2020).

The participants of the UN Global Compact commit to making the ten principles an integral part of their business as well as making annual financial contributions to the work of the UN Global Compact. In addition, participants are required to submit an annual communication on progress (COP) report, which is shared with the participants's stakeholders and published in the Global Compact database. If a participant fails to submit a COP report in time, its status is changed to non-communicating. If the requirements are not fulfilled within a year of becoming a non-communicating participant, the undertaking is expelled from the Global Compact (United Nations Global Compact, 2012).

In addition to voluntary human rights guiding principles applicable to all enterprises, the United Nations World Tourism Organization (UNWTO) adopted in 1999 a Global Code of Ethics for Tourism (GCET). The GCET incorporates many of the principles of international human rights law in its principles. Tourism activities should promote human rights and in particular, the individual rights of the most vulnerable groups, such as children, the elderly, the handicapped, ethnic minorities and Indigenous Peoples (art. 2(2)). In the event of a dispute concerning the interpretation or application of the GCET, two or more tourism stakeholders may jointly submit the matter to the World Committee on Tourism Ethics for dispute settlement. The committee shall then submit its recommendations on the settlement of the dispute to the parties. However, the committee has no enforcement powers. If one or more of the parties to the dispute refuse to implement the recommendations, the committee can only take action by holding renewed consultations with the parties or by issuing a press release containing its conclusions (World Committee on Tourism Ethics, n.d.).

The soft law status of voluntary codes has been criticized by commentators, who point to the practice of corporations who publicly commit to voluntary human rights guidelines but do not incorporate them into their business models (Mock, 2000; Etzioni, 2010; Park, 2014; Härkönen, 2018). As a result of the problems with voluntary corporate human rights obligations, human rights proponents have increasingly focused their attention on legally binding corporate human rights obligations as the next step in the evolution of corporate human rights obligations. This can be done in the form of international human rights conventions, which become legally binding for the states who ratify such conventions. For example, the UNWTO did in 2019 approve a proposal from the World Committee on Tourism Ethics to convert the aforementioned GCET into an international convention, in order to make it more effective (Framework Convention on Tourism Ethics, 2019). Legally binding human rights obligations can also be adopted at the national level, in laws and other regulations. This is the topic of the next section.

2.4 Legally enforceable corporate human rights obligations

In addition to international principles addressing the responsibility corporations have to respect human rights, human rights are often protected at the national level. In Chapter 1, a distinction was made between human rights, articulated in international human rights documents, and civil rights, articulated in national legislation. In this book, we are focusing on both international and national legislation covering human rights, thus covering both human and civil rights. Business accountability can, in addition to voluntary measures, be achieved through criminal liability, civil liability and transparency legislation. This type of legislation is generally adopted at the national level (see however the discussion on the International Criminal Court, ICC, in Chapter 1). Criminal liability involves state prosecution for acts that have been classified as crimes. Civil liability on the other hand involves individuals or businesses that in the legal system can obtain redress for injuries they have sustained as a result of another person's conduct, while transparency regulation involves the mandatory publication of certain facts in a corporation's annual reports or similar documents.

Corporate criminal liability can either be directed towards the corporate structure, in jurisdictions acknowledging corporate criminal liability, or encompass the board of directors and managers of the corporation, in their personal capacity (Härkönen, 2018). The concept of corporate criminal liability was recognized early on in common law countries (Criminal Law Act of 1827, England & Wales; the Queen v. Great North of England Railway Co., 1846; N.Y. Cent. & Hudson River v. United States, 1909; Gilchrist, 2012), while civil law countries were more hesitant to the idea of holding corporations criminally responsible. However, since the 1970s, more and more civil law countries have embraced the concept. Corporate criminal liability provisions have for example been introduced in the Netherlands in 1976, Norway in 1991, France in 1994, Finland in 1995, Denmark in 1996, Iceland in 1998, Belgium in 1999, Slovenia in 1999, Estonia in 2001, Poland in 2002, Lithuania in 2002, Spain in 2003, Romania in 2004, Austria in 2006, Portugal in 2007 (limited in 1984), and Luxembourg in 2010 (European Council, 1988; Swedish Government, 1997; Gobert and Pascal, 2011; Härkönen, 2015b).

Some countries still reject the concept of corporate criminal liability, arguing that criminal law is a reflection of the moral values in society. Since only physical persons can have a conscience and understand moral values, corporations should not be held criminally responsible for the conduct of individuals. In Sweden, for example, human rights violations committed in a business context are attributed to the persons in charge in their personal capabilities. The board of directors or the chief executive officer can for example be held liable for corporate human rights violations (Härkönen, 2015b).

Corporate civil liability is a less invasive procedure than attaching criminal liability to corporate conduct. Corporate civil liability was acknowledged in the United States courts in the late 19th century in two cases concerning banks and employees who had misappropriated funds. In both cases the United States Supreme Court held that the actions of the employees could be attributed to the bank, thus holding the bank liable for the loss (Merchants Nat. Bank v. State Nat. Bank, 1870; First Nat'l Bank of Carlisle v. Graham, 1879). There are several advantages with civil liability, compared to corporate criminal liability, from a procedural perspective. Firstly, the burden of proof is lower in a civil case, often requiring that the conduct is "more likely than not", while the criminal system requires that the conduct is proven "beyond reasonable doubt". It can be argued that human rights crimes, which are notoriously difficult to prove, are best enforced in the civil system with its lesser burden of proof. Furthermore, a civil case verdict can provide for monetary compensation to the victims, who often suffer from a lack of opportunities and a lack of access to other means of support (Härkönen, 2015a).

More recently, it seems that the preferred mode of regulation in the context of business responsibility for human rights violations is regulation requiring mandatory corporate disclosures. Normally, disclosure regulation does not require businesses to commit to any risk assessments, due diligence procedures or preventive measures. Instead, such regulation requires businesses to disclose if they work with human rights issues in the corporate context. Transparency has long been hailed as an efficient method of nudging businesses towards more sustainable business models where human rights violations are not tolerated in the business entity or its supply chains. Empirical evidence by Kaufmann and Bellver (2005) shows that transparency is associated with better human development and socio-economic indicators, lower corruption and higher competitiveness. A weakness with transparency regulation is however that such regulation is dependent on investors who require a certain business conduct, or consumers, who take action, when the information is disclosed (Etzioni, 2010, p. 392; Härkönen, 2018). Transparency regulation is therefore an effective tool to regulate behaviour in sectors with many end-users but may be less efficient in industries where the business is not affected by consumer or shareholder sentiments. Tourism could be categorized as a business sector, which is highly dependent on end-users, i.e., tourists. If a tourism destination or a tourism enterprise becomes known for human rights violations, there is a great likelihood that tourists choose to direct their business elsewhere. Transparency regulation thus has the potential to become an efficient tool in the fight against human rights violations in the tourism sector.

Formal reporting has been established in many fields, where the society has deemed there to be an unethical or otherwise unwanted corporate behavioural pattern. Non-financial reporting requirements can be divided into general CSR transparency requirements and targeted CSR transparency requirements. The EU non-financial reporting directive is an example of a general CSR transparency regulation (European Parliament and the Council directive 2014/95, 2014). Large undertakings exceeding an average number of 500 employees, which are considered public interest entities, are required to publish a non-financial statement according to the directive. The statement shall contain information on the business entity's "development, performance, position and impact of its activity, relating to, as a minimum, environmental, social and employee matters, respect for human rights, anti-corruption and bribery matters" (art. 19a). The requirements were applied for the first time for the financial year starting in 2017 (art. 4).

There are also several regulatory initiatives, focusing specifically on human rights disclosures. The UK Modern Slavery Act (2015) requires UK commercial organizations of a certain size to prepare "a statement of the steps the organisation has taken during the financial year to ensure that slavery and human trafficking is not taking place – (i) in any of its supply chains, and (ii) in any part of its own business". It is also possible to publish a statement that the organization has not taken any steps to ensure that slavery and human trafficking has not taken place in the organization or in its supply chains (s. 54). Similarly, the California Transparency in Supply Chains Act requires California-based large retailers and manufacturers to provide consumers information on their efforts to eradicate slavery and human trafficking (California Senate, 2010).

Other targeted human rights disclosure regulations include the EU regulation on conflict minerals, which requires importers of conflict minerals to disclose their supply chain policy. In addition to committing to mandatory disclosures, importers are required to identify and assess the risks for adverse impacts, implement a strategy to prevent adverse impacts and carry out third-party audits of their supply chains (European Parliament and the Council regulation 2017/821, 2017; Härkönen, 2018). The French "Duty of Vigilance law" of 2017 (loi no 2017–399 relative au devoir de vigilance des sociétés mères et entreprises donneuses d'ordre) is similar to the EU conflict minerals regulation in that it covers both disclosures and contains additional requirements on business entities. Large enterprises are required to establish a publicly disclosed vigilance plan, including due diligence measures to identify risk areas and prevent serious harm to human rights and fundamental freedoms, human health and safety and the environment.

> The French Duty of Vigilance Law seems to have had an effect in the actions taken by tourism companies subject to the obligations of the law. The Air France-KLM Group (2020) for example has included a section dedicated to "Monitoring of Act No. 2017–399 known as the Duty of Vigilance Law" in its Universal Registration Document. The company undertakes to "scrupulously respect Human Rights, oppose child and forced labour, apply laws and ask its service providers and suppliers to uphold these principles." It states that "[s]ince 2018, in response to the regulatory requirements, the Group has implemented a vigilance plan in compliance with the legal provisions, it being understood that the Group already had processes in place enabling it to comply directly or indirectly with the requirements of the new Act. In particular, having established verification processes in the areas required to be covered by the vigilance plan, the Group has ensured that it is in a position to benefit, as effectively as possible, from the contributions of its various entities" (p. 214). The company also notes that a supplier selection process has been implemented to respond to the duty of vigilance requirements. For all new contracts, suppliers have to commit to environmental, social, ethical and supply chains sustainability. Suppliers in risk areas are asked to submit an evaluation of their sustainability performance. Independent audits may also be conducted. In 2019, 414 suppliers had their sustainability performance evaluated at the company's request.

The French law is the first law with such a broad objective in the field of human rights. Hitherto, all laws have either targeted specific problems, like the conflict minerals supply chain, or only required disclosures, without any required actions on the part of the business entity, like the EU non-financial reporting directive.

As mentioned in Section 2.3, in addition to mandatory transparency legislation, tourism businesses can adopt voluntary guidelines, undergo voluntary certification procedures or follow recommendations for businesses that aspire to improve the approach of the corporation to human rights. The Global Reporting Initiative (GRI), developed by U.S. non-profit organizations, publishes a widely used set of sustainability reporting standards covering economic, environment and social reporting (GRI, 2019). Furthermore, in an effort to help companies report on their compliance with the UNGP, the United Nations launched in 2015 a comprehensive guidance for companies on human rights issues reporting. The UN Guiding Principles Reporting Framework (UNGPRF) consists of three parts; a set of human rights related questions a business entity should strive to answer and disclose in its corporate social responsibility reporting, an implementation guidance and an assurance guidance for auditors and external assessors (Shift & Mazars, 2015; 2017). The UNGPRF project also includes a searchable database (actively maintained until March 2020), where users can view how the disclosures of the world's largest companies compare to the expectations of the UNGPRF.

2.5 Jurisdiction over corporate human rights violations

According to international public law, the right to adopt legislation and prosecute crimes is dependent on the interests the country has in the matter. This interest shall be weighed against the interests of other countries in the same matter (Härkönen, 2012). The territorial principle, allowing states to adopt laws and prosecute offences where the constituent acts occur on territory controlled by a state, is a fundamental principle of international law. Many human rights offences discussed in this book are litigated under the territorial principle. In addition to the territorial principle, states can also claim jurisdiction over matters which take place outside its territorial boundaries, so called extraterritorial jurisdiction.

> In the case of the S.S. Lotus (France v. Turkey, 1927), a French steamer, Lotus, collided with a Turkish steamer, Boz-Kourt, on the high seas. The Turkish vessel sank, and eight Turkish sailors and passengers died. The French captain was later prosecuted in Turkey for involuntary manslaughter. France objected to the prosecution, since the collision took place on the high seas and the offence was committed by a French national outside the territorial boundaries of Turkey. Both Turkey and France agreed to let the Permanent Court of International Justice solve the jurisdictional dispute. The court declared that failing a permissive rule to the contrary, derived from international custom or a convention, a state may not exercise its power in any form inside the territory of another state (¶45). However, it does not follow that international law prohibits a state from exercising jurisdiction in its own territory, in respect of a case which relates to acts taken place abroad, unless permitted

by international law. On the contrary, a state has wide discretion in how it exercises its jurisdiction in its own territory, only limited by prohibitions in international law. Each state remains free to adopt jurisdictional principles, which it regards as best and most suitable (¶46).

There are several accepted principles for when extraterritorially applicable laws and prosecution of human rights offences are accepted according to international public law (Harvard Research in International Law, 1935; see Chapter 4). According to international public law, states can claim jurisdiction over extraterritorial offences according to *the nationality principle*, when the perpetrator of the human rights offence is a national of the state in question. It is thus acceptable to prosecute a national in his/her country of origin even if the offence took place in another country. Many states have chosen to prosecute tourism-related offences, such as child sex tourism and human trafficking offences, according to the nationality principle (see Chapter 13). According to *the protective principle*, states can also assert jurisdiction over offences where the security, territorial integrity or political independence of the state is threatened. The protective principle is seldom applicable in cases involving the tourism sector. Additionally, some states assert jurisdiction over an offence according to *the passive personality principle*, when the victim of the offence is a national of the state. Finally, some offences are so blameworthy that any state can assert jurisdiction over the perpetrators, according to *the principle of universal jurisdiction*. Under international public law, universal jurisdiction can be asserted over piracy, war crimes, crimes against humanity, genocide and torture. Some countries have prosecuted other crimes, such as child sex tourism crimes, under universal jurisdiction (Härkönen, 2015), but it is doubtful if such assertions of jurisdiction constitute an accepted practice according to international public law.

> The Council of Europe Convention on Action against Trafficking in Human Beings (2005) provides an example of jurisdictional clauses in international conventions.
>
> Each party shall adopt such legislative and other measures as may be necessary to establish jurisdiction over any offence established in accordance with this Convention, when the offence is committed:
>
> a in its territory; or
> b on board a ship flying the flag of that Party; or
> c on board an aircraft registered under the laws of that party; or
> d by one of its nationals or by a stateless person who has his or her habitual residence in its territory, if the offence is punishable under criminal law where it was committed or if the offence is committed outside the territorial jurisdiction of any State;
> e against one of its nationals.
>
> *(Art. 31(1))*

Corporate liability is a more recent addition to international conventions and many conventions do not contain any sections on corporate liability. However, when such rules are added to conventions, they follow the general rules on jurisdiction. A corporation can thus be held liable for offences committed on the territory of the state asserting jurisdiction or in their state of origin. Corporate liability usually attaches to business entities when a person in a leading position either commits or approves of the offence.

> The Council of Europe Convention on Action against Trafficking in Human Beings (2005) provides an example of corporate criminal liability clauses in international conventions.
>
> "1. Each Party shall adopt such legislative and other measures as may be necessary to ensure that a legal person can be held liable for a criminal offence established in accordance with this Convention, committed for its benefit by any natural person, acting either individually or as a part of an organ of the legal person, who has a leading position within the legal person, based on:
>
> a a power of representation of the legal person;
> b an authority to take decisions on behalf of the legal person;
> c an authority to exercise control within the legal person.
>
> 2. Apart from the cases already provided for in paragraph 1, each Party shall take measures necessary to ensure that a legal person can be held liable where the lack of supervision or control by a natural person referred to in paragraph 1 has made possible the commission of a criminal offence established in accordance with this Convention for the benefit of that legal person by a natural person acting under its authority.
>
> 3. Subject to the legal principles of the Party, the liability of a legal person may be criminal, civil or administrative.
>
> 4. Such liability shall be without prejudice to the criminal liability of the natural persons who have committed the offence."
>
> *(Art. 22)*

In certain cases, a human rights violation is committed partly in one country, where the offence was initiated, and partly in another country, where the offence was concluded. An example would be a tourism enterprise, where the board of directors or the chief executive officer of the enterprise, located in the country of origin of the business, decides to employ members from a paramilitary group in another country in order to provide security during the construction of a new hotel. The paramilitary group clears the area for the hotel construction, forcibly displacing the local population, killing those who protest or refuse to relocate. According to the territorial principle, the offence can be prosecuted in the state where the human rights violations took place. Unfortunately, many states where human rights violations occur, are weakly governed. The offence can however also be prosecuted in the home country of the tourism enterprise, according to the nationality principle.

In practice, businesses are seldom if ever prosecuted for human rights violations in the tourism sector according to the nationality principle. When tourism enterprises are accused of human rights violations, the state where the legal process takes place usually asserts jurisdiction according to the territorial principle. This is problematic since human rights violations often occur in states with weak governance structures, and victims of human rights violations have to face corrupt and/or weak legal systems, where redress is difficult. As a result, although international public law allows states to assert jurisdiction over human rights violations when the conduct has taken place outside the territorial boundaries of the state, there are few cases concerning extraterritorial corporate liability for human rights violations.

2.6 Conclusion

Throughout history, there has been a tension between the private motives of owners of business enterprises and the expectations of the society that such enterprises contribute to public purposes. In recent years, it seems that more emphasis has been placed on the public purpose of business entities. The notion of corporate social responsibility has become an accepted, if not required, part of the management of businesses. This is in particular relevant for large businesses, which are increasingly covered by laws requiring disclosure as well as an expectation from the society that they engage in public purposes. The expectations of society are reflected in several new laws and voluntary guidelines requiring corporations to protect affected individuals and communities from adverse human rights reactions emanating from their business activities. However, there are still many challenges in how regulation should be drafted to achieve their purpose.

At the international level, the focus has been on soft law, i.e., rules that are not legally enforceable. Such voluntary initiatives have proven remarkably popular among business entities. Many industry-leading tourism enterprises have committed to initiatives such as UN Global Compact and UNGP. In addition, at the national level, several countries have in the past decade adopted either transparency regulation, requiring large companies to disclose how they work with human rights issues, or more intrusive regulation, such as requirements that part of the profits need to be invested in CSR activities, or that the business enterprises enacts a plan of vigilance to prevent human rights violations. A combination of soft law at the global level, supported by legislation covering large corporations at the national level, is likely to be the most viable approach in the fight to eradicate human rights violations.

Permissions

1 Box 2.1 is composed of material from Protect, Respect and Remedy: A Framework for Business and Human Rights. Report of the Special Representative of the

Secretary-General on the issue of human rights and transnational corporations and other business enterprises, John Ruggie by Human Rights Council, ©2008, United Nations. Reprinted with the permission of the United Nations.
2 Box 2.2 is composed of material from United Nations Global Compact Progress Report 2018 by United Nations Global Compact, ©2018, United Nations. Reprinted with the permission of the United Nations.

References

Air France–KLM, 2020. *Universal Registration Document 2019 Including the Annual Financial Report (unofficial translation from Document d'Enregistrement Universel)*. Available at: <www.airfranceklm.com/en/system/files/universalregistrationdocument2019va.pdf> [Accessed 18 July 2020].

Balcerowicz L. and Fischer, S., eds., 2006. *Living Standards and the Wealth of Nations: Successes and Failures in Real Convergence*. Cambridge, MA. MIT Press.

Bowen, H.R., 1953. *Social Responsibilities of the Businessman*. Reprint 2013. Iowa City. University of Iowa Press.

California Transparency in Supply Chains Act [2012] Senate Bill No. 657.

Commission of the European Communities, 2001. *Green Paper Promoting a European framework for Corporate Social Responsibility*. COM (2001) 366 final.

Companies Act (2013) (Ind.).

Council of Europe. *Liability of enterprises for offences, Recommendation No. R (88) 18*. Strasbourg: Council of Europe.

Council of Europe Convention on Action against Trafficking in Human Beings, 2005. CETS No. 197. (May 16, 2005).

Criminal Law Act of 1827, England & Wales 1827 (c. 28).

David, J.P., 1897. The Nature of Corporations, *Political Science Quarterly*, 12(2), pp. 273–94.

Declaration on Fundamental Principles and Rights at Work and its Follow-up, 86th session of the General Conference of the International Labour Organisation (June 18, 1998) (Annex revised June 15, 2010).

Dodge v. Ford Motor Co. [1919] 204 Mich. 459, 170 N.W. 668.

European Commission, 2011. *A renewed EU strategy 2011–14 for Corporate Social Responsibility, Communication from the Commission to the European Parliament, the Council, the European Economic and Social Committee and the Committee of the Regions*. p. 6. COM (2011) 681 final.

European Parliament and the Council directive 2014/95/EU of 22 October 2014 amending Directive 2013/34/EU as regards disclosure of non-financial and diversity information by certain large undertakings and groups, 2014. *Official Journal*, L330, pp. 1–9 [online]. Available at: <http://data.europa.eu/eli/dir/2014/95/oj> [Accessed 18 May 2020].

European Parliament and the Council regulation (EU) 2017/821 of 17 May 2017 laying down supply chain due diligence obligations for Union importers of tin, tantalum and tungsten, their ores, and gold originating from conflict-affected and high-risk areas, 2017. *Official Journal*, L130, pp. 1–20. [online]. Available at: <http://data.europa.eu/eli/reg/2017/821/oj> [Accessed 18 May 2020].

Etzioni, A., 2010. Is Transparency the Best Disinfectant? *Journal of Political Philosophy*, 18(4), pp. 389–404.

First Nat'l Bank of Carlisle, Pa., v. Graham [1879] 100 U.S. 699.

Framework Convention on Tourism Ethics, Sep. 9–13, 2019, UNWTO 110th session, resolution 707(XXII).

France v. Turkey (the case of the S.S. Lotus) [1927] P.C.I.J. (ser. A) No. 10. Leyden. Netherlands.
Friedman, M., 1970. The Social Responsibility of Business is to Increase its Profits. *New York Times Magazine*, 13, pp. 32–3, 122–4.
Garriga E. and Melé D., 2004. Corporate Social Responsibility Theories: Mapping the Territory. *Journal of Business Ethics*, 53(1–2), pp. 51–71.
Gilchrist, G.M., 2012. The Expressive Cost of Corporate Immunity. *Hastings Law Journal*, 64(1), pp. 1–57.
Global Code of Ethics for Tourism. WTO General Assembly Res. 406 (XIII), U.N. Doc. A/RES/406(XIII) (Sep. 27–Oct. 1, 1999).
Gobert J. and Pascal, A., eds., 2011. *European Developments in Corporate Criminal Liability*. New York: Routledge.
GRI, 2019. *Consolidated Set of GRI Sustainability Reporting Standards 2019.* [pdf] Available at: <www.globalreporting.org/standards/gri-standards-download-center/?g=ecbf 219d-44e7-44b9-9cd4-520d97f60c34> [Accessed 18 May 2020].
Härkönen, E., 2012. Amerikansk övervakning av europeiska värdepappersmarknader. In: J. Kellgren, (ed.), *Vänbok till Ingrid Arnesdotter*. Stockholm. Jure.
Härkönen, E., 2015a. Corporate Liability and International Child Sex Tourism-With Special Reference to the Regulation in the Nordic Countries. *Scandinavian Journal of Hospitality and Tourism*, 16(3), pp. 315–332.
Härkönen, E., 2015b. Juridiska personers ansvar för brott. *Juridisk Tidskrift*, 1, pp. 145–158.
Härkönen, E., 2018. Conflict Minerals in the Corporate Supply Chain: Is Transparency the Solution to Human Rights Violations in the Tantalum, Tin, Tungsten and Gold Supply Chains? *European Business Law Review*, 29(5) pp. 691–727.
Harvard Research in International Law, 1935. Draft Convention on Jurisdiction with Respect to Crime. *The American Journal of International Law*, 29(S1) (Supplement: Research in International Law), pp. 439–442.
Human Rights Council, 2008. *Protect, Respect and Remedy: A Framework for Business and Human Rights. Report of the Special Representative of the Secretary-General on the issue of human rights and transnational corporations and other business enterprises, John Ruggie.* [pdf] A/HRC/8/5. Available at: <www.business-humanrights.org/sites/default/files/reports-and-materials/Ruggie-report-7-Apr-2008.pdf> [Accessed 18 May 2020].
Human Rights Council, 2011. *Report of the Special Representative of the Secretary-General on the issue of human right and transnational corporations and other business enterprises, John Ruggie. Guiding Principles on Business and Human Rights: Implementing the United Nations "Protect, Respect and Remedy" Framework.* [pdf] A/HRC/17/31. 21 Available at: <www.business-humanrights.org/sites/default/files/media/documents/ruggie/ruggie-guiding-principles-21-mar-2011.pdf> [Accessed 18 May 2020].
ILO, 2017. *ILO Guidelines on Decent Work and Socially Responsible Tourism.* [pdf] Geneva: ILO Sectoral Policies department. Available at: <www.ilo.org/wcmsp5/groups/public/---ed_dialogue/---sector/documents/normativeinstrument/wcms_546337.pdf> [Accessed 7 July 2020].
ILO, 2020. The impact of COVID-19 on the tourism sector. *ILO Sectoral Brief.* [pdf] May. Available at: <www.ilo.org/wcmsp5/groups/public/---ed_dialogue/---sector/documents/briefingnote/wcms_741468.pdf> [Accessed 18 July 2020].
Kaufmann D. and Bellver A., 2005. Transparenting Transparency: Initial Empirics and Policy Applications. Draft Discussion Paper. *IMF Conference on Transparency and Integrity*, 6–7 July. World Bank, Washington, United States.
Loi no 2017–399 relative au devoir de vigilance des sociétés mères et entreprises donneuses d'ordre 2017 [online]. Available at: <www.legifrance.gouv.fr/affichTexte.do?cidTexte=JORF TEXT000034290626&categorieLien=id> [Accessed 18 May 2020].

Merchants Nat. Bank v. State Nat. Bank [1870] 77 U.S. 604.

Mills v. Williams [1850] 33 N.C. 558.

Mock, W.B.T., 2000. Corporate Transparency and Human Rights. *Tulsa Journal of Comparative and International Law* 8(1), pp. 15–26.

N.Y. Cent. & Hudson River R.R: Co. v. United States, [1909] 212 U.S. 481.

OECD, 1976. *OECD Declaration on International Investment and Multinational Enterprises.* [online]. C (76)99/FINAL, Available at: <https://legalinstruments.oecd.org/en/instruments/OECD-LEGAL-0144> [Accessed 18 May 2020].

OECD, 2011. *Guidelines for Multinational Enterprises, 2011 edition.* [pdf] Paris: OECD Publishing. Available at: <http://dx.doi.org/10.1787/9789264115415-en> [Accessed 18 May 2020].

Office of the High Commissioner for Human Rights, 2011. *New Guiding Principles on Business and human rights endorsed by the UN Human Rights Council–News Release.* [pdf] Geneva: OHCHR. Available at: <www.business-humanrights.org/sites/default/files/media/documents/ruggie/ruggie-guiding-principles-endorsed-16-jun-2011.pdf> [Accessed 18 May 2020].

Park, S.K., 2014. Targeted Social Transparency as Global Corporate Strategy. *Northwestern Journal of International Law & Business*, 35(1), pp. 87–137.

Pepelasis, I.S. and Emmanouilidi, E., 2013. Joint Stock Company births: historical coincidence and economic causality (Greece, 1830–1909). *MPRAA Paper No. 51614* [pdf] Available at: <https://mpra.ub.uni-muenchen.de/51614/1/MPRA_paper_51614.pdf> [Accessed 18 May 2020].

Rio Declaration on Environment and development. G.A. Res. 47/190, U.N. Doc. A/CONF.151/26 (June 3–14, 1992).

Ruggie J., 2010. *The UN "Protect, Respect and Remedy" Framework for Business and Human Rights, Background.* United Nations. [pdf] Available at: <www.business-humanrights.org/sites/default/files/reports-and-materials/Ruggie-protect-respect-remedy-framework.pdf> [Accessed 18 May 2020].

Ruggie, J., 2011. *Application of the U.N. "Protect, Respect and Remedy" Framework. 30 June 2011.* [pdf] Available at: <www.business-humanrights.org/sites/default/files/media/documents/applications-of-framework-jun-2011.pdf [Accessed 18 May 2020].

Shift and Mazars LLP, 2015. *UN Guiding Principles Reporting Framework with Implementation Guidance.* [pdf] Available at: <www.ungpreporting.org/wp-content/uploads/UNGPReportingFramework_withguidance2017.pdf> [Accessed 18 May 2020].

Shift and Mazars LLP, 2017. *UN Guiding Principles Reporting Framework with Implementation Guidance. Guidance Part II: Assurance of Human Rights Performance and Reporting.* Available at: <www.ungpreporting.org/wp-content/uploads/UNGPRF_AssuranceGuidance.pdf> [Accessed 18 May 2020].

Shleifer A., 2009. The Age of Milton Friedman, *Journal of Economic Literature* 47(1), pp. 123–135.

Swedish Government. Official Report of the Swedish Government. SOU 1997:127.

Telfer, D. J. and Sharpley, R., 2016. *Tourism and Development in the Developing World*, 2nd Edition. London and New York: Routledge.

The Queen v. Great North of England Railway Co. [1846] 9 Q.B. 315.

The Secretary of State, 2016. Responsible Business Conduct, First National Action Plan for the United States of America. Washington. Available at: <https://2009-2017.state.gov/documents/organization/265918.pdf> [Accessed 18 May 2020].

The UK Modern Slavery Act, 2015 (c.30) [online]. Available at: <www.legislation.gov.uk/ukpga/2015/30/contents/enacted> [Accessed 18 May 2020].

United Nations, 2011. *Guiding Principles on Business and Human Rights*. [pdf] HR/PUB/11/04. New York and Geneva: United Nations. Available at: <www.ohchr.org/Documents/Publications/GuidingPrinciplesBusinessHR_EN.pdf> [Accessed 18 May 2020].

United Nations Convention against Corruption, Oct. 31, 2003, 2349 U.N.T.S. 41.

United Nations General Assembly, 2010. *Report of the Special Representative of the Secretary-General on the issue of human rights and transnational corporations and other business enterprises, John Ruggie*. [pdf] A/HRC/14/27. Available at: <www2.ohchr.org/english/issues/trans_corporations/docs/A-HRC-14-27.pdf> [Accessed 18 May 2020].

United Nations Global Compact, 2012. *After the Signature. A guide to Engagement in the United Nations Global Compact* [pdf] Available at: <https://d306pr3pise04h.cloudfront.net/docs/news_events%2F8.1%2Fafter_the_signature.pdf> [Accessed 18 May 2020].

United Nations Global Compact, 2018. *United Nations Global Compact Progress Report 2018*. [pdf] NewYork: United Nations Global Compact. Available at: <https://d306pr3pise04h.cloudfront.net/docs/publications%2FUN-Global-Compact-Progress-Report-2018.pdf> [Accessed 18 May 2020].

United Nations Global Compact, 2019. *United Nations Global Compact Progress Report 2019*. [pdf] New York: United Nations Global Compact. Available at: <https://d306pr3pise04h.cloudfront.net/docs/publications%2F2019-UNGC-Progress-Report.pdf> [Accessed 18 May 2020].

United Nation Global Compact, 2020. *Our participants*. [online]. Available at: <www.unglobalcompact.org/what-is-gc/participants/search?utf8=✓&search%5Bkeywords%5D=&search%5Bper_page%5D=50&search%5Bsort_field%5D=&search%5Bsort_direction%5D=asc> [Accessed 18 May 2020].

Universal Declaration of Human Rights, G.A. Res. 217 (III) A, U.N. Doc. A/RES/217(III) (Dec. 10, 1948).

World Committee on Tourism Ethics, n.d., *Procedures for consultation and conciliation for the settlement of disputes concerning the application of the Code of Ethics for Tourism*. [pdf] Available at: <https://webunwto.s3.eu-west-1.amazonaws.com/s3fs-public/2019-12/wctetextofprocedures.pdf> [Accessed 18 July 2020].

World Travel & Tourism Council, 2020. *Travel & Tourism Economic Impact 2020 World*. [pdf] London: World Travel and Tourism Council.

Wright, R.E., 2010. The Rise of the Corporation Nation. In: D. Irwin and R. Sylla, (eds.), *Founding Choices: American Economic Policy in the 1970s*. London: University of Chicago Press, pp. 217–258.

3
HUMAN RIGHTS, DEVELOPMENT, AND THE SUSTAINABLE DEVELOPMENT GOALS

3.1 Introduction

As Currie-Alder (2016, p. 6) notes, "concern of over development has been with us as long as people have existed, for it is fundamentally about improving the human condition." In the evolution of the development paradigm, there have been waves of scholarly attention on development, which combines concern over the presence of poverty in society and the pursuit to comprehend and shape how society changes over time (Currie-Alder, 2016). It is during these waves that various ideas have come to the forefront on how to best achieve development. Initial thinking focused on economic growth, and in time, other dimensions including society, the environment, and sustainability have come to the forefront. Writing in 1999, Sen postulated that development should be regarded in terms of freedom, and noted the rise in discussion on political liberties and human rights. Past ideas on development do not completely disappear, but continue alongside new avenues of the development paradigm (Telfer, 2015). Currie-Alder (2016, p. 9) notes "ideas that describe the ends and means of development both inform and inspire the actions of individuals, organisations and states in the continuous efforts to invent a better world." While the private sector tends to regard tourism as a business, the public sector also sees tourism as a means of regional or national development. Moreover, the United Nations World Tourism Organization (UNWTO) and various agencies within the United Nations have endorsed tourism as a means of sustainable development, which focus on human rights-based approaches to development (e.g. OHCHR, 2010; UNWTO, 2017; UNDP 2007; UNEP and WTO, 2005). However, the incorporation of human rights issues in the concept of tourism development is a relatively recent phenomenon.

This chapter will explore changes in the development paradigm, and how it has begun to incorporate a human rights-based approach. The chapter will begin by reviewing how the United Nations Universal Declaration of Human Rights (UN UDHR) ushered in the concept of a human rights-based approach to development, principally through United Nations' initiatives. In particular, the 1986 UN Declaration on the Right to Development adopted this approach and called for states to take steps to end "the massive and flagrant violations of the human rights of peoples and human beings" (Article 5). Secondly, the chapter will trace the evolution of how this human rights-based approach to development became manifested in the UN Millennium Goals, which then transformed into the Sustainable Development Goals (SDG). Given this evolution, this chapter then turns to examine how the tourism industry's understanding of sustainable tourism development transitioned from a natural resource-oriented view to a more human-oriented view. In line with the 2030 Sustainable Development Goals, over 290 signatories adopted the Berlin Declaration in 2017 in order to transform tourism. The same year was also declared the International Year of Sustainable Tourism for Development by the United Nations. This chapter links the transition in the development paradigm towards human rights approaches and its incorporation in sustainable tourism.

3.2 UN declaration of human rights and UN declaration to the rights to development

Witnessing the atrocities of World War II raised global concerns over human rights, and thus stirred social movements to address human rights issues. The post War trials in Nuremberg and Tokyo for war crimes were the beginnings of humanitarian intervention, which recognised not only national leaders, but also individuals as being responsible in times of war (Mansbach and Rafferty, 2008). It was during this social and political climate, the United Nations Universal Declaration of Human Rights (UN UDHR) was adopted in 1948, followed by many other human rights related declarations and documents. The history of human rights ideology and the formation of the UDHR are covered in detail in Chapter 1. Here, the evolution of development paradigms is outlined, along with how the approach of the United Nations has responded to such changes to raise the profile of human rights.

The United Nations has been the institution spearheading the installation of human rights issues within the concept of "development." The United Nations Commission on Human Rights was founded in 1946 as a key UN Intergovernmental body, later replaced by The Human Rights Council in 2006. In 1993, the Office of the United Nations High Commissioner for Human Rights (OHCHR) was established by the UN General Assembly. The OHCHR assisted other UN agencies dealing with human rights (OHCHR, 2017). Today the UDHR, together with the International Covenant on Civil and Political Rights (and its two Optional

Protocols) (ICCPR) and the International Covenant on Economic, Social and Cultural Rights (ICESCR), are known as the International Bill of Human Rights (OHCHR, 2017). Within the Bill, individual entitlements of rights can be understood as negative rights or positive rights (Mansbach and Rafferty, 2008). Negative rights are for individuals not to suffer from state actions/interference; in contrast, positive rights are for states to look after individuals' essential needs for life. Securing positive rights, such as food, education, health care, and jobs, is viewed as a prerequisite to exercising negative rights, such as political rights, civil rights, and liberty. However, in many developing countries where negative rights are compromised or lacking, individuals tend to be subject to structural violence (Galtung, 1969; Sen, 1999; Sachs, 2005; Ho, 2007). In this case, equality, liberty, and human rights are physically and psychologically violated by structures, but not by individuals. For instance, the global trading system under the current structure of supranational agencies, e.g. International Monetary Fund and World Trade Organization, is often criticised for causing more injustices than benefits to the developing world. After establishing a universal understanding of human rights, shortcomings were identified, requiring the UN to further establish that human rights should be the foundation of "development." The evolution in the development paradigm as it came to embrace human rights is traced below.

After World War II, the priority of "development" was modernisation (c.f. Rostow's Stages of Modernisation), until approximately the 1960s. Rebuilding war-ravaged nations and bringing the so-called Third World or Less Developed Countries (LDCs) to higher stages of modernisation – in which the nation is ready for export-led economic activities – was the focus. Yet, many of the processes of modernisation were deemed dysfunctional fairly quickly. Disturbing overdependence of LDCs on developed countries was not helping the LDCs to become economically self-sufficient, but rather trapped them in a vicious cycle of debt and poverty. Concerned parties condemned modernisation theory, and called this problematic reality "dependency theory" (Mansbach and Rafferty, 2008; Britton, 1989; Harrison, 1995). It was at about this time that Galtung (1969) advocated the theory of structural violence in line with dependency theory. Meanwhile, development theory in the following decade (1970s to 1980s) shifted to economic neoliberalism based on free and open markets, and limited state involvement in global economies all setting the foundations for globalisation of today. Economic neoliberalism purported to provide equal opportunities and leverage to every player in a capitalist economy to access markets and trade (Mansbach and Rafferty, 2008); however, the LDCs faced too many disadvantages to enjoy these opportunities (Sen 1999; Sengupta 2000), leaving them once more in a vulnerable position. In part based on the criticism of neoliberalism, development theorists and practitioners shifted development thinking again by proposing Alternative Development, which focuses on people-centred development, increased role of women in development (see Box 3.1), satisfying basic needs, and sustainable development (c.f. Telfer, 2015 for more details).

BOX 3.1 WOMEN'S RIGHTS, DEVELOPMENT, AND TOURISM

Approaches to the role of women in the development process have evolved over time since the end of the Second Word War. Beginning as Women in Development in the early 1970s, the paradigm shifted to Woman and Development, and then Gender and Development. The Basic Needs approach also highlighted the important role of women. The UN has played an active role in raising the profile of women's rights in development through a variety of ways. The UN Declared the Decade from 1975 to 1985 as the Decade for Development. In 1979, the UN issued the Convention on the Elimination of all Forms of Discrimination against Women. The UN has also held four world conferences on women with the last one being in Beijing in 1995, and this has been followed up with meetings every five years. The Beijing Declaration and the Platform for Action set out the following 12 strategic objectives:

- Women and the environment
- Women in power and decision-making
- The girl child
- Women and the economy
- Women and poverty
- Violence against women
- Human rights of women
- Education and training of women
- Institutional mechanisms for the advancement of women
- Women and health
- Women and the media
- Women and armed conflict

Goal 3 in the UN MDG was to promote gender equality and empower women, and Goal 5 in the UN SDG is to achieve gender equality and empower all women and girls. Both the MDS and SDG also incorporate maternal health. In 2014, the UN published Women's Rights are Human Rights (OHCHR, 2014) which provides an introduction to women's human rights alongside provisions in international human rights law, and how they relate to specific women's human rights issues. The rights and roles of women have also been explored in tourism development ranging from exploitation (see Chapter 13 on exploitation through sex tourism) to empowerment. In Spain, recent changes in government regulations have resulted in the work of chambermaids at major hotel chains being outsourced to private cleaning companies. Workers have seen their wages fall by up to 40% and their workload has also increased (Burgen, 2017). They have taken to social media and protesting in front of hotels to increase awareness of the negative impacts this has had on their lives. In a more positive light, women have been empowered through access to initiatives such as microfinance programs and community-based tourism. In rural Japan, Hashimoto and Telfer (2011) found that the introduction of tourism has empowered rural female farmers, giving them the opportunity to make their own income and new opportunities to socialise with other women in the agritourism industry. In a very male-dominated society, tourism has opened up new opportunities for women. However even with initiatives such as microfinance, Lynne (2001) found in women's craftwork in the Upland Philippines, it was mainly women with existing businesses or entrepreneurs that were benefitting, and not the "poor." Lynne (2001) argues that microfinance programs need to evolve beyond just providing credit, and involve social initiatives. Microfinance tourism does bring tourists into direct contact with those living in poverty, and therefore has the potential to raise awareness and contribute to global citizenship to varying degrees (Thi Phi, et al., 2017). Raising awareness is one avenue tourism can contribute to promote women's rights. With the tourism industry beginning to incorporate a human rights-based approach to tourism development, there are early signs that the rights of women are increasingly being recognised in the industry – although there are still significant challenges. "Women around the world nevertheless regularly suffer violations of their human rights throughout their lives, and realizing women's rights has not always been a priority."

Source: (OHCHR, 2014).

Sustainable Development has become a major focus of development planning since the 1970s, especially after the release of the Brundtland Report in 1987. From the 1970s through the 1990s, sustainable development put priority on environmental management, with particular interest in the prevention of the depletion of natural resources as described in the Brundtland Report. However, the Earth Summits in Brazil in 1992, in New York in 1997, and in South Africa in 2002, brought changes to the fundamental views of sustainable development. Through these Summits, the enforcement of human rights was viewed as a precondition to Sustainable Development (UN-NGLS, 2002; Orellana and Azoulay, 2012). In 1986, the UN Declaration on the Rights to Development proclaimed that everyone is "entitled to participate in, contribute to, and enjoy economic, social, cultural and political development, in which all human rights and fundamental freedoms can be fully realized." The development thought continued to evolve in the 1990s focusing on Human Development, which focused on issues such as human rights, poverty reduction, good governance (see Chapter 4), and utilised the Human Development Index. In 1997, then UN Secretary-General Kofi Anan established human rights across the UN system, which endorsed a rights-based approach. The rights-based approach to development was proposed as a result of the poor achievement of the goals of the UN Stockholm Conference on Environment and Development in 1972. This approach focuses on (1) the right to a healthy environment, (2) access to information and public participation in decision-making, and (3) the right to promote and defend the protection of the environment and human rights (UN-NGLS, 2002; OHCHR, 2006).

3.3 From the millennium development goals to the Sustainable Development Goals

The Millennium Declaration was signed in September of 2000 by 189 world leaders entering into a new global commitment to reduce extreme poverty, as well as achieve human development and human rights (UNDP, 2007). The Millennium Declaration set the groundwork for the establishment of the eight UN Millennium Development Goals with a target date of 2015.

Although the main focus of the Millennium Development Goals (MDGs) was on sustainable gains in Human Development, the guidelines were based on social, environmental, and economic aspects of sustainable development. The Goals included:

1. Eradicate extreme poverty and hunger
2. Achieve universal primary education
3. Promote gender equality and empower women
4. Reduce child mortality
5. Improve maternal health
6. Combat HIV/Aids, malaria, and other diseases
7. Ensure environmental sustainability
8. Develop a global partnership for development

The UNDP (2007) mapped each of the eight goals, alongside key related human rights standards. These standards relate not only to the UDHR, but also to documents on economic, social and cultural rights, civil and political rights, racial discrimination, discrimination against women, and the rights of the child. The documents cited included:

- Universal Declaration of Human Rights
- International Covenant on Economic, Social and Political Rights
- International Covenant on Civil and Political Rights
- International Convention on the Elimination of all Forms of Racial Discrimination
- International Convention on the Elimination of all Forms of Discrimination Against Women
- Convention on the Rights of the Child

A report by Sengupta (2000) to the UN General Assembly, echoed Galtung's theory of structural violence, and advocated strongly for international cooperation in order to achieve the rights to development. The Commission of the European Communities at the same time was endorsing Corporate Social Responsibility (CSR), "a concept whereby companies integrate social and environmental concerns in their business operations and in their interaction with their stakeholders on a voluntary basis" (Euro-Lex, 2011). This initiative on CSR went further, reinforcing human rights and that for enterprises to fully meet their corporate social responsibility, they "should have in place a process to integrate social, environmental, ethical, human rights and consumer concerns into their business operations and core strategy in close collaboration with their stakeholders ..." (Euro-Lex, 2011). It was clear that human rights-based development was moving beyond the responsibility of not only states, but also private enterprises. The United Nations adopted the "UN Guiding Principles Reporting Framework (UNGPRF)" in 2015, providing enterprises and lawyers comprehensive guidelines to identify, access, and take action on human rights issues in their businesses (Shift and Mazars, 2017) (see Chapter 2 for further details on human rights and business).

After the MDGs were implemented in 2000, the Earth Summit in Johannesburg, South Africa assigned the Commission on Sustainable Development to follow up on the MDGs; in response, the Earth Summit Rio+20 in 2012 crafted a framework on how to further achieve the MDGs. The results of the 2013 *MY World Survey* launched by the UN to collect the voices of over 7 million people, served as a foundation for the post-2015 development agenda (UN, 2017a). Furthermore, a session of the Working Group on the Right to Development from the 2014 UN General Assembly reported that 38 states expressed a sense of urgency about sustainable development and the crucial nature of the realisation of the rights to development. The overwhelming majority of developing nations requested shared responsibility and the coordinated efforts of the international community. There were also requests to include the Rights to Development in the post-2015 development agenda and calls for legally binding instruments (UN, 2014). The well-timed 2014 People's Climate March in New York, in which the then Secretary-General Ban Ki-moon participated, doubtlessly contributed to the finalisation of the SDGs. The MDGs expired in 2015, and while improvements had been made, there was recognition that there was still much work to be done. In 2015, the UN General Assembly adopted 2030 SDGs, bringing it into effect as of 1 January 2016 (UN, 2015b).

The eight MDGs were then replaced by the 2030 Sustainable Development Goals (SDGs) with an expanded 17 Goals. The New Goals are based on the three core elements of sustainability, namely, economic growth, social inclusion, and environmental protection. These elements are inseparable in order to foster "inclusive and equitable economic growth, creating greater opportunities for all, reducing inequalities, raising basic standards of living, fostering equitable social development and inclusion, and promoting integrated and sustainable management of natural resources and ecosystems" (UN, 2017a). These 17 goals are divided into three groups:

Goals 1 to 6

- *Poverty*: End poverty in all its forms everywhere
- *Hunger and Food Security*: End hunger, achieve food security and improved nutrition, and promote sustainable agriculture
- *Health*: Ensure healthy lives and promote well-being for all at all ages
- *Education*: Ensure inclusive and quality education for all, and promote lifelong learning
- *Gender Equality and Women's Empowerment*: Achieve gender equality, and empower all women and girls
- *Water and Sanitation*: Ensure access to water and sanitation for all

Goals 7 to 12

- *Energy*: Ensure access to affordable, reliable, sustainable, and modern energy for all
- *Economic Growth*: Promote inclusive and sustainable economic growth, employment, and decent work for all
- *Infrastructure, Industrialisation*: Build resilient infrastructure, promote sustainable industrialisation, and foster innovation
- *Inequality*: Reduce inequality within and among countries
- *Cities*: Make cities inclusive, safe, resilient, and sustainable
- *Sustainable Consumption and Production*: Ensure sustainable consumption and production patterns

Goals 13 to 17

- *Climate Change*: Take urgent action to combat climate change and its impacts
- *Oceans*: Conserve and sustainably use the oceans, seas, and marine resources
- *Biodiversity, Forests, Desertification*: Sustainably manage forests, combat desertification, halt and reverse land degradation, halt biodiversity loss
- *Peace, Justice, and Strong Institutions*: Promote just, peaceful, and inclusive societies
- *Partnerships*: Revitalize the global partnership for sustainable development

The first SDG, "eradicating in all forms and dimensions," of poverty according to UN (2017a), is an imperative prerequisite for sustainable development. Even though the MDGs had succeeded in decreasing global poverty by 50%, still 836 million people live in "extreme poverty"; and the vast majority of them are found in South Asian countries and Sub-Saharan African countries (2017a). Sachs (UN, 2015c) commended the MDGs for giving new visions of implementing sustainable development and eradicating extreme poverty; he estimated less than 1% of the income of rich countries could solve many of the problems of poverty. In July 2015, the 3rd International Conference on Financing for Development in Addis Ababa agreed to overhaul and change global finance practices that have been inflicting structural violence to the developing world, which has links to Goal 17 on partnerships (UN 2017a). Each of the 17 Goals has more specific targets, and as with the MDGs noted above, the SDGs have been mapped with specific human rights indicators. The OHCHR "regards the majority of the SDGs indicators as being directly relevant to the implementation and measurement of human rights including the right to development." Nonetheless, the language used in the SDGs has met an unexpected challenge. As commented in Chapter 1, the gendered language – i.e. describing a person as he/his/him – was used in the 1948 UDHR and in other UN documents. In the UN SDGs, Goal 5 reads: "Achieve gender equality and empower all women and girls." It is true that gender equality challenges are deep-rooted and widespread. Gender issues in the 21st century, however, do not only concern binary genders (male-female). LGBTQ+ people are trying to apply their rights within the SDGs, being not mentioned explicitly in the goals. While the overall aim of the UN SDGs is for a better and more sustainable life for all which includes LGBTQ+ people, additional attentiveness is required to avoid (unintentional) discrimination by the language used (see Chapter 8 for more discussion).

3.4 The tourism industry's path to sustainability

Although the UDHR has existed since the late 1940s and the additional Covenants (ICCPR and ICESCR) related to human rights were added in the 1960s, the tourism industry, like many others, was not quick to pick up on human rights issues. The tourism industry followed a winding path to sustainable tourism principles, not to mention embracing a human rights-based approach to sustainable tourism development. Although the history of travel and tourism itself has long roots, contemporary tourism did not emerge until the 1930s when the League of Nations realised the impacts of international tourism on the balance of payments and expenditures (Lanfant, Allcock and Bruner, 1995). Passenger airline development was in its infancy during the pre-World War I era. The International Air Transport Association (IATA) recognises the period of the late 1940s and 1970s as when the civil air transportation shifted from "a scientific phenomenon to a public utility at the disposal of the entire world" (IATA, 2017). The competition for improvements in civil passenger airliners during the 1950s led to the so-called jet age (Burns and McDonnel, 2017; Belstein, 2017; Boyne, 2017). With the availability of air transport to the general population in the 1960s, rapid growth in international tourism had begun (Lanfant, Allcock and Bruner, 1995). This launch of contemporary forms of tourism coincided with the rise of the Green Movement in Europe and North America, which had begun to raise concerns over the growing Consumer Society.

As with many social movements beginning in the 1960s, immediate concerns were about the degradation of the natural environment caused by rapid recovery from the devastation of World War II, as well as the unprecedented scale of global industrialisation. High mass consumption was also considered to be a primary cause of environmental exploitation. The unparalleled scale and speed of global economic development was happening so quickly that there was a lack of understanding of the complexities of the problems it was causing for the environment. Health and living condition issues associated with environmental problems were often discussed independently, and there was not a focus of examining the problems under the umbrella of human rights. In a capitalist economic system where economic development is paramount, tourism was an ideal business for many countries with abundant social, cultural, and environmental resources. The industry was viewed as not requiring a great deal of initial capital, and could result in quick economic returns. In particular, many developing countries chose tourism as a development option as it was perceived to be smokeless industry, or a quick foreign currency earner compared to other export sectors. In addition, tourism provides opportunities to revive and maintain otherwise forgotten traditions and is also a job creator for the less skilled segments of the population. Furthermore, tourism was promoted by some under the politically correct motivation of promoting world peace through furthering people's mutual understanding. Nonetheless, tourism destinations require sound economic and social systems, and attractive natural environments at the destination for their success. The tourism industry increasingly became cognisant of the unfavourable impacts of tourism on destinations; "the problems of physical environmental degradation and destruction seem to be aggravated by tourism development; resentment and antagonism between tourists and hosts are ever growing; social problems induced by tourism development are increasing; tourist generating countries' demands on the destinations do not always encourage sustainable tourism development" (Hashimoto, 1996, p. 6). The Green Movement in the 1960s and the 1970s influenced the shift towards "green tourism" (Shaw and Williams, 1992), and thus forms of low-impact tourism to natural environments in contrast to mass tourism were sought. When Ceballos-Lascurain coined the term "eco-tourism" in 1987, it originally meant "travel to natural areas" (Wild, 1994); however, this was later expanded by Boo (1992) to a form of nature-based tourism that includes nature conservation and sustainable development. De Kadt (1992, p. 48) summarised that "political hostility to transnational capitalism mingles with cultural and ecological unease over modern mass consumption society" as reasons for seeking alternative forms of tourism. The new favoured forms of tourism in this political climate should (1) have a less negative impact on the environment; (2) consist of small-scale attractions run by the community; (3) benefit local people; and (4) emphasise cultural sustainability (de Kadt, 1992). The types of tourism often discussed were "green tourism," "nature-oriented tourism," "soft tourism," "defensive tourism," "ecotourism," and "alternative tourism" (Hashimoto, 1996).

The UNWTO released the Manila Declaration on World Tourism in 1980. It stated tourism can contribute to the establishment of a new international economic order, generating world peace and security, "equity, sovereign equality … improvement of the quality of life and the creation of better living conditions for all peoples, worthy of human dignity …" (p. 1). Though not in the language of human rights of today, the Manila Declaration on World Tourism was clearly aware of the need to improve human rights issues in tourism, not just about the *Rights to Tourism* (see Chapter 9 for discussion on legitimacy of Rights to Tourism). In contrast, at the 1992 Earth Summit, then Secretary General of the World Tourism Organization, Savignac, presented three proposals related to sustainable tourism (1992):

1. Travel promotes environmental awareness;
2. Well managed tourism is a good friend of the environment;
3. A successful tourism industry needs a high quality environment.

These proposals were much more natural environment focused than the sustainable tourism development insinuated in the Manila Declaration. Based on Agenda 21, which was derived from the 1992 Earth Summit, the UNWTO and the World Travel and Tourism Council (WTTC) suggested the following guideline principles for sustainable tourism development:

- *Travel and tourism assist people in leading healthy and productive lives in harmony with nature;*
- *Tourism should contribute to the conservation, protection, and restoration of the Earth's ecosystem;*
- *Travel and tourism should be based upon sustainable patterns of production and consumption;*
- *Nations should cooperate to promote an open economic system in which international trade in travel and tourism services can take place on a sustainable basis;*
- *Protectionism in trade in tourism services should be halted or reversed;*
- *Tourism, peace, development, and environmental protection are interdependent;*
- *In order to achieve sustainable development, environmental protection shall constitute an integral part of the tourism development process;*
- *Tourism development issues should be handled with the participation of concerned citizens, with planning decisions being adopted at the local level;*
- *Nations shall warn one another of natural disasters that could affect tourists or tourist areas;*
- *Since the full participation of women is necessary to achieve sustainable development, advantage should be taken of travel and tourism's capacity to create employment for women;*
- *Tourism development should recognise and support the identity, culture, and interests of Indigenous peoples;*
- *International laws protecting the environment should be respected by the worldwide travel and tourism industry.* (WTO, 1997)

In the early 1990s, primary concerns were still focused on the degradation of the natural environment and exploitation of natural resources. Reflecting on the priorities of the time, these 12 guidelines were heavily influenced by environmental concerns. The social environment and socio-cultural resources in destinations were only taken into consideration as an attraction. The industry started to incorporate early environmental certification schemes in the 1990s such as Green Globe. Along with the "greening of the tourism industry," Codes of Conduct for tourists to behave more responsibly were also suggested in many different formats, yet the primary purpose of these Codes of Conducts was to reduce resource input, establish more efficient waste management, and give tourists and staff more environmental awareness (Goodall, 1992). Nevertheless, in the Twelve Guideline Principles, the precursors of human rights issues in tourism can be seen in Principles #8, 10, and 11, which incorporate the inclusion of locals, women, and Indigenous peoples.

Early understanding of Sustainable Development was based on the Brundtland Report in 1987, and hence the management of the natural environment and resources took precedence. However, social injustice and inequalities in the relationships between tourists and hosts or between tourist-generating countries and tourist-receiving countries raised by concerned lobbying groups became more evident by 1990 (ECPAT, 2015). Many Non-governmental Organisations (NGOs) or Non-profit Organisations (NPOs) and various faith-based organisations were raising the alarm on the exploitation of the poor, particularly those in extreme poverty and especially on issues of sexual exploitation in developing nations. The expansion of sex tourism in developing nations became well known, albeit sometimes masked under the disguise of recreation and entertainment. Just before the 1980 World Tourism Organization (WTO) Conference on Tourism in Manila, Christian groups denounced "economic imperialism, domination by transnational corporations, political exploitations, organized prostitution of women and children, the degradation of traditional cultures, and other ills" caused by foreign investment and international tourism (Lanfant and Graburn, 1992, p. 90). This incident led to creation of the Ecumenical Coalition on Third World Tourism (ECTWT, founded in 1982) (Brot für die Welt, 2001), followed by the *Tourism European/ Ecumenical Network* (TEN) in Stuttgart in 1984 (TEN, n.d.) in partnership with ECTWT. Later in the 1990s, a campaign to "End Child Prostitution in Asian Tourism (ECPAT)" was started in Thailand in consultation with ECTWT (ECPAT, 2015). These organisations and their campaigns also took aim at the roots of such exploitation. They argued that social injustice and violations of human rights are invariably linked to the unbreakable cycle of utter poverty. There is also a lack of education and job opportunities in these societies leaving women, children, and Indigenous populations frequently at a disadvantage. In such societies, traditional social class systems tend to reinforce vicious cycles and authorities had done little to address the social injustices and violations of human rights. An early publication on Tourism and Human Rights from the lobbying organisation Tourism Concern, UK, was based on the assumptions of the vicious cycle of poverty in developing nations (Keefe and Wheat, 1998). As social movements to address and eliminate exploitation in tourism progressed, the realisation that human rights violations associated with tourism were not only an issue in developing nations, but also in developed nations (e.g. UN, 2017b; Tourism Concern, 2017a; Perrin, 2010; Skinner, 2008). When discourse on social injustice and exploitation in tourism began to emerge in the context of human rights language, various concerns about tourists themselves also came into the spotlight. For instance, inequalities in accessibility to holiday experiences (Morgan and Cole, 2010; Buhalis and Darcy, 2011); tourists' security, safety and privacy (Nkyi and Hashimoto, 2015); tourists' mobility rights and citizenship rights (Bianchi and Stephenson, 2014), among others.

3.5 From the UNWTO declarations to the Berlin Declaration – tourism in the Sustainable Development Goals

The idea of incorporating aspects of human rights into tourism development and business operations has slowly been gaining ground amongst tourism stakeholders. Between 1980 and 2016, the UNWTO issued 64 declarations, statements, and letters (UNWTO, 2016). The first declaration in the list is the Manila Declaration and while the UNWTO did not explicitly affirm the full document of the UDHR, it supported the respect of human rights; and agreed with the Rights to Leisure, Recreation and Paid Holiday (Article 24), Right to Freedom of Movement (Article 13), and Right to Work (Article 23) in the UDHR.

In a further analysis of the *Compilations of UNWTO Declarations* (UNWTO, 2016), only 12 Declarations acknowledged the UDHR and recognised the UNWTO's obligation to observe human rights (see the following Declarations: Manila, 1980; Hague, 1989; St Vincent, 1995; Charter for Sustainable Tourism, 1995; Statement on the Prevention of Organized Sex Tourism, 1995; Québec, 2002; Aswan, 2011; Yerevan, 2012; Ninh Binh, 2013; Santiago de Compostela, 2014; San Marino, 2014; and Beijing, 2016). Although the UNWTO made efforts to clarify the organisation's stance on respecting human rights, there is no specific document from the UNWTO until 1999 on human rights (Global Code of Ethics for Tourism -Resolution adopted by UN in 2001) to guide national tourism organisations or tourism and hospitality businesses. The UNWTO declarations and statements (1980–2016) clearly suggest the tourism industry should provide education and training to employees, integrate the means to strengthen cultural identities, and ensure an equitable distribution of financial benefits. Where there are suggestions in the UNWTO's documents for inter-governmental organisations, financial institutions, or the international community (see Québec Declaration, 2002 for instance), they are written to assist in developing national policy frameworks that will respect human rights. It is important to note that the UNWTO Declarations do not have legally binding power, and it is up to an individual organisation as to whether human rights are respected and related policies implemented.

The Global Code of Ethics for Tourism was adopted by the UNWTO in 1999, and while it is non-binding, several sections raise the status of human rights in tourism, and it was a major breakthrough for the UNWTO (Hemingway, 2004). These include Article 1(5) which prohibits tourists from committing crimes or offensive acts towards host communities, Article 2 focuses on non-discrimination and the elimination of exploitation – especially sexual exploitation, and other

Articles address resources, cultural preservation, and behaviour of transnational corporations (Hemingway, 2004). In line with the Human Development paradigm, which includes a focus on poverty reduction, the UNWTO launched the ST-EP (Sustainable Tourism – Eliminating Poverty) at the World Summit on Sustainable Development in Johannesburg in 2002 (Scheyvans, 2015). This along with other initiatives helped promote pro-poor tourism (see Box 3.2).

BOX 3.2 POVERTY REDUCTION, PRO-POOR TOURISM, AND A HUMAN RIGHTS APPROACH

Kofi Annan, the former United Nations Secretary General stated: "Wherever we lift one soul from a life of poverty, we are defending human rights. And whenever we fail in this mission, we are failing human rights." Pro-poor tourism is a poverty reduction strategy for tourism to assist those facing the harsh reality of poverty and, by extension, a way to potentially "defend human rights." The UN Office of the High Commissioner for Human Rights (OHCHR) (2006) published a document entitled Principles and Guidelines for a Human Rights Approach to Poverty Reduction Strategies. In the document, one of the compelling reasons to adopt a human rights perspective to poverty reduction is that it has the potential to empower the poor. Empowerment occurs when the concept of rights is introduced into policy making, and so the rational for poverty reduction is no longer just based on people living in poverty that have needs, but rather they have rights and entitlements giving rise to the legal obligations of others (OHCHR, 2006). Key features of the human rights normative framework that can add to empowerment include: "the principles of universality, non-discrimination and equality, the principle of participatory decision making, the notion of accountability, and the recognition of the interdependence of rights" (OHCHR, 2006, p. 5).

Pro-poor tourism first gained in popularity in the 1990s, with the shift towards Human Development and the focus on poverty reduction. Pro-poor tourism is not a type of tourism, but rather an approach that can be used so that the benefits of tourism go towards the poorest segments of the population. There are several initiatives in pro-poor tourism that have emerged including Fair Trade in Tourism, Corporate Social Responsibility in Tourism, NGOs supporting pro-poor tourism and the UNWTO's ST-EP programme (Scheyvens, 2015). Scheyvens (2015 based on Ashley 2002) outlined some of the benefits of pro-poor strategies. Economic benefits include an expansion of employment and wages by job creation and training the poor, expansion of entrepreneurial opportunities, and the development of collective community income. Non-cash benefits include capacity building, training, mitigation of negative environmental impacts of tourism on the poor, and improved access to services and infrastructure. Finally, policy, process, and participation benefits include frameworks, which enable the participation of the poor, more participation by the poor in decision-making, and the encouragement of partnerships and enhanced communication. Ghelli (2018) notes a number of examples of pro-poor tourism in Laos, Uganda, and Kenya. Ecotourism Laos, under the Asian Development Bank, offers interactive hiking experiences with a considerable portion of the income going to guides and villagers. In Uganda, Byoona Amagara is a non-profit organisation that links tourism around Lake Bunyonyi to a variety of pro-poor programs including healthcare, literacy and rural education, indigenous forestry, and organic agriculture. Finally, in Kenya, the African Pro-poor Tourism Development Centre focuses on sustainable safaris, reinvesting the profits into regional economies. By adopting a human rights approach to poverty reduction through pro-poor tourism, there is the potential to empower individuals and communities. Many case studies on pro-poor tourism focus on the benefits of the strategy; however, focusing on the human rights dimension has the potential to further enhance the benefits for those most in need.

From the beginning of 2016, the UN launched the 2030 Agenda for Sustainable Development (UN, 2015d). The 17 goals with 169 targets are to be monitored by a set of Global Indicators. It was made clear that despite progress made on the MDGs, there were many goals left unfulfilled and the SDGs are to further improve the achievement rates on these challenges. The UN's adoption of the MDGs unquestionably influenced the policy of the UNWTO. The UNWTO published "Tourism and the Millennium Development Goals" in 2010, followed by "How Tourism can Contribute to the Sustainable Development Goals (SDGs)" in 2015 (UNWTO, 2015). The joint publication from the UNWTO and UNEP (2017) reviewed how much work has been done in the tourism sector – both in public and in private – two years into the implementation of the 2030 Agenda. Although the study identified all 17 SDG have been tackled to various degrees, the Public sector and Private sector have had different priorities. The Private sector's Corporate Social Responsibility (CSR) activities emphasised business operations and local community support through SDG 12, 13, 1, 4, and 8 (in order of priority); while the Public sector focused on SDG 17, 12, 11, 9, and 14, to actively engage various stakeholders and improve co-operation. While the language and key phrases used in earlier documents, e.g. UNWTO's 2015 brochure, did not provide exact instructions on how to achieve specific goals, the information provided broad ideas of "what" possibly might be achieved. Each individual destination and country in turn needs to formulate how they might be able to achieve the various SDG, and what role tourism can play. The difference in the UNWTO and UNEP's 2017 document is provision of concrete examples, best practices, and future indicators from the study findings for the tourism sector to achieve SDG.

One of the SDG in the above list that has significant implications not only for sustainable tourism but also human rights is climate change. Scott, Hall, and Gössling (2016) state there are strong interconnections between the Paris Climate Agreement and the SDG 2030 agenda to which the UNWTO sees tourism contributes in a significant manner. The WTTC made a commitment in 2009 to cutting emissions of the tourism sector by 50% from 2005 to 2035 (WTTC 2015). In 2015 the WTTC proposed the following priority areas to help meet their 2035 target and they include:

- Integrating climate change and related issues into business strategy
- Supporting the global transition to a low carbon economy
- Strengthening local resilience
- Promoting the value of responsible travel
- Engaging across the value chain

While tourism has the potential to contribute to the SDG and reduce its contribution to climate change, it is important to recognise the human rights dimension. "Those who have contributed least to climate change unjustly and disproportionally suffer its harms" (OHCHR, 2015). The OHCHR (2015) highlighted the following essential obligations and responsibilities for states and other duty-bearers, including businesses, so that mitigation and adaptation programs of climate change are compliant with human rights obligations:

- To mitigate climate change and to prevent its negative human rights impacts
- To ensure that all persons have the necessary capacity to adapt to climate change
- To ensure accountability and effective remedy for human rights harms caused by climate change
- To mobilise maximum available resources for sustainable human-rights development
- International cooperation
- To ensure equity in climate action
- To guarantee that everyone enjoys the benefits of science and its applications
- To protect human rights from business harm
- To guarantee equality and non-discrimination
- To ensure meaningful and informed participation

The World Charter for Sustainable Tourism +20 was signed in 2015, and it recognised a range of important documents including the SDG and the Davos Declaration on climate change and tourism, as well as advocating for the strengthening of legislation and policy frameworks for sustainable development to protect human and labour rights (World Charter for Sustainable Tourism +20, 2015).

In 2017, a concerned party of "19 countries in Africa, Asia, Europe and Latin America, representatives of non-governmental organizations, people's movements and academia" (Tourism Concern, 2017b, p. 1) gathered to discuss how to transform the tourism industry so that tourism stakeholders can contribute to achieving Agenda 2030 of the SDGs. Their concerns were over the current consumptive business model of tourism, and how the industry was selecting easy-to-achieve SDGs, and therefore, true sustainable development would never be achieved. In the "Berlin Declaration on Transforming Tourism," it is acknowledged in the Preamble that the current form of tourism is "exploiting people, harming communities, violating human rights and degrading the environment" (Tourism Concern, 2017b, p. 1). This document expresses concern over: the shrinking space in civil society for human rights defenders and others; the need for the implementation of human rights-based approaches in tourism policy and development; the enforcement of the UN Guiding Principles on Business and Human Rights; and it made calls for tourists to respect the human rights of their hosts. The number of signatures on the Berlin Declaration representing individuals, organisations, and regions reached 290 at the end of July 2017. The accompanying document, "Transforming Tourism – Tourism in the 2030 Agenda" (Alba sud et al., 2017) details projects for tourism stakeholders. Recognising that Agenda 2030 is based on a human rights-based approach, it goes through the 17 SDGs and for each goal it identifies related problems and cases in the tourism and hospitality industry. It also examines major challenges and possible causes of problems, and outlines potential action plans. In this document, human rights are mentioned 53 times. The emphasis of the document is on the structural violation of human rights, and suggestions are made on how to right the wrongs. On 8 March 2017, the Berlin Declaration was presented at ITB Berlin (Internationale Tourismus-Börse Berlin), the world's largest tourism trade fair.

While advancements have been made towards the UN SDGs, and the UNWTO maintains a platform on their website "Tourism for SDGs," there is no question that the COVID-19 pandemic has a major impact on the past successes related to the SDGs, including those made by tourism. The pandemic has taken an immense human toll in terms of loss of life and infections, and combined with the sharp economic decline, the targets for the SDGs will be even harder to achieve and human rights harder to protect. In a Policy brief (#78) on 11 June 2020 the UN Department of Economic and Social Affairs (UN/DESA) provided a dire assessment on the impact of COVID-19 on the SDGs (UN DESA, 2020). With a global drop in GDP between 3.2% and 5.2% in 2020, the worst contraction since the Great Depression, COVID-19 could push millions (35–60) into extreme poverty. Approximately 1.6 billion work in the informal sector, including many in tourism. The report indicates that these people are at risk of losing their livelihoods, with many not having any access to social protection. The UN/DESA is calling for greater collaboration and coordination among nations along the following three priorities as a way to reinforce the SDGs through the period of crisis response and recovery: (1) maintain past progress towards eradicating basic deprivations, (2) accelerate the universal provisions of quality essential services, and (3) reverse course on the degradation of nature. While it may take years to know the impacts of COVID-19, the UN/DESA stresses how central the UN SDGs are for building resilience against shocks and backslides into poverty (see Chapter 14).

3.6 Conclusion

This chapter has provided background information in regard to the chronological evolution of development theory, along with concepts of human rights, Sustainable Development, and a human rights-based approach to development. The fusion of all these separate movements came to fruition in the MDGs and the SDGs. Led by various UNWTO initiatives, tourism has embraced human rights-based Sustainable Tourism Development.

Concerns over human rights have been raised for centuries (Chapter 1). The UN Universal Declaration of Human Rights in 1948 was a turning point in modern history. Fresh with memories of the atrocity of war, the world was ready to accept the idea that every human being deserves dignity and a safe life. Yet, some of the UDHR articles did not agree with some nations' values, traditions, religious practices, and worldviews – not to mention existing laws. Moreover, some of the UDHR articles were quite unpalatable for corporations that were benefiting from the exploitation of their labour force. As a result, accepting the UDHR fully and implementing or incorporating human rights clauses in national Constitutions and laws has not been an easy task.

In the interim, the discourse on sustainable development evolved from the green movement in the 1960s, yet it seemed to evolve as a separate issue from human rights and focused on the environment. At its core, the protection of the natural environment and resources is closely related to human rights to life, livelihood, and resources; however, the eco-centric idealism of the protection of nature was overpowering and some radical groups, often dubbed "Environmental Terrorists," became prominent. These groups' ideology was more radical, and operated in the vein of protecting "Mother Earth" (see Chapter 11). The international community was more concerned about the state of the natural environment and ecosystems, than considering the situation in terms of nature's connection to human rights. Consequently, the emphasis of sustainable development at this point of time was more towards environmental protection.

The human rights movement and the sustainable development movement evolved separately yet in parallel, until the Millennium Development Goals were proposed in 2000. After 15 years of human rights-based development projects, the UN proposed the revised Sustainable Development Goals in 2016. This 2030 Agenda of the SDGs is based on a renewed understanding that sustainable development cannot be achieved without respect of the human rights of citizens.

The tourism and hospitality industries have begun to recognise the value of a human rights approach. As seen in the various declarations and documents issued by the UNWTO, it respects human rights as declared in the UDHR, endorses environmentally friendly sustainable tourism development, and advocates the incorporation of the MDGs and SDGs into tourism development. Destination countries, various organisations, and businesses signed on to the Berlin Declaration on Transforming Tourism in 2017, in a pledge to eliminate the structural violence inherit in many forms of current tourism development and business operations. The degree to which the 2030 Agenda of SDGs and the Berlin Declaration will be implemented is up to the various stakeholders in tourism. Nevertheless, while a lot more work is required, it is encouraging to know that more concerned stakeholders in tourism are taking action to respect human rights. Collaboration will be essential in the recovery from COVID-19 and the protection of human rights.

References

Alba sud, et al., eds., 2017. *Transforming Tourism – Tourism in the 2030 Agenda* [pdf]. Available at: <www.transforming-tourism.org/fileadmin/baukaesten/sdg/downloads/sdg-complete.pdf> [Accessed 10 May 2017].

Belstein, R.E., 2017. History of Flight – The Jet Age. *Encyclopædia Britannica Online.* [online]. London: Encyclopædia Britannica (UK). Available at: <www.britannica.com/technology/history-of-flight/General-aviation> [Accessed 19 July 2017].

Bianchi, R.V. and Stephenson, M.L. 2014. *Tourism and Citizenship: Rights, Freedom and Responsibilities in the Global Order.* London: Routledge.

Boo, E., 1992. *Ecotourism: The Potentials and Pitfalls (two volumes).* Washington, DC: World Wildlife Fund.

Boyne, W.J., 2017. History of Flight – General Aviation. *Encyclopædia Britannica Online.* [online]. London: Encyclopædia Britannica (UK). Available at: <www.britannica.com/technology/history-of-flight/The-jet-age> [Accessed 19 July 2017].

Britton, S., 1989. Tourism, dependency and development: A model of analysis. In: T.V. Singh, H.L. Theuns and F.M. Go, (eds.), *Towards Appropriate Tourism: The Case of Developing Countries.* Frankfurt: Peter Long, pp. 167–187.

Brot für die Welt, 2001. Open Letter from the Conference of the Ecumenical Coalition on Third World Tourism (ECTWT) "Mission Perspective in Tourism" Pen. *Tourism Watch: Informationdienst Tourismus und Entwicklung.* [online]. Available at: <www.tourism-watch.de/content/open-letter-conference-ecumenical-coalition-third-world-tourism-ectwt-mission-perspective> [Accessed 19 July 2017].

Brot für die Welt, 2016. Human Rights. *Tourism Watch: Informationdienst Tourismus und Entwicklung.* [online]. Available at: <www.tourism-watch.de/en/meta-themen/human-rights> [Accessed 12 May 2017].

Brot für die Welt, 2017. Human Rights. *Tourism Watch: Informationdienst Tourismus und Entwicklung.* [online]. Available at: <www.tourism-watch.de/en/meta-themen/human-rights> [Accessed 17 July 2017].

Buhalis, D. and Darcy, S., eds., 2011. *Accessible Tourism: Concepts and Issues.* Bristol: Channel View Publications.

Burgen, S., 2017. Chambermaids' revolt aims to shame Spain's rogue employers. *The Guardian.* [online]. 15 July. Available at: <www.theguardian.com/travel/2017/jul/15/spanish-hotel-cleaners-fightback-exploitation> [Accessed 21 August 2019].

Burns and McDonnel, 2017. *Timeline of Commercial Aviation.* [online]. Available at: <www.burnsmcd.com/insightsnews/insights/aviation-special-report/2011/timeline-of-commercial-aviation> [Accessed 19 July 2017].

Currie-Alder, B., 2016. The state of development studies: origins, evolution and prospects. *Canadian Journal of Development Studies,* 37(1) pp. 5–26. DOI: https://doi.org/10.1080/02255189.2016.1135788

De Kadt, E., 1992. Making the Alternative Sustainable: Lessons from Development for Tourism. In: V.L. Smith and W.R. Eadington, (eds.), *Tourism Alternatives: Potentials and Problems in the Development of Tourism*. Chichester: John Wiley & Sons, pp. 47–75.

ECPAT, 2015. *ECPAT 25 Years: Rallying the World to End Child Sexual Exploitation*. [pdf]. Available at: <www.ecpat.org/wp-content/uploads/2016/04/ECPAT%2025%20Years_FINAL.pdf> [Accessed 11 November 2016].

EURO-Lex, 2011. *Communication from the Commission to the European Parliament, the Council, the European Economic and Social Committee and the Committee of Regions A renewed EU strategy 2011–14 for Corporate Social Responsibility /* COM/2011/0681 final */* [online]. Available at: <http://eur-lex.europa.eu/legal-content/EN/TXT/?uri=celex%3A52011DC0681> [Accessed 4 August 2017].

IATA, 2017. *Two-tier IATA*. [online]. Available at: <www.iata.org/about/Pages/history-two-tier-IATA.aspx> [Accessed 19 July 2017].

Galtung, J., 1969. Violence, Peace, and Peace Research. *Journal of Peace Research* [e-journal] 6(3), pp. 167–191. https://dx.doi.org/10.1177/002234336900600301.

Ghelli, N., 2018. Reinvesting in Locals: The Benefits of Pro-poor. *Borgen Magazine*. [online]. 16 May. Available at: <www.borgenmagazine.com/reinvesting-in-locals-the-benefits-of-pro-poor-tourism/> [Accessed 19 August 2019].

Goodall, B., 1992. Environmental auditing for tourism. In: C.P. Cooper and A. Lockwood, (eds.), *Progress in Tourism, Recreation and Hospitality Management (Volume Four)*. London: Belhaven Press, pp. 60–74.

Harrison, D., ed., 1995. *International Tourism and the Less Developed Countries*. Chichester: John Wiley.

Hashimoto, A., 1996. *A cross-cultural study of attitudes towards the natural environment and tourism development: Northern Europe and East Asia*. PhD. University of Surrey.

Hashimoto, A. and Telfer, D., 2011. Female empowerment through argitoursim in rural Japan. In: R. Torres and J. Momsen, (eds.), *Tourism and Agriculture: New Geographies of Consumption, Production and Rural Restructuring*. Oxford: Routledge, pp. 72–84.

Hemingway, S., 2004. The Impact of Tourism on the Human Rights of Women in South East Asia. *International Journal of Human Rights*, 8(3), pp. 275–304. DOI: https://doi.org/10.1080/1364298042000255216.

Ho, K., 2007. Structural Violence as a Human Rights Violation. *Essex Human Rights Review*. [e-journal] 4(2), pp. 1–17. Available at: <http://projects.essex.ac.uk/ehrr/V4N2/ho.pdf> [Accessed 21 July 2017].

Keefe, J. and Wheat, S., 1998. *Tourism and Human Rights*. London: Tourism Concern.

Lanfant, M.-F., Allcock, J.B. and Bruner, E.M., 1995. *International Tourism: Identity and Change*. London: Sage Publications.

Lanfant, M.F. and Graburn, N.H., 1992. International tourism reconsidered: The principle of the alternative. In: Valene L. Smith, William R. Eadington, (eds.), *Tourism Alternatives: Potentials and Problems in the Development of Tourism*. Philadelphia: University of Pennsylvania Press, pp. 88–112.

Lynne, M., 2001. Organizing microfinance: Women and Craft Work in Ifugao, Upland Philippines. *Human Organisation*, 60(3), pp. 212–224.

Mansbach, R.W. and Raggerty, K.L., 2008. *Introduction to Global Politics*. London: Routledge.

Morgan, N. and Cole, S., (eds.), 2010. *Tourism and Inequality: Problems and Prospects*. Wallingford: CAB International.

Nkyi, E. and Hashimoto, A., 2015. Human Rights Issues in Tourism Development. In: R. Sharpley and D.J. Telfer, (eds.), *Tourism and Development: Concepts and Issues*, 2nd Edition. Bristol: Channel View Publications, pp. 378–399.

OHCHR, 2006. *Frequently Asked Questions on a Human Rights-based Approach to Development Cooperation.* [pdf] Geneva: United Nations. Available at: <www.ohchr.org/Documents/Publications/FAQen.pdf> [Accessed 6 February 2017].

OHCHR, 2010. *Human Rights and the Millennium Development Goals in Practice: A review of country strategies and reporting.* [pdf] New York and Geneva: United Nations. Available at: <www.ohchr.org/Documents/Issues/MDGs/Human_rights_and_MDGs_in_practice_ML.pdf> [Accessed 6 February 2017].

OHCHR, 2014. *Women's Rights are Human Rights.* [pdf] Available at: <www.ohchr.org/Documents/Events/WHRD/WomenRightsAreHR.pdf>.

OHCHR, 2015. *Understanding Human Rights and Climate Change.* [online]. Available at: <www.ohchr.org/Documents/Issues/ClimateChange/COP21.pdf> [Accessed 21 August 2019].

OHCHR, 2017. *Brief History.* [online]. Available at: <www.ohchr.org/EN/AboutUs/Pages/BriefHistory.aspx> [Accessed 5 February 2017].

OHCHR, n.d. *Human Rights Indicators Tables Updated with the Sustainable Development Goals (SDG) indicators.* [online]. Available at: <www.ohchr.org/Documents/Issues/HRIndicators/SDG_Indicators_Tables.pdf> [Accessed 17 August 2019].

Orellana, M.A. and Azoulay, D., 2012. *Human Rights & Environment in the Rio+20 UN Conference on Sustainable Development.* Centre for International Environmental Law (CIEL) Issue Brief [pdf] 15 February. Available at: <www.ciel.org/Publications/Rio+20_IssueBrief_Feb2012.pdf> [Accessed 17 July 2017].

Perrin, B., 2010. *Invisible Chains: Canada's Underground World of Human Trafficking.* Toronto: Penguin Canada.

Sachs, J., 2005. *The End of Poverty: Economic Possibilities for Our Time.* New York: Penguin Books.

Scheyvans. R. 2015. Tourism and Poverty Reduction In: R. Sharpley and D.J. Telfer, (eds.), *Tourism and Development: Concepts and Issues*, 2nd Edition. Bristol: Channel View Publications, pp. 118–139.

Scott, D., Hall, C.M., and Gössling, S., 2016. A Report on the Paris Climate Change Agreement and its implications for tourism: why we will always have Paris. *Journal of Sustainable Tourism*, 24(7), pp. 933–948. https://doi.org/10.1080/09669582.2016.1187623.

Sen., A., 1999. *Development as Freedom.* Oxford: Oxford University Press.

Sengupta, A., 2000. *The Right to Development: Report of the Independent Expert on the Right to Development, General Assembly resolution 54/175 and Commission on Human Rights resolution E/CN.4/RES/2000/5.* [pdf] Geneva: United Nations. Available at: <http://ap.ohchr.org/documents/E/CHR/report/ECN42000WG18CRP1.pdf.> [Accessed 21 July 2017].

Shaw, G. and Williams, A., 1992. Tourism, development and the environment: the eternal triangle. In: C.P. Cooper and A. Lockwood, (eds.), *Progress in Tourism, Recreation and Hospitality management (Volume Four)*. London: Belhaven Press, pp. 47–59.

Shift and Mazars, LLP., 2017. *UN Guiding Principles Reporting Framework.* [online]. Available at: <www.ungpreporting.org> [Accessed 4 August 2017].

Skinner, B., 2008. *A Crime So Monstrous: Face-to-Face with Modern-Day Slavery.* New York: Free Press.

Telfer, D.J., 2015. The Evolution of Development Theory and Tourism, In: R. Sharpley and D.J. Telfer, (eds.), *Tourism and Development: Concepts and Issues*, 2nd Edition. Bristol: Channel View Publications, pp. 31–71.

TEN, n.d. *Declaration. Tourism European/Ecumenical Network.* [online] 20 October 1984. Available at: <www.ten-tourism.org> [Accessed 9 January 2017].

Thi Phi, G., Whitford, M., Dredge, D., and Reid, S., 2017. Educating tourists for global citizenship: a microfinance tourism perspective. *Tourism Recreation Research*. 42 (2), pp. 235–247.

Tourism Concern, 2017a. *Campaigns*. [online]. Available at: <www.tourismconcern.org.uk/campaigns/> [Accessed 9 January 2017].

Tourism Concern, 2017b. *Berlin Declaration "Transforming Tourism."* [pdf] Available at: <www.tourismconcern.org.uk/wp-content/uploads/2017/03/Berlin_Declaration.pdf> [Accessed 10 March 2017].

UN, n.d. *We can end poverty: Millennium Development Goals and Beyond 2015*. [online]. Available at: <www.un.org/millenniumgoals/> [Accessed 9 January 2017].

UN, 2014. *Report of the Working Group on the Right to Development on its fifteenth session (Geneva, 12–16 May 2014): Human Rights Council, Twenty-seventh session, Agenda item 3* [online doc]. Available at: <www.ohchr.org/EN/HRBodies/HRC/RegularSessions/Session27/Documents/A_HRC_27_45_ENG.doc> [Accessed 21 July 2017].

UN, 2015a. *The Millennium Development Goals Report 2015 - Summary*. [pdf] Available at: <www.un.org/millenniumgoals/2015_MDG_Report/pdf/MDG%202015%20Summary%20web_english.pdf> [Accessed 17 August 2016].

UN, 2015b. *Resolution adopted by the General Assembly on 25 September 2015. A/RES/70/1* [pdf] Available at: <www.un.org/ga/search/view_doc.asp?symbol=A/RES/70/1&Lang=E> [Accessed 21 July 2017].

UN, 2015c. *A Conversation with Jeffrey Sachs: 2015 a 'unique opportunity for our generation' to set new goals for a more prosperous world*. [video online]. Available at: <www.youtube.com/watch?v=_p-0H8E0Zu8> [Accessed 21 July 2017].

UN, 2015d. *Launch of new sustainable development agenda to guide development actions for the next 15 years*. [press release] 31 December. Available at: <www.un.org/sustainabledevelopment/blog/2015/12/launch-of-new-sustainable-development-agenda-to-guide-development-actions-for-the-next-15-years/> [Accessed 2 August 2017].

UN, 2017a. *The Sustainable Development Agenda. Sustainable Development Goals: 17 Goals to Transform Our World*. [online]. Available at: <www.un.org/sustainabledevelopment/development-agenda/> [Accessed 21 July 2017].

UN, 2017b. *International Day of the World's Indigenous Peoples - 9 August*. [online]. Available at: <www.un.org/en/events/indigenousday/> [Accessed 19 July 2017].

UN DESA, 2020. *UN/DESA Policy Brief #78: Achieving the SDGs through the COVID-19 response and recovery*. [online] 11 June. Available at <www.un.org/development/desa/dpad/publication/un-desa-policy-brief-78-achieving-the-sdgs-through-the-covid-19-response-and-recovery/> [Accessed 12 June 2020].

UNDP, 2007. *Human Rights and the Millennium Development Goals: Making the Link*. [pdf] Oslo: United Nations Development Programme, Oslo Governance Centre. Available at:<www.undp.org/content/dam/aplaws/publication/en/publications/poverty-reduction/poverty-website/human-rights-and-the-millennium-development-goals/Human%20Rights%20and%20the%20MDGs.pdf> [Accessed 6 February 2017].

UNEP and WTO, 2005. *Making Tourism More Sustainable: A Guide for Policy Makers*. [pdf] Paris and Madrid: United Nations Environmental Programme and World Tourism Organization. Available at: <www.unep.fr/shared/publications/pdf/DTIx0592xPA-TourismPolicyEN.pdf> [Accessed 5 February 2017].

UN-NGLS, 2002. *Human Rights Approaches to Sustainable Development* [press release] May. Available at: <www.un-ngls.org/orf/pdf/ru90hrsd.pdf> [Accessed 6 February 2017].

UN OHCHR, 2014. *Women's Rights are Human Rights.* [online]. Available at: <www.ohchr.org/Documents/Events/WHRD/WomenRightsAreHR.pdf> [Accessed 21 August 2019].

UN OHCHR, 2006. *Principles and Guidelines for a Human Rights Approach to Poverty Reduction Strategies.* [online]. Available at: <www.refworld.org/docid/46ceaef92.html> [Accessed 19 August 2019].

UNWTO, 1980. *Manila Declaration on World Tourism.* Madrid: World Tourism Organization.

UNWTO, 1995. *Sustainable Tourism Development; Background Paper by WTO Secretariat, (UNWTO Asian Tourism Conference, Technical Session, 13 January 1995, Islamabad, Pakistan).* Madrid: WTO.

UNWTO, 2015. *Tourism and the Sustainable Development Goals.* [pdf] www.e-unwto.org/doi/pdf/10.18111/9789284417254.

UNWTO, 2016. *Compilation of UNWTO Declarations.* July. [pdf] DOI: https://doi.org/10.18111/9789284419326.

UNWTO, n.d. *Sustainable Development of Tourism.* [online]. Available at: <http://sdt.unwto.org> [Accessed 6 February 2017].

UNWTO and UNDP, 2017. *Tourism and the Sustainable Development Goals – Journey to 2030.* Madrid: UNWTO.

Wild, C., 1994. Issues in Ecotourism. In: C.P. Cooper and A. Lockwood, (eds.), *Progress in Tourism, Recreation and Hospitality management (Volume Six).* Chichester: John Wiley & Sons, pp. 12–21.

World Charter for Sustainable Tourism +20. 2015. *World Charter for Sustainable Tourism +20.* [pdf] Available at: <www.skal.org/sites/default/files/media/Public/Web/PDFs/1015_peterclaesen_english.pdf> [Accessed 21 August 2019].

WTO, 1997. *Agenda 21 for the Travel and Tourism Industry* (English version). Madrid: WTO.

WTTC, 2015. *Travel and Tourism 2015 Connecting Global Climate Action.* [online]. Available at: <www.wttc.org/-/media/files/reports/policy-research/tt-2015—connecting-global-climate-action-a4-28pp-web.pdf> [Accessed 21 August 2019].

4
POLITICS, HUMAN RIGHTS, AND TOURISM

4.1 Introduction

The integration of international human rights treaties into domestic laws, and the implementation of related policies and legislation at various levels in a political system, can have a profound impact on the political environment. As noted in Chapter 1, the political environment in a country is the arena where regulations on rights are established. While the conceptual analysis of "rights" is an important theme in political theory, until recently, the topic of human rights has been relatively marginal in political science (Beetham, 1995; Cardenas, 2009; Carey, Gibney and Poe, 2010). Evans (2005) outlined three perspectives on human rights including: (1) the philosophy of rights, (2) the legal discourse on human rights, and (3) the political discourse on human rights. He argued that politics has played a lesser role in 'human rights talk' than either philosophy or law. The political discourse on human rights asks questions about power and interests, which are associated with a particular conception of rights. It also raises questions in regards to how and why dominant forms of legal reason and philosophy can sustain these interests (Evans, 2005, 2011). While the abstract, moral, and utopian approach of philosophy allows us to glimpse a better future, the neutral, empirical, and norm-driven approaches of international law reassure us that action is being taken on behalf of human rights (Evans, 2005, 2011). Together, these two perspectives have marginalised political discourse, whereby consideration of economic, social, and political structures and practices, which supports certain interests that sustain conditions for the continuous violations of human rights, are excluded (Evans, 2005, 2011). While the area may have been marginalised in the past, fields such as comparative politics – the study of political life inside countries (Cardenas, 2016), and the global politics of human rights (Salvador, 2019) have contributed significantly to the understanding of human rights, illustrating the evolving and important role for political approaches.

The political dimensions of tourism have also received less attention in literature (Richter, 2009) in the past, including those that intersect with human rights. An important element in regards to the politics of human rights and tourism is power and control – which is vital in considering the nature of government policies, how the tourism industry operates in various destinations, and to what extent human rights may be violated or upheld. A range of actors including government, industry, local communities, NGOs, international organisations, and tourists themselves, influence the operation of tourism. Like most businesses, tourism thrives in a stable and peaceful political environment. Factors such as political regimes, governmental policies, economic systems, laws, security, and human rights affect every business; tourism is no exception. Tourism developers, investors, and most tourists may show limited interest in places that are engulfed in protracted political crises, despite being endowed with great tourism potential. Insecurity issues and human rights violations tend to be very common in countries that experience political turmoil and other forms of instability. Civil protests may result in mass arrests, detentions, and crackdowns. Insurgencies and counter-insurgencies may result in states of emergencies, thereby affecting human rights and human security of the people in a given destination and cause travel restrictions. In destinations with a history of human rights violations, tourism has been used to try and legitimise the state. By attracting tourist investors and tourists, regimes have attempted to portray an element of international legitimacy, whilst human rights violations continue. Understanding the political environment and the political economy of tourism is central to examining the power relationships that impact human rights. Multinational tourism corporations, for example, may seek out destinations with government policies of lower minimum wages or less strict environmental regulations, resulting in negative impacts for the local communities. As noted by Bowen, Zubair, and Altinay (2016), it is not only important to make the connections between policy making, structures, values, and power in terms of tourism development, but also to understand how the patterns of dominance of stakeholder power, subservience, and decline evolve over time.

This chapter will focus on the intersection of the political dimensions of human rights and tourism. It begins by exploring the broader aspects of the politics of human rights, and setting out the concept of the political environment as it relates to the tourism industry. Threats to human rights are often intertwined with an unfavourable political environment, characterised by elements of political insecurity and the corruption of good governance, which all impact tourism. The comparative politics of human rights records of various nations and tourism businesses is highlighted; some countries and tourism enterprises host a significant number of tourists, yet have policies or operational procedures which result in human rights violations. As a foundation for understanding national policy in relation to tourism, the chapter explores human rights issues in the context of laws, and the principles of good governance. The chapter then examines a range of political issues with respect to tourism indicating how they impact human right, including political instability, the use of tourism to legitimise a state, tourism policy, political boycotts, the political economy of tourism, and tourism operations and working conditions.

4.2 Dimensions of the politics of human rights and the political environment

As noted by Beetham (1995), the conceptual analysis of "rights" is an important theme in political theory and some of these related issues have been addressed in Chapters 1–3. Balibar (2013) explores the "politics of human rights" in detail, and raises the quasi-tautological notion "apart from politics, or without a political system of institutions and actions, not only is there no implementation of human rights, but there is also no 'right' within these rights." Kistner (2014) notes that there has been a plethora of debates on the theoretical questions of the politics of human rights (see also Balibar, 2013; Beetham, 1995; Regilme Jr., 2018; Steinberg, 2015) including: human rights being premised on an hypothetical, isolated human being without any authority, which could guarantee these rights through reference to any source of legitimacy outside themselves (see Arendt, 2004); the gap between the "Rights of Man" and the "Rights of the Citizen"; depoliticisation of rights; role of the nation state; rights under different political regimes; linkages between human rights and democracy; right to politics; the right to have rights; universalism vs. relativism; cultural imperialism; women's rights; and human rights activism as anti-political (see Brown, 2004), to just name a few.

A further detailed conceptual analysis of the politics of human rights is beyond the scope of this chapter. Here, the focus will be on a broader range of political issues that are linked to issues of power and control within governments and tourism – which influences not only how the tourism industry is governed and operates but also, ultimately, to what extent human rights are upheld or violated. Ingram (2008) outlines three points of the politics of human rights, which include coercive power, law and institutions, and political action. The first focuses on the use of power to achieve certain ends and the politics of human rights, then using power to promote the moral imperative of advancing these rights. The second point is that human rights are a moral imperative, and should be embodied in institutions and taken up by the law. The third point on political action, is that rights arise from, and should be based on, the activities of the bearers. In this context, the politics of human rights is a creative, democratic politics of contestation, which challenges exclusions and inequalities in the name of the principles of equal freedom.

Political action occurs within the *political environment*, which can be quite broad in scope. In simple terms, the political environment refers to all government actions and inactions (policies), activities, institutions, laws, systems, security, human rights, and the prevailing political regimes that either facilitate or obstruct business activities and development. Such factors and activities may occur at the regional, national, subnational, or local level, to either facilitate or impede business activities and development (WebFinance, 2019). Moreover, Kuklinski, et al. (2001) construed the term political environment as "the totality of politically relevant communication to which citizens are exposed (p. 411)" that helps citizens to make political decisions, as well as help authorities finalise policies and political actions. Such a notion of political environment is strongly anchored to the concept of good governance examined later in this chapter.

The political environment has a strong influence on the economics and businesses of tourism (Dwyer, 2018). Business activities including tourism often require, and perform well, in a very stable political environment, where the factors noted above work positively to support their operations. Conversely, few business activities perform well in a volatile political environment, which are often characterised by protracted civil wars, political unrest, insecurity conditions, flagrant disregard of laws and institutions, unjust economic systems, poor human rights conditions, and unstable political regimes, to mention only a few (see also Saha and Yap, 2014). Klein (2007) referred to these businesses in the context of disaster capitalism (see Chapter 7 for discussion on disaster capitalism germane to tourism). A stable political environment which is more opened to business activities provides a congenial atmosphere for businesses to flourish by: (i) boosting investors' confidence, (ii) providing equal playing fields for businesses to compete, (iii) ensuring openness and accountability of businesses, and (iv) providing the framework to address business disputes and grievances. Businesses and investors pay key attention to risk analysis in the political environment, and such analysis often informs where businesses may decide to operate (WebFinance, 2019). The political environment of a nation often sets the tone for whether human rights are upheld or not.

4.3 Comparative politics: human rights records of nations and tourism businesses

In the context of comparative politics, comparing human rights practices or human rights records is an essential tool to understand the sources of both abuse and reform (Cardenas, 2016). Once-popular tourism hubs in the Middle East, North Africa, Turkey, Egypt, Tunisia, and many other countries have experienced plummeting tourist activities after political instability occurs – especially during and in the aftermath of the Arab Spring in the early 2010s (see Chapter 5). Deadly civil protests, and in some cases civil war (as exemplified in the case of Syria), create unstable political conditions which may result in government travel warnings, withdrawal of travel insurance, cancellation of travel plans, and the reduction of other tourist activities. As a corollary, other protests such as the labour demonstrations that engulfed Greece in 2011 and 2012; the 'Occupy Wall Street' movement in the USA; political protests against human rights violations at the Beijing Olympics in 2008 (quickly dismantled by the Chinese authorities) (CBC, 2008); student protests in Hong Kong; and the "Black Lives Matter" protests which began in the USA and spread around the globe particularly in 2020 to mention a few – all raise critical issues, but also tend to have potential impacts on tourism and tourist activities, at least for a certain period of time. These types of situations may affect foreign tourist inflow, revenue, and capital mobilisation into those countries, as well as impacting potential domestic tourism.

Mansbach and Lafferty (2008) identify a range of reasons for why governments violate the rights of individuals, including promoting their ideology and inducing fear. Dictators have forced citizens to accept ideological, religious, and political views while persecuting objectors. Rulers have also arbitrarily jailed opponents, used torture on political prisoners, denied justice and equality to ethnic and racial groups, treated women as chattel, killed opponents, and, in general, abused citizens (Mansbach and Lafferty, 2008). Various organisations, such as Amnesty International and Human Rights Watch, have sought to bring the world's attention to human rights abuses. Amnesty International has focused on freeing political and religious prisoners, assuring fair trials, eliminating torture, executions, harsh punishments, and bringing those who abuse human rights to justice through publicity, education, and political pressure (Mansbach and Lafferty, 2008). While it is beyond the scope of this chapter to discuss individual nations in detail, both Amnesty International and Human Rights Watch have country profiles on their websites, outlining human rights violations. Burnell and Randall (2005) identified barriers to human rights implementation in developing countries, which include: lack of finances; a lack of power in the global economy, leaving governments vulnerable to policies of powerful states, and non-state actors that can be unfriendly to human rights; corruption and an incompetent government; traditional cultures, where human rights may have had limited traction; ethnic divisions predisposed to conflict in times of scarcity, and subsequent repression; and the inability to meet growing expectations for economic progress can stimulate protests and repression. The complexity of the situation is revealed in the context of contemporary Brazil, a country aiming to boost visitor numbers by relaxing visa requirements (CTV News, 2019). While the state has committed the country to relevant international and regional human rights treaties, Brazilian society has become more violent, leading the state to undertake heavy-handed approaches to criminal suspects, especially in poor communities – resulting in a strong dualism in human rights (Martins and Pereira, 2018). Human Rights abuses also occur in developed countries; Amnesty International cites the USA as having policies seeking to narrow human rights protections for sexual and reproductive rights, LGBTQ+ related issues and protections, and there have been human rights violations in relation to asylum seekers along the US–Mexico border (Amnesty International, 2020). Human Rights Watch (2019a) notes some of Canada's long-standing human rights challenges as the right to safe drinking water of Indigenous peoples; mistreatment of Indigenous women and girls; and the Canadian government not taking effective action on abuses in overseas operations of Canadian extractive and apparel companies. Cuba depends heavily on international tourism, and especially the Canadian market; however, Amnesty International has raised concerns over the arbitrary detainment of independent artists, journalists, and members of the political opposition (Amnesty International, 2020).

The tourism industry has also been directly or indirectly responsible for human rights violations in regard to their operations (see Chapter 2). NGOs such as Tourism Concern, have raised human rights concerns over the operations of the industry linked to exploitation, displacement, poor pay, and poor working conditions. In Spain, legislative reforms by the government have allowed outsourcing, which hotels have taken advantage of. This has had negative impacts on the working conditions of hotel maids – such as reduction in salary, increase of workload, and an increase in health problems among others (Cañada, 2018). The cruise ship industry has come under intense criticism for flying flags of convenience (registering their vessels in a country with less stringent environmental and labour regulations), resulting in lower pay and long working hours (Terry, 2011; see Chapter 9 and 10). While the UN has called on states to ensure that enterprises in their territory respect human rights in their extraterritorial operations, to date, there are not many domestic laws specifically addressing the liability of parent or subcontracting companies for the violations of "just" working conditions of employees in foreign companies (Bueno, 2017). The Canadian mining corporation Nevsun in Eritrea faced a lawsuit in 2014 for human rights violations through its Eritrean sub-contractor. This case reached the Supreme Court of Canada (SCC) in 2020, and the SCC in a preliminary hearing stated all customary international law is part of Canadian common law; Canadian courts have jurisdiction on corporate liability of MNE like Nevsun[1] (SCC, 2020; Nwapi, 2017). Elsewhere in 2017, France's Duty of Vigilance Law was enacted, and hailed as a pioneering law – the first national legislation in the world to legally bind corporations for human and environmental rights violations (Cossart and Chatelain, 2019). NGOs (Friends of the Earth France, Survie and four Ugandan associations) filed a lawsuit against Total Uganda for violation of the Duty of Vigilance law; however, the Nantarre High Court (France) did not review the case, as it was determined that it fell within the jurisdiction of the Commercial Court (Friends of the Earth International, 2020). Thus, one of the central elements of human rights are the legal frameworks set out to protect human rights (see Chapters 2 and 10). Insights from comparative politics illustrate it is critical to understand the domestic and international linkages which can be determinants of human rights practices (Cardenas, 2016). Domestic politics can help explain why regimes commit differently to international human rights treaties, while international actors can either prolong human rights violations, or, on a positive note, empower societal groups while "building the state's institutional capacity to implement human rights" (Cardenas, 2016, p. 90). The following section explores human rights issues in politics and laws by examining international human rights laws and the importance of good governance for protecting human rights at the national level.

4.4 Human rights issues in laws and good governance

The emergence and evolution of the concepts of human rights, particularly in the Western world, were examined in Chapter 1. It is important to note that recognising human rights alone does not necessarily protect human rights. Without civil rights, the state, organisations, industries, groups, or individuals can threaten an individual's rights and freedoms. Many scholars consider a "declaration of human rights" as a form of political invention (c.f. Hunt, 2007 and Goodhart, 2016 for discussion). Throughout history, declarations of natural rights or freedoms were necessary in order to protect these rights. Other scholars consider a declaration of human rights as giving opportunities to the state or authorities to mask their political power through the use of language (c.f. Frankenberg, 2014 for arguments). The language of the UN Bill of Rights allows states and rights holders to justify their wrongdoings and atrocities by claiming the "unjust" conduct of others, i.e. a *just* war, a *civilising* mission, *rescue* torture, detaining *illegal* combatants, or a war on *terror*, etc. (Frankenberg, 2014, p. 40). It is also important to note that the declaration of human rights is clearly a political invention, as it defines what is "civilised" and "uncivilised" through the measures of practicing human rights in a certain way (Liu, 2014; Frankenberg, 2014). Having said that, it is undeniable that the declaration of human rights has led to changes in international and domestic laws (see Chapter 1).

Today, human rights are an important part of International Law, and states asseverate that they promote key human rights and freedoms. Showing respect for human rights is viewed as a reflection of a state's commitment to their citizens, as well as a reflection of the states' "acknowledgement of pre-eminence of rule of law" (Smith, 2016, p. 61). However, not all states embrace all of the human rights articles articulated in the International Bill of Rights. It has always been a major challenge as to how to transform the rhetoric of law into a functional mechanism to protect and enforce human rights; there are always legal means to avoid the state's full responsibility (Smith, 2016; White, 1985).

Achieving a human rights standard through international law and global governance can be extremely challenging. One argument is that the human rights articulated in the UDHR is a catalogue of "*desiderata*", which imposes obligations and duties onto a third party to ensure one's claim for rights; as such, authorities or states apply different interpretations and different principles in the arbitration of a rights conflict (Davis, 2012). Some warn that different nations do not discernibly respond to the global rights-based regimes in the same way in the global regimes of security or economic governance (Hathaway, 2002, cited in Grugel and Piper, 2007, p. 8). Thus, international coordination surrounding human rights can be incoherent. Another dimension to consider, is an individual state's political inclinations and domestic legal institutions – such as a democratic system or the inclination to liberalism – which all have a bearing on how human rights are regarded and operationalised.

After the declaration of the UDHR, the principle of global governance became paramount, with an emphasis on rights-based governance (Robinson, 2018). However, various institutional structures of states presented unique challenges in terms of human rights implementation (Robinson, 2018; Cardenas, 2016). Governance requires structures, systems, and practices in which participating groups and actors can make decisions, and take actions to achieve an end. Usually, the government/state oversees this role. Governance "determines who has power, who makes decisions, how other players make their voice heard and how account is rendered" (IOG, 2020). However, in global governance, there is no single entity that can act as a governing body to represent every participating nation's interests. The UN is an innately political entity and cannot be an impartial governing body; its unequal representation by population of the states, e.g. in the UN Security Council, cannot achieve fair and equal representation when it comes to voting (Peters, 2009). Yet, successful global governance that encompasses the principles of good governance is non-negotiable, if human rights standards are to be implemented successfully on a global level.

Lewis (2016, p. 179) argues that good governance is crucial to establishing the conditions that are conducive to the fulfilment of human rights. Human rights principles provide a "set of values which can guide a state or institution towards stronger governance, and the framework of international human rights laws serve to strengthen this relationship through enforcement mechanisms" (Lewis, 2016, p. 180). The definition of "good governance" is ambiguous, or flexible at the best, though the OHCHR (2019) stated it should encompass:

> full respect of human rights, the rule of law, effective participation, multi-actor partnerships, political pluralism, transparent and accountable processes and institutions, an efficient and effective public sector, legitimacy, access to knowledge, information and education, political empowerment of people, equity, sustainability, and attitudes and values that foster responsibility, solidarity and tolerance.

The measure of good governance is the degree to which a state delivers on its promise of human rights protection, and its ability in enforcement for its citizens (OHCHR, 2019). Without good governance, human rights cannot be delivered within the territory, as well as within the global community.

The two International Covenants of Human Rights (the International Covenant on Civil and Political Rights and the International Covenant on Economic, Social and Cultural Rights) recognise each participatory government's commitment to ensure human rights standards, and implicitly endorse a global rights-based development approach (OHCHR, 2019; Robinson, 2018). Nevertheless, some critics argue that global governance – which in principle, should enhance individual autonomy, an individual's political participation, and the more effective delivery of human rights – is incoherent and illegitimate (Davis, 2012). Thus, a failure to deliver good governance is a failure to present a favourable political environment. Lewis (2016), however, argues that a good governance framework built on human rights principles should be applied to the international climate regime in the fight against climate change. Good governance establishes the framework (laws, policies, institutions, programmes, etc.) for respective societies, economies, and environments. This framework, and to what degree it is enforced, has a significant impact then on the tourism industry and on human rights.

The Office of the UN High Commissioner for Human Rights (OHCHR 2007) published the "Good Governance Practices for the Protection of Human Rights," which explored the link between human rights and good governance in four areas: democratic institutions; the delivery of state services; the rule of law; and anti-corruption measures. Democratic reforms involve public participation, including multiple social groups in the decision-making process, and encouraging civil society and local communities to express their opinions on issues that are important to them. In the delivery of state services to the public, reforms focus on improving the state's capacity to provide essential public goods (e.g. right to education, health, and food), as well as improving mechanisms for accountability, transparency, and developing culturally sensitive policy tools to ensure public participation. Under the rule of law, human rights-sensitive initiatives include legislative reforms and assisting institutions (e.g. penal systems, courts, parliaments) to implement new legislation. Examples include: advocacy for legal reform, raising public awareness about national and international legal frameworks, capacity building, and the reformation of institutions. The final dimension is anti-corruption measures which focus on the principles of transparency, accountability, and participation to shape anti-corruption measures. Examples include creating anti-corruption commissions, developing mechanisms for sharing information, and monitoring governments' use of public funds and their implementation of policies (OHCHR, 2007).

The extent to which policies of good governance that protect human rights are adopted is an important question in the context of tourism destinations. For example, do destination governments operate in a transparent and accountable manner in establishing policies, legislative frameworks, and employment standards in regards to tourism? Good governance can not only be applied to governments, but it can also be applied in the operation of tourism enterprises. The following section will explore the political dimensions of tourism as they relate to human rights.

4.5 Politics, tourism, and the relationship to human rights

Richter (2009, p. 189) has argued that while tourism has not been explored to a great extent in the context of political science, concepts such as "legitimacy, power, stakeholder analysis, sovereignty, democracy, equity, political development, colonialism, risk analysis, heritage preservation, sustainability, and gender roles" have been applied to tourism. This section will examine a variety of perspectives on the role of politics in tourism, and how this relates to human rights. Two of these perspectives are closely connected. The first perspective relates to the role of the state, in terms of political stability and security, and whether human rights are upheld. In 2019, Sri Lanka was named as the world's number one tourist destination by Lonely Planet; however, both Amnesty International and Human

Rights Watch have raised a number of human right concerns in their respective profiles of the country (Amnesty International, 2020; Wilson, 2018). States establish the political environment of the destination, including setting out policies, laws, and plans related to tourism investment, and how tourism operates in the country. NGOs continue to bear down pressure on states and tourism enterprises to uphold human rights. The second perspective this section will consider is the operations of the tourism industry. The final section of the chapter focuses on the political economy of tourism, illustrating who has power in the industry, and how the tourism industry if controlled, can have a significant impact on human rights.

4.5.1 Political stability, state policy, tourism, and human rights

Political stability and security play an enormous role in the tourism industry, and often illustrates how fragile the industry can be. Global security has undergone tremendous change with the dawn of the new Millennium. Shortly after the 9/11 terrorist attacks on the United States in 2001, the tightening of national security became vital, and technology has improved in this area very rapidly. Innovative security techniques – such as the collection of biometric information, facial recognition, body scanners, surveillance cameras, voice/speech recognition, and e-passports with radio frequency identification – at points of entry and exit have emerged to identify potential criminals who pose risks to national security (See Chapters 5 and 9). Despite these security innovations, concerns relating to the rights of individual/personal privacy, racial and religious profiling, as well as discrimination against travellers who have different beliefs and values – including those against the use of technology – are still major issues of concern to the post-9/11 security regime.

Additionally, global security has witnessed many new developments in public safety measures such as: travel bans, visa suspensions of certain nationalities and individuals, governmental travel alerts/advisories for visitation to certain countries, no-fly lists, and the presence of armed guards at ports, stations, public places, road check-points, and borders – as well as at departure and arrival points for flights and vessels (see Chapters 5 and 9 for more discussion). On Easter in 2019, a terrorist group attacked three luxury hotels and three churches in Sri Lanka, targeting not only tourists but locals as well. Many countries around the world immediately issued travel warnings, but for some countries – including Australia, these were relaxed a few months later (Browning, 2019).

All these developments have had different impacts on mobility, and on travel and tourism – both nationally and internationally. The following are some political stability and security issues affecting travel and tourism: (i) conflicts and civil unrest, (ii) terrorism, (iii) diseases and epidemics/pandemics, (iv) violent crimes, (v) transportation safety, (vi) piracy, (vii) natural disasters, (viii) food safety, (ix) human rights abuses, (x) clash of cultures, (xi) personal safety, (xii) public safety measures, (xiii) immigration policies, (xiv) economic policies, and (xv) gross human rights violations. The intractable conflict and insecurity in places such as

Somalia, Afghanistan, Libya, and Iraq have made many of these destinations not only unattractive to many travellers, but also impossible to access due to travel restrictions. As a corollary, violent civil unrests – such as the Arab Spring protests in Egypt, Tunisia, Bahrain, and many other places negatively impacted tourism flow. Even social activism movements have had impacts on travel and tourism. Egypt, Tunisia, and other countries that experienced the Arab Spring had plummeting international tourist arrival numbers due to violent civil protests (see Chapter 5). Box 4.1 illustrates the examples of Somalia and Ethiopia in the context of political instability, human rights, and tourism. Croatia, on the other hand, is an example of a state that has rebuilt its tourism industry after war. Political stability and security issues surrounding the outbreak of disease, such as Ebola, SARS, and COVID-19, are further covered in the context of human security in Chapter 5.

BOX 4.1 POLITICAL INSTABILITY, HUMAN RIGHTS, AND TOURISM IN SOMALIA AND ETHIOPIA

Somalia was once known as the "Pearl of the Indian Ocean," and a haven for tourists seeking relaxation and natural beauty; it offered wonderful and attractive beaches, waterfalls, historical sites, parks, and culture for tourism in the 1960s, 1970s, and 1980s before civil war erupted in 1991 (UNSOM, 2018). Two decades of strife between militia and Islamic groups followed, and subsequently the Al-Qaida-affiliated group Al-Shabaab terrorised the Mogadishu area (Hatcher, 2012). Meanwhile, desperately poor fishermen began pirating along the country's coast (Lucas, 2013). For over 25 years since the civil war, the foreigners who visited Somalia were largely diplomats, aid workers, African Union Peacekeepers, employees of the United Nations, and other international charity and humanitarian groups (UNSOM, 2018). Most of the tourists were expatriate Somalis (Hatcher, 2012). Years of civil war and political violence saw the country witnessing serious human rights violations (killings, arbitrary arrests, degrading human treatment, etc.), coupled with an increase in violent crimes such as robbery, kidnapping, rape, hijacking, piracy, terrorism, killing – to list only a few. During the 1990s and early 2000s, several governments issued travel alerts warning citizens to avoid non-urgent visits to Somalia. These security advisories, coupled with the civil war (which brought everything in the country to a standstill) – as well as negative international press on human rights and security – negatively affected tourism in Somalia.

Efforts have been made to return the country to its lost glory. Key amongst these efforts was the admission of Somalia as the 157th member of the United Nations World Tourism Organization in 2017 (UNSOM, 2018). At the end of 2018, there were over 150 travel agencies operating within Somalia; there are some limited foreign flights to facilitate the movement of tourists and visitors (UNSOM, 2018), despite several travel advisories issued against travelling to

Somalia by several states. Present concerning human rights issues in this "relative" peacetime in Somalia include gendered violence; abuse of children's rights, religious rights, and personal liberties (see Human Rights Watch, 2017). In sum, the tourism industry in Somalia virtually collapsed for almost 25 years due to intractable insecurity conditions and gross human rights violations experienced by the country during – and in the aftermath – of the civil war.

Interestingly, the history of the tourism industry in Ethiopia (Somalia's western border neighbour) is very different. Both Somalia and Ethiopia have had their own security and human rights challenges, but the tourism industry in Ethiopia did not collapse as it did in Somalia. Like Somalia, Ethiopia also went through a civil war between 1974 and 1991, and also warred with its neighbour – Eritrea – between 1961 and 1991 (the Eritrean War of Independence), and then again in 1998 and 2000 (Eritrean–Ethiopian War). Both wars created several security and human rights challenges for Ethiopia – just as the Somalian civil war did for Somalia. Furthermore, another difficulty Ethiopia experienced was severe famine in 1984, claiming the lives of more than a million of its population (Smith, 2014). Despite these challenges, tourism in Ethiopia did not collapse as it did in Somalia.

With sustained efforts to maintain security, develop an aviation industry (Ethiopian Airlines became known as one of Africa's best airlines to offer regional and global flights), and the development of Adis Ababa as a regional hub, Ethiopia's travel and tourism economy has grown over the years (Government of Ethiopia, 2019). As noted above, the incessant wars, political unrest, famine, unfavourable economic policies, and poor infrastructure influenced tourism development in Ethiopia negatively (Asmara, 2016). Fortunately, Ethiopia's natural beauty won UNESCO Heritage sites, as well as the hearts of ecotourists and adventure tourists. According to the World Travel and Tourism Council (WTTC, 2019), the travel and tourism economy in Ethiopia grew by 48.6% in 2018; representing the largest growth of any country in the world (i.e. surpassing the global average growth rate of 3.9% and the African average of 5.6%, see Government of Ethiopia, 2019). The WTTC 2019 annual review stated that the tourism sector in Ethiopia in 2018 contributed US$7.4 billion to the economy – which represented an increase of US$2.2 billion against 2017 figures; the travel and tourism sector employed 2.2 million of the population or representing 8.3% of total employment (WTTC, 2019). The country, however, will see a decline in the context of the COVID-19 pandemic.

Countries with poor human rights records have used tourism in an attempt to win support for their regime; examples include the Marcos dictatorship in The Philippines, Franco's Spain, and Taiwan under Chiang Kai-Shek (Richter, 2009). When human rights violations are brought to the attention of tourists and agencies such as NGOs, it had led to boycotts of tourism destinations and companies (see Box 4.2).

BOX 4.2 TOURISM BOYCOTTS: HUMAN RIGHTS AND POLITICS

Tourism boycotts have been enacted against destinations, attractions, and service providers for a variety of reasons – including human rights violations, social causes (i.e. violation of animal rights), and political statements (see Shaheer, Insch and Carr, 2017; Yu, et al., 2020; Mowforth and Munt, 2016) – leading to a decrease in market share (loss of tourists), as well as damage to the image of the company or destination. Yu, et al. (2020) identified the main aspects for studies on boycotts including: the motivations for the boycott, the purpose of the boycott, boycott actions, and the effects of boycotts including changes in public policy, corporate practices, and financial impacts. After examining 146 boycotts between 1948 and 2015, Shaheer, Insch and Carr (2017) found that over 90% were initiated between 2003 and 2015. They found the increase in destination boycotts was a result of: innovation of new technology, including social media platforms; increase in social movements; emphasis on ethical consumerism; and using tourism as a vehicle for social change. An important boycott of note directly related to human rights involved Myanmar, also known as Burma. In 1990 when the National League for Democracy (NLD) won 81 percent of the vote, the generals (State Law and Order Council) imprisoned most of the newly elected parliamentarians. Later in 2007, the military regime used a brutal crackdown on prodemocracy uprisings (see Mowforth and Munt, 2016). In terms of tourism, the regime had been attracting hotel investors, declared 1996 as the "Visit Myanmar Year," and drew a growing number of visitors; together which they hoped would collectively lend a claim of political legitimacy for the regime. The leader of the NDL, Aung San Suu Kyi, asked visitors to stay away in 1996, and Tourism Concern (UK-based NGO focused on ethical tourism), initiated a Burma Campaign in the year 2000; the campaign urged people to stop buying all Lonely Planet guidebooks, as the company had been publishing a guidebook on Burma. In 2010, when Aung San Suu Kyi was released, the boycott ended (Mowforth and Munt, 2016). Recently, there have been renewed calls for a boycott of the country due to the ongoing persecution of the Rohingya people.

In a detailed analysis of seven events leading to Chinese tourists to boycotting other countries, Yu, et al. (2020) found that four of the seven exhibited political animosity. These examples are linked to the occurrence of an international bilateral political incident, which can then be connected to a dyadic political hazard, national/regional conflict (i.e. involving territory/resources), or political ideology. An example used in the article was the Chinese boycott of the Philippines, over the country's handling of an incident where Chinese tourists were hijacked. The political animosity cases had longer-term impacts on visitor numbers.

> The growing use of tourism boycotts raises many issues, including whether boycotts can influence change on human rights issues, what the role of civil society in promoting boycotts is, and if tourists and tourism investors will heed boycotts.

State policies and regulations linked directly or indirectly to tourism can have a profound impact on human rights – with implications for tourists, tourism developers, the industry, host communities, and those people whose lives depend either directly or indirectly on tourism. Government policies allowing tourism development to displace locals (see Chapter 7) may generate economic development but deprive local and Indigenous residents access to resources (Jennings, 2017; see Chapter 12). Tourism planning decisions that favour resort enclaves may further exclude local participation. Regulations, or lack thereof, of the sharing economy has led to gentrification and overtourism – forcing out local residents as rent and the cost of living continue to increase (Telfer, 2019). Policies related to employment, either formally or informally, in the tourism industry can raise human rights issues related to job insecurity, poor working conditions, low wages, lack of benefits and severance packages, intimidation and abuse, labour exploitation, underage employment (child labour), child exploitation, trafficking, safety and security concerns. According to the WTTC, an estimated 5.5 million children are victims of human trafficking, and are part of the larger number of an estimated 40 million people who are victims of human trafficking globally (see ECPAT, 2019). In the case of migrant workers in the tourism industry, some of the common issues they face are exploitation, abuse and violence, lack of access to proper healthcare, discrimination, low wages, lack of benefits and severance packages, occupational hazards (unsafe working conditions), employment insecurity, tolerance and acceptance of intimidation due to fear of losing immigration statuses (deportation), physical and mental health issues, and legal and immigration barriers (Faraday, 2019; Global News, 2019; see Chapter 10). Despite the fact that women play a significant role in the labour force in tourism, their disadvantageous positions in social and political spheres (see Chapter 8) have resulted in discrimination which can be political, and based on social demands built upon traditions, customs, and religions. Sex workers in the tourism industry face a significant number of human rights issues including: stigmatisation, vulnerability to violence and abuse, exploitation, physical and mental health issues, exposure to sexually transmitted diseases, marginalisation, occupational hazards, and a lack of access to proper reproductive healthcare (Rapaport, 2016; see Chapter 13). Richter (2009, p. 197) argues that tourism has been politicised at the international level by its association with prostitution at international sporting events.

Boonabaana (2014) reviewed the literature on tourism employment and gender, and notes the inequalities that impact women include the gender pay gap; women missing out on formal employment as a result of religious norms restricting their movement in public spaces; sex-stereotyped occupations; and the combination of tourism work with household responsibilities. Traditions and customs in a society can limit the participation of women in the tourism industry, and it is important to investigate whether these traditions are supported by states. From a feminist perspective, Enole (2014) notes that sexist stereotyping in tourism has prevented women from gaining the empowerment and development benefits that tourism can potentially generate. In her study in Uganda, Boonabaana (2014) notes the customs of polygamy, bride wealth, and later Christianity, have resulted in perpetuating male dominance and the subordination of women in society. Further, one of the main constraints on women looking to work in the industry was seeking male permission; however, those that have been able to participate in tourism note the financial autonomy, mobility, and networking opportunities as a result of tourism (Boonabaana, 2014). In exploring the interconnection between the SDGs and tourism from a gender perspective, Alarcón and Cole (2019) state that there cannot be sustainability for tourism without gender equality. They suggest the inclusion of Human Rights Impact Assessments, Women's Empowerment Principles, and Gender Audits as some of the preliminary steps businesses can take towards the SDGs; they also note issues of sexual harassment, intersectional issues, and the additional burdens tourism places on women as needing more detailed analysis (see Chapter 8 for further discussion).

4.5.2 *The political economy in tourism operations and human rights*

Tourism companies operate within the policies and regulations set out by various governments, but depending on the nature of the tourism enterprise they may also be governed or influenced by the powerful forces of the globalised tourism industry (see Chapter 2). How a company navigates the political, economic, social, and environmental milieu it operates in – along with a company's own operational policies – will have an impact on human rights. A political economy lens is useful in investigating power relations in the tourism industry as outlined by Bianchi (2015). Bianchi (2015, p. 291) defines political economy in tourism as "the examination of the systematic sources of power which both reflect and constitute the competition for resources and the manipulation of scarcity, in the context of converting people, places and histories into objects of tourism consumption." Bianchi (2015) argues the key concepts of the political economy of tourism over the past three decades have shifted. Capitalist restructuring, and economic globalisation – facilitated by neoliberal economics – have reconfigured power relations, resulting in the increasing dominance of transnational tourism corporations, as well as the growing structural power of market forces at global and regional levels. Cross border foreign direct investment, and investment in tourism sub-industries, is occurring alongside the growth of tourism regions, which are becoming relatively autonomous actors competing for mobile tourism capital. Bianchi (2015) claims the dominance and influence of transnational tourism corporations over particular tourism subsectors and distribution chains need to be considered in the context of the arrangements of enterprises and labour. Although there has been a trend in deregulation and privatisation, suggesting a weakening of the state, state actors still play a central role in restructuring places, which are in accordance with the interests of tourism capital (Bianchi, 2015). Transnational tourism corporations have the ability to dictate the scope of product diversification and innovation, while externalising risk through contractual relations with suppliers, thereby distributing the balance of power in favour of capital rather than that of local destination workers and businesses (Bianchi, 2015). The balance of power is often lopsided, with the power being held by foreign ownership or domestic elites (Richter, 2009). As Richter (2009, p. 194) suggests, tourism developers too often create lucrative deals with elites in power, and then are often left to the changing fortunes of the elites. Given the structure of the tourism industry, it is important to consider how this impacts human rights. Jacobs (2018) argues that the modern development of Dubai – with its luxurious hotels, skyscrapers, and shopping malls – has mainly been built by migrant workers. These same workers have complained of harsh working conditions, long shifts, and companies that withhold paychecks or worker's passports so that they are not able to quit or return home. Many workers are brought to Dubai on a visa sponsorship programme, the costs of which are passed on to the workers (Jacobs, 2018). While Human Rights Watch and the United Nations have acknowledged improvements in laws related to migrant workers, they indicate labour abuses continue (Jacobs, 2018). With the potential for a globalised workforce, tourism enterprises can draw on migrant workers for construction or to work in the cruise ship industry, where similar concerns about working conditions and rates of pay have been raised. It is important to note that tourism is a luxury product, which coexists alongside poverty in both developing and developed countries (Telfer, 2019). From a developed country perspective, Krenn (2012) observed that while Austria is known for beautiful landscapes and high-quality infrastructure, the tourism sector suffers from low income levels, low wage satisfaction, limited career opportunities, unfavourable working conditions, significant use of over-qualified workers, and a high level of career breaks. Given the political economy of tourism, enterprises have the opportunity to take advantage of globalisation, yet this may impact human rights. Pressures are being brought to bear for tourism enterprises to behave in a more responsible manner, and ensure human rights are protected. The OECD policy statement *Tourism Policies for Sustainable and Inclusive Growth* (2017), called for the industry to "use tourism as an engine for inclusive growth, to create quality jobs, businesses and regional development opportunities, mitigate the negative impacts on local communities, and spread the benefits to all people and territories." Arguably, some forms of tourism – such as community-based tourism – are based on the premise that politically, control is in the hands of the local community. In developing a framework for cultural sustainability for Aboriginal tourism in British Columbia, Thimm (2019, p. 206) argued that the protection of human rights, good self-governance, identity, control of the land, the tourism products' authenticity, and a market-ready tourism product – must all be taken into account.

4.6 Conclusion

Richter argues that the twenty-first century may be "the era where political scientists belatedly recognize that the core issues of political science inquiry are germane and compelling for the world's largest industry [tourism]" (2009, p. 198). Many of the political dimensions of tourism, including state policy and how the tourism industry operates, have direct implications on human rights. Human rights records are, in part, linked to the type of government in power and the type of governing system. As Harari (2018) suggests, it appeared liberalism had won an overwhelming victory in the ideological battles between fascism, communism, and liberalism at the end of the twentieth century. "Democratic politics, human rights and free-market capitalism seemed destined to conquer the entire world" (Harari, 2018, p. xvi). But as often is the case, history has taken an unexpected turn and as fascism and communism collapsed, liberalism is now in trouble (Harari, 2018). While there have been tremendous advancements in human rights, there have been some steps backwards in terms of human rights – even in liberal democratic systems. As Kistner (2014) suggests, "the confrontation between human rights and politics is ubiquitous in political modernity" (p. 122). How international human rights treaties and laws are integrated into domestic laws, and how various national, regional, and local political systems establish and enact policies and laws through good governance, have a profound impact on the political environment and on human rights. Even where human rights laws are passed, it still requires the political will of implementation and enforcement for them to take effect. This, combined with a globalised economy in which multinational corporations illustrate the complexity of the politics, relates to human rights. "If tourism developers ever laboured under the illusion that their fate was dependent only on economics, they have been increasingly made aware of their vulnerability to politics" (Richter 2009, p. 194). While there will continue to be debates on the conceptual analysis of "rights" in political theory (Beetham 1995; Evans 2005, 2011), this chapter has taken a broad approach in examining the relationship between politics, human rights, and tourism. Tourism is used as an economic development tool, where governments offer investment incentives to attract investors. Where human rights have been at the centre of this process, whole communities can benefit. As noted above, adopting the principles of good governance can protect human rights. Where there has been exploitation, and instances of the tourism industry taking advantage through mechanisms human rights abuses are found. It sometimes falls to NGOs and individual tourists to raise the alarm to boycott destinations. de la Dehesa (2006) examines the *Winners and Losers in Globalization* and notes the process of "social dumping" – whereby poor countries exploit their comparative advantage via cheap labour, non-existent social protections, excessive workhours, and despicable working conditions. Richter (2009) argues that the political issues raised by tourism require greater regulations, strict standards, not *laissez-faire* trade, and levels of political commitment to international protocols that guarantee heightened levels of scrutiny both among and above nations. Within this context, the commitment to international human rights protocols needs to be enhanced. It is important tourism adopts a human rights approach (Tourism Concern, 2014). The structure of tourism, and whether it operates on the principles of sustainability and empowers communities and individuals, is key to understanding its relationship to human rights. The following chapter will further explore the concepts of human rights by focusing on human security.

Note

1 Nevsun vs Araya case raised the issue that international law traditionally focuses on the crime of the state, not of corporations. Notwithstanding, Canadian Common law has jurisdiction over allegations and claims of human rights violation abroad by sub-contractors. This February 2020 ruling opens the possibility of lawsuits against MNE for human rights crimes committed abroad (Jones, 2020; Volterra Fietta, 2020; Lam, Bridges and Chen, 2020).

References

Alarón, D. and Cole, S., 2019. No sustainability for tourism without gender equality. *Journal of Sustainable Tourism* [e-journal] 27(7), pp. 903–919. https://doi.org/10.1080/09669582.2019.1588283.

Amnesty International, 2020. *Countries*. [online] 5 March. Available at: <www.amnesty.org/en/countries/>. [Accessed 16 April 2020].

Arendt, H., 2004. The origins of totalitarianism. Reprint of the origins of totalitarianism by Hannah Arendt, 1951. Introduction by Samantha Power. New York: Harvest-Harcourt.

Asmare, B.A., 2016. Pitfalls of tourism development in Ethiopia: the case of Bahir Dar town and its surroundings. *Korean Social Science Journal* [e-journal] 43(6), pp. 15–28. DOI: 10.1007/s40483-016-0029-1.

Balibar, E., 2013. On the politics of human rights. *Constellations* [e-journal] 20(1), pp. 18–26. DOI: https://doi.org/10.1111/cons.12018.

Beetham, D., 1995. Introduction: human rights in the study of politics. *Political Studies* [pdf] XLIII, pp. 1–9. DOI: https://onlinelibrary.wiley.com/doi/pdf/10.1111/j.1467-9248.1995.tb01696.x.

Bianchi. R., 2015. Towards a new political economy of global tourism revisited. In: R. Sharpley and D. Telfer, (eds.), *Tourism and Development Concepts and Issues*, 2nd Edition. Bristol: Channel View Publications, pp. 287–331.

Boonabaana, B. 2014. Negotiating gender and tourism work: women's lived experiences in Uganda. *Tourism and Hospitality Research* 14(1–2), pp. 27–36. https://doi.org/10.1177/1467358414529578.

Bowen, D., Zubair, S. and Altinay, L., 2016. Politics and tourism destination development: the evolution of power. *Journal of Travel Research* 56(6), pp. 725–743. DOI: https://doi.org/10.1177/0047287516666719.

Brown, W., 2004. "The most we can hope for…": human rights and the politics of fatalism. *South Atlantic Quarterly*, 103 (2–3), pp. 297–310. [online]. Available at: <https://muse.jhu.edu/article/169139#info_wrap> [Accessed 16 April 2020].

Browning, M., 2019. Sri Lanka declared safe to travel after terror attacks. *Escape*. [online]. 14 June. Available at: <www.escape.com.au/destinations/asia/sri-lanka/sri-lanka-declared-safe-to-travel-after-terror-attacks/news-story/2730bebf6dcbb4fc381f2e6fd11ac4bb> [Accessed 19 April 2020].

Bueno, N, 2017. Corporate liability for violations of the human right to just conditions of work in extraterritorial operations. *International Journal of Human Rights* [e-journal] 21(5), pp. 565–588. DOI: https://doi.org/10.1080/13642987.2017.1298092.

Burnell, P. and Randall, V., 2005. *Politics in the Developing World*. Oxford: Oxford University Press.

Cañada, E., 2018. Too precarious to be inclusive? Hotel main employment in Spain. *Tourism Geographies* [e-journal] 20(4), pp. 653–674. DOI: https://doi.org/10.1080/14616688.2018.1437765.

Cardenas, S., 2009. Mainstreaming Human Rights: publishing trends in political science. *PS: Political Science and Politics* [PDF] 42(1), pp. 161–166. DOI: 10.1017/S1049096509090143.

Cardenas, S., 2016. Human rights in comparative politics. In: M. Goodhart, (ed.), 2016. *Human Rights: Politics and Practice*, 3rd Edition. Oxford: Oxford University Press, pp. 77–92.

Carey, S., Gibney, M. and Poe, S., 2010. *The Politics of Human Rights: The quest for Dignity*. Cambridge: Cambridge University Press.

CBC News, 2008. Protesters interrupt ceremony for Beijing Olympics. *CBC News*. [online]. 24 March. Available at: <www.cbc.ca/news/world/protesters-interrupt-ceremony-for-beijing-olympics-1.699907> [Accessed 19 September 2018].

Conrad, C. and Moore, W., 2010. What stops the torture? *American Journal of Political Science*, 54 (2), pp. 459–476. [online]. Available at: <www.jstor.org/stable/25652217> [Accessed 8 April 2020].

Conrad, C.R., 2013. Why democracy doesn't always improve human rights. *LSE European Politics and Policy (EUROPP)*[Blog].18 October. Available at: <https://scholars.org/contribution/why-democracy-does-not-always-improve-human-rights> [Accessed 8 April 2020].

Cossart, S. and Chatelain, L., 2019. What lessons does France's Duty of Vigilance law have for other national initiatives? *Business and Human Rights Resource Centre*. [online] 27 June. Available at: <www.business-humanrights.org/en/what-lessons-does-frances-duty-of-vigilance-law-have-for-other-national-initiatives> [Accessed 23 May 2020].

CTV News, 2019. Brazil to allow Canadians to visit visa-free for 90 days. *CTV News*. [online] 19 March. Available at: <www.ctvnews.ca/lifestyle/brazil-to-allow-canadians-to-visit-visa-free-for-90-days-1.4342621> [Accessed 20 April 2020].

Davis, J. W., 2012. A critical view of global governance. *Swiss Political Science Review* 18(2), pp. 272–286. doi:10.1111/j.1662-6370.2012.02069.x.

dela Dehesa, G., 2006. *Winners and Losers in Globalization*. Oxford: Blackwell Publishing.

Dwyer, L., 2018, Economics of tourism, In: C.Cooper, S.Volo, W.C.Gartner and N. Scott, (eds.), *The Sage Handbook of Tourism Management: Theories, Concepts and Disciplinary Approaches to Tourism*. London: Sage Publications Ltd, pp. 173–189. doi: 10.4135/9781526461452.n11.

ECPAT, 2019. World travel & tourism council takes action against human trafficking. End Child Prostitution & Trafficking. [online] 9 April. Available at: <www.ecpat.org/news/travel-tourism-council-human-trafficking/> [Accessed 26 December 2019].

Enole, C., 2014. *Bananas, Beaches and Bases: Making Feminist Sense of International Politics*. Berkley: University of California Press.

Evans, T., 2005. *The Politics of Human Rights: A Global Perspective*, 2nd Edition. London: Pluto Press.

Evans. T., 2011. Castles in the air: "universal" human rights in the global political economy. In: G. Teeple and S. McBride, (eds.), *Relations of Global Power: Neoliberal Order and Disorder*. Toronto: University of Toronto Press. Chapter 8.

Faraday, F., 2019. We can no longer ignore the exploitation of migrant workers in Canada. Opinion. *The Globe and Mail*. [online] 8 April. Available at: <www.theglobeandmail.com/opinion/article-we-can-no-longer-ignore-the-exploitation-of-migrant-workers-in-canada/> [Accessed 9 December 2019].

Frankenberg, G., 2014. Human rights and the belief in a just world. *International Journal of Constitutional Law* 12(1), pp. 35–60. DOI: https://doi.org/10.1093/icon/mot068.

Friends of the Earth International, 2020. 6 NGOs file lawsuit against Total over alleged failure to respect French Duty of Vigilance law in its operations in Uganda. *Business and Human Rights Resource Centre*. [online] 31 January. Available at: <www.business-humanrights.org/en/6-ngos-file-lawsuit-against-total-over-alleged-failure-to-respect-french-duty-of-vigilance-law-in-its-operations-in-uganda> [Accessed 23 May 2020].

Global News, 2019. Calls for reform after Ontario migrant workers claim they worked in terrible conditions. *Global News*. [online] 16 March. Available at: <https://globalnews.ca/news/5063850/migrant-workers-reform-ontario/> [Accessed 9 December 2019].

Goodhart, M., 2016. Introduction. In: M. Goodhart, (ed.), *Human Rights: Politics and Practice*, 3rd Edition. Oxford: Oxford University Press, pp. 1–8.

Government of Ethiopia, 2019. Ethiopia scores highest tourism growth in the world. [online] 12 April. Available at: <www.ethioembassy.org.uk/ethiopia-records-biggest-growth-in-world-travel-and-tourism/> [Accessed 12 February 2020].

Grugel, J. and Piper, N., 2007. *Critical Perspectives on Global Governance: Rights and Regulation in Governing Regimes*. Abingdon, Oxon: Routledge.

Harari, Y. N., 2018. *21 Lessons for the 21st Century*. Toronto: Signal (Penguin Random House Canada).

Hatcher, J., 2012. Somalia: does tourism stand a chance in Mogadishu? *The Telegraph*. [online] 2 August. Available at: <www.telegraph.co.uk/travel/news/Somalia-does-tourism-stand-a-chance-in-Mogadishu/> [Accessed 23 April 2020].

Human Rights Watch, 2017. *World Report 2018. Somalia: events of 2017*. [online]. Available at: <www.hrw.org/world-report/2018/country-chapters/somalia> [Accessed 9 February 2020].

Human Rights Watch, 2019a. *Canada*. [online] 9 December. Available at: <www.hrw.org/americas/canada> [Accessed 17 April 2020].

Human Rights Watch, 2019b. *World Report 2019*. [online] Available at: <www.hrw.org/sites/default/files/world_report_download/hrw_world_report_2019.pdf> [Accessed 15 December 2019].

Hunt, L., 2007. *Inventing Human Rights: A History*. New York: WW Norton & Company.

Ingram, J.D., 2008. What is a "Rights to Have Rights'? Three images of the politics of human rights. *American Political Science Review* [e-journal] 102(4), pp. 401–416. DOI: https://doi.org/10.1017/S0003055408080386.

IOG, 2020. Defining governance. *Institute on Governance*. [online]. Available at: <https://iog.ca/what-is-governance/> [Accessed 7 April 2020].

Jacobs, H., 2018. Dubai's glittering, futuristic metropolis came at the cost of hundreds of thousands of workers, and recommending it as a tourist destination feels wrong.

Business Insider. [online] 15 December. Available at: <www.businessinsider.com/dubai-development-tourism-workers-problem-2018-12> [Accessed 19 April 2020].

Jennings, H., 2017. *Indigenous people & tourism. Tourism Concern Research briefing.* [pdf] Available at: <www.tourismconcern.org.uk/wp-content/uploads/2016/02/Indigenous-Peoples-Tourism-1.pdf> [Accessed 9 December 2019].

Jones, B., 2020. Commentary: Canadian Court ruling opens the way for lawsuits against companies for human rights abuses committed abroad. *Business and Human Rights Resource Centre.* [online] 1 May. Available at: <www.business-humanrights.org/en/commentary-canadian-court-ruling-opens-the-way-for-lawsuits-against-companies-for-human-rights-abuses-committed-abroad> [Accessed 23 May 2020].

Kistner, U., 2014. A politics of human rights – The right to rights as universal right to politics? *Acta Academica* [pdf] 46(3), pp. 122–133. Available at: <https://repository.up.ac.za/bitstream/handle/2263/43447/Kistner_Politics_2014.pdf?sequence=1> [Accessed 16 April 2020].

Klein, N., 2007. *The Shock Doctrine: The Rise of Disaster Capitalism.* New York: Henry Holt Company.

Krenn, M., 2012. Working conditions – the dark side of tourism. European foundation for the improvements of living and working conditions. *European Foundation.* [online] 14 March. Available at: <www.eurofound.europa.eu/publications/article/2012/working-conditions-the-dark-side-of-tourism> [Accessed 19 April 2020].

Kuklinski, J.H., Quirk, P.J., Jerit, J. and Rich, R.F., 2001. The political environment and citizen competence. *American Journal of Political Science,* 45(2), pp. 410–424. DOI: 10.2307/2669349.

Lam, M., Bridges, M.S. and Chen, E., 2020. Supreme Court of Canada cracks open the door for international human rights tort claims in Nevsun Resources Ltd. v. Araya. *McCarthy Tétrault.* [online] 4 March. Available at: <www.mccarthy.ca/en/insights/blogs/canadian-appeals-monitor/supreme-court-canada-cracks-open-door-international-human-rights-tort-claims-nevsun-resources-ltd-v-araya> [Accessed 24 May 2020].

Lewis, B., 2016. Enhancing good governance within the international climate regime through human rights principles. In: T. Cadman, R. Maguire and C. Sampford, (eds.), *Governing Climate Change Regime.* London: Routledge, pp. 177–196.

Liu, L. H., 2014. Shadows of universalism: The untold story of human rights around 1948. *Critical Inquiry* 40(4), pp. 385–417. DOI: 10.1086/676413.

Lucas, E.R., 2013. Somalia's "Pirate Cycle": The Three Phases of Somali Piracy. *Journal of Strategic Security* [e-journal] 6(1), pp. 55–63. DOI: http://dx.doi.org/10.5038/1944-0472.6.1.5.

Mansbach, R. and Lafferty, K., 2008. *Introduction to Global Politics.* London: Routledge.

Martins, J. and Pereira, A., 2018. The politics of human rights. In: B. Ames, (ed.) *Routledge Handbook of Brazilian Politics.* New York: Routledge, pp. 503–518.

Mowforth, M. and Munt. I., 2016. *Tourism and Sustainability Development, Globalization and New Tourism in the Third World.* London: Routledge.

Nwapi, C., 2017. Accountability of Canadian Mining Corporations for their overseas conduct: can extraterritorial corporate criminal prosecution come to the rescue?. *Canadian Yearbook of International Law/Annuaire canadien de droit international,* [e-Journal] 54, pp. 227–275. DOI: https://doi.org/10.1017/cyl.2017.9.

OECD, 2017. *Policy Statement – Tourism Policies for Sustainable and Inclusive Growth.* Paris: OECD, [pdf] Available at: <www.oecd.org/cfe/tourism/OECD-Policy-Statement-Tourism-Policies-for-Sustainable-and-Inclusive-Growth.pdf.> [Accessed 19 April 2020].

OHCHR, 2003. *Professional Training Series No. 9. Human Rights in the Administration of Justice: A Manual on Human Rights for Judges, Prosecutors and Lawyers*. New York and Geneva: United Nations.

OHCHR, 2007. Good Governance Practices for the Protection of Human Rights. [online]. Available at: <www.ohchr.org/Documents/Publications/GoodGovernance.pdf> [Accessed 27 June 2020].

OHCHR, 2019. Good Governance and Human Rights. [online]. Available at: <www.ohchr.org/EN/Issues/Development/GoodGovernance/Pages/GoodGovernanceIndex.aspx> [Accessed 8 April 2020].

Peters, A., 2009. The merits of global constitutionalism. *Indiana Journal of Global Legal Studies* 16(2), pp. 397–411. DOI: 10.2979/gls.2009.16.2.397.

Rapaport, L., 2016. Health risks for female sex workers and their children. *Reuters* [online] 26 May. Available at: <www.reuters.com/article/us-health-publichealth-sexworkers-childr-idUSKCN0YH20D> [Accessed 9 December 2019].

Regilme Jr, S., 2018. The global politics of human rights: From human rights to human dignity? *International Political Science Review* [e-journal] 40(2), pp. 279–290. DOI: https://doi.org/10.1177/0192512118757129.

Richter, L., 2009. Power, politics, and political science: the politicization of tourism. In: T. Jamal and M. Robinson, (eds.), *The Sage Handbook of Tourism Studies*, London: Sage, pp. 188–202.

Robinson, M., 2018. Human rights in global health governance. In: B.M. Meier and L.O. Gostin, (eds.), *Human Rights in Global Health: Rights-based Governance for a Globalizing World*. Oxford: Oxford University Press. Foreword.

Saha, S. and Yap, G., 2014. The moderation effects of political instability and terrorism on tourism development: A cross-country panel analysis. *Journal of Travel Research* [PDF] 54(4), pp. 509–521. DOI: 10.177/0047287513496472.

Salvador, S. S., 2019. The global politics of human rights: From human rights to human dignity? *International Political Science Review* [PDF] 40(2), pp. 270–290. DOI: 10.1177/0192512118757129.

SCC, 2020. Cases Decisions and Resources Supreme Court Judgments Nevsun Resources Ltd. v. Araya. *Supreme Court of Canada* [online] 28 February. Available at: <https://decisions.scc-csc.ca/scc-csc/scc-csc/en/item/18169/index.do> [Accessed 23 May 2020].

Shaheer, I., Insch, A. and Carr, N., 2017. Tourism destination boycotts – are they becoming a standard practice? *Tourism Recreation Research*. [e-journal] 43(1), pp. 129–132. DOI: https://doi.org/10.1080/02508281.2017.1377385.

Smith, D., 2014. Ethiopia, 30 years on from the famine. *The Guardian*. [online] 22 October. Available at: <www.theguardian.com/world/2014/oct/22/-sp-ethiopia-30-years-famine-human-rights> [Accessed 28 May 2019].

Smith, R.K.M., 2016. Human Rights in International Law. In: M. Goodhart, (ed.), *Human Rights: Politics and Practice*, 3rd Edition. Oxford: Oxford University Press, pp. 60–76.

Steinberg, G.2015. NGOs, The UN and the politics of human rights in the Arab-Israeli Conflict. *Israel Journal of Foreign Affairs* [e-journal] 5(1), pp. 73–88. DOI: https://doi.org/10.1080/23739770.2011.11446444.

Telfer, D. J., 2019. Tourism and (re)development in developed nations. In: R. Sharpley and D. Harrison, (eds.), *A Research Agenda for Tourism and Development*. Cheltenham: Edward Elgar, pp. 206–232.

Terry, W. C., 2011. Geographic limits to global labor market flexibility: the human resources paradox of the cruise industry. *Geoforum* 42, pp. 660–670. doi:10.1016/j.geoforum.2011.06.006.

The Advocate for Human Rights, 2020. *Human Rights & the U.S.: How has the Unites States handled the human rights issues in the past and today?* [online]. Available at: <www.theadvocatesforhumanrights.org/human_rights_and_the_united_states> [Accessed 11 April 2020].

Thimm, T., 2019. Cultural sustainability – a framework for Aboriginal tourism in British Columbia. *Journal of Heritage Tourism* [e-journal] 14(2019), pp. 205–218. DOI: https://doi.org/10.1080/1743873X.2018.1484469.

Tourism Concern, 2014. Why the tourism industry needs to take a human rights approach: The business case. *Industry Briefing* [pdf]. Available at: <www.tourismconcern.org.uk/wp-content/uploads/2014/10/TourismConcern_IndustryHumanRightsBriefing-FIN-4.pdf> [Accessed 24 October 2019].

UNSOM, 2018. After years of conflict, Somalia eager to recapture former glory as tourism destination. *United Nations Assistance Mission in Somalia.* [online] 7 January. Available at: <https://unsom.unmissions.org/after-years-conflict-somalia-eager-recapture-former-glory-tourism-destination> [Accessed 5 February 2020].

Volterra Fietta, 2020. Canadian courts assert jurisdiction over allegations against Canadian mining company for alleged complicity in modern slavery and human rights abuses in Eritrea. *Lexiology.* [online] 20 April. Available at: <www.lexology.com/library/detail.aspx?g=db271d88-10e3-4339-8bdf-7d85df19d56e> [Accessed 24 May 2020].

WebFinance, 2019. Business Dictionary "Political Environment". [online]. Available at: <www.businessdictionary.com/definition/political-environmental.html>.

White, J.B., 1985. Law as Rhetoric, Rhetoric as Law: The Arts of Cultural and Communal Life. *The University of Chicago Law Review* [pdf] 52(3), pp. 684–702. Available at: <www.jstor.org/stable/1599632>.

WHO, 2020. *Coronavirus (Covid 19).* [online] 19 April. Available at https://covid19.who.int/. [Accessed 19 April 2020].

Wilson, A., 2018. Sri Lanka ranked top country for travel in 2019 by Lonely Planet. *The Guardian.* [online] 23 October. Available at: <www.theguardian.com/travel/2018/oct/23/sri-lanka-ranked-top-country-for-travel-in-2019-by-lonely-planet> [Accessed 19 April 2020]

WTTC, 2019. Ethiopia records biggest growth in world travel & tourism. World Travel & Tourism Council. [online] 15 March. Available at: <www.wttc.org/about/media-centre/press-releases/press-releases/2019/ethiopia-records-biggest-growth-in-world-travel-tourism/> [Accessed 12 February 2020].

Yu, Q., McManus, R., Yen, D. and Li, X., 2020. Tourism boycotts and animosity: A study of seven events. *Annals of Tourism Research.* [e-journal] 80, p. 102792. https://doi.org/10.1016/j.annals.2019.102792.

SECTION 2
Human rights issues in tourism

5
HUMAN SECURITY, HUMAN RIGHTS, AND TOURISM

5.1 Introduction

Poverty, unemployment, unfulfilled basic needs, disease, conflict, violent crime, pollution and climate change are a few of the threats, real or perceived, to human life. Threats to human life and security are inevitably linked to human rights violations and can be examined from perspectives of individuals residing in tourist destinations, those employed or dependent upon the tourism industry and tourists themselves. A risk analysis of threats for individuals reveals repercussions for families, communities, regions and nations, impacting the tourism industry and those who rely on it. Tourism can enhance human security and human rights, but it can simultaneously have the opposite effect.

Absolute and relative poverty is a major threat to human security and poverty reduction is the first goal in the 2030 UN SDGs. Tourism is used as a poverty reduction strategy, yet poverty sits next to the affluence of tourism in both developing and developed nations (Telfer, 2019). According to the UN, poverty has:

> various manifestations, including lack of income and productive resources sufficient to ensure sustainable livelihoods; hunger and malnutrition; ill health; limited or lack of education and other basic services; increased morbidity and mortality from illness; homelessness and inadequate housing; unsafe environments; and social discrimination and exclusion.
> *(UN DESA, 1995)*

The realities of poverty experienced by many poor have been described as local, complex, diverse, dynamic, uncontrollable and unpredictable (lcdduu) (Chambers, 2010). One approach to address poverty through tourism is the sustainable livelihood strategy (Tao and Wall, 2009). As tourism seldom occurs in isolation, Tao and Wall note particularly in marginal economies, individuals and communities support themselves through multiple activities rather than discrete jobs. Although not without criticisms, pro-poor tourism or volunteer tourism has been endorsed to help those most in need and enhance human security. Tourism has also embraced the shift towards human development advocating links to civil society and social capital, highlighting tourism-related NGOs as agents that can enhance human security (Telfer, 2015).

Koehn (2019, p. 2) raises concerns over global health in terms of mobility, noting, "anyone can be health-secure today and health-vulnerable tomorrow." In an era of transnational migration, people and particularly the vulnerable (e.g. refugees and migrant labour) are compelled to move (see Chapter 7). At the same time, those with financial means, voluntarily seek out health care in foreign places through medical tourism (Koehn, 2019). As with any human security issue, it is important to consider vulnerability, resilience and adaptability of individuals and communities to events which may appear suddenly such as a natural disaster, terrorist attack or a pandemic, or evolve slowly like a steady decline in currency rates. Disasters, conflict, crisis and crisis response need to be understood within the context of the societies in which they occur (Hilhorst, 2013). Urbain (2013, p. xvii) notes the importance of challenging "the global dominance of neoliberalism that has allowed the social welfare aspects of tourism to be overshadowed by its financial market potential and enable peace advocates to review tourism's capacity to contribute to human well-being, human rights recognition, conflict resolution, and to the worldwide enhancement of justice and a culture of peace."

Human security is a relatively new concept, first officially articulated in the 1994 United Nations Development Programme (UNDP) Human Development Report (see UNDP, 1994). Human security emerged in an attempt to broaden traditional security (which emphasises the protection of the state, its sovereignty and territorial integrity) to include individual security (Krause, 2009). The concept includes individual security, group security, common security, societal security, global security, cooperative security and more (Krause, 2009, p. 147). Human security places emphasis on the security of the people. In its broadest sense, human security includes the factors embodying individual needs in society, in addition to basic human needs like food, shelter, water, healthcare, personal protection, freedom from fear, freedom from want, etc. (Tadjbakhsh and Chenoy, 2007). Sen's (1999) influential work *Development as Freedom* called for expanding freedoms in the areas of economic opportunity, political freedoms, social facilities, transparency guarantees and protective security. Human security extensively relates and overlaps in so many areas with human rights – so much so that many people often use the two concepts interchangeably (Owen, 2008). However, as will be seen later, scholars (e.g. Benedek, 2008) warn that they are not the same concept.

This chapter will first explore the evolution of the concept of security and probe the relationship between human rights and human security. The chapter will then examine human security issues facing tourists, host communities and tourism stakeholders and highlight how these threats intersect with human rights. While it is beyond the scope of this chapter to include all dimensions of human security, the focus will be on issues with immediate impacts on tourists and tourism.

5.2 Brief evolution of the concept of security

The concept of "security" in ancient times is not the same as today. In ancient Greece, security was primarily connected to spirit and spirituality; in the Roman Empire, security was closer to contemporary meanings of safety (Burgess, 2008). However, the idea of protection from physical violence started when humans began to form bands, communities, villages, kingdoms and eventually nation-states (McCrie, 2006) as there have always been conflicts and struggles between communities.

As communities grew, the state accumulated wealth and resources. In the 12th and 13th centuries, security took political form, as security became "safe-making and safe-keeping of material things" (Burgess, 2008, p. 54). Thus, the relationship between the state and individuals through the provision of security progressed. Codes (laws) were established to deal with external forces, ensuring peaceful co-existence, and to stimulate economic and social activities within community boundaries (McCrie, 2006). Defence mechanisms, including the armed forces emerged. From Medieval times to modern society, warfare developed, followed by technical innovation (McCrie, 2006).

5.2.1 From "security" to "human security" in the UN system

In President Roosevelt's State of Union Address in 1941, he included "freedom from want" and "freedom from fear" in his Four Freedoms speech. Some scholars consider this one of the forerunners of the conception of Human Security (Benedek, 2008). After the Cold War, the rise in non-violent threats to the most vulnerable at local, national, regional or international levels prompted the UN to publish Boutros Boutros-Ghali's 1992 report: *An Agenda for Peace* (Owen, 2008). Dealing with "compounded impacts of intra-state conflicts, degradation of the environment, worsening of extreme poverty, spreading of pandemics and political exploitation of cultural and ethnic differences" (Sané, 2008, p. 5) became a driving force to define, identify and strategise for Human Security. The UN published multiple agendas and reports on security, peace and human security between 1992 and 2005 (see Owen, 2008, p. 114 for the full list). The 1993 UNDP *Human Development Report – People's Participation* first recorded the conceptual shift from protection of the state to protection of the people (Owen, 2008). The 1994 UNDP's *New Dimensions of Human Security Report* is the first document to attempt to define human security. The report used three categories: first, temporal (short-term vs. long-term) vulnerability; second, human security as "freedom from want" and "freedom from fear"; third, the compartmentalisation of threats (Owen, 2008; Burgess, 2008), using seven components of human security including economic, food, health, environmental, personal, community and political security (UNDP,

1994). However, after many debates, the UN has still not produced a universally accepted definition of Human Security since the release of the Report. UNESCO produced the following working definition of Human Security:

> [a] paradigm in the making, for ensuring both a better knowledge of the rapidly evolving large-scale risks and threats that can have a major impact on individuals and populations, and a strengthened mobilisation of the wide array of actors actually involved in participative policy formulation in the various fields it encompasses today.
>
> *(2000, cited in Sané, 2008, p. 6)*

Human security is highly politicised, and with considerable reluctance from many UN member states, especially on the Security Council, led to a secession of further discussions (Benedek, 2008; Owen, 2008). UN Secretary-General Annan's 2005 report dropped human security as part of the major UN agenda (Owen, 2008).

Wars, globalisation, transnational economic arrangements and transnational terrorism began to erode Peace of Westphalia state sovereignty, a state's responsibility for security as well as recognition that a single nation state could not handle the immediate consequences of security (Burgess, 2008). After the Cold War in the mid-1990s, the UN had to reassess its role as peacekeeper; the issue of human security became its core concern, as human security is considered part of human rights, i.e. the protection of dignity of a person (Sané, 2008). Yet, the concept of human security remained a questionable political concept by many UN member states without justifiable obligation (Benedek, 2008).

5.3 Human rights and human security

In many respects, human rights and human security have similar historical origins. Human rights are believed to have been influenced by the development of natural/divine law, natural rights theories and positivism (Nkyi and Hashimoto, 2015). Human security, on the other hand, is believed to have largely been influenced by the development of international humanitarian law (the laws of war), the work of the International Committee of the Red Cross, the United Nations (Krause, 2009) and the UN's reassessment of its role as a peacemaker and peacekeeper after the Cold War (Owen, 2008). After the Cold War and the paradigm shift from "high politics" to "low politics" and the influx of intrastate conflicts, human security largely emerged as a response to address the shortfalls of human rights, drawing its foundations on humanitarian norms. The term "human security" officially emerged in UN reports in the 1990s (UNDP, 1994), whereas the term "human rights" is believed to have emerged after the French Revolution of 1789 but popularised after the end of the Second World War and the formation of the UN in 1945 (Sepúlveda, et al., 2004 cited in Icelandic Human Rights Centre, 2014; Nkyi and Hashimoto, 2015, p. 383).

Both concepts have been embroiled in debates with no universally accepted definition for either. The preamble of the United Nations Universal Declaration of Human Rights (UDHR, 1948) defines human rights as "the inherent dignity and of the equal and inalienable rights of all members of the human family ..." (UDHR, 1948). Viewed in this context, human rights are those inherent and inalienable entitlements that enable every human being to pursue life choices with respect, self-esteem and dignity. Every person enjoys these entitlements by virtue of being part of the human race (Tremblay, et al., 2008). Conversely, human security can be defined in simple and general terms as the "absence of insecurity and threats" (Tadjbakhsh and Chenoy, 2007, p. 39).

Tadjbakhsh and Chenoy (2007, pp. 125–6) underscore five similarities between human rights and human security: (i) they are people centred in approach, thereby recognising individuals as subjects of international law (a situation which hitherto was not the case before 1945); (ii) they focus on freedoms and pursuit of human dignity (i.e. human rights addresses the violation of human dignity whereas human security addresses the threats to human rights); (iii) Similar content: both concepts stress "freedom from fear" – civil and political rights or first generation rights and "freedom from want" – second generation rights or social and economic rights); (iv) mutual interdependence, i.e. they call for collaboration for action between state and non-state actors, which is directly opposite to the state-centric approach prior to 1945; (v) mutual reinforcement, i.e. human security policies promote and enhance human rights whereas human rights violations undermine human security. In other words, human security can be a "warning mechanism" for human rights violations. Where human security is lacking, human rights violations most likely occur; while human rights violations could cause conflicts and threaten human security (Benedek, 2008; Owen, 2008).

Notwithstanding their similarities, human rights and human security are two different concepts. Tadjbakhsh and Chenoy (2007, p. 127) also identified the following three differences between human rights and human security: (i) human rights are legal documents which are subject to court interpretations, whereas human security is a non-legal concept and lacks any court interpretations; (ii) human rights imposes a duty on states to protect individual and community rights, whereas human security argues for the right to protect individuals and states; (iii) human security is an analytical framework (tool) for analysing and identifying threats to human rights, whereas human rights is a legal document to enforce individual and community rights. Human security is a precondition of human rights – only within a secure environment can individuals exercise their human rights (Owen, 2008). It is also noted that many human rights instruments allow the state to set aside human rights in the case of a public emergency; however, human security cannot be disregarded in the case of emergency and is the last resort in protecting human dignity (Benedek, 2008). Box 5.1 explores the relationship between human rights, human security and tourism while the remainder of the chapter examines human security issues affecting tourism.

BOX 5.1 INTERSECTION OF HUMAN SECURITY, HUMAN RIGHTS AND TOURISM

Although the concept of human security is new to tourism studies, equality and social justice studies have raised similar issues about tourism. Hall and Brown (2010) pointed out how tourism can contribute to "welfare" in a variety of dimensions:

- Health (freedom from disease and ill health)
- Physical safety and security
- Emotional and spiritual well-being (freedom from stress and anxiety)
- Financial security (freedom from poverty)
- Mutual respect and support (freedom from exploitation)
- A healthy environment
- Access to appropriated accommodation (housing provision)
- Access to other necessary services. (p. 145)

In most cases, tourism's contribution to welfare was discussed from the viewpoint of benefits to tourists. For instance, taking a vacation greatly improves stress-related ailments of tourists. The tourism industry's concern for tourists' safety and security has been sharpened as acts of terrorism, kidnapping or crimes against tourists increased (Hall and Brown, 2010). Security and safety issues in tourism are also examined by:

- Criminal activities directed against tourists.
- Crimes committed by tourists.
- Crimes that occur through illegal services for tourists.
- Criminal activities that occur within a tourist-dependent economic base.
- Criminal activities directed against the residents but independent of the tourist destination.

(Hall and Brown, 2010, pp. 158–159)

Higgins-Desbiolles (2010) argues that in an era of globalisation, justice must be discussed beyond socio-political borders unlike past research on ethics/moral/social justice in tourism that was focused on justice within social boundaries. Human insecurities and inequalities are caused by the inherently unjust and inequitable nature of tourism. Poverty may push locals to sell sexual services to tourists, organs for transplant surgeries, and live their lives in poverty hosting slum tourism (Higgins-Desbiolles, 2010, p. 195). Tourism is even considered to be a contributor to social inequality (Cole and Morgan, 2010). International tourism between more economically developed countries (MEDS) and less economically developed countries (LEDS), facilitated

> by multinational enterprises exercising substantial political influences in LEDS, generates class polarisation between tourists and local hosts (Cole and Eriksson, 2010). It has been argued that the affluent population of the world has a moral duty to spend their income to help vulnerable populations who are in life-threatening danger rather than enjoying luxuries, such as holidaymaking (Singer, 1972 cited in Higgins-Desbiolles, 2010, p. 198). With the expansion of international tourism through globalisation, affluent populations are also arguably faced with the moral obligation to assist those in less fortunate situations internationally. Citing Pogge (2005), Lash and Urry (1994), Hutnyk's (1996), and Enloe (1989), Higgins-Desbiolles (2010) also argue that class polarised tourism is guilty of creating degrading poverty in some parts of the world through a system of post-colonial tourism development, mindless consumption of "other" places, and a "tourism formula for development" that leads to perpetual economic leakage and dependence (pp. 198–199).

5.4 Human security issues affecting tourism

Conflicts of various kinds and human rights abuses perpetuated by state and non-state actors continue to affect and threaten the safety of millions of people in the world. Such insecurity issues have significant ramifications for human life and tourism. Liberia and Sierra Leone, located in the western part of Africa, had their tourism industries virtually collapse during long civil wars. Insecurity and gross human rights violations were recorded during civil wars in both Sierra Leone (1991–2002) and Liberia (1989–1997; 1999–2003). In addition to insecurity caused by political elements, disease, conflict, poverty, crime, labour exploitation, human trafficking, sexual exploitation, shortages of basic needs (housing, food, and water), pollution and climate change are just a few human security issues affecting the tourism industry today. In the Caribbean, Griffin (2005, p. 27) highlighted concern over increasing levels of crime generally as well as crime and harassment of tourists. The safety and security issues identified as overlapping with tourism were: borders and ports; infrastructure (facilities and accommodations, transportation and communications systems); roads and signage; food; health care; crisis response and disaster preparedness/response/mitigation; education and training; employment and distribution of tourism benefits; terrorism; crime and harassment.

Tourism should not just be considered in isolation but is part of wider social, cultural, political, economic, and ecological processes. This is reflected in the UNDP's (1994) interlinked seven realms of human security: personal, health, food, community, political, economic, and environmental security. In developing guidelines on human security, Gómez and Gasper (2014) posed a number of important questions noted in Table 5.1. The answers may be different based on whether those asked are employed or dependent upon the tourism industry, tourists themselves and the degree of power a person/organisation has. For example, an expansion of the

TABLE 5.1 Questions for Designing a UN Human Development Report Focused on Human Security

Whose security?	What specific groups should the report be focused on – e.g. vulnerable groups?
Security of what?	What values are in need of protection? Which of the UNDP (1994) seven realms of security (economic; food; health; environmental; personal; community; political) are in need of protection?
Security from what?	What are the threats most relevant at a particular time and place? What is the number of threats/issues to be considered and how are they interrelated? What is the perception of threats compared to their actual occurrence?
Who can play a role?	What are the roles of individuals, businesses, communities, states and international organisations in promoting human security?
What means for promoting security can be used?	What strategies should be used (e.g. principles of being comprehensive, contextual, participatory, preventative)? Reports should be creative, innovative and differentiate by context.
Target levels – are there examples of too little or too much (human) security?	Can a form of cost-benefit analysis be used to explore trade-offs implicit in focusing on one type of threat rather than another or one type of resource response compared to another?

Source: (Gómez and Gasper, 2014).

sharing economy may provide inexpensive accommodation for tourists and additional rental income for some locals while other residents may be deprived of housing as property values soar, gentrification occurs and the community changes. Opportunities for some may represent direct security threats and human rights violations for others. While there is debate on the scope of human security with some focusing only on "violent threats", Section 5.4.1 will focus on the broader seven human security categories outlined by the UNDP (Owen, 2013). Due to the highly interconnectedness of the categories, examples used could highlight threats from a variety of different perspectives.

5.4.1 Personal safety and tourism

Every individual has the right to live and stay safe, devoid of real or perceived fears, danger, intimidation and attacks, regardless of where one lives, works or travels. Personal safety is both a human right and a human security issue. Despite the efforts of the UN system since the Cold War, human security has not been respected or implemented in many parts of the world. In 2002 the World Health Organization published the first World report on violence and health indicating over 1.6 million people were losing their lives each year as a result of violence (Krug, et al., 2002). The first two targets of the 2030 UN SDG 16 aim to reduce all forms of violence and resulting deaths and end abuse, exploitation, trafficking and violence against children. UN Women (2019) state violence against women and girls (VAWG) is one of the "most widespread and persistent and devastating human rights violations today remains largely unreported due to the impunity, silence, stigma and shame surrounding it."

Exploitation against human beings in tourism

Incidents of tourism-related exploitation include slavery and inhuman treatment, as well as human trafficking. Sex tourism is not always a form of exploitation so long as sex workers chose their profession, are fairly paid, and the work is regulated. However, when people are forced into sex work against their will or forced by abject poverty, and experience unfair work condition or no wages, then it is an exploitation of human rights. House maids, hotel cleaners, tour guides, trekking porters and any type of job that people have been coerced into, are bonded to, or have had their travel documents and work permits withheld, or were trafficked from other regions of the country or across borders, can all be a part of modern slavery. International organisations such as ECPAT, Salvation Army, World Vision, Save the Children, and Tourism Concern – to name only a few – have been tirelessly fighting against modern-day slavery, and are raising awareness among citizens and tourists (see Chapter 13 for more discussion on sexual exploitation). Countries such as the UK and Australia have also recently passed Modern Day Slavery Legislation. Campaigns have also been developed warning tourists of the potential exploitation of children in orphanage tourism. Noting the growth in orphanages in Cambodia, Guiney (2018, p. 125) argues that with volunteer tourism, "children are now a tourist commodity, utilizing their love and emotions and creating a space for exploitation." Other forms of exploitation are linked to low rates of pay and poor working conditions such as those endured by porters whether they are climbing the Inca Trail to Machu Picchu or up Kilimanjaro.

Terrorist attacks

Another form of threat to human security is terrorist attacks impacting both locals and tourists. The terrorist attack on September 11 (9/11) in the United States in 2001 was a wake-up call to Western nations. Al-Qaeda – an Islamist terrorist group – launched a series of four co-ordinated attacks against the US by hijacking commercial planes and killing a total of 2,753 people. After the incident, tourism to the US mainland dropped sharply (Hetter, 2012). In 2000, New York received 6.8 million tourists. Tourist numbers declined in the following two years, taking five years to recover to pre-9/11 levels (Wolfe and Corasaniti, 2017). Wide ranging security measures were introduced globally following these attacks (see Chapters 6 and 9).

The Middle East and North Africa (MENA) region states affected by the Arab Spring (pro-democracy uprising – more discussion in Chapter 4 and later in this chapter) have also suffered terrorist attacks. In Tunisia, for example, a terrorist attack at a museum in Bardo in March 2015 resulted in at least 23 deaths and several injured; another attack in June 2015 left 38 dead and many injured at a beachfront hotel (see Cullinane, 2015; Botelho, 2015). This culminated in the declaration of a state of emergency by Tunisia on 4 July 2015 (Sanchez, 2015). In Egypt, a tour bus carrying Vietnamese tourists near the Giza Pyramids was attacked in December 2018, resulting in three deaths and 11 victims sustaining various degrees of injuries (BBC, 2018). Several other terrorist attacks targeted at tourists, security forces and people of faith (BBC, 2018; Ragahavan and Mahfouz, 2018; Walsh and Youssef, 2017), as well as violent crackdown on protests (see United Nation News, 2016; Ismail, 2016) have complicated the security situation of the country; especially after the Arab Spring creating fears, thereby deterring tourists from visiting Egypt.

In contrast to Egypt, Tunisia, and other MENA countries, the situation in France is quite different. Notwithstanding the many deadly terrorist attacks that have rocked the country since 2014, France continued to attract tourists maintaining its spot as one of the leading destinations for global tourism (Government of France, 2015, 2016). Deadly terror activities include the Charlie Hebdo attack which left 12 people dead in January 2015 (Bilefsky and de la Baum, 2015); the November 2015 attacks at 6 locations in Paris, resulting in 130 deaths and 494 injured led to an extension of a 3-month national state of emergency (CNN, 2015); and the Nice attack in July 2016, killed 86 people and wounded many (Rubin and Breeden, 2016). Other terrorist attacks occurred throughout France between 2014 and 2018 (see The Telegraph, 2018). In 2013, France recorded 84.7 million foreign tourists (La France au Vanuatu, 2014). After the terrorist attacks the international tourism growth rate was stunted, yet tourist arrival numbers in 2017 reached 87 million (Government of France, 2018), and 89 million in 2018 (Government of France, 2019).

Despite insecurity conditions between 2014 and 2018, France was able to assure tourists that the country still remained safe. For instance, in its 2018 budget, France devoted US$30 billion to security and another $64 billion to defense (CBC, 2018). Since 2015, about 7,000 troops have been deployed to guard French tourist sites, while another 3,000 troops are on standby for emergencies with another 2,000 anti-terror police to protect residents and visitors across the country (CBC, 2018). In contrast, countries in the MENA region have been unable to assure tourists of their safety resulting in plummeting international tourist numbers. While attacks on tourists are highlighted in the media, Bianchi (2006) notes it is important to put this into perspective. Risk is an almost continuous fact of everyday existence for a large majority of the world's population, and the vast majority of the terrorism victims are local populations living far from tourist destinations (Bianchi, 2006).

Violence towards tourists and residents

Violent crimes as well as extortion, unlawful arrests and detention all affect the human security of tourists and people in the host community. In 2017, Brazil recorded 63,880 homicide cases, which equates to 175 deaths per day (Darlington, 2018; Embury-Dennis, 2018). Other crimes including, but not limited to, armed robbery, rape, gang warfare, and pickpocketing are also on the rise in Brazil (see Embury-Dennis, 2018; Darlington, 2018; Phillips, 2017). Between 2016 and 2017, multiple international tourists were shot dead at a police roadblock point at the Rocinha favela in Brazil (Phillips, 2017). An upsurge in violent crimes has also been seen in Mexico, South Africa, and Columbia. In an effort to protect personal safety, governments issue travel alerts and provide security updates cautioning their citizens to either avoid non-essential travel or exercise a high degree of caution when travelling to certain countries. For example, the governments of Canada, the USA, the UK, and Australia continuously updated their travel advisory websites providing security information to their citizens. Travel alerts range from weather and environmental conditions to petty crimes, violent crimes, terrorist activities, civil wars, political instability, flagrant abuse of human rights, and infectious diseases.

5.4.2 Health security and tourism

Every individual has the right to live, remain safe and healthy, devoid of fears of contracting diseases, and being able to access quality and affordable healthcare regardless of where an individual lives or travels. The 1946 Constitution of the WHO states:

> a state of complete physical, mental and social well-being and not merely the absence of disease or infirmity...the enjoyment of the highest attainable standard of health is one of the fundamental rights of every human being without distinction of race, religion, political belief, economic or social condition (Preamble).
>
> *(WHO, 2017; OHCHR, 2008)*

The 1948 UDHR Article 25 also mentions "health as part of the right to an adequate standard of living." Recognising health as a human right:

> creates a legal obligation on states to ensure access to timely, acceptable, and affordable health care of appropriate quality as well as to providing for the underlying determinants of health, such as safe and potable water, sanitation, food, housing, health-related information and education, and gender equality.
>
> *(WHO, 2017)*

Potable water, sanitation, hygiene, and safe food preparation are important human safety components for locals and tourists, and states have an obligation to provide them. Despite these obligations, inequality and lack of access to health care are realities in both developed and developing countries representing threats to human security.

Communicable diseases and health care

Highly infectious and communicable diseases continue to spread to which tourism contributes, putting at risk those in destinations, at home and along the transit route. Communicable diseases, or infectious diseases are usually caused by microorganisms – e.g. bacteria, viruses, and parasites – spreading from person to person; others are spread through insect bites, infected animals or contaminated surface areas, water and food. The WHO states that waterborne diarrhoeal diseases are responsible for two million deaths per year. Examples of diseases include COVID-19, Ebola, Severe Acute Respiratory Syndrome (SARS), Cholera, Zika, HIV/AIDS, H1N, Avian Influenza, Malaria, Dengue Fever, Hepatitis, Polio, and Typhoid representing significant health security concerns. Some diseases are treatable with medicines or preventable with immunisations (see WHO Travel Vaccination Website) along with hygiene and sanitation programmes. Sexually transmitted infections and HIV/AIDS can be spread through sex tourism (see Chapter 13). Depending on the destination and type of outbreak, medical services may not be prepared or have the capacity to treat the infected.

The recent novel coronavirus (COVID-19) pandemic has threatened human security at a global level (see Chapter 14 for more discussion). The WHO declared COVID-19 a pandemic in March 2020. As the death toll increased, the UN Secretary General stated the COVID-19 pandemic is a "human crisis", the worst test the world has faced since the last World War (BBC News, 2020a; France 24, 2020). At the time of writing this book, COVID-19 had still not been contained. In the first 3 months, there were over 3 million confirmed cases, and 218,000 deaths (WHO, 2020a). International flights were cancelled, tourists were trapped in destinations or on cruise ships in quarantine (WHO, 2020b; BBC News, 2020b), and 72% of all tourist destinations completely closed their borders to international tourists (UNWTO, 2020) (see Chapters 9 and 14). Cruise ships around the world were stranded or quarantined offshore, as docking rights were refused (Amos, 2020; BBC, 2020a; BBC, 2020b). Many destinations imposed a 14-day quarantine period for arriving tourists. In Hawaii, tourists were arrested for breaking the quarantine and visiting beaches putting locals at risk (Kelleher, 2020). Travel advisories were issued under COVID-19 such as the Canadian Government's global travel advisory for all its citizens to avoid all non-essential travel outside of the country. As COVID-19 shut down tourism, it has led to major impacts on economic security.

Past outbreaks have caused severe health outcomes and disruption to the tourism industry although nothing on the scale of COVID-19. While efforts were underway to recover from civil wars, and redevelop travel and tourism, Ebola swept through countries in West Africa in 2014 and 2015, affecting over 28,000 people recording over 11,000 deaths (Van Bortel, et al., 2016; WHO, 2016). Liberia, Sierra Leone and Guinea were the worst affected; forcing the closure of schools and other social services for several months (The World Bank, 2015). Countries like South Africa, Canada, United States, Australia placed visa restrictions on Liberia, Sierra Leone and Guinea (Thompson and Torre, 2014) while some scheduled international flights to those affected countries were cancelled (Anderson, 2014). Airlines, hotels, tour companies, travel agents, and people whose livelihoods depended on the tourism industry – as well as the countries at large were all affected negatively by the Ebola crisis (Gayle, 2014; Brock, 2014).

In many countries, it is very expensive to access quality healthcare. Health insurance premiums, services and prescription drugs are simply not affordable. Few nation-states provide universal health care. In some places, healthcare facilities are very scarce compelling many sick people to travel long distances to access healthcare. Inadequate healthcare facilities are sometimes exacerbated by the lack of adequately trained healthcare professionals and medical equipment. A preventable disease such as Malaria kills about 3,000 children each day, and over a million people every year (UNICEF, 2020). While some destinations struggle to provide basic care for locals, medical tourism is rapidly growing providing new revenue streams. Mun and Musa (2013) examined the challenges with medical tourism in Thailand, Singapore, Malaysia and India and found a rise in privatisation and commodification of many medical facilities putting these services out of reach for many locals due to costs. They also raised concerns over illegal organ transplants going to foreign tourists. While medical tourism may enhance opportunities for some, it may raise health security issues for others.

Hygiene and sanitation

There are 2.2 billion people in the world without access to safe drinking water and 4.2 billion lack safe sanitation (UN SDG, 2019). There are tremendous social (e.g. vulnerable groups) and spatial (e.g. rural versus urban) inequalities in access to drinking water (Hirai and Graham, 2019). The 2030 UN SDG 6 is to ensure access to clean water and sanitation for all with a focus on WASH (water, sanitation, and hygiene) by monitoring the availability of hand washing facilities. Without proper hygiene and sanitation, it can lead to an increase in waterborne diseases. In destinations where accommodation is of poor quality, sanitation and hygiene is inadequate, clean water is unavailable and medical facilities do not exist can all pose a threat to the health of travellers (WHO, 2020c). Linked to poor hygiene and sanitation is food poisoning. Food security can be compromised through the process of food production, food supply, preparation, and delivery of food and drink to consumers. The Dominican Republic and Cuba are very popular tourist destinations in the Caribbean but are also infamous for poor sanitation, leading to numerous cases of food poisoning and subsequent deaths (Fantz, 2019; Cain, 2019; Foundation for Human Rights for Cuba, 2018; Steinmetz, 2019). However, it is not always a destination in developing countries that have food poisoning problems. Food related deaths in developed nations include Canada reporting 240 deaths per year (Government of Canada, 2019), the UK 500 per year (Sustain, 2020), the US 3,000 per year (Gamarra, 2018) and Australia 86 per year (Food Safety Information Council, 2020). Those who react more seriously and are hospitalised may develop complications and long-term effects, some of which are irreversible (Centers for

Disease Control and Prevention, 2017). Tourists' perceptions of a destination's ongoing occurrences of foodborne and waterborne insecurity can influence travel decisions. Improvements in the areas of safe and accessible water, affordable healthcare, proper sanitation controls, public health education and awareness, and proper disease control systems (detection, treatment and containment) are measures needed to address health insecurity issues for locals and the tourism sector. While access to safe water and hygiene is improving globally there are still tremendous inequalities putting health security at risk.

5.4.3 Food, shelter, basic needs security and tourism

By far, poverty remains one of the greatest security threats to many of the world's population threatening the lives of about 1.3 billion people in the world (UNDP, 2018). Severe poverty can contribute to the spread of diseases, poor quality of life, and lack of access to basic needs including food, water, housing, clothing and healthcare. The inability to access these basic human needs is a human security issue infringing on Article 25 of the UDHR (1948) which entitles every person "the right to a standard of living adequate for the health and well-being of himself and of his family, including food, clothing, housing and medical care and necessary social services, ..." (UDHR, 1948). In St Lucia, Thornburg (2011) criticised market-led government policy where much of its revenue was being spent on tourist-oriented infrastructure at the expense of a social security system. The development policies had failed to solve the problem of maldistribution of economic resources, poverty, skewed income distribution and underemployment. Thornburg (2011) advocated a basic-needs approach focusing on the welfare of the population.

Food insecurity is a matter of life-and-death. Man-made activities like civil wars, poor farming practices and natural disasters, such as severe droughts and desertification, have resulted in famine and food insecurity in places like Ethiopia, Yemen, Eritrea, and South Sudan. In 1984, severe famine resulted in an estimated one million deaths in Ethiopia (Smith, 2014). To date, the country continues to battle with food insecurity issues. Likewise, in South Sudan, an estimated 7.1 million people were experiencing severe food insecurity in early 2018 (United Nations News, 2018). In Yemen in 2019, international assistance was estimated to have prevented about 10 million people from experiencing famine (United Nations News, 2019).

In light of increased food insecurity and rising food prices, Telfer and Sharpley (2016) examined the complex relationship between tourism and food. Food is produced, packaged, transported and consumed by both tourists and residents representing a possible source of income for local farmers as well as being the attraction. However, tourism is a luxury product and countries such as Kenya which attract the safari tourism market also import a significant amount of food aid. The tourism industry which is known to waste a significant quantity of food (e.g. cruise ships) may end up competing for land and water (e.g. golf courses and land for hotels) and labour that are needed for local agricultural production (Telfer and Sharpley, 2016). While there is the potential to increase backward linkages by using local agricultural product in tourism, there remain substantial challenges in doing so (Telfer and Wall, 1996).

Another life-and-death issue is access to shelter and housing. In a capitalist economy, speculation of property values evicts many people from their rental properties, or their own houses. In large cities like Toronto, New York, London, Tokyo, Beijing, Nairobi, Accra and so on, people in the lower income tier are struggling to keep up with rising rent, as purchasing houses are completely out of the equation. Unattainable housing prices in cities have resulted in a higher number of homeless; while several thousand others are precariously housed or face imminent risks of homelessness. In Canada in 2016, it was estimated that 235,000 people became homeless every year, while 35,000 people are estimated to be homeless on any given night (CTV News, 2016). The Department of Housing and Urban Development in the United States estimated 553,000 people were homeless in 2018, with half of this figure coming from five states: New York, California, Florida, Texas and Washington (McCarthy, 2018). In the United Kingdom, an estimated 320,000 people were considered homeless in 2018 (Richardson, 2018). Tourism-related inflation of land and property values that displaces local populations to more remote areas is a documented phenomenon (see Chapter 7). In cases, such as in Iceland, the government had to intervene so that locals can remain in their properties. The popularity of the Stockholm archipelago attracts tourists to buy their second home or immigrate; as a result, property values soar (Marjavaara, 2009). Investors and landlords convert properties in Toronto into Airbnbs to rent out to tourists rather than stable local tenants, causing an inflation of property values (Grisdale, 2019). Locals are, consequently, unable to afford housing in these cities. The problems when people are not properly housed include exposure to bad weather, crimes and other social vices. The lack of access and affordability of housing has given rise to the development of slums in some locations. Slum tourism has emerged which focuses on human poverty. While it may provide needed income, it puts people's lives in poverty on display.

5.4.4 Community security and tourism

Since the publication of the UNDP report in 1994, the definition of community security has expanded. The initial definition focused on a breakdown of communities and looked specifically at the security of ethnic minorities and Indigenous groups (Caballero-Anthony, 2015). Over time it has broadened to encapsulate social cohesion and other vulnerable groups, e.g. women and children, as well as being linked to social identity theory (Caballero-Anthony, 2015). Security studies defined societal security as the sustainability, manifestation of culture, religious and national identity (Buzan 1991 cited in Caballero-Anthony, 2015). Potential societal threats include:

- Migration: host society is changed by influx of outsiders
- Horizontal competition: groups must change their ways due to overriding linguistic/cultural influence of another

- Vertical competition: through integration or disintegration groups are forced towards narrower or wider identities
- Military: depopulation – enough members of a society are killed or deported to inhibit identity being transmitted to the next generation
- Political: likely from their own government usually suppressing a minority group
- Economic: capitalism can undermine cultural distinctiveness through globalisation and consumerism replacing traditional identities; free market can result in depression and unemployment impacting traditional ways of life
- Environmental: when identity is tied to a territory, threats to the landscape can threaten culture and lives. (Buzan, Waever and de Wilde 1998 in Caballero-Anthony, 2015)

Tourism can threaten societies on a number of these fronts and thereby impact human rights. The original focus of community security on Indigenous communities is explored in depth in Chapter 12 while displacement of communities by tourism is covered in Chapter 7. Environmental threats to community are highlighted later in this chapter as well as in Chapter 11. Economic threats from tourism to community security are evident through globalisation and consumerism. Cultural change over time is inevitable through globalisation. Many cultures borrow desirable parts of different cultures to improve their own through the process of acculturation. Cultural displacement may occur through cultural dilution and adulteration, gross cultural appropriation, and cultural assimilation. However, changes by force or coercion – for example, tourists and tourist-generating countries demand changes in destinations or denying a community's wish to change – are forms of exploitation. The wish of Kayan women to remove their traditional brass coils around their necks was denied by the tourism industry and Thai government; it was thought that such a change would devalue the Kayan women as a tourist attraction (see Chapter 7). The Kayan women's human rights, a life with dignity, choice of work, and choice of a place to live were systematically denied.

Communities are also becoming more vocal in their opposition to tourism development. Civil society groups at times linked with NGOs have led protest movements in European cities linked to the process of overtourism. In Barcelona, residents have been campaigning against the negative impact of the tourism economy on their neighbourhoods including a growing number of short-term rental apartments, noise and anti-social behaviour (e.g. drunkenness), and the commodification and occupation of public spaces by café terraces (Novy and Colomb, 2016). Urban community groups have been raising concerns over the quality of life, public space, neighbourhood restructuring, heritage protection, gentrification, urban density and social impacts of mega-events, employing forms ranging from new collective mobilisations to using existing community activities, and to micro-practices of resistance (Novy and Colomb, 2016). Community protests have also occurred in Bali, Indonesia over proposed tourism developments near religious sites; and in Goa, India against disruptions and noise from rave tourism. While some forms of tourism may represent threats to community security, other forms of tourism try to promote empowerment and sustainability. Community-based tourism or village tourism is focused on enhancing communities and the distribution of benefits. The extent to which communities can maintain control over the development of the tourism process may mitigate the threats to community security.

5.4.5 Political security and tourism

A central foundation of political security is it underlines many freedoms enjoyed in democratic societies (McEldowney, 2005). The notion of political security has also undergone significant changes since the 1994 UNDP report. Initially it was defined as the prevention of government repression, the systematic violations of human rights and threats from militarisation (Hassan, 2015). The concept has evolved in both theory and practice with the emergence of various crises and changes in international relations (Hassan, 2015). While the fundamental principles remain, debates rose about the nature and legitimacy of humanitarian intervention which later evolved into the Responsibility to Protect agenda (Hassan, 2015). As noted in Chapter 4 on the political environment, Amnesty International continues to alert the international community about states that violate human rights and are involved in political repression. Political conditions can have a significant impact on tourism as is explored through the Arab Spring below.

Pro-democracy uprising: The Arab Spring

Many tourists who use to patronise tourism activities in the nation-states affected by the Arab Spring (Tunisia, Egypt, Libya, Syria, Yemen, Bahrain, etc.) have either stopped visiting these places, or considered other destinations. The Arab Spring began in Tunisia in 2010, before spreading to other countries in the Middle East and North African (MENA) region. Protests began with peaceful demonstrations, with links to social media "mainly fuelled by dissatisfied and unemployed youth looking for more rights, improved living conditions and a better future for themselves and for their children" (Magablih and Mustafa, 2018). Al-Shammari and Willoughby, (2019) identified determinant factors of the Arab Spring as: (i) the region is sensitive to food price inflation. It is hypothesised that internal policies on food and energy prices were not sustainable and created more social instability; (ii) an extremely high youth unemployment rate is closely related to an increase in instability; (iii) the regime durability in the region is connected to greater social upheaval. In the cases of Syria, Libya and Yemen, these protests escalated into full-scale civil wars; in other countries conflicts lingered in different forms of oppression (Murphy, 2012; Amnesty International, 2016). In contrast, monarchies in Jordan and Morocco have gradually undertaken political reforms after the Arab Spring (Magablih and Mustafa, 2018).

International tourist arrival numbers have plummeted since the beginning of the Arab Spring in the MENA region (Tomazos, 2017). For example, Egypt recorded 14 million tourist arrivals in 2010 (the last year before the crisis), which dropped to 9.5 million in 2011 (HURGHADA, 2013). Five years later, while tourism in some of other MENA region states began to recover, Egypt's numbers continued to drop. It received 4.8 million tourists in 2016, a 40% drop from 2015 (Middle East Monitor, 2017). Part of the reason is an Egyptair crash in May 2016 and controversy over the kidnapping of an Italian student (Tomazos, 2017). Even in 2018, the tourist number only reached 11.3 million (UNWTO, 2019). Similarly, the Tunisian National Tourist Office recorded the number of foreign arrivals fell by 45% in 2011 due to the uprising (BBC 2011). In 2010 before the uprising, 6.9 million tourists visited but by 2011, the number fell to 4.8 million. By 2014, numbers recovered to 7.1 million visitors, but in 2016 dropped to 5.7 million (Ministry of Tourism and Handicraft, 2020) due to multiple terrorist attacks and bombings involving tourists in 2015 (BBC, 2017; Walker, 2015; Reuters, 2015). Like Egypt and other states affected by the Arab Spring, the Tunisian tourism industry has been struggling to recover from the shock of the revolution. It was only in 2017 that Tunisia received 7 million tourists, back to the pre-Arab Spring level (Reuters, 2017).

The Kingdom of Jordan implemented gradual political change after the Arab Spring and showed a steady increase in tourist arrival numbers. In 2010, 4.2 million tourists visited Jordan; dropping to 3.9 million in 2011 and quickly recovering in 2012 to 4.1 million. Jordan's strategy was to target other Arab tourists who might have visited Syria or Egypt; and tourists from Russia, Ukraine and Poland replacing lost Western tourists (Magablih and Mustafa, 2018). Jordan has been involved in the fight against the Islamic State since 2014, and suffered a terrorist attack in 2016, killing ten people – including tourists (BBC, 2018; Nahhas, 2018). Jordan tourism is slowly regained its footing receiving over 4.1 million tourists in 2018 (UNWTO, 2019).

5.4.6 Economic security and tourism

Tourism is a type of business where price elasticity often determines business success. In order to ensure low prices, human rights are often set aside resulting in sweatshop like working conditions (see Chapter 10). In the context of tourism, Dwyer and Cavlek (2019, p. 15) note that "economic globalisation is causing people in developed countries to lose their livelihood because of outsourcing and many people in developing countries face poor working conditions and poor compensation." The tourism sector in 2018 offered both direct and indirect employment to about 319 million people globally (WTTC, 2019). Nkyi and Hashimoto (2015) noted that while employment in the tourism sector does not always result in exploitation, underage employment, poor working conditions, seasonal and unguaranteed jobs, gendered roles, and child labour in tourism hospitality have violated human rights according to the UDHR (1948), the International Labour Organization Equal Remuneration Convention (1951), the International

Covenant on Economic, Social and Cultural Rights (1966) and the Convention on the Rights of the Child (1989).

Recent changes, and the rising awareness of global consumers about ethical business practices and fair work conditions, have driven some consumers to avoid destinations where such practices – i.e. violation of human rights in the work environment – occur (see Chapter 4 on boycotting destinations). Baum and Hai (2019) advocate applying sustainable employment principles as a way to mediate human rights violations. Winchenbach, Hanna and Miller (2019) support the concept of dignity in tourism employment. As one of the leading global employment sectors, it is important for tourism stakeholders to acknowledge, address and prevent human exploitation such as unethical business practices (see Chapters 2 and 10). While tourism generates revenues for large corporations and for governments through taxes and development fees, tourism is largely made up of micro, small and medium-sized enterprises (MSME). As observed during the COVID-19 pandemic, these MSME are often the first one to be hit, and various states have been enacting emergency financing to save MSME from bankruptcy. Other government loan programs such as the Price Edward Island (Canada) Tourism Assistance Loan programme or microcredit loans in developing countries such as through Kiva, an international non-profit organisation supporting entrepreneurs operated through the Internet can help MSME succeed (Kiva, 2020; Government of PEI, 2020).

5.4.7 Environmental security and tourism

Increasingly, the overuse of natural resources and degradation of ecosystems are understood to play a role in increasing human vulnerability, undermining livelihoods and human well-being, and potentially generating conflict all augmented by climate change (Renner and French, 2004). Environmental security has evolved from a focus on environmental problems and conflict in the 1990s to climate change and security (Busby, 2018). The environment and tourism are intertwined, with environmental degradation a major concern for host communities, the tourism industry, and tourists. Tourism is often blamed for undue appropriation of land, and excessive use of natural resources in destinations at the cost of local people's needs. Environmental issues are highly integrated with social considerations as evident in the UNDP's *Social and Environmental Standards* (UNDP 2014). The seven project-level standards include: biodiversity conservation and sustainable natural resource management; climate change mitigation and adaptation; community health, safety and working conditions; cultural heritage; displacement and resettlement; Indigenous People; and pollution prevention and resource efficiency. As noted in the various chapters throughout this book, degradation in any of these seven integrated factors in relation to tourism can lead to human rights violations. For example, with worsening climate change, and the unprecedented scale of natural disasters in recent years, people around the world have been displaced by earthquakes, tsunamis, flooding, tornadoes, hurricanes, and volcano eruptions. Displacement causes the loss of livelihood, access to their lands and resources, and reduced access to a safe and healthy environment where people can exercise their life with dignity. Politically motivated investors and politicians in some cases have used the opportunity of natural disasters and subsequent evacuation of locals, to rebuild disaster-struck areas quickly for tourism and consequently locals cannot return to their villages (see Chapters 4 and 7 on disaster capitalism and land grabbing). Tourism destinations in developing countries are also some of the most vulnerable locations for climate change and tourism has been a significant CO_2 emission contributor from long-haul air travel, transportation, and operation of hotels and other facilities (see Chapter 11). Another example of integration can be seen in the volatile situation in the MENA region before and after the Arab Spring. Shortages of food, water, shelter, or the needed natural resources for livelihood have produced socially and politically unstable situations leading to declines in tourism. Today, understanding such volatility caused by environmentally induced stress has become an important part of the defense strategy of nation-states (Goodman, 2012) as well as for crisis management in tourism. Protection of natural environments and resources and combatting climate change will be a priority in order to prevent worst-case scenarios such as armed conflict fighting for scarce resources, increasing number of climate refugees and decimation of regions by natural disasters. Tourism's shift towards sustainability and adapting to climate change are critical towards protecting human rights.

5.5 Conclusions

Higgins-Desbiolles and Whyte (2015) argue that much of tourism discourse has been centred on the needs of tourists and the industry and that a human rights perspective would necessitate a shift to a 'host' community-centred approach. It is evident that human rights and human security – though both alike and distinct – highly complement each other. Like human rights, human security places the focus of security on the individual or a group of individuals, as opposed to the security of the state, and examines issues which present threats to the security of the individual. Human security issues hitherto have been downplayed and given less attention by a national security approach, have now taken centre stage in global politics; they are influencing policy decisions affecting individuals across the globe. The concept of human security has evolved over time and has become an indispensable concept in every human activity. The chapter has explored the relationship between tourism and the UNDP's (1994) seven realms of human security. The integration of these seven categories can be seen in the context of climate change and tourism illustrating the imperative to further examine all human security issues along with human rights and tourism.

References

Al-Shammari, N. and Willoughby, J., 2019. Determinants of political instability across Arab Spring countries. *Mediterranean Politics* [pdf] 24(2), pp. 196–217. DOI: https://doi.org/10.1080/13629395.2017.1389349

Amnesty International, 2016. *The 'Arab Spring': Five Years On.* [online] 20 January. Available at: <www.amnesty.org/en/latest/campaigns/2016/01/arab-spring-five-years-on/> [Accessed 20 April 2020].

Amos, O., 2020. Coronavirus journey: The 'last cruise ship on Earth' finally comes home. *BBC News.* [online] 20 April. Available at: <www.bbc.com/news/world-52350262> [Accessed 20 April 2020].

Anderson, M., 2014. Ebola: airlines cancel more flights to affected countries. *The Guardian.* [online] 22 August. Available at: <www.theguardian.com/society/2014/aug/22/ebola-airlines-cancel-flights-guinea-liberia-sierra-leone> [Accessed 19 April 2019].

Baum, T. and Hai, N.T.T., 2019. Applying sustainable employment principles in the tourism industry: righting human rights wrongs?. *Tourism Recreation Research*, [e-Journal] 44(3), pp. 371–381. Available at: <https://doi.org/10.1080/02508281.2019.1624407> [Accessed 5 May 2020].

BBC, 2011. Arab nations aim to win back tourists. *BBC.* [online] 10 November. Available at: <www.bbc.com/news/business-15651730> [Accessed on 2 March 2019].

BBC, 2017. Tunisia attack: What happened. *BBC.* [online] 1 February. Available at: <www.bbc.com/news/world-africa-33304897> [Accessed 20 April 2020].

BBC, 2018. Jordan profile – Timeline. *BBC.* [online] 5 June. Available at: <www.bbc.com/news/world-middle-east-14636713> [Accessed 20 April 2020].

BBC, 2020a. Coronavirus: How did Cambodia's cruise ship welcome go wrong? *BBC.* [online] 20 February. Available at: <www.bbc.com/news/world-asia-51542241> [Accessed 20 February 2020].

BBC, 2020b. Coronavirus: Tourists quarantined on cruise ship Aidamira off South Africa *BBC.* [online] 18 March. Available at: <www.bbc.com/news/world-asia-51542241> [Accessed 18 March 2020].

BBC News, 2020a Coronavirus: Greatest test since World War Two, says UN chief. *BBC.* [online] 1 April. Available at: <www.bbc.com/news/world-52114829> [Accessed 1 April 2020].

BBC News, 2020b. Coronavirus: Beijing orders 14-day quarantine for returnees. *BBC.* [online] 15 February. Available at: <www.bbc.com/news/world-asia-china-51509248> [Accessed 16 February 2020].

Benedek, W., 2008. Human security and human rights interaction. *International Social Science Journal,* [e-journal] 59(S1), pp. 7–17. Available at: <https://onlinelibrary.wiley.com/toc/14682451/2008/59/s1> [Accessed 7 March 2019].

Bianchi, R., 2006. Tourism and the globalisation of fear: Analysis and the politics of risk and (in)security in global travel. *Tourism and Hospitality Research*, [e-Journal] 7(1), pp. 64–74. Available at: <www.jstor.org/stable/23745382> [Accessed 4 May 2020].

Bilefsky, D. and de la Baum, M., 2015. Terrorists strike Charlie Hebdo Newspaper in Paris, leaving 12 dead. *The New York Times.* [online] 8 January. Available at: <www.nytimes.com/2015/01/08/world/europe/charlie-hebdo-paris-shooting.html> [Accessed 9 March 2019].

Botelho, G., 2015. Terror attacks on 3 continents; ISIS claims responsibility in Tunisia, Kuwait. *CNN.* [online] 27 June. Available at: <www.cnn.com/2015/06/26/africa/tunisia-terror-attack/index.html> [Accessed 2 March 2019].

Brock, J., 2014. Ebola fears slow tourists flow to Africa. *Reuters.* [online] 20 August. Available at: <www.reuters.com/article/us-health-ebola-africatourism/ebola-fears-slowing-tourist-flow-to-africa-idUSKBN0GK1GG20140820> [Accessed 30 June 2019].

Burgess, J.P., 2008. The ethical challenges of human security in the age of globalisation. *International Social Science Journal* [e-journal] 59(S1), pp. 49–63. Available at: <https://onlinelibrary.wiley.com/toc/14682451/2008/59/s1> [Accessed 7 March 2019].

Busby, J., 2018. Environmental Security. In: A. Gheciu and W. Wohlforth, (eds.), *The Oxford Handbook of International Security*. Oxford Online Handbooks [PDF] <DOI: 10.1093/oxford/9780198777854.012.31> [Accessed 10 May 2020].

Caballero-Anthony, M., 2015. Community security: human security at 21. *Contemporary Politics* 21(1), pp. 53–69. <http://dx.doi.org/10.1080/13569775.2014.994812.> [Accessed 9 May 2020].

Cain, Á., 2019. Over 1,000 people reported falling ill while staying in the Dominican Republic on a popular food-safety site as reports of mysterious tourist deaths and rampant sickness plague the Caribbean island. *Business Insider*. [online] 21 June. Available at: <www.businessinsider.com/dominican-republic-i-was-poisoned-reports-2019-6> [Accessed 21 June 2019].

CBC, 2018. The staggering scale of France's battle against terror, by the numbers. *The National Newsletter*. [online] 12 December. Available at: <www.cbc.ca/news/thenational/national-today-newsletter-terrorism-implant-registry-rice-1.4939071> [Accessed 12 June 2019].

Centers for Disease Control and Prevention, 2017. *Food Poisoning Symptoms*. [online] 22 November. Available at <www.cdc.gov/foodsafety/symptoms.html> [Accessed 21 June 2019].

Chambers, R., 2010. *Paradigms, poverty and adaptive pluralism (IDS Working Paper 344)*. DOI: https://onlinelibrary.wiley.com/doi/epdf/10.1111/j.2040-0209.2010.00344_2.x.

CNN, 2015. 2015 Paris terror attacks fast facts. *CNN*. [online] 19 December 2018. Available at: <www.cnn.com/2015/12/08/europe/2015-paris-terror-attacks-fast-facts/index.html> [Accessed 9 March 2019].

Cole, S. and Eriksson, J., 2010. Tourism and Human Rights In: S. Cole and N. Morgan, (eds.), *Tourism and Inequality: Problems and Prospects*. Wallingford: CAB, pp. 107–125. eBook. DOI: 10.1079/9781845936624.0000.

Cole, S. and Morgan, N., 2010. Introduction: Tourism and Inequalities. In: S. Cole and N. Morgan, (eds.), *Tourism and Inequality: Problems and Prospects*. Wallingford: CAB, pp. 1–21 eBook. DOI: 10.1079/9781845936624.0000.

CTV News, 2016. Homelessness in Canada: Key statistics. *The Canadian Press*. [online] 16 March. Available at: <www.ctvnews.ca/canada/homelessness-in-canada-key-statistics-1.2819986> [Accessed 27 June 2019].

Cullinane, S., 2015. Tunisia museum attackers wore suicide vests, President says. *CNN*. [online] 23 March. Available at: <www.cnn.com/2015/03/23/africa/tunisia-museum-attack/index.html> [Accessed 2 March 2019].

Darlington, S., 2018. A year of violence sees Brazil's murder rate hit record high, *The New York Times*. [online] 10 August. Available at: <www.nytimes.com/2018/08/10/world/americas/brazil-murder-rate-record.html> [Accessed 15 June 2019].

Dwyer, L. and Cavlek, N., 2019. Economic globalisation and tourism. In: D. Timothy, (ed.) *Handbook on Globalisation and Tourism*. Cheltenham: Edward Elgar Publishing Limited. DOI 10.4337/9781786431295.

Embury-Dennis, T., 2018. Brazil breaks own record for number of murders in a single year as deaths hit 63,880. *The Independent*. [online] 10 August. Available at: <www.independent.co.uk/news/world/americas/brazil-murder-rate-record-homicides-killings-rio-de-janeiro-police-a8485656.html> [Accessed 15 June 2019].

Fantz, A., 2019. After deaths, more tourists to Dominican Republic say they were stricken with illness. *CNN Investigates*. [online] 24 June. Available at: <www.cnn.com/2019/06/24/health/dominican-republic-sickness-deaths-invs/index.html> [Accessed 24 June 2019].

Food Safety Information Council, 2020. World Food Safety Day 7 June. [online] 11 March. Available at: <https://foodsafety.asn.au/topic/australias-food-safety-report-card-released-for-the-inaugural-world-food-safety-day-7-june-2019/> [Accessed 11 March 2020].

Foundation for Human Rights for Cuba, 2018. *British tourists in Cuba are treated on IV drips after 'food poisoning' bug at ANOTHER Thomas Cook resort – just weeks after UK couple died at Egyptian hotel*. [online] 5 September. Available at: <www.fhrcuba.org/2018/09/british-tourists-in-cuba-are-treated-on-iv-drips-after-food-poisoning-bug-at-another-thomas-cook-resort-just-weeks-after-uk-couple-died-at-egyptian-hotel/> [Accessed 24 June 2019].

France 24, 2020. UN chief says coronavirus worst global crisis since World War II. *France 24*. [online] 1 April. Available at: <www.france24.com/en/20200401-un-chief-says-coronavirus-worst-global-crisis-since-world-war-ii> [Accessed 1 April 2020].

Gamarra, R.M., 2018. What is the prevalence of food poisoning in the US? *Medscape*. [online] 19 June. Available at: <www.medscape.com/answers/175569-114358/what-is-the-prevalence-of-food-poisoning-in-the-us> [Accessed 11 March 2020].

Gayle, E., 2014. Ebola virus affecting tourism say travel agents. *EuroNews*. [online] 20 August. Available at: <www.euronews.com/2014/08/20/ebola-virus-affecting-tourism-say-travel-agents> [Accessed 30 June 2019].

Gómez, O. and Gasper, D., 2014. Human Security A Thematic Guide Note for Regional and National Human Development Report Teams. *UNDP*. [PDF] Available at: <http://hdr.undp.org/sites/default/files/human_security_guidance_note_r-nhdrs.pdf> [Accessed 6 May 2020].

Goodman, S., 2012. What is environmental security? *Yale Insights*. [online] 15 April. Available at: <https://insights.som.yale.edu/insights/what-is-environmental-security> [Accessed 20 June 2019].

Government of Canada, 2019 Infographic: Food-related illnesses, hospitalizations and deaths in Canada. [online] 24 September. Available at: <www.canada.ca/en/public-health/services/publications/food-nutrition/infographic-food-related-illnesses-hospitalizations-deaths-in-canada.html> [Accessed 11 March 2020].

Government of France, 2015. France still world's No. 1 tourist destination in 2014. [online] 8 April. Available at: <www.gouvernement.fr/en/france-still-world-s-no-1-tourist-destination-in-2014> [Accessed 12 March 2019].

Government of France, 2016. France remains the world's leading tourist destination. [online] 11 April. Available at: <www.gouvernement.fr/en/france-remains-the-world-s-leading-tourist-destination> [Accessed 12 March 2019].

Government of France, 2018. *Le 4 pages de la DGE: 87 million foreign tourists in France in 2017* [pdf] 5 July. Available at <www.entreprises.gouv.fr/etudes-et-statistiques/4-pages-84-87-millions-de-touristes-etrangers-france-2017> [Accessed 12 July 2019].

Government of France, 2019. *Le 4 pages de la DGE: More than 89 million foreign tourists in France in 2018* [pdf] 3 July. Available at: <www.entreprises.gouv.fr/etudes-et-statistiques/4-pages-ndeg88-plus-de-89-millions-de-touristes-etrangers-france-2018> [Accessed 12 July 2019].

Government of PEI, 2020. *Tourism Assistance Loan Program*. [online]. Available at: <www.princeedwardisland.ca/en/service/tourism-assistance-loan-program> [Accessed 8 May 2020].

Griffin, C., 2005. The imperatives of regional governance: Securing the tourism sector and enhancing human security. *Social and Economic Studies* 54(4), pp. 13–41. Available at: <www.jstor.org/stable/27866443> [Accessed 12 July 2019].

Grisdale, S., 2019. Displacement by disruption: short-term rentals and the political economy of "belonging anywhere" in Toronto. *Urban Geography* [e-journal] pp. 1–27. <https://doi.org/10.1080/02723638.2019.1642714 >.

Guiney, T., 2018. "Hug-an-orphan vacations": "Love" and emotion in orphanage tourism. *The Geographical Journal*, [e-Journal] 184(2), pp. 125–137. https://doi:10.1111/geogj.12218.

Hall, D. and Brown, F., 2010. Tourism and Welfare: Ethics, Responsibility and Well-being. In: S. Cole and N. Morgan, (eds.), *Tourism and Inequality: Problems and Prospects*. Wallingford: CAB eBook. DOI: 10.1079/9781845936624.0000. Chapter 9.

Hassan, O. 2015. Political security from the 1990s to the Arab Spring. *Contemporary Politics* 21(1), pp. 89–99. <https://doi.org/10.1080/13569775.2014.993907> [Accessed 9 May 2020].

Hetter, K., 2012. Who's afraid to fly on September 11? CNN Travel. [online] 11 September. Available at: <www.cnn.com/2012/09/11/travel/fear-travel-september-11/index.html> [Accessed 20 April 2020].

Higgins-Desbiolles, F., 2010. Justifying Tourism: Justice through Tourism. In: S. Cole and N. Morgan, (eds.), *Tourism and Inequality: Problems and Prospects*. Wallingford: CAB eBook. DOI: 10.1079/9781845936624.0000. Chapter 12.

Higgins-Desbiolles, F. and Whyte, K., 2015. Tourism and human rights. In: C.M. Hall, S. Gössling and D. Scott, (eds.), *The Routledge Handbook of Tourism and Sustainability*. Oxon: Routledge, pp. 105–116.

Hilhorst, D. ed., 2013. *Disaster, Conflict And Society in Crises: Everyday Politics of Crisis Response*. Abingdon, Oxon: Routledge.

Hirai, M. and Graham, J., 2019. Toward Universal access to basic and safely managed drinking water: remaining challenges and new opportunities in the era of sustainable development goals. In: J. Selendy, (ed.), *Water and Sanitation- Related Diseases and the Changing Environment: Challenges, Interventions, and Preventative Measures*. Hoboken, NJ: Wiley. Chapter 1.

HURGHADA, 2013. Tourism in Egypt: Arab spring break. *The Economist*. [online] 4 May. Available at: <www.economist.com/business/2013/05/04/arab-spring-break> [Accessed 2 March 2019].

Icelandic Human Rights Centre, 2014. Human Rights Concepts, Ideas and Fora. [online] Available at: <www.humanrights.is/en/human-rights-education-project/human-rights-concepts-ideas-and-fora> [Accessed September 2014].

International Labour Organization, 1951. *Equal remuneration Convention, 1951 (No.100)* [pdf] Available at: <www.ilo.org/wcmsp5/groups/public/---ed_norm/---declaration/documents/publication/wcms_decl_fs_84_en.pdf> [Accessed 23 July 2019].

Ismail, A., 2016. After university crackdown, Egyptian students fear for their future. *Reuters*. [online] 1 June. Available at: <www.reuters.com/article/us-egypt-students-specialreport/special-report-after-university-crackdown-egyptian-students-fear-for-their-future-idUSKCN0YN3YV> [Accessed 7 March 2019].

Kelleher, J., 2020. Rogue tourists arrested as Hawaii tries to curb virus spread. *Associated Press*. [online] 7 May. Available at: <https://apnews.com/86c1327cd4630d745176078828787373> [Accessed 8 March 2020].

Kiva, 2020. *Homepage*. [online]. Available at: <www.kiva.org/> [Accessed 8 May 2020].

Koehn. P.H., 2019. *Transnational Mobility and Global Health: Traversing Borders and Boundaries*. Abingdon, Oxon: Routledge.

Krause, K., 2009. Human security, In: V. Chetail, (ed.), *2009. Post-Conflict Peacebuilding: A Lexicon*. Oxford: Oxford University Press, pp. 147–57.

Krug, E.G., Mercy, J.A., Dahlberg, L.L. and Zwi, A.B., 2002. The world report on violence and health. *The Lancet* [e-journal] 360(9339), pp. 1083–1088. DOI: https://doi.org/10.1016/S0140-6736(02)11133-0.

La France au Vanuatu, 2014. *Tourisme - les statistiques sur le tourisme pour 2013.* [online] 8 October. Available at: <https://vu.ambafrance.org/Tourisme-les-statistiques-sur-le> [Accessed 12 March 2019].

Magablih, K.M.A. and Mustafa, M.H., 2018. How the "Arab Spring" Influenced Tourism and Hospitality Industry in Jordan: Perceptions of Workers in Tourism and Hospitality Business. *Journal of Tourism and Hospitality Management*, [e-Journal] 6(2), pp. 132–139. DOI: 10.15640/jns.v6n2a11

Marjavaara, R., 2009. Cases and Issues 8.5. Second home tourism and displacement in the Stockholm archipelago. In: C.M. Hall, D.K. Müller and J. Saarinen, (eds.), *Nordic Tourism: Issues and Cases*. Bristol: Channel View Publication, pp. 192–193.

McCarthy, N., 2018. The U.S. cities with the most homeless people in 2018. *Forbes*. [online] 20 December. Available at: <www.forbes.com/sites/niallmccarthy/2018/12/20/the-u-s-cities-with-the-most-homeless-people-in-2018-infographic/#30bc842e1178> [Accessed 27 June 2019].

McCrie, R.D., 2006. A history of security. In: M.L. Gill, (ed.), *The Handbook of Security*. New York: Palgrave Macmillan, pp. 21–44.

McEldowney, J. 2005. Political security and democratic rights, [e-Journal] 12(5), pp. 766–782. DOI: https://doi.org/10.1080/13510340500322249

Middle East Monitor, 2017. *Tourism to Egypt plummets by 40 per cent in 2016.* [online] 5 January. Available at: <www.middleeastmonitor.com/20170105-tourism-to-egypt-plummets-by-40-per-cent-in-2016/> [Accessed 20 April 2020].

Mun, W. and Musa, G., 2013. Medical Tourism in Asia: Thailand, Singapore, Malaysia, and India. In: C. M. Hall, (ed.), *Medical Tourism: The Ethics, Regulation and Marketing of Health Mobility*. London: Routledge. Chapter 11.

Murphy, C., 2012. The Arab Spring: The uprising and its significance. *Trinity Magazine 2012.* [online] Spring. Available at: <www.trinitydc.edu/magazine-2012/the-arab-spring-the-uprising-and-its-significance/> [Accessed 20 April 2020]

Nahhas, R., 2018. Jordan's tourist arrivals, revenue show improvement. *The Arab Weekly* [online] 9 December. Available at: <https://thearabweekly.com/jordans-tourist-arrivals-revenue-show-improvement> [Accessed 20 April 2020]

Nkyi, E. and Hashimoto, A., 2015. Human rights issues in tourism development. In: R. Sharpley and D.J. Telfer, (eds.), *Tourism and Development: Concepts and Issues*. Bristol: Channel View Publications. Chapter 13.

Novy, J. and Colomb, C., 2016. Urban tourism and its discontents: an introduction. In: C. Colomb and J. Novy, (eds.), *Protest and Resistance in the Tourist City*. London: Routledge. Chapter 1.

OHCHR, 2008. *The Rights to Health: Fact Sheet No. 31* [pdf] Available at: <www.ohchr.org/Documents/Publications/Factsheet31.pdf> [Accessed 20 Aril 2020]

Owen, T., 2008. The uncertain future of human security in the UN. *International Social Science Journal,* [e-journal] 59(S1), pp. 113–127. Available at: <https://onlinelibrary.wiley.com/toc/14682451/2008/59/s1> [Accessed 7 March 2019].

Owen, T. ed., 2013. *SAGE Library of International Relations: Human security* (Vols. 1–4). London: SAGE Publications Ltd. doi: 10.4135/9781446286418.

Phillips, D., 2017. Brazil police shoot dead Spanish tourist in Rio de Janeiro favela. *The Guardian*. [online] 23 October. Available at: <www.theguardian.com/world/2017/oct/23/brazil-police-shoot-dead-spanish-tourist-rio-de-janeiro-favela> [Accessed 15 June 2019].

Ragahavan, S. and Mahfouz, H.S., 2018. Gunmen in Egypt attack bus carrying Christians, killing at least 8 and wounding 13. *The Washington Post.* [online] 2 November. Available at: <www.washingtonpost.com/world/gunmen-in-egypt-attack-bus-carrying-christians-killing-at-least-7-and-wounding-14/2018/11/02/cadb679b-ab2f-4e28-98f0-47abd40f32fd_story.html> [Accessed 7 March 2019].

Renner, M. and French, H., 2004. The United Nations and Environmental Security: Recommendations for the Secretary-General's High-level Panel on Threats, Challenges and Change. *ESCP Report, 10.* [pdf]. Available at: <www.wilsoncenter.org/sites/default/files/media/documents/publication/ecspr10_unf.pdf> [Accessed 15 May 2020].

Reuters, 2015. Tunisia identifies bus suicide bomber as Tunisian national. *Reuters.* [online] 26 November. Available at: <www.reuters.com/article/us-tunisia-security/tunisia-identifies-bus-suicide-bomber-as-tunisian-national-idUSKBN0TF1FT20151126> [Accessed 20 April 2020].

Reuters, 2017. Foreign tourist numbers up 23 percent in Tunisia in 2017. *Reuters.* [online] 27 December. Available at: <www.reuters.com/article/us-tunisia-tourism/foreign-tourist-numbers-up-23-percent-in-tunisia-in-2017-idUSKBN1EL0LT> [Accessed 20 April 2020].

Richardson, H., 2018. At least '320,000 people homeless in Britain'. *BBC.* [online] 22 November. Available at: <www.bbc.com/news/education-46289259> [Accessed 27 June 2019].

Rubin, A.J. and Breeden, A., 2016. France remembers the Nice attack: 'we will never find the words.' *The New York Times.* [online] 14 July 2017. Available at: <www.nytimes.com/2017/07/14/world/europe/nice-attack-france-bastille-day.html> [Accessed 9 March 2019].

Sanchez, R., 2015. Tunisian President declares emergency: new terror attack would cause 'collapse'. *CNN.* [online] 4 July. Available at: <www.cnn.com/2015/07/04/world/tunisia-state-of-emergency/index.html> [Accessed 2 March 2019].

Sanchez, R., Williams, D. and Flores, R., 2019. After mysterious tourist deaths and shooting of David Ortiz, Dominican officials try to reassure travelers. *CNN.* [online] 13 June. Available at: <www.cnn.com/2019/06/12/us/dominican-republic-deaths-tourism/index.html> [Accessed 15 June 2019].

Sané, P., 2008. Rethinking human security. *International Social Science Journal,* [e-journal] 59(S1), pp. 5–6. Available at: <https://onlinelibrary.wiley.com/toc/14682451/2008/59/s1> [Accessed 7 March 2019].

Sen, A., 1999. *Development as Freedom.* New York: Anchor Books.

Smith, D., 2014. Ethiopia: 30 years on from the famine. *The Guardian.* [online] 22 October. Available at: <www.theguardian.com/world/2014/oct/22/-sp-ethiopia-30-years-famine-human-rights> [Accessed 28 May 2019].

Steinmetz, J.T., 2019. Is this Hard Rock Hotel Cafe slowly poisoning guests? *eTurbo News.* [online] 11 June. Available at: <www.eturbonews.com/254961/is-this-hard-rock-hotel-restaurant-slowly-poison-guests/> [Accessed 11 June 2019].

Sustain, 2020. Fears new trade deals with US will increase UK food poisoning. [online] 3 March. Available at: <www.sustainweb.org/news/feb18_US_foodpoisoning/> [Accessed 11 March 2020].

Tadjbakhsh, S. and Chenoy, A., 2007. *Human Security: Concepts and Implications.* London: Routledge. DOI: https://doi.org/10.4324/9780203965955.

Tao, T. and Wall, G., 2009. Tourism as a sustainable livelihood strategy. *Tourism Management* 30(1), pp. 90–98. DOI: https://doi.org.10.1016/j.tourman.2008.03.009.

Telfer, D.J., 2015. The evolution of development theory and tourism. In: R. Sharpley and D.J. Telfer, (eds.), *Tourism and Development: Concepts and Issues*, 2nd Edition. Bristol: Channel View Publications. pp. 31–74.

Telfer, D.J., 2019. Tourism and (re)development in developed nations. In: R. Sharpley and D. Harrison, (eds.), *A Research Agenda for Tourism and Development*. Cheltenham: Edward Elgar, pp. 206–232.

Telfer, D.J. and Sharpley, R., 2016. *Tourism and Development in the Developing World*, 2nd Edition. Abingdon, Oxon: Routledge.

Telfer, D. J. and Wall. G., 1996. Linkages between tourism and food production. *Annals of Tourism Research*, [e-Journal] 23(3), pp. 635–653. http://doi.org/10.1016/0160-7383(95)00087-9.

The Telegraph, 2018. Terror attacks in France: from Toulouse to the Louvre. *The Telegraph*. [online] 24 June. Available at: <www.telegraph.co.uk/news/0/terror-attacks-france-toulouse-louvre/> [Accessed 9 March 2019].

The World Bank, 2015. Back to School After the Ebola Outbreak. *News*. [online] 01 May. Available at: <https://www.worldbank.org/en/news/feature/2015/05/01/back-to-school-after-ebola-outbreak> [Accessed 20 April 2020].

Thompson, N. and Torre, I., 2014. Ebola virus: Countries with travel restrictions in place. *CNN*. [online] 4 November. Available at: <www.cnn.com/2014/11/04/world/ebola-virus-restrictions-map/index.html> [Accessed 18 April 2019].

Thornburg, J., 2011. Market-led development versus Basic Needs: Common Property and the Common Good in St. Lucia. *Journal of International and Global Studies* 2(2), pp. 1–20. Available at: <www.lindenwood.edu/files/resources/1-20-2.pdf> [Accessed 8 May 2020].

Tomazos, K., 2017. Egypt's tourism industry and the Arab Spring. In: R. Butler and W. Suntikul, (eds.), *Tourism and Political Change*, 2nd Edition. [e-book] Oxford: Goodfellow Publishers. Chapter 15. DOI: 10.23912/9781910158814-3160.

Tremblay, R., Kelly, J., Lipson, M. and Mayer, J.F., 2008. *Understanding Human Rights: Origins, Currents, and Critiques*. Toronto: Thomson Nelson.

UN DESA, 1995. *WSSD 1995 Agreement*. Available at: <www.un.org/development/desa/dspd/world-summit-for-social-development-1995/wssd-1995-agreements/> [Accessed 5 May 2020].

UNDP, 1994. New dimensions of human security. *Human Development Report 1994*. Oxford: Oxford University Press. Chapter 2.

UNDP, 2014. UNDP Social and Environmental Standards. Available at: [PDF] <www.undp.org/content/dam/undp/library/corporate/Social-and-Environmental-Policies-and-Procedures/UNDPs-Social-and-Environmental-Standards-ENGLISH.pdf> [Accessed 10 May 2020].

UNDP, 2018. *Beyond income: A broader picture of poverty*. [online]. Available at: <https://feature.undp.org/multidimensional-poverty/> [Accessed 9 February 2019].

UNICEF, 2020. *The reality of Malaria*. [pdf]. Available at: <https://www.unicef.org/media/files/MALARIAFACTSHEETAFRICA.pdf> [Accessed 23 April 2019].

UN SDG, 2019. *Goal 6 Ensure access to water and sanitation for all*. Available at: <www.un.org/sustainabledevelopment/water-and-sanitation/> [Accessed 8 May 2020].

UN Women, 2019. *International Day for the Elimination of Violence Against Women*. Available at: <www.un.org/en/events/endviolenceday/> [Accessed 8 May 2020].

United Nations News, 2016. *Egypt: UN experts report worsening crackdown on protest*. [online]. 9 May. Available at: <www.news.un.org> [Accessed 7 March 2019].

United Nations News, 2018. *South Sudan: A year after averting famine, 'food insecurity outlook has never been so dire' UN warns*. [online] 26 February. Available at: <https://news.un.org/en/story/2018/02/1003552> [Accessed 29 May 2019].

United Nations News, 2019. *10 million Yemenis 'one step away from famine', UN food relief agency calls for 'unhindered access' to frontline regions*. [online] 26 March. Available at: <news.un.org/en/story/2019/03/1035501> [Accessed 28 May 2019].

Universal Declaration of Human Rights (UDHR), 1948. G.A. Res. 217 (III) A, U.N. Doc. A/RES/217(III) (December 10, 1948).

UNWTO, 2019. *International Tourism Highlights 2019 Edition*. [pdf] Available at: <www.e-unwto.org/doi/pdf/10.18111/9789284421152> [Accessed 20 April 2020].

UNWTO, 2020. World Tourism Remains at a Standstill as 100% of Countries Impose Restrictions on Travel. *UNWTO News*. [online] 11 May. Available at: <www.unwto.org/news/Covid-19-world-tourism-remains-at-a-standstill-as-100-of-countries-impose-restrictions-on-travel> [Accessed 11 May 2020].

Urbain, O., 2013. Prologue: envisioning peace tourism. In: L.A. Blanchard and F. Higgins-Desbiolles, (eds.), *Peace through Tourism: Promoting Human Security through International Citizenship*. Abingdon, Oxon: Routledge.

Van Bortel, T., Basnayake, A., Wurie, F. Jambai, M., Koroma, A.S., Muana, A.T., Hann, K., Eaton, J., Maring, S. and Nellumsa, L.B., 2016. Psychosocial effects of an Ebola outbreak at individual, community and international levels. *Bulletin of the World Health Organization*, 94 (3), pp. 210–214. [online]. DOI: doi: 10.2471/BLT.15.158543.

Walker, J., 2015. Terrorists Kill Tourists as Costa Fascinosa and MSC Splendida Visit Tunis. *Cruise Law News*. [online] 18 March. Available at: <www.cruiselawnews.com/2015/03/articles/terrorism/terrorists-kill-tourists-as-costa-fascinosa-and-msc-splendida-visit-tunis/> [Accessed 20 April 2020].

Walsh, D. and Youssef, N., 2017. Militants kill 305 at Sufi Mosque in Egypt's deadliest terrorist attack. *The New York Times*. [online] 24 November. Available at: <www.nytimes.com/2017/11/24/world/middleeast/mosque-attack-egypt.html> [Accessed 7 March 2019].

WHO, 2016. *Ebola outbreak 2014–2016*. [online] June 2016. Available at: <www.who.int/csr/disease/ebola/en/> [Accessed 20 April 2020].

WHO, 2017. *Human Rights and Health*. [online] Available at: <www.who.int/news-room/fact-sheets/detail/human-rights-and-health> [Accessed 20 April 2020].

WHO, 2020a. *Coronavirus disease 2019 (COVID-19) Situation Report – 72*. [pdf] 1 April. Available at: <www.who.int/emergencies/diseases/novel-coronavirus-2019/situation-reports> [Accessed 1 April 2020].

WHO, 2020b. Coronavirus disease (COVID-19) outbreak. *World Health Organization*. [online]. Available at: <www.who.int/> [Accessed 16 February 2020].

WHO, 2020c. *International travel and health*. Available at: <www.who.int/ith/precautions/travel_related/en/> [Accessed 8 May 2020].

Winchenbach, A., Hanna, A. and Miller, G., 2019. Rethinking decent work: the value of dignity in tourism employment. *Journal of Sustainable Tourism*, [e-Journal] 27(7), pp. 1026–1043. DOI: https://doi.org/10.1080/09669582.2019.1566346.

Wolfe, J. and Corasaniti, N., 2017. New York Today: terrorism and tourism. *The New York Times*. [online] 3 November. Available at: <www.nytimes.com/2017/11/03/nyregion/new-york-today-terrorism-and-tourism.html> [Accessed 20 April 2020].

WTTC, 2019. Travel and tourism economic impact 2019 world. *World Travel and Tourism Council*. [online]. Available at: <www.wttc.org> [23 Accessed July 2019].

6
RIGHT TO PRIVACY AND TOURISM

> Always the eyes watching you and the voice enveloping you. Asleep or awake, working or eating, indoors or out of doors, in the bath or bed- no escape. Nothing was your own except the few cubic centimeters inside your skull.
> *(Orwell, 1949, p. 27)*[1]

6.1 The right to privacy: an introduction

The topic of this chapter is the human right to privacy in tourism, travel and hospitality establishments. Privacy concerns can be raised in the tourism and hospitality context for example when a person has his/her cell phone searched by customs and border agents at a border crossing, when a person is filmed by security cameras in a hotel room where there is an expectation of privacy, when a person is subjected to body scans in concert venues or when there is a transfer or publication of personal data, for example regarding lodging or travel arrangements.

The origins of the right to privacy can be traced to several ancient legal systems and legal concepts. Traces of the legal concept of a right to privacy can be observed in Classical Hindu Law (Ashesh and Acharaya, 2014), Islamic Law (Aslam Hayat, 2007), Roman law (Periñán, 2012) and common law (Cooley, 1879). Although not explicitly defined as a right to privacy or recognized as a legal concept in all of the mentioned legal systems, the concept of protection of the private sphere from unwarranted invasions was present early on in different legal systems, manifested as a right to property, right to virtue, right to honour, sanctity of the home or a right to be left alone.

The demands of modern society have led to some aspects of the ancient legal concept being defined anew and expanded into new spheres of human interaction.

With the evolvement of society, there is a need to redefine legal principles, such as the protection of privacy. As Warren and Brandeis (1890) noted more than a hundred years ago, the changing nature of law is an inevitable part of a well-functioning society. More recently, the spread of the Internet and other technological innovations have led to a redefined sphere of privacy, for example encompassing an expanded protection of personal data.

This chapter is divided into a discussion on three main themes. First, sections 6.2 and 6.3 include a general discussion on the right to privacy from an international human rights law perspective, followed by a discussion of how the human right is implemented at the national level. Constitutional guarantees to a right to privacy as well as more recently developed data privacy laws implemented at the national level have advanced the position of those advocating for a far-reaching right to privacy. These developments are discussed in Section 6.3. Secondly, Sections 6.4 and 6.5 focus on the accommodation industry, where guests can experience both a physical invasion of privacy as well as an invasion of privacy consisting of disclosure of personal data. Thirdly, Sections 6.6 and 6.7 include a discussion about privacy in the travel industry. The travel sector faces some unique challenges in an effort to balance the right to privacy with the societal goal of safe travel, a topic which is explored more in depth in these sections. Finally, Section 6.8 includes some concluding remarks on the topic.

6.2 The right to privacy in international human rights law

In international public law, the traces of a legally enforceable right to privacy from ancient legal systems have evolved into a fundamental human right. It is recognized both in international conventions, as well as at the regional and national levels. At the international level, the right to privacy is recognized in fundamental human rights instruments, such as the Universal Declaration of Human Rights (UDHR) (art. 12), the International Covenant on Civil and Political Rights (ICCPR) (art. 17) and the Convention on the Rights of the Child (CRC) (art. 16).

> According to the UDHR (art. 12):
>
> No one shall be subjected to arbitrary interference with his privacy, family, home or correspondence, nor to attacks upon his honour and reputation. Everyone has the right to the protection of the law against such interference or attacks.

At the regional level, the European Convention for the Protection of Human Rights and Fundamental Freedoms (ECHR) (1950, art. 8), the American Convention on Human Rights (art. 11) and the ASEAN Human Rights Declaration (art. 21) similarly protect the right to privacy. The African Charter on Human and Peoples' Rights does not explicitly protect the right to privacy or private life but includes protection of human integrity (art. 5). The European Court of Human Rights

(ECtHR) has categorized the right to privacy as a classical negative right, with its core provision affording protection from arbitrary interferences by the public authorities (Kroon and others v. Netherlands, § 31). Interferences by public authorities can consist of interferences in family life or other spheres where an individual has a reasonable expectation of privacy.

As mentioned, the right to privacy is only offering protection from arbitrary interferences. The right to privacy can therefore not be classified as an absolute right, since it can be subjected to limitations that are not arbitrary. However, according to the ECHR, public authorities can only interfere with the right to privacy under certain circumstances.

> There shall be no interference by a public authority with the exercise of this right except such as is in accordance with the law and is necessary in a democratic society in the interests of national security, public safety or the economic well-being of the country, for the prevention of disorder or security, for the protection of health or morals, or for the protection of the rights and freedoms of others.
>
> *(ECHR, art. 8)*

Although the protection from negative government interference constitutes the core provision of the right to privacy, states also have positive obligations to protect individuals from third-party interferences.

> In Moreno Gómez v. Spain (2004), the applicant alleged that the Kingdom of Spain had breached her right to respect for her home according to article 8 of the ECHR by permitting bars, pubs and discotheques to open in the vicinity of her home in a residential quarter of Valencia, Spain. The entertainment facilities did not follow time limits or decibel restrictions and noise levels exceeded permitted levels for years. The ECtHR held that the article 8 right to privacy had been breached since the Valencia City Council had tolerated, and thus contributed to the repeated flouting of the rules on noise levels. The right to privacy applies in cases where state responsibility arises from the failure to regulate private industry properly or enforce existing regulations. In the case, the State had failed to discharge its obligation to guarantee the applicant's right to respect for her home and private life.
>
> On the other hand, in Hatton and Others v. The United Kingdom (2003), the court held that the U.K. government had not failed to strike a fair balance between the right of individuals and the conflicting interests of others and the community as a whole. The applicants in the case alleged that the government policy on night flights at Heathrow airport, the busiest airport in Europe, was disturbing their night sleep and thus violated their article 8 right to privacy. The court held that considering that the U.K. government had continuously monitored the situation and placed certain restrictions on night

flights it had, in the circumstances applicable, struck a fair balance between the economic interests of the operators of airlines as well as the country as a whole and the individuals affected by the night flights. There had thus been no violation of article 8 ECHR.

(Hatton and Others v. The United Kingdom, ¶129–130)

6.3 The human right to privacy codified at the national level

Many countries have codified the human right to privacy as part of legislation at the national level. The Spanish Constitution for example protects the right to honour, to personal and family privacy and guarantees the secrecy of postal, telegraphic and telephonic communications (Constitución Española, 1978, art. 18). Other countries do not explicitly protect the right to privacy or the protection of personal information as a civil/human right but infer such protection from other explicitly stated rights. For example, the Indian Supreme Court has recently confirmed that the right to privacy is "an incident of a fundamental freedom or liberty" and is an intrinsic part of life, personal liberty and the other liberties guaranteed by the Indian Constitution (Justice K.S. Puttaswamy (Retd) v. Union of India, 2017, p. 158). The Court emphasizes that "[e]very individual in a society irrespective of social class or economic status is entitled to the intimacy and autonomy which privacy protects" (p. 157). Similarly, the United States Supreme Court has affirmed that the protection offered by the Fourth Amendment in the United States Constitution includes the right to privacy. The Fourth Amendment provides for "the right of the people to be secure in their persons, houses, papers and effects" as well as the right to be free from "unreasonable searches and seizures". The protections of the Fourth Amendment have been liberally constructed to protect individual privacy against certain kinds of instrusions by the government. For example, in Katz v. United States (1967), the government had listened and recorded the defendant's phone conversation in a public phone booth. The United States Supreme Court held that the search violated the defendant's expectation of privacy and was thus a violation of the Fourth Amendment of the United States Constitution.

In the realm of private law, the right to privacy has mainly developed in a tort law setting. Tort law provides for an avenue for redress, when the invasion of privacy is committed not by the government, but by private individuals. Cooley's Tort Treatise from 1879 contains one of the earliest descriptions of the tort:

> The right to one's person may be said to be a right of complete immunity: to be left alone. The corresponding duty is, not to inflict an injury, and not, within such proximity as might render it successful, to attempt the infliction of an injury.

(Cooley, p. 29, 1879)

Warren and Brandeis (1890) expand on the concept in their seminal article on privacy, where they conclude that the law should evolve to recognize a separate legal principle, a "right to privacy", defined independently of the law of slander and libel, right to property or rights arising from a breach of contract or trust (p. 213). Shortly thereafter, courts in the United States started applying the new principle in case law (Pavesich v. New England Life Ins. Co., 1905). Since the late 19th century, when it was first discussed in legal doctrine, protection of privacy has evolved into a recognized concept in the United States.

In addition to defining the right to privacy as a human right in international conventions, constitutional law and private law, many countries have enacted legislation protecting the right to privacy and personal data. The European Union (EU), with its supranational legislation, has been at the forefront when it comes to protection of privacy, especially when it comes to protection of personal data. The supranational Charter of Fundamental Rights of the European Union (2000/C 364 01), which is directly applicable in EU member states both when EU institutions adopt union law as well as when member states of the union implement EU law (art. 51(1)), explicitly protects "private and family life, home and communications" (art. 7). The Charter also includes the right to protection of personal data (art. 8), an aspect of the right to privacy of increased importance in today's society. In addition to the Charter protection of personal data, the EU adopted in 2018 the General Data Protection Regulation (GDPR) (European Parliament and Council Regulation 2016/679, 2016), which includes wide-ranging protection for personal data. The GDPR is based on an earlier EU directive (European Parliament and Council directive 95/46/EC, 1995), but contains more stringent requirements on data processors to guard personal data they have access to. According to article 5, personal data shall be "processed lawfully, fairly and in a transparent manner," "limited to what is necessary" and collected only "for specified, explicit and legitimate purposes." Processing is lawful only if the individual has consented to the processing, it is necessary for the performance of a contract with the party, it is done to comply with a legal obligation, or is necessary in order to protect the vital interests of the individual, the performance of a task carried out in the public interest or in the exercise of official authority or the legitimate interests of the processor, except where such interests of the processor are overridden by the interests of the individual (art. 6).

As mentioned, the GDPR is directly applicable in all 27 EU member states. It is also extraterritorially applicable in other countries if it involves the processing of personal data of data subjects who are in the EU, and the processing is related to the offering of goods or services to data subjects in the Union (art. 3). This means that if a tourism or hospitality enterprise offers its goods or services to persons in the EU, it will have to follow the GDPR on protection of personal data, regardless of if the tourism enterprise is physically located in the EU or if the processing of data takes place in the EU. The maximum administrative fines for infringements of the GDPR amount to €20,000,000 or 4% of worldwide annual turnover, whichever is higher (art. 83). The dissuasive nature of the administrative fines in GDPR has led to increased awareness of data protection requirements among tourism and hospitality companies.

Several tourism and hospitality enterprises have been mired in legal processes involving infringements of the EU data protection rules at the national level in member states. In 2015 and 2016, the ride-hailing company Uber's cloud-based storage service was subject to a cyber-attack where the hackers downloaded personal information (names, mobile phone numbers, sign-up location data and user passwords) from its users. The United Kingdom Information Commissioner's Office (ICO) determined that Uber had failed to take reasonable steps to safeguard its user data and issued a £385,000 monetary penalty in accordance with the UK data protection rules (based on the European Parliament and Council directive 95/46/EC, which was in force at the time) (ICO, 2018).

In March 2020, the Hong Kong carrier Cathay Pacific was fined £500,000 in accordance with the UK data protection rules (based on the European Parliament and Council directive 95/46/EC, which was in force at the time) by the ICO for a large-scale data breach involving 9.4 million data subjects. The breach involved various passenger data such as names, nationalities, dates of birth, phone numbers, addresses, passport numbers and historical travel information. The ICO determined that Cathay Pacific had a number of basic security inadequacies across its systems, which gave easy access to hackers. "Under data protection law organisations are required to have appropriate security measures and robust procedures in place to ensure that any attempt to infiltrate computer systems is made as difficult as possible." The airline had failed to take such reasonable steps to prevent the data breaches. (ICO, 2020).

The hotel chain Marriott International and the airline British Airways are in the midst of similar breach of personal data investigations. According to the ICO notice (ICO, 2019a), it intends to fine Marriott International £99,200,396 for infringements of the GDPR relating to a personal data breach where 339 million guest records were exposed. Around 30 million of those records were related to residents in the European Economic Area, why the GDPR is applicable. According to the investigation, Marriott had failed to undertake due diligence when it bought a rival hotel chain, Starwood, which had compromised personal data management systems. The British Airways cyber incident involved traffic which was diverted from British Airways website to a fraudulent site, where customers' personal information was harvested by the attackers (ICO, 2019b). Approximately 500,000 customers were affected by the incident. Information Commissioner Elisabeth Denham noted that: "People's personal data is just that–personal. When an organisation fails to protect it from loss, damage or theft it is more than an inconvenience. That's why the law is clear–when you are entrusted with personal data you must look after it. Those that don't will face scrutiny from my office to check they have taken appropriate steps to protect fundamental privacy rights" (ICO, 2019b). British Airways risks a fine of £183,390,000, one of the largest fines to date under GDPR. It remains to be seen how the COVID-19 pandemic affects the proposed fines. Both British

Airways and Marriott International have been struggling and the fines might be reduced due to the financial impact of the pandemic on the corporations concerned.

The adoption of the GDPR in the EU has had a vast impact globally, with other countries adapting to the extraterritorial parts of the regulation as well as reviewing and revising their own data privacy legislation. Similar legislation exists outside the EU, although the sanctions for violations of other countries' privacy laws tend to be less severe. The European Commission has recognized that Andorra (2010a), Argentina (2003a), Canada (2002) (only commercial organisations), Faroe Islands (2010b), Guernsey (2003b), Israel (2011), Isle of Man (2004), Japan (2019), Jersey (2008), New Zealand (2013), Switzerland (2000) and Uruguay (2012) have comparable legislation providing adequate protection of personal data.

6.4 Physical invasion of privacy in tourism accommodation establishments

All customers in tourism establishments expect a certain level of privacy when they are engaging with a tourism establishment such as a hotel or a tour operator. The level of privacy is dependent on the type of tourism establishment as well as the specific circumstances of the case. For example, there is a lower expectation of privacy in a bed and breakfast establishment, where the owners rent out a spare room in their home, compared to a luxury hotel, with several hundred rooms. The right to privacy is also dependent on the specific circumstances in each case. For example, most customers in a hotel establishment do not expect that other third parties have access to the hotel room night-time. On the other hand, there is a limited expectation of privacy, when it comes to employees engaged in room cleaning or room service, who access the same room during the morning hours.

A right to privacy can also involve personal information, instead of an intrusion into the physical space of a customer. When a guest books a room or checks into a lodging establishment, the establishment regularly includes in its records a number of personal details about the hotel guest. Usually guests are required to provide personal information including name and address of each guest, the total number of guests, the make, type and license number of a vehicle parked on premises, identification documents, the date of arrival and departure, the rate charged and the method of payment for the room. Most guests would object to the sharing to third parties of at least some of the information, while others would consider the sharing of any information an invasion of privacy.

There can be many legitimate reasons why a person would not want to share personal information with third parties. A person using a hotel room for a romantic rendezvous would likely object to the invasion of her/his privacy. A person fleeing an abusive spouse would also likely object to the disclosure of information about her/his whereabouts to the spouse. In addition, customers in tourism and hospitality enterprises often share personal information of economic value, such as credit card numbers or other payment information. There are many other legitimate reasons, why guests of a tourism establishment would not want to share personal information with any third parties. However, hotels and motels also provide for a site for criminal activity ranging from drug dealing, prostitution, child sex trafficking (see Chapter 13) and illegal migrant smuggling. It is therefore of interest to balance the right to privacy with other interests, such as avoiding criminal activity in society.

An invasion of privacy by government actors can be either a physical intrusion into the space of the individual or an invasion of privacy through the request for disclosures containing personal data. Most jurisdictions try to balance the right to privacy with the need to fight crime and gather evidence in a dwelling by introducing procedural safeguards, to protect from unreasonable government searches and seizures of property. The determining factor for when information can be disclosed is if a person has a reasonable expectation of privacy in the specific situation concerned. Heightened protection is provided when it comes to a person's dwelling. A hotel room or other similar accommodation is considered analogous to an apartment or a house in this context. A person can thus have a heightened legitimate expectation of privacy in a hotel room, during the period when they have rented the hotel room. The procedural requirements before government actors can search a hotel room vary between different jurisdictions. In some jurisdictions, a search can be decided by the investigation leader or a prosecutor, while other countries require a court to issue a warrant before a search is conducted. However, when a search is likely to be extensive or cause a major invasion of privacy to the person whose dwelling is searched, most jurisdictions require additional procedural safeguards, such as a court order allowing the search (see for example Swedish Code of Judicial Procedure, 1942, Ch.28 §4). Most countries allow warrantless searches when there are exigent circumstances present, for example when police officers believe that a person is in immediate need of medical attention (see for example Mincey v. Arizona, 1978, p. 392).

> In Stoner v. State of California (1964), a grocery store in California was robbed. The police developed a lead which led them to a hotel nearby. They had neither search nor arrest warrants when they approached the night clerk of the hotel and asked if they could gain access to the hotel room. The hotel clerk agreed to give them permission to search the room, and the police obtained evidence, which was used in the ensuing trial where the hotel guest was convicted of armed robbery. The United States Supreme Court held that the hotel clerk had no authority to permit the search and since the hotel guest was entitled to constitutional protection against unreasonable searches, the verdict against the hotel guest had to be reversed.

The repercussions of an illegal warrantless search differ depending on the country concerned. Evidence gathered during an illegal warrantless search is suppressed and cannot usually be used during an ensuing trial in the United States (Mapp v. Ohio,

1961). Most other countries are more liberal in allowing the presentation of evidence at trial, even if the search violated procedural safeguards.

An invasion of privacy can also be committed by non-governmental actors, either by owners of lodging or other tourism establishments, employees in such establishment or other third parties, such as guests or visitors to the complex. Such incidents are often litigated under tort law, either under the common law tort "invasion of privacy," applicable in the United States, the similar tort "misuse of private information," applicable in the United Kingdom, (Campbell v. MGN Ltd, 2004; Vidal-Hall v. Google, 2015) or under privacy legislation, applicable in both civil and common law countries. Privacy legislation usually contains complaints procedures or damages clauses for breaches of the law. According to the Restatement (Second) of Torts standard, followed in many states in the United States:

> one who intentionally intrudes, physically or otherwise, upon the solitude or seclusion of another or his private affairs or concerns, is subject to liability to the other for invasion of his privacy, if the intrusion would be highly offensive to a reasonable person.
>
> *(REST 2d TORTS § 625B)*

The intrusion can consist of a physical intrusion into a hotel room, despite the objections or without the knowledge of the hotel guest, but it can also consist of a non-physical intrusion, by using the defendant's senses, such as when a person spies on a hotel guest through a "peep hole" or communicates private information about the hotel guest to a third party.

> One of the most famous "peeping Tom" cases concerns a well-known sports television reporter, E.A., who was required to travel across the United States to perform her job. During several separate hotel stays, another guest, M.B., called the hotels in question in advance, asked if E.A. would be staying at the hotel and was provided, at his request, a room next to E.A.'s room. M.B. then altered the peepholes and recorded E.A. while she was undressing/changing clothes. The videos were posted on the internet where they were viewed more than 300 million times by nearly 17 million people. E.A. sued the hotels on a theory of negligence. The hotels had erred by, amongst other things, revealing that she was going to be a guest at the hotels, by intentionally placing M.B. in the room next to E.A.'s room and by failing to discover that M.B. altered the peephole to allow the recording of the videos. A jury awarded E.A. $55 million in damages, finding M.B. at 51 percent at fault and the hotel at 49 percent at fault (E. A. v. West End Hotel Partners et al., 2006). The hotel and E.A. later settled and reached an undisclosed verdict.

A hotel has a duty to exercise due care and protect guests from foreseeable harm from any third parties on premises. However, the duty does not extend to unforeseeable or unanticipated criminal acts by third persons.

> In Cangiano v. Forte Hotels (2000) two hotel guests found a nail-sized hole in the bathroom mirror and filed suit against the hotel under theories of invasion of privacy and negligence. The hotel guests testified that when they were having intercourse in the hotel bathroom, they heard mechanical noises coming from behind the mirror. Upon investigation, a nail-sized hole in the mirror was found. Behind the mirror there was hole in the wall, through which the adjoining bathroom could be seen. The court held that the innkeeper's duty to protect patrons "does not extend to unforeseeable or unanticipated criminal acts by independent third persons". Since there was no evidence that the employees of the hotel knew about the spying device in the bathroom, they could not be held liable for the invasion of privacy of the hotel guests.

A hotel has an affirmative duty to protect the privacy of a hotel guest against any kind of third-party invasions, even if the invasion of privacy is from friends or family members of the guest.

> In Campbell v. Womack (1977), a married couple brought suit against a motel and its desk clerk for breach of contract when the desk clerk refused to allow the wife to enter her husband's hotel room. In the case, Mr. Campbell had rented a double room on a month to month basis when he needed temporary accommodation in the area where he was working. On occasion, his wife, Mrs. Campbell, joined him during weekends and holidays. However, the room was registered in Mr. Campbell's name only. On one weekend, Mrs. Campbell arrived at the motel before her husband and asked for the key to the room. Her request was denied by the desk clerk, allegedly in a rude and abusive manner. Mrs. Campbell became distressed and left the premises and together with her husband filed suit against the motel and the desk clerk. The Court of Appeal held that the motel clerk had no duty to give the wife of a hotel guest the key to the hotel room. "In fact, the motel had an affirmative duty, stemming from a guest's rights of privacy and peaceful possession, not to allow unregistered and unauthorized third parties to gain access to the rooms of its guest...The mere fact of marriage does not imply that the wife has full authorization from her husband at all times and as to all matters."

6.5 Invasion of privacy in tourism accommodation establishments by access to personal records

Most jurisdictions allow hotels and other entertainment facilities to gather personal data from guests, subject to limits established by privacy legislation. Many jurisdictions not just allow, but require that such information is gathered. For example, a hotel operator on Norfolk Island, Australia, shall keep a register of guests, including their name and address, number in party, the date of arrival and departure as well as a signature of the guest (Tourist Accommodation Regulations,

2007, § 31(1), 2007). More information is often required when a hotel receives foreign guests. In the United Kingdom, non-British, Irish or Commonwealth guests have to provide their passport number and place of issue as well as details of their next destination (Immigration (Hotel Records) Order 1972, §§ 4–5). In Sweden, hotels are only required to register foreign guests (Police Ordinance PMFS 2015:6). There are limits on the amount of information that can be recorded as well as the amount of time such information can be kept by the hotel operator or entertainment establishment.

> In a Canadian case, the Office of the Privacy Commissioner of Canada (OPC), a government agency in charge of investigating complaints against the Canadian privacy legislation (PIPEDA) investigated a hotel chain, which operated a number of night clubs in Manitoba. The establishment scanned and stored the drivers' licenses or other identification cards of bar patrons in its identification machines. The motive to collect the information was to verify the age of customers as well as to ensure an appropriate level of security in the clubs. The company also gathered personal information of patrons who were prohibited to enter the establishment. The OPC filed suit before the Canadian Federal Court, whereafter the parties reached a settlement. As part of the settlement, the company agreed to stop collecting information via its identification machines, destroy all information collected with the machines and limit the amount of personal information on its "barred persons list" as well as to ensure that the information on the list is securely stored. The OPC agreed that it was not unreasonable to gather the names, dates of births and photos from bar patrons and to retain that information for 24 hours.
>
> *(Office of the Privacy Commissioner of Canada, 2010)*

An invasion of privacy by government actors can be concluded by a request to access private records of the customer. Up until recently, many lodging establishments routinely shared hotel records with third parties, such as law enforcement or any other third parties having a legitimate interest in the information. However, more and more jurisdictions have extended the protection afforded by the right to privacy and right to personal data to include lodging records.

> One of the most important United States Supreme Court cases regarding privacy in tourism accommodation eastablishments is City of Los Angeles v. Patel (2015), where several hotel and motel owners challenged a Los Angeles Municipal Code provision requiring every operator of a hotel to keep a record with guest information and to make the record available for inspection to any Los Angeles police officer on demand (Los Angeles Municipal Code §§ 41.49 (2015)). The hotel owners had been subjected to mandatory record inspections under the ordinance without consent or a warrant. The court held that the provision of the Los Angeles Municipal Code that required hotel operators to turn over their records to police officers without a warrant

or consent was unconstitutional under the Fourth Amendment of the United States Constitution and therefore invalid. The hotel owners had not been afforded any opportunity to question the reasonableness of the request in a pre-compliance review before a neutral decisionmaker, and the ordinance did therefore not fulfil the requirements of the Fourth Amendment.

The United States Supreme Court in City of Los Angeles v. Patel only held that hotel owners be afforded an opportunity to have a neutral decisionmaker review the request, in the rare instances when a hotel owner objects to the request from the police officer. It did not hold the actual disclosure of hotel records a violation of the Fourth Amendment, if the hotel owner voluntarily disclosed the information to the law enforcement. The Los Angeles Municipal Code was in 2017 amended to reflect this. A police officer of the Los Angeles Police Department may now request that a hotel operator consents to an inspection of the records. Guests are thus not protected by the Constitution of the United States from voluntary disclosures of hotel records by hotel operators to law enforcement.

In a Canadian case, a hotel had disclosed the check-in and check-out times of an individual to a private security service that worked for the individual's employer. The apparent motive to request such information seemed to be to determine if the employee had claimed unnecessary overtime expenses from the employer. The disclosure led to the individual being terminated from his employment, after which he filed a complaint with the OPC. The OPC concluded its investigation by finding that the complaint was well-founded, but since the hotel had undertaken to revise its disclosure policies in the wake of the incident it concluded that the complaint was resolved (Office of the Privacy Commissioner of Canada, 2013).

As mentioned, the constitutional protection of privacy in most countries only protects from government invasions of privacy. A situation where a guest objects to the fact that a hotel operator voluntarily discloses personal information to any third party would not be covered by the human rights charters or the constitution, which only concerns government invasions of privacy. However, a voluntary disclosure by the hotel operator could be subjected to the aforementioned laws governing personal data processing by any private parties (see Section 6.3). Also, such disclosures could be covered by tort law if the disclosure in question constitutes an invasion of guest privacy.

6.6 Security screenings and physical searches before air travel

During the past decades, airport security has been upgraded across international airports in all jurisdictions (see Chapter 9). National authorities screen passengers, luggage, flight crews and other persons with access to restricted areas in airports, such as airport workers. Today's travellers are accustomed to security screenings by metal detectors, physical searches and full-body scanners. Passengers' luggage is screened in X-ray machines and random swipes of luggage and passengers are made in an effort to find gun powder residue or other chemicals. Laptops and cell phones can be searched in an effort to find incriminating evidence of a violation of safety, immigration or taxation regulations.

> In the case of Gillan and Quinton v. the United Kingdom (2010), the two applicants were stopped and searched by British police officers under the Terrorism Act 2000 (sec. 44–45). The ECtHR held that legislation permitting police officers to search individuals without reasonable suspicion "anywhere and anytime, without notice and without any choice as to whether or not to submit to the search" violated the right to privacy (¶64, ¶87). The controversial sections in the Terrorism Act 2000 were subsequently repealed by the Protection of Freedoms Act 2012 (sec. 59).

Airports and border crossing are different from other public places in that there is a reduced expectation of privacy for persons travelling by air or crossing a national border. In this context, privacy rights are weighed towards public safety concerns as well as other public interests such as national sovereignty, immigration control and taxation. Even if many of the security measures are agreed upon at the international level, courts have struggled at striking a proper balance between individual rights and national security.

Since the terrorist attacks of 9/11 in the United States, several countries have enacted sweeping anti-terrorism legislation, giving law enforcement broad rights to interfere with the expectation of privacy if the person is suspected for terrorism-related crimes. The United States Congress enacted the USA Patriot Act of 2001, giving new powers to law enforcement agencies and Australia amended its Criminal Code Act 1995, by creating offences relating to international terrorism activities as well as increased its border security (Suppression of Terrorist Bombings Act 2002; Border Security Legislation Amendment Bill 2002). The European Council has stated that the main responsibility to combat terrorism rests with the member states, but the European Union adds value by strengthening national capabilities as well as facilitating European cooperation (Council of the European Union, 2005, p. 3).

In Europe, the ECtHR has decided several cases where the applicants alleged violations of their right to privacy when confronted with anti-terrorism legislation.

> In Murray v. United Kingdom (1993) a claim was brought by a family of Irish citizens, resident in Northern Ireland, against the United Kingdom. One of the applicants was arrested for a couple of hours, suspected of involvement in the purchase of arms for the IRA, an offense under United Kingdom anti-terrorism legislation. During the short interrogation, photographs of her were taken without her knowledge or consent and personal details about her family and home were kept on record. The applicant alleged that the treatment of her was in violation of the art. 8 right to privacy in the ECHR,

while the government of the United Kingdom argued that the measures were necessary in the context of the fight against terrorism in Northern Ireland. The ECtHR held that the measure pursued a legitimate aim and that the interferences were proportionate to the aim and necessary.

In Brogan, Coyle, McFadden and Tracey v. the United Kingdom (1988), the ECtHR noted that "[i]t is against the background of a continuing terrorist threat in Northern Ireland and the particular problems confronting the security forces in bringing those responsible for terrorist acts to justice that the issues in the present case must be examined. In such a situation the Convention organs must remain vigilant that a proper balance is struck between the protection of individual rights and the need to defend democratic society against the threats posed by organized terrorism. In the Commission's opinion it is inherent in the whole of the Convention that a fair balance has to be struck between the general interest of the community and the interests of the individual (¶80)...In so doing, the Commission takes into account that the struggle against terrorism may require a particular measure of sacrifice by each citizen in order to protect the community as a whole against such crimes".

(¶106, see also ¶82 Murray v. United Kingdom, 1993)

Searches of passengers and luggage at airports have become a part of air travel during the past 50 years. Such searches became part of routine inspections after the number of hijackings of commercial airplanes from the United States increased in the 1960s (United States v. Davis, 1973, pp. 897–898). In 1972, the U.S. Federal Aviation Administration issued a rule requiring air carriers to screen all airline passengers either by "behavioral profile, magnetometer, identification check or physical search" (Id., p. 890). By 1973, U.S. aircrafts were required to conduct searches of all carry-on luggage as well as screen all passengers by magnetometer (Id., p. 904). With the September 11 terrorist attacks, the security procedures at airports have been further enhanced, creating new tension between the public goal of safe travel and the right to privacy of individual passengers.

In addition to air travel, other transport providers have increased their security procedures when transporting passengers in a commercial setting.

> The Office of the Privacy Commissioner of Canada investigated an incident where sales agents for a transportation company were asking for personal information including name, date of birth, and citizenship from individuals making train travel bookings for the Toronto-to-New York train run. The information was disclosed to the United States Customs and the United States Naturalization and Immigration Service (USNIS). The transportation company confirmed that the practice had been taking place since December 2000, after an agreement between the company, Canadian customs, U.S. customs and USNIS. The Privacy Commissioner recommended that the company advises its sales agents that the collection of personal information is

voluntary in order to facilitate customs clearance at the border and that the company should not collect information without the informed, voluntary consent of the customer.

(Office of the Privacy Commissioner of Canada, 2001)

The ECtHR has stated that a search of passengers at an airport cannot be compared to random searches in other public places, since an air passenger can be seen to consent to a search by choosing to travel. "He knows that he and his bags are liable to be searched before boarding the aeroplane and has freedom of choice, since he can leave personal items behind and walk away without being subjected to a search" (Gillan and Quinton v. the United Kingdom, 2010, ¶64). However, U.S. courts have held that a search conducted at an airport cannot be upheld on the basis of consent, since the alternative, to forgo air travel altogether, is in many situations a form of coercion. Some mitigating factors of an airport search are that there is no compulsion and that there are many passengers who undergo the search, thus reducing the social stigma of a search. Furthermore, passengers have prior knowledge of the search. Despite the mitigating factors, a physical search at an airport is normally considered an invasion of a passenger's privacy. A search is thus permissible only if there is a reasonable suspicion that other passengers' safety is in danger (United States v. Albarado, 1974). The courts have reasoned that it is clear that innocent passengers are not resenting the intrusion of privacy but instead are welcoming the reassurance of safety physical inspections before boarding an aircraft brings. A search is thus more than reasonable; "it is a compelling necessity to protect essential air commerce and the lives of passengers" (United States v. Epperson, 1972). A passenger has the right to refuse an airport security search before the screening process has commenced (United States v. Mendenhall, 1980, p. 555). However, once the screening process commences, there is no possibility for a passenger to voluntarily withdraw from the screening, but a screening process is allowed to run its full course, despite the objections of the passenger (United States v. Pulido-Baquerizo, 1986).

It is generally established that individuals must tolerate some violations of their right to privacy for the common good of the society, for example in airport screening processes. The technological revolution of the past decade has however raised new questions of how far-reaching intrusions an individual has to tolerate in the interest of the common good. Would it for example be acceptable to retain images of full body scans after the screening or can a border agent search through a cell phone for evidence? Would it be acceptable to search a passengers' social media accounts or photographs available on the phone, for evidence of terrorist or other criminal activity? The technological advances have complicated the legal landscape and there is not yet a clear international standard for how to solve questions between individual rights to privacy and societal interests of safe travel, when it comes to many of the recent technological inventions. However, it is important to balance the rights of privacy of passengers with the need for safe air travel, by minimizing the intrusion, for example by not retaining images from scans or copies from phone searches longer than necessary (see Chapter 9 for more discussions on the subject).

6.7 Collection of personal information– advance passenger information programs and no-fly lists

In addition to the enhanced screening processes at airports involving passengers and their luggage, which can be directly traced to the hijackings of U.S. airplanes in the 1960s, airports have implemented additional security processes after the September 11 attacks on airplanes. Two of the most notable features are advance passenger information required by airplane carriers and so-called no-fly lists.

Many countries implemented voluntary advance passenger information systems (APIS) in the 1990s. However, following September 11, these voluntary systems became mandatory. The United States was the first country to implement APIS requirements in the Aviation and Transportation Security Act of 2001 and the Enhanced Border Security and Visa Entry Reform Act of 2002 for all passengers and crew members who arrived or departed from the United States on a commercial air or sea carrier. In addition, since 2009, citizens from countries who do not require an advance visa to visit the United States have to apply for a travel authorization through the Electronic System for Travel Authorization (ESTA) at least 72 hours before travel to the United States. In Australia, mandatory APIS requirements were introduced for all international commercial airplanes flying into Australia in 2003. In 2004, these requirements were extended to cover international passenger cruise ships (Migration Act of 1958). In the European Union, the Council of the European Union adopted in 2004 a directive on the obligation of carriers to communicate passenger data (Council directive 2004/82/EC, 2004).

Advance passenger information (API) is now required when travelling to a number of different countries, such as Australia, Canada, Great Britain, Indonesia, India, Japan, Mainland China, New Zealand, United States of America, South Africa and South Korea. The APIS have allowed for faster processing of passengers at border controls, faster check-in times as well as prevented unauthorized travel. However, the systems also collect pre-arrival passenger information, which many travellers object to on the basis of privacy concerns. The EU passenger data directive for example requires member states to establish an obligation for carriers to transmit, at the request of authorities, information on the number and type of travel documents used, nationality, full names, the date of birth, the border crossing point of entry into the EU, departure and arrival time of transportation, code of transport, the total number passengers carried on that transport and the initial point of embarkation (Council directive 2004/82/EC, art. 3, 2004). Lately, the APIS have been extended to cover outbound passengers from a country. For example, in 2015, Australia introduced new requirements on outbound advance passenger information (Migration Act 1958). The effectivity of the APIS depends on sharing of information between countries. In an effort to acknowledge privacy concerns, countries usually sign an agreement on the responsibilities of the parties using such information. Such agreements often contain safeguards ensuring that personal data is protected against unlawful or unauthorized use (see for example Agreement on the use and transfer of passenger name records to the United States Department of Homeland Security, 2012, art. 5) (see Chapter 9 for more discussions on the subject).

In response to the September 11 terrorist attacks, some countries have in addition to advance screening of passengers, created so-called no-fly lists. The persons on such lists are barred from flying in the air space or boarding airplanes destined to the countries where they are included on the lists. The United States Terrorist Screening Center, administered by the FBI, develops and maintains a "watch list" of persons with suspected international and domestic terrorism links. The U.S. Government's central repository of information on international terrorist identifiers (TIDE) supplies identities to the watchlist. As of February 2017, TIDE contained records of about 1.6 million persons, with approximately 0.5% U.S. persons of the total. Approximately 81,000 individuals on the general "watch list" are included in a no-fly list, which is sent to other government agencies and prevents the individuals on the list from boarding commercial aircrafts to or from the United States or flying over United States airspace. An additional 28,000 individuals are on the Selectee list, subjecting them to secondary screening before a decision is made if they can board an aircraft (National Counterterrorism Center, 2017; Kahan, 2017). Canada has introduced a similar programme, called Passenger programme, including the names of individuals where there are reasonable grounds to suspect that the individual will engage in an act that would threaten transportation security or they are attempting to travel abroad to commit terrorism offences (Secure Air Travel Act, 2015, sec. 8–9).

> An individual does not receive any notice when they are added to the United States no-fly list, but usually discover that at the airport when they are denied boarding without any explanation. In *Latif et al v. Holder et al.* several plaintiffs had good reason to believe that they were on the United States no-fly list. After trying to unsuccessfully find out if they were on the list and the basis for their apparent inclusion from the Transportation Security Authority, which refused to confirm or deny their inclusion, they filed an action against the Director of the Terrorist Screening Center, the Director of the FBI and the Attorney General. The District Court for the District of Oregon held that the government failed to afford them any meaningful opportunity to contest their apparent inclusion on the list and ordered them to devise new procedures to provide the plaintiffs due process without risking national security, a balancing act between individual rights and the rights of the community as a whole.
>
> *(Latif et al. v. Holder et al., 2014, p. 63; see also Latif et al v. Holder et al., 2012)*

In an effort to further increase security, the United States has entered into information sharing arrangements where the Terrorist Screening Center in 2013 shared watchlist information with 22 countries (Latif et al. v. Holder et al., 2014, p. 25). The U.S.-Canadian tip off programme, TUSCAN, and the similar U.S.-Australia programme, TACTICS, are two examples of programmes where border and immigration officers in Canada and Australia share information on incoming persons with United States authorities. The exact content of the bilateral agreements and the content of the information shared is classified information, which makes it hard to evaluate the agreements from a privacy perspective.

6.8 Conclusion

The right to privacy is sometimes framed as a Western idea, but it is clear that the right to privacy can be found as a general principle in many ancient legal systems worldwide. The right to privacy as a human right is also included in international human rights law. The right to privacy can be described as a qualitative human right, since it can be restricted in certain ways, if there are more pressing concerns to access personal data or violate the right to privacy. At the national level, certain jurisdictions are still to recognize the right to privacy or have just recently recognized the right to privacy as part of national legislation. Other countries have recognized the concept for a long time and protect both the right to privacy as well as the right to personal data at the national level. The recent renewed interest in the right to privacy can be explained by the fact that there has been an exponential growth in the amount of data which can be processed, due to the technical revolution in society. This has increased the possibilities for government authorities to place persons under surveillance or collect data which can be analysed. The increased possibilities to process personal data raise questions of how to balance the rights of individuals to privacy and personal data and the necessities of the society to get access to personal data in an effort to create a safe society.

Tourism travel and hospitality enterprises are particularly affected by the evolving scope and content of the right to privacy. New data privacy laws have already had an impact on how passenger and customer records are stored and disclosed in tourism and hospitality establishments. In the travel industry, the recent technological developments have also had an effect on the ease of human movement, particularly at ports, airports, train stations and borders (see further discussions in Chapter 9), which raises human rights concerns. Such human rights concerns have to be weighed against human security concerns. The security of nations is no longer solely the concern of individual nation-states but concerns the global community. The tourism and travel industry is particularly affected by global security threats. Airlines, trains, soccer stadiums, hotels and other tourism locations have been the scene of violent terrorist attacks. Global threats require global responses, which is an argument for increased co-operation and harmonization between different countries regarding the requirements for when, how and in which circumstances an invasion of privacy is justified. It is likely that the content of the right to privacy as well as the justifications for a restriction of the right to privacy will continue to evolve in the coming years, which will be of great interest for the tourism industry.

Permission

1 Quote by George Orwell, *Nineteen Eighty-Four* by George Orwell (Copyright © George Orwell, 1949). Reprinted by permission of Bill Hamilton as the Literary Executor of the Estate of the Late Sonia Brownell Orwell.

References

African Charter on Human and Peoples' Rights, June 27, 1981, 1520 U.N.T.S. 217.
Agreement on the use and transfer of passenger name records to the United States Department of Homeland Security, U.S.-E.U., 2012 OJ L 215.
American Convention on Human Rights, Nov. 22, 1969, 1144 U.N.T.S 123.
ASEAN Human Rights Declaration, Nov. 18, 2012 [pdf] Available at: <www.asean.org/storage/images/ASEAN_RTK_2014/6_AHRD_Booklet.pdf> [Accessed 17 July 2020].
Ashesh, A. and Acharaya, B., 2014. *Locating Constructs of Privacy within Classical Hindu Law.* [White Paper], The Centre for Internet and Society. Available at: <https://cis-india.org/internet-governance/blog/loading-constructs-of-privacy-within-classical-hindu-law> [Accessed 19 June 2020].
Aslam H. M., 2007. Privacy and Islam: From the Quran to data protection in Pakistan. *Information & Communication Technology Law*, 16(2), pp. 137–148.
Aviation and Transportation Security Act of 2001 (Pub. L. No 107–71, sec. 115).
Border Security Legislation Amendment Bill 2002 (schedule 1, no. 64) (Austl.).
Brogan and others v. The United Kingdom, App. Nos. 11209/84, 11234/84, 11266/84 and 11386/85, 11 Eur. H.R. Rep. 117 (1989).
Campbell v. MGN Ltd [2004] UKHL 22.
Campbell v. Womack, 345 So.2d 96 (La. Ct. App. 1977).
Cangiano v. Forte Hotels, 772 So.2d 879 (La. Ct. App. 2000).
Charter of Fundamental Rights of the European Union (2000/C 364 01). [online]. Available at: <www.europarl.europa.eu/charter/pdf/text_en.pdf> [Accessed 19 June 2020].
City of Los Angeles, California v. Patel, 576 U.S. ___, 135 S. Ct. 2443 (2015).
Constitución Española (1978) (Spain).
Convention for the Protection of Human Rights and Fundamental Freedoms, Nov. 4, 1950, 213 U.N.T.S. 221.
Convention on the Rights of the Child, Nov. 20, 1989, 1577 U.N.T.S. 3.
Cooley T. M., 1879. *A Treatise on the Law of Torts or the Wrongs Which Arise Independent of Contract*. Chicago: Callaghan.
Council directive 2004/82/EC of 29 April 2004 on the obligation of carriers to communicate passenger data, 2004. *Official Journal*, L261 pp. 24–27. [online]. Available at: <https://eur-lex.europa.eu/legal-content/EN/TXT/PDF/?uri=CELEX:32004L0082&from=NL> [Accessed 20 June 2020].
Council of the European Union, 2005. *The European Union Counter-Terrorism Strategy*, 14469/4/05 REV 4.
Criminal Code Act (1995) (Austl.).
E. A. v. West End Hotel Partners et al., No. 11C-4831 (Cir. Ct. Davidson Cnty. Tenn., 2006).

Enhanced Border Security and Visa Entry Reform Act of 2002 (Pub. L. No. 107–173).

European Commission, 2000. Commission Decision 2000/518/EC of 26 July 2000 pursuant to Directive 95/46/EC of the European Parliament and of the Council on the adequate protection of personal data provided in Switzerland. [2000] OJ L 215/1.

European Commission, 2002. Commission Decision 2002/2/EC of 20 December 2001 pursuant to Directive 95/46/EC of the European Parliament and of the Council on the adequate protection of personal data provided by the Canadian Personal Information Protection and Electronic Documents Act. [2002] OJ L 2/13.

European Commission, 2003a. Commission Decision 2003/490/EC of 30 June 2003 pursuant to Directive 95/46/EC of the European Parliament and of the Council on the adequate protection of personal data in Argentina. [2003] OJ L 168/19.

European Commission, 2003b. Commission Decision 2003/821/EC of 21 November 2003 on the adequate protection of personal data in Guernsey. [2003] OJ L 308/27.

European Commission, 2004. Commission Decision 2004/411/EC of 28 April 2004 on the adequate protection of personal data in the Isle of Man. [2004] OJ L 151/48.

European Commission, 2008. Commission Decision 2008/393/EC of 8 May 2008 pursuant to Directive 95/46/EC of the European Parliament and of the Council on the adequate protection of personal data in Jersey. [2008] OJ L 138/21.

European Commission, 2010a. Commission Decision 2010/625/EU of 19 October 2010 pursuant to Directive 95/46/EC of the European Parliament and of the Council on the adequate protection of personal data in Andorra. [2010] OJ L 277/27.

European Commission, 2010b. Commission Decision 2010/146/EU of 5 March 2010 pursuant to Directive 95/46/EC of the European Parliament and of the Council on the adequate protection provided by the Faeroese Act on processing of personal data. [2010] OJ L 58/17.

European Commission, 2011. Commission Decision 2011/61/EU of 31 January 2011 pursuant to Directive 95/46/EC of the European Parliament and of the Council on the adequate protection of personal data by the State of Israel with regard to automated processing of personal data. [2011] OJ L 27/39.

European Commission, 2012. Commission Implementing Decision 2012/484/EU of 21 August 2012 pursuant to Directive 95/46/EC of the European Parliament and of the Council on the adequate protection of personal data by the Eastern Republic of Uruguay with regard to automated processing of personal data. [2012] OJ L 227/11.

European Commission, 2013. Commission Implementing Decision 2013/65/EU of 19 December 2012 pursuant to Directive 95/46/EC of the European Parliament and of the Council on the adequate protection of personal data by New Zealand. [2013] OJ L 28/12.

European Commission, 2016. Commission Implementing Decision (EU) 2016/1250 of 12 July 2016 pursuant to Directive 95/46/EC of the European Parliament and of the Council on the adequacy of the protection provided by the EU-U.S. Privacy Shield. [2016] OJ L 207/112.

European Commission, 2019. Commission Implementing Decision (EU) 2019/419 of 23 January 2019 pursuant to Regulation (EU) 2016/679 of the European Parliament and of the Council on the adequate protection of personal data by Japan under the Act on the Protection of Personal Information. [2019] OJ L 76/1.

European Parliament and Council directive 95/46/EC of 24 October 1995 on the protection of individuals with regard to the processing of personal data and on the free movement of such data, 1995. *Official Journal*, L281 pp. 31–50. [online]. Available at:

<https://eur-lex.europa.eu/legal-content/en/TXT/?uri=CELEX%3A31995L0046> [Accessed 20 June 2020].

Gillan and Quinton v. the United Kingdom, ECLI:CE:ECHR:2010:0112JUD000415805 (2010).

Hatton and Others v. The United Kingdom, App. No. 36022/97, 34 Eur. H.R. Rep. 1 (2003).

ICO, 2018. *Monetary Penalty Notice, Uber.* [pdf] Available at: <www.ico.org.uk/media/action-weve-taken/mpns/2553890/uber-monetary-penalty-notice-26-november-2018.pdf> [Accessed 19 June 2020].

ICO, 2019a. *Statement: Intention to fine Marriott International, Inc more than £99 million under GDPR for data breach.* [online]. Available at: <https://ico.org.uk/about-the-ico/news-and-events/news-and-blogs/2019/07/statement-intention-to-fine-marriott-international-inc-more-than-99-million-under-gdpr-for-data-breach/> [Accessed 19 June 2020].

ICO, 2019b. *Intention to fine British Airways £183.39m under GDPR for data breach.* [online]. Available at: <https://ico.org.uk/about-the-ico/news-and-events/news-and-blogs/2019/07/ico-announces-intention-to-fine-british-airways/> [Accessed 19 June 2020].

ICO, 2020. *Monetary Penatly Notice, Cathay Pacific Airways Limited.* [pdf] Available at: <https://ico.org.uk/media/action-weve-taken/mpns/2617314/cathay-pacific-mpn-20200210.pdf> [Accessed 19 June 2020].

Immigration (Hotel Records) Order 1972. [online]. Available at: <http://www.legislation.gov.uk/uksi/1972/1689/made> [Accessed 20 June 2020].

International Covenant on Civil and Political Rights, Dec. 16, 1966, 999 U.N.T.S. 171.

Justice K.S. Puttaswamy (Retd) v. Union of India, Writ Petition (Civil) No. 494 of 2012, (2017) 10 SCC 1.

Kahan, J. H., 2017. Quis Custodiet Ipsos Custodies?: Who Watches the Watchlisters? *Harvard Law School National Security Journal* [online]. Available at: <www.harvardnsj.org/2017/02/who-watches-the-watchlisters/> [Accessed 19 June 2020].

Katz v. United States, 389 U.S. 347 (1967).

Kroon and others v. Netherlands, App. No. 18535/91, 19 Eur. H. R. Rep. 263 (1994).

Latif et al. v. Holder et al., No. 3:10-CV-00750-BR (D. Or., June 24, 2014).

Latif et al v. Holder et al, No. 3:10-CV-00750-BR (9th. Cir. Co., May 11, 2012).

Los Angeles Municipal Code (2015) (USA).

Mapp v. Ohio, 367 U.S. 643 (1961).

Migration Act of 1958 (Austl.).

Mincey v. Arizona, 437 U.S. 385 (1978).

Moreno Gómez v. Spain, App. No. 4143/02, 41 Eur. H. R. Rep. 40 (2005).

Murray v. United Kingdom, App. No. 14310/88, 19 Eur. H.R. Rep. 193 (1994).

National Counterterrorism Center, 2017. *Terrorist Identities Datasmart Environment (TIDE).* [pdf] Available at: <www.dni.gov/files/NCTC/documents/features_documents/TIDEfactsheet10FEB2017.pdf> [Accessed 19 June 2020].

Office of the Privacy Commissioner of Canada, 2001. *Transportation company collects, discloses passengers' personal information.* PIPEDA Incident Summary #2001-1 Available at: <www.priv.gc.ca/en/opc-actions-and-decisions/investigations/investigations-into-businesses/incidents/2001/cf-dc_010420/> [Accessed 19 June 2020].

Office of the Privacy Commissioner of Canada, 2010. *Settlement between the Privacy Commissioner of Canada and Canada Corporation of Manitoba Ltd.* PIPEDA Case Summary #2008–296. Available at: <www.priv.gc.ca/en/opc-actions-and-decisions/investigations/investigations-into-businesses/2008/pipeda-2008-396/> [Accessed 19 June 2020].

Office of the Privacy Commissioner of Canada, 2013. *Hotel check-in/check-out times are personal information and must not be disclosed without consent.* PIPEDA Report of Findings #2013-007. Available at: <www.priv.gc.ca/en/opc-actions-and-decisions/investigations/investigations-into-businesses/2013/pipeda-2013-007/> [Accessed 19 June 2020].

Orwell, G., 1949. *Nineteen Eighty-Four.* Reprint 2000. London: Penguin Books.

Pavesich v. New England Life Ins. Co., 122 Ga. 190, 50 S.E. 68 (1905).

Periñán, B., 2012. The Origins of Privacy as a Legal Value: A Reflection on Roman and English law. *American Journal of Legal History*, 52(2), pp. 183–201.

Police Ordinance PMFS 2015:6, 2015. FAP 279-1 (Swed.).

Protection of Freedoms Act 2012 (c. 9). [online]. Available at: <www.legislation.gov.uk/ukpga/2012/9/contents> [Accessed 19 June 2020].

Regulation (EU) 2016/679 of the European Parliament and of the Council of 27 April 2016 on the protection of natural persons with regard to the processing of personal data and on the free movement of such data, and repealing Directive 95/46/EC, 2016. *Official Journal*, L119 pp. 1–88. [online]. Available at: <http://data.europa.eu/eli/reg/2016/679/oj> [Accessed 19 June 2020].

Restatement (Second) of Torts (USA).

Secure Air Travel Act (S.C. 2015, c. 20, s. 11). [online]. Available at: <www.laws-lois.justice.gc.ca/eng/acts/S-6.7/page-1.html> [Accessed 19 June 2020].

Stoner v. State of California, 376 U.S. 483 (1964).

Suppression of Terrorist Bombings Act 2002 (Criminal Code Amendment no. 58). (Austl.).

Swedish Code of Judicial Procedure, 1942. [online]. Available at: <www.government.se/49e41c/contentassets/a1be9e99a5c64d1bb93a96ce5d517e9c/the-swedish-code-of-judicial-procedure-ds-1998_65.pdf> [Accessed 20 June 2020].

Terrorism Act 2000 (c. 9). [online]. Available at: <www.legislation.gov.uk/ukpga/2000/11/contents> [Accessed 19 June 2020]

Tourist Accommodation Regulations, 2007. [online]. Available at: <www.norfolkisland.gov.nf/sites/default/files/public/documents/Pre2015Legis/ConsolidatedRegs/TouristAccommodationRegulations.pdf> [Accessed 20 June 2020].

United States v. Albarado, 495 F.2d 799 (2d Cir. 1974).

United States v. Davis, 482 F.2d 893 (9th Cir. 1973).

United States v. Epperson, 454 F.2d 769 (4th Cir., 1972).

United States v. Mendenhall, 446 U.S. 544 (1980).

United States v. Pulido-Baquerizo, 800 F.2d 899 (9th Cir. 1986).

Universal Declaration of Human Rights, G.A. Res. 217 (III) A, U.N. Doc. A/RES/217(III) (Dec. 10, 1948).

U.S. Const. amend. IV (USA).

USA Patriot Act of 2001 (USA).

Vidal-Hall v. Google [2015] EWCA Civ 311.

Warren, S. D. and Brandeis, L. D., 1890. The Right to Privacy. *Harvard Law Review*, 4(5), pp. 193–220.

7
DISPLACEMENT IN TOURISM

7.1 Introduction

Due to the on-going worldwide refugee crises, the terms 'displacement' and 'relocation' have become familiar words. The UN High Commissioner for Refugees (UNHCR) (2019) places the number of people forcibly displaced worldwide at 70.8 million. The term 'Displacement' in human rights discourse is often used to describe the physical removal of a person from a place. Yet, it can also mean the displacement of businesses and cultures. Whatever the form of displacement, it can lead to violations of human and civil rights. Political and economic strife, conflict, poverty, natural disasters, epidemics/pandemics, and loss of livelihood – among other impacts – reveals the interrelationship and complexity of issues generating flows of refugees and internally displaced peoples. Asylum seekers may also face human rights violations in new locations where feelings of antagonism, xenophobia, aggression, and intolerance do not foster a dignified life for those who are displaced. Those who end up in temporary camps often do not have rights to physical and mental health care, the right to work or to freedom of movement. Displacement and the violation of human rights are also evident in tourism. The driving force of displacement in tourism is not only the development of infrastructure such as new hotels, parks or airports but also other forces such as globalisation, government and corporate policy, overtoursim, gentrification, natural disasters, and other factors which accelerate change in the destination, and the movement of people. From an economic perspective, people are also displaced from tourism business opportunities or other business opportunities, due to the growth of tourism. Conversely, COVID-19 has caused major economic displacement, with the rapid decline in tourism. Indigenous and marginalised people are often the most vulnerable to displacement in tourism, resulting in the loss and commodification of cultures. In this chapter, displacement will be approached from three intertwined areas: the physical displacement of peoples, the displacement of businesses, and the displacement of cultures. While one can look at the issues of displacement and human rights from various angles, these three are closely related to the development of tourism, and therefore they are of special interest here.

7.2 Physical displacement of peoples

Displacement of people, or 'population displacement', means a forcible movement of people from their regular place of habitation. According to UNESCO (2017), this social change is caused by many factors – including armed conflict, natural disasters, famine, disease, development, and economic changes. UNESCO (2017) recognises two distinct forms of population displacement: (1) direct displacement and (2) indirect displacement. Direct displacement involves the physical removal of people from their usual place of residency or habitat; indirect displacement involves loss of livelihood, and subsequent impoverishment. People in their usual place of residence have knowledge about their environment and resources, and access to resources for their livelihood. However, once removed from their usual place of residence, they would no longer have the same knowledge or access, and thus their lives will be impoverished. UNESCO (2017) makes it clear that such social costs must be taken into consideration, and proper policies must be put in place if a development project will inevitably result in population displacement. There is growing concern about internally displaced persons (IDPs) worldwide; those who do not cross an international border – unlike refugees fleeing their homes and countries. UNESCO (2017) is concerned that the number of IDPs is increasing rapidly due to armed conflict, and has categorised IDPs under the same criteria as refugees. A displaced population caused by a tourism-related development project is often displaced within recognised political boundaries; and thus, like IDPs, they are highly unlikely to receive the same level of protection or privileges as many international refugees. The recent exodus of the Rohingya ethnic minority from Myanmar (Burma) to surrounding countries and to other regions of Myanmar has received global attention in the media. The majority of the Rohingya refugees are part of the Muslim minority in Myanmar. After Myanmar won independence from the British Empire in 1948, the boundary between India and Myanmar was demarcated, and the Rohingya Muslim minority group was trapped between the states. Myanmar's oppression of the Muslim minority has been known since the 1970s; however, the violent incidents between the military and civilians in 2016 and 2017 led to the destruction of over 300 villages, and an exodus of over 671,000 Rohingya. The villages were burnt and bulldozed so that refugees no longer have a home to return to. The UN investigated this gross violation of human rights and humanitarian law, warning about the continued threat of genocide (Government of Canada, 2018; Mathieson, 2009; OHCHR, 2019, 2017).

Tourism Concern, an NGO, has been campaigning to combat the objectionable displacement of residents to make room for tourism. Indigenous peoples, ethnic minorities, people living in informal or illegal settlements, homeless people living in the streets, street children, or people without legal deeds to their lands tend to be severely affected once they are displaced. Tourism Concern (2014) listed examples of displacement in tourism development:

> Governments and private companies have forced many tribal peoples from their ancestral lands to make way for national parks and 'eco-tourism'. Fishing communities are removed from their coastal villages and blocked from accessing the sea as hotels are built and beaches are privatised, destroying livelihoods and traditional ways of life. Informal settlements are bulldozed under beautification projects in the lead up to major international sporting events.
>
> This often happens with little or no warning, compensation or alternative provision.

Tourism Concern (2014) also warns that direct and indirect displacement do not happen overnight. Local residents are frequently more euphoric about the social and economic prospects resulting from tourism during the initial phases of development. Once the facilities for mass tourism are complete, the rapid influx of tourists soon begins to cause various forms of disruption to the local communities and their lifestyles. Overtourism is an exasperating competition for resources, with locals protesting in response. Historically, resorts have been depicted as notorious natural resource exploiters – depriving local population's access to, and the use of, natural resources such as beachfronts. In particular, the tourism industry is a large consumer of water; in Bali, Indonesia for example, increased demand from tourism put pressure on local water supplies (Cole, 2012). Land prices and everyday living costs also inflate, as multinational tourism corporations capable of paying higher prices than local residents and businesses take control. In Vanuatu, land leases in coastal areas are given to expatriate tourism developers, restricting resident's access to beachfront areas and fishing grounds that have historically been important for women's livelihoods (Neef, 2019). Moreover, local businesses are involuntarily forced into competition over access to necessary resources against multinational corporations with international networks (see Tourism Concern, 2014 for more details).

Neef (2019) examined the 'Practices of Dispossession in Tourism', under Eviction, Enclosure, Extraction, and Erasure. Under eviction, Neef (2019) cites examples such as Cambodia – a large-scale tourism project on coastal land in Koh Kong Province forced hundreds of families from their land with meagre compensation; and Tanzania – the expansion of national parks and wildlife sanctuaries for safari tourism forced thousands of pastoralist Maasai out from their lands with no compensation or alternative settlement. This would violate the UN Declaration on the Rights of Indigenous Peoples (2007), Article 10 "Indigenous peoples shall not be forcibly removed from their lands or territories," amongst others. Under enclosure, Neef (2019) includes the Boracay Island, Philippines; the delineation of tourism economic zones and large-scale resort expansion have pushed locals to the fringes, making coastal areas inaccessible to subsistence farmers and fisher folk. At the heart of many of these forms of dispossession is the resulting impact on local livelihoods. Once a group of people is forced to move, or declined access to resources, it can put traditions and even languages under threat. Vulnerable populations are especially at risk of being deprived of their rights to life, water, and natural resources and the environment. Such discrimination and inequality are clearly facilitated by neoliberal market-led development, involving not only the private sector, but also through state-led development projects.

In recent years, multiple legal cases have been reported concerning the displacement of those in residential areas (including slums) and businesses, to build facilities for mega-events – such as the Olympics. These cases have often been ruled as violations of the rights to life (see IHRB, 2013 for details). Hosting mega-events is important for many countries in terms of economic development, place promotion, and the associated social development that may lead to tourism growth. However recent cases of abandoned facilities after the Olympics have some countries considering whether the overall costs are worth the investment (see Box 7.1).

BOX 7.1 HOSTING MEGA EVENTS AND DISPLACEMENT OF LOCAL PEOPLE – BRAZIL

Brazil hosted the 2007 Pan-American Games, the 2014 Football World Cup, and the 2016 Summer Olympic Games. Hosting these mega-sporting events quickly and consecutively had tremendous impact on the urban planning of Rio de Janeiro. In order to expand the road system and construct the Olympic facilities, residents in certain communities of the city, notably the *favelas* (informal settlements), faced eviction.

In Rio, nearly 18% of the population live in *favelas*, and this population increased by 53% between 1980 and 1991 (Oliveira, 1996). Some well-established *favelas* received Special Zone of Social Interest status to protect them in the 1980s (Smith, 2017). Nonetheless, the Law of World Cup Brazil was passed in 2012, and virtually overrode the Special Zone status (Smith 2017), so that the government could evict residents. The government saw the *favelas* as the 'dark side of Rio' and sent in the militarised Police Pacification Unit (UPP). They removed the *favela* residents to peripheral areas away from the city as soon as 2014 World Cup and 2016 Olympic Games were announced (Smith, 2017).

In April 2011, the World Cup and Olympics Popular Committee of Rio de Janeiro submitted a letter of human rights violations to the UN Special Rapporteur for Adequate Housing Rights, condemning the government-sanctioned violence against the *favela* residents. Forcible evictions in West Rio for the 2016 Summer Olympic drew international media attention. In West Rio, public residences were demolished rapidly, marginalising about 3,000 residents in a *favela*, Vila Autódromo. This community was neighbouring the prime development area for the Olympic Park, with major sport venues and housing for the international media. From Vila Autódromo and several communities, over 500 families were either evicted, accepted financial compensation, or resettled in other areas (Silvestre and de Oliveira, 2012). Some claim 77,000 people lost their homes (Talbot, 2016). The negotiations for relocation were characterised by a lack of information distributed to the residents, coercion, and intimidation (Silvestre and de Oliveira, 2012) – and in some cases resulted in homelessness.

The case of Vila Autódromo is a 'Displacement Decathlon' where "well-trained residents competed for the right to remain in their homes and on their land" (Vale and Gray, 2013). With the news of future evictions from Vila Autódromo, residents drew the attention of the international media and activists. Legal advisors and well-trained activists among the residents, helped the residents fight against rapidly changing tactics by the city such as (1) the global media image of Rio, (2) public safety, (3) environmental risk, and (4) time pressure (see Vale and Gray for details). The legal advisors filed an injunction for eviction postponement, and the communities petitioned the IOC on the basis of human rights violations of forcible eviction in 2011 (Vale and Gray, 2013). Such activism proved that the *favelas* could resist and postpone eviction for a while.

The gentrification of areas in Rio de Janeiro is another force for displacement of the poor. The announcement of hosting the World Cup and Summer Olympics drastically increased property prices (Gaffney, 2016). Communities in South Rio, such as Vidigal, Santa Marta, Babilônia, Cantagalo, and Cabritos, become highly desirable locations (Robertson and Williamson, 2016). The Police presence in these areas also improved perceived safety of these communities, adding to property speculation. For instance, retail residential sales price per square metre of Vidigal increased 598% from 2008 to 2014; while the city of Rio de Janeiro's increase was 256% (Gaffney, 2016). The *favelas* and existing affordable public housing experienced a hike in rents and utility service fees. The government decision to convert old and affordable residential buildings into expensive apartments, hotels, medical clinics, and other facilities, put pressure on the residents in the area to relocate (Gaffney, 2016).

During the Opening Ceremony of Olympic Games, the depiction of non-white-Brazilians was criticised as whitewashed, and their aesthetic and culture misrepresented; in addition, the culture of non-white-Brazilians was criticised as being viewed as valuable for entertainment, but not valuable enough to be protected (Robertson, 2016).

Hosting mega-sporting events also had a profit motive. The main sources of Olympic revenues are TV broadcasting money, sponsorships (domestic and international), ticket sales, and licensing. The IOC reported that the Rio Olympics lured 6.6 million foreign tourists, and earned US$6.2 billion in the year of 2016 (Chavez, 2017). The sponsorship rights brought US$1.3 billion (Chapman, 2016). The largest portion of the Olympic Game revenue comes from TV broadcasting money – estimates vary from $4.1 billion (King, 2016) collected by the IOC (Chapman, 2016) to $4.4 billion as the amount NBC paid for broadcast rights for the Olympics until 2020 (Settimi, 2016); yet, how much of the revenue actually goes to the host nation is often questioned. For instance, McBride (2018) estimates half of the TV revenue goes to the IOC.

However, the Rio Olympics illustrates the long-standing discourse of cost-and-benefit of hosting the Olympic games. Brazil invested over US$20 billion in necessary infrastructure. The federal government had to lend the state $900 million to cover the policing fee; and the chaotic political and economic situation brought the worst economic recession in decades (McBride, 2018). Financial mismanagement, and government officials' corruption left Rio with BRL$62 billion (US$16 billion) debt after the Olympics. The Olympic Park and facilities became a ghost town and was left to decay; financial debts forced the government to privatise social services such as the water supply. As a result, residents – particularly the *favela* residents – cannot afford their bills. Even as recently as 2017, residents were not free from the risk of forced eviction and displacement (Smith, 2017).

7.2.1 *Physical displacement of people and 'gentrification'*

Inequality and rising property values can cause displacement in communities where gentrification takes hold. Ruth Glass introduced the term gentrification in 1964 in London, UK, to describe middle-class (higher income) people displacing working class (lower income) residents in downtown areas, to rejuvenate and uplift disinvested areas of urban centres (Brown-Saracino, 2014). Today, gentrification occurs not only in urban areas, but also rural communities. Tourism development causes inflation in living expenses and property speculation, subsequently displacing local residents who can no longer afford to live in the area. In New Orleans, the growth of tourism has driven up property values; resulting in the conversion of affordable family homes to high-end condominiums (Neef, 2019). Gentrification happens in the name of beautification or betterment of an area. Impoverished areas – such as tent cities or makeshift habitats – are frequently considered eyesores for visitors that need dismantling. Government revitalisation schemes, including waterfront redevelopments, are done through changing zoning regulations or the demolition of poor neighbourhoods (Neef, 2019). Gentrification can cause residential displacement, commercial displacement, and place-based displacement (Neef, 2019). Place-based displacement is the loss of a sense of place and belonging for residents. More recently, this phenomenon has intensified through the sharing economy, which will be discussed later. Many Latin American cities have received funds from international agencies to revitalise historical centres for cultural tourism – including

Mexico City, Lima, and Santiago de Chile – dislocating groups from lower socio-economic classes (Neef, 2019).

7.2.2 Disasters and displacement of people

Both natural and human-made disasters have had significant impact on tourism destinations, causing major displacement. While more attention has been placed on humanitarian assistance, less attention has been given to human rights protections (Brookings–Bern Project, 2011). Table 7.1 contains examples of human rights challenges in the aftermath of natural disasters. Da Costa and Pospieszna (2015) argue that the vulnerability of individuals to disasters could be reduced if laws and policies were to adopt a human rights-based approach (HRBA), contributing to better accountability and empowerment.

Global climate change is becoming a serious threat to human settlement, and is a looming disaster for many tourism destinations. The Intergovernmental Panel on Climate Change (IPCC) (2018) indicates vulnerable and disadvantaged populations, including some Indigenous populations and local communities dependent on coastal or agricultural livelihoods, are the populations disproportionally at higher risk of the negative consequences of global warming; an increase in average global temperatures by 1.5°C can result in ecological systems no longer being sustainable. Human activities, including tourism, are unquestionably contributing to global warming – and very likely quickening the cycle of El Niño Southern Oscillation (ENSO) (see Chapter 11 on human activities and the natural environment). The cycling of El Niño and La Niña is affecting the occurrences of typhoons/hurricanes/cyclones, drought/desertification, and raising global temperatures.

TABLE 7.1 Examples of Human Rights Challenges after a Natural Disaster

• Lack of safety and security (e.g. rampant crime, secondary impacts of natural disasters, etc.);	• Inadequate law enforcement mechanisms, and restricted access to a fair and efficient justice system;
• Gender-based violence;	• Lack of effective feedback and complaint mechanisms;
• Unequal access to assistance, basic goods and services, and discrimination in aid provision;	• Unequal access to employment and livelihood opportunities;
• Abuse, neglect, and exploitation of children;	• Forced relocation;
• Family separation, particularly for children, older persons, persons with disabilities;	• Unsafe or involuntary return or resettlement of persons displaced;
• Loss/destruction of personal documentation and difficulties to replace them (e.g. birth registration mechanisms);	• Lack of property restitution and access to land.

Source: (Brookings–Bern Project, 2011).

A few notable examples in the years of 2017 to 2019 include: numerous typhoons and heavy monsoon rains resulting in the worst flooding in decades in some Asian countries (e.g. India, Nepal, and Bangladesh); consecutive hurricanes devastating the Caribbean, the Gulf Coast, and Florida; dry weather bringing wild fires in the USA, Canada, Greece, and Australia; drought conditions occurring in Brazil and Somalia; a combination of heavy rain and typhoons, and heat waves occurring across Australasia; and record breaking hot summers in Europe. These unusual conditions can force locals from their place of residence, tourists to evacuate destinations, and have significant impacts on livelihoods. Developing countries that could most benefit from the economic benefits of tourism are also the most vulnerable to climate changes, leading to a cycle of tourism growth, emission growth, and an increase in vulnerability (Scott, Hall and Gössling, 2019). Beachfront tourist areas and their surrounding communities, and small island nations face rising sea levels and land erosion. The Island Nation of Kiribati in the Pacific is predicted to be uninhabitable by 2050 due to the rise in sea levels. In 2014, the Kiribati government purchased 6,000 acres of land in Fiji as an evacuation site for the Kiribati people. The current government, however, is hoping people will remain as long as the island is liveable, and that by an increased focus on tourism, international aid, fishing, and the coconut trade there will be a boost in income and resilience (Walker, 2017).

Governments and businesses have also been known to taken advantage of disasters. In the context of disaster capitalism, Klein (2007; ShockDoctrine, 2018) and Rice (2005) reported on tsunami-devastated coastal regions, including Thailand and Sri Lanka, which were sealed off from previous residents under the pretext of reconstruction; in reality, new tourism facilities or hospitals were built so the original residents and fisher folk could not return to their coastal village, but were resettled inland. There are parallels to the global land-and-resource-grab predicament (Neef, 2019), whereby governments are allowing the displacement of local communities for tourism development. Not only are Indigenous populations seriously affected by these land grab practices, the local poor are unprotected due to weak civil rights, laws and protections.

Recovery in the aftermath of disasters takes time. Those displaced may be housed in shelters and temporary housing or asked to move some distance away. The unprecedented scale of disasters – such as the 1995 Great Hanshin Earthquake and the 2011 Northeast Great Earthquake in Japan – saw the evacuation of thousands into temporary housing projects that lasted five to ten years (NHK, 2019; Maly and Shiozaki, 2012; Edgington, 2010). According to the World Bank, more recent refugees have been in exile for 4 years, but other cohorts have been in exile for 5 to 37 years (Devictor and Do, 2016). The longer they are displaced, the more complicated the violations of human rights the refugees suffer. In the case of Australian asylum-seeker detention centres on islands of Manus Island and Nauru, Papua New Guinea – refugees are held in isolated locations – most of them since 2013. Loewenstein (2015) called the privatisation of the Australian refugee detention system 'Disaster Capitalism'. These asylum seekers came, fleeing from a mix of reasons, including but not limited to, politics, civil war, and disasters; they are traumatised by direct and indirect displacement. They are suffering from human rights abuses, including sexual and physical assaults, and a mental health crisis in refugee camps is on the rise (BBC, 2019). With such long-term displacement, those impacted suffer from basic human rights violations, including loss of heritage; loss of access to water, resources, land, and adequate standard of living; loss of the choice of residence or freedom of movement, etc. (McNamara, et al., 2016; OHCHR, 2016). It can also cause a medical condition called 'relocation damage', leading to a lack of self-determination, loneliness, loss of hope, desperation, depression, suicidal thoughts, social isolation, and unnoticed death (NHK, 2019).

When the traumatic experience of a natural disaster is combined with disaster capitalism policies, the displaced peoples' physical and mental health is further at risk. The loss of family members, friends, and acquaintances may be combined with the loss of home and businesses. Unable to return to their village or ancestral land for an indefinite period of time, some also encounter new residents or tourists already occupying their land when they do attempt to return. Rights to land and property, rights to resources and livelihood, right to freedom of movement, right to work, right to health, and right to life are all at stake, and may be a matter of life-or-death.

7.3 Economic displacement of businesses and industries

Growth in tourism is usually accompanied by increased competition in destinations – accelerated by the arrival of external business interests – typically at the expense of local enterprises. Changes in one sector of the economy can result in displacement in another. According to Optimal Economics and TNS Research International (2012), displacement and additionality are closely related. Additionality occurs when an intervention of economic policy or activity (e.g. marketing campaign) promotes additional economic activities that would not have occurred without the intervention. However, displacement of regular economic activities may happen, because of additional tourism-related economic activities elsewhere. For example, in the summer of 2018, Cornwall, England stopped marketing two beaches as a severe heat wave triggered overcrowding. Cornwall has a large number of self-employed people who were unable to make enough money, as traffic congestion had an impact on travel times, which is not paid for when self-employed (Dury, 2018). Creative destruction is another aspect of economic displacement, whereby original businesses are replaced by new tourism businesses – incorporating dimensions of gentrification. In addition, the recent phenomenon of the sharing economy has generated new economic opportunities for homeowners; however, it has also had the negative effect of pushing locals out of the rental market. Finally, COVID-19 has led to significant employment displacement and layoffs, as the tourism industry struggles with the impacts of the pandemic. This section will examine the concept of economic displacement that potentially leads to direct population displacement, and the indirect displacement of livelihoods.

7.3.1 Economic displacement and creative destruction

Joseph Schumpeter, an American political economist, coined the term 'creative destruction' in 1942. Creative destruction was considered to be a fundamental fact of a capitalist economy – continuous product and process innovation in order to replace out-dated, unproductive segments with new production units (Caballero and Hammour, 2000; Caballero, n.d.). This concept even asserts that impeding this process is likely to be an obstacle to development (Caballero and Hammour, 2000, pp. 2–3). Harvey (2006) also argues that the neo-liberalism accompanying capitalism is a force for creative destruction. Neo-liberalism urges massive class restructuring, typically only successful with the upper classes. When it works, it encourages competition and innovation to stimulate growth. However, Harvey (2006) also illustrates that neo-liberalism through the process of neo-colonialism, appropriates land and natural resources – by commodifying and privatising the land and natural resources, resulting in the forceful expulsion of local populations and businesses. By replacing native forms of production and consumption as being out-dated, creative destruction suppresses local peoples' rights to the commons.

In tourism, creative destruction often results from efforts made to diversify a sluggish economy or rejuvenate non-functioning economic activities. In a well-documented longitudinal study by Mitchell on the Mennonite community of St. Jacobs, Ontario, Canada, the process of creative destruction was evident (Mitchell and Vanderwerf, 2010; Mitchell and de Waal, 2008; Mitchell, 1998). In the pre-commodification stage of St. Jacobs, there was a Mennonite community where few visitors came to shop. St. Jacobs represented a romanticised pre-industrial era, with an ideal community in an ideal rural environment. It was not long before tourism overtook the community, as outside investment turned St. Jacobs into a heritage village for tourists.

The concept of creative destruction can also be linked to land grabbing or disaster capitalism, which licenses governments and authorities to replace a devastated local economy with more prospective economic activities – namely tourism and hospitality. Harvey (2006, 2003) examined neo-liberalism's Accumulation by Dispossession process in which states and élites orchestrate financial crises, through the power of monopoly and legality, and accumulate wealth through privatisation, appropriation of assets and resources, suppression of rights to the commons, and usury. Eviction and displacement of local people follow, allowing the displacement of marginalised people from tourism and hospitality business opportunities to be replaced with multinational corporations or international business chains (Braganza, 2015).

7.3.2 Economic displacement and the sharing economy

Since the early 2000s, the sharing economy had seen tremendous growth in tourism and hospitality. Instead of licensed taxi services, tourists began using Uber, a "ride share company"; and Airbnb had gained a significant share of the accommodation sector. Many providers of these services started as unregulated businesses to earn additional income, and are now facing tougher regulations, licensing, and taxation in many countries. Clashes between licensed taxi companies and Uber, budget motels and guesthouses against Airbnb, and disputes over the evasion of taxes, all illustrate emerging challenges as this new economy grows. The introduction of the sharing economy opened up opportunities for people without much initial capital or business means to enter the global tourism market. On the other hand, the success of companies like Airbnb has led to gentrification, rising property values, loss of income for traditional licensed taxis and hotels, and expansion of tourist accommodation into residential areas. Locals are being displaced, as inexpensive residential rental units are being converted into tourist accommodation units. Airbnb is not only competing with hotels for travellers, it is competing with locals for space. "The company has shifted the burden of rising prices in crowded downtown areas from travellers to residents – pushing down prices for hotel rooms while rising rents for city dwellers" (Thompson, 2018). Anti-tourism protests have spread across Europe to locations such as Venice, Barcelona, Majorca, and Amsterdam – citing overcrowding, increasing numbers of unlicensed accommodation establishments, and cruise ships (Coldwell, 2017). In Iceland, locals were evicted as rental properties were converted into tourist accommodation, and property values rose (Ástvaldsson, 2018) – violating their rights to housing. The sharing economy is also displacing local businesses. In Australia, short-term backpacker hostels were struggling to compete with the rise of Airbnb, and in some cases, forcing them out of business – such was the case for two hostels in Victoria (Irving-Guthrie, 2018). Restrictions on Airbnb now include a reduction in rental nights per year (e.g. Amsterdam and New York), and licensing restrictions (e.g. Barcelona) (Boztas, 2019). Since the onset of COVID-19, the sharing economy – along with all other types of accommodation – has struggled as borders closed and travel stopped. As some countries begin to reopen only time will tell what the long-term impact will be on the sharing economy.

7.3.3 Economic displacement in tourism caused by COVID-19

The tourism industry has been one of the hardest hit sectors as a result of COVID-19, with the closure of businesses. The UNWTO (2020) is predicting a fall between 60–80% in international tourism numbers in 2020, resulting in significant job losses. With widespread layoffs in the tourism industry, many face economic displacement. Airlines, for example, have been hard hit with some declaring bankruptcy and most laying off workers, grounding planes and cutting routes. In the UK, over 12,000 jobs were cut over the span of two days at the end of June 2020, including 1,300 crew and 727 pilots at EasyJet and 1,700 at Airbus (airliner manufacturer). The government programme to keep people employed in the UK (paying 80% of wages for over 9 million workers) was to be phased out; companies are realising they need to make significant structural changes, and have begun reducing their numbers of workers (Jack, 2020). In Niagara Falls, Ontario,

Canada, 98% of approximately 40,000 tourism workers have been laid off during the pandemic (Dunne, 2020), and the Niagara Region is hoping domestic tourism will help reverse the trend. The shift to online conferences and meetings, may permanently reduce the number of business trips negatively impacting the conference and event sector. Different destinations are showing different success rates containing the virus and are at different stages in reopening. While some tourism-related businesses have begun to reopen, the future is uncertain and others have closed permanently. The critical issues for tourism include: when restrictions and border closures will be lifted, what new regulations will be imposed (e.g. social distancing and operation capacity), whether tourists feel safe to travel and comfortable patronising tourism businesses (led by domestic tourists), and whether employees will feel safe to return to work. Chan, Morissette and Qui (2020) examined COVID-19 and job displacement in Canada with a focus on the longer term. The number of Canadian workers that will lose their job as a result of the pandemic and how the workers will fare after a job loss is unknown. The authors proposed a set of interrelated factors in understanding the degree to which the pandemic will adversely affect Canadian workers over the long term, including the degree to which the pandemic will:

- affect consumption expenditures, as households try to work to improve their balance sheets;
- reduce exports, as Canada's trading partners work towards re-opening their economies;
- stifle investment, as firms face uncertainty about the speed of the recovery and the possibilities of subsequent lockdowns;
- reduce firm entry and increase firm closures (e.g. conventional retail trade stores);
- lead firms to automate certain tasks through the use of robots and computer algorithms;
- promote firms to expand their telework and online sales capacity, adopt shift work, and modify the workspace to protect workers against subsequent waves of the virus;
- affect employment by generating new business costs related to the implementation of sanitary and physical distancing measures in the workplace;
- reduce world oil process and employment in the energy sector;
- induce displaced workers to retire early or to upgrade their skills and move to dynamic regions as the pandemic subsides.

Many of the above factors apply to the tourism industry, and it will be important to understand the differences in job displacement between the formal and informal sectors, as well as differences between countries. While some governments have been able to help workers laid off with emergency wage programmes, others have not, forcing workers to seek out employment that potentially puts their health at risk.

The loss of employment due to COVID-19 impacts workers' right to livelihood. A further discussion on COVID-19 can be found in Chapter 14.

7.4 Displacement of culture

Cultural displacement comes in many forms. Lubuguin (1998) classified culturally displaced people as: refugees (forced or involuntary move), immigrants (voluntary move), sojourners (temporary displacement), returning veterans (second displacement upon returning home), and ethnic minorities (no geographical movement). Similarly, Bammer (1994, xi) suggests two forms of cultural displacement: the first form of displacement occurs through physical dislocation such as refugees, immigrants, exiles, and expatriates; the second form is the "colonizing imposition of a foreign culture". Both forms of cultural displacement can infringe on a variety of human rights, especially of Indigenous or local cultures. For example, in the Chittagong Hill Tracts of Bangladesh, the military has forcefully evicted hundreds of Indigenous families for a military-owned tourist resort used by domestic tourists (Neef, 2019). Alternatively, a common form of cultural displacement in tourism involves people who do not geographically move out of their place of residency, yet are forced to live with other groups of people (such as tourists) of contrasting cultures. The host population – particularly in non-western nations – must live within tourist culture, rather than their own. Mollett (2014) refers to displacement-in-place in describing the Afro-Indigenous Garifuna, on the north coast of Honduras, who farm and fish as their main livelihood. The state government is opening up coastal landownership to foreigners for tourism, threatening the integrity of their communal land titles and way of life. Gentrification and creative destruction noted earlier, both transform physical structures, change communities, and subsequently alter the cultural heritage of the area. Other critics advocate that even supranational agencies and initiatives, like UNESCO, creating heritage designations facilitate the displacement of cultural values. In the case of Accumulation by Dispossession (Harvey, 2003, 2006), those who have economic control benefit the most, and cultural displacement is often a by-product. Local culture and heritage can be deemed valuable as a tourist attraction, and therefore a source of tourism revenue. However, in the pursuit of revenue, oftentimes local customs, amenities, and service levels are not satisfactory for tourists, and therefore must be replaced with western services and standards. UN UDHR Article 22 (cultural rights indispensable to his/her/their dignity and personality) and various articles in ICESCR and UNDRIP never mentioned forced change of heritage and cultural activities for the benefit of economic development. Many states aiming to achieve economic success through tourism support or even lead local cultural displacement, replacing it with the type of culture tourists demand (Oliver-Smith, 2001). Further commodification of culture occurs when elements of culture become commodities, such as souvenirs – yet this also raises debates over authenticity. As seen below, assigning financial values to tangible and intangible culture and heritage is to select which parts are worthy to represent the culture and people.

7.4.1 Cultural displacement and the colonial past

Historically, various forces have caused cultural displacement in developing nations, including the homogenisation of culture during colonial eras, and the more contemporary force of neo-colonial tourism development. Indigenous people's cultural heritage has been notably displaced and influenced by new settlers, such as European colonists or other immigrants. According to Stephens, et al. (2006), two of the factors that characterise Indigenous people are:

- Culture in general, or in specific manifestations (such as religion, living under a tribal system, community membership, dress, means of livelihood, lifestyle, etc.),
- Language (whether used as the main, preferred, habitual, general, or normal language) (p. 2020).

Culture and cultural manifestations of Indigenous peoples have been suppressed or banned when they do not fit into colonists' religious teachings. For instance, the Hawai'ian monarchs who were influenced by missionaries banned the Hula dance in Hawai'i (HawaiiHistory, 2019; Young, 2013). Similarly, missionaries to Papua New Guinea forbade native culture, including the use of drums (TakeCareOfOurCulture, 2007). These cultural manifestations have been displaced and replaced by more acceptable forms – e.g. ukulele and guitars in place of drums; more westernised clothing for traditional clothing. Language plays a key role in self-identity of Indigenous peoples. However, linguists have the bleak view that 50% of the 7,105 plus spoken languages today will disappear by the end of the 21st century (Mirza and Sundaram, 2016). Furthermore, legal protection of minority languages does not seem to provide much protection. Using the Native American Languages Act (NALA) of 1990 in the US as an example, Romaine (2002) shows that even policies with explicit statements "to preserve, protect, and promote the rights and freedom of Native Americans to use, practice, and develop Native American languages" (p. 195) can have no implementation plans. With bans or neglect by external agents or governments, cultural expressions in groups where storytelling, dance, songs, and musical instruments are used instead of a written language, can lead to the total annihilation of native cultures. Colonial policies including the restriction of physical mobility and landownership, economically shifts to industry that benefits colonialists, and misappropriation of the local culture, have caused massive displacement among Indigenous peoples (Bammer, 1994, see Chapter 12). Hyra's urban study (2014, p. 7) identified the relationship between political and cultural displacement, and noted "feelings of resentment, alienation and civic withdrawal among some long-standing residents". By assimilation or acculturation Indigenous or local residents adopt the tourist culture (demonstration effect) to the point that their original culture can be displaced. The strength of the local culture or targeted initiatives may, however, help offset pressures to change from outside cultures. Nevertheless, as discussed below, Indigenous culture is also commoditised.

7.4.2 Cultural displacement through cultural commodification

The commodification process turns elements of culture such as art, music, and performances into a commodity for tourists. Box 7.2 demonstrates how the Padaung Long Neck women have become a commodified tourism product. Cultural commodification can lead to violation of privacy rights. Tapia (2019) calls for an end to western tourists, particularly celebrities, taking photos of children without permission in poverty-stricken nations, and posting them on social media. Even if it is for charity, she argues it perpetuates the "white saviour" stereotype, and is a violation of their privacy. Article 12 of the UDHR states "No one shall be subjected to arbitrary interference with his privacy, family or home or correspondence nor to attacks upon his honour and reputation." Often the "museumisation and the commodification" of a heritage site is created by the loss of unique local culture and characteristics, and replaced by the "needs and tastes of international tourists" (Pleumarom, 2015). *Museumisation* of cultural performances for tourists, though habitually criticised, can also be a means to preserve otherwise disappearing cultural manifestations and heritage. The Hawai'ian Polynesian Culture Centre on Oahu Island is a very popular tourist attraction, largely staffed by students from Brigham Young University. Students are mostly Polynesian descendants, and are aware that they are performing for tourists; yet at the same time, they are learning or re-learning their culture and heritage, which instils pride in them (Stanley, 1998). The famous Inuit (Canadian and US) art form of soapstone carving is a case of cultural displacement used to combat economic displacement. Traditional bone and tusk carvings became popular trading goods with white settlers in the 19th century. Through cultural manipulation, the carved objects became *pinguaq* or 'toy-like representations' to cater to the tastes of white settlers (Swinton, 2016). These items were often not for sale but used as a gift or for exchange (Anselmi, 2017). The 1940s and 1950s saw a drastic change in the promotion of Inuit Art, when the Canadian government was seeking a way to establish uniquely Canadian Art in the world (Anselmi, 2017). The arctic military project, the Distant Early Warning Line (DEW), built in the midst of the Cold War, displaced and changed Inuit lifestyle, and pulled them into a "wage" economy (Contensa, 2012). A young artist named Houston, from Toronto, encouraged the Inuit to use their artistic talents to solve economic problems, and the Inuit Cooperative was established (Swinton, 2016). The Hudson's Bay company (originally a fur trading company in Canada, currently a large retail company) introduced sandpaper to the Inuit artisans (McCormack, n.d.) that further advanced the craft. Suddenly many Inuit artists found a decent way to make a living with their carvings. The challenge, however, is for Indigenous groups to maintain intellectual property rights and control of their artistic works (c.f. UDHR 27(2); ICESCR, 15(1-c, 2)). The Indigenous art community in Australia is lobbying the government to make it illegal to import and sell fake Aboriginal souvenirs (Michelmore, 2017). The Australian Competition and Consumer law only requires a sticker of the place of origin on the souvenir, and that it does not claim to be authentic. As a result, mass produced Aboriginal-style souvenirs/art are being imported from places such as Indonesia, India, and China.

BOX 7.2 THE PADAUNG LONG NECK WOMEN – THAILAND/MYANMAR

The Padaung tribe, are a branch of the Burmese Karen or Karenni ethnic group, also a sub-group of the Red Karen people (Maunati, 2018; Wilson, 2017; Grundy-Warr and Wong, 2002) who call themselves Kayan (Mirante, 1990). The Padaung tribe lived in Eastern Myanmar before they became refugees from political turmoil. The Karenni people are the victim of militarily motivated displacement by the authorities, to quell possible insurgents and political dissent. For more details on the geopolitical strife and geographical displacement in the border area of Myanmar and Thailand, see Grundy-Warr and Wong (2002).

The Padaung tribe is known for their tradition of women wearing metal rings around their necks and legs. These women are also referred to as Giraffe women or Long-neck women. A spirit doctor selects a providential day to put the brass coils around the neck of a girl (Mirante, 1990) The coils are added to intermittently, up to the age of marriage; the coils can be one foot (30 cm) in height, and weigh 20 pounds (9 kg) (Mirante, 1990). The origins of the custom vary, though the most common explanations are: (1) to protect women from a tiger's attack; (2) "a symbol of wealth and status, which in turn enhances marriageability, and as an assertion of a woman's identity and beauty"; (3) the rings make women unattractive and thus protect women from slave traders; (4) the Padaung are descendants of a "female dragon who mated with a male human angel" and the brass rings are meant to connect them to their dragon mother; (5) and finally the brass rings are a portable family shrine for magic-to-cure-illness or blessings for a journey (Wilson, 2017; Theurer, 2014; Mirante, 1990). The leg brass coils shackle women's mobility, which is a considerable challenge for people who live on the hillside (Mirante, 1990). Whatever the origin of the custom, it must be considered a privilege to wear them. Theurer (2014) described when parents could not afford the rings for their daughters, the girls were reduced to tears.

Once the brass rings are placed, they are seldom removed. Removal was used as punishment for adultery in the past, but some Padaung women who converted to Christianity began to remove their rings: some women removed the rings because they considered the tradition antiquated (Mirante, 1990), and some believed the brass rings have shackled them as a tourist attraction in Thailand (Theurer, 2014).

By the 1930s, the Padaung women were already known as the giraffe women to curious explorers and tourists. In 1931 French photographer Philip Charliat published in Le Figaro Magazine photographs of scenery and the Padaung women from the Inle Lake area (Puech, 2015).

In 1962, after a military coup, the junta launched "the Burmese Way to Socialism", which fostered a xenophobic and racist ideology to drive 'unclean' ethnic groups out of the country (Theurer, 2014). The Burman national claim was meant to deny ethnic diversity – even though these ethnic groups were the majority population in geographically peripheral states (Grundy-Warr and Wong, 2002). Since 1968, the military dictatorship has forced minority groups to flee from their homeland into the Myanmar-Thai border area (Mirante, 1990).

In 1985, three young Padaung women with neck rings were kidnapped and brought to the Karenni rebel base near the Pai River, as they were recognised as a valuable tourist attraction (Mirante, 1990). The Karenni rebels made arrangements with Thai tour operators to bring in tourists for a "Special Tour to Burma," crossing the Pai River. In addition to the tour price, "each tourist had to pay a Thai 'departure tax'" at a small customs post on the river, and then ante up an additional $20 to the Karenni rebel administration. Most of that payment was then kicked back to the Thai authorities by the Karenni (Mirante, 1990).

The Mae Hong Son community in Thailand was situated across the Pai River from the Karenni rebel base. Every year when the Mae Hong Son Fair is held, the Padaung women were forced to participate in the "Miss Hill Tribe" beauty pageant and sold at "the post-contest auction of teenaged contestants to provincial administrators and police" (Mirante, 1990). When the Karenni rebels refused further demands from Thais to send more Padaung women, the base was attacked by Burmese troops in 1987 in retaliation (Mirante, 1990).

From 1988 onwards, an additional 30% of the rural Karen population have been displaced (Grundy-Warr and Wong, 2002). Many Karenni refugees, including the Padaung tribe, crossed the Pai River and fled to Thailand. Grundy-Warr and Wong (2002) pointed out that the refugees had: "little knowledge about the broader geopolitical context and conflicts that have led to their forced migration into Thailand and remain perplexed at their predicament," (p. 110).

When Thailand repatriated the Karenni refugees, only the Padaung tribe was allowed to stay. The Mae Hong Son Resort sponsored the Padaung tribe, clearly intending to profit from using the Padaung women as a tourist attraction. Their popularity increased as a tourist attraction, and they were promoted as a Thai minority tribe (Mirante, 1990). In 1997, *The Times* magazine featured a place near the Thailand-Myanmar border, in which a Thai businessman runs a tourist attraction exhibiting the kidnapped Padaung refugees. The refugees were on the way to the Baan Na Soi Refugee camp near Mae

Hong Son, put into a minivan and driven away. The guide – who use to be a Mae Hong Son tourist guide – had sold the women. They were forced to work against their will, surrounded by armed guards (Drummond, 1997).

Direct and indirect displacement has changed the Padaung way of life. They can no longer live as hillside farmers or foragers. Traditionally men worked in the fields, and the women and children stayed at home engaging in cottage industries; but today, the women and children serve the tourists (Maunati, 2018). They live in a re-created village, rather than in a concealed refugee camp (Grundy-Warr and Wong, 2002). The village is kept as "primitive" as possible to be "authentic"; the Padaung girls are punished if they attempt to get an education, use technology such as mobile phones, or leave the village (Theurer, 2014). Theurer's (2014) interview with the Padaung women revealed that the women are not allowed to speak to the tourists but to smile; the tour guides explain to the tourists that the Padaung do not want a modern and convenient lifestyle, and prefer to live in a primitive way; and tourists received false information about medical and education assistance the Padaung receive. In another village, the Padaung women's wages were reduced when they were seen riding motorcycles (Levett, 2008).

The Padaung tribe were also denied their refugee relocation rights. The UN's High Commissioner for Refugees (UNCHR) began the registration process in 2005 to relocate the Burmese refugees in the Mae Hong Son. The UNHCR and the Thai Ministry of Interior jointly conducted the refugee registration, yet the Thai government denied exit permits to the applicants, claiming they are registered Thai Hill Tribes; or that they are economic refugees who do not qualify for refugee relocation (Levett, 2008). The Thai authorities even argued the Padaung tribe is like "an endangered species on the verge of extinction which needed protection," (Levett, 2008) hence they should stay in Thailand. The then-governor of Mae Hong Son said: "The Long Necks are very popular among European tourists. The Mae Hong Son administration had requested the Ministry of Interior to withhold their exit permits and set up this Long Neck Cultural Conservation Village" (Levett, 2008). The plight of the Padaung has been broadcasted globally. The UNHCR and the ASEAN will have to correct the current situation, especially for the Padaung families whose applications were already accepted through the 2005 Refugee relocation programme.

7.5 Conclusion

When displacement in tourism development is discussed, the first thing that comes to mind is population displacement. Indigenous or local people are evicted from their usual habitats in order to make space for tourism and hospitality facilities. However, the challenges associated with displacement and tourism can be quite complex. This chapter examined the displacement issues from different concepts and perspectives, including political migration, gentrification, economics, creative destruction, land grabbing, disaster capitalism, and acculturation and assimilation. Population displacement may be politically motivated, or it can be militarily motivated to control certain group of peoples within a political boundary. Environmental problems and natural disasters can impact tourism destinations, displacing peoples and businesses. Economic motivations of authorities or élites are also used to justify population displacement; and the pressure from globalisation and multinational tourism enterprises to replace local economic activities are done under the promise of better economic conditions. The recent economic phenomenon of the sharing economy, facilitated by technological advancements in online booking platforms, has displaced traditional economic activities as out-dated modes of exchange. Overtourism, the sharing economy, and gentrification combined, enhance the pressure for further displacement. As a result of geographical and/or economic displacement, the culture and heritage of displaced peoples may be altered. These types of displacements inevitably infringe on the basic human rights of displaced peoples. To evict and displace peoples from their natural habitats for potentially long durations uproots people from their culture, way of life, livelihood, jobs, professions, peace, and safety. During the transition and resettlement, or returning home, the life of displaced people is not the same as what they remember. It can be a long and hard process to regain what was lost.

Tourism and hospitality development as an economic driving force displaces and replaces traditional and Indigenous ways of production and consumption. Frequently, multinational enterprises replace local small-and-medium sized businesses. Expatriates or immigrant workers compete against local people for job opportunities. Tourism not only accelerates the change of local culture by introducing tourist culture, but also commercialises local culture and manifestations of heritage as moneymaking entities. The entanglement of displacement issues impacts various human rights, legal issues, and the social fabric of communities in the most complex ways.

References

Anselmi, E., 2017. Carving Out A Career. *Up Here.* [online] 2 October 2017. Available at: <https://uphere.ca/articles/carving-out-career> [Accessed 15 May 2019].

Ástvaldsson, J., 2018. Poverty and Inequality. *Iceland Review*, 1, pp. 15–16.

Bammer, A., 1994. *Displacements: Cultural Identity in Question*. Bloomington & Indianapolis: Indiana University Press.

BBC News, 2019. Hassan al-Kontar: Who is the man trapped in an airport helping now? *BBC News*. [online] 12 August 2019. Available at: <www.bbc.com/news/world-middle-east-49296093> [Accessed 12 August 2019].

Boztas, S. 2019. Airbnb is Accused of Destroying Cities. This Company Says it's the Ethical Alternative. *Huffpost* 2 June 2019 Available at: <www.huffingtonpost.ca/entry/airbnb-affordable-housing-gentrification- tourism-fairbnb_n_5c5949c3e4b00187b554828d?guccounter=1&guce_referrer=aHR0cHM6Ly93d3cuZ29vZ2xlLmNvbS8&guce_referrer_sig=AQAAAEQ5VRn6zpIUo5SPOhC4BK6Y7jW_Eaaowt178lzNjzY0N0TBZ11HnEjAbZCjwN8I7a3tl_0M3sVpqV6M3z2nsFCshkiq5AkGv7ptikyg6bTUSHXwBFTeu_DDAyRJ7a9W_qeyb4UoNSSUrpbCyT1LxjBCyw2LDbgfM-IuEi-yWBRB> [Accessed 6 August 2019].

Braganza, F., 2015. *Corporatization of Tourism Spaces.* Centre for Responsible Tourism, Goa. [pdf] 12 February 2015. Available at: <http://responsibletourismgoa.com/corporatization-tourism-spaces/> [Accessed 29 March 2019].

Brookings – Bern Project 2011. IASC Operational Guideline on the Protection of Persons in Situations of Natural Disasters. *Washington: The Brookings – Bern Project on Internal Displacement.* [pdf] Available at: <www.ohchr.org/Documents/Issues/ IDPersons/OperationalGuidelines_IDP.pdf> [Accessed 7 August 2019].

Brooks, S., Spierenburg, M., Van Brakel, L., Kolk, A. and Lukhozi, K.B., 2011. Creating a Commodified Wilderness: Tourism, Private Game Farming, and 'Third Nature' Landscapes in Kwazulu-Natal. *Journal of Economic and Social Geography,* [e-Journal] 102(3), pp. 260–274. DOI: https://doi.org/10.1111/j.1467-9663.2011.00662.x

Brown-Saracino, J., 2014. Gentrification. In: J. Manza, (ed.), *Oxford Bibliographies.* Oxford: Oxford Univsrsity Press. DOI: 10.1093/OBO/9780199756384-0074.

Caballero, R. J. and Hammour, M.L., 2000. *Massachusetts Institute of Technology Department of Economics Working Paper Series: Creative Destruction and Development: Institutions, Crises, and Restructuring. Working Paper 00-17. August 2000* [pdf] Available at: <https://poseidon01.ssrn.com/delivery. php?ID=265092002101091123002090097097 1141110000520610 060040091021240901030810311240220670290830760250 800040030350190180041 230011180820181011220220041080941160040910081008 02911808912111511901109930 05122&EXT=pdf> [Accessed 30 January 2018].

Caballero, R. J., n.d. *Creative destruction.* [pdf] Available at: <https://economics.mit.edu/files/1785> [Accessed 30 January 2018].

Chan, P., Morissette, R. and Qui, H., 2020. COVID-19 and job displacement: Thinking about the longer term. *Statcan COVID-19.* [online] 10 June 2020. Available at: <www.150.statcan.gc.ca/n1/ pub/45-28-0001/2 020001/article /00030-eng.htm> [Accessed 1 July 2020].

Centre on Housing Rights and Evictions, 2007. Fair Play for Housing Rights: Mega-Events, Olympic Games and Housing Rights. [pdf] Available at: <www.ruig-gian.org/ressources/Report %20Fair%20Play% 20FINAL%20FINAL %20070531.pdf> [Accessed 20 May 2018].

Chamberlain, G., 2012. Andaman Islands tribe threatened by lure of mass tourism. *The Observer.* [online] 7 January. Available at: <www.theguardian.com/world/2012/jan/07/andaman-islands-tribe-tourism-threat?> [Accessed 15 February 2012].

Chamberlain, G., 2013. 'Human safaris' to end for Andaman tribe. *The Observer.* [online] 27 January 2013. Available at: <www.theguardian.com/world/2013/jan/27/jarawa-tribe-andaman-islands-human-safaris-to-end> [Accessed 10 February 2013].

Chamberlain, G., 2014. Jarawa tribe now face sexual abuse by outsiders on Andaman Islands. *The Observer.* [online] 1 February. Available at: <www.theguardian.com/world/2014/feb/01/andaman-islands-jarawa-sex-abuse-outsiders> [Accessed 22 February 2014].

Chapman, B., 2016. Rio 2016: The richest Games in 120 years of Olympic history. *The Independent.* [online] 04 August 2016. Available at: <www.independent.co.uk/news/business/analysis-and-features/rio-2016-olympic-games-richest-ever-usain-bolt-mo-farah-a7171811.html> [Accessed 20 May 2019]

Chavez, N., 2017. Olympic Games Rio 2016 – Economic Legacy. *ICO Olympic News.* [online] 16 March. Available at: <www.olympic.org/news/olympic-games-rio-2016-economic-legacy> [Accessed 11 May 2019].

Cho, R., 2016. *El Niño and Global Warming—What's the Connection? State of the Planet: Earth Institute| Columbia University.* [blog] 2 February. Available at: <https://blogs.ei.columbia.edu/2016/02/02/el-nino-and-global-warming-whats-the-connection/> [Accessed 6 August 2019].

Climate Signals beta, 2018. *Extreme El Niño Frequency Increase.* [online] 10 July. Available at: <www.climatesignals.org/climate-signals/extreme-el-niño-frequency-increase> [Accessed 6 August 2019].

Coldwell, W., 2017. First Venice and Barcelona: now anti-tourism marches spread across Europe, *The Guardian,* 10 August, Available at: <www.theguardian.com/travel/2017/aug/10/anti-tourism-marches-spread-across-europe-venice-barcelona> [Accessed 6 August 2019].

Cole, S., 2012. A Political Ecology of Water Equity and Tourism A Case Study from Bali. *Annals of Tourism Research.* 39(2), pp. 1221–1241. DOI: https://doi.org/10.1016/j.annals.2012.01.003.

Contensa, S., 2012. DEW Line: Canada is cleaning up pollution caused by Cold War radar stations in the Arctic. *The Star.* [online] 4 August. Available at: <www.thestar.com/news/insight/2012/08/04/dew_line_canada_is_cleaning_up_pollution_caused_by_cold_war_radar_stations_in_the_arctic.html> [Accessed 15 May 2019].

da Costa, K., and Pospieszna, P., 2015. The Relationship between Human Rights and Disaster Risk Reduction Revisited: Bringing the Legal Perspective into the Discussion. *Journal of International Humanitarian Legal Studies* [e-journal] 6(1), pp. 64–86. DOI: https://doi.org/10.1163/18781527-00601005.

Devictor, X. and Do, Q.T., 2016. How many years do refugees stay in exile? *The World Bank Development for Peace.* [blog] 15 September. Available at: <http://blogs.worldbank.org/dev4peace/how-many-years-do-refugees-stay-exile> [Accessed 26 March 2019].

Drummond, A., 1997. Prisoners in a Human Zoo. The Original Story. *The Times.* [online] 22 November. Available at: <www.andrew-drummond.com/1997/11/22/prisoners-in-human-zoo-original-story_21/> [Accessed 30 September 2012].

Dunne, J. 2020. Saving summer: The Niagara Falls region hopes to recover from COVID-19 with Canadian tourists' help. Will it work? *CBC News.* [online] 1 July. Available at: <https://newsinteractives.cbc.ca/longform/niagara> [Accessed 2 July 2020].

Dury, C., 2018. Cornwall stops telling people to come to tourists beaches after heatwave triggers severe overcrowding. *The Independent.* [online] 12 August. Available at: <www.independent.co.uk/news/uk/home-news/cornwall-struggling-visitors-tourism-weather-heat-social-media-a8488211.html> [Accessed 6 August 2019].

Edgington, D. W., 2010. *Reconstructing Kobe: The Geography of Crisis and Opportunity.* Vancouver: University of British Columbia Press.

Gaffney, C., 2016. Gentrifications in pre-Olympic Rio de Janeiro. *Urban Geography*, [e-Journal] 37(8), pp. 1132–1153. DOI: http://dx.doi.org/10.1080/02723638.2015.1096115.

Government of Canada, 2018. *"Tell them we're human" What Canada and the world can do about the Rohingya crisis. Report of Special Envoy to Myanmar. Bob Rae.* [online] 3 April. Available at: <www.international.gc.ca/world-monde/issues_development-enjeux_developpement/response_conflict-reponse_conflits/crisis-crises/rep_sem-rap_esm.aspx?lang=eng#a2_1> [Accessed 10 August 2019].

Grundy-Warr, C. and Wong, E., 2002. Geographies of Displacement: the Karenni and the Shan across the Myanmar-Thailand Border. *Singapore Journal of Tropical Geography*, [e-Journal] 23(1), pp. 93–122. DOI: https://doi.org/10.1111/1467-9493.00120.

Harvey, D., 2003. *The New Imperialism.* Oxford: Oxford University Press.

Harvey, D., 2006. Neo-liberalism as creative destruction, *Geografiska Annaler: Series B, Human Geography*, [e-Journal] 88(2), pp. 145–158. DOI: https://doi.org/10.1111/j.0435-3684.2006.00211.x.

HawaiiHistory.org, 2019. Missionaries and the Decline of Hula. [online]. Available at: <www.hawaiihistory.org/index.cfm?fuseaction=ig.page&CategoryID=253> [20 May 2019].

Hyra, D., 2014. The back-to-the-city movement: Neighbourhood redevelopment and processes of political and cultural displacement. *Urban Studies*, 52(10), 1753–1773. [online]. DOI: 10.1177/0042098014539403.

IHRB, 2013. *Striving for Excellence: Mega-Sporting Events and Human Rights. Institute for Human Rights and Business (IHRB)*. [pdf] October. Available at: <www.ihrb.org/pdf/2013-10-21_IHRB_Mega-Sporting-Events-Paper_Web.pdf> [Accessed 12 August 2019].

IPCC, 2018 Special Report Global Warming of 1.5°C IPCC Geneva. [online]. Available at: <www.ipcc.ch/sr15/download/> [Accessed 6 August 2019].

Irving-Guthrie, A., 2018. Airbnb blamed for closure of short-term hostel accommodation with YHA calling for level playing field. *ABC News*. [online] 29 January. Available at: <www.abc.net.au/news/2018-01-29/regional-accommodation-closures-due-to-airbnb/9361930> [Accessed 6 August 2019].

Jack, S., 2020. Coronavirus: UK firms slash more than 12 000 jobs in two days. *BBC News*. [online] 1 July. Available at: <www.bbc.com/news/business-53247787> [Accessed 2 July 2020].

King, H., 2016. Rio Olympics 2016: economic gain or loss? World Finance – the Voice of the Market. [online] 7 June. Available at: <www.worldfinance.com/infrastructure-investment/rio-olympics-2016-economic-gain-or-loss> [Accessed 13 May 2019].

Klein, N., 2007. *The Shock Doctrine: The Rise of Disaster Capitalism*. Toronto: Knopf Canada.

Leowenstein, A., 2015. *Disaster Capitalism: Making a Killing Out of Catastrophe*. London: Verso Books.

Levett, C., 2008. Imprisoned in Rings of Brass. *Sydney Morning Herald*. [online] 12 January. Available at: <www.smh.com.au/world/imprisoned-in-rings-of-brass-20080112-gdrwin.html> [Accessed 12 October 2012].

Lubuguin, F.S.A., 1998. The Acculturation of Culturally Displaced Persons: The Case of Pilipino-Americans. *Advances in Descriptive Psychology*, 7, 167–233. [online]. Available at: <www.sdp.org/wp-content/uploads/2019/01/ADP-7-Lubuguin-Acculturation-pp-167_233.pdf> [Accessed 1 May 2019].

Maly, E. and Shiozaki, Y., 2012. Towards a Policy that Supports People-Centered Housing Recovery—Learning from Housing Reconstruction after the Hanshin-Awaji Earthquake in Kobe, Japan. *International Journal of Disaster Risk Science*, [e-Journal] 3(1), pp. 56–65. doi: 10.1007/s13753-012-0007-1.

Mathieson, D.S., 2009. Plight of the Damned: Burma's Rohingya. *Global Asia*, 4 (1). [online]. 20 March. Available at: <www.globalasia.org/v4no1/feature/plight-of-the-damned-burmas-rohingya_david-scott-mathieson> [Accessed 1 May 2019].

Maunati, Y., 2018. Diaspora and Ethnic Identities in the Border Areas of Thailand-Myanmar and Thailand-Laos. In: B.R. Sari, (ed.), *Borders and Beyond: Transnational Migration and Diaspora in Northern Thailand Boarder Area with Myanmar and Laos*. Jakarta: Yayasan Pustaka Obor Indonesia. pp. 89–151.

McBride, J., 2018. The Economics of Hosting the Olympic Games. *Council on Foreign Relations*. [online] 19 January. Available at: <www.cfr.org/backgrounder/economics-hosting-olympic-games> [Accessed 10 May 2019].

McCormack, K., n.d. History of Soapstone Carving. Artwork by Kay McCormack. [online]. Available at: <www.artworkbykm.com/history-of-soapstone-carving.html> [Accessed 29 May 2019].

McNamara, K.E., Bronen, R., Fernando, N., and Kelpp, S., 2016. The complex decision-making of climate-induced relocation: adaptation and loss and damage. *Climate Policy*, [e-Journal] 18 (1), pp. 111–117. Doi: https://doi.org/10.1080/14693062.2016.1248886.

Met Office, 2018. *What is El Niño?* [online] 25 May. Available at: <www.metoffice.gov.uk/learning/ocean/el-nino >.

Michelmore, K., 2017. Indigenous arts community lobby Government to make it illegal to sell fake Aboriginal-style souvenirs, *ABC News*. [online] 16 January. Available at: <www.abc.net.au/news/2017-01-17/calls-to-make-fake-aboriginal-style-souvenirs-illegal/8187042> [Accessed 10 August 2019].

Mirante, E. T., 1990. Hostage to Tourism. *Cultural Survival Quarterly Magazine*. [online] March. Available at: <www.culturalsurvival.org/publications/cultural-survival-quarterly/hostages-tourism >. [Accessed 30 January 2008].

Mirza A., and Sundaram D., 2016. Harnessing Collective Intelligence to Preserve and Learn Endangered Languages. In: P. Vinh and L. Barolli, (eds.), *Nature of Computation and Communication. ICTCC 2016. Lecture Notes of the Institute for Computer Sciences, Social Informatics and Telecommunications Engineering*, [e-Journal] 168, pp. 224–236. DOI: https://doi.org/10.1007/978-3-319-46909-6_21.

Mitchell, C.J.A., 1998. Entrepreneurialism, Commodification and Creative Destruction: a Model of Post-modern Community Development. *Journal of Rural Studies*, [e-Journal] 14(3), pp. 273–286. DOI: https://doi.org/10.1016/S0743-0167(98)00013-8.

Mitchell, C.J.A. and de Waal, S.B., 2008. Revisiting the model of creative destruction: St. Jacobs, Ontario, a decade later. *Journal of Rural Studies*, [e-Journal] 25, pp. 156–167. DOI: https://doi.org/10.1016/j.jrurstud.2008.09.003.

Mitchell, C.J.A. and Vanderwerf, J., 2010. Creative destruction and trial by space in a historic Canadian village. *Geographical Review*, 100(3), pp. 356–374. DOI: https://doi.org/10.1111/j.1931-0846.2010.00041.x.

Mollett, S., 2014. A modern paradise: Garifuna land, labor, and displacement-in-place. *Latin American Perspectives*, [e-Journal] 41(6), pp. 27–45. DOI: https://doi.org/10.1177/0094582X13518756.

Neef, A., 2019. *Tourism, Land Grabs and Displacement: A Study with Particular Focus on the Global South*. [pdf] 14 February. Available at: <www.tourism-watch.de/system/files/document/Neef_Tourism_Land_Grab_Study.pdf> [Accessed 29 March 2019].

NHK, 2019. *8 Years from Great East Japan Earthquake Documentary Series*. NHK News Web. [online]. Available at: <www3.nhk.or.jp/news/special/shinsai8portal/document/> [Accessed 12 March 2019].

NOAA, 2018. *What are El Niño and La Niña? National Oceanic and Atmospheric Administration, U.S. Department of Commerce*. [online] 25 June. Available at: <https://oceanservice.noaa.gov/facts/ninonina.html> [Accessed 7 August 2018].

Odin, J. K., 1998. *The Performative and Processual: A Study of Hypertext/Postcolonial Aesthetic*. [online]. Available at: <www.postcolonialweb.org/poldiscourse/odin/odin14.html> [Accessed 7 August 2018].

OHCHR, 2016. *Discussion Paper: Human rights, migration, and displacement related to the adverse impacts of climate change*. [pdf] 30 September. Available at: <www.ohchr.org/Documents/Issues/ClimateChange/EM2016/HumanRightsMigrationDisplacement.pdf.> [Accessed 26 March 2019].

OHCHR, 2017. *Statement to the Special Session of the Human Rights Council on the "Situation of human rights of the minority Rohingya Muslim population and other minorities in Rakhine*

State of Myanmar." [online] 5 December. Available at: <www.ohchr.org/EN/HRBodies/HRC/Pages/NewsDetail.aspx?NewsID=22495&LangID=E> [Accessed 27 December 2017].

OHCHR, 2019. *UN Independent International Fact-Finding Mission on Myanmar calls on UN Member States to remain vigilant in the face of the continued threat of genocide.* [online] 23 October. Available at: <www.ohchr.org/EN/NewsEvents/Pages/DisplayNews.aspx?NewsID=25197&LangID=> [Accessed 30 October 2019].

Oliveira, N.D.S., 1996. Favelas and Ghettos: Race and Class in Rio de Janeiro and New York City. *The Latin American Perspectives Issue 91.* [pdf] 23(4), pp. 71–89. Available at: <www.jstor.org/stable/2634130> [Accessed 12 May 2019].

Oliver-Smith, A., 2001. *Displacement, Resistance and the Critique of Development: From the Grassroots to the Global. Final Report Prepared for ESCOR R7644 and the Research Programme on Development Induced Displacement and Resettlement.* [pdf] Available at: <https://reliefweb.int/sites/reliefweb.int/files/resources/93DBFB51B743EBE5C1256C3700537385-Grass_roots.pdf> [Accessed 13 August 2018].

Optimal Economics and TNS Research International, 2012. *Tourism Marketing Return on Investment: The Impact of Displacement Final Report: October 2012. Report Prepared for Department for Culture, Media and Sport.* [pdf] Available at: <https://assets.publishing.service.gov.uk/government/uploads/system/uploads/attachment_data/file/77592/Displacement_Final_Report.pdf> [Accessed 13 August 2018].

Pleumarom, A., 2015. Tourism - a driver of inequality and displacement. *The Third Word Network/Third World Resurgence.* [online]. Available at: <www.twn.my/title2/resurgence/2015/301-302/cover01.htm> [Accessed 9 June 2018].

Puech, M., 2015. L'éblouissement birman de Philippe Charliat. *L'OEIL?* [online] 25 November. Available at: <www.a-l-oeil.info/blog/2011/02/18/l'eblouissement-birman-de-philippe-charliat/> [Accessed 23 May 2019].

Rice, A., 2005. *Post-tsunami reconstruction and tourism: a second disaster? A report by Tourism Concern October 2005.* [pdf] Available at: <www.tourismconcern.org.uk/wp-content/uploads/2014/12/Post-tsunami-reconstruction-and-tourism-a-second-disaster.pdf> [Accessed 13 August 2018].

Robertson D., 2016. Olympic Opening Ceremony Spectacle Draws Criticism from Favelas on Social Media. *RioOnWatch.* [online] 8 August. Available at: <www.rioonwatch.org/?p=31545> [Accessed 01 May 2019].

Robertson D., and Williamson, T., 2016 The Favela as a Community Land Trust: A Solution to Eviction and Gentrification? *RioOnWatch.* [online] 15 November. Available at: <www.rioonwatch.org/?p=25330> [Accessed 1 May 2019].

Romain, S., 2002. The Impact of Language Policy on Endangered Languages. *International Journal on Multicultural Societies UNESCO,* 4 (2), pp. 194–212. [pdf]. Available at: <www.unesco.org/shs/ijms/vol4/issue2/art3> [Accessed 1 April 2019].

Scott, D., Hall, C.M. and Gössling, S., 2019. Global tourism vulnerability to climate change. *Annals of Tourism Research* 77, pp. 49–61. DOI: https://doi.org/10.1016/j.annals.2019.05.007.

Settimi, C., 2016. The 2016 Rio Summer Olympics: By The Numbers. *Forbes.* [online] 5 August. Available at: <www.forbes.com/sites/christinasettimi/2016/08/05/the-2016-summer-olympics-in-rio-by-the-numbers/#3070e7f3fa18> [Accessed 12 May 2019].

ShockDoctrine, 2018. The Shock Doctrine. [online] 28 April. Available at: <www.naomiklein.org/shock-doctrine> [Accessed 1 May 2019].

Silvestre, G., de Oliveira, N.G., 2012. The revanchist logic of mega-events: community displacement in Rio de Janeiro's West End. *Visual Studies*, 27 (2), pp. 204–210. DOI: 10.1080/1472586X.2012.677506.
Smith, S., 2017. Rio de Janeiro residents protest World Cup and Olympics 2011–2016. *Global Nonviolent Action Database*. [online] 8 February. Available at: <https://nvdatabase.swarthmore.edu/content/rio-de-janeiro-residents-protest-world-cup-and-olympics-2011-2016> [Accessed 11 May 2019].
Stanley, N., 1998. *Being Ourselves for You: Global Display of Cultures*. London: Middlesex University Press.
Stephens, C., Porter, J., Nettleton, C. and Willis, R., 2006. Indigenous Health 4: Disappearing, displaced, and undervalued: a call to action for Indigenous health worldwide. *The Lancet*, 367 (9527), pp. 2019–2028. [online]. DOI: https://doi.org/10.1016/S0140-6736(06)68892-2.
Swinton, G., 2016. Inuit Art. *The Canadian Encyclopedia*. [online]. Available at: <www.thecanadianencyclopedia.ca/en/article/inuit-art> [Accessed 15 May 2019].
TakeCareOfOurCulture, 2007. *Beware of the white man*. [video online] Available at: <www.youtube.com/channel/UCUpHkclVa6WtDnrP0M_SLZQ> [Accessed 12 September 2010].
Talbot, A., 2016. Reflecting on the Games: A Look Behind the Olympic Smokescreen and the Rio 2016 'Success Story'. *RioOnWatch*. 22 August. [online]. Available at: <www.rioonwatch.org/?p=32012> [Accessed 11 May 2019].
Tapia, A., 2019. Dear westerners, please stop taking pictures of other people's children while travelling in developing countries. Independent 16 April, Available at: <www.independent.co.uk/voices/western-photography-tourism-black-children-white-people-a8872316.html> [Accessed 6 August 2019].
The Jarawa Foundtion, 2019. Who are the Jawara People? Available at: https://organicthejarawas.com/pages/who-are-the-jarawa-people> [Accessed 21 May 2019].
Theurer, J., 2014. Trapped in Their Own Rings: Padaung Women and Their Fight for Traditional Freedom. *International Journal of Gender and Women's Studies*, 2(4), pp. 51–67. DOI: 10.15640/ijgws.v2n4a3.
Thompson, D., 2018. Airbnb and the Unintended Consequences of 'Disruption.' *The Atlantic*. [online] 17 February. Available at: <www.theatlantic.com/business/archive/2018/02/airbnb-hotels-disruption/553556/> [Accessed 6 August 2019].
Tourism Concern, 2014. *Displacement caused by tourism*. [blog] 14 September. Available at: <www.tourismconcern.org.uk/displacement-caused-by-tourism/ >.
UN, 2007. United Nations Declaration on the Rights of Indigenous Peoples. [online]. Available at: <www.un.org/development/desa/indigenouspeoples/wp-content/uploads/sites/19/2018/11/UNDRIP_E_web.pdf> [Accessed 6 August 2019].
UNESCO, 2017. *Displaced Person / Displacement*. [online]. Available at: <www.unesco.org/new/en/social-and-human-sciences/themes/international-migration/glossary/displaced-person-displacement/> [Accessed 6 August 2019].
UNHCR, 2019. Figures at a Glance. [online]. Available at: <www.unhcr.org/figures-at-a-glance.html/> [Accessed 6 August 2019].
UNWTO, 2020. *International Tourist Numbers Could Fall 60–80% in 2020, UNWTO Reports*. [online] 7 May. Available at: <www.unwto.org/news/covid-19-international-tourist-numbers-could-fall-60-80-in-2020> [Accessed 8 May 2020].
Vale, L., and Gray, A., 2013. The Displacement Decathlon. *Places Journal*. [online] April. DOI: https://doi.org/10.22269/130415.

Walker, B., 2017 An Island Nation Turns Away from Climate Migration, Despite Rising Seas. *Inside Climate News*. [online] 20 November, Available at: <https://insideclimatenews.org/news/20112017/kiribati-climate-change-refugees-migration-pacific-islands-sea-level-rise-coconuts-tourism> [Accessed 6 August 2019].

Wilson, B., 2017. *The reality behind Thailand's Kayan Long Neck Hill Tribe will make you rethink your trip.* [online] 14 November. Available at: <https://matadornetwork.com/read/reality-behind-thailands-karen-long-neck-hill-tribe-will-make-rethink-trip/> [Accessed 14 May 2019].

Young, P.T., 2013. Hula – How the Missionaries Felt. *Hoʻokuleana*. [online] 8 December. Available at: <https://totakeresponsibility.blogspot.com/2013/12/hula-how-missionaries-felt.html> [Accessed 20 May 2016].

8
DISCRIMINATION OF PATRONS IN TOURISM ESTABLISHMENTS

> All human beings are born free and equal in dignity and rights
> *Universal Declaration of Human Rights, art. 1*

8.1 Discrimination of patrons in tourism establishments – an introduction

A fundamental principle of human rights legislation is that all humans should have equal opportunities to pursue their life goals, without being hindered by discriminatory practices based on any ground such as race, ethnic origin, gender, sex, religion, age, disability, political opinion or sexual orientation. The Universal Declaration of Human Rights (UDHR) is one of the most important international human rights documents denouncing discrimination. Article 2 in the UDHR proclaims the equality of every person:

> Everyone is entitled to all the rights and freedoms set forth in this Declaration, without distinction of any kind, such as race, colour, sex, language, religion, political or other opinion, national or social origin, property, birth or other status.

Similar declarations denouncing discrimination can also be found in the International Covenant on Civil and Political Rights (ICCPR) (art. 2(1)) and the International Covenant on Economic, Social and Cultural Rights (ICESCR) (art. 2(2)) adopted in 1966. The UDHR and the two covenants have been followed by other international agreements and resolutions, covering specific forms of discrimination more in detail. Most countries have implemented non-discrimination legislation at the national level covering all or a majority of the protected grounds in international human rights law.

In the tourism sector, discrimination can consist of a wide variety of different actions, ranging from denial of services and the rendering of services of lower quality to discrimination in an employment relationship or a hostile working environment. In this chapter, the topic is limited to discrimination in the access to facilities and services in the tourism sector, while discrimination in an employment relationship is covered in Chapter 10. The tourism and travel industry has historically struggled with diversity and there are many examples of overt and more subtle discriminatory policies in the provision of accommodation and travel services. For example, tourism and travel destinations can be marketed in a stereotypical way, marginalizing minorities and their experiences (Martin, 2004). Discrimination can also be more overt, where certain groups are denied services or made feel unwelcome during travel or at the destination. Alderman contends that "[t]he tourism industry, both inside and outside the United States, has traditionally adopted a white male gaze that obscures the experiences of racial and ethnic minorities while also perpetuating racist stereotypes" (2013).

There is ample evidence that tourists from groups that are regularly discriminated against adapt their travel patterns to avoid situations where they might be discriminated against during their travels. One of the earliest documentations of changed travel patterns due to discrimination is the *"The Travelers' Green Book,"* an annual publication published from 1936 to 1967 in the United States. The guidebook gave advice to African American tourists about relatively safe towns, hotels and restaurants, where they would experience less discrimination. Past research (Philipp, 1994) shows that African American tourists are less likely than whites to go to unfamiliar places, such as unknown streets, travel alone or in small groups or engage in unplanned activities. It can be argued that if a group of individuals have experienced hostility, they would prefer to travel in large secure groups to known areas, make fewer unplanned stops and patronize familiar restaurants and hotels, why the differences in travel patterns between white and African American tourists may be linked to discrimination. Other examples are the travel agencies and guides catering to other groups that may experience discrimination while travelling (see for example IGLTA, a travel association that has catered to the LGBTQ+ community since 1983, or the more recent halal travel guides, catering to Muslim travellers). Discrimination in the tourism and travel industry causes immense personal suffering to the persons who experience discrimination. In addition, it has a significant economic impact, resulting in job losses, lost revenue for tourism businesses as well as hampering the ability to attract, retain and recruit top talent to the destination (Texas Association of Business, 2017).

The chapter is divided into five sections; Section 8.2 contains a discussion of discrimination based on race, national or ethnic origin, followed by a discussion of discrimination based on sex/gender in Section 8.3, sexual orientation and gender identity in Section 8.4 religious orientation in Section 8.5 and disability in Section 8.6. Each section includes an overview of international human rights law as well as many examples of legislation at the national level prohibiting the particular ground of discrimination. As will be noted in this chapter, the effectiveness of legal rules prohibiting discrimination is dependent on the cultural and social context where the rules are adopted, interpreted and enforced. Finally, the chapter includes a section (8.7) where the tension and interaction between, as well as the compatibility of legislation in different countries, is discussed. The different themes of Chapter 8 are summarized in the concluding Section 8.8.

8.2 Discrimination in tourism establishments based on race, national or ethnic origin

Racial, national and ethnic orientation discrimination impedes the lives of millions of people every day. It consists of everything from milder forms of intolerance to more sinister forms of racial/ethnic hatred fuelling ethnic genocide and hate crimes.

> The Declaration on Race and Racial Prejudice defines "racism" as including: "racist ideologies, prejudiced attitudes, discriminatory behaviour, structural arrangements and institutionalized practices resulting in racial inequality as well as the fallacious notion that discriminatory relations between groups are morally and scientifically justifiable; it is reflected in discriminatory provisions in legislation or regulations and discriminatory practices as well as in anti-social beliefs and acts; it hinders the development of its victims, perverts those who practise it, divides nations internally, impedes international co-operation and gives rise to political tensions between peoples; it is contrary to the fundamental principles of international law and, consequently, seriously disturbs international peace and security."
>
> *(Declaration on Race and Racial Prejudice, 1978, art. 2)*

Discrimination based on a person's race or ethnic origin is one of the earliest discrimination grounds acknowledged in international human rights law. It was included as one of the protected grounds in the UDHR as well as in the ICCPR and ICESCR. Furthermore, in 1965, the UN General Assembly adopted the International Convention on the Elimination of All Forms of Racial Discrimination (Race Convention) strengthening the position of race and ethnic origin as a protected class. The Race Convention enjoys considerable international support, with 181 state parties to the Convention. Racial discrimination is in the Convention defined as:

> any distinction, exclusion, restriction or preference based on race, colour, descent, or national or ethnic origin, which has the purpose of effect of nullifying or impairing the recognition, enjoyment or exercise, on an equal footing, of human rights and fundamental freedoms in the political, economic, social cultural or any other field of public life.
>
> *(National Convention on the Elimination of All Forms of Racial Discrimination, 1966, art.1)*

Distinctions made between citizens and non-citizens are not covered by the definition. Also, the Race Convention explicitly allows states to implement affirmative action measures, to ensure that certain racial or ethnic groups can equally enjoy human rights and fundamental freedoms (art. 1).

It is well established that some groups are more vulnerable to and experience a higher rate of discrimination based solely on their race or ethnic origin. People of African and Asian descent have for centuries been victims of racism and racial discrimination (see Box 8.1). According to the U.N. Durban Declaration, people of African and Asian descent still "face barriers as a result of social biases and discrimination prevailing in public and private institutions" in many parts of the world (World Conference against Racism, Racial Discrimination, Xenophobia and Related Intolerance, 2001, ¶35–36).

BOX 8.1 CASE STUDY: SOUTH AFRICA

One of the most known examples of institutional racial discrimination is the apartheid system in force in South Africa until 1992. The origins of the apartheid system can be traced back to the Dutch East India company, which founded a settlement in Cape Town, South Africa, as a trade outpost between the Netherlands and the East Indies more than 350 years ago. The settlement was populated by Dutch ancestors of the present-day Afrikaners. During the following years, Afrikaners gained near complete economic and political power in the territory of South Africa and a system of racial segregation begun. The Natives Land Act of 1913 forced black South Africans to live in segregated settlements, later in the 1950s divided into ten "homelands" or "Bantustans", to prevent them from interacting with white Afrikaners. The homelands were either independent or self-governing entities inside South Africa. They consisted of approximately 13% of the land area, although black South Africans were the majority population of the country (see for example Hall, 2014). Furthermore, the land allotted for the homelands was of poor agricultural quality, why many black South Africans had to leave their homelands and work in the mines, as house maids or with other non-skilled work in the areas allocated for whites in South Africa. The racial segregation policies were incorporated under a system of legislation called apartheid, when the Afrikaner-dominated National Party gained power in South Africa in 1948. The goal was to separate whites from non-whites as well as to separate the black majority population along tribal lines. All mixed-race relationships were prohibited, and the government established separate public facilities for whites and non-whites. Resistance to the apartheid system grew during the 20th century both domestically and at the international level. The United Nations introduced several sanctions, such as an oil embargo in 1963, a mandatory arms embargo in 1977, as well as suspension of cultural, educational, sporting and other exchanges with the racist regime in 1968. After increased pressure on the South African regime in the 1980s, reforms were introduced inside the country, culminating in the abolition of the apartheid system in 1994, when a new constitution, embracing equality, took effect.

According to research undertaken by Grundligh (2006), the tourism market in South Africa consisted mainly of whites from neighbouring countries until the late 1950s. In the 1960s, with the advancement of air transportation, there was an increase of overseas tourism, with the government focusing on high-income tourists, instead of mass market tourism. Part of the reasoning was that mass market tourism might have sparked social incidents, when tourists unintentionally breached apartheid regulations. In the 1970s, the government increased its efforts to attract all types of tourists, from high-income to mass market tourists. Up until the mid-1970s, the apartheid system did not seem to have any significant effect on the willingness of tourists to experience the wildlife, sunshine, beaches and mountains of the country. In fact, South Africa had an increase of 11.4 per cent arrivals for the period 1965 to 1970, while the world showed a 7.2 per cent growth rate. From the mid-1970s and onwards, domestic as well as international pressure against the apartheid regime grew more vocal, which had an effect on tourist arrivals. The tourism industry did not experience the same type of exponential growth as earlier from the mid-1970s and onwards. However, a steady flow of overseas tourists continued to visit the country during the later years of apartheid. A distinct feature of domestic tourism from the mid-1970s and onwards was the promotion of casino-gaming resorts in the homelands. After awarding "independence" to certain homeland areas, the South African government wanted to wean them off revenue dependency from white South Africa by allowing the building of casino resorts (Crush and Wellings, 1983; Rogerson, 2015). Tourists were lured by gambling, pornographic films and multiracial prostitution, which was allowed in the homelands but forbidden in white South Africa (Grundligh, 2006).

Black tourism in South Africa was severely restricted by discriminatory legislation during the apartheid era. Black tourists were systematically denied access to hotels, beaches, hiking trails and had to use separate public facilities. There were very few tourist facilities geared towards the black population (Grundlingh, 2006). Although the tourism industry in South Africa abandoned its segregation policies when the apartheid system was abolished in 1994, challenges in ensuring black participation in the tourism industry still exist, although such challenges are now based on socio-economic marginalization, rather than racist government policies (Goudie, Khan and Kilian, 1999; Rogerson, 2015).

At the national level, many countries have domestic legislation prohibiting racial and ethnic origin discrimination. The United States has a long history with racial discrimination. Although the United States Constitution outlawed slavery (U.S. Const. 13th amendment, 1865), provided for the equal protection of laws (U.S. Const. 14th amendment, 1868) and the right to vote irrespective of race, colour or previous condition of servitude (U.S. Const. 15th amendment, 1870) in the second half of the 19th century, states continued to segregate persons based on race.

> In 1896, the Supreme Court tried a case concerning the right of states to continue providing separate but equal facilities to persons of different races (Plessy v. Ferguson, 1896). In the case, a statute in the state of Louisiana required railway companies to provide equal but separate accommodations for the "white and colored races." No person was permitted to occupy seats in coaches other than the ones assigned to the race they belonged to. Plessy, a person of mixed descent, with "seven eighths Caucasian and one eighth African blood" was forcibly moved from a carriage assigned to the "white race" and charged with criminally violating the Louisiana segregation act. The Supreme Court upheld the Louisiana law, stating that "[l]egislation is powerless to eradicate racial instincts or to abolish distinctions based upon physical differences, and the attempt to do so can only result in accentuating the difficulties of the present situation. If the civil and political rights of both races be equal, one cannot be inferior to the other civilly or politically. If one race be inferior to the other socially, the Constitution of the United States cannot put them upon the same plane" (p. 551–552). Plessy v. Ferguson was later overturned in Brown v. Board of Education of Topeka in 1954, where the Supreme Court held that separate public school for students of different races were in fact inherently unequal and a violation of the 14th amendment of the U.S. Constitution.

It was first in the 1960s that the United States received a comprehensive anti-discrimination legislation in the Civil Rights Act of 1964. According to section 201 of the Act "[a]ll persons shall be entitled to the full and equal enjoyment of the goods, services, facilities, privileges, advantages, and accommodations of any place of public accommodation, as defined in this section, without discrimination or segregation on the ground of race, colour, religion, or national origin." Public accommodations are in the Civil Rights Act (sec. 201) defined as any inn, hotel, motel or other establishment which provides lodging to transient guests, any restaurant, cafeteria or other facility principally engaged in selling food for consumption on premises as well as any movie theatre, concert hall, sports arena or other place of entertainment, when the operations of the establishment affect commerce, or if discrimination or segregation by it is supported by State action.

> In Heart of Atlanta Motel Inc. v. United States (1964), an owner of a large motel in Atlanta, Georgia restricted its clientele to white persons only. The owner contended that the prohibition on racial discrimination in places of public accommodation affecting commerce adopted in the Civil Rights Act

of 1964 exceeded Congress' powers to regulate interstate commerce. The challenge was based on the fact that the federal Congress can only regulate in certain matters enumerated in the U.S. Constitution, while states regulate all areas not left to the federal Congress in the U.S. Constitution. The Supreme Court held that the interstate movement of persons is "commerce", whether or not the transportation of persons between States is "commercial". Furthermore, the power of Congress to remove the disruptive effect of racial discrimination was not invalidated just because the Congress also considered racial discrimination to be a moral wrong. "How obstructions in commerce may be removed–what means are to be employed– is within the sound and exclusive discretion of the Congress. It is subject only to one caveat–that the means chosen by it must be reasonably adapted to the end permitted by the Constitution. We cannot say that its choice here was not so adapted. The Constitution requires no more" (p. 261–262). The Civil Rights Act of 1964 was thus upheld by the Supreme Court and still constitutes a fundamental part of United States anti-discrimination legislation.

In recent years, different activist groups in the United States, such as the well-known National Association for the Advancement of Colored People (NAACP) as well as chapters of the national movement of Black Lives Matter (focusing on police brutality as well as other racially motivated violence directed towards black persons) have issued travel advisories in an effort to bring attention to police brutality, hate crimes and discriminatory laws affecting non-Caucasian persons (NAACP, 2017; Black Lives Matter Minnesota, 2018; 2019).

In other parts of the world, similar legislation as in the United States exists, limiting discrimination based on race in public life. In Australia, the federal Racial Discrimination Act (RDA) of 1975 provides for similar safeguards as the U.S. Civil Rights Act. According to the RDA, it is unlawful for a person who supplies goods or services to the public to refuse or fail on demand to supply those goods on similar terms as he or she would otherwise have done, if the refusal or less favourable terms are by reason of race, colour or national or ethnic origin of the other person (sec. 13). The act also covers any other act involving a distinction, restriction or preference based on the abovementioned characteristics if it impairs the recognition, enjoyment or exercise of any human right in the political, economic, social or cultural field of public life (sec. 9).

Likewise, in the European Union, the Charter of Fundamental Rights (2000, art. 21) prohibits discrimination based on "sex, race, colour, ethnic or social origin, genetic features, language, religion or belief, political or other opinion, membership of a national minority, birth, disability, age or sexual orientation." In addition to the charter, which is addressed to the EU institutions and national authorities when they implement EU law, a directive on the principle of equal treatment between persons irrespective of racial or ethnic origin (Council directive 2000/43/EC, 2000) requires member states to put into place laws, regulations and administrative provisions necessary to ensure the principle of equal treatment. The directive applies to all persons, both in the public and private sectors, including in relation to access to and supply of goods and services available to the public (art. 3(1)(h)).

The anti-discrimination regulation covering race and ethnic origin has often been adopted earlier and is more wide-reaching than anti-discrimination legislation protecting several other vulnerable groups. For example, when the Civil Rights Act in the United States was enacted, it covered discrimination based on race, colour, religion or national origin both in relation to access to and supply of goods and services as well as in an employment context, while discrimination based on sex was only covered in an employment context (compare Civil Rights Act sec. 703 with sec. 201). Similarly, the European Union directive against discrimination on grounds of race and ethnic origin (Directive 2000/43/EC, 2000) applies to all persons, and covers both access to employment as well as access to and supply of goods and services available to the public, while the Directive 2000/78/EC (2000), covering discrimination on grounds of religion or belief, disability, age or sexual orientation, only applies in the employment context. Both the fact that anti-discrimination legislation covering race and ethnic origin was adopted early in history, as well as the reach of such legislation makes such legislation a fundamental part of anti-discrimination legislation.

Despite the longstanding legal protection from discrimination based on race, colour and ethnic origin both at the international and national level, it is clear that such discrimination is still persistent in society. A recent example is the COVID-19 pandemic, which has exposed xenophobia as well as led to scaremongering and anti-Asian hate crimes on a global scale. Although it is clear that the spread of the SARS-CoV-2 virus is not connected to any particular group of people, but affects everybody without discrimination, Chinese and other Asian origin persons are blamed for the spread of the virus in Europe, North America and Africa. There are several reported incidents of animosity, denial of services, hate crimes as well as orientalist and racist descriptions of Chinese and Asian origin persons in North America, Europe and Africa in connection with the COVID-19 pandemic (Human Rights Watch, 2020).

8.3 Discrimination in tourism establishments based on sex/gender

Women's rights and sex discrimination have long been on the global human rights agenda. Already in 1948, the UDHR included sex as one of the protected classes from discrimination (art. 2). Furthermore, both the ICCPR and ICESCR obligate state parties to ensure the equal right of men and women to the enjoyment of civil, political, economic, social and cultural rights (ICCPR, art. 3; ICESCR, art. 3). The International Bill of Rights was later complemented by a convention specifically addressing sex discrimination, the Convention on the Elimination of All Forms of Discrimination against Women (CEDAW), which was adopted in 1979 by the United Nations General Assembly. CEDAW has 189 countries as state parties to the convention, making it the second most widely ratified human rights convention after the Convention on the Rights of the Child. Countries that are parties to the Convention shall embody the principle of equality between men and women in their national legal systems, ensure the effective protection of women against discrimination and provide for a right to redress and sanctions where appropriate. Furthermore they shall take appropriate steps to eliminate all acts of discrimination by any person, organization or enterprise (art. 2). The Convention also recognizes culture and tradition as influential in shaping gender roles and family relations and requires state parties to take appropriate measures to:

> modify the social and cultural patterns of conduct of men and women, with a view to achieving the elimination of prejudices and customary and all other practices which are based on the idea of the inferiority or the superiority of either of the sexes or stereotyped roles for men and women.
> *(Convention on the Elimination of All Forms of Discrimination against Women, art. 5)*

Although most countries in the world are parties to the Convention, many countries have made reservations to the Convention or do not follow through on the obligations to assure equality of men and women and prevent discrimination of women. On a global scale, women still face many challenges in their daily life, and are discriminated against solely based on their gender.

> A lawsuit against Starwood Hotels & Resorts (A.F. v. Starwood Hotels and Resorts Worldwide, 2012) illustrates the potential for sexual harassment women face when travelling alone (there is no publicly available judgment in the case, why the case may have been dismissed or settled). According to the complaint: "On January 15, 2011, Plaintiff A…F…–an accomplished investment banker and Princeton University and Harvard Business School graduate–was sexually assaulted inside her locked Starwood hotel room. The perpetrator had not broken the lock to get into her room. Ms. F… had not opened the door for him. Instead, he had been handed the key by the desk clerk just moments before at the four-star hotel marketed under the renowned Starwood brand–which caters to and lures high-end business travellers–in blatant violation of the most basic security protocols. As a direct result of the assault, Ms. F…'s life and career unravelled. She was unable to return to work as a banker, feeling unsafe in the most ordinary circumstances. This action seeks to redress Starwood Hotel and Resorts Worldwide Inc.'s gross violations of its obligations to Ms. F… as its guest and customer, and to ensure that professional women travelling for business are not subjected to such gross negligence in the future" (see also Marchionda v. Embassy Suites, 2018, with similar facts, settled out of court).

In the provision of goods and services in the tourism sector, women can be denied service in all-male drinking clubs, refused entry to certain entertainment venues geared towards "gentlemen" as well as receive inferior service or experience sexual harassment in the provision of services. It is also common that the issue of sex discrimination rises in an employment context, something which is covered more in depth in Chapter 10. However, women may also receive preferential treatment in the hospitality sector. It is a common practice in many jurisdictions to market bars and dancing establishments with promotions for "ladies' nights" and similar marketing campaigns, letting women enter the establishment without a cover charge or allowing them to buy discounted drinks at the bar.

> In Maclean v. the Barking Frog (2013), a Canadian case from the Human Rights Tribunal of Ontario, a young man, K.M., stated that he was asked to pay a higher cover charge than the females in the group at a local bar. He argued that by charging men twice what was being charged to women, the bar was perpetuating a belief in society that men are less worthy than women and that a higher cover charge for men discouraged them from entering the bar and made them feel excluded and unwelcome. The Human Rights Tribunal of Ontario dismissed the case stating that "[t]here are many things that could be said about societal beliefs in Ontario, but the notion that men are less worthy than women is not among them. In fact, the entire history of gender discrimination in this province reveals the opposite." The tribunal continued with noting that the purpose of ladies' nights is not to exclude men. Instead, the primary function of ladies' nights is to try to increase the attendance of men because of the presence of more women. Thus, there was no substantive discrimination in the overall societal context, considering the privileged position that men hold in the society.

Despite the ladies' night ruling of the Human Rights Tribunal of Ontario, the marketing of tourism and hospitality enterprises to a specific sex is bound to raise difficult issues of the application of discrimination laws. As an example of a different outcome, the Bella Sky Comwell in Copenhagen, Denmark lost a lawsuit on discrimination grounds when it offered a female-only hotel floor, with 20 rooms out of the hotel's total 812 rooms dedicated to female travellers (Bella Sky Comwell, 2014 see also Koire v. Metro Car Wash, 1985, where discounts and free admission offered to women by a nightclub and a carwash were considered discriminatory). The hotel was forced to open up the female-only floor to both female and male guests of the hotel.

8.4 Discrimination in tourism establishments based on sexual orientation or gender identity

> *As nought diff'rent can make me,*
> *As I am thou must take me!*
> *If I'm not good enough,*
> *Thou must cut thine own stuff,*

> *As nought diff'rent can make me,*
> *As I am thou must take me!*
> (Goethe, 1885, p. 15)

The lesbian, gay, bisexual, transgender, queer and other sexuality and gender identity communities (LGBTQ+), who do not identify themselves as part of the heterosexual cisgender community, have long faced discrimination all around the world. The United Nations High Commissioner for Human Rights noted as late as in 2011 that homophobic and transphobic crimes had been reported in all regions of the world. Violence against the LGBTQ+ community may be physical (including murder, torture and rape) or psychological (threats and coercion). The LGBTQ+ population may be subject to unprovoked violent attacks on the street or more organized violence by right-wing groups or religious extremists. Such violence tends to be particularly vicious, showing a high degree of cruelty and hate.

At the national level, many countries maintain laws criminalizing same-sex sexual relations between consenting adults as well as other discriminatory laws penalizing the LGBTQ+ community. However, there has also been progress in the last decades. For example, since 2000, laws criminalizing homosexual acts between consenting adults have been repealed in Armenia, Azerbaijan, Bosnia and Hercegovina, Cape Verde, Georgia, Fiji, India, the Marshall Islands, Nepal, Nicaragua and Panama (United Nations High Commissioner for Human Rights, 2011, ¶43). In the United States, the United States Supreme Court held in Lawrence v. Texas (2003) that state laws criminalizing sexual contact between consenting adults in private violated the constitutional right to privacy, thus overruling Bowers v. Hardwick (1986), its own previous ruling from 1986, where it held that the constitution did not confer a "fundamental right to engage in homosexual sodomy" (p. 191).

In the tourism and hospitality industry, discrimination based on sexual orientation can affect both employees as well as customers. Many countries have during the last decades expanded their national discrimination laws to cover discrimination of LGBTQ+ persons in an employment setting (see Chapter 10). However, it is less clear what kind of protection is afforded to persons who are discriminated against based on sexual orientation or gender identity when it comes to access to and supply of goods and services available to the public.

> In United States, courts have long adhered to a 1990 Supreme Court case (Employment Division, Department of Human Resources of Oregon v. Smith, 1990), involving two defendants who worked as drug rehabilitation counsellors. Both of them had smoked peyote, a powerful drug prohibited by the state of Oregon's drug laws and as a result of the use were fired by the drug rehabilitation organization. When they filed a claim for unemployment benefits, their claim was denied, based on the fact that their dismissal was work-related misconduct. The two employees claimed that the decision

violated their constitutional right under the First Amendment to freely exercise their religion. Both of the defendants were members of the Native American Church and had ingested the drug as part of a religious ceremony. The Supreme Court held that a religious motivation did not constitute a valid excuse to not obey generally applicable laws that did not specifically target the exercise of a religion. The peyote case was believed to be applicable to persons who on religious grounds discriminated against LGBTQ+ persons. However, when same-sex marriages where increasingly recognized at the state-level in the United States in the early 2000s (the Supreme Court of the United States recognized in Obergefell v. Hodges, 2015, that the right to marry is a fundamental right guaranteed to same-sex couples in all fifty states), many LGBTQ+ couples became aware that they were refused services connected to the wedding ceremony.

In 2018, the U.S. Supreme Court considered a case (Masterpiece Cakeshop Ltd. v. Colorado Civil Rights Commission, 2018), where the right to be free from disparate treatment on grounds of sexual orientation was in conflict with the right to free exercise of religion (Free Exercise Clause). In 2012, a same-sex couple, C.C. and D.M., visited Masterpiece Cakeshop, a bakery in Colorado, owned by J.P., a devout Christian. One of J.P.'s beliefs was that God's intention for marriage from the beginning of history was that it is and should be the union of man and woman. When C.C. and D.M asked him to bake a wedding cake for them, J.P. explained that he does not create wedding cakes for same-sex weddings, although he could sell them other cakes on offer in the store. He later explained his belief that to create wedding cake that "directly goes against the teachings of the Bible, would have been a personal endorsement and participation in the ceremony and relationship that they were entering into". According to the Colorado Anti-Discrimination Act it was a discriminatory practice to deny the full and equal enjoyment of goods and services in places of public accommodation because of a disability, race, creed, colour, sex, sexual orientation, marital status, national origin, or ancestry. The Colorado Court of Appeals affirmed the order from the Colorado Civil Rights Commission, according to which the Colorado Anti-Discrimination Law did not violate the Free Exercise Clause and J.P. was to cease and desist discriminating against same-sex couples by refusing to sell them wedding cakes. J.P. sought review in the U.S. Supreme Court, which stated that J.P. was entitled to a neutral and respectful consideration of his claims. In this case, a neutral review was compromised by the treatment of the case by the Civil Rights Commission, which showed hostility to J.P.'s religious beliefs. For example, the Commission described J.P.'s views as "one of the most despicable pieces of rhetoric that people can use–to use religion to hurt others." Also, the Civil Rights Division had on at least three other occasions determined that bakers acted lawfully when they refused to bake cakes that conveyed disapproval of same-sex marriages, treating similar cases differently. The Supreme Court held that the Commission's hostility was inconsistent with the constitutional guarantee that laws be applied in a manner that is neutral towards religion and reversed the Colorado Court of Appeals judgment, thus allowing for bakeries to refuse to bake wedding cakes for same-sex couples. It did however state that a case against a baker that refused to sell *any* cakes for a gay wedding would be a different matter and that the State would have a strong case that it would be a denial of goods and services. The Court concluded by stating that *"[t]he outcome of cases like this in other circumstances must await further elaboration in the courts, all in the context of recognizing that these disputes must be resolved with tolerance, without undue disrespect to sincere religious beliefs, and without subjecting gay persons to indignities when they seek goods and services in an open market"*.

There are several similar undecided cases in the courts in the United States at the moment. In Klein v. Oregon Bureau of Labor and Industries (2019) a couple refused to bake a wedding cake to a same-sex couple, on the basis of their sincerely held religious beliefs. The case was remanded back to the Oregon state courts by the Supreme Court of the United States in June 17, 2019 for reconsideration in light of Masterpiece Cakeshop. Similarly, in State of Washington v. Arlene's Flowers Inc. (2019) a flower shop refused to provide floral arrangements to celebrate a same-sex wedding ceremony. The Supreme Court of Washington held that the flower shop had discriminated the same-sex couple, but the case is still pending after the flower shop filed a petition to the U.S. Supreme Court to hear the case. It is thus at the moment unclear if religious concerns can be invoked as a defence to a discrimination charge. A recent decision by the U.S. Supreme Court (Bostock v. Clayton County, Georgia, 2020) prohibiting sexual orientation discrimination in employment on the basis that it is sex discrimination, might have an impact on the provision of goods and services (see Chapter 10). On the other hand, since the Civil Rights Act only covers sex discrimination in employment, and not in the provision of public services, the issue is likely to be further litigated in the U.S. courts.

At the same time as the majority of Western countries have made great strides towards full equality in all spheres of public life for the LGBTQ+ community, matters are much worse in other parts of the world. For LGBTQ+ persons living in those countries the "wedding cake battles" of United States are trivial, compared to the oppression in their home countries. In March 2019, 70 UN member states (35 per cent) criminalized consensual sexual acts between individuals of the same sex. Six UN member states impose the death penalty on consensual same-sex sexual acts. In Africa, Asia and the Middle East, the majority of countries criminalize same-sex relations between consenting adults (Mendos, 2019, pp. 15, 179). Many gay cruise lines avoid certain destinations for fear of homophobic attitudes and violence towards, and police arrest and temporary custody of their patrons (Skelly Gilmer, 2012). However, there are signs that at least some of these countries are reconsidering the criminalization of the LGBTQ+ community. In 2018, the India Supreme Court decriminalized all sexual conduct between consenting adults, including between persons of the same sex, holding that the Indian penal code, which in effect criminalized sexual relationships between same-sex couples, violated the constitutional guarantees of liberty and equality (Navtej Singh Johar v. Union of India, 2018). Similarly, the African countries Mozambique (2015), Angola (2019) and Botswana (2019) have recently decriminalized consensual sexual acts between same-sex couples.

8.5 Discrimination in tourism establishment based on religious orientation

In addition to race, ethnic origin, national origin and sex discrimination, discrimination based on religion has long been included in anti-discrimination legislation, both internationally and at the national level. It was included in the 1948 UDHR (art. 2, 18) as well as the ICCPR (art. 18).

> Everyone shall have the right to freedom of thought, conscience and religion. This right shall include freedom to have or to adopt a religion or belief of his choice, and freedom, either individually or in community with others and in public or private, to manifest his religions of belief in worship, observance, practice and teaching.
>
> *(ICCPR, art. 18)*

In 1981, the UN General Assembly adopted the Declaration on the Elimination of All Forms of Intolerance and of Discrimination Based on Religion or Belief. At the national level, discrimination based on religious orientation was included in early anti-discrimination legislation, such as the Civil Rights Act in the United States (sec. 201, sec. 703).

In Western Europe and North America, the divisive question of public displays of religious symbols has during recent years become a topical question. According to the ICCPR:

> [f]reedom to manifest one's religion or beliefs may be subject only to such limitations as are prescribed by law and are necessary to protect public safety, order, health, or morals of the fundamental rights and freedoms of others.
>
> *(ICCPR, art. 18)*

In the summer of 2016, several towns in France passed ordinances prohibiting access to beaches and swimming places to all persons without a correct dress adapted to laicity standards, hygiene rules and security concerns. The ordinances were adopted after the Nice terrorist attacks on July 14th, 2016, and in effect banned the "burkini," a body covering swimwear popular among the Muslim population of the country. The *Conseil d'État*, the highest administrative court in France, however held that the ordinances encompassed serious infringements on the right of mobility as well as the freedom of conscience. French courts have either suspended or only upheld the ordinances for a limited time on public security grounds in municipalities where there were documented security concerns connected to women in burkinis on public beaches (see *Conseil d'État*, 2016; where the court suspended a burkini ban in the seaside resort of Villeneuve-Loubet, on the grounds that there was no evidence of public disturbances caused by the attire worn by certain people while swimming; compare with the appellate court judgment of *Cour Administrative d'Appel de Marseille*, 2017, upholding the ordinance of the city of Sisco after an incident where the local police had to avert a lynching by locals of three families where the women wore a "burka"/"hijab" to the beach).

In North America, the National Assembly of Quebec, a Canadian province, recently passed a law prohibiting employees at public bodies, such as government departments, municipalities, public transit authorities, school boards as well as public institutions providing health and social services from wearing religious symbols in the workplace. In addition, the law mandates that they exercise their functions with their face uncovered. Persons presenting themselves to receive a service from a covered body must also have their face uncovered, where it is necessary to allow their identity to be verified or for security reasons (Act respecting the laicity of the State, 2019). It remains to be seen if the Quebec law is upheld in courts, when challenged on human rights grounds.

8.6 Discrimination in tourism establishments based on disability

There are an estimated one billion persons, consisting of 15 per cent of the world's population, that experience some form of disability. Nearly 200 million persons have considerable difficulties in functioning. In the coming years, these numbers are set to rise due to ageing populations and more advanced health care enabling persons with disabilities to live longer. People with disabilities are more often poor, they have lower education and worse health outcomes. These outcomes are exacerbated in the developing world, where a majority of the disabled people live (World Health Organization and World Bank, 2011).

The World Health Organization (2001) defines in its International Classification of Functioning, Disability and Health (ICF) disability as a difficulty encountered in any or all of three areas: impairments in body functions (for example seeing, hearing, pain), activity and participation limitations (difficulty communicating, moving around, washing oneself or eating) or limitations due to environmental factors (features and attitudes in the environment that can either lower or raise the capacity to participate in society, such as products and technology for personal use, communication technology or attitudes by family members, health care professionals or strangers). A disability is thus an umbrella term for impairments of bodily functions and activity and participation limitations, with environmental factors and personal characteristics, such as motivation or self-esteem, that interact with the other components.

Although disability was mentioned as early as in 1948 in international human rights law (UDHR, art. 25), it was first in the late 1960s that the international community recognized more widely that the society creates barriers to the full participation in society by disabled persons. In the 1960s and 1970s, the emphasis shifted from separation of disabled persons, to inclusion and participation on equal basis with other groups in the community (United Nations, 2019, pp. 23–24). A key milestone in the development of the rights of disabled persons is the adoption of the Convention on the Rights of Persons with Disabilities (CRPD) in 2006. The CRPD has gained near universal support, with 177 state parties to the Convention. More recently, the General Assembly of the United Nations pledged in the 2030 Agenda for Sustainable Development (2015) to empower and promote the social and economic and political inclusion of all, including persons with disabilities (goal 10.2, p. 21).

Discrimination based on a disability in the tourism industry can affect persons applying for employment, persons employed in the sector as well as tourists visiting tourism establishments. According to the CRPD, parties to the Convention undertake to adopt all appropriate laws to implement the rights recognized in the Convention (art. 4), such as prohibiting discrimination on the basis of disability. The CRPD obligates state parties to ensure persons with disabilities get access, on equal basis with others, to the physical environment, including ensuring that private entities with facilities and services open to or provided to the public take into account accessibility for persons with disabilities (art. 9).

Tourism enterprises, such as restaurants, hotels, movie theatres and sports arenas, are generally covered by national legislation prohibiting discrimination. For example, in the United States, the Americans with Disabilities Act of 1990 (ADA) prohibits discrimination in places of public accommodation, including restaurants, bars, theatres, concert halls, convention centres, museums, parks, zoos, amusements parks, health spas, golf courses as well as hotels, motels and inns. Discrimination includes the imposition of eligibility criteria that screens out individuals with disabilities, the failure to make reasonable modifications in policies, practices or procedures, a failure to take the steps necessary to ensure that a person with a disability is not excluded and a failure to remove architectural barriers, where such removal is readily achievable (§12182(b)(2)(A)).

Some examples on how a tourism enterprise can take into account people with disabilities are provided by the United States Code of Federal Regulations (CFR), which is supplementing ADA (2020). Public accommodations must allow mobility devices, such as walkers, wheelchairs (see Chapter 9), canes and crutches on premises, unless a business can demonstrate legitimate safety concerns based on actual risks. They must also allow a disabled person to bring his or her service animal to premises, even if a business has a "no pets" policy. Businesses may ask for credible assurances that a service animal or a mobility device is needed by the customer, but it is not permissible to ask individuals about the nature and extent of their disability. Furthermore, businesses are required to take steps in an effort to communicate effectively with customers with vision, hearing and speech impairments. Also, a business must remove barriers, when it can be done without much difficulty. The requirements are based on the size and resources of the business, with higher expectations placed on multinational corporations compared with small enterprises. Examples of readily achievable barrier removal include installing entrance ramps, widening doorways or moving tables to provide for accessible seating in a restaurant. New facilities must be constructed in such a manner that they are readily accessible to individuals with disabilities. Similar requirements as in the United States exist in other countries with disability discrimination legislation.

8.7 Discrimination in tourism establishments and conflicts between different principles

Legislation is generally based on the territoriality principle, letting each country adopt laws in the territory they control. Tourism on the other hand is often transcending national boundaries. This creates an inherent conflict between the laws of different countries, which is a difficult problem to solve for tourism establishments operating at a global level. On the one hand, tourism establishments are obligated to follow the laws of the country where the operations are based, but on the other hand, this sometimes means that they have to break the law in their own country of origin, or the country where the tourists originate from.

An interesting example is the conflict created by the travel, export and trading prohibitions of the Trading with the Enemy Act 2018. The law was introduced in the United States during the First World War and gives the President the power to restrict all trade between the U.S. and its enemies. As of 2019, the U.S. embargoes trade with Cuba, including banning tourism travel and export of goods. The embargo is broadly constructed, including financial transactions between any person subject to U.S. jurisdiction and any person who acts on behalf of the Cuban military, intelligence or other person on the State Department's "Cuba Restricted List", when the U.S. entity is either the originator or the ultimate beneficiary of the transaction (31 C.F.R. § 515.209). The embargo on Cuba has an effect on cruise vessels, airplanes and other travel providers, since travel to Cuba is severely restricted. Furthermore, U.S.-owned hotels are affected, since they are prohibited from engaging in financial transactions with persons on the "Cuba Restricted List." This can sometimes lead to conflicts with other countries' anti-discrimination laws.

> In 2006, Cuban officials were meeting with representatives of American oil companies at Sheraton Maria Isabel Hotel & Towers, in Mexico City, Mexico. The hotel was at the time owned by Starwood Hotels and Resorts Worldwide, an American company organized at the time under the laws of Maryland (Starwood Hotels, 2006). Since the hotel was owned by a U.S. company, they had to follow the federal laws imposing a trade embargo with Cuba. When the U.S. Treasury Department's Office of Foreign Asset Control contacted the company, the hotel expelled the 16 Cuban representatives and sent the guest deposits to the U.S. Treasury Department.

The incident caused an international controversy, with demonstrations outside the hotel as well as Mexican government officials threatening to fine or close the hotel, for violations of legislation prohibiting the discrimination based on national origin.

(McKinley Jr., 2006)

Many countries consider the U.S. unilateral sanctions against certain countries to be contrary to international law and have adopted blocking measures to counter any fines imposed by U.S. courts. The European Union has for example adopted legislation introducing retaliatory measures allowing companies sued in the U.S. to recover any damages in the European Union courts (Council Regulation 2271/96, 1996).

The inconsistent laws of the country where the corporation is incorporated, and the destination country, can both cause business risks for a tourism establishment as well as lead to ethical dilemmas. An example is the restrictive laws on sexual acts between consenting adults of the same sex in some countries, which can lead to conflicts with other countries' anti-discrimination laws. In North America and Europe, all countries have decriminalized consensual sexual acts between same sex adults. As mentioned above, many states have in addition to decriminalizing sexual acts, protected sexual orientation under anti-discrimination legislation. However, same-sex sexual relations were in 2019 still banned in 33 African states, 21 Asian states, 6 states in the Oceania and 9 Latin American states. In some countries the penalties amount to lengthy prison terms, lashes, caning or the death penalty (Mendos, 2019, pp. 197–202; see Chapter 1). Another example is the conflicting norms on gender orientation. Some countries allow persons to identify their gender as unspecified in their passports, while this might not be accepted in other countries.

> The Government of Canada states in its travel advisory for LGBTQ+ persons: "If you identify your gender as "X" in your passport, or if your Canadian passport has an observation indicating "the sex of the bearer should read as X, indicating that it is unspecified, check with the Embassy, High Commission of consulate of all the countries you intend to visit or transit through to enquire about their entry requirements."
>
> *(Government of Canada, 2020)*

It is difficult for a tourism enterprise to navigate the legal landscape, when they are located in countries banning anti-discrimination, while at the same time advising customers of the discriminatory legislation in the destination countries they market. The state departments in some countries post information specific for LGBTQ+ communities, warning about local laws criminalizing LGBTQ+ activities, but this is not common practice in all countries with anti-discrimination legislation covering sexual orientation. Tourism enterprises usually refer to the official information available by the country of origin state departments, but do not have any stated policies of how to deal with such situations.

8.8 Conclusion

Great strides have been made in achieving full equality for all humankind. During the 20th century, the right to be free from discrimination has been established as a fundamental human right. Most countries have in addition to ratifying international human rights conventions on the subject implemented legislation providing protection from discrimination at the national level. The extent of actual protection for different vulnerable groups however varies depending on resources as well as cultural norms. According to international human rights law, all persons have the right to the full enjoyment of all human rights, without any discrimination. However, at the national level, despite the positive trajectory in legislation protecting different groups, there still exist state-sponsored discrimination and discriminatory attitudes in the tourism sector as well among the general population. The COVID-19 pandemic in particular has shown that discriminatory attitudes towards Asian people are still, despite anti-racism legislation, prevalent in society. Also, the Black Lives Matter movement has highlighted systematic racism towards African-origin persons in many societies. The tourism and travel sector is not immune to such attitudes in the society, and there is a concern that racial stereotypes and attitudes prevent certain groups of people from the full enjoyment of tourism and travel services.

Discrimination based on sex is similarly to race and ethnic origin discrimination prohibited according to international human rights law. In recent years, the overt discrimination of women customers in the travel and hospitality industry is becoming less common. However, new challenges have emerged. It is questionable if gender-segregated services, such as women-only hotel rooms, are in accordance with the prohibition of discrimination based on sex. The issue becomes even more complicated if other public accommodations, such as public pools with women-only swimming hours, are discussed from a sex/gender discrimination perspective. Discrimination legislation at the national level is necessary interpreted in different cultural and societal contexts, which is certain to affect the outcome of such discussions.

Discrimination affecting the LGBTQ+ community is differing from the other discrimination grounds in that there is no international human rights convention specifically addressing such discrimination. Instead, legislation prohibiting discrimination of LGBTQ+ communities has mainly evolved in a national setting. As noted in this chapter, there are still substantial differences in the protection offered to LGBTQ+ persons in different countries. In recent decades, the public opinion in the Western world has become more and more supportive of LGBTQ+ rights, which is reflected in added legal protections for the LGBTQ+ community. Major strides have also been made in other parts of the world, such as in India. However, there still exist discriminatory laws and policies in many countries and the travel patterns of the LGBTQ+ community are in practice severely restricted by the hostile environment existing in many parts of the world. The rights of the LGBTQ+ community have in particular been hampered by persons objecting to the full enjoyment of such rights based on religious grounds. In this chapter, several court cases have illustrated the difficult balance between two fundamental human rights, the right to freedom of religion and the right to live a life free from discrimination. It is too early to say how the conflict between these two competing human rights is going to be solved in the context of provision of travel and hospitality services, but it should be noted that most human rights are qualified, as opposed to absolute rights, and restrictions can be placed on such rights.

Freedom of religion is a fundamental right, which was included in the core human rights promulgated in the UDHR. Despite the widespread acknowledgment of the right to freedom of religion as a core human right, there has in recent years been an increase of incidents where persons with religious symbols have been threatened and attacked. It is clear that the public opinion in many countries is hostile to the public displays of religious affiliation. This can be evidenced by the recent French local bans on burkinis as well as the Quebec ban on public displays of religious symbols. On a more positive note, persons with disabilities have in recent decades received added legal protection, both at the national level as well as in an international convention condemning discrimination based on disability. It is no longer a public policy to separate persons with disabilities and keep them hidden and away from public spaces. Instead, persons with disabilities have in recent decades, at least in more economically advanced countries, gained the right to full enjoyment of public spaces, including services in the travel and hospitality sector. It is a solemn hope that similar opportunities can in the future be afforded to disabled persons in the developing world, where most disabled persons live.

References

Act respecting the laicity of the State, 2019, R.S.Q., c. L-0.3 (Can.).
A.F. v. Starwood Hotels & Resorts Worldwide Inc., Complaint filed in the United States District Court, Southern District of New York, 12 CV 0148 (Jan. 12, 2012).
Alderman, D., 2013. Introduction to the Special Issue: African Americans and Tourism. *Tourism Geographies*, 15(3), pp. 375–379.
Americans with Disabilities Act of 1990, 42 U.S.C. §12101–12213 (2018).
Bella Sky Comwell, 2014. Østre Landsret (Apr. 2014) (Den.).
Black Lives Matter Minnesota, 2018. *Travel Alert St. Paul, February 1st, 2018* [Facebook]. 20 June. Available at: <www.facebook.com/BlackLivesMatterMN/posts/991568424325891> [Accessed 20 June 2020].
Black Lives Matter Minnesota, 2019. *Travel Warning St. Paul, April, 2019* [Facebook]. 20 June. Available at: <www.facebook.com/BlackLivesMatterMN/posts/black-lives-matters-minnesota-issues-st-paul-travel-warningapril-6-2019-having-b/1284375205045210/> [Accessed 20 June 2020].
Bostock v. Clayton County, Georgia, No. 17–1618 (June 15, 2020).
Bowers v. Hardwick, 478 U.S. 186 (1986).

Brown v. Board of Education of Topeka, 347 U.S. 483 (1954).

Charter of Fundamental Rights of the European Union, 2000. *Official Journal*, C364, pp. 1–22. [online]. Available at: <www.europarl.europa.eu/charter/pdf/text_en.pdf> [Accessed 24 June 2020].

Civil Rights Act of 1964, Pub. L. No. 88–352, 78 Stat. 241 (codified as amended in 42 U.S.C. 2000a–h-6).

Code of Federal Regulations, 28 CFR § 36.301–311 (2020).

Conseil d'État, N° 402742, Aug. 26, 2016, ECLI:FR:CEORD:2016:402742.20160826.

Convention on the Elimination of All Forms of Discrimination against Women, Dec. 18, 1979, 1249 U.N.T.S 13.

Convention on the Rights of Persons with Disabilities, Dec. 13, 2006, 2515 U.N.T.S. 3.

Council Directive 2000/43/EC of 29 June 2000 implementing the principle of equal treatment between persons irrespective of racial or ethnic origin, 2000. *Official Journal*, L180, pp. 22–26. [online]. Available at: <https://eur-lex.europa.eu/legal-content/EN/TXT/PDF/?uri=CELEX:32000L0043&from=GA> [Accessed June 25 2020].

Council Directive 2000/78/EC of 27 November 2000 establishing a general framework for equal treatment in employment and occupation. *Official Journal*, L303, pp. 16–22. [online]. Available at: <https://eur-lex.europa.eu/legal-content/EN/TXT/PDF/?uri=CELEX:32000L0078&from=EN> [Accessed June 25 2020].

Council Regulation (EC) No. 2271/96 of 22 November 1996 protecting against the effects of the extra-territorial application of legislation adopted by a third country, and actions based thereon or resulting therefrom. *Official Journal*, L309, pp. 1–6. [online]. Available at: <https://eur-lex.europa.eu/legal-content/EN/TXT/PDF/?uri=CELEX:01996R2271-20180807&from=EN> [Accessed 25 June 2020].

Cour Administrative d'Appel de Marseille, N° 17MA01337, Jul. 3, 2017. Leave to appeal to the Conseil d'État denied on January 14th, 2018. Available at: <http://marseille.cour-administrative-appel.fr/content/download/104768/1049245/version/1/file/17MA01337%20arrêt.pdf> [Accessed 25 June 2020].

Crush, J. and Wellings, P., 1983. The Southern African Pleasure Periphery, 1966–83. *The Journal of Modern African Studies*, 21(4), pp. 673–698.

Declaration on Race and Racial Prejudice, UNESCO, 20th. Sess. (Nov. 27, 1978).

Declaration on the Elimination of All Forms of Intolerance and of Discrimination Based on Religion or Belief, G.A. Res. 36/55, U.N. Doc. A/RES/36/55 (Nov. 25, 1981).

Employment Division, Department of Human Resources of Oregon v. Smith, 494 U.S. 872 (1990).

Goethe, J.W., 1885. Lover in All Shapes. In: Goethe, J.W., (ed.), *Goethe's Works, vol. 1 (Poems)*. Philadelphia: George Barrie.

Goudie, S. C., Khan, F. and Kilian, D., 1999. Transforming Tourism: Black Empowerment, Heritage and Identity Beyond Apartheid. *South African Geographical Journal*, 81(1), pp. 22–31.

Government of Canada, 2020. *Lesbian, gay, bisexual, transgender, queer and two-spirit Canadians abroad*. [online] 20 June. Available at: <www.travel.gc.ca/travelling/health-safety/lgbt-travel> [Accessed 20 June 2020].

Grundlingh, A., 2006. Revisiting the 'Old' South Africa: Excursions into South Africa's Tourist History under Apartheid 1948–1990. *South African Historical Journal*, 56(1), pp. 103–122.

Hall, R., 2014. The Legacies of the Natives Land Act of 1913. *Scriptura*, 1, pp. 1–13.

Heart of Atlanta Motel, Inc. v. United States, 379 U.S. 241 (1964).

Human Rights Watch, 2020. *Covid-19 Fueling Anti-Asian Racism and Xenophobia Worldwide*. [online]. Available at: <www.hrw.org/news/2020/05/12/covid-19-fueling-anti-asian-racism-and-xenophobia-worldwide> [Accessed 25 June 2020].

International Covenant on Civil and Political Rights, Dec. 16, 1966, 999 U.N.T.S. 171.

International Covenant on Economic, Social and Cultural Rights, Dec. 16, 1966, 993 U.N.T.S. 3.

International Convention on the Elimination of All Forms of Racial Discrimination, Mar. 7, 1966, 660 U.N.T.S. 195.

Klein v. Oregon Bureau of Labor and Industries, 139 S.Ct. 2713 (2019).

Koire v. Metro Car Wash, 40 Cal. 3d 24 (Cal. 1985).

Lawrence v. Texas, 539 U.S. 558 (2003).

Maclean v. The Barking Frog, 2013 HRTO 630 (Apr. 16, 2013).

Marchionda v. Embassy Suites Franchise, LLC, 359 F.Supp. 3d 681 (S.D. Iowa, 2018).

Martin D.C., 2004. Apartheid in the great outdoors: American advertising and the reproduction of a racialized outdoor leisure identity. *Journal of Leisure Research*, 36(4), pp. 513–535.

Masterpiece Cakeshop Ltd. v. Colorado Civil Rights Commission, 584 U.S. _ (2018).

McKinley, Jr., 2006. Mexico and Cuba Protest Hotel's Expulsion of Havana Delegation, *The New York Times*, 7 Feb. p. 11.

Mendos, L.R., 2019. *State-Sponsored Homophobia 2019 Global Legislation Overview Update. ILGA World*. [PDF] December. Available at: <https://ilga.org/downloads/ILGA_World_State_Sponsored_Homophobia_report_global_legislation_overview_update_December_2019.pdf> [Accessed 12 June 2020].

NAACP, 2017. *Travel Advisory for the State of Missouri, August 2, 2017*. [online]. Available at: <www.naacp.org/latest/travel-advisory-state-missouri/> [Accessed 20 June 2020].

Natives Land Act of 1913 (S. Afr.).

Navtej Singh Johar v. Union of India, 2018, W. P. (Crl.) No. 76 of 2016; D. No. 14961/2016.

Obergefell v. Hodges, 576 U.S. 644 (2015).

Plessy v. Ferguson, 163 U.S. 537 (1896).

Philipp, S., 1994. Race and tourism choice: legacy of discrimination? *Annals of Tourism Research*, 21(3), pp. 479–488.

Racial Discrimination Act of 1975 (Austl.).

Rogerson, C. M., 2015. Tourism and regional development: The case of South Africa's distressed areas. *Development Southern Africa*, 32(3), pp. 277–291.

Skelly Gilmer, S., 2012. Cruising for a Bruisin' When Cruise Lines Dock at Anti-Gay Ports. *EDGE Media Network*. [online] 23 December. Available at: <www.edgemedianetwork.com/story.php?ch=news&sc=local&sc2=&id=140099> [Accessed 1 September 2016].

State of Washington v. Arlene's Flowers Inc., 441 P.3d 1203 (Wash. 2019).

Starwood Hotels, 2006. *Annual Report 2006*. [pdf] Available at:<www.annualreports.com/HostedData/AnnualReportArchive/s/NYSE_HOT_2006.pdf> [Accessed 16 July 2020].

Texas Association of Business, 2017. *The Economic Impact of Discriminatory Legislation on the State of Texas*. [pdf] Available at: <www.courthousenews.com/wp-content/uploads/2017/01/Bathroom-study.pdf> [Accessed 16 July 2020].

Trading with the Enemy Act of 1917, ch. 106, 40 Stat. 411, Pub.L. 65–91 (1917), 50 U.S.C. § 4301–41 (2018).

United Nations, 2015. Transforming our world: the 2030 Agenda for Sustainable Development, G.A. Res. 70/1, U.N. Doc. A/RES/70/1 (Sep. 25, 2015).

United Nations, 2019. *Disability and Development Report 2018*. New York: United Nations.

United Nations High Commissioner for Human Rights, *Annual Report of the United Nations High Commissioner for Human Rights, Discriminatory laws and practices and acts of violence against individuals based on their sexual orientation and gender identity,* U.N. Doc. A/HRC/19/41 (Nov. 17, 2011).

Universal Declaration of Human Rights, G.A. Res. 217 (III) A, U.N. Doc. A/RES/217(III) (Dec. 10, 1948).

U.S. Const. amend. XIII, XIV, XV (USA).

World Conference against Racism, Racial Discrimination, Xenophobia and Related Intolerance, Aug. 31-Sep. 8, 2001, *Durban Declaration and Programme of Action,* U.N. Doc. A/CONF.189/12 (Sep. 8, 2001).

World Health Organization, 2001. *International Classification of Functioning, Disability and Health*. Geneva: World Health Organization.

World Health Organization and World Bank, 2011. *World Report on Disability*. Geneva: World Health Organization.

9

RIGHTS TO FREEDOM OF MOVEMENT AND TOURISM

9.1 Introduction and Overview of Mobility

The impact of globalisation on mobilities has compressed worldwide distances, whereby Bauman refers to this phenomenon as the "death of distance" (2000 cited in Sheller and Urry, 2004, p. 3). Advancements in technology have contributed to the intensification of the movement of information, images, capital, goods, waste, animals, and people (Cook and Butz, 2019a; Sheller, 2011); and in particular, in tourism, leading to the rapid physical movement of tourists from place to place (Sheller and Urry, 2004).

Increasingly, there is evidence of the intersection of people's right to the freedom of movement and national security concerns (see Chapter 5). Some restrictions are warranted, such as in the case of safety and security (c.f. ICCPR), while others may be motived by more political or economic reasons (see Chapter 4), and others reflect bias – all of which interfere with the ability of people to travel. In this era of pandemics, threats of terrorism, and increased security measures, borders are becoming more stringent and difficult for some to cross. US Executive Order 13769 (Issued January 2017), also known as a travel ban, was superseded by Executive Order 13780 (March 2017, revised April 2018) "Protecting the Nation from Foreign Terrorist Entry into the United States", which identified countries (Iran Syria, Libya, Yemen, Somalia, North Korea and Venezuela, and all refugees without proper travel documentation), and restricted the movements of peoples between these countries and the US (Federal Register, 2017a, 2017b; BBC, 2017; Goodman, 2017). This was met with many legal challenges, including critics calling it an anti-Muslim ban (University of Michigan Law School, 2017). On the other hand, in news articles akin to "Deadly export: Canadians responsible for hundreds of terrorism deaths and injuries overseas", Bell (2019) argues that Section 6 of the Charter of Rights and Freedoms (Canada) prevents the state from stopping potential terrorists from travelling abroad without providing legitimate reasons. It is becoming increasingly more difficult to balance the need for security and people's right to free movement. However, blanket travel bans may prevent those not involved in criminal activity from crossing borders not only from banned countries, but these restrictions may directly impact travellers from other nations.

The COVID-19 global pandemic brought never before seen restrictions to the movement of people due to public health. Governments closed borders to non-citizens, enforced lockdowns, and urged citizens to return. Prime Minister Trudeau of Canada issued the following statement on 16 March 2020:

> I am asking all Canadians that they should avoid all nonessential travel outside of our country until further notice. Canadian travellers should return to Canada via commercial means while it is still possible to do so. Let me be clear, if you are abroad, it is time to come home. If you have just arrived, you must self isolate for 14 days.
>
> *(Heart FM.ca, 2020)*

The pandemic brought the tourism industry to a standstill, and restricted mobility both within, and between, nations.

Historically, mobility studies stemmed from sociology, with a focus on human mobilities in society, i.e. occupation, education, income, etc. (Urry, 2010). The world transformed drastically in the latter half of the 20th century, with globalisation challenging assumptions of geographical, economic, political, and cultural boundaries. The world of today "seems to be on the move. Asylum seekers, international students, terrorists, members of diasporas, holidaymakers, business people, sports stars, refugees, backpackers, commuters, the early retired, young mobile professionals, prostitutes, armed forces … and many others …" (Sheller and Urry, 2006 p. 207). As human movement increases, so too must the mobilities of objects, goods, waste, information, and images be supported by infrastructure, software/applications, and networks. Without "immobile platforms (transmitters, roads, stations, satellite dishes, airports, docks, factories)," (Hannam, et al., 2006 cited in Sheller, 2011, p. 4), human mobility could not occur.

Today, mobility studies cover migration, transportation, infrastructure, transnationalism, mobile communications, corporeal/imaginative/virtual travel and tourism (Sheller, 2011; Urry, 2010), and social justice (Cook and Butz, 2019a). Interested disciplines have expanded to include anthropology, cultural studies, geography, migration studies, science and technology studies, tourism studies, sociology (Sheller and Urry, 2006), philosophy, transport planning, urban studies, media studies, and inequality studies (gender, race, sexuality, disability, etc.) (Cook and Butz, 2019a).

Interest in mobilities in tourism studies is increasing to include research on infrastructure development, cultural studies, displacement issues, and the development of tourist destinations. More importantly, the discourse of social justice, i.e. inequality, accessibility, exclusion, human rights, etc., needs to be discussed beyond impact assessment. Travel and tourism is a highly polarising social phenomenon. A small proportion of the world's population has sufficient disposable income to enjoy the mobility of holidaymaking. But rapid changes are underway, with a growth in the middle class and super rich in some developing countries. Out of an estimated world population of 8.5 billion by 2030 (UNDESA, 2015), the World Travel and Tourism Council (WTTC) predicted there will be 1.8 billion international arrivals recorded (WTTC, 2019). Questions arise from these figures: Who are these tourists? Will everyone have an equal opportunity to travel? Will tourists be able to travel to anywhere in the world they want? What will travel look like post-COVID-19?

The colonial world economy necessitated global mobilities (Sheller, 2011). It was not tourists, but colonisers/colonists, slaves, explorers, religious groups, capital, goods, and commodities that moved across regions. Eurocentric colonialism transformed natural and political landscapes of colonised nations, altering fundamental values, as well as justifying forms and patterns of travel. Eurocentric colonialism dominated travel writing, while ignoring non-European expeditions and scholars (Bianchi and Stephenson, 2014). D'Hauteserre (2008) calls today's tourist experience "a thin parody of colonial experiences" (p. 237).

Globalisation is a phenomenon and a process connecting the world. It has accelerated technological development, collapsed the space-time continuum, and tourism owes its success to globalisation. However, the privileges of movement are not fairly distributed around the world, leading to discrimination. This chapter will examine the meaning of Freedom of Movement and its relevance to tourism, and its relationship to human rights. The chapter will also explore the right to freedom of mobility in a range of issues linked to globalisation, including the impact of COVID-19 on mobility, accessibility, rise of nationalism, travel visas, national security and technology, and migrant workers.

9.2 Mobility as a symbol of freedom of movement

Mobility over large distances used to be a luxury, yet in the 20th Century, it has become a significant part of Western modernity (Paris, 2011). Sheller (2011) cautioned that such a change in the mobility paradigm is "grounded in masculine subjectivities… and ignored the gendered production of space" (p. 3). In June 2018, Saudi Arabia finally allowed women to drive (Hubbard, 2017; Al Jazeera, 2017) and in August 2019, a Royal Decree announced women over the age of 21 could hold a passport and travel without a male chaperon, although without mentioning an effective date (RT, 2019; Al Jazeera, 2019). In Saudi Arabia – which exercises one of the world's tightest restrictions on women – a male family member as her guardian must grant permission for a woman to study, travel, and engage in other activities. Although new freedoms of movement for women are a sign of progress, inevitably they will face many challenges from the guardianship system. Mobility – as illustrated here – is a symbol of power and control, rather than of true freedom. Factors that hinder access to the benefits of the freedom of movement include: "residence location, knowledge of the transport system, gender, household composition, access to transport funds and physical ability" (Cook and Butz, 2019a, p. 13). Has globalisation transformed the mobility paradigm? How has the UDHR influenced people's understanding of the Freedom of Movement and accessibility? The following sections will examine the emergence of the concept of the Freedom of Movement, and the understanding of the Rights to Travel in the context of globalisation.

9.3 Freedom of movement and rights to travel

Since ancient times, limited groups of people have been moving across borders: i.e., on pilgrimages to sacred sites, travelling for trade, participating in the Grand Tour, or making recreational visits to the seaside and countryside. Holidaymaking and travelling were once reserved for Aristocrats and well-to-do people in the upper classes, yet after the two World Wars, advancements in flight technology, rising ownership of automobiles, and increased availability of petroleum-based fuel made mass tourism possible (see Urry and Larsen, 2011 for further discussion).

Surging second home ownership in the past few decades in North America, Europe, and Australasia has also spurred increases in mobility (cf. Paris, 2011; Hall and Müller, 2004) although this is nothing new – in ancient times, wealthy Romans had multiple countryside residences (Villas) in addition to urban dwellings (Wasson, 2018; McKay, 1975), as did the European upper class in later times. The development of spa resorts and ease of transportation contributed to second home ownership (cf. Hall and Müller, 2004; Müller, 2004). Paris (2011) argues that rising second home ownership popularity is a reflection of massive inequalities in the living standards of countries. If domestic second home vacations increased travel by private car, international second home vacations have increased the demand for cheap flights (Paris, 2011).

Whether it is a second home vacation or not, tourists travelling to destinations reinforce the relationship between the unequal distribution of wealth and access to the benefits of mobility. The flow of tourists is still predominantly from economically affluent nations to more affordable destinations. Second homeowners move from country to country, where purchasing real estate property is easier for non-nationals, and travel is easier for tourists (Paris, 2011). Within this highly mobile globalised society, divisions are evident between those who belong to the global élite culture and the localised others who do not (Aronsson, 2004), thereby illustrating the inequality in the distribution of mobility.

9.3.1 Definition of "freedom of movement"

Arendt (1968) asserted the freedom of movement is "historically the oldest and also the most elementary" (p. 9) liberty. Freedom of movement is a gesture of being free, and the constraint of freedom of movement is a precondition to enslavement. In Article 13 of the UNDHR, the right to freedom of movement is enshrined as:

1. Everyone has the right to freedom of movement and residence within the borders of each State.
2. Everyone has the right to leave any country, including his own, and to return to his country.

Czaika and Mayer (2017) pointed out, however, Article 13 only refers to entering one's own country – not a foreign country. Bianchi and Stephenson (2014) support the idea that this Article guarantees automatic return to one's country, but does not endorse crossing a border from one country to another. In international law, there is no right to enter a foreign country (Sassen 1998 cited in Neumayer, 2006).

Children's right to the freedom of movement is essentially the same liberty as that of adults, and is contained in the Convention on the Rights of the Child (Article 10). ICCPR (Article 12) also protects the right to freedom of movement:

1. Everyone lawfully within the territory of a State shall, within that territory, have the right to liberty of movement and freedom to choose his residence.
2. Everyone shall be free to leave any country, including his own.
3. The above-mentioned rights shall not be subject to any restrictions except those which are provided by law, are necessary to protect national security, public order (ordre public), public health or morals or the rights and freedoms of others, and are consistent with the other rights recognized in the present Covenant.
4. No one shall be arbitrarily deprived of the right to enter his own country.

De Genova (2010) points out issues of power and control by the "state", in Article 13 of the UNDHR. Under claims of sovereignty and spatial jurisdiction, the laws, regulations, and policies of each state dictate citizens' or visitors' – right to freedom of movement. ICCPR Article 12–3 sanctions extra power to the state to further control human mobilities for the purpose of national security (see United Nations Human Rights Committee, 1999 for further comments on how to interpret ICCPR Article 12). In addition, the first half of ICCPR Article 13 states:

> An alien lawfully in the territory of a State Party to the present Covenant may be expelled therefrom only in pursuance of a decision reached in accordance with law and shall, except where compelling reasons of national security otherwise require, …

The article requires that the competent authority shall review expulsion cases. Since the mid-2010s, national security measures have escalated to militarised border policing in many countries, making travel and tourism – including transiting a country – incredibly more complex. This has also led to deportations of people at a global scale, without having their cases reviewed by authorities (see Chapter 7 for displacement discourse). Further, De Genova (2010) even argues that freedom of movement must not be understood as a human right or natural right, but rather, it is an essential part of a human being's creative and productive powers that distinguishes the human species from other species. Therefore, it is not for the state to control.

9.3.2 Is there a right to tourism?

Article 24 of the UDHR is also called the Right to Rest or the Right to Rest and Leisure. This article reads:

> Everyone has the right to rest and leisure, including reasonable limitation of working hours and periodic holidays with pay.

Unlike the UDHR Article 13, on the Right to Freedom of Movement, this right (Article 24) is not mentioned in any other UN covenants. Article 24 concerns fair and just work conditions and is meant to be read in conjunction with Article 22, the Right to Social, Economic and Cultural Rights (Melander, 1992, cited in Danchin, n.d.). From a different perspective, Article 24 reminds employers their duty to "offer the employee options to have the time off without losing wages or using vacation time" or "If the workplace or the employee's individual circumstances are such that the employee cannot make up the time that they must miss ... other forms of accommodation must be explored" (Ontario Human Rights Commission, n.d.). However, Article 24 does not endorse an individual's entitlement to holidaymaking. Only in the Convention on the Rights of Persons with Disabilities (CRPD) Article 30 does it state that the State Party ensures persons with disabilities, "[enjoy] access to places for cultural performances or services, such as theatres, museums, cinemas, libraries and tourism services, and, as far as possible, enjoy access to monuments and sites of national cultural importance" (1-c); and the State Party takes measures to "ensure that persons with disabilities have access to sporting, recreational and tourism venues" (5-c).

Bianchi and Stephenson (2014) pointed out that this misconception of the right to tourism probably came from the UNWTO's interpretation of UDHR Article 13 on the Right to Freedom of Movement as a "right to tourism," as shown in its Code of Ethics (p. 89). The Code of Ethics, Article 8 is entitled "Liberty of tourist movement" (UNWTO, n.d.). The first paragraph of this Article reads:

1. Tourists and visitors should benefit, in compliance with international law and national legislation, from the liberty to move within their countries and from one State to another, in accordance with Article 13 of the Universal Declaration of Human Rights; they should have access to places of transit and stay and to tourism and cultural sites without being subject to excessive formalities or discrimination;

In the Code of Ethics Article 7 on the "Right to tourism", paragraph two is clearly adopting Article 24 of the UDHR:

1. The prospect of direct and personal access to the discovery and enjoyment of the planet's resources constitutes a right equally open to all the world's inhabitants; the increasingly extensive participation in national and international tourism should be regarded as one of the best possible expressions of the sustained growth of free time, and obstacles should not be placed in its way;
2. The universal right to tourism must be regarded as the corollary of the right to rest and leisure, including reasonable limitation of working hours and periodic holidays with pay, guaranteed by Article 24 of the Universal Declaration of Human Rights and Article 7.d of the International Covenant on Economic, Social and Cultural Rights;

As stated, an individual has the right to enjoy tourism activities as a natural result of their right to rest and leisure. In some societies, Article 24 may be incorporated in their constitution, yet it is hardly persuasive to call this link between the right to rest-and-leisure and the right to holidaymaking as a "corollary." The UNWTO (2017) claims various declarations and covenants including the UDHR, Rio Summits, and GATS, "affirm the right to tourism and the freedom of tourist movements," (p. 13) though how they affirm the Western concept of Travel and Tourism as a universal "right to tourism" has never been explained. What is more concerning, as noted by Bianchi and Stephenson (2014), the rights to tourism and the liberty of tourist movement focuses on the tourists' and the tourism industry's "right to enter and consume other places and cultural sites" (p. 89). In reality, tourism is a highly polarising form of consumption creating a clear division between tourists and hosts. As reviewed earlier, mobility is not something fairly distributed to everyone – it is a matter of power and wealth. While the UDHR enshrines everyone's rights, the UNWTO's right to tourism and the liberty of tourist movement strongly favours a specific group of the world's population – the wealthy.

9.4 Globalisation and the rights to freedom of movement

Neither the UDHR nor the ICESCR mention national security as a justification for restrictions of the right to the freedom of movement. Only the ICCPR has included such clauses in Articles 12, 13, and 14 (the right to freedom of movement), Article 19 (right to opinion), Article 21 (right to peaceful assembly), and Article 22 (freedom of association with others). Although none of the above declarations and covenants has legally binding power, many member States have incorporated them in their constitutions, laws, and business contracts.

Prior to COVID-19, growth in tourist numbers led some nation-states to control the flow of tourists – particularly for destinations threatened by overtourism. Diverting tourist flows to lesser-known areas has the potential to spread tourism income, as well as reviving community culture. However, a nation-state also has the power to exclude an area from tourist itineraries. Dangerous areas must be sealed off for the safety of tourists. For example, after the nuclear explosion in Fukushima,

Japan in 2011, nearby towns were evacuated and sealed off from the public until 2018. Military zones and politically sensitive areas are also off most tourist itineraries. Some governments do not allow tourists to explore local villages, in order to protect these areas from cultural contamination. The Indian government had prohibited tourists from travelling to the islands of the Sentinelese in the Bay of Bengal in order to protect the inhabitants, known as the last pre-Neolithic tribe in the world. However, in 2018 the government removed the requirement for foreign nationals to have special permits to visit two dozen islands, including North Sentinel, raising concerns that the area will be opened up for tourism (ABC News, 2018) (see also Chapters 7 and 12). Before the Myanmar/Burma government transitioned to a form of democracy in 2015 following decades of military dictatorship, only a handful of travellers had been allowed to visit areas the then-government identified as tourist areas, and the facilities were controlled by military personnel. Locals were instructed not to associate with foreigners in any way, subject to punishment (Norman, personal communication 1997). North Korea places severe restrictions on the movements of locals and international tourists. In nation-states where governments or religion has tight control, locals may be prohibited from moving to tourist areas to seek employment, where the work requires contact with foreigners or with persons of opposite sex. Saudi Arabia, however, has proposed relaxing gender segregation restrictions in order to attract more Western tourists (Corderoy, 2017). Under COVID-19, entire countries, provinces, regions, or villages have closed their borders citing public health concerns. For example, the Italian village of Nerola was declared a red zone, and sealed off by the army due to a spike in COVID-19 in early April 2020 (Mackenzie, Monetta and Smythe, 2020). There can be tension between the role of states and the process of globalisation, including over the rights to the freedom of movement. The following sections will explore various facets of globalisation in the context of mobility and human rights.

9.4.1 Influence of globalisation on mobility

While it is beyond the scope of this chapter to discuss globalisation in detail, it is interesting to note that many readers cannot imagine the world before globalisation. The concept of globalisation is often confused with the concept of internationalisation. Unlike internationalisation, in which the fundamental unit is an independent state with the assumption that capital and labour force remain within the bounds of the state, globalisation breaks the boundaries of the state, becoming interregional where capital and labour move freely (Daly, 2004). Globalisation is strongly imbedded in connectedness through digital technology. The mobilities of information, ideology, goods, technology, and people have become much easier and faster. Financial transactions are increasingly done online, especially on credit, without the participants seeing "real" money. Websites, social media, e-books, e-newspapers, and other PDF documents have all multiplied online. Tsagarousianou (2004) suggests that globalisation fuelled by digital connectivity has transformed transnational flows of human mobilities, finance, politics, and cultural production.

Globalisation accelerated by the advancement of digital technologies has realised "time-space compression" (Harvey, 1990), allowing a small group of the world's population to enjoy greater mobility, including travel and tourism. The advent of low-cost carriers and high-speed trains are taking tourists further and faster than ever before. Tourists can book complex itineraries online without the need of a traditional brick-and-mortar travel agency. Interpersonal connections through technology have also changed how human beings interact with each other. However, while it is shrinking, the digital divide continues to leave those without Internet access at a disadvantage in the highly competitive tourism economy.

9.4.1 COVID-19 and the impact on global mobility

The recent global phenomenon that has severely constrained physical movement is COVID-19. This SARS-like illness was first recognised in China at the end of 2019, and within 3 months of its discovery, the WHO declared it to be a pandemic. The global movement of people came to halt – even the international movement of goods and postal services were disrupted. Nations exercised their political power to ban travel, cancel and ground flights, limit commuting by automobiles, reduce non-essential business operations, and enforce quarantines of individuals and communities. The impact of COVID-19 is the worst crisis to hit tourism and hospitality. The International Civil Aviation Organization (ICAO, 2020) examined the effects of COVID-19 on civil aviation compared to business as usual (i.e. originally planned) and predicted (as of 25 May 2020): (1) a reduction in seat offerings by airlines from 33 per cent to 60 per cent; (2) a reduction of 1,878 to 3,227 million passengers; and (3) a loss in gross operating revenues between US$244 and 420 billion. As the virus spread globally and new hotspots emerged, further restrictions were put in place in some countries, while other locations eased restrictions as case numbers waned. In many countries, arriving visitors were forced to self-isolate for 14 days. When there was a surge of cases in Brazil in late May 2020, the USA banned travel from Brazil to the USA. Other countries were considering air corridors between nations with low infection rates, allowing these passengers to forgo the 14-day self-isolation period. The pandemic affected not only the freedom of movement, but also severely impacted the rights to livelihood, work, and life. In countries such as Spain, Germany, Poland, the UK, and the USA protests emerged as the lockdowns continued. This pandemic illustrates how individuals and communities in a globalised world are interconnected physically and virtually; while also impacting the mobility of humans, goods, and non-mobile entities (see Chapter 14 for further discussion).

9.4.3 Mobility and accessibility of persons with special needs

Globalisation has helped raise awareness of accessibility issues and the rights of people with disabilities, as well as generating international standards to accommodate their needs. As human mobilities are facilitated by technology, social perceptions of the mobilities of people with disabilities have also drastically changed. Mobility challenges are not limited to physical mobility, yet in this chapter, the main focus will be on physical mobility in regard to tourism. People with physical and mental challenges, or disabilities and impairment that require medical attention and equipment are becoming increasingly visible, active, and travelling in societies. The disabilities and impairment can be temporary due to injuries or episodic in nature. As the world's population ages, more and more senior tourists will require assistance for both physical and mental needs. The Convention on the Rights of Persons with Disabilities (ICRPD) outlines that persons with disabilities should be given opportunities and support to enjoy the rights of everyone else as much as possible. Articles 9 and 18 are about freedom of movement (see Box 9.1), endorsing better accessibility by removing barriers and obstacles, and the rights to freedom of movement within and between states. Government policies supporting human rights of peoples with disabilities have enabled some tourist destinations to be more accessible (see detailed discussions in Buhalis, Darcy and Ambrose, 2012; see Chapter 8 for legal discourse).

BOX 9.1 THE CONVENTION ON THE RIGHTS OF PERSONS WITH DISABILITIES 2006 – ARTICLES 9 AND 18

The UN Convention on the Rights of Persons with Disabilities was the first comprehensive human rights treaty of the 21st century, and had the highest number of signatories in history for a UN Convention on its opening day (30 March 2007). It changed "viewing persons with disabilities as 'objects' of charity, medical treatment, and social protection, towards viewing persons with disabilities as 'subjects' with rights, who are capable of claiming those rights, and making decisions for their lives based on their free and informed consent, as well as being active members of society." Articles 9 and 18 below are about the freedom of movement (UNDESA, n.d.)

Article 9

1. To enable persons with disabilities to live independently, and participate fully in all aspects of life, State Parties shall take appropriate measures to ensure to persons with disabilities access, on an equal basis with others, to the physical environment, to transportation, to information and communications, including information and communications technologies and systems, and to other facilities and services open or provided to the public, both in urban and in rural areas. These measures, which shall include the identification and elimination of obstacles and barriers to accessibility, shall apply to, inter alia:

(a) Buildings, roads, transportation and other indoor and outdoor facilities, including schools, housing, medical facilities and workplaces;
(b) Information, communications and other services, including electronic services and emergency services.
2. States Parties shall also take appropriate measures to:
   (a) Develop, promulgate and monitor the implementation of minimum standards and guidelines for the accessibility of facilities and services open or provided to the public;
   (b) Ensure that private entities that offer facilities and services which are open or provided to the public take into account all aspects of accessibility for persons with disabilities;
   (c) Provide training for stakeholders on accessibility issues facing persons with disabilities;
   (d) Provide in buildings and other facilities open to the public signage in Braille and in easy to read and understand forms;
   (e) Provide forms of live assistance and intermediaries, including guides, readers and professional sign language interpreters, to facilitate accessibility to buildings and other facilities open to the public;
   (f) Promote other appropriate forms of assistance and support to persons with disabilities to ensure their access to information;
   (g) Promote access for persons with disabilities to new information and communications technologies and systems, including the Internet;
   (h) Promote the design, development, production and distribution of accessible information and communications technologies and systems at an early stage, so that these technologies and systems become accessible at minimum cost.

Article 18

1. States Parties shall recognize the rights of persons with disabilities to liberty of movement, to freedom to choose their residence and to a nationality, on an equal basis with others, including by ensuring that persons with disabilities:
   (a) Have the right to acquire and change a nationality and are not deprived of their nationality arbitrarily or on the basis of disability;
   (b) Are not deprived, on the basis of disability, of their ability to obtain, possess and utilize documentation of their nationality or other documentation of identification, or to utilize relevant processes such as immigration proceedings, that may be needed to facilitate exercise of the right to liberty of movement;
   (c) Are free to leave any country, including their own;

> (d) Are not deprived, arbitrarily or on the basis of disability, of the right to enter their own country.
> 2. Children with disabilities shall be registered immediately after birth and shall have the right from birth to a name, the right to acquire a nationality and, as far as possible, the right to know and be cared for by their parents.
>
> Source: (OHCHR, n.d.).[1]

Nevertheless, different states have different laws and policies that often contradict support for securing the freedom of movement of persons with disabilities. For instance, Heritage and Culture Protection laws may not allow alteration of historical buildings or cobblestone roads, or the additions of an elevators/lifts or ramps. In many countries, the awareness and importance of building accessibility is receiving more attention, yet, buildings of historic value are often exempted from complying with accessibility codes. Even if historic buildings have added accessibility measures, building codes are not universal. Wheelchair manufacturers are already aware of the discrepancies in elevator car dimension codes and wheelchair sizes in different countries (see Table 9.1).

The International Organization for the Standardization of wheelchairs (ISO 7176-5:2008) provides a standard measurement of occupied width and depth which individual states are encouraged to use. US wheelchair standards allow 24–27 inches of seat width, which consequently makes the overall occupied width to 32–35 inches or more (Scootaround, 2019; References, 2019) and is the largest in Table 9.1. Door and pathway width standards also vary from one country to another, and it can be a challenge for tourists on a wider wheelchair to access places as freely in a destination as they may have at home with larger width standards.

Even when governments are ready to support travellers with special needs, individual business sectors may not be able to fully accommodate accessibilities. Support and equipment for tourists travelling with medical oxygen tanks for example, is not as widespread as there is demand. There were some 45 airlines in 2014 that have policies to allow passengers to use portable oxygen (Oxygen Solutions, 2014). Some airlines charge extra for bringing medical oxygen equipment or for the provision of oxygen on-board (Pulmonary Hypertension Association UK, 2018; Cooper, 2009). Travel insurance may not cover tourists using oxygen treatments (Trip Advisor Canada, 2019). Hotels and attractions may not be equipped with an oxygen supply system or oxygen recharging stations at hand (Trip Advisor Canada, 2019).

Accessibility issues are not only applicable to people with special needs or disabilities. Tourists carrying heavy suitcases, pregnant or injured persons, and people of different physical sizes may be also deprived of opportunities of their freedom of

TABLE 9.1 Accessibility Elevator (Public) Minimum Dimensions

Region	Conditions	Width	Depth	Door Clear Width
UN	Accessibility elevator for the Disabled	39 inches (1000 mm)	51 inches (1300 mm)	31 inches (800 mm)
USA	New elevator	42 inches (1065 mm)	54 inches (1370 mm)	36–42 inches (925–1065 mm)
	Existing elevator	36 inches (915 mm)	54 inches (1370 mm)	
European Union	With an accompanying person	43 inches (1100 mm)	55 inches (1400 mm)	No explicit figures provided
	Without an accompanying person	35 inches (900 mm)	47 inches (1200 mm)	
Japan	Multiple passengers including wheelchair passenger use	55 inches (1400 mm)	53 inches (1350 mm)	31–35 inches (800–900 mm)

Source: (UN enable, 2004) (USA: Department of Justice, 2010) (Europe: CCPT, 1996) (Japan: MILT, n.d.).

movement by so called standard building codes and safety codes. It is important to note that accessibility also involves other people's perceptions towards special needs and societies' willingness to provide accommodations.

9.4.4 Globalisation and the rise of nationalism

Globalisation has had a tremendous influence on human mobilities, and a building block of globalisation is regionalisation. Nations in geographical proximity often form a Region by pooling resources for economic or political security reasons. Neighbouring nations often share fundamental values. Kacowicz (1998) notes that globalisation is not a single force affecting the entire world, but multiple imbalanced forces affecting different regions of the world. Examples of Interregional organisations are: the European Union (EU), the Association of Southeast Asian Nations (ASEAN), the African Union (AU), the North Atlantic Treaty Organization (NATO), and The Commonwealth of Nations. There are many positive effects of Regionalisation on human movements, such as the EU members signing the Schengen Agreement in 1985 to create a passport-free area for the member states' citizens (Schengen Visa Info, 2018).

Globalisation, on the other hand, is a compilation of various regions interacting with the rest of the world, and there is an intensification of connectedness bringing about changes in economies, ideologies, technology, and cultures. Some parts of the world see globalisation as "the triumph of US values" (Kacowicz, 1998) particularly in the domains of economies and political democracy. This is also linked to the neoliberal policies of the Washington Consensus. There have been numerous discourses on whether globalisation has diminished nationalism, stemming from the argument that a single nation-state cannot survive the post-war world, thus the needs for alliances leading to Regionalism and Globalisation. Kacowicz (1998) proposed seven scenarios on how globalisation, regionalisation, and nationalism interact with each other:

1. Nation-states oppose globalisation
2. Nationalism and the formation of new states are encouraged by the forces of globalisation
3. Nation-states oppose the forces of globalisation
4. Nationalism and nation-states can be strengthened through regionalism
5. Regionalisation co-exists with nationalism and with globalisation
6. Nation-states mediate between trends of regionalisation and globalisation
7. Nation-states oppose globalisation through regionalisation (see Kacowicz, 1998 for more details)

Nationalism is no longer a simple feeling of pride and attachment to a people and a nation-state where they live. Contemporary nationalism is "the desire of the members of the nation to control and govern the territory in which they live" (Kacowicz, 1998). Reinforcing this argument, Pickel (2005) found there is a strong relationship between national identity and economic nationalism. In the process of globalisation, nation-states are becoming obsolete, as economies are turning progressively more international; yet, ironically each nation-state contributes to the process of globalisation. Anderson (2006) argues the origin of nation-states is based on three factors: the spread of a common language (e.g. Latin in the pre-Christian Roman Empire and Mandarin in the Chinese Empire) that led to a national consciousness; the success of print-capitalism through the Reformation; and lastly, the "well-positioned would-be absolutist monarchs" (p. 42) that could control administrative centralisation. Others consider the origin of nation-states can be traced back to The Peace of Westphalia/The Treaty of Westphalia in 1648, which articulates the concept of territorial sovereignty (Augustyn, 2019). Nation-states can simply be a geographically bounded legal entity (Kacowicz, 1998) or imagined community (Anderson, 2006). Nation-states can also be linked to postcolonial nations that won independence after WWII, or a nation-state could be an amalgamation of different pre-colonial nations. New World nations are built upon the appropriated lands of Indigenous nations, and being a legal entity as such, is faced with contentious land disputes with Indigenous Peoples. Each nation state's government has the authority to forge diplomatic ties with other nation-states, release a Travel Advisory on a certain country, issue passports to its citizens, and issue visas and other travel documents to allow tourists' movements.

In the 20th century, nationalism has led to many wars. In the 21st century, economic nationalism is becoming more evident. At one point, regionalism through initiatives like the EU or the North American Free Trade Agreement (NAFTA – now Canada-United States-Mexico Free Trade Agreement) or the Trans-Pacific Partnership (TPP) seemed to be continued steps towards more successful globalisation. However, the Brexit movement to remove the UK from the EU, the withdrawal of the USA from the Trans-Pacific Partnership (TPP), and US Executive Order 13780, illustrate how nation-states are opposing the forces of globalisation. The rise of nationalism has been used in some cases to justify nation-states pursuing their own interests. In some situations, this has led to an alarming number of extreme right-wing activities with deep-rooted xenophobic attitudes, controlling to the point of discrimination, whereby certain nationalities or religious groups are prevented from entering into a country. In Canada, a new political party, the People's Party of Canada, put up controversial election billboards with the message "Say NO to mass immigration" (The Canadian Press, 2019) and did not win any seats in the 2019 election. Still in other instances, access to information is repressively controlled, even isolating the nation-state from the outside world, which is essentially undermining the positive aspects of globalisation. As discussed earlier, the Right to Freedom of Movement can be compromised for the need of national security. Nevertheless, how a growing sense of nationalism is used to protect the state, and how it can also protect human rights to the freedom of movement is yet to be seen.

9.4.5 Inequality of mobilities through passports and travel visas

Mobilities is at the heart of globalisation, yet, the distribution of the freedom of mobility has never been fair. Historically, physical mobility – particularly travelling or luxury holidaymaking – were signs of wealth. Long before globalisation became a buzzword in the 1990s, so called Élite Cosmopolitans of unparalleled wealth – a handful of people who controlled most of the global economy – moved around the world. These super rich cosmopolitans are also dubbed "duty free citizens," (Prideaux, 2004, cited in Bianchi and Stephenson, 2014, p. 49) purchasing properties around the world and avoiding paying the full amount of tax.

The earliest record of a travel document is from about 450 B.C.E. in ancient Persia, in the form of a letter requesting safe passage of the bearer (The Guardian, 2006; Government of Canada, 2014). In Medieval Europe, citizens were a source of labour and military recruitment, and therefore, controlling the movement of a population became paramount. States also 'pursued ethnic and cultural homogeneity' by creating 'national foundation myths and unitary languages', through propaganda and education systems, and the prosecution of people who did not fit into the ethnic or cultural profile of the state (Czaika, de Haas and Villares-Varela, 2018). Records show that the English monarch Henry V in the 15th century issued a "safe conduct" letter (The Guardian, 2006). Such letters of request became popular during the reign of King Louis XIV of France in the 17th century

(Government of Canada, 2014), and many other European nations followed suit. Through the Treaty of Westphalia, the formation of nation-states allowed each sovereign state to exercise the power to control the movement of people. This concept is still evident today when it comes to the issuance of passports and travel visas. In the mid-19th century with unprecedented growth in tourist numbers, European countries could not handle border checks and by 1914, passport requirements were abolished in Europe (Government of Canada, 2014). After WWI, the League of Nations, and after WWII, the Council of Europe, reminded member states to revisit the need for visa restrictions on international trade and tourism (Czaika and Neumayer, 2017). The Schengen Treaty in Europe realised freedom of movement for EU citizens within the Region, accompanied by the visa-waiver programme for non-EU Schengen members. The EU Harmonisation Law however does not allow for the harmonisation of national laws in certain areas, including tourism activities.

The passport is not, as people often take for granted, issued to every citizen who applies for one (Bianchi and Stephenson, 2014). In some countries, the issuance or not of a passport was used to restrict and control the movement of citizens. In a similar token, obtaining a visa to enter other countries is not always straight-forward. Today, many countries require airlines to deny boarding if the passenger does not possess a valid visa over concerns some asylum seekers may destroy their travel documents so they have no country to be deported to (Neumayer, 2006). Nonetheless, it is the issuing of travel visas that signifies the power and the relationship of the states involved. Some countries' passports are more powerful than other countries' passports. With stronger diplomatic relations with other countries, passport holders of such countries do not need visas to enter a number of countries, compared to a country with a weaker passport.

Contemporary population growth, the spread of capitalism, as well as a decline in autocratic states has shifted the focus of control from emigration to immigration (Czaika, de Haas and Villares-Varela, 2018). Subsequently, the number of exit visas issued is on the decline. However, the issuance of travel entry visas is often politically motivated, and reflects nation-states' immigration regimes (Vezzoli and Flahaux, 2016). The issuing country can deny a visa application without giving reason (Neumayer, 2006). Due to the usually reciprocal nature of diplomatic relations among nation-states, if one country has lifted travel visa requirements from a certain nationality, the benefiting country will likely remove its visa requirements in return. Similarly, if one country introduces visa requirements, the other country will impose visa requirements in retaliation. Visa retaliation can also be connected to geopolitics and foreign policy. Such diplomatic relations can be observed in the recent travel ban by US Executive Orders 13769/13770 – for example, Iran temporarily stopped issuing travel visas to US citizens when it was included in the list of countries in the US Executive order. Czaika, de Haas, and Villares-Varela (2018) argue these US Executive Orders are a good example of how a nation uses visa regulations as "a convenient means by which to back up migration rhetoric and regulations." The US Executive Orders impact not only tourists and businesspeople, but also legal immigrants, citizens of dual nationalities, Green-card (permanent residency) holders, international students, scholars, and others.

Economic regions of the world have achieved some degree of freedom of movement by implementing visa-free travel agreements. Under the Schengen agreement, EU citizens and non-EU members with visa waiver status can travel freely within the EU. In contrast, citizens of other nations must apply for an entry visa through a lengthy process or wait in a long queue to be approved to enter EU countries. Vezzoli and Flahaux (2016) found that there are favourable mutual policies and arrangements in terms of the freedom of movement of former colonists and post-colonial nations, when there is low migration potential from post-colonial nations to their former colonial states. Other regions where citizens enjoy visa-free intraregional movement include the Economic Community of West African States (ECOWAS), the Gulf Cooperation Council (GCC), and the South African Development Community (SADC), whereas citizens from non-member countries need an entry visa (Czaika, de Haas and Villares-Varela, 2018). The most successfully integrated economic regions are: the EU/European Free Trade Association (EFTA) and the GCC; and regions where visa restrictions are below 20%, including the Caribbean Community (CARICOM), the Southern African Customs Union (SACU), the Southern Common Market (MERCOSUR for its Spanish initials), the Commonwealth of Independent States (CIS), the Central American Common Market (CACM), ECOWAS, and the Central European Free Trade Agreement (CEFTA). In contrast, regions that still experience a very high level of restriction include: the Pan-Arab Free Trade Area (PAFTA), the South Asian Free Trade Agreement (SAFTA), the Asia Pacific Trade Agreement (APTA), and the Common Market for Eastern and Southern Africa (COMESA) (Czaika, de Haas and Villares-Varela, 2018).

A travel visa is a symbol of diplomatic power, and wealthy countries – in particular those in the Organization for Economic Cooperation and Development (OECD) – typically have gained more visa-free mobility. Czaika, de Haas and Villares-Varela's study (2018) showed that the gap between Outbound Restrictiveness (the ability of their own citizens to travel freely to other countries) and Inbound Restrictiveness (ability of foreign citizens to enter their territory) has been widening over the decades, and the inequality in visa waiver policies is rising. The mobility rights of many African citizens are diminishing; thus the global divide of mobility rights is widening. However, in addition to Advance Passenger Information (API) for national security reasons (see Chapter 6), visa and visa waiver programmes also have an economic benefit in the form of application/processing fees. Advancements in automation and online systems have reduced the human costs of processing visa applications. Many countries have adopted Electronic Travel Authorisations (ETA) applied for online and include: ESTA (USA), eTA (Canada), Australia ETA, e-Visa (India & Turkey), and ETIAS (EU from 2021). Many countries have begun to introduce e-passports embedded with a microchip with biometric data. Technology can be used to prevent of entrance of visitors who may be a threat to national security, which will be discussed in the following section.

9.4.6 Impact of national security technology on rights

Any form of threat to the nation raises alarms, often resulting in further security measures. Civil unrest and political conflicts always affect tourism negatively (see Chapters 4 and 5). After the 9/11 terrorist attacks in the US, the tightening of national security became vital, and technology has improved in this area rapidly. While advances in technology include collecting biometric information, other related security innovations at points of entry have enhanced mobility for most travellers, it has also raised questions over the rights to privacy, and discrimination against travellers with different values and beliefs – including those against the use of technology (see Chapter 6).

During the Britain and Ireland conflict, numerous attacks in the UK by the Provisional Irish Republican Army (IRA) led to the positioning of armed guards at airports and on streets, the removal of garbage bins in public places, and strict security checks at airports and international railway stations. The 9/11 attacks were a wake-up call to the world, resulting in a significant surge in national security measures. The failed terrorist attack at Amsterdam's Schiphol Airport in Christmas of 2009 led to the reorganisation of security teams and systems (Schouten, 2014). Security measures such as travel bans, visa suspensions to certain nationalities, the issuing of governmental travel advisories not to visit certain countries, and the presence of armed guards at ports, stations, public places, and road checkpoints, would all influence the movements of citizens (see Chapter 5).

After the 9/11 attacks, security measures became increasingly strict, with a visible shift towards a reliance on technology (Schouten, 2014), although technology is never 100% fool-proof (Shaikh, n.d.). Security technology examples include CCTV surveillance cameras combined with facial recognition, iris or retina recognition, fingerprints, voice/speech recognition, and ePassports with Radio Frequency Identification (RFID) with biometric information (Bakštein, 2016; Pankanti, 2003). COVID-19 tracking apps are a more recent development in biometric information used in some countries. The collection and use of biometric information, and the use of full-body scanners at airports raised discussion over privacy violations. Taylor (2010) argued with the support of various court cases in the US that the use of pre-flight screening by Magnetometer is reasonable under the Fourth Amendment that guarantees the protection against unreasonable searches and seizures, while individualised strip searches without cause and the use of full–body scanners at airports is an unacceptable violation of the protections under the Fourth Amendment. Biometric information, on the other hand, is also used to combat counterfeit passports and visas (Neumayer, 2006). By 2008, 84% of travellers have used biometrics (Burt, 2019). As of 2018, 800 million biometric passports are in circulation, and 240 airports in Europe have installed biometric scanners (Airport technology, 2018). Travellers must voluntarily provide their biometric information and register in this system. However, a new generation of in-motion identification technology is currently in development. So-called "Smart Security" Airports are recommended by the International Air Transport Association

(IATA) and the Airports Council International (ACI). These systems will: keep inconvenience to travellers to a minimum, allow security forces to be allocated based on risk factors, and a network of information will share information with various parties around security checkpoints (Airport Council International, n.d., 2017). Major international airports in the world have already adopted this Smart Security system, especially in luggage check-in security areas to provide efficient travel experiences to tourists. Facial recognition technology is being incorporated in the latest walk-through security systems at various locations around the world, including at major airports such as Heathrow, Shanghai, and major international airports in the US, as well as at European border security check points. In 2019, major Japanese airports began adopting a new type of facial recognition technology incorporated within mobile phone apps so registered passengers can check-in their luggage, security check their carry-on luggage, walk through automated security gates, complete duty-free shopping, proceed through customs and exit security gates all through the stored facial recognition and other biometric information in their phone, i.e. travellers will seamlessly walk-through the airport (VARINDIA, 2019). While this sounds like an ideal and effortless travel experience at an airport, IATA and WTTC are trying to harmonise various stakeholder efforts (Burt, 2019), although a universal standard on such technology is still unresolved. One possible concern such as at an airport is the registration of biometric information becoming obligatory in order to proceed to travel. Nations that consider crime prevention as one of the purposes behind the use of facial recognition and collecting other biometric information (e.g. US Department of Homeland Security, 2019), argue that the collection of this information even without individualised suspicion is necessary, and is therefore not a violation to the human right to privacy. The Biometrics Institute (2019) outlines collected, stored, and processed biometric data are sharable, and an individual traveller who provides the data does not completely own the data. Shaikh (n.d.) summarised the major challenges of biometric technology as (1) concerns with personal privacy, (2) conflict with one's belief and values, and (3) concern with data collection, protection, and use of the biometric data. Biometric information was designed to identify people with a criminal history, politically dissenting ideology, or people who do not belong to certain groups – the means of social exclusion (Wickins, 2007). Wickins warns that the misuse of biometrics can create social exclusion or discrimination against certain groups of people, however, the justification that this exclusion is for the good of people, i.e. "the rights of many outweigh the rights of the few" is the "wrong argument" (see Chapter 6 for more discussions).

9.4.7 Issues of migration of labour in tourism

Globalisation has opened the door to labour migration around the world. As of 2012, the number of worldwide migrant workers is estimated at 105 million, and the number in the hospitality industry (i.e. HoReCa) is growing rapidly (Joppe, 2012). In the past, going abroad to find a job was often stigmatised as it was interlocked with poverty, powerlessness, and exploitation (Glick Schiller and Salazar, 2013). Although in the globalised world, and the increase in countries having immigration regimes, the perception of labour migration has gradually changed. In the case of the EU, citizens can move to another EU country to find employment and purchase real estate property. Cohen, Duncan and Thulemark (2013) argue a better way to examine the increased fluidity between travel, leisure, and migration is through Lifestyle Mobilities. Contemporary life-style led mobility patterns have broken down the concepts of home and away. Brexit, however, has ignited concerns about work opportunities for British citizens in Europe, and for European citizens currently working in the UK – whether their right to the freedom of movement and their right to work will be seriously threatened as the UK moves towards leaving the EU remains to be seen. Asylum seekers and refugees may find a host nation where they can stay and work in a fixed location, with a work permit limited to one employer. Whereas illegal migrants without proper travel documents and work permits or those unfortunate workers whose employers have confiscated their documents (see Chapter 10), often must move from one location to another to avoid surveillance, arrest, or deportation (Glick Schiller and Salazar, 2013). In these particular circumstances, mobility is not a sign of freedom of movement, but a trap where people are forced to work illegally with no protection from the state.

Migrant labourers often find jobs in tourism and hospitality (Joppe, 2012). Tourism is known for its seasonality and fluctuations, and some employers prefer easily-hired and easily-fired contract employees. Globalisation has also opened up global labour markets and tourism businesses can tap into low-wage developing nations. For example, the Hurtigruten cruise company in Norway employs 21% of its workers on a seasonal basis, of which a significant number are foreign workers (Chen and Wang, 2015). Most of the cruise ship companies are registered in countries like the Bahamas or Liberia, using flags of convenience (FOC). Terry (2011) explains FOC as:

> open registrations that provide ship owners with strategic flexibility of operations by eliminating restrictions on crew and owner citizenship, reducing or eliminating certain taxes, and drastically reducing other forms of regulation on environmental and labor controls... an FOC ship registered (flagged) in the Bahamas may be built in Finland, owned by an American, crewed by a mixture of Asians, Europeans, and Latin Americans, subject to Bahamian regulations ... (p. 663)

Although FOC allows cruise ship operators to recruit workers through recruitment companies with access to various countries, the dilemma is to find people who possess the necessary skill set needed (Terry, 2011). Many tourism jobs, including those on cruise ships, involve emotional labour and require excellent interpersonal skills, not to mention communication skills. Unsuccessful employment is often linked to language barriers, education, and skill-levels (Joppe, 2012).

Contract-based seasonal jobs are driven by the desire to minimise the cost of labour. Cruise ship companies prefer to hire workers from developing nations where wages are low. The British HoReCa has used migrant workers to fill low-end positions not filled by the local workforce (Terry, 2011). There has always been a debate whether migrant workers are stealing jobs from locals, or whether the migrant workers are needed to do the jobs the locals do not want. By implication, does the mobility of migrant workers deprive locals from the right to work? Considering the case of the US as an example, Open Borders (n.d.) demonstrates that one stance argues that the US needs migrant workers "to do work that Americans won't do," i.e. low skill jobs with low wages; while the other side argues that Americans tend to be at the middle skill-level and migrant workers fill in both high skill level jobs and low skill level jobs, to "do jobs that wouldn't exist if the immigrants weren't there to do them." The cruise ship companies, and by extension other tourism businesses, often prefer hiring flexible labourers: i.e. work by contract, no labour unions, without full benefits, minimum cost, and able to perform duties outside their job descriptions (Terry, 2011). Approximately 70% of cruise ship employees come from Asia, Latin America, and Eastern Europe and certain ethnic groups tend to do specific work, especially menial jobs (Terry, 2011). The estimated difference between hiring a European crew and an Asian crew was $700,000 per annum in 2006 (Terry, 2011). Young workers behind the scenes (e.g. kitchen help) earn US$350 per week; waiters/bartenders earn tips so their income could be US$2,500 per month (Artini, Nilan and Threadgold, 2011). Although globalisation and the ease of mobility has expanded the size of the labour market, a lack of training and skill sets limit the availability of migrant workers. Other tourism businesses such as HoReCa are also using recruitment agencies, and the competition between tourism businesses to procure skilled migrant workers will invite inevitable labour shortages.

The question of more freedom of movement for migrant workers often leads to a fear of the loss of rights to work, unfair wages, and a harsher work environment than local workers experience. The COVID-19 pandemic has revealed the crowded living conditions some migrant workers are living in, as there have been outbreaks at farms in Ontario, Canada (Xing, 2020). In many cases, it is migrant workers who face higher unemployment rates (Joppe, 2012), lower wages (Terry, 2011), and racial, gender-based, and hierarchical discrimination (Artini, Nilan and Threadgold, 2011). Nevertheless, some nation-states react to citizens' fear in terms of migrant workers. Policy makers in wealthy nations, i.e. OECD member states, are taking progressively anti-immigration stances for economic reasons and for threats to state identity (Neumayer, 2006), while simultaneously OECD member state citizens are receiving greater freedom to travel to other countries (Czaika, de Haas and Villares-Varela, 2018).

9.5 Conclusion

This chapter has attempted to examine the meaning of the Freedom of Movement and its relevance to tourism, and how the current political climate has impacted people's rights to the freedom of movement. As discussed in Chapters 1 and 4, even though every person has human rights, for the UN UDHR to be effective, each nation-state must ratify the Declaration and implement laws to protect human rights. The freedom of movement is considered to be a primary liberty of human life. However, the nation-state can have other agendas, and use their power to control the movement of people. This impacts travel and tourism, and migrant workers, leading to inequality in the freedom of movement.

This chapter also drew attention to the influence of globalisation on the (un)fairness of the distribution of the right to freedom of movement. In this era of globalisation, political climate, and technological advancement all seem to enhance the human right to freedom of movement in the global community. Cross-border procedures have greatly improved, and been simplified for tourists with the proper travel documents. International standards have facilitated the travel of those with disabilities. Information technology has given potential tourists a wide variety of destinations to choose from, and even to book their holiday online. A cross-border job search has been made simpler. The use of biometric information at the airport has made the travel experience convenient, seamless, quick, and efficient. Yet, the latent effects of such improvements can create social exclusion, separating wealthy travellers from undesirable travellers or migrant workers. For instance, wealthy countries – especially OECD member states – have increasingly gained more freedom of movement by visa-free or visa-waiver programmes, while less developed/economically disadvantaged countries face harsher restrictions and obstacles to travel to other countries, for fear tourists may turn into asylum seekers or fear of illegal migrant workers. States can exercise powers to issue passports and visas, as well as prohibit certain groups of peoples from travelling or working abroad. There are times however, when human rights enshrined in a constitutional law must be suspended in the case of national security. The globalisation of travel has enabled the transmission of COVID-19, which has led to the introduction of unprecedented travel restrictions.

This chapter has also posed questions on the rights to tourism. Citizens from the global North or Western societies often take it for granted that they have the right to the freedom of movement, the freedom to rest, and even justify there is the right to tourism. The right to holidaymaking, nonetheless, in the eyes of international law or in the UDHR, does not exist. It is a privilege, yet contemporary society has tended to imagine it is a human right. Article 13 of the UDHR enshrines the right to freedom of movement, albeit the language used is controversial. It does not protect people's freedom of movement from one country to another. In a similar light, Article 24 of the UDHR on the right to rest, leisure, and paid holidays was originally meant to prevent unethical working conditions, though somehow it was interpreted as the right to holidaymaking.

Lastly this chapter considered migration of labour in light of the freedom of movement. Migrant workers often find jobs in tourism and hospitality. Article 24 of the UDHR can be applied to prevent sweatshop-like working conditions in the tourism industry. Ironically, tourism still has a notorious reputation for exploiting workers with biases in job types, low wages, and discrimination on the basis of race, gender, and beliefs all being reported (cf. UDHR Articles 2, 8, 18, 23, and 24). While globalisation has enhanced mobility for migrant workers, working conditions may violate other human rights. Although the income earned can represent a vital lifeline for workers and their families back home, it is clear more work needs to be done to implement a human rights-based approach to the Freedom of Movement in the tourism industry. These issues will be further examined in the following chapter, with an additional focus on labour conditions and human rights in tourism.

Permission

1 Box 9.1 is composed of material from *Convention on the Rights of Persons with Disabilities*, by Office of the High Commissioner of Human Rights (OHCHR), ©1996–2020, United Nations. Reprinted with the permission of the United Nations.

References

ABC News, 2018. *Sentinelese incident shines spotlight on India's 'fragmented and contradictory' indigenous protections*. [online] Available at: <www.abc.net.au/news/2018-11-28/calls-for-more-indigenous-land-rights-protection-after-sentinel/10560600/> [Accessed 25 August 2019].

Airports Council International, n.d. *Smart Security Guidance Document*. [online]. Available at: <https://aci.aero/About-ACI/Priorities/Security/Smart-Security/Smart-Security-Guidance-Documents/> [Accessed 3 August 2019].

Airports Council International, 2017. *Smart Security Flyer* [pdf] Available at: <https://aci.aero/Media/9143959c-91ed-4115-87bf-ee5250ec43ec/CKgoCg/About%20ACI/Priorities/Security/Smart%20Security/Flyers/Smart_Security_flyer_20170118.pdf> [Accessed 3 August 2019].

Airport Technology, 2018. *Complete Biometric Solutions Key to Streamlining Airport Check-in and Security*. [online] 23 January. Available at: <www.airport-technology.com/features/complete-biometric-solutions-key-streamlining-airport-check-security/> [Accessed 3 August 2019].

Al Jazeera, 2017. Saudi Arabia to allow women to drive. *Al Jazeera News*. [online] 27 September. Available at: <www.aljazeera.com/news/2017/09/saudi-arabia-women-drive-170926190857109.html> [Accessed 4 August 2019].

Al Jazeera, 2019. Saudi Arabia lifts travel restriction on its women. *Al Jazeera News*. [online] 1 August. Available at: <www.aljazeera.com/news/2019/08/saudi-arabia-lifts-travel-restriction-women-190802010707868.html> [Accessed 4 August 2019].

Anderson, B., 2006. *Imagined Communities: Reflections on the Origin and Spread of Nationalism (Revised Version)*. London: Verso.

Arendt, H., 1968. On Humanity in Dark Times: Thoughts about Lessing (Translated by C. and R. Winston). *Men in Dark Times*. San Diego, CA: Harcourt Bryce Co., pp. 3–32.

Aronsson, L., 2004. Place Attachment of Vacation Residents: Between Tourists and Permanent Residents. In: C.M. Hall and D.K. Müller, (eds.), *Tourism, Mobility and Second Homes: Between Elite Landscape and Common Ground*. Clevedon: Channel View Publications. Chapter 5.

Artini, L.P., Nilan P. and Threadgold, S., 2011. Young Indonesian Cruise Workers, Symbolic Violence and International Class Relations. *Asian Journal of Social Science*, [e-journal] 7(6), pp. 3–14. DOI: 10.5539/ass.v7n6p3.

Augustyn, A., 2012. Peace of Westphalia. *Encyclopædia Britannica Online*. [online] London: Encyclopædia Britannica (UK). Available at: <www.britannica.com/event/Peace-of-Westphalia> [Accessed 12 July 2019].

Bakštein, E., 2016. *Iris Recognition*. [pdf] Available at: <www.mlmu.cz/wp-content/uploads/2014/09/Iris-MLMU.pdf> [Accessed 4 August 2019].

BBC, 2017. Trump's executive order: Who does travel ban affect? *BBC News*. [online] 10 February. Available at: <www.bbc.com/news/world-us-canada-38781302> [Accessed 10 February 2017].

Bell, S., 2019. Deadly export: Canadians responsible for hundreds of terrorism deaths and injuries overseas. *Global News*. [online] 9 April. Available at: <https://globalnews.ca/news/5117211/deadly-export-canadian-terrorists/> [Accessed 09 April 2019].

Bianchi, R.V. and Stephenson, M.L., 2014. *Tourism and Citizenship: Rights, Freedoms and Responsibilities in the Global Order*. Abingdon, Oxon: Routledge.

Biometrics Institute, 2019. *Ethical Principles for the Biometrics Institute*. [online] March. Available at: <www.biometricsinstitute.org/ethical-principles-for-biometrics/> [Accessed 3 August 2019].

Buhalis, D., Darcy, S. and Ambrose, I. eds., 2012. *Best Practice in Accessible Tourism: Inclusion, Disability, Ageing Population and Tourism*. Bristol: Channel View Publication.

Burt, C., 2019. Airport biometrics adoption itinerary explored by diverse stakeholders. *Biometrics Update*. [online] 13 June. Available at: <www.biometricupdate.com/201906/airport-biometrics-adoption-itinerary-explored-by-diverse-stakeholders> [Accessed 4 August 2019].

Central Coordinating Commission for the Promotion of Accessibility (CCPT), 1996. *European Concept for Accessibility*. [pdf] March. Available at: <www.eca.lu/index.php/documents/eucan-documents/14-1996-european-concept-for-accessibility-1996/file> [Accessed 25 July 2019].

Chen, J.S. and Wang, W., 2015. Foreign labours in Arctic destinations: seasonal workers' motivations and job skills. *Current Issues in Tourism*, [e-journal] 18(4), pp. 350–360, DOI: http://dx.doi.org/10.1080/13683500.2014.894499.

Cohen, S.A., Duncan, T, and Thulemark, M., 2013. Lifestyle Mobilities: The Crossroads of Travel, Leisure and Migration. *Mobilities*, [e-journal] 10(1), pp. 155–172. DOI: 10.1080/17450101.2013.826481.

Cook, N. and Butz, D., 2019a. Moving toward mobility justice. In: N. Cook and D. Butz, (eds.), *Mobilities, Mobility Justice and Social Justice*. Abingdon, Oxon: Routledge. Chapter 1.

Cook, N. and Butz, D., 2019b. Theorizing mobility justice. In: N. Cook, and D. Butz, (eds.), *Mobilities, Mobility Justice and Social Justice*. Abingdon, Oxon: Routledge. Chapter 2.

Cooper, C., 2009. Airlines censured for 'tax on breathing'. *The Guardian*. [online] 17 January. Available at: <www.theguardian.com/money/2009/jan/17/airline-charge-oxygen> [Accessed 25 July 2019].

Corderoy, J., 2017. Saudi Arabia may Ease Rules for Tourists as It Tries to Attract More Western Visitors. *News (Australia)*. [online] 2 August. Available at: <www.news.com.au/travel/world-travel/middle-east/saudi-arabia-may-ease-rules-for-tourists-as-it-tries-to-attract-more-western-visitors/news-story/29fb02304fe9802c0fdcf085579bf555> [Accessed 4 August 2019].

Czaika, M., de Haas, H. and Villares-Varela, M., 2018. The Global Evolution of Travel Visa Regimes. *Population and Development Review*, [e-Journal] 44(3), pp. 589–622. doi: 10.1111/padr.12166.

Czaika, M. and Neumayer, E., 2017. Visa Restrictions and Economic Globalisation. *Applied Geography*, [e-journal] 84, pp. 75–82. https://doi.org/10.1016/j.apgeog.2017.04.011.

Daly, H.E., 2004. Population, Migration, and Globalization. (Population and its Discontent: One of 12 features in this special issue) *World Watch Magazine.* September/October. pp. 41–44.

Danchin, P., n.d. Article 24: Introduction. Universal Declaration of Human Rights. [online]. Available at: <http://ccnmtl.columbia.edu/projects/mmt/udhr/article_24.html> [Accessed 19 July 2019].

De Genova, N., 2010. The Deportation regime: sovereignty, space and the freedom of movement. In: N. De Genova and N. Peutz, (eds.), *The Deportation Regime: Sovereignty, Space, and the Freedom of Movement.* Durham, NC: Duke University Press, pp. 33–68.

Department of Justice, 2010. *2010 ADA Standards for Accessible Design.* [pdf] Available at: <www.ada.gov/regs2010/2010ADAStandards/2010ADAStandards.pdf?utm_medium=website&utm_source=archdaily.com> [Accessed 25 July 2019].

D'Hauteserre, A.M., 2008. Postcolonialism, colonialism and tourism. In: A. A. Lew, C. M. Hall, and A. M. Williams, (eds.), *A Companion to Tourism.* Oxford: Blackwell Publishing. Chapter 19.

Federal Register, 2017a. *Protecting the Nation from Foreign Terrorist Entry into the United States: Executive Order 13769 of January 27, 2017. 2017–02281.* [online] 1 February. Available at: <www.federalregister.gov/d/2017–02281> [Accessed 5 September 2017].

Federal Register, 2017b. *Protecting the Nation from Foreign Terrorist Entry into the United States: Executive Order 13780 of Mar 6, 2017. 2017–04837.* [online] 9 March. Available at: <www.federalregister.gov/d/2017–04837> [Accessed 5 September 2017].

Glick Schiller, N. and Salazar, N.B., 2013. Regimes of Mobility Across the Globe. *Journal of Ethnic and Migration Studies*, [e-journal] 39(2), pp. 183–200, http://dx.doi.org/10.1080/1369183X.2013.723253.

Goodman, J., 2017. US travel ban: Why these seven countries? *BBC News.* [online] 30 January. Available at: <www.bbc.com/news/world-us-canada-38798588> [Accessed 30 January 2017].

Government of Canada, 2014. *History of Passports.* [online] 10 April. Available at: <www.canada.ca/en/immigration-refugees-citizenship/services/canadians/celebrate-being-canadian/teachers-corner/history-passports.html> [Accessed 31 July 2019].

Hall, C.M. and Müller, D.K., 2004. Introduction: second homes, curse or blessing? Revisited. In: C.M. Hall and D.K. Müller, (eds.), *Tourism, Mobility and Second Homes: Between Elite Landscape and Common Ground.* Clevedon: Channel View Publications. Chapter 1.

Harvey, D., 1990. *The Condition of Postmodernity: An Enquiry into the Origins of Cultural Change.* Cambridge, MA: Blackwell.

Heart FM.ca, 2020. Government Urges Canadians Abroad to Come Home. *104.7 Heart FM.* [online] 16 March. Available at: <www.heartfm.ca/news/local-news/government-urges-canadians-abroad-to-come-home/> [Accessed 16 March 2020].

Hubbard, B., 2017. Saudi Arabia Agrees to Let Women Drive. *New York Times.* [online] 26 September. Available at: <www.nytimes.com/2017/09/26/world/middleeast/saudi-arabia-women-drive.html> [Accessed 4 August 2019].

ICAO, 2020. *Effects of Novel Coronavirus (COVID-19) on Civil Aviation: Economic Impact Analysis.* [pdf] Available at: <www.icao.int/sustainability/Documents/COVID-19/ICAO%20COVID%202020%2005%2025%20Economic%20Impact.pdf> [Accessed 25 May 2020].

Joppe, M., 2012. Migrant Workers: Challenges and Opportunities in Addressing Tourism Labour Shortages. *Tourism Management*, [e-journal] 33, pp. 662–671. DOI: doi:10.1016/j.tourman.2011.07.009.

Kacowicz, A.M., 1998. *Regionalization, Globalization and Nationalism: Convergent, Divergent or Overlapping? Working Paper #262. The Helen Kellogg Institute of International Studies*. [pdf] Available at: <https://kellogg.nd.edu/sites/default/files/old_files/documents/262.pdf> [Accessed 25 July 2019].

Mackenzie, J., Monetta, S. and Smythe, A., 2020. Coronavirus: Quarantined Italian village turned into human laboratory. *BBC News*. [online video] 6 April. Available from <www.bbc.com/news/av/world-europe-52159316/coronavirus-quarantined-italian-village-turned-into-human-laboratory> [Accessed 6 April 2020].

McKay, A.G., 1975. *Houses, Villas, and Palaces in the Roman World*. Reprint 1998. Baltimore, MD: Johns Hopkins University Press.

Ministry of Land, Infrastructure, Transport and Tourism (MILT), n.d. 2.6. *Elevator/Escalator*. [pdf] Available at: <www.mlit.go.jp/common/001179669.pdf> [Accessed 25 July 2019].

Müller, D.K., 2004. Mobility, tourism, and second homes. In: A. A. Lew, C. M. Hall, and A. M. Williams, (eds.), *A Companion to Tourism*. Oxford: Blackwell Publishing. Chapter 31.

Müller, D.K., Hall, C.M. and Keen, D., 2004. Second home tourism impact, planning and management. In: C.M. Hall and D.K. Müller, (eds.), *Tourism, Mobility and Second Homes: Between Elite Landscape and Common Ground*. Clevedon: Channel View Publications. Chapter 2.

Neumayer, E., 2006. Unequal Access to Foreign Spaces: How States Use Visa Restrictions to Regulate Mobility in a Globalised World. *Transactions of the Institute of British Geographers*, 31(1), pp. 72–84. DOI: 10.2139/ssrn.695122.

OHCHR, n.d. *Convention on the Rights of Persons with Disabilities*. [online] www.ohchr.org/EN/HRBodies/CRPD/Pages/ConventionRightsPersonsWithDisabilities.aspx.

Ontario Human Rights Commission, n.d. Frequently Asked Questions. *Ontario Human Rights Commission*. [online]. Available at: <www.ohrc.on.ca/en/faqs> [Accessed 21 July 2019].

Open Borders, n.d. *Immigrants Do Jobs Natives Won't Do*. [online]. Available at: <https://openborders.info/immigrants-do-jobs-natives-wont-do/> [Accessed 4 August 2019].

Oxygen Solutions, 2014. List of Airlines that Allow Portable Oxygen. *Oxygen Solutions*. [online] 26 March. Available at: <https://oxygensolutions.com.au/the-list-of-portable-oxygen-loving-airlines/> [Accessed 25 July 2019].

Pankanti, S., 2003. Biometric Recognition: Security and Privacy Concerns. *IEEE Security and Privacy Magazine,* [e-journal] 1(2), pp. 33 – 42. DOI: 10.1109/MSECP.2003.1193209.

Paris, C., 2011. *Affluence, Mobility and Second Home Ownership*. London: Routledge. https://doi.org/10.4324/9780203846506.

Pickel, A. 2005. Introduction. False oppositions: reconceptualising economic nationalism in globalizing world. In: E. Helleiner and A. Pickel, (eds.), *Economic Nationalism in Globalizing World*. New York: Cornell University Press. pp. 1–18.

Pulmonary Hypertension Association UK, 2018. Travelling with Oxygen. *Living with Pulmonary Hypertension*. [online]. Available at: <www.phauk.org/living-with-pulmonary-hypertension/travelling-with-ph/travelling-with-oxygen/> [Accessed 25 July 2019].

References, 2019. *What Are the Dimensions of a Standard Wheelchair?* [online]. Available at: <www.reference.com/health/dimensions-standard-wheelchair-45f8c65bc8b23f29> [Accessed 25 July 2019].

RT, 2019. Saudi Arabian women can now hold passports and travel alone without men's blessing. *Russia Today.* [online]. Available at: <www.rt.com/news/465630-saudi-arabian-women-passports-travel/> [Accessed 4 August 2019].

Schengen Visa Info., 2018. *The Schengen Agreement - History and the Definition.* [online]. updated 18 October. Available at: <www.schengenvisainfo.com/schengen-agreement/> [Accessed 25 July 2019].

Schouten, P., 2014. Security as Controversy: Reassembling Security at Amsterdam Airport, *Security Dialogue.* [e-journal] 45(1), pp. 23–42, DOI: 10.1177/0967010613515014.

Scootaround, 2019. *The Best Narrow Wheelchairs for Tight Spaces and Doorways.* Available at: <www.scootaround.com/blog/mobility/216-the-best-narrow-wheelchairs-for-tight-spaces-and-doorways> [Accessed 25 July 2019].

Shaikh, A., n.d. *Ethical Issues in the Use of Biometric Technology.* [pdf] Available at: <www.bcs.org/upload/pdf/ashaikh.pdf> [Accessed 3 August 2019].

Sheller, M., 2011. Mobility, *Sociopedia.isa.* [online]. DOI: 10.1177/205684601163

Sheller, M. and Urry, J., 2004. Places to play, places in play. In: M. Sheller and J. Urry, (eds.), *Tourism Mobilities: Places to play, places in play.* Abingdon, Oxon: Routledge. Chapter 1.

Sheller, M. and Urry, J., 2006. The New Mobilities Paradigm. *Environment and Planning A: Economy and Space.* [e-journal] 38(2), pp. 207–226. DOI: https://doi.org/10.1068/a37268

Taylor, M.M., 2010. Bending Broken Rules: The Fourth Amendment Implication of Full-Body Scanners in Preflight Screening. *Richmond Journal of Law and Technology,* [pdf] 17(1), 1–38. Available at: <http://jolt.richmond.edu/v17i1/article4.pdf>.

Terry, W. C., 2011. Geographic Limits to Global Labor Market Flexibility: The Human Resources Paradox of the Cruise Industry. *Geoforum,* [e-journal] 42, pp. 660–670. doi:10.1016/j.geoforum.2011.06.006.

The Canadian Press, 2019. Ad firms says controversial Bernier billboards staying up. *CityNews.* [online]. Available at: <https://toronto.CityNews.ca/2019/08/25/ad-firm-says-controversial-billboards-promoting-berniers-party-staying-up-2/> [Accessed 25 August 2019].

The Guardian, 2006. A Brief History of the Passport: From a Royal Letter to a Microchip. *The Guardian.* [online] 17 November. Available at: <www.theguardian.com/travel/2006/nov/17/travelnews> [Accessed 31 July 2019].

Trip Advisor Canada, 2015. *Travelling with Disabilities Forum.* [online]. Available at: <www.tripadvisor.ca/SearchForums?q=oxygen&scope=2&sub-search=Search&ff=12336&geo=1&returnTo=__2F__ShowForum__2D__g1__2D__i12336__2D__Traveling__5F__With__5F__Disabilities__2E__html> [Accessed 25 July 2019].

Tsagarousianou, R., 2004. *Rethinking the concept of diaspora: mobility, connectivity and communication in a globalised world. Westminster Papers in Communication and Culture (University of Westminster, London),* 1(1), pp. 52–65.

United Nations, Department of Economic and Social Affairs, Population Division (UNDESA), n.d. *Convention on the Rights of Persons with Disabilities (CRPD).* [online]. Available at: <www.un.org/development/desa/disabilities/convention-on-the-rights-of-persons-with-disabilities.html> [Accessed 18 June 2019].

United Nations, Department of Economic and Social Affairs, Population Division (UNDESA), 2015. *Population 2030: Demographic challenges and opportunities for sustainable development planning* [pdf] Available at: <www.un.org/en/development/desa/population/publications/pdf/trends/Population2030.pdf> [Accessed 18 June 2019].

UN enable, 2004. II. Architectural Design Considerations, 2. Elevators. *Accessibility for the Disabled - A Design Manual for a Barrier Free Environment.* [online]. Available at: <www.un.org/esa/socdev/enable/designm/AD2-02.htm> [Accessed 18 September 2018].

United Nations Human Rights Committee, 1999. Human Rights Committee, General Comment 27, Freedom of movement (Art. 12), U.N. Doc CCPR/C/21/Rev.1/Add.9 (1999). [online] Available at: <hrlibrary.umn.edu/gencomm/hrcom27.htm >.

University of Michigan Law School, 2017. Special Collection: Civil Rights Challenges to Trump Refugee/Visa Order. *University of Michigan Law School, Civil Rights Litigation Clearinghouse.* [online]. Available at: <www.clearinghouse.net/results.php?searchSpecial Collection=44> [Accessed 5 September 2017].

UNWTO, 2017. *Global Code of Ethics for Tourism.* [pdf] 21 September 2017. Available at: <cf.cdn.unwto.org/sites/all/files/docpdf/gcetpassportglobalcodeen.pdf> [Accessed 20 October 2017].

Urry, J., 2010. Mobile Sociology. *British Journal of Sociology.* [e-journal] 61(s1), pp. 347–366. DOI: https://doi.org/10.1111/j.1468-4446.2009.01249.x.

Urry, J. and Larsen, J., 2011, *The Tourist Gaze 3.0.* London: SAGE Publications Ltd. doi: 10.4135/9781446251904.n1.

US Department of Homeland Security, 2019. *Biometrics.* [pdf] 9 May. Available at: <www.dhs.gov/biometrics> [Accessed 3 August 2019].

VARINDIA, 2019. *NEC to Install Customs Procedure System with Face Recognition for Six Major Airports in Japan* [pdf] 11 July. Available at: <www.varindia.com/news/nec-to-install-customs-procedure-system-with-face-recognition-for-six-major-airports-in-japan> [Accessed 3 August 2019].

Vezzoli, S. and Flahaux, M.-L., 2017. How Do Post-Colonial Ties and Migration Regimes Shape Travel Visa Requirements? The Case of Caribbean Nationals, *Journal of Ethnic and Migration Studies,* [e-journal] 43(7), pp. 1141–1163, DOI: 10.1080/1369183X.2016.1228446.

Wasson, D.L., 2018. Roman Daily Life. Ancient History Encyclopaedia. [online]. 23 April. Available at: <www.ancient.eu/article/637/roman-daily-life/> [Accessed 29 December 2018].

Wickins, J., 2007. The Ethics of Biometrics: The Risk of Social Exclusion from the Widespread Use of Electronic Identification. *Science and Engineering Ethics,* [e-journal] 13, pp. 45–54, DOI 10.1007/s11948-007-9003-z.

WTTC, 2019. World Travel & Tourism Council: World, Transformed. [pdf] Available at: <www.wttc.org/publications/2019/megatrends-2019/> [Accessed 18 June 2019].

Xing, L., 2020. Ottawa 'remotely' inspected Ontario farms while COVID-19 infected hundreds of migrant workers. *CBC News.* [online]. 1 July. Available at: <www.cbc.ca/news/canada/toronto/migrant-workers-covid-coronavirus-inspections-1.5633737> [Accessed 1 July 2020].

10
HUMAN RIGHTS AND LABOUR CONDITIONS IN TOURISM ESTABLISHMENTS

10.1 Employees in tourism establishments

The travel and tourism sectors are highly labour intensive. In 2019, travel and tourism created more than 119 million jobs directly. If wider effects are included, more than 330 million persons were supported by the sectors. This translated to one in ten jobs globally, and a total contribution of more than ten per cent to global GDP in 2019 (World Travel & Tourism Council, 2020). Unfortunately, the 2019–20 COVID-19 pandemic has had a disastrous impact on employment in travel and tourism. According to the United Nations World Tourism Organization's (UNWTO) projected impact on tourism in 2020, 100 to 120 million direct tourism jobs are at risk due to the COVID-19 induced decline in tourism arrivals (UNWTO, 2020a). Despite the gloomy outlook, the crisis could also represent an opportunity to promote human rights and build better tourism for people, planet and prosperity. The UNWTO envisions that "[t]he principles of decent work and safety at a workplace should guide measures aiming at enhancing job security in tourism and at providing formal employment" during the recovery (UNWTO, 2020b, p. 7). The tourism sector provides for many entry-level jobs for migrants and other groups who might otherwise have a difficult time to enter the workforce. It is also a major employer of young people. According to the International Labour Organization (ILO), most tourism workers are under 35 years of age and half of them globally are under 25 years of age (ILO, 2017a; see also Stacey, 2015). In addition, the tourism sector provides for many jobs, where higher education is not necessary. Data from European OECD countries (Stacey, 2015) show that the number of workers with tertiary level education is much lower than in the economy as a whole. Many tourism workers are self-employed or employed in small and medium-sized enterprises. Approximately every second worker in the tourism sector is employed in enterprises employing less than ten persons, while more than 70 per cent work in enterprises employing less than 50 persons. With the number of people working in the travel and tourism sector, it has strong potential to be a driving force in reaching the Agenda 2030 Sustainable Development Goals (SDG) of full and productive employment for all (see Box 10.1).

BOX 10.1 AGENDA 2030 SUSTAINABLE DEVELOPMENT GOALS

Goal 8 Promote sustained, inclusive and sustainable economic growth, full and productive employment and decent work for all

...

8.5 By 2030, achieve full and productive employment and decent work for all men and women, including for young people and persons with disabilities, and equal pay for equal value.

8.6 By 2020, substantially reduce the proportion of youth not in employment, education or training.

8.7 Take immediate and effective measures to eradicate forced labour, end modern slavery and human trafficking and secure the prohibition and elimination of the worst forms of child labour, including recruitment and use of child soldiers, and by 2025 end child labour in all its forms.

8.8 Protect labour rights and promote safe and secure working environments for all workers, including migrant workers, in particular women migrants, and those in precarious employment.

8.9 By 2030, devise and implement policies to promote sustainable tourism that creates jobs and promotes local culture and products.

...

Source: (United Nations, 2015).[1]

Although employment in the tourism sector can create opportunities to countless persons, and in particular to women, migrants and youth, tourism workers also get exploited by unscrupulous employers. The specific features of the tourism sector in comparison with the economy as a whole create a favourable environment for human rights violations. Workers in the tourism sector work part-time more often than in other sectors. They are also often employed in temporary positions and have no job security. In addition, the turnover of employees is high. Data from OECD countries show that more than 45 per cent of tourism workers stay less than 2 years with the same employer, compared with less than 25 per cent for the total economy (Stacey, 2015, p. 10). Problems in the sector range from forced and child labour, collective bargaining issues, dangerous work, gender inequality as well as other violations of human rights. In the following, these issues are discussed more in detail, with a focus on how international human rights law has responded to the challenges present in the travel and tourism labour force. First, the chapter starts with a general overview of international human rights and labour standards in the travel and tourism sector in Section 10.2. Secondly, the right to freedom of association and collective bargaining among tourism and travel workers is addressed in Section 10.3. The chapter continues with sections concentrating on the problems with forced labour in Section 10.4 and child labour in Section 10.5, the right to decent work for all in Section 10.6, the problems with discrimination of employees in the tourism and travel industry in Section 10.7 and the rights of migrant workers in Section 10.8. Finally, a conclusion in Section 10.9 summarizes the main themes in the chapter.

10.2 Human rights and labour standards in the travel and tourism sector

It is a fundamental human right to be allowed to work. According to the Universal Declaration of Human Rights (UDHR) "[e]veryone has the right to work, to free choice of employment, to just and favourable conditions of work and to protection against unemployment" (art. 23). Furthermore, everyone has the right to equal pay for equal work, the right to just and favourable remuneration allowing an existence of human dignity, the right to join trade unions and the right to rest and leisure, including a reasonable limitation of working hours and periodic holidays with pay (art. 23–24 UDHR). The non-binding declarations in the UDHR were later included in two of the core human rights conventions, the International Covenant on Civil and Political Rights (ICCPR) (art. 8, 22) and the International Covenant on Economic, Social and Cultural Rights (ICESCR) (art. 6–9). Both of the conventions are legally binding for the 170 (ICESCR) and 173 (ICCPR) state parties to the convention.

The fundamental labour-related human rights from the International Bill of Rights (the UDHR, ICCPR and ICESCR) are further elaborated upon in specific conventions addressing labour rights. The ILO is a specialized agency under the United Nations, bringing together governments, employers and employees to set globally applicable labour standards. The ILO, with its 187 member countries, plays a central role in advancing international human rights in the employment context. According to the Declaration of Philadelphia (1944), the ILO has the obligation to promote rights at work, decent working conditions, policies in regard to wages and earnings as well as other conditions of work where a "just share of the fruits of progress" is shared by all workers. In its Declaration on Fundamental Principles and Rights at Work (1998), ILO declared that:

> Members, even if they have not ratified the Conventions in question, have an obligation arising from the very fact of membership in the Organization to respect, to promote and to realize, in good faith and in accordance with the Constitution, the principles concerning the fundamental rights which are the subject of those Conventions, namely:
>
> (a) Freedom of association and the effective recognition of the right to collective bargaining;
> (b) the elimination of all forms of forced or compulsory labour;
> (c) the effective abolition of child labour; and
> (d) the elimination of discrimination in respect of employment and occupation
>
> *(Declaration on Fundamental Principles and Rights at Work, 1998, p. 2)*

In addition to the non-binding declarations, the ILO has developed several fundamental conventions, addressing working conditions globally. Furthermore, ILO has adopted conventions applicable specifically to the travel and tourism industry (see Box 10.2).

BOX 10.2 FUNDAMENTAL ILO CONVENTIONS

- Convention (No. 87) Concerning Freedom of Association and Protection of the Right to Organise (1948)
- Convention (No. 98) concerning the application of the principles of the right to organise and to bargain collectively (1949)
- Convention (No. 29) concerning Forced or Compulsory Labour (1930), and Protocol of 2014 to the Forced Labour Convention (2014)
- Abolition of Forced Labour Convention (No. 105) (1957)
- Convention (No. 138) Concerning Minimum Age for Admission to Employment (1973)
- Convention (No. 182) Concerning the Prohibition and Immediate Action for the Elimination of the Worst Forms of Child Labour (1999)
- Equal Remuneration Convention (No. 100) (1951)
- Discrimination (Employment and Occupation) Convention (No. 111) (1958)

ILO CONVENTIONS & GUIDELINES APPLICABLE TO THE TRAVEL AND TOURISM INDUSTRY

- Convention (No. 172) Concerning Working Conditions in Hotels, Restaurants and Similar Establishments (1991) and Working Conditions (Hotels and Restaurants) Recommendation (No. 179) (1991).
- ILO Guidelines on Decent Work and Socially Responsible Tourism (2017b)

ILO (2019).

In addition to the ILO conventions and guidelines, voluntary initiatives, such as the United Nations Guiding Principles on Business and Human Rights (UNGP) and the United Nations Global Compact promote labour rights as part of human rights (see Chapter 2 for further discussions).

10.3 Freedom of association and collective bargaining in tourism establishments

The right to freedom of association, including the right to form and join trade unions for the protection of a person's collective interests, is a well-established human right. It is acknowledged in the UDHR (art. 23(4)), ICCPR (art. 22) and ICESCR (art. 8). The ICCPR guarantees the right to form and join trade unions without elaborating further on the subject, while the ICESCR includes a right for trade unions to establish national federations and to function freely subject to no limitations, other than those prescribed in law and necessary in a democratic society. Most importantly, the ICESCR establishes a right to strike, provided that it is exercised in conformity with the laws of the country. The right to strike is an integral part of collective bargaining. If there is no threat of any type of consequences for employers who refuse to negotiate in good faith, trade unions have no bargaining power.

> In 2015, the Supreme Court of Canada elaborated on the right to strike in the groundbreaking case of Saskatchewan Federation of Labour v. Saskatchewan (2015): "this Court [has] recognized that the [Canadian] Charter [of Rights and Freedoms] values of "[h]uman dignity, equality, liberty, respect for the autonomy of the person and the enhancement of democracy" supported protecting the right to a meaningful process of collective bargaining within the scope of s. 2(d). The right to strike is essential to realizing these values through a collective bargaining process because it permits workers to withdraw their labour in concert when collective bargaining reaches an impasse. Through a strike, workers come together to participate directly in the process of determining their wages, working conditions and the rules that will govern their working lives. The ability to strike thereby allows workers, through

collective action, to refuse to work under imposed terms and conditions. This collective action at the moment of impasse is an affirmation of the dignity and autonomy of employees in their working lives.

The right to strike also promotes equality in the bargaining process. This Court has long recognized the deep inequalities that structure the relationship between employers and employees, and the vulnerability of employees in this context. While strike activity itself does not guarantee that a labour dispute will be resolved in any particular manner, or that it will be resolved at all, it is the possibility of a strike which enables workers to negotiate their employment terms on a more equal footing."

In addition to the provisions on freedom of association and collective bargaining in fundamental human rights conventions, the ILO has adopted two additional conventions covering the same subject; the Convention (No. 87) Concerning Freedom of Association and Protection of the Right to Organise (1948) and the Convention (No. 98) Concerning the Application of the Principles of the Right to Organise and to Bargain Collectively (1949). According to the freedom of association convention, workers have the right to establish and join organizations of their own choosing without previous authorization (art. 2) as well as to undertake "all necessary and appropriate measures to ensure that workers and employers may exercise the right to freely organize" (art. 11). The Convention on collective bargaining protects workers against anti-union discrimination in their employment. Member states who are parties to the Convention shall protect against all discrimination based on trade union membership, and in particular to acts calculated to make the employment of a worker subject to the condition that he or she shall not join a union or shall leave a trade union, or acts that cause the dismissal or the prejudice of a worker by reason of union membership (art. 1). The two conventions have been ratified by 155 countries (Convention Concerning Freedom of Association) respectively 166 countries (Convention Concerning the Application of the Principles of the Right to Organise and to Bargain Collectively). However, several populous countries, such as United States, China, Iran and India, are not state parties to the conventions, leaving more than 40 per cent of global workers living in countries that have not signed the conventions (ILO, 2019, p. 3). As an example of strike activity in the tourism accommodation industry, approximately 1,500 hotel workers in Vancouver, Canada went on strike in 2019 for better wages and working conditions when they could not reach an agreement during collective bargaining negotiations; strike action at seven downtown hotels and one airport hotel lasted for a month, before unionized hotel workers reached an agreement with the hotels (Korstrom, 2019; Lazaruk, 2019).

10.4 Forced and compulsory labour in tourism establishments

The prohibition on subjecting another human to forced labour is a deeply rooted human rights principle. No one shall be required to perform forced or compulsory labour, no one shall be held in servitude and no one shall be held in slavery. Despite these fundamental rights, proclaimed in the UDHR (art. 4) as well as IICPR (art. 8), a substantial number of the people in the world are subjected to forced and compulsory labour. In 2016, it was estimated that approximately 21 million adults and 4 million children were victims of forced labour at any given time during the year. Out of the 25 million victims, 16 million were working in the private sector. Women are disproportionally affected. They represent 99 per cent of forced labour in the commercial sex industry and 58 per cent of the victims in other sections of the economy (ILO, 2017c).

According to the Forced Labour Convention (1930), forced or compulsory labour is defined as "all work or service which is exacted from any person under the menace of any penalty and for which the said person has not offered himself voluntarily" (art. 2). All members to the Convention undertake to suppress the use of forced or compulsory labour in all its forms (art. 1). The 1930 Convention was later supplemented by the Abolition of Forced Labour Convention (1957), expanding the forms of prohibited forced labour, and the Protocol of 2014 to the Forced Labour Convention (2014). According to the supplementing protocol, member states shall in addition to prohibiting forced labour, take effective measures to prevent forced labour by educating people, enforce appropriate legislation and strengthen labour inspection services. Victims, and in particular migrant workers, shall be protected from abuse and have access to effective remedies. In addition, state parties shall ensure that there are appropriate measures in place to sanction the perpetrators of forced labour (art. 1–2) (see Box 10.3).

Forced labour in the tourism sector can take many forms, from exploitation of undocumented migrants as housekeeping staff members, to sex trafficking in hotel rooms. With the transient nature of travel and tourism employment and the high number of temporary jobs, the sector is at high-risk and particularly vulnerable to exploitative business practices. The problems with sex trafficking and children working in the adult entertainment sector are further developed in Chapter 13.

BOX 10.3 CASE STUDY: THE MYANMAR TOURISM BUSINESS

Myanmar has had a long history of forced labour by the military government, which ruled the country from the 1960s until the first elections were held in 2010. The military government systematically made use of the forced labour of thousands of civilians on development projects, such as roads and military camps. Ethnic minorities, such as the Shan, Karen, Karenni, Rakhine and Rohingya groups were particularly vulnerable when the military requested villagers to perform labour. In the 1990s, the government implemented many large infrastructure projects. Forced labour was linked to the building of airports, hotels, golf courses, roads and other facilities built in an effort to develop tourism in the country (U.S. Department of Labor, 2000). According to the findings of the ILO (1998), large infrastructure projects "appeared to be constructed in large part with the use of forced labour, sometimes involving hundreds of thousands of workers". The findings led to the unprecedented action of ILO imposing sanctions on the country in 2000 (ILO, 2000). The sanctions were lifted in 2012, after key reforms in Myanmar's executive, legislative and judiciary framework (ILO, 2012; 2013). However, despite the reforms, forced labour continues to be a problem in the country. An estimated 4.1 million people in Myanmar were forced to work in state-imposed forced labour in 2016. This includes civilians who were forced to work in agriculture and construction as well as military conscripts who were forced to do non-military work. Globally, a majority of the workers in the public sector were involved in compulsory labour for the purpose of economic development (ILO, 2017c, p. 40–41). The Independent Fact-Finding Mission on Myanmar, established by the Human Rights Council of the Unites Nations, reported as late as in September 2018 that the use of forced labour by the military still continues on a systematic scale, particularly in villages close to military compounds (Human Rights Council, 2018).

10.5 Child labour in tourism establishments

Children who work deserve special measures of protection and assistance. The United Nations Convention on the Rights of the Child of 1989 (CRC) is the most widely adopted human rights convention in the world. With its 196 state parties, the convention has been adopted by every single country, except for the United States. According to article 32, state parties undertake to recognize "the right of the child to be protected from economic exploitation and from performing any work that is likely to be hazardous or to interfere with the child's education, or to be harmful to the child's health or physical, mental, spiritual, moral or social development" (art. 32). State parties shall also provide for a minimum age for admission to employment, appropriately regulate hours and conditions of employment and provide for appropriate sanctions for violations of article 32 (see also ICESR, art. 10(3)).

In addition to the more general principles in the CRC, the ILO adopted Convention (No. 138) Concerning Minimum Age for Admission to Employment in 1973 (see also Minimum Age Recommendation, 1973). The state parties to the convention undertake to create a national policy to ensure the effective abolition of child labour as well as to raise the national minimum age for employment, so that it is consistent with the emotional and physical development of children (art. 1). The minimum age shall not be less than the age of completion of compulsory schooling, and in any case, not less than 15 years of age (art. 2). Children between the age of 13 and 15 years of age are allowed to undertake light work, which is not harmful to their development and does not interfere with their schooling (art. 7). The minimum age for hazardous work is set at 18 years of age (art. 3). Developing countries are allowed to lower the minimum age to 14 years during a transitional period (art. 2). They are also allowed to initially limit the application of the convention to certain sectors, such as mining, manufacturing, electricity, gas and water (art. 5).

In 1999, the Convention (No. 138) Concerning Minimum Age for Admission to Employment (1973) was supplemented by the Convention (No. 182) Concerning the Prohibition and Immediate Action for the Elimination of the Worst Forms of Child Labour (1999) (see also Worst Forms of Child Labour Recommendation, 1999). The 1999 convention defines "worst forms of child labour" as all forms of slavery and forced labour, the use, procurement or offering of a child for prostitution, the production of pornography or pornographic performances, the use, procurement or offering of a child for illicit activities, and in particular the production or trafficking in drugs and other work which by its nature is likely to harm the health, safety or morals of children, defined as all persons under the age of 18 (art. 2–3). Each member state undertakes to take action to eliminate as a priority all worst forms of child labour (art. 6).

The Convention (No. 138) Concerning Minimum Age for Admission to Employment (1973) has 172 ratifications (the convention has not been ratified by Australia, New Zealand or the United States) while the Convention (No. 182) Concerning the Prohibition and Immediate Action for the Elimination of the Worst Forms of Child Labour (1999) has 186 ratifications, making the conventions almost universally accepted as principles of international law. Four countries limit the application of the minimum age convention to certain sectors, with the rest of the state parties setting the minimum age at either 14 or 15 years of age. Although the principles in both conventions enjoy widespread support globally, state parties have not always succeeded in protecting children from economic and social exploitation in employment. ILO estimates that there are 152 million children between the age of 5–17 years involved in child labour. Out of these children, 72 million children perform hazardous work and work categorized as "worst forms of child labour", while another 80 million are below the minimum age for work. There is a gender disparity in child labour. Although there are more boys than girls in child labour, boys and girls perform different types of work. Girls often have to carry out heavy household work, which prevents them from attending school (ILO, 2019, p. 3).

> According to the Constitution of India (art. 32) a person can move the Indian Supreme Court to enforce any of the fundamental rights enshrined in the Constitution of India. In Bachpan Bachao Andolan v. Union of India & Others (2011) a public interest petition was filed by a non-governmental organisation, Bachpan Bachao Andolan (BBA), on behalf of children working in circuses. At the time, organized crime, in the form of trafficking of young girls from Nepal to Indian circuses, was rampant. The young girls were

working from dawn to around midnight, received inadequate amounts of food and were confined to small spaces in the circus compounds. Accidents were common, when some of the girls were forced to engage in high-risk activities, such as ring of death performances, sword performances and rope dancing at high altitudes. The child artists were bound by contracts of 3 to 10 years and had no means of escape, if they wanted to leave the circus. The BBA argued that considering the conditions for children working in circuses, the children were deprived of their fundamental human rights according to the Indian Constitution. The Indian Supreme Court agreed and directed the Indian government to prohibit the employment of children in circuses, to conduct simultaneous raids at all circuses and rescue the children in the circuses as well as to design a proper rehabilitation programme for the children who were rescued. The case is noteworthy for its enforcement of labour laws and the protection of children's fundamental human rights in a developing country. The founder of BBA, Kailash Satyarthi, received the Nobel Peace Prize in 2014 for his work with children's rights.

Most children involved in child labour tend to work in the agricultural sector (70.9 per cent) and help out with family chores (69.1 per cent are contributing family workers). However, the extent of children working in the travel and tourism sector is still substantial. An estimated 17.2 per cent of the 152 million child workers work in the services sector. Despite the grim reality for many children exploited in child labour, progress has been made in recent years. According to ILO estimates, there were almost 94 million fewer children working in 2016 than in 2000. The number of children working in hazardous jobs fell by more than half during the same period (ILO, 2017d, pp. 11, 35–37).

10.6 Decent work for all in the travel and tourism sector

The right to decent work is a fundamental human right, recognized in several international conventions. The ILO has defined decent work as "productive work in which rights are protected, which generates an adequate income, with adequate social protection. It also means sufficient work, in the sense that all should have full access to income-earning opportunities" (ILO, 1999, p. 13). The right to decent work is included as a fundamental human right in the ICESCR. The 170 state parties to the ICESCR have undertaken to recognize the right of everyone to just and favourable conditions at work, including fair equal wages, safe and healthy working conditions, rest, leisure and reasonable limitation of working hours and periodic holidays with pay (art. 7). Furthermore, the state parties to the convention recognize the right of everyone to social security, including social insurance (art. 9). The economic and social rights in the ICESCR are however often not implemented at the national level, due to a lack of resources or political will. Furthermore, many workers work under exploitative labour conditions, experiencing decent work deficits, such as inappropriate periods for rest between work periods, low wages or a work environment that is dangerous to the health or safety of a worker.

The ILO has adopted two flagship conventions, one covering occupational safety and health and one covering social security issues, in an effort to improve the work conditions for the majority of the global workforce. The state parties to the Occupational Safety and Health Convention (1981) undertake to implement a coherent national policy on occupational safety, health and the working environment, with the object to minimize the causes of hazards inherent in the working environment. They also undertake to adequately enforce laws and regulations on occupational safety and health at the national level as well as to provide for adequate penalties for occupational safety and health violations (art. 4, 8–9). The second flagship convention, the Social Security (Minimum Standards) Convention (1952), is a comprehensive social security convention, covering all nine branches of social security standards, i.e., standards for medical care, sickness benefits, unemployment benefits, old-age benefits, employment injury benefits, family benefits, maternity benefits, invalidity benefits and survivor's benefits. Ratifying countries are required to introduce at least three of the nine benefits in the convention at the national level (see Chapter 5).

In addition to the flagship conventions, several conventions cover more specific social security matters, such as the principle of a forty-hour week (Forty-Hour Week Convention, 1935), holiday pay (Holidays with Pay Convention, 1970), maternity leave (Maternity Protection Convention, 2000), part-time work (Part-Time Work Convention, 1994), night work (Night Work Convention, 1990), protection against unemployment (Employment Promotion and Protection against Unemployment Convention, 1988) as well as adequate times for weekly rest (Weekly Rest (Commerce and Offices) Convention, 1957). Despite the numerous conventions on social security-related matters, major differences still exist between countries. None of the ILO social security conventions have been widely ratified by state parties, leaving a majority of the global workforce without a comprehensive social security safety net. Out of the global population, the ILO estimates that only 27 per cent enjoy full access to comprehensive social benefit systems (ILO, 2017e).

Sector-specific initiatives to improve the conditions of workers include the Convention (No. 172) Concerning Working Conditions in Hotels, Restaurants and Similar Establishments (1991), which covers establishments providing lodging as well as establishments providing food, beverages or both. According to the Hotels and Restaurants Convention, workers shall be entitled to normal hours of work and rest periods as well as annual leave with pay. Regardless of tip, workers shall receive a basic salary (art. 4–6). The Convention does not establish any minimum wages or include a definition of "normal" working hours. Instead, such matters shall be determined according to collective bargaining or national law and practice. So far, the convention has only been ratified by 16 state parties.

The adoption of ILO Guidelines on Decent Work and Socially Responsible Tourism (2017b) is an additional attempt to come to terms with the labour protection problems in the tourism sector. The guidelines urge actors in the tourism sector as well as governments to promote full and productive employment, decent jobs for youth in the tourism sector, the transition of tourism workers from the informal to the formal economy as well as investments in human resource development in the sector. In addition, all parties should promote fundamental international labour standards, labour protection and basic social security measures. The guidelines provide for a comprehensive framework for the regulation of the tourism workforce. However, they are non-binding, without any enforcement mechanisms, why the success of the guidelines is dependent on voluntary adoption by stakeholders in the industry. Despite all the efforts to improve the work conditions of tourism workers, exploitative work in the tourism sector is still rampant. A large number of tourism workers are neither covered by social security programs, nor experience a safe and healthy work environment. The Agenda 2030 goal of "full and productive employment and decent work for all men and women" and "safe and secure working environments for all workers" (United Nations, 2015) is thus at present more a vision than reality for the majority of the global tourism workforce.

10.7 Discrimination of tourism and travel employees

One of the fundamental principles of international human rights law is the elimination of discrimination in respect of employment and occupation. This principle is reiterated in foundational human rights conventions such as the ICCPR and ICESCR, as well as in ILO conventions such as the Discrimination (Employment and Occupation) Convention (1958). In addition to the personal suffering of those affected by discriminatory policies, discrimination also carries an economic cost to businesses affected. If people do not reach their full potential due to discrimination at work, the value of their economic output decreases. International human rights law includes several different discrimination grounds, covering persons who are discriminated in an employment relationship based on any of these grounds (see Chapter 8 for discussions on discrimination of guests in tourism establishments).

Firstly, discrimination based on race or ethnic origin is prohibited in international human rights law. The International Convention on the Elimination of All Forms of Racial Discrimination (1965) is adopted by 182 countries. State parties to the Convention agree to "condemn racial discrimination and undertake to pursue by all appropriate means and without delay a policy of eliminating racial discrimination in all its forms" (art. 2). Racial discrimination in the convention includes any distinction, exclusion, restriction or preference based on race, colour, descent, or national or ethnic origin. Most countries have implemented similar legislation at a national level, prohibiting discrimination based on race and other similar characteristics (see Chapter 8).

> In Australia, the federal Racial Discrimination Act (RDA) of 1975 provides for similar safeguards as international human rights law. According to the RDA it is unlawful for a person to discriminate in employment (sec. 15). In

the Australian case Gama v. Qantas Airways, 2006 (damages order upheld in Gama v. Qantas Airways, 2008) the applicant, a licensed aircraft mechanical engineer with Indian ethnic origin, alleged that Qantas Airways had discriminated against him on grounds of race during the course of his employment. The allegations involved racist comments by co-workers as well as discrimination in regard to work conditions and reporting requirements. The court was satisfied that remarks comparing his appearance to a "Bombay taxi driver" and work colleagues suggesting that "you should be walking up the stairs like a monkey", and "ask Willie" when referring to him were made during his employment with Qantas, distinguishing him based on race and impairing his right to work free of discriminatory comments from his colleagues. In conclusion, the court found that "there was a general culture inimical to persons of Asian background" (¶97), based on workmates making racially insensitive remarks in breach of section 9 of the RDA.

Secondly, discrimination based on sex is prohibited in international human rights law (UDHR, art. 2). State parties to the ICCPR and ICESCR have a legal obligation to undertake to ensure that both men and women are afforded the equal right of enjoyment of civil, political, economic, social and cultural rights, applicable in all member states to the conventions (ICCPR, art. 3, ICESCR, art. 3). According to the UDHR (art. 23.2), everyone, without discrimination, has the right to equal pay for equal work. The non-legal commitment from UDHR is reinforced in the Equal Remuneration Convention (1951), according to which state parties shall ensure the application of the principle of equal remuneration for men and women workers for work of equal value (art. 2). Furthermore, the Convention on the Elimination of All Forms of Discrimination against Women (1979, art. 11), guarantees women the same employment opportunities, the right to free choice of employment, the right to equal remuneration and the right to a safe working environment and the right to social security. State parties to the Convention also undertake to prohibit the dismissal of women on the grounds of pregnancy or maternal leave.

Despite the laudable aspirations in international human rights law, gender inequality persists in the world economy. On average, women are paid 23 per cent less than males holding the same position or performing the same job functions (ILO, 2019). In the tourism industry, although women make up more than 50 per cent of the workforce, discriminatory policies differentiating female employees are common. Sometimes such policies include gender-specific work titles, which are used to justify a wage gap between female and male employees, for example female air hostesses and cooks compared to male cabin attendants/stewards and chefs. In particular, airline carriers have historically maintained different types of discriminatory policies towards female cabin employees.

In 1975, the European Union Court delivered an important judgment concerning the effect of European Union treaties in Case C-43/75 (1976).

The case concerned an action between an air hostess and her employer Sabena, a Belgian air carrier. According to the employment contract, adopted under the terms of a collective agreement, female air hostesses could not continue to work beyond the age of 40 years. There were no similar requirements for male cabin stewards, although the work of a cabin steward and an air hostess was identical. The effect of the mandatory retirement age for female employees was that their pensions could not be calculated on the basis of the longer service period of their male colleagues. Furthermore, cabin crew who remained in active service until 55 were entitled to a special pension. The discriminatory policies resulted in a significantly lower pension for female crew members. According to the European Union treaty in force at the time, men and women were to receive equal payment for equal work. However, it was unclear at the time if the principle that men and women should receive equal pay for equal work was directly applicable in member states and if private individuals could institute proceedings before national courts, independently of any national legislation. The court held that the principle of equality is a fundamental principle of European Union law and that the treaty provisions indeed did have direct effect, i.e., could be relied upon by individuals, irrespective of any national legislation, why the air hostess was entitled to the protection of the treaty provisions. Later on, two directives, guaranteeing equal treatment for men and women in matters of employment (now recast as European Parliament and Council Directive 2006/54/EC, 2006) and in the access to and supply of goods and services (now recast as Council Directive 2004/113/EC, 2004) have been adopted.

Similarly, in Helen Tsang v. Cathay Pacific Airways (2000) the subject was a discriminatory policy concerning the retirement age of female and male cabin attendants. According to the "Standard Conditions of Service for Cabin Attendants" of Cathay Pacific Airways (a Hong Kong-based air carrier), which Ms. Tsang agreed to in 1979, the normal retirement age for male cabin attendants was 55 years, while the services of female cabin attendants would not normally be extended beyond the age 40. Cathay Pacific later made changes to its standard contract terms, and for crew recruited after 1 July 1993, the retirement age for all cabin crew, male and female, was 45 years. The Hong Kong District Court concluded that Ms. Tsang had not received the same treatment as a male cabin attendant hired in 1979, and therefore the air carrier was liable for sex discrimination in violation of the Hong Kong Sex Discrimination Ordinance (1996).

According to the first Global Report on Women in Tourism (UNWTO, 2011), tourism employment can be described as a pyramid, with a large number of women at the bottom. Women are overrepresented in lower paid occupations, such as housekeeping and customer service areas. In addition to low-status jobs, women face gender stereotyping in the tourism sector. For example, women in the airline industry dominate sales, ticketing and flight crew positions, while the majority of CEOs, managers and pilots are men. A second example is the work of a tour guide. A majority of tour guides in many societies are men, which can be explained by the fact that in the developing world, tour guiding is a desirable position due to the generous tips from foreign tourists. Also, women are overrepresented in informal and exploitative work in the tourism sector. Although there still exist huge challenges when it comes to gender equality, the second edition of the Global Report on Women in Tourism (UNWTO, 2019) shows that tourism offers greater opportunities for women's entrepreneurship than the wider economy. Moreover, tourism policies increasingly address gender equality and more and more women are challenging stereotypes in the sector.

Thirdly, discrimination based upon a worker's religious orientation is prohibited according to international human rights law. Questions about discrimination based on religion often arise in the employment context, when an employer either harasses an employee, does not act against a hostile working environment or does not accommodate an employee's religious beliefs or practices. An employer who takes action based on the discriminatory preferences of others is also unlawfully discriminating.

> The United States Equal Employment Opportunities Commission Compliance Manual (2008, section 12–II (B) gives the following example regarding employment discrimination under the Civil Rights Act (sec.701–703): *"Harinder, who wears a turban as part of his Sikh religion, is hired to work at the counter in a coffee shop. A few weeks after Harinder begins working, the manager notices that the work crew from the construction site near the shop no longer comes in for coffee in the mornings. When he inquires, the crew complains that Harinder, whom they mistakenly believe is Muslim, makes them uncomfortable in light of the September 11th attacks. The manager tells Harinder that he has to let him go because the customers' discomfort is understandable. The manager has subjected Harinder to unlawful religious discrimination by taking an adverse action based on customers' preference not to have a cashier of Harinder's perceived religion. Harinder's termination based on customer preference would violate Title VII [of the Civil Rights Act, author's note] regardless of whether he was Muslim, Sikh, or any other religion."*

Fourthly, discrimination of a disabled worker or a person applying for employment is prohibited. According to the Convention on the Rights of Persons with Disabilities (CRPD) (2006), parties to the convention undertake to adopt all appropriate laws to implement the rights recognized in the Convention (art. 4), including prohibiting discrimination on the basis of disability. State parties also undertake to take steps to ensure that "reasonable accommodation" is provided to disabled persons (art. 5), an important right for persons with disabilities looking to get hired or working in a gainful employment. Reasonable accommodation is defined as "necessary and appropriate modification and adjustments not imposing a disproportionate or undue burden, where needed in a particular case, to ensure to persons with disabilities the enjoyment or exercise on an equal basis with others of all human rights and fundamental freedoms" (art. 2).

At the national level, disability legislation tends to incorporate and closely follow the wording of the CRPD. In some countries, the disability rights legislation only applies to employers of a certain size, while other countries include all employers. For example, the Americans with Disabilities Act of 1990 (ADA), applicable in the United States, only includes employers who have 15 or more employees (42 U.S.C. § 12111 (5) (a)), while the Canadian Employment Equity Act (1995), the Australian Disability Discrimination Act 1992 (DDA) as well as the European Union Directive on Equal Treatment in Employment and Occupation (Council Directive 2000/78/EC, 2000) are applicable in most types of work places.

In a national setting, the two central tenets of employment disability discrimination law are the prohibition on discrimination and the duty of an employer to reasonably accommodate a disabled person. A fundamental requirement is however that the disabled person is able to carry out the "inherent duties" (sec.21A, DDA), "essential functions" (ADA, 42 U.S.C. § 12111 (8), § 12112 (a)) or "essential qualifications" (Employment Equity Act, 1995, sec. 5) of the work to be performed (see Box 10.4). A disabled person must therefore be qualified for the position and must be able to perform any essential functions of the job, whether unaided or with reasonable accommodation. In workplaces with many employees, certain tasks can be delegated to other workers, while in a small enterprise it might be essential that all workers can perform all tasks related to the position, so a determination of the essential functions in a job position is fact-dependent. A determination of undue hardship can never take into account the prejudices, irrational fears or discriminatory attitudes of customers or other employees. For example, an employer cannot refuse to hire a disabled person as a waitress solely because customers would object to being served by a person in a wheelchair (Code of Federal Regulations, USA, 29 C.F.R. § 1630 app. 2020).

An employer that denies a request to provide a reasonable accommodation, may have a defense in that the accommodation causes an unjustifiable hardship for the employer. The determination of what is considered an unjustifiable hardship is dependent on the nature of the benefit or detriment likely to accrue to or be suffered by any person concerned, the nature and cost of the accommodation, the overall financial resources of the facility making the adjustment, the overall financial resources of the employer, the type of operation of the employer as well as the impact of the accommodation on other employees and the impact of the facility's ability to conduct business. When considering the cost of the accommodation, the relevant factor is the net cost, taking into account any financial assistance available (DDA, section 11; ADA 42 U.S.C. § 12111 (10) (B); Code of Federal Regulations, USA, 29 C.F.R. § 1630.2 (p) (2) (i)).

BOX 10.4 EXAMPLES OF REASONABLE ACCOMMODATIONS

1. Changing recruitment and selection procedures.

Examples: Providing sign language interpreters for people for are deaf, readers for people for are blind, making recruiters aware of a disability and how it relates to the work requirements.

2. Modifying work premises.

Examples: Making physical changes, installing a ramp for a wheelchair, modifying a workspace or restroom, providing flashing lights to alert deaf people, providing a quiet workspace for a person with a mental disability, providing a chair to someone who cannot stand for long periods of time.

3. Making changes to job design, work schedules or other work duties.

Examples: Providing modified work schedules for someone who needs time off for treatment of a disability, changing schedules to allow for longer breaks, allocating work differently between employees.

4. Providing additional training or other assistance.

Examples: Providing a mentor for a person with a mental disability, modifying the workspace to allow service animals on premises, providing training and other written materials in accessible formats, communicating instructions through a tape-recorded message instead of a written memorandum.

Source: (Australian Human Rights Commission, 2014; United States Equal Employment Opportunity Commission, 2002).

In addition to "reasonable accommodation" provided to disabled persons, the CRPD obligates state parties to ensure persons with disabilities access, on equal basis with others, to the physical environment, including ensuring that private entities with facilities and services open to or provided to the public take into account accessibility for persons with disabilities (art. 9). Tourism enterprises, such as restaurants, hotels, movie theatres and sports arenas, are generally covered by national legislation prohibiting discrimination.

Fifthly, age discrimination in employment has in recent years become an important consideration for employers. Age discrimination as a discrimination ground has received a subdued response in international human rights law. Age discrimination is not mentioned in the UDHR, ICCPR or the ICESCR, even if it can technically be included in the "other status" usually included in legal instruments addressing discrimination. In fact, out of the nine core human rights instruments, only the International Convention on the Protection of the Rights of All Migrant Workers and Members of Their Families (1990) prohibits discrimination of migrant workers based on age. However, at the national level, many countries include age in the prohibited discrimination grounds. The United States was one of the first countries to recognize age discrimination, when the United States Congress in 1967 adopted the Age Discrimination in Employment Act of 1967 (ADEA). ADEA covers employers with 20 or more employees (§ 630) and prohibits age discrimination of any employee who is at least 40 years of age (§ 623, 631). It is not unlawful for an employer to consider age "where age is a bona fide occupational qualification reasonably necessary to the normal operation of the particular business" (§ 623 (f)).

In other countries, age discrimination was included as a protected class much later. At the European Union level, a directive covering age discrimination in employment was adopted in 2000 (Council Directive 2000/78/EC). The prohibition on discrimination does not apply according to the directive if the difference in treatment is based on occupational requirements and such a characteristic constitutes a genuine and determining occupational requirement (art. 4(1)). Member states may also provide that differences of treatment based on age do not constitute discrimination if the differences are objectively and reasonably justified by a legitimate aim, including employment policy, labour market and vocational training opportunities and if the means to achieve that aim are appropriate and necessary (art. 5). Australia adopted its federal legislation covering age discrimination in 2004. The Australian Age Discrimination Act 2004 is more far-reaching than its U.S. and European Union counterparts. The act covers most aspects of public life, including employment and public access to products and services. There are no exclusions for small businesses or employees younger than 40 years of age. Equivalent to U.S. and European Union legislation, it is not unlawful to discriminate against another person on the grounds of age if the other person is unable to carry out the inherent requirements of the particular job (sec. 18).

> Many of the landmark age discrimination cases concern discrimination in the airline industry. In the United States, in Western Air Lines v. Criswell (1985), the petitioner, Western Air Lines, required its flight engineers to retire at age 60. The airline required three persons in the cockpit, the pilot, a co-pilot and a flight engineer. The flight engineer did not operate the aircraft, unless the other two persons in the cockpit became incapacitated. The Federal Aviation Administration (FAA) required all pilots to retire at age 60, but there was no mandatory retirement age for flight engineers. The District Court entered a judgment, according to which Western Air Lines mandatory retirement age did not qualify as a bona fide occupational requirement. The judgment

was affirmed by the Circuit Court and the United States Supreme Court. The Supreme Court stated that: "[u]nless an employer can establish a substantial basis for believing that all or near all employees above an age lack the qualifications required for the position, the age selected for mandatory retirement less than 70 must be an age at which it is highly impractical for the employer to insure by individual testing that its employees will have necessary qualifications for the job." (p. 422–423). In a similar case, Trans World Airline v. Thurston (1985), the United States Supreme Court held that if the airline provided transfer privileges to some employees, it could not refuse to provide it to pilots who had reached the FAA mandatory retirement age.

In Australia, the Australian High Court considered age discrimination in Qantas Airways Ltd v. Christie (1988) a case considered under workplace legislation enacted before the federal Age Discrimination Act of 2004. The respondent in the case, a pilot, was discharged on his 60th birthday, in accordance with Qantas policy. Qantas argued that state parties to the Convention on International Civil Aviation were not allowed to permit a pilot who had attained the age of 60 to be in command of an international air service. The court found that since the pilot could not be in command of an international air service, he was no longer able to perform the inherent requirements of the job, and the Qantas dismissal was therefore lawful. In 2014, the requirements in the Convention on International Civil Aviation were amended. Now, pilots who are 60 years of age, but less than 65 years of age are allowed to fly airplanes with more than one pilot if they conduct a medical examination every six months. For single-pilot airplanes, the age limit remains at 60 years.

In the United States, where the ADEA only covers discrimination of persons who have attained the age of 40 or above, the question of reverse age discrimination, i.e., discrimination of someone based on the person being too young, has become a topical subject.

The United State Supreme Court has clearly stated that the ADEA does not intend to stop an employer from favouring an older employee over a younger one in General Dynamics Land Systems v. Cline (2004). However, at the state level, many states prohibit discrimination against the young as well as against the old. For example, the New York State Human Rights Law prohibits discrimination based on age in both employment and in places of public accommodation, regardless of the age of the person. One of the first cases of reverse age discrimination is the New York case of People by Koppell v. Alamo Rent A Car (1994), where the state of New York successfully sued several car rental agencies for refusing to rent cars to persons between the age of 18 and 25 years of age. The car rental firms argued that it was impossible to insure such young drivers, but the court held that insurance was available and that any extra costs associated with renting to younger customers could be passed on to them. The opportunity to rent should therefore be made available to the young drivers, no matter the cost.

Lastly, discrimination based on sexual orientation or gender identity is prohibited according to international human rights law. The UDHR guarantees the same rights and equality to all human beings (art. 2). Several United Nations bodies have confirmed in declarations and decisions that discrimination of LGBTQ+ employees is contrary to international human rights principles.

In Toonen v. Australia (1994), the applicant claimed to be a victim of violations by Australia of the ICCPR. At the time, the criminal code of Tasmania criminalized various forms of sexual contacts between men, including sexual contacts between consenting adult men in private. The complaint was heard by the Human Rights Committee of the United Nations under the optional protocol to the convention, allowing individual complaints against state parties. Although the Tasmanian code had not been used at the time of the complaint in the mid-1990s, the Tasmanian public prosecutors had announced that proceedings would be initiated if there was sufficient proof of a commission of a crime. The Human Rights Commission held that the criminal law provisions of Tasmania violated the right to equal rights, without distinction of any kind. It held that the reference to "sex" in the examples of prohibited discrimination also included discrimination based on sexual orientation, thus prohibiting discrimination based on sexual orientation. Furthermore, the applicant's right to not be subjected to arbitrary or unlawful interference with his privacy, family, home or correspondence was also violated by the criminalization of adult consensual sexual activity in private.

Similarly, in Young v. Australia (2003), the applicant raised a complaint against Australia under the optional protocol to the ICCPR, alleging that he was a victim of a violation of the covenant by Australia. The applicant had been in a same-sex relationship with another man for 38 years. When his partner died, he applied for a pension under the Veteran's Entitlement Act, as a veteran's dependant. However, his claim was denied in that he was not a person of the opposite sex living with the person in a marriage-like relationship. The Human Rights Committee concluded that there had been a violation of the covenant and that the applicant was entitled to reconsideration of his pension application, without discrimination based on his sex or sexual orientation, if necessary, through the amendment of the law. Also, the state party was under an obligation to ensure that similar violations did not happen in the future.

The same principle of non-discrimination has also been upheld at the national level. In El-Al Israel Airlines Ltd v. Jonathan Danielwitz (1994), an Israeli Supreme Court decision from 1994, the applicant was employed by El-Al as a flight attendant. The airline awarded every employee and his/her companion free aeroplane tickets each year. The flight attendant was in a stable relationship with another man but was not awarded the employment benefit of a free airplane ticket for his partner. The Israeli Supreme Court, applying national Israeli law, held that not giving the employee a free ticket for his same-sex partner amounted to discrimination, since he was treated differently from heterosexual couples.

In the European Union, the previously mentioned Council Directive 2000/78/EC (2000) guarantees protection against discrimination at work on grounds of sexual orientation. Similarly, the United States Equal Employment Opportunity Commission (EEOC) has in several recent decisions held that discrimination against transgender persons as well as on the basis of a person's sexual orientation can be viewed as sex discrimination based on non-conformance with gender norms and stereotypes (Macy v. Dep't of Justice, 2012; Baldwin v. Dep't of Transportation, 2015). This position was recently reiterated by the U.S. Supreme Court.

> The United States Supreme Court delivered a landmark decision for LGBTQ+ rights in its 2020 decision, Bostock v. Clayton County, Georgia (2020). In each of three joint cases, an employer allegedly fired a long-term employee for being homosexual or transgender. The court held that the Civil Rights Act prohibition on discrimination based on sex necessary included discrimination of homosexuals and transgender persons. "If the employer intentionally relies in part on an individual employee's sex when deciding to discharge the employee-put differently, if changing the employee's sex would have yielded a different choice by the employer–a statutory violation has occurred … An individual's homosexuality or transgender status is not relevant to employment decisions. That's because it is impossible to discriminate against a person for being homosexual or transgender without discriminating against that individual based on sex. Consider, for example, an employer with two employees, both of whom are attracted to men. The two individuals are, to the employer's mind, materially identical in all respects, except that is a man and the other a woman. If the employer fires the male employee for no reason other than the fact he is attracted to men, the employer discriminates against him for traits or actions it tolerates in his female colleague … Or take an employer who fires a transgender person who was identified as a male at birth but who now identifies as a female. If the employer retains an otherwise identical employee who was identified as female at birth, the employer intentionally penalizes a person identified as male at birth for traits or actions that it tolerates in an employee identified as female at birth."

The U.S. Supreme Court decision in Boston v. Clayton County (2020) could have wide-reaching implications for the LGBTQ+ community. Many countries lack specific protection from sexual orientation or transgender discrimination at the national level, while at the same time they have laws on protection from sex discrimination. If legal protection from sex discrimination is interpreted to include sexual orientation and transgender discrimination, in line with the U.S. Supreme Court decision, it could open up for more protection from discrimination in the labour context for LGBTQ+ individuals.

10.8 Migrant workers in tourism establishments

In addition to other vulnerable groups covered by discrimination legislation, migrant workers are often of particular importance for the tourism sector. The tourism sector is extremely labour intensive, requiring large numbers of workers, who often work on part-time, seasonal, on-call or other temporary contracts. Migration can offer a solution to labour shortages in the tourism sector, with migrants bringing in new skills and diversity to the work force. However, migrants can also be exploited in the tourism sector. Undeclared labour and foreign workers in irregular status are common in the tourism sector. Also, ethnic and cultural minority groups tend to be overrepresented in the tourism workforce. Many migrant workers face unsafe working conditions, long hours and lower pay than their native colleagues (ILO, 2010, pp. 16, 37). In 1990, the United Nations General Assembly adopted the International Convention on the Protection of the Rights of All Migrant Workers and Members of Their Families (1990) in an effort to strengthen migrant workers position in the global economy. Furthermore, a Declaration on the Rights of Persons Belonging to National or Ethnic, Religious and Linguistic Minorities was adopted in 1992.

> According to art. 25 in the International Convention on the Protection of the Rights of all Migrant Workers (1990):
>
> "1. Migrant workers shall enjoy treatment not less favourable than that which applies to nationals of the State of employment in respect of remuneration and:
>   (a) Other conditions of work, that is to say, overtime, hours of work, weekly rest, holidays with pay, safety, health, termination of the employment relationship and any other conditions of work which, according to national law and practice, are covered by these terms;
>   (b) Other terms of employment, that is to say, minimum age of employment, restriction on work and any other matters which, according to national law and practice, are considered a term of employment.
> 2. It shall not be lawful to derogate in private contracts of employment from the principle of equality of treatment referred to in paragraph 1 of the present article.
> 3. States Parties shall take all appropriate measures to ensure that migrant workers are not deprived of any rights derived from this principle by reason of any irregularity in their stay or employment. In particular,

employers shall not be relieved of any legal or contractual obligations, nor shall their obligations be limited in any manner by reason of such irregularity."

Article 25 in the International Convention on the Protection of the Rights of all Migrant Workers does in theory preclude the exploitation of migrant workers in tourism establishments. However, the convention has not gained widespread support in the receiving countries of migrant workers. The 54 signatories to the convention consist mainly of Latin American, as well as North and West African countries while the United States, Canada, Australia and Western European countries are notably absent from the list of signatory countries, despite the fact that high-income countries absorb most of the estimated 258 million current migrants (United Nations, 2017). In addition, national immigration legislation is often drafted in an effort to attract highly skilled immigrants. This poses a problem for the tourism and travel industry, which has a high number of low-skilled jobs as well as a lower salary range. Immigrants who want to work in the tourism industry have a difficult time meeting the high education and salary requirements for immigration, while tourism employers in more economically developed countries have difficulties filling low-wage positions with domestic employees.

> With the exit of United Kingdom (UK) from the EU (the so-called Brexit), many sectors in the UK are worried about labour shortages due to new immigration rules. According to UKInbound, a trade association representing the interests of UK's inbound tourism sector, the UK tourism and travel sector is likely to be severely impacted by Brexit. According to the organization, approximately 10 % of the total tourism workforce in the UK are EU nationals. London has considerably higher concentrations of EU nationals in its tourism and hospitality workforce. Nearly half of tourism and hospitality enterprises in London rely on EU nationals for over half of their staff. The retention of EU nationals in the UK tourism sector may prove difficult. Most tourism employees earn less than the government's proposed salary level for immigration purposes. In addition, "skill" is in the proposed immigration system translated to formal qualifications, which is disadvantageous for many tourism employees. UKInbound predicts that "[t]he sector is facing a perfect storm created by high levels of skills shortages, high employment rates and low perceptions of the industry as a career of choice. When considered alongside its higher than average reliance on EU workers, this conjunction places the industry in an extremely vulnerable position when faced with the end of Free Movement post-Brexit."
>
> (UKInbound, 2019, p. 5)

The need to create international norms for the orderly migration of workers is necessary. The number of international migrants has grown more than 49 per cent from year 2000 to 2017. A large majority of the migrants (74 per cent) are of working age. Migrant workers can contribute to a competitive tourism sector in all countries, as well as to the development of their countries of origin. In 2016, migrants from developing countries sent home remittances totalling an estimated US $413 billion (United Nations, 2017, p.1). International migrant workers are however also one of the most vulnerable and exploited groups in the global tourism workforce, why there is a need to create a global framework for migrant workers human rights.

10.9 Conclusion

As shown in this chapter, there is an abundance of international legal instruments protecting workers from human rights violations. In particular, the ILO has been instrumental in forming international human rights law covering labour rights. During the past century, the ILO has adopted conventions, declarations and guidelines in various areas covering workers' rights. Although the coverage of international human rights law is nearly universal, when it comes to the existence of legal instruments addressing different labour-related issues, the actual coverage, measured as ratification and compliance with the legal instruments, is less encouraging.

When it comes to freedom of association and the right to organize and to bargain collectively, more than 40 per cent of global workers are not covered by the conventions guaranteeing these rights. The principles of decent work, including standards on occupational safety, health and the working environment, standards for medical care, sickness benefits, unemployment benefits, old-age benefits, employment injury benefits, family benefits, maternity benefits, invalidity benefits and survivor's benefits, are clearly regulated in several international conventions. Despite the extensive legal protection offered to workers in theory, the ILO estimates that only 27 per cent of the global population enjoy full access to comprehensive social benefit systems at the national level. Similarly, although there exists a convention protecting the rights of migrant workers, countries receiving a large number of migrant workers are notably absent from the signatories of the convention.

There are other areas where workers' human rights are at risk, not because of the fact that states have not agreed on following international human rights conventions, but because of a lack of enforcement of the generally agreed upon principles. Despite the widespread denunciation of forced labour and exploitative child labour by a majority of states, violations of human rights in the form of forced labour and exploitative child labour are still numerous. The nature of employment in the travel and tourism sectors makes the sector particularly vulnerable to forced and child labour. It is therefore of uttermost importance that the sector is taking an active stand in the efforts to eradicate forced labour and exploitative child labour.

On a more positive note, major strides have been made when it comes to worker's rights to live free from discrimination of any kind. Most workers are covered by some form of legislation prohibiting discrimination at the national level. In addition, recent developments in the area of LGBTQ+ rights mean that the ambit of discrimination legislation is expanding to cover more workers. Globally, the tourism and travel industry is a major employer, which is why it is important that workers' rights are embraced at the firm level in the sector. In addition to international human rights law, which has a role in creating global minimum standards, workers' rights can be promoted at the firm level by the introduction of internal guidelines and reporting mechanisms, by educating the workforce and by staying vigilant in noticing and denouncing violations of workers' rights, as articulated in international human rights agreements.

Permission

1 Box 10.1 is composed of material from Transforming our world: the 2030 Agenda for Sustainable Development by United Nations General Assembly ©2015, United Nations. Reprinted with the permission of the United Nations.

References

Abolition of Forced Labour Convention (No. 105), June 25, 1957. 320 U.N.T.S. 291.
Age Discrimination Act 2004 (Austl.).
Age Discrimination in Employment Act of 1967, 29 U.S.C. § 621–634 (USA).
Americans with Disabilities Act of 1990, .S.C. §12101–12213 (2018) (USA).
Australian Human Rights Commission, 2014. *Disability Discrimination Know Your Rights.* [pdf] s.l.: Australian Human Rights Commission. Available at: <https://humanrights.gov.au/sites/default/files/Disability%20Discrimination_2014_Web.pdf> [Accessed 7 July 2020].
Bachpan Bachao Andolan v. Union of India & Others (2011) (July 15, 2015) (Ind.).
Baldwin v. Dep't of Transportation, EEOC Doc. No. 0120133080 (EEOC July 15, 2015).
Bostock v. Clayton County, Georgia, 590 U.S. _ (2020).
Case C-43/75, *Defrenne v. Société anonyme belge de navigation aérienne Sabena*, EU:C:1976:56, [1976] ECR 455.
Civil Rights Act of 1964, Pub. L. No. 88–352, 78 Stat. 241 (codified as amended in 42 U.S.C. 2000a–h-6).
Code of Federal Regulations, 29 CFR § 1630 (2020) (USA).
Constitution of India (1949) (Ind.).
Convention (No. 29) Concerning Forced or Compulsory Labour, June 28, 1930, 39 U.N.T.S 55.
Convention (No. 87) Concerning Freedom of Association and Protection of the Right to Organise, July 9, 1948, 68 U.N.T.S. 17.
Convention (No. 98) Concerning the Application of the Principles of the Right to Organise and to Bargain Collectively, July 1, 1949, 96 U.N.T.S. 257.
Convention (No. 138) Concerning Minimum Age for Admission to Employment, June 26, 1973, 1015 U.N.T.S. 297.
Convention (No. 172) Concerning Working Conditions in Hotels, Restaurants and Similar Establishments, June 25, 1991, 1820 U.N.T.S. 445.
Convention (No. 182) Concerning the Prohibition and Immediate Action for the Elimination of the Worst Forms of Child Labour, June 17, 1999, 2133 U.N.T.S. 161.
Convention on the Rights of Persons with Disabilities, Dec.13, 2006, 2515 U.N.T.S. 3.

Convention on the Elimination of All Forms of Discrimination against Women, Dec. 18, 1979, 1249 U.N.T.S. 13.

Convention on the Rights of the Child, Nov. 20, 1989, 1577 U.N.T.S. 3.

Council Directive 2000/78/EC of 27 November 2000 establishing a general framework for equal treatment in employment and occupation. *Official Journal*, L303, pp. 16–22. [online]. Available at: <https://eur-lex.europa.eu/legal-content/EN/TXT/PDF/?uri =CELEX:32000L0078&from=EN> [Accessed 25 June 2020].

Council Directive 2004/113/EC of 13 December 2004 implementing the principle of equal treatment between men and women in the access to and supply of goods and services. *Official Journal*, L373, pp. 37–43. [online]. Available at: https://eur-lex.europa.eu/ legal-content/EN/TXT/HTML/?uri=CELEX:32004L0113&from=EN [Accessed 30 June 2020].

Declaration of Philadelphia (Declaration concerning the aims and purposes of the International Labour Organisation), ILO Constitution, Annex, 26th session of the General Conference of the International Labour Organisation (May 10, 1944).

Declaration on Fundamental Principles and Rights at Work and its Follow-up, 86th session of the General Conference of the International Labour Organisation (June 18, 1998) (Annex revised June 15, 2010).

Declaration on the Rights of Persons Belonging to National or Ethnic, Religious and Linguistic Minorities, G.A. Res. 47/135, U.N. Doc. A/RES/47/135 (Feb. 3, 1993).

Disability Discrimination Act 1992, No. 135 (Austl.).

Discrimination (Employment and Occupation) Convention (No. 111), June 25, 1958, 362 U.N.T.S. 31.

El-Al Israel Airlines Ltd v. Jonathan Danielwitz (HCJ721/94) (Isr.).

Employment Equity Act (S.C. 1995 c. 44) (Can.).

Employment Promotion and Protection against Unemployment Convention (No. 168), June 21, 1988, 1654 U.N.T.S. 67.

Equal Remuneration Convention (No. 100), June 29, 1951, 165 U.N.T.S. 303.

European Parliament and Council Directive 2006/54/EC of 5 July 2006 on the implementation of the principle of equal opportunities and equal treatment of men and women in matters of employment and occupation, 2006. *Official Journal*, L204 pp. 23–36. [online]. Available at: <https://eur-lex.europa.eu/legal-content/EN/TXT/HTML/ ?uri=CELEX:32006L0054&from=EN> [Accessed 30 June 2020].

Forced Labour Convention (No. 29), June 28, 1930, 39 U.N.T.S. 55.

Forty-Hour Week Convention (No. 47), June 22, 1935, 271 U.N.T.S. 199.

Gama v. Qantas Airways [2006] FMCA 1767 (Austl.).

Gama v. Quantas Airways [2008] FCAFC 69 (Austl.).

General Dynamics Land Systems v. Cline, 540 U.S. 581 (2004).

Helen Tsang v. Cathay Pacific Airways, [2000] HKEC 1590 (H.K.).

Holidays with Pay Convention (Revised) (No. 132), June 24, 1970, 883 U.N.T.S. 97.

Human Rights Council, 2018. Report of the detailed findings of the Independent International Fact-Finding Mission on Myanmar, 39th Sess., Sep. 10–28, 2018, A/ HRC/39/CRP.2 (Sep. 17, 2018).

ILO, 1998. Report of the Commission of Inquiry appointed under article 26 of the Constitution of the International Labour Organization to examine the observance by Myanmar of the Forced Labour Convention, 1930 (no. 29), July 2, 1998. 81 ILO Official Bulletin 1 (Spec. Suppl.).

ILO, 1999. *Decent Work. Report of the Director-General*. [pdf] Geneva: ILO. Available at: <www.ilo.org/public/libdoc/ilo/P/09605/09605(1999-87).pdf> [Accessed 7 July 2020].

ILO, 2000. Resolution concerning the measures recommended by the Governing Body under article 33 of the ILO Constitution on the subject of Myanmar, 88th session of the General Conference of the International Labour Organisation (June 2000).

ILO, 2010. Developments and Challenges in the hospitality and tourism sector. *Global Dialogue Forum for the Hotels, Catering, Tourism Sector.* Geneva, Switzerland, 23–24 November. Geneva: ILO.

ILO, 2012. Resolution concerning the measure on the subject of Myanmar adopted under article 33 of the ILO Constitution, 101st session of the General Conference of the International Labour Organisation (May–June 2012).

ILO, 2013. Resolution concerning the measure on the subject of Myanmar adopted under article 33 of the ILO Constitution, 102nd session of the General Conference of the International Labour Organisation (June 18, 2013).

ILO, 2017a. *Tourism- An Important Driving Force for Inclusive Socio-Economic Development, Economic Diversification, Enterprise and Job Creation, Fact Sheet.* [pdf] s.l.: ILO Sectoral Policies Department. Available at: <www.ilo.org/wcmsp5/groups/public/---ed_dialogue/---sector/documents/publication/wcms_544196.pdf> [Accessed 7 July 2020].

ILO, 2017b. *ILO Guidelines on Decent Work and Socially Responsible Tourism.* [pdf] Geneva: ILO Sectoral Policies department. Available at: <www.ilo.org/wcmsp5/groups/public/---ed_dialogue/---sector/documents/normativeinstrument/wcms_546337.pdf> [Accessed 7 July 2020].

ILO, 2017c. *Global Estimates of Modern Slavery.* [pdf] Geneva: ILO. Available at: <www.ilo.org/wcmsp5/groups/public/---dgreports/---dcomm/documents/publication/wcms_575479.pdf> [Accessed 7 July 2020].

ILO, 2017d. *Global Estimates of Child Labour, Results and Trends 2012–2016.* [pdf] Geneva: ILO. Available at: <www.ilo.org/wcmsp5/groups/public/---dgreports/---dcomm/documents/publication/wcms_575499.pdf> [Accessed 7 July 2020].

ILO, 2017e. *World Social Protection Report 2017–19.* [pdf] Geneva: ILO. Available at: <www.ilo.org/wcmsp5/groups/public/---dgreports/---dcomm/---publ/documents/publication/wcms_604882.pdf> [Accessed 7 July 2020].

ILO, 2019. *Integrated Strategy on Fundamental Principles and Rights at Work 2017–2023.* [pdf] s.l.: ILO. Available at: <www.ilo.org/wcmsp5/groups/public/---ed_norm/---ipec/documents/publication/wcms_648801.pdf> [Accessed 7 July 2020].

International Convention on the Elimination of All Forms of Racial Discrimination, Dec. 21, 1965, 660 U.N.T.S. 195.

International Convention on the Protection of the Rights of All Migrant Workers and Members of Their Families, Dec. 18, 1990, 2220 U.N.T.S. 3.

International Covenant on Civil and Political Rights, Dec. 16, 1966, 999 U.N.T.S. 171.

International Covenant on Economic, Social and Cultural Rights, Dec. 16, 1966, 993 U.N.T.S. 3.

Korstrom, G., 2019. Vancouver hotel strike disrupting corporate events. *Business Vancouver.* [online] 8 October 2019. Available at: <www.biv.com/article/2019/10/vancouver-hotel-strike-disrupting-corporate-events> [Accessed 17 July 2020].

Lazaruk, S., 2019. Job action possible after Vancouver hotel workers deliver strike vote. *Vancouver Sun.* [online] 25 August. Available at: <https://vancouversun.com/news/local-news/job-action-possible-after-vancouver-hotel-workers-deliver-strike-vote> [Accessed 17 July 2019].

Macy v. Dep't of Justice, EEOC Appeal No. 0120120821, 2012 WL 1435995 (April 20, 2012).

Maternity Protection Convention (No. 183), June 15, 2000, 2181 U.N.T.S. 253.
Minimum Age Recommendation (No. 146), 58th session of the General Conference of the International Labour Organisation (June 26, 1973).
New York State Human Rights Law (Executive law, art. 15, sec. 291) (USA).
Night Work Convention, June 26, 1990, 1855 U.N.T.S. 305.
Occupational Safety and Health Convention (No. 155), June 22, 1981, 1331 U.N.T.S. 22345.
Part-Time Work Convention (No. 175), June 24, 1994, 2010 U.N.T.S. 51.
People by Koppell v. Alamo Rent A Car, 620 N.Y.S.2d 695 (1994) (USA).
Protocol of 2014 to the Forced Labour Convention, 1930, 103rd session of the General Conference of the International Labour Organisation (June 11, 2014).
Qantas Airways Ltd v. Christie, [1988] 193 CLR 280 (Austl.).
Racial Discrimination Act of 1975 (Austl.).
Saskatchewan Federation of Labour v. Saskatchewan, [2015] 1 SCR 245 (Can.).
Sex Discrimination Ordinance, Cap. 480 (1996) (H.K.).
Social Security (Minimum Standards) Convention (No. 102), June 28 1952, 210 U.N.T.S. 131.
Stacey, J., 2015. Supporting Quality Jobs in Tourism, *OECD Tourism Papers*, 2015/02, pp. 1–99. [online]. https://doi.org/10.1787/5js4rv0g7szr-en.
Toonen v. Australia, Communication No. 488/1992, U.N. Doc. CCPR/C/50/D/488/1992 (1994).
Trans World Airline v. Thurston, 469 U.S. 111 (1985).
UKInbound, 2019. *A Perfect Storm? The end of Free Movement and its impact on the UK tourism workforce* [pdf]. Available at: <www.ukinbound.org/wp-content/uploads/2019/10/UKinbound-Perfect-Storm-Long-Report-FINAL.pdf> [Accessed 9 July 2020].
UN Global Compact, 2020. Leadership for the Decade of Action. *UN Global Compact*. [online] 16 July. Available at: <www.unglobalcompact.org/> [Accessed 17 July 2020]
United Nations, 2015. Transforming our world: the 2030 Agenda for Sustainable Development, G.A. Res. 70/1, U.N. Doc. A/RES/70/1 (Sep. 25, 2015).
United Nations, 2017. *International Migration Report 2017*. [pdf] New York: United Nations. Available at: <www.un.org/en/development/desa/population/migration/publications/migrationreport/docs/MigrationReport2017_Highlights.pdf> [Accessed 7 July 2020].
United States Equal Employment Opportunity Commission, 2002. Enforcement Guidance on Reasonable Accommodation and Undue Hardship Under the ADA. [online]. Available at: <www.eeoc.gov/laws/guidance/enforcement-guidance-reasonable-accommodation-and-undue-hardship-under-ada> [Accessed 30 June 2020].
United States Equal Employment Opportunities Commission, 2008. *EEOC Compliance Manual*. [online]. Available at: <www.eeoc.gov/laws/guidance/section-12-religious-discrimination> [Accessed 30 June 2020].
Universal Declaration of Human Rights, G.A. Res. 217 (III) A, U.N. Doc. A/RES/217(III) (Dec. 10, 1948).
UNWTO, 2011. *Global Report on Women in Tourism 2010*. [pdf] Madrid: UNWTO. Available at: <www.e-unwto.org/doi/pdf/10.18111/9789284413737> [Accessed 7 July 2020].
UNWTO, 2019. *Global Report on Women in Tourism-Second edition*. [pdf] Madrid: UNWTO. Available at: <www.e-unwto.org/doi/pdf/10.18111/9789284420384> [Accessed 7 July 2020].
UNWTO, 2020a. *Global Guidelines to Restart Tourism*. [pdf] Madrid: UNWTO. Available at: <https://webunwto.s3.eu-west-1.amazonaws.com/s3fs-public/2020-05/UNWTO-Global-Guidelines-to-Restart-Tourism.pdf> [Accessed 7 July 2020].

UNWTO, 2020b. *One Planet Vision for a Responsible Recovery of the Tourism Sector*. [pdf] s.l.:UNWTO. Available at: <https://webunwto.s3.eu-west-1.amazonaws.com/s3fs-public/2020-06/one-planet-vision-responsible-recovery-of-the-tourism-sector.pdf> [Accessed 7 July 2020].

U.S. Department of Labor (Bureau of International Labor Affairs, U.S. International Child Labor Program), 2000. *2000 Report on Labor Practices in Burma*. [pdf] s.l.: U.S. Department of Labor. Available at: <https://digitalcommons.ilr.cornell.edu/cgi/viewcontent.cgi?article=1165&context=key_workplace> [Accessed 7 July 2020].

Weekly Rest (Commerce and Offices) Convention (No. 106). June 26, 1957, 325 U.N.T.S. 279.

Western Air Lines v. Criswell, 472 U.S. 400 (1985) (USA).

Working Conditions (Hotels and Restaurants) Recommendation (No. 179), 78th session of the General Conference of the International Labour Organisation (June 25, 1991).

World Travel & Tourism Council, 2020. *Travel & Tourism Economic Impact 2020 World*. [pdf] London: World Travel and Tourism Council.

Worst Forms of Child Labour Recommendation (No. 190), 87th session of the General Conference of the International Labour Organisation (June 17, 1999).

Young v. Australia, Communication number 941/2000, U.N. Doc. No. CCPR/C/78/D/941/2000 (2003).

11
HUMAN RIGHTS, THE ENVIRONMENT, AND TOURISM

11.1 Introduction

The UN Special Rapporteur on human rights and the environment stated "All human beings depend on the environment in which we live. A safe, clean healthy and sustainable environment is integral to the full enjoyment of a wide range of human rights, including the rights to life, health, food, water and sanitation" (OHCHR, 2019). Growing threats to the environment on multiple fronts, including tourism, are impinging on human rights. Inspired by Swedish activist Greta Thunberg, millions around the world took part in the largest climate change protest to date, on the 20th of September 2019 in advance of a UN Environmental Summit in New York (Weston and Osborne, 2019). Many of the protesters were school-aged children. Thunberg and 15 other children from 12 countries presented an official complaint to the UN Committee on the Rights of the Child, arguing that Member States' failure to act on the climate crisis is a violation of children's rights (Wylie, 2019). Concerns over raging forest fires in the Amazon Rainforest in Brazil took centre stage at the G7 meeting in France in 2019, and clean-up campaigns for plastics and micro-plastic pollution in the air, lakes, rivers, and oceans are gaining traction. About 700 marine species are affected by plastic garbage (Ocean Conservancy, 2019), which is wreaking havoc in ocean ecosystems (National Ocean Service, n.d.). Plastics can entangle marine life or be ingested, ending up in the human food chain. The Honduran beach is covered in plastic garbage; the only exception being tourist resorts where garbage is actively removed. Locals are also continuing to tackle this Sisyphean task as every tide washes up more plastic (Osterath, 2018). If ecosystems are not protected from local to global levels, the impacts on the land, water, and the atmosphere will severely affect human lives, and the human right to a clean and healthy environment.

An excess of 2 million deaths and billions of cases of diseases annually are ascribed to pollution (UNEP, n.d.). Economic-growth centred development has been traded for environmental degradation and resource depreciation. Sagoff (1981) questioned if economists and policymakers got the priority of development right by asking, "[w]hat about the trade-off between efficiency and self-respect, efficiency and the magnificence of our natural heritage, efficiency and quality of life?" (p. 1417) – implicating other values, rather than efficiency, need to be prioritised. For human beings to live a healthy and dignified life, they need access to "a clean, healthy and functional environment" (UNEP, 2015). Every human being has rights to life, health, food, and an adequate standard of living (c.f. UDHR Articles 3, 25(1), UNDRIP Articles 7(1), 24 (1), 25, 26, 29, ICCPR Articles 1(2), 47, ICESC Articles 1(2), 11(2), 25). Lockdowns imposed under COVID-19 have revealed improvements in water and air quality, highlighting the impacts human activity is having on the environment (see Chapter 14). Indigenous Peoples face serious health issues from environmental pollution and environmental change. In 2005, an Inuit petition on sea-change caused by greenhouse gas emissions emanating from the US was submitted to the Inter-American Human Rights Commission, and was initially considered "quixotic" (UNEP, 2015). Later, the petition was successful in the context of violation of human rights to life (Earthjustice, 2005). A more recent case involves the planned disposal of radioactive waste by Canadian Nuclear Laboratories; Indigenous communities and other concerned citizens are calling for the auditor general to investigate the planned nuclear waste disposal facility in Chalk River near the Ottawa River for environmental and health risks (Lamirande and Scholey, 2018).

Global climate change discourse focuses on anthropogenic causes and the impending climate crisis. The World Meteorological Society has reported the period 2014–19 as the warmest on record, with sea level rise increasing 5 mm per year and carbon emissions increasing by 20% over the previous five-year period (McGrath, 2019). Tourism has been contributing to climate change, with many destinations at risk from rising sea levels relying on tourists arriving on long-haul flights. Tourism and hospitality benefit from attractive natural resources and healthy natural environments. However, tourism development and tourist activities have exploited natural resources and local environments. Destination development has involved the felling of forests, the destruction of natural habitats, overdevelopment along beachfronts, and the destruction of the natural aesthetic. Tourism has also denied local populations' access to their natural environment and resources, caused overcrowding in heritage cities and excluded locals from environmental protection processes.

This chapter will begin by first studying important human rights related declarations, covenants, and articles on the environment and exploring if humans have rights to environment. After considering anthropocentric climate change, the chapter will turn to a historical account of the relationship between human activities and the environment. The nature of human rights will then be explored in relation to government, and the industry response to environmental issues in tourism.

11.1.1 Influence of three major UN documents on environmental law

Three UN documents are known to have had significant impact on international environmental law, thereby influencing discussions on development, climate change, natural disasters, and pollution in relation to human rights. Handl (2012) argues the Stockholm Declaration (1972), combined with the Rio Declaration (1992) from the United Nations Conference on Environment and Development (UNCED), were major milestones in the evolution of international environmental law. Subsequent policy documents such as Agenda 21 are strongly based on these two Declarations (Handl, 2012). The third UN document of note, The Brundtland Commission Report, also known as "Our Common Future," published in 1987, instilled the concept of sustainable development in environmental thought, echoed in various UN human rights documents and subsequent environmental policies.

The Stockholm Declaration (1972) forged a universal basic outlook among various nation-states, so they could come to a consensus on broad environmental policy goals and objectives (Handl, 2012). The declaration was meant to be a guideline for governments and peoples "to exert common efforts for the preservation and improvement of the human environment, for the benefit of all the people and for their posterity" (UNEP, 1972). After lengthy deliberations, the final Preamble declares, "Man is both creature and moulder of his environment." The first Principle enshrines that a quality environment is a "pre-condition" (Shelton, 2009) to achieve human rights, but humans have "a solemn responsibility to protect and improve the environment for present and future generations." Throughout this declaration, governments and individuals have responsibilities to safeguard the environment, stop pollution, and improve the quality of environment. The Stockholm Declaration linked human rights and environmental protection, affirming states' responsibility in developing international laws collaboratively – to ensure a safe environment and adequate living standard, as well as rewarding liability and compensation for victims of environmental harm (Shelton, 2008, 2009).

While the Stockholm Declaration had significant impact on legal developments internationally (Shelton, 2009), it is debatable if international communities appreciate the inexplicable relationship between human rights and the environment. The Brundtland Commission Report (1987) awakened and reinforced the essence of sustainable development focused on the responsible use of natural and cultural resources, without compromising the needs of future generations. For decades, human rights, environmental protection, economic development, and sociocultural development were dealt with independently. However, under sustainability principles – laws must work in synchronisation for current generation and future generations (Brown Weiss, 1990).

What the Brundtland Report identified was the need for legal and political development frameworks, which consequently altered the focus of future UNCED conferences (Shelton, 2008). The Rio summit in 1992 – the first in the series of UNCED – sought to build upon the Stockholm Declaration (UN, 1992). The rights-based approach of the Stockholm Declaration is reflected in Principle 1 of the Rio Declaration: that human beings are "entitled to a healthy and productive life in harmony with nature" (UN, 1992). Yet, the final Rio Declaration shifted slightly from the original Stockholm Declaration. Human beings are central to sustainable development in the Rio Declaration, and the development process must consider environmental protection as integral; the Rio Declaration also introduced the precautionary principle (Principle 15); the "polluter pays" principle (Principle 11); and procedural rights by public participation to achieve more effective environmental protection (Principle 10) (see UN 1992 for final Rio Declaration). More importantly, the Rio Declaration represents "a carefully negotiated balance between the priorities and interests of the developed and developing States" (Shelton, 2008). While nation-states pledged to strive to achieve Sustainable Development Goals, developed and developing nations have differentiated levels of allowance for natural resource exploitation, and environmental protection. This is due to "standards applied by some countries may not be appropriate to others because of the economic and social costs involved" (Shelton, 2008).

The Stockholm Declaration initiated the process of integrating international law and environmental law. The Brundtland Report provided guidelines for sustainable development, and how environmental laws and human rights laws must work as one. The Rio Declaration further expanded upon the idea that environmental protection is a part of the sustainable development process (see Sand, 1993 and Helman, 1995 for further discussion). The concept of sustainable development implies all humans are entitled to human rights, as well as being responsible for protecting the dignity of all people and the equality of their rights. The question arises, what has permitted human beings to an *entitlement* to the environment.

11.1.2 Do people have "rights to environment"?

The UDHR claimed that human beings have rights to a healthy and dignified life, or an adequate life; states must ensure that a clean, healthy environment is provided so that no one will be deprived of subsistence. How did this then become interpreted and solidified into "rights to the environment"? Shelton (2008) and Handl (2012) agree that Principle 1 of the Stockholm Declaration can be misinterpreted. Shelton (2008) points out:

> Read narrowly, it restates pre-existing international human rights guarantees of liberty, equality and an adequate standard of living, but innovates in adding that the exercise of these rights depends upon environmental conditions, reflecting the perception that environmental degradation can impair the full enjoyment of human rights. Read more broadly, Principle 1 Stockholm Declaration supported a growing movement to recognize the right to a safe and healthy environment as a human right ... improvement of living and working environments; protection of human health ... and improvement of the quality of life.

Depending on the reader's interpretation, Principle 1 refers to fundamental human rights to a quality of environment where a life of dignity and well-being can be achieved, and thus "rights to the environment" (Shelton, 2008; Handl, 2012). In the Brundtland Report and the Rio Declaration, human beings are an integral part of the environment or have a responsibility to environmental protection, rather than having natural rights to a quality environment.

According to Boyle (2012), three theoretical approaches on the relationship between human rights and the environment have emerged. The first, in the Stockholm Declaration, views the environment as a "precondition" to the enjoyment of human rights (i.e. the rights to life, private life, health, water, and property). The second, in the Rio Declaration, human rights are a "tool to address environmental issues." The third, in the Brundtland Report, sustainable development desegregates human rights and the environment (Boyle, 2012). Together, these approaches confirm there are relationships between human rights and the environment, though none of them explicitly affirms humanity's generic rights to the environment.

Handl (2012) further argues that the generic human right to a quality environment has failed to earn general international support or become enshrined in global human rights treaties. Shelton (2009) however, counter argues that the legal experts claim the right to a safe and healthy environment exists as "an independent substantive human right." She also refutes that the right to environment was not expressed in global human right treaties because these treaties were drafted before human rights issues were discussed as part of environmental protection. Boyle (2012) points out that human rights were discussed as a means to move states to "regulate environmental risks, enforce environmental laws, or disclose environmental information" in treaties such as the International Covenant on Civil and Political Rights (ICCPR), the International Covenant on Economic Social and Cultural Rights (ICESCR), the European Convention on Human Rights (ECHR), the American Convention on Human Rights (AmCHR), and the African Convention [sic] on Human and Peoples' Rights (AfCHPR). In particular, AmCHR and AfCHPR contain articles that enshrine generic human rights to the environment (Shelton, 2009). It is important to mention that the rights of Indigenous Peoples extensively reference the links between human rights and environmental protection. The ILO Convention No. 169 (Indigenous and Tribal Peoples in Independent Countries, 1989) has numerous mentions of Indigenous People's rights to lands, resources, and the environment.

The Rio Declaration's key influence was its rights-based approach to development. Human rights law in this context should safeguard conditions and environmental quality in order to protect "the substantive rights to life, the rights to health, the rights to a family and private life, the rights to culture, and other human rights" (Shelton, 2006). Sachs (2003, p.3) explains environmental justice as human rights for a dignified life in six situations: (1) extraction of raw materials, (2) alteration of ecosystems, (3) reprogramming of organisms, (4) destabilisation as a result of climate change, (5) pollution of urban living space, and (6) effects of resource prices.

The relationship between environmental risk and social considerations is discussed in the UNDP *Social and Environmental Standards* (UNDP, 2014). Deprivation of a healthy environment is considered to be a human security issue, not just a human right issue (see Chapter 5).

However, *rights* always come with *responsibilities*. Brown Weiss (1990) emphasised intergenerational equity, in which, "rights are always associated with obligations," but "the reverse is not always true" (pp. 202–203). She advocates that every generation and every state must ensure that every human being gains equitable access to economic benefits from resources on the planet; i.e. breathable air, clean and safe water, no pollution, and access to natural and cultural resources. Helman (1995) critically reviewed the 1992 Rio Summit as having failed to change conventional environmental law to sustainable development law; the main reasons were twofold. First, what was demanded was beyond a typical updating of environmental law; second, many developed nations resisted the shift in focus to natural resource enhancement, rather than man-made resources and capital. Conca (2015), on the other hand, argued that the UN failed to achieve its targets in the Millennium Development Goals, and then moved on to 2016 UN Sustainable Development Goals. He observed that many countries neglected the idea of accessing a safe and healthy environment as a necessary part of human rights. Conca (2015) suggests that: "Environmental protection works best when citizens' rights...have real meaning in the corridors of environmental policy, project planning and economic decision-making... Rights-based approaches make it possible for people to secure access to natural resources for sustainable livelihoods."

Boyd conducted research on environmental rights in constitutional frameworks (see Boyd, et al., 2017; Boyd, 2013, 2012, 2011). In 2013, 182 out of 193 UN member nations recognised "human rights to [a] healthy environment" are part of generic human rights in one of the following forms: constitutions, environmental laws, court decisions, or ratification of international laws (Boyd, 2013, p.3). Over 100 countries from Europe, Latin America and the Caribbean, Asia and Africa explicitly or implicitly recognise the rights to a healthy environment through their constitutions. Boyd also identified the effectiveness of strengthening environmental laws and policies if the "right to environment" was incorporated into the constitutional framework (Boyd, 2013, 2017). However, developed countries such as the USA, Canada, Australia, New Zealand, Japan, and emerging economies like The People's Republic of China, did not recognise the "human rights to environment" in the legal forms mentioned (Boyd, 2013). The US made its position clear in their "Explanation of Position by the United States of America" submitted to the UN Human Rights Council 34th session, 2017. The excerpt reads:

> Pending review of U.S. policies relating to climate change and the Paris Agreement, the United States reserves its position on language in this resolution relating to these issues.
>
> At the same time, we remain concerned about the general approach of placing environmental concerns in a human rights context and about addressing

them in fora that do not have the necessary expertise. For related reasons, while we recognize the efforts of the Special Rapporteur and UN bodies in this area, we do not agree with a number of aspects of their work.

(US Mission Geneva, 2017)

In Canada there have been several attempts to pass into law a Canadian Environmental Bill of Rights, however it has yet to be achieved. A recommended amendment to the Canadian Environmental Protection Law in December of 2017 recognised everyone's rights to a healthy environment (Bill C-202) (David Suzuki Foundation, 2018), however its status as of August 2018 was labeled as "Introduction and First Reading" (Parliament of Canada, 2018) or "dormant" (Mulley, 2018). Subsequently, Bill C-438 to enact the Canadian Environmental Bill of Rights also included the right to a healthy and ecologically balanced environment, received first reading on April of 2019; however, this too has yet to be passed (Parliament of Canada, 2019).

UN documents have unquestionably influenced contemporary environmental law. The incorporation of human rights into environmental law has led to tremendous improvements in dealings with environmental pollution and damage. However, the interpretation of the severity of harm to the "right to an adequate environment" or the "right to life" depends on the court of law and how the applicants present their issues. See Box 11.1 for two contrasting European cases of rights-based hearings.

BOX 11.1 EUROPEAN CONVENTION ARTICLE 8: TWO CONTRASTING CASES

Article 8 of the European Convention guarantees the right to private life and the home and is often applied in court cases. Below are two contrasting cases under Article 8. In *Kyrtatos v. Greece* (2003) the applicants complained of noise and lights resulting from tourism development near their home, in addition to the deterioration of nearby protected areas and changes in wildlife. These complaints were – even assuming that the damage to the environment by the tourism development in the vicinity was as severe as alleged – not considered sufficiently detrimental or serious to bring the case within the scope of Article 8; the impacts did not constitute an attack on the private or family life of the applicants, or show disturbance to their own rights under Article 8 of the Convention. The case was rejected.

The second case, *Tatar v. Romania* (2009), was brought to the European court by two Romanians, father and son, after they were unable to receive accountability or redress through the Romanian justice system. An ecological disaster at a Romania gold mine washed high levels of sodium cyanide and heavy metals into freshwater systems. It also polluted rivers in Hungary, into the

> Black Sea, and Serbia. The applicants alleged violations of Convention Articles 2 (rights to life) and 8, but the European Court decided to proceed under only Article 8, after consideration of Romania laws. Evidence relied on reports from the UNEP and the WHO, due to a lack of domestic reports. The Stockholm Declaration, the Aarhus Convention, and the Gabčikovo-Nagymaros judgment about environmental protection were heavily quoted. The Court unanimously found a violation of Article 8, nevertheless rejected any compensatory damages to the applicants. From this case, two of the findings were considered to be particularly significant: that Europe's Precautionary Principle had become the juridical norm; therefore the Romanian government must take action to adopt measures to meet European standards, and prove it is capable of protecting individuals' rights against serious risk to their health and well-being; and that Romania must remember its obligation under Stockholm Principle 21 and Rio Principle 14 to prevent significant trans-boundary harm.
>
> Source: (Shelton, 2009).

11.1.3 Impacts of anthropogenic climate change on human rights

A recent challenge in the rights to environment discourse is climate change. The world has observed changing weather patterns, and an increase in the frequency and severity of natural disasters around the world. The effects of global warming are being experienced everywhere, i.e. on the land, in the sea, and in the atmosphere. Agriculture and wildlife habitats are impacted due to temperature and precipitation pattern changes: marine life and aquaculture are similarly impacted, and there are threats of rising sea levels. In the atmosphere, greenhouse gases are accumulating, causing warming and melting sea ice, glaciers, permanent snow on the top of mountains, and permafrost, as well as contributing to the disappearance of inland seas, lakes, and rivers. Shifting seasons, and changes to the extent that wildlife range are also linked to global temperature changes (c.f. NASA, 2018; UN Library, 2018). The cycling of El Niño and La Niña is called the El Niño Southern Oscillation (ENSO), and is a normal phenomenon, recorded since the 1600s (NOAA, 2018). Changes in the ENSO cycle are contributing to global warming, and these changes are unquestionably coming from human activities. (Di Liberto, 2018; NOAA, 2018). Human-induced global warming has been a contributing factor to the increasing number of super El Niños or more extreme ENSO events (Climate Signals beta, 2018). ENSO has brought typhoons and super-typhoons, heavy rains and flooding, an increasing number of wildfires, and desertification – in other words, the changing weather patterns are generating detrimental impacts on primary industries (i.e. agriculture, fisheries, and forestry), causing the loss of habitats, and the destruction of ecosystems (see Cho, 2016 for details). These changes are having significant impacts on ways of life, and we are witnessing the emergence of "climate" refugees. In light of these changes, in 2016, the Paris Agreement on climate change came into force, limiting temperature rise to well below two degrees Celsius above pre-industrial levels, yet there are significant challenges in meeting this goal. The Intergovernmental Panel on Climate Change is in the process of undertaking its 6th Assessment Report on climate change for 2022, and temperatures continue to rise.

International law recognises climate change as a common concern of humanity (Boyle 2012). The 2008 OHCHR Resolution 7/23 "Human rights and climate change" states that the Human Rights Council (HRC) is: "Concerned that climate change poses an immediate and far-reaching threat to people and communities around the world and has implications for the full enjoyment of human rights" (OHCHR, 2008). In the following year, the OHCHR Annual Report (A/HRC/10/61) emphasised that climate change is "attributed directly or indirectly to human activity" and "with more than 90 per cent certainty, most of the warming observed over the past 50 years is caused by man-made greenhouse gas emissions," with the main source from "the combustion of fossil fuels" (OHCHR, 2009a). In this document, it was acknowledged that climate change has apparent impacts on the "enjoyment of human rights." What is more interesting is that even after acknowledging this, the OHCHR (2009a) indicated it is not evidently certain whether climate change is a direct violation of human rights; yet the OHCHR stressed the provision of the protection of human rights affected by climate change as the dispositive fact (A/HRC/10/61, para. 71). These points were also emphasised in the 2016 OHCHR report (A/HRC/31/52, para. 35&36) (OHCHR, 2016). In the 2009 report, the OHCHR examined some of the human rights that are deemed most directly impacted by any form of climate change activity: the right to life, rights to adequate food, water, health, adequate housing, and self-determination. Scholars like Boyle (2012) and Shelton (2009a) express concerns that the precautionary approach adopted by the UN is not yet well integrated or may even be not well suited in international human rights laws – unlike international environmental laws. Laws and strategies for climate change are based on risk assessment, while human rights violations are based on what has happened.

11.2 The human–environment relationship

Human beings depend on a healthy environment for survival. Human rights, such as rights to life, food, water, health, and sanitation, cannot be achieved without clean air and water, and a sustainable natural environment. However, human rights issues and environmental protection issues were historically discussed as separate concerns (c.f. Chapter 3), and as such, the harmonisation of human rights laws and environmental laws has not yet materialised. Concerned citizens and scholars have advocated that human beings are an integrated part of the natural system, and thus human behaviours and the natural system interact with each other. However, as Brown Weiss expressed, humans "have no rights to destroy… [the natural system's] integrity" (1990, p. 199). In this quid pro quo relationship between human beings and the natural system, many societies have understood for centuries that if human societies protect and care for the well-being of the natural system, then it provides humans with a critical life-support system – making human life possible. Nevertheless, the balance in the human–environment relationship has been rapidly deteriorating, and climate change is threatening the only liveable environment for human beings.

Environmental concerns and protection are not only a 20th-century social phenomena; for example, the Babylonians had hygiene laws (1800 BCE), and sewer systems were found in Mohenjo-daro, Pakistan (2500 BCE) and in ancient Rome (500 BCE) (Koloski-Ostrow, 2015; Jansen, 2010). India claims its religious and customary norms have protected the diverse ecosystem of India from the Himalayan mountain range to the coastlines for over 5000 years by animistic worship of individual dharma (some of the translations are: "protection" (About Dharma, n.d.), and "religious and moral law" (Encyclopædia Britannica, 2012; CPREEC, 2015). England had the Smoke Abatement Act in 1273 (Tsuru, 1989), long before the 1956 Clean Air Act was passed. In England, King William the Conqueror displaced local inhabitants and communities to establish his hunting forest – "New Forest" in 1079, thus forbidding his subjects from hunting in his forests with heavy penalties under Forest Law. Yet, this seemingly self-centred action allowed 570 km^2 of woodlands and wilderness heath to be managed and protected by stakeholders for nearly 1000 years (The New Forest, 2017; National Parks UK, 2017; New Forest National Park, 2017). A similar logic was employed in colonial territories, predominantly in Africa, where European colonists barred native populations from poaching wildlife, so that hunting (although unfairly) was reserved for the colonists. Many other countries have regulated air pollution from burning coal, animal and human waste management, animal abuse, hygiene, and sanitation (c.f. Environmental history timeline, 2017; de Melo, Vaz and Costa Pinto, 2017) since ancient times. Indigenous populations have long known the importance of environmental conservation. Yet while humankind is aware of the dangers of mistreating the environment, it continues to cause irreparable damage. Westra (2011) explored the relationship between human rights, the commons, and the collective. Increasingly with the primacy of economic motives, it is the poor and disposed that are being shut out of the natural global commons. "Whatever is left of the commons has become someone's property ... Even the simplest "natural goods" – for example clean air, pure water, safe sunlight and safe foods – are no longer freely available, and all are unavailable to the poor" (Westra, 2011, p. 7). Drawing on the work of Vašák who postulated three generations of rights, Westra (2011) notes that the third generation of rights focuses more on collective rights, and are referred to as "rights of solidarity" (c.f. Chapter 1). They incorporate the right to self-determination, development, a healthy environment, natural resources, as well as participation in cultural heritage (Vašák in Domaradzik, Khvostova and Pupovac 2019). These collective rights have also been mentioned in the Stockholm Declaration and the Rio Declaration (Domaradzik, Khvostova and Pupovac 2019).

11.2.1 Agriculture, industrialisation, and environmental changes

As humans evolved, the beginnings of agriculture and an agrarian lifestyle began to impact the global climate. During the Palaeolithic Era of *Homo sapiens* migration, humans travelled on land and sea, spreading to the four corners of the world, adapting to their new environments and ecosystems (Christian, 2011). As humans settled and started farming about 11,000 years ago, the Agrarian Era emerged, and lasted until about the 17th century when industrialisation began. There is evidence that agriculture started in Southwest Asia about 10,000 years ago; 8,000 years ago in The Middle East; and in approximately 600 BCE in Europe (Civitello, 2004). According to Kinnear and Rhode (1987), the first wave of climate change began to occur when European ecosystems were drastically affected by sedentary agriculture – the Neolithic Revolution – with the burning and clearing of land, and domestication of wild animals. Agriculturalists around the world used various farming technologies to manipulate the plants, animals, and landscape around them; whatever humans found useful was selected, protected, and efforts were made to increase the production of those species; meanwhile what was not useful was discarded (Christian, 2011). This unnatural and anthropocentric selection of species greatly impacted ecosystems (Standage, 2009). During the Agrarian Era, the human population multiplied from an estimated six million people 10,000 years ago, to 250 million 1,000 years ago (Christian, 2011). In 2019, this number had grown to 7.7 billion people worldwide (Worldometers, 2019). With rapid population growth, humans require more resources, and agriculture had to be more efficient at producing enough food supplies. With intensive farming, atmospheric levels of methane and carbon dioxide have been rising. These factors associated with the expansion of agriculture and human activities have been contributing to changes in the biosphere (Christian, 2011; Standage, 2009).

The second shock to the world's ecosystems was industrialisation from the 18th to the 20th century. Industrialisation began in England and spread quickly, prompting rapid urbanisation and large-scale population mobility. It brought medical improvements and resulting population growth, and the widespread use of chemical fertilisers and pesticides (Kinnear and Rhode, 1987). During the medieval period in England, 75–90% of the population were involved in subsistence agriculture (Clark, 2002; Staples, 1999 cited in Whitheridge, 2006). Evidence of declining participation is reflected in the number of males employed in agriculture falling to 37% (1800s) and then to 10% (1900s) (Clark, 2002, p.12), as industrialisation changed farming methods. The two World Wars hastened the evolution of agricultural technology in order to keep up with demand. After WWII, rapid technological change and a sudden surge in the world's population increased humanity's capacity to destroy the environment (Janssen, et al., 1992). It was after WWII that modern tourism started to evolve with the rise in commercial aircraft. Industrial agriculture started in the USA after WWII, with chemically intensive mono-crop farming. While initially embraced as technological achievement, its resulting environmental damage, negative impacts on public health, and unexpected mutations of organisms and bacteria became the focus of environmental discourse (Union of Concerned Scientists, 2017). Belated industrialisation in Asian countries meant that developments of advanced technologies and chemicals caused far more environmental damage – this along with the rapid recovery of war-ravaged nations added to the fast-pace of environmental degradation. To fuel industrialisation and national recovery efforts, coal was extracted and burnt as an inexpensive fuel source; untreated waste, and polluted effluents were released unchecked; chemical run-off from agricultural lands contaminated water and soil, and dangerous materials entered the food chain.

Another wake-up call was the emergence of diseases previously unknown before industrialisation, especially linked to heavy industries. In 17th century France, 18th century England, and 19th century USA, mercury poisoning in the hat making industry resulted in a neurological disorder known as "Mad Hatter's Syndrome" (Wedeen, 1989; A Unity College, n.d.). Other Mercury-induced poisonings included, "Hunter-Russell Syndrome" identified in the 1940s (Grandjean, et al., 2010) in the UK; and "Minamata Disease" in Japan in the 1950s, caused by the methyl mercury compound poisoning the central nervous system due to contamination of marine life from a nitrogen fertiliser processing company in the area (Minamata City, 2007). Cadmium poisoning from a sphalerite mine between 1910 and 1970 in Toyama, Japan, led to the rise of "*Itai-Itai* Disease" (literally translated as "it hurts, it hurts") which was officially acknowledged in 1955 (Nordberg, et al., 2007; Iijima, Watanabe and Fujikawa, 2007). In the 1970s, in Niagara Falls, New York, USA, residents of a community built upon a waste disposal site of 21,000 tons of toxic chemicals dumped between 1942 and 1953, suffered from a series of perplexing illnesses; eventually becoming known as the Love Canal tragedy (Kleiman, 2017; Beck, 1979). There is also a correlation between polluted air in industrial areas, and the number of reported respiratory diseases (e.g., Wang and Chau, 2013), and possible links between Parkinson's Disease and exposure to heavy metals (e.g., Uversky, Li and Fink, 2001). Other disasters such as Bhopal (1984), Chernobyl (1986), and Fukushima (2011) all illustrate the potential environmental damage industrial disasters can cause. Reflecting on the collective rights and the environment, Westra (2011) argues the right to development is often that of corporations and neoliberal states, and not the local and Indigenous communities who suffer harm rather than reap the benefits. The rise of tragic health problems resulting from environmental pollution in recent history has led to campaigns and activism around the world to clean up the environment and restore conditions for a healthy life.

11.2.2 Environmentalism and environmental movements

Publications such as *Silent Spring* by Rachel Carson (1962), *Population Bomb* by Paul Ehrlich (1968), and the *Tragedy of Commons* theory by William Forster Lloyd (1833)/Garrett Hardin (1968) all sparked concern and inflamed environmental movements. Similarly, the UN began spearheading less sensational contributions to the environmental movement over the past half-century (Conca, 2015), publishing major treaties and declarations on the environment. Numerous organisations, associations, and NGOs operating on a local to global scale along with concerned citizens throughout the world have all played important roles contributing to environmentalism and environmental rights.

Environmentalism is a political, social, or ethical movement to bring about change to harmful human activities towards nature, or to improve the quality of the natural environment by altering the current human–nature relationship. The two ends of the environmentalism spectrum are: Anthropocentric (alias: human-centred, soft ecology, or technocentrism) and Biocentric (alias: life-centred, deep ecology, or ecocentrism). Environmental groups are located somewhere on this spectrum, with some believing that if natural resources and the environment have no use to humans, they have no value at all. Thus, species selection and the prioritisation of environmental protection measures are calculated by the degree of usefulness to humans. Technology can also contribute to this process of selection. Biocentric environmentalists tend to be more extreme in their beliefs, and some groups are referred to as eco- or green-terrorists. They claim humans are one small part of nature; and thus, their belief in saving nature, may in the end, compromise human wellbeing and even human lives. To a certain extent, many ancient religions share similar views of biocentrism; all creatures have equal value and all life forms must be revered. The responsibility of good stewardship is a task bestowed upon all human beings if they want to survive and live in harmony with nature. King William the Conqueror's Forest Law was purely anthropocentric, and even punitive to the peasant population who cut down any trees, yet over the course of history, it can now be interpreted as part of the biocentric environmental movement.

Although many countries and societies boast about environmental guardianship and protection, rapid industrialisation, overuse of chemicals, rapid technological advancement, together with exponential population growth, has nullified Indigenous methods of stewardship for the natural environment. Reactionary management of environmental problems is often characteristic of the approach in Western societies. Industrialised or developed countries witnessed environmental pollution and problems in more urbanised areas, where a larger number of victims were present; e.g. in industrialised Victorian England, where increasing numbers of slums or poor neighbourhoods in urban areas were fraught with recurring epidemics, poor health, and poverty, leading to the Poor Law Amendment Act of 1834 (Wilde, 2018; Henrique, 1979). The pursuit of wealth and progress has been paid at the cost of human and animal welfare through air and water pollution, and pharmaceutical tragedies. For example, Thalidomide, touted as a breakthrough in medical science, was introduced as a tranquiliser and as a sleeping pill in post-war Germany in 1957. When Thalidomide's effectiveness as a morning sickness remedy was noticed, it was sold in 46 countries. However, Thalidomide children were born with phocomelia or did not survive. As soon as the correlation between Thalidomide and children with shortened or absent limbs was confirmed, it was banned by 1962. This tragedy led to tighter legislation in the approval of new medicines in many countries (Fintel, Samaras and Carias, 2009).

Rutherford and Williams (2015) examined a range of actors linked to the environmental movement, which have influenced both norms of behaviour and political choices. These include: influential individuals (e.g. Rachel Carson), independent pressure groups (e.g. NGOs like Greenpeace), corporate businesses (e.g. multinational corporations supplying consumer demand and creating environmental impacts), governments (e.g. making policy decisions and applying legislation), and intergovernmental bodies (e.g. United Nations holding Earth Summits). The modern mindset of environment gained traction in the 1960s. Environmentalism today has seen increased research on biodiversity loss and climate change, leading to greater action to protect the environment and encourage sustainability from individuals, corporations, and governments (Rutherford and Williams, 2015). In light of climate change, the concepts of vulnerability, risk, resilience, adaption, mitigation, and good governance have all come to the forefront.

11.3 Environmental issues in tourism

The relationship between tourism and the environment has been considered in Chapter 3 (SDG) and Chapter 5 (environmental security). Goodall (1992) pointed out that tourists are consumers of an attractive environment, and the tourism industry has been using the "environment" as a core feature of many of its tourism products. As early as the 1960s, the shift towards "environmentally friendly", "green", and "eco-(logical)" tourism products has been observed, and Green Consumerism movements pushed tourism businesses to become more environmental friendly or "green." Numerous conferences and seminars on environmental issues in tourism have been held, and business codes, i.e. Corporate Social Responsibility (CSR) and Responsible Business Conduct (RBC) have become more and more common in the industry – particularly in developed nations (see Chapter 2). Yet the CSR and RBC are over and above the legal requirements in many countries (Global Affairs Canada, 2018). CSR first appeared as a result of pressure from the Green Consumerism movement. However, many parties are sceptical, believing that CSR is merely a superficial gesture to enhance corporate image (Hashimoto, 1996). Over time, CSR shifted from simply a "greening" of businesses, towards making more visible contributions to the wellbeing of the local population. RBC emphasises responsible business behaviours – particularly abroad where legal regulations of the home country may not always apply. For example, the Canadian government emphasises that these corporate behavioural codes include "respect for human rights," being "consistent with applicable laws and internationally recognised standards," and "the positive voluntary contributions that businesses can make to sustainable development and inclusive growth" (Global Affairs Canada, 2018; see Chapter 2 for further discussion).

Asadzadeh and Mousavi (2017) summarise tourisms' negative environmental impacts into six categories: water pollution, visual pollution, waste management problems, ecological disturbance of natural areas, damage to archaeological and historical sites, problematic use planning, and construction and poor engineering that threatens the environment. Pollution of air and water, and the deprivation of natural resources such as water in tourism areas have been a source of conflict for a long time. In 2010, a UN Resolution (Resolution 64/292) "explicitly recognized the human right to water and sanitation and acknowledged that clean drinking water and sanitation are essential to the realisation of all human rights" (UN/DESA, 2014). Tourists are known for overusing water resources in destinations (c.f. Parkes, 2018; Hickman, 2012; Becken, 2014), where water is diverted from local communities for tourist use. Water shortages in destinations often result in a lack of drinking water, drought, spread of disease, and serious health problems for locals. Tourist facilities provide plenty of shower and bath water, swimming pools, and well-watered lawns and gardens. Watering gardens and golf courses also causes run-off of chemical fertilisers, herbicides, and pesticides into local water systems (see Gössling, Hall and Scott 2015 for further discourse). Unplanned tourism development opens up forested areas, levels hills and mountains, and changes the landscape; which becomes more prone to erosion, landslides, and other natural hazards. Ecotourism continues to open up even more remote destinations with fragile environments.

Pollution from air, ground, and water transportation (including cruise ships which often use lower quality fuel) has been affecting the health of residents and tourists while also contributing to global warming. From data in 2007, the UNWTO concluded that tourism is responsible for 5% of the world's CO_2 emissions, and 4.6% of global warming, while the transportation sector generates 75% of CO_2 emission (UNWTO, n.d.). In Lenzen, et al.'s study (2018), between 2009 and 2013, tourism was responsible for 8% of global warming gas emission (CO_2 and CH_4) – four times higher than earlier estimates.

Flying to and from destinations, travelling by luxurious cruise ships, and staying in comfortably air-conditioned accommodation facilities with Western style amenities (including flush toilets) is often expected. Prior to COVID-19, airline companies were trying to reduce their CO_2 emissions, as the popularity of travel and tourism had seen an increase in the numbers of flights and passengers. In a similar vein, the number of automobiles was increasing, but trips were significantly reduced under COVID-19 lockdowns. While smart cars and hybrid cars are becoming more popular, as of yet, there are relatively few electronic cars in use globally, and alternative fuels for automobiles and accompanying support systems are not in place. The use of air conditioning and central heating systems to satisfy tourists' needs for comfort, and the provision of luxury facilities – such as swimming pools or golf courses – all add to the worsening effect of global warming. Without altering mass consumerism in contemporary society, the over-reliance on modern technologies to solve environmental issues presents more challenges.

11.3.1 Tourism's contribution to global warming

The grounding of airlines and docking of cruise ships under COVID-19 restrictions has significantly reduced the tourism industry's emissions and contributions to global warming (see Chapter 14). This section will highlight recent trends, and briefly comment on the impact of COVID-19. Prior to the COVID-19 outbreak and the closure of borders and tourism companies, the number of tourist arrivals had been continuing to grow. High-income countries (per capita GDP is >US$10,000), generated 656.7 million tourists in 2013: middle-income countries (US$3,000 – US$10,000) generated 281.5 million tourists in the same year, and low-income countries (<US$3,000) generated 53.9 million tourists (Lenzen, et al., 2018). In 2019, international tourism arrivals reached 1.5 billion, a 4% growth from the previous year, and a similar forecast was predicted for 2020 (UNWTO, 2020a). In 2021, outbound tourist growth rates were estimated to be distributed as: Americas 3.3%, Europe 3.5%, Asia Pacific 4.7%, Africa 4.9%, and the Middle East 5.4% (Lock, 2019). Major European cities such as Barcelona, Venice, and Amsterdam, were experiencing overtoursim as the numbers of visitors grew, multiplying the negative impacts of tourism on the environment.

Damage to the environment compromises human rights to a healthy and adequate environment in which to live. Global carbon movements illustrate tourism has been a high-income affair. Carbon embodied in tourism predominantly moves between high-income nations. Approximately half of the global total footprint had been a result of travel between high-income countries (per capita GDP greater than US$25,000). High-income nations such as the USA, Canada, and the UK exert a higher carbon footprint in destinations (Lenzen, et al., 2018). Tourism's total global carbon footprint contribution was 8.1% of global CO_2 emissions, 5.3% of global CO_2-e (CO_2 equivalent) emissions or 4.5 Gt CO_2-e (Gigatons of CO_2 equivalent): of which 3.2 Gt CO_2-e (Gigatons of CO_2 equivalent) came from "emissions for moving planes and road vehicles, electricity for running hotels and restaurants, and from the combustion of various fuels required to manufacture consumer goods purchased by tourists" (Lenzen, et al., 2018). Half of the tourism carbon footprint growth rate (1.1 Gt CO_2-e) from 2009–13 happened in higher-income countries, and was due to higher-income visitors. The changes in tourism's carbon footprint revealed that middle-income countries had the highest growth rate of 22.6% p.a. Lenzen, et al. (2018) also examined changes in visitors' carbon footprint. Chinese visitors contributed an average annual increase of 75 Metric ton CO_2 equivalent (Mt CO_2-e) to the global tourism carbon footprint, while Indian visitors' contribution is 19 Mt CO_2-e. Examples of visitors from high-income countries include the USA (25 Mt CO_2-e), and Canada (12 Mt CO_2-e). Low-income countries, particularly island nations, had seen a rise in carbon emission growth rates due to the distance flights must cover to reach the islands and the shipping of goods and food to the islands (Lenzen, et al., 2018). In an analysis of the vulnerability of global tourism to climate change Scott, Hall and Gösling (2019) found that areas of high vulnerability were in Africa, the Middle East, South Asia, and Small

Island Developing States. Further, vulnerability is highest where tourism comprises the highest proportion of GDP, and areas where tourism growth is expected to be highest in the coming decades. Developing island nations in the Pacific – for example, Kiribati – face rising costs as they confront extreme threats from rising sea levels.

Recent trends in emissions, however, have been largely negated by the lockdowns due to COVID-19, with the tourism industry projected to be one of the hardest economically hit sectors. The UNWTO (2020b) notes a 22% decrease in international arrivals in the first quarter of 2020, with arrivals in March down by 57%, equating to a loss of 67 million international arrivals and US$80 billion in receipts. The UNWTO stresses the outlook is extremely uncertain, with various scenarios estimating declines in international arrivals between 58–78%. The decline in travel has reduced emissions and environmental impacts, but has come with associated health and economic costs. Global CO_2 reduction estimates due to COVID-19 for 2020 could range from 4 to 7% (Le Quéré, et al., 2020). As some nations begin to reopen, what the recovery from COVID-19 will look like is still unknown but steps must continue to be made to protect the natural environment. Tourism development, like any other forms of development, must ensure that the local population – regardless of their involvement in tourism – have rights to the environment, rights to natural resources, and rights to livelihood. The following section explores what the industry and governments have done to combat pollution and reduce its impact.

11.3.2 Government and the tourism industry's response to environmental issues in tourism

The tourism industry and governments have been taking various actions to minimise the negative environmental impacts of tourism. There have been attempts to reduce CO_2 emissions in the air transportation sector. In 2015, a Member of the European Parliament proposed a tax on frequent flyers, who represent 15% of the population, but occupy 70% of flights (Taylow, 2015). This taxation idea is a form of demand management – reducing frequent flyers while non-frequent flyers such as family holidaymakers were not to be impacted. By using demand management, Taylor argues that there is no need for airport expansions that would further deteriorate surrounding environments for residents. The Dutch government is planning to introduce a flight tax in January 2021. The amount will be determined later but it is small – below €7.50 (Government of the Netherlands, 2019). France will introduce a tax on airlines leaving from French airports from 2020 (Pennetier and De Clercq, 2019). Many other destination cities and countries are already applying a tourist tax, e.g. Catalonia since 2012, Barcelona, and Paris; and many more are planning to introduce a levy, e.g. Bali (Erviani, 2019) and Edinburgh (BBC, 2019). However, some argue that such a small sum is not painful enough to deter tourists (Francis, 2019); or if the money will be actually used for environmental or cultural protection (Erviani, 2019). The "*flygaskam* (flight shaming)" movement started in

Sweden in the Spring of 2019, and has slowly been spreading among European tourists, encouraging them to take more environmentally friendly trains (Coffey, 2019). The International Air Transport Association (IATA) took note of this anti-flying movement. The aviation industry defended itself, saying aircrafts are cutting 1 to 2% of their emissions each year (Coffey, 2019). Trans-Atlantic Finnair aircraft began flying with a biofuel mix in August 2019, and many other major airlines – such as Lufthansa, KLM, Thomson Airways, and Singapore Airlines – are also working on alternative fuels (Graham, 2019). In Germany, the government plans to double taxes on domestic and intra-European flights, while simultaneously reducing taxes on train tickets as part of their plan for the country to be carbon neutral by 2050 (Hummel, 2019). However, US airline experts say that the anti-flying movement does not stand a chance of making a lasting change in the US because "[s]peedy train travel across the United States is a dream that may never come true" and driving is not a good alternative option: the only option is not to fly, and travelling is a social good that Americans do not want to be deprived of (Sampson, 2019). COVID-19 has caused a rapid decline in the number of flights, and consequently emissions. Airlines took planes out of service, cut routes, and reduced their number of employees as they tried to remain in operation. While some airlines have collapsed, others such as Lufthansa required a major bailout from the German Government (9 billion Euro) due to COVID-19. As countries begin to reopen, it will be important to monitor the growth rate of emissions and if past travel patterns will return.

Supranational organisations and nation-states have been incorporating principles from the Stockholm Declaration, the Brundtland Report (see Telfer, 2013), and the Rio Declaration into operations or Environmental Law so that human rights are reflected. These principles are: (1) The Precautionary principle (see Box 11.2), (2) The Prevention principle, (3) The "Polluters Pay" principle (see Box 11.2), (4) The Integration principle, (5) The Public Participation principle, and (6) Sustainable Development (Campbell-Mohn and Cheever, 2016). The UN also outlined guidelines for governments and private actors: (a) procedural obligations, (b) substantive obligations to protect human rights, (c) unique obligation to certain groups, e.g. women, children, and Indigenous People, and (4) private actors' obligations to follow UN guidelines on Human Rights and Business (UNEP, 2015). Codes of Ethics, Corporate Social Responsibility Statements (CSR), Certification Programs, and Indicators have been adopted by the tourism industry in attempt to reduce their negative impacts (see Chapters 2 and 10). For example, the Global Sustainable Tourism Council has established industry criteria (for hotel and tour operators) and destination criteria (for managing tourism destinations) around four pillars: sustainable management, socioeconomic impacts, cultural impacts, and environmental impacts (including consumption of resources, reducing pollution, and conserving biodiversity and landscapes) (GSTC, 2019). The operations criteria specifically mention human rights, and the entire programme is framed around the UN Sustainable Development Goals. However, Buckley and de Vasconcellos Pegas (2013) argue that CSR is very weak in the mainstream tourism industry, and few companies do significantly more than the minimum required by law, while many others do not even comply with the legal minimal standards.

> **BOX 11.2 POLLUTER'S RESPONSIBILITY: THE CASE OF INDIA**
>
> In the wake of the UN Conference on the Human Environment in 1972, where countries agreed on taking all possible steps to prevent pollution, several countries adopted laws to protect deteriorating conditions of the environment (Report of the UN Conference on the Human Environment, A/CONF.48/14/Rev. 1, June 1972). For example, the Indian Constitution imposes on its citizens to protect the natural environment as one of the fundamental duties of the constitution (art. 51, Indian Constitution). The Indian Supreme Court has in several cases enforced the Constitution, and ordered polluting companies to set up effluent treatment plants, close hazardous industries, and relocate polluting industries from residential areas (see for example M.C. Mehta v. Union of India, WP 3727/1985, Sep. 22, 1985).
>
>> In *M.C. Mehta v. Kamal Nath* (Supreme Court of India, May 12, 2000, see also M.C. Mehta v. Kamal Nath & Ors, 1996 INSC 1608, Dec. 13, 1996) a motel company had been granted a commercial 99-year lease on environmentally fragile protected forest land, owned by the Himachal Pradesh state government in India. Kamal Nath, whose family owned almost all the shares in the motel company, was also the Minister of Environment and Forests in charge of granting of the lease. The motel company started an ambitious project, the Span Club. As part of the realization of the project, the management used bulldozers to turn the course of an adjacent river, the Beas River, as well as letting untreated water enter the river. These activities caused floods along the river as well as pollution. M.C. Mehta, a public interest lawyer, filed a petition to stop the activities of the company. The Indian Supreme Court relied partly on the Indian Constitution and held that *"Article 48-A of the Constitution provides that the State shall endeavour to protect and improve the environment and to safeguard the forests and wildlife of the country. One of the fundamental duties of every citizen as set out in Article 51-A(g) is to protect and improve the natural environment, including forests, lakes, rivers and wildlife and to have compassion for living creatures. These two articles have to be considered in the light of Article 21 of the Constitution which provides that no person shall be deprived of his life and liberty except in accordance with the procedure established in law. Any disturbance of the basic environmental elements, namely air, water and soil, which are necessary for "life" would be hazardous to "life" within the meaning of Article 21 of the*

Constitution." (¶8). Furthermore, in the matter of enforcement of fundamental rights under Article 21, the court could award damages against those who were responsible for disturbing the ecological balance by conducting an activity which polluted the environment. The court held that motel company's lease was cancelled, and the riverbank and the river basin had to be left open for public use. The motel was also ordered to stop discharging untreated effluent into the river, and to pay compensation for the restitution of the environment and ecology of the area.

In 1984, M.C. Mehta, the abovementioned public interest lawyer, visited the Taj Mahal, one of the most popular tourist destinations in the world. He saw that the marble had turned yellow with black fungus patches, and that pollutants from nearby industries caused acid rain, having a corroding effect on the marble of the Taj Mahal. This prompted him to file a petition with the Supreme Court of India, seeking the court to take effective measures against the pollutants (*M.C Mehta (Taj Trapezium Matter) v. Union of India & Ors*, (1997 2 SCC 353 Dec. 30, 1996). The Indian Supreme Court noted that *"[t]he Taj, apart from being a cultural heritage, is an industry by itself. More than two million tourists visit the Taj every year. It is a source of revenue for the country...The old concept that development and ecology cannot go together is no longer acceptable. Sustainable development is the answer ... The pollution created as a consequence of development must be commensurate with the carrying capacity of our ecosystems"* (p. 42). Relying partly on the Constitutional right to life and the duty to protect the environment, the court ordered industries in the area to switch their energy supply to environmentally sustainable alternatives, or to relocate to areas outside the zone of impact on the Taj Mahal. The court noted that pollution has to be eliminated at all costs. *"Not even one per cent chance can be taken when – human life apart – the preservation of a prestigious monument like the Taj is involved"* (p. 45).

In recent years, human rights litigation focusing on environmental concerns has been more prevalent, as public rights activists have focused on climate change and the challenges it brings.

Other examples highlight the challenges with environmental law. In Egypt, Shaalan (2005) found the government willing to adopt sustainable development concepts for the Red Sea area, yet the economic reality of the nation (need of economic boost, high unemployment, etc.) inhibited attempts to fully realise environmental law. A study by Hernádez, et al. (2010) on an island where environmental law is salient, found personal norms are a strong predictor of environmental transgression. If the community or groups hold the norm that environmental protection is insignificant, they tend to break environmental laws. Understanding and acceptance of the need for environmental law is critical for the local population and the protection of their environment – and as a consequence, rights to environment. In Antarctica, no single nation-state is responsible for environmental protection, yet the protection of Antarctica is of utmost importance for minimising climate change. Bastmeijer and Roura (2004) found that the complication of sovereignty of laws impeded the ability to implement environmental protection. Chile, for example, had been operating Antarctic tours and claimed it could continue to operate its hotel that opened in the 1980s adjacent to its research station prior to the Antarctic Treaty System and its Protocol coming into effect. Meanwhile, other countries operating in the region like Germany, Norway, and New Zealand argued land-based tourism activities do not comply with the Antarctic Treaty System and their own domestic laws. These cases show the difficulties dealing with jurisdiction rights and environmental law, as well as implementing the precautionary principle (see Chapters 1 and 2 for more discussions).

11.4 Conclusion

Sachs (2003) wrote that "human dignity" is a form of justice. Justice takes the form of (1) fairness, (2) equitable distribution, and (3) human dignity. International environmental justice is a human right in a sense, and it is an absolute necessity for a dignified existence. UN Special Rapporteur Knox's Statement in 2017 concludes that states have the obligation to protect the environment, provide environmental information, and facilitate public participation in decision-making – while also fulfilling human rights obligations. Development and environmental policies, in regard to human rights to life, water and food, and health must benefit everyone without discrimination.

In accordance with the UN Sustainable Development Goals, the UNWTO has also proactively been strategising how tourism can contribute to the SDGs. In the documents, *Tourism for Development Volume 1* (UNWTO, 2018a), the language used in the strategies never mentions rights to the environment, however, *Tourism for Development Volume 2* (2018b), and *Tourism and the Sustainable Development Goals – Journey to 2030* (UNWTO and UNDP, 2017) focus on the human right to a healthy environment through tourism development. In *Tourism for Development Volume 2* (2018b), environment-related issues are examined in "Pillar 3: Resource efficiency, environmental protection and climate change":

> As a sector that heavily depends on the natural environment, tourism has a special responsibility towards the planet ... This section discusses tourism's relationship with resource efficiency, environmental protection, biodiversity conservation and climate change, with a view to better understanding how tourism can mitigate negative environmental impacts and contribute to protecting our planet's invaluable natural resources.
>
> *(pp. 63–64)*

The UNWTO documents illustrate that approaches to environment-related issues are often based on the assumption of the tourism industry's rights and responsibilities to natural resources and the environment in a destination. This rhetoric, however, does not focus on the local population and local businesses' rights to a healthy environment, and how tourism can fulfil its obligation to satisfy their rights to environment.

Earlier discourse on the human right to environment in this chapter must be considered, along with the discussion of the human right to travel (see Chapter 9). UN documents argue that human beings do not have rights to environment or to tourism; rather human beings require a healthy and adequate environment and natural resources so that they can attain a dignified and healthy life. To attain this, rights to a dignified life can be used as a tool to push states to provide the necessary means to ensure a healthy and adequate environment. The same logic goes to the rights to tourism. Successful tourism development can achieve many things outlined in the UN SDGs, such as poverty alleviation, rights to work with adequate wages, work conditions, rights to equality, and so on (see UNWTO and UNDP, 2017; UNWTO 2015 for details). However, the right to tourism is not enshrined in any UN documents, except in the UNWTO's Code of Ethics Article 13 (see Chapter 9). Rights to enjoy cultural events, and rights to rest and leisure are noted in UN documents, but not the right to tourism. The recent COVID-19 pandemic has also proved that tourism is a luxury and privilege, but not a basic human right.

It is important to realise that rights to a healthy environment is not simply a matter of protecting the natural environment and resources from degradation. Protecting the natural environment and resources also means the protection of human rights, i.e. a dignified life with access to a healthy livelihood and resources. It is also not simply about combatting poverty. A symbiotic relationship between nature and human beings, built on careful stewardship, has the potential to create a sustainable relationship for the future. Nature can survive without human beings; however, humans cannot survive without nature.

This chapter has examined human rights and environmental issues at a macro level. What the UN, scientists, lawmakers, and governments are concerned with, and what they have achieved so far, clearly indicate that human rights cannot be achieved without an adequate environment to live in. Climate change is not just part of a natural cycle, but is also a human-induced phenomenon, and tourism has been contributing to global warming. Climate change has been referred to as a threat multiplier. Nation-states have been disputing whose responsibility it is to reduce emissions to combat climate change. While they did come together in the Paris Climate Accord, global temperatures continue to rise. When the Swedish government claimed that implementing stronger climate policies is improbable if the public does not make the issue a priority, young activist Greta Thunberg responded that world leaders and politicians have done nothing and have failed the public (Watts, 2019). Activist organisations, such as Extinction Rebellion, continue to push for change. Global development paradigms must be altered, so that the priority of governments and businesses in tourism is not solely focused on economic growth. In a new development paradigm, individuals must realise that the right to environment is not something just to be given – but it is something to be earned and protected by law (see Chapter 1 for absolute and qualified rights). Collective action must be taken to ensure these rights are protected. Living in a healthy environment where people can live with health, dignity, and equality is essential for all.

References

About Dharma, n.d. *What is Dharma?* [online]. Available at: <www.aboutdharma.org/what-is-dharma.php/> [Accessed 13 September 2017].

Asadzadeh A, Mousavi MSS., 2017. The Role of Tourism on the Environment and its Governing Law. *Electronic Journal of Biology*, 13:1. [online]. Available at: <http://ejbio.imedpub.com/the-role-of-tourism-on-the-environment-and-its-governinglaw.php?aid=19002> [Accessed 14 May 2018].

A Unity College, n.d. *Mercury/History: A Unity College Student-Faculty Project*. [online]. Available at: <www.environmentalhistory.org/mercury/history> [Accessed 24 January 2018].

BBC, 2019. Edinburgh 'tourist tax' backed by council. *BBC News*. [online]. 7 February. Available at: <www.bbc.com/news/uk-scotland-47157011> [Accessed 16 August 2019].

Beck, E.C., 1979. The Love Canal Tragedy. *EPA Journal*. [online]. Available at: <https://archive.epa.gov/epa/aboutepa/love-canal-tragedy.html> [Accessed 24 January 2018].

Becken, S., 2014. Water Equity – Contrasting Tourism Water Use with That of the Local Community. *Water Resources and Industry*, 7/8 (September), pp. 9–22. https://doi.org/10.1016/j.wri.2014.09.002.

Bastmeijer, C.J. and Roura, R., 2004. Regulating Antarctic Tourism and the Precautionary Principle. *American Journal of International Law*, 98(October), pp. 763–781. https://doi.org/10.2307/3216699.

Boyd, D.R., 2011. The Implicit Constitutional Right to Live in a Healthy Environment. *Review of European Community & International Environmental Law*, 20(2), pp. 171–179. https://doi.org/10.1111/j.1467-9388.2011.00701.x.

Boyd, D.R., 2012. *The Environmental Rights Revolution: a Global Study of Constitutions, Human Rights, and the Environment*. Vancouver: UBC Press.

Boyd, D.R., 2013. Effectiveness of Constitutional Environmental Rights. *Yale UNITAR Workshop*. [online]. Available at: <https://environment.yale.edu/content/documents/00003438/Boyd-Effectiveness-of-Constitutional-Environmental-Rights.docx?1389969747> [Accessed 14 August 2018].

Boyd, D.R., Boisvert, A., Collins, L.M. and Mitchell, K., 2017. The Case for Constitutional Environmental Rights. *National Magazine* (Canadian Bar Association). [online]. 8 March. Available at: <www.nationalmagazine.ca/Articles/March-2017/The-case-for-constitutional-environmental-rights.aspx> [Accessed 11 August 2018].

Boyle, A., 2012. Human Rights and the Environment: Where Next? *The European Journal of International Law*, 23(3), pp. 613–642. doi:10.1093/ejil/chs054.

Brown Weiss, E., 1990. *Our Rights and Obligations to Future Generations for the Environment*. [pdf] Georgetown University Law Center. Available at: <http://scholarship.law.georgetown.edu/cgi/viewcontent.cgi?article=2639&context=facpub> [Accessed 8 May 2017].

Buckley, R. and de Vasconcellos Pegas, F., 2013. Tourism and CSR. In: A. Holden and D. Fennell, (eds.), *The Routledge Handbook of Tourism and Environment*. Abingdon: Routledge, pp. 521–530.

Campbell-Mohn, C.I. and Cheever, F., 2016. Environmental Law. *Encyclopædia Britannica Online*. [online]. 19 September. London: Encyclopædia Britannica (UK). Available at: <www.britannica.com/topic/environmental-law> [Accessed 26 January 2018].

Cho, R., 2016. El Niño and Global Warming—What's the Connection? *State of the Planet | Earth Institute* [blog] 02 February. Available at: <https://blogs.ei.columbia.edu/2016/02/02/el-nino-and-global-warming-whats-the-connection/> [Accessed 30 September 2018]

Christian, D., 2011. World Environmental History. In: J.H. Bentley, (ed.), *The Oxford Handbook of World History*. Oxford: Oxford University Press. DOI: 10.1093/oxfordhb/9780199235810.013.0008.

Civitello, L., 2004. *Cuisine and Culture: A History of Food and People*. New Jersey: John Wiley & Sons.

Clark, G., 2002. *The Agricultural Revolution and the Industrial Revolution: England, 1500–1912*. [pdf] June 2002. Available at: <http://faculty.econ.ucdavis.edu/faculty/gclark/papers/prod2002.pdf> [Accessed 2 October 2017].

Climate Signals beta, 2018. Extreme El Niño Frequency Increase. *Climate Signals*. [online]. 08 June. Available at: <www.climatesignals.org/climate-signals/extreme-el-ni%C3%B1o-frequency-increase> [Accessed 30 September 2018]

Coffey, H., 2019. Flygskam: What is the Flight Shaming environmental Movement That's Sweeping Europe? *The Independent*. [online] 5 June. Available at: <www.independent.co.uk/travel/news-and-advice/flygskam-anti-flying-flight-shaming-sweden-greta-thornberg-environment-air-travel-train-brag-a8945196.html> [Accessed 16 August 2019].

Conca, K., 2015. United Nations Opinion: A Healthy Environment is a Human Right. *The Guardian*. [online] 1 October. Available at: <www.theguardian.com/commentisfree/2015/oct/01/a-healthy-environment-is-a-human-right> [Accessed 10 May 2017].

CPREEC, 2015. *Environmental Law in India - Part I, C.P.R. Environmental Education Centre*. [online]. Chennai, India: A Centre of Excellence of the Ministry of Environment and Forests, *Government of India*. Available at: <http://cpreec.org/168.htm> [Accessed 13 September 2017].

Curtis, V.A., 2007. A Natural History of Hygiene. *Canadian Journal of Infectious Diseases and Medical Microbiology* [e-journal] 18(1), pp. 11–14. Available at: <www.ncbi.nlm.nih.gov/pmc/articles/PMC2542893/pdf/jidmm18011.pdf> [Accessed 26 January 2018].

David Suzuki Foundation, 2018. *Environmental Protection Act report could signal breakthrough for Canadian environmental law*. [online]. 15 June 2017. Available at: <https://davidsuzuki.org/press/environmental-protection-act-report-signal-breakthrough-canadian-environmental-law/?nabe=5392362493968384:0&utm_referrer=https%3A%2F%2Fwww.google.com%2F> [Accessed 22 August 2017].

Di Liberto, T., 2018. Changes in ENSO impacts in a warming world. *Climate.gov*. [Blog] 27 September. Available at: <https://www.climate.gov/news-features/blogs/enso/changes-enso-impacts-warming-world> [Accessed 30 September 2018].

Domaradzki, S., Khvostova, M. and Pupovac, D., 2019. Karel Vasak's Generations of Rights and the Contemporary Human Rights Discourse. *Human Rights Review*, 20(4), pp. 423–443. https://doi.org/10.1007/s12142-019-00565-x.

Earthjustice, 2005. *Inuit Human Rights Petition Filed Over Climate Change*. [online] 7 December. Available at: <https://earthjustice.org/news/press/2005/inuit-human-rights-petition-filed-over-climate-change> [Accessed 12 May 2016].

Encycopaedia Britannica, 2012. *Dharma. Encyclopædia Britannica Online.* [online]. London: Encyclopædia Britannica (UK). Available at: <www.britannica.com/topic/dharma-religious-concept> [Accessed 13 September 2017].

Environmental history timeline, 2017. *Ancient – Middle Ages 5th – 15th Centuries.* [online]. Available at: <http://environmentalhistory.org/ancient/middle-ages/> [Accessed 13 September 2017].

Erviani, N.K. 2019. Tourists support Bali tax plan. But where will the money go? *Jakarta Post.* [online]. 20 February. Available at: <www.thejakartapost.com/news/2019/02/20/tourists-support-bali-tax-plan-but-where-will-the-money-go.html> [Accessed 16 August 2019].

Fintel, B., Samaras, A.T. and Carias, E., 2009. The Thalidomide Tragedy: Lessons for Drug Safty and Regulation. *Helix.* [online] 28 July. Available at: <https://helix.northwestern.edu/article/thalidomide-tragedy-lessons-drug-safety-and-regulation> [Accessed 14 August 2019].

Francis, J., 2019. Why Tourist Taxes will Never Solve the Problem of Overtourism, According to a Responsible Travel Expert. *The Independent.* [online] 2 August. Available at: <www.independent.co.uk/travel/news-and-advice/tourist-taxes-edinburgh-venice-amsterdam-overtourism-responsible-travel-a8769561.html> [Accessed 16 August 2019].

Global Affairs Canada, 2018. *Responsible Business Conduct Abroad.* [online]. 23 April. Available at: <www.international.gc.ca/trade-agreements-accords-commerciaux/topics-domaines/other-autre/csr-rse.aspx?lang=eng >.

Goodall, B., 1992. Environmental auditing for tourism. In: C. Cooper and A. Lockwood, (eds.), 1992. *Progress in tourism, recreation and hospitality management, Vol. 4.* Wallingford, UK: CAB International, pp. 60–74.

Gössling, S., Hall, C. M., and Scott, D. 2015. *Tourism and Water.* Bristol: Channelview Publications.

Government of the Netherland, 2019. *Dutch Government Tables National Flight Tax Bill* [press release] 14 May. Available at: <www.government.nl/latest/news/2019/05/14/dutch-government-tables-national-flight-tax-bill> [Accessed 16 August 2019].

Graham, R., 2019. Finnair Brings Low Carbon Biofuel to Long Haul Flights. *Euronews.* [online] 7 August. Available at: <www.euronews.com/living/2019/08/07/finnair-brings-low-carbon-biofuel-to-long-haul-flights> [Accessed 16 August 2019].

Grandjean, P., Satoh, H., Murata, K. and Eto, K., 2010. Adverse effects of methylmercury: environmental health research implications. *Environmental Health Perspectives*, 118(8), pp. 1137–1145. doi: 10.1289/ehp.0901757

GSTC, 2019. *GSTC Criteria Overview.* [online]. Available at: <www.gstcouncil.org/gstc-criteria/> [Accessed 18 November 2019].

Handl, G., 2012. *Declaration of the United Nations Conference on the Human Environment (Stockholm Declaration), 1972 and the Rio Declaration on Environment AND Development, 1992* [pdf] United Nations Audiovisual Library of International Law. Available at: <www.un.org/law/avl> [Accessed 22 August 2017].

Hashimoto, A., 1996. *A cross-cultural study of attitudes towards the natural environment and tourism development – Northern Europe and East Asia.* PhD. University of Surrey (UK).

Helman, U., 1995. Sustainable development: strategies for reconciling environment and economy in the developing world. *Washington Quarterly*, 18(4), pp. 189–208 [Academic OneFile] Available at: <go.galegroup.com/ps/i.do?p=AONE&sw=w&u=st46245&v=2.1&id=GALE%7CA18148207&it=r&asid=f4aaa767cbb7e011fef8f1bd65b6708f> [Accessed 13 September 2017].

Henriques, U.R.Q., 1979. *Before the Welfare State: Social Administration in Early Industrial Britain*. London: Longman.

Hernández, B., Martín, A.M., Ruiz, C. and del Carmen Hidalgo, M., 2010. The role of place identity and place attachment in breaking environmental protection laws. *Journal of Environmental Psychology*, 30, pp. 281–288. doi:10.1016/j.jenvp.2010.01.009.

Hickman, L., 2012. Charity condemns tourists' use of fresh water in developing countries. *The Guardian*. [online] 8 July. Available at: <www.theguardian.com/global-development/2012/jul/08/fresh-water-tourist-developing> [Accessed 10 August 2018].

Hummel, T., 2019. Germany plans to nearly double taxes on short-haul flights. *Reuter*. [online] 15 October. Available at: <www.reuters.com/article/us-climate-change-germany-flights/germany-plans-to-nearly-double-taxes-on-short-haul-flights-idUSKBN1WU1US> [Accessed 15 October 2019].

Iijima, N., Watanabe, S. and Fujikawa, K., 2007. Neglect of Pollution Victims – Environmental *Sociology of Itai-itai disease and Cadmium Pollution Problem* –. In Japanese. Tokyo: Tōshindō.

Jansen, M., 2010. Water supply and sewage disposal at Mohenjo-Daro. *World Archaeology: Archaeology of Public Health* [e-journal] 21(2), pp. 177–192. DOI: https://doi.org/10.1080/00438243.1989.9980100.

Janssen, H., Keirs, M. and Nijkamp, P., 1992. Private and Public Development Strategies for Sustainable Development for Island-Economies. *International Conference: Tourism and the Environment Proceedings 1992*. Mytilini, Greece.

Joanez de Melo, C., Vaz, E. and Costa Pinto, L.M. eds., 2017. *Environmental History in the Making, Volume II: Acting*. Berlin: Springer International Publishing.

Kinnear, R. and Rhode, B., 1987. Europe: its environmental identity. In: G. Enyedi, A.J. Gijswijt and B. Rhode, (eds.), *Environmental Policies in East and West*. London: Taylor Graham, pp. 5–21.

Kleiman, J., 2017. *Love Canal: A Brief History*. [online]. GENESCO The State University of New York. Available at: <www.geneseo.edu/history/love_canal_history> [Accessed 24 January 2018].

Knox, J.H., 2017. *Statement of United Nations Special Rapporteur John H. Knox on the conclusion of his mission to Uruguay*. [online] 28 April. Available at: <www.ohchr.org/EN/NewsEvents/Pages/DisplayNews.aspx?NewsID=21559&LangID=E#sthash.eRJWvyME.dpuf> [Accessed 8 May 2017].

Koloski-Ostrow, A.O., 2015. Talking heads: What toilets and sewers tell us about ancient Roman sanitation. *The Conversation*. [online] 19 November. Available at: <https://theconversation.com/talking-heads-what-toilets-and-sewers-tell-us-about-ancient-roman-sanitation-50045> [Accessed 26 January 2018].

Lamirande T. and Scholey, L., 2018. First Nations, citizen groups call for auditor general to investigate nuclear waste disposal. *APTN National News*. [online] 21 August. Available at: <https://aptnnews.ca/2018/08/21/first-nations-citizen-groups-call-for-auditor-general-to-investigate-nuclear-waste-disposal/> [Accessed 8 August 2019].

Lenzen, M., Sun, Y.Y., Faturay, F., Ting, Y.P., Geschke, A. and Malik, A., 2018. The Carbon Footprints of Global Tourism. *Nature Climate Change* 8, pp. 522–528. DOI: 10.1038_s41558-018-0141-x.ris.

Le Quéré, C., Jackson, R.B., Jones, M.W., Smith, A.J.P., Abernethy, S., Andrew, R.M., De-Gol, A.J., Willis, D.R., Shan, Y., Canadell, J.G., Friedlingstein, P., Creitzig, F. and Peters, G.P., 2020. Temporary reduction in daily global CO_2 emissions during COVID-19 forced confinement. *Nature Climate Change* [e-juornal]. DOI: https://doi.org/10.1038/s41558-020-0797-x.

Lock, S., 2019. Outbound Tourism Visitor Growth Worldwide from 2008 to 2021, by Region. *Statista*. [online] 29 July. Available at: <www.statista.com/statistics/274011/outbound-visitor-growth-forecast-worldwide-by-region/> [Accessed 14 August 2019].

McGrath, M. 2019 Climate change: Impacts 'accelerating' as leaders gather for UN talks. *BBC News* [on-line] 22 September. Available at: <www.bbc.com/news/science-environment-49773869/> [Accessed 22 September 2019].

Minamata City, 2007. *Minamata Disease – Its History and Lessons – 2007. Edited by Minamata Disease Municipal Museum*. [pdf] Minamata City Planning Division. Available at: <www.minamata195651.jp/pdf/kyoukun_en/kyoukun_eng_all.pdf> [Accessed 24 January 2018].

Mulley, M., 2018. Bills & Votes. *Open Parliament*. [online]. Available at: <https://openparliament.ca/bills/> [Accessed 14 August 2018].

NASA, 2018. *Global Climate Change: Vital Sign of the Planet*. [online] 8 August. Available at: <https://climate.nasa.gov/effects/> [Accessed 12 August 2018].

National Ocean Service, n.d. A Guide to Plastic in the Ocean. *National Ocean and Atmospheric Administration, U.S. Department of Commerce*. [online]. Available at: <https://oceanservice.noaa.gov/hazards/marinedebris/plastics-in-the-ocean.html> [Accessed 18 August 2019].

National Parks UK, 2017. *National Park facts and figures*. [online]. Available at: <www.nationalparks.gov.uk/students/whatisanationalpark/factsandfigures> [Accessed 13 September 2017].

New Forest National Park, 2017. *Fascinating history*. [online]. Available at: <www.newforestnpa.gov.uk/info/20088/fascinating_history> [Accessed 13 September 2017].

NOAA, 2018. What are El Niño and La Niña? *National Ocean and Atmospheric Administration, U.S. Department of Commerce*. [online]. Available at: <https://oceanservice.noaa.gov/facts/ninonina.html> [Accessed 20 May 2018].

Nordberg, G.F., Nogawa, K., Nordberg, M. and Friberg, L.T., 2007. 7.2.8. Itai-Itai Disease. Chapter 23: Cadmium. In: G.F. Nordberg, B.A. Fowler, M. Nordberg and L. Friberg, (eds.), *Handbook on the Toxicology of Metals (Third Edition)*. Burlington, MA: Academic Press, pp. 468–469.

Ocean Conservancy, 2019. *Fighting for Trash Free Seas*, [online]. Available at: <https://oceanconservancy.org/trash-free-seas/plastics-in-the-ocean/> [Accessed 18 August 2019].

OECD, 2018. *OECD Tourism Trends and Policies 2018: Highlights* [pdf]. Available at: <www.oecd.org/cfe/tourism/2018-Tourism-Trends-Policies-Highlights-ENG.pdf> [Accessed 13 August 2018].

OHCHR, 2008. *Resolution 7/23 Human Rights and Climate Change*. [pdf] 28 March. Available at: </www2.ohchr.org/english/issues/climatechange/docs/Resolution_7_23.pdf> [Accessed 8 May 2017].

OHCHR, 2009a. *Annual Report of the United Nations High Commissioner for Human Rights and Reports of the Office of the High Commissioner and the Secretary-General A/HRC/10/61. Report of the Office of the United Nations High Commissioner for Human Rights on the relationship between climate change and Human Rights*. [online] 15 January. Available at: <www2.ohchr.org/english/issues/climatechange/docs/A.HRC.10.61_AUV.pdf> [Accessed 8 May 2017].

OHCHR, 2009b. *Resolution 10/4 Human Rights and Climate Change*. [online] 25 March. Available at: <www2.ohchr.org/english/issues/climatechange/docs/resolution10_4.doc> [Accessed 8 May 2017].

OHCHR, 2016. *Report of the Special Rapporteur on the issue of human rights obligations relating to the enjoyment of a safe, clean, healthy and sustainable environment A/HRC/31/52.* [online] 1 February. Available at: <www.ohchr.org/Documents/Issues/Environment/A.HRC.31.52_AEV.docx> [Accessed 8 May 2017].

OHCHR, 2019. *Special Rapporteur on the issue of human rights and the environment.* [online]. Available at: <www.ohchr.org/EN/Issues/Environment/SREnvironment/Pages/SRenvironmentIndex.aspx> [Accessed 17 November 2019].

Osterath, B., 2018. Plastic pollution: Do beach cleanups really make a difference? *Deutsche Welle.* [online] 20 December. Available at: <https://p.dw.com/p/37pwV> [Accessed 18 August 2019].

Parkes, L., 2018. World Water Day: Is it ethical to holiday in water-starved countries? *The Independent.* [online] 22 March. Available at: <www.independent.co.uk/travel/news-and-advice/world-water-day-holidays-drought-responsible-tourism-cape-town-cyprus-jordan-a8268556.html> [Accessed 10 August 2018].

Parliament of Canada, 2018. LEGISinfo: Private Member's Bill. C-202 An Act to establish a Canadian Environmental Bill of Rights and to make a related amendment to another Act. [online] 8 August. Available at: <www.parl.ca/LegisInfo/BillDetails.aspx?Language=E&billId=8061008&View=6> [Accessed 14 August 2018].

Parliament of Canada, 2019. Bill C-438 An Act to enact the Canadian Environmental Bill of Rights and make related amendments to other Acts. [online] 5 April. Available at: <www.parl.ca/DocumentViewer/en/42-1/bill/C-438/first-reading#enH851> [Accessed 1 October 2019].

Pennetier, M. and De Clercq, G., 2019. France to tax flights from its airports, airline shares fall. *Reuters.* [online] 9 July. Available at: <www.reuters.com/article/us-france-airlines-tax/france-plans-new-tax-on-outbound-flights-airline-shares-fall-idUSKCN1U412B> [Accessed 14 August 2019].

Rutherford, J. and Williams, G. 2015. *Environmental Systems and Societies.* Oxford: Oxford University Press.

Sachs, W., 2003. *Environment and Human Rights. Wuppertal Paper No. 137 · November 2003.* [pdf] Available at: <http://hdl.handle.net/10419/49131> [Accessed 21 January 2018].

Sagoff, M., 1981. Economic theory and environmental law. *Michigan Law Review,* 79(7), pp. 1393–1419.

Sampson, H., 2009. Europe's 'flight shame' movement doesn't stand a chance in the U.S. *The Washington Post.* [online] 9 July. Available at: <www.washingtonpost.com/travel/2019/07/09/europes-flight-shame-movement-doesnt-stand-chance-us/?noredirect=on> [Accessed 14 August 2019].

Sand, P., 1993. International Environmental Law After Rio. *European Journal of International Law,* 4 (October), pp. 377–389. DOI:10.1093/oxfordjournals.ejil.a035836.

Scott, D., Hall, C.M., and Gösling, S. 2019. Global tourism vulnerability to climate change. *Annals of Tourism Research,* 77, pp. 49–61. https://doi.org/10.1016/j.annals.2019.05.007.

Shaalan, I.M., 2005. Sustainable tourism development in the Red Sea of Egypt threats and opportunities. *Journal of Cleaner Production,* 13, pp. 83–87. doi:10.1016/j.jclepro.2003.12.012.

Shelton, D., 2006. Human rights and the environment: What specific environmental rights have been recognized? *Denver Journal of International Law and Policy* [pdf] 31(1), pp. 129–171. Available at: <http://djilp.org/wp-content/uploads/2011/08/Human-Rights-Environment-What-Specific-Environmental-Rights-Been-Recognized-Dinah-Shelton.pdf> [Accessed 8 May 2017].

Shelton, D., 2008. Stockholm Declaration (1972) and Rio Declaration (1992). *Max Planck Encyclopedia of Public International Law*. [online]. Available at: <https://opil.ouplaw.com/view/10.1093/law:epil/9780199231690/law-9780199231690-e1608> [Accessed 4 August 2019].

Shelton, D., 2009. Human Rights and Environment: Past, Present and Future Linkages and the Value of a Declaration (Draft Preparation). In: UNEP and OHCHR, *High Level Expert Meeting on the New Future of Human Rights and Environment: Moving the Global Agenda Forward*. Nairobi, Kenya, 30 November-1 December. [pdf] Available at: <https://jak.ppke.hu/uploads/articles/719134/file/Shelton%20paper.PDF> [Accessed 4 August 2019].

Standage, T., 2009. *An Edible History of Humanity*. London: Walker Books.

Taylor, K., 2019. Instead of airport expansion, a 'frequent flyer tax'. *The Ecologist*. [online] 10 October 2015. Available at: <https://theecologist.org/2015/oct/10/instead-airport-expansion-frequent-flyer-tax> [Accessed 16 August 2019].

Telfer, D.J., 2013. The Brundtland Report (Our Common Future) and tourism. In: A. Holden and D. Fennell, (eds.), *The Routledge Handbook of Tourism and Environment*. Abingdon: Routledge, pp. 213–227.

The New Forest, 2017. *New Forest History*. [online]. Available at: <www.thenewforest.co.uk/discover/history.aspx> [Accessed 13 September 2017].

Tsuru, S., 1989. History of pollution control policy. In: S. Tsuru and H. Weidner, (eds.), *Environmental Policy in Japan* (Wissenschaftcentrum Berlin für Sozialforschung: Research Unit Environmental Policy). Berlin: Edition Sigma Bohn Verlag, pp. 15–42.

UN, 1992. *Report of the United Nations Conference on Environment and Development A/CONF.151/26 (Vol. I)*. [online]. Last update 12 January 2000. Available at: <www.un.org/documents/ga/conf151/aconf15126-1annex1.htm> [Accessed 4 August 2019].

UN/DESA, 2014. The human right to water and sanitation. *Water for Life Decade*. [online] 29 May. Available at: <www.un.org/waterforlifedecade/human_right_to_water.shtml> [Accessed 11 November 2019].

UNDP, 2014. UNDP Social and Environmental Standards [PDF]. Available at: <www.undp.org/content/dam/undp/library/corporate/Social-and-Environmental-Policies-and-Procedures/UNDPs-Social-and-Environmental-Standards-ENGLISH.pdf> [Accessed 10 May 2020].

UNEP, 2015. *Climate Change and Human Rights*. [pdf] Nairobi: UNEP in corporation with Columbia Law School. Available at: <http://web.unep.org/divisions/delc/human-rights-and-environment> [Accessed 8 August 2019].

UNEP, n.d., Human Rights and the Environment. [online] Available at: <http://web.unep.org/divisions/delc/human-rights-and-environment> [Accessed 8 August 2019].

UNEP, 1972. *Declaration of the United Nations Conference on the Human Environment* [pdf]. Available at: <www.soas.ac.uk/cedep-demos/000_P514_IEL_K3736-Demo/treaties/media/1972%20Stockholm%201972%20-%20Declaration%20of%20the%20United%20Nations%20Conference%20on%20the%20Human%20Environment%20-%20UNEP.pdf> [Accessed 8 August 2019].

UN Library, 2018. *Climate Change - A Global Issue*. [online] 1 August. Available at: <https://research.un.org/en/climate-change> [Accessed 12 August 2018].

Union of Concerned Scientists, 2017. Industrial Agriculture. *Food and Agriculture. Union of Concerned Scientists: Science for a healthy planet and safer world*. [online]. Available at: <www.ucsusa.org/our-work/food-agriculture/our-failing-food-system/industrial-agriculture#.WdJ4XhT_7-0> [Accessed 2 October 2017].

UNWTO, 2015. *Tourism and Sustainable Development Goals* (brochure) [pdf] Available at: <http://cf.cdn.unwto.org/sites/all/files/pdf/sustainable_development_goals_brochure.pdf> [Accessed 2 July 2016].
UNWTO, 2017. *UNWTO Tourism Highlights: 2017 Edition* [pdf] Available at: <www.e-unwto.org/doi/book/10.18111/9789284419029> [Accessed 13 August 2018].
UNWTO, 2018a. *Tourism for Development – Volume I: Key Areas for Action*. Madrid: UNWTO. DOI: https://doi.org/10.18111/9789284419722.
UNWTO, 2018b. *Tourism for Development – Volume II: Good Practices*. Madrid: UNWTO, DOI: https://doi.org/10.18111/9789284419746.
UNWTO, n.d. *FAQ - Climate Change and Tourism: Sustainable Development of Tourism.* [online]. Available at: <http:// sdt.unwto.org/content/faq-climate-change-and-tourism> [Accessed 14 August 2019].
UNWTO, 2020a. *International tourism growth continues to outpace the global economy.* [online]. 20 January. Available at: <https://unwto.org/international-tourism-growth-continues-to-outpace-the-economy> [Accessed 5 April 2020].
UNWTO, 2020b. *International tourism and COVID-19.* [online]. Available at: <www.unwto.org/international-tourism-and-covid-19> [Accessed 19 May 2020].
UNWTO and UNDP, 2017. *Tourism and the Sustainable Development Goals – Journey to 2030*. Madrid: UNWTO.
US Mission Geneva, 2017. *Explanation of Position by the United States of America.* [online] 24 March. Available at: <https://geneva.usmission.gov/2017/03/24/u-s-explanation-of-position-on-human-rights-and-the-environment/> [Accessed 14 August 2018].
Uversky, V.N., Li, J. and Fink, A.L., 2001. Metal-triggered structural transformations, aggregation, and fibrillation of human α-Synuclein. *Journal of Biological Chemistry*, 276(42), pp. 44284–44296. DOI 10.1074/jbc.M105343200.
Wang K.-Y., Chau T.-T., 2013. An association between air pollution and daily outpatient visits for respiratory disease in a heavy industry area. *PLoS ONE*, [e-Journal] 8(10), p. e75220. doi:10.1371/journal.pone.0075220.
Watts, J. 2019. Greta Thunberg, schoolgirl climate change warrior: 'Some people can let things go. I can't'. *Canada's National Observer*. [online] 11 March. Available at: <www.nationalobserver.com/2019/03/11/features/greta-thunberg-schoolgirl-climate-change-warrior-some-people-can-let-things-go-i> [Accessed 14 August 2019].
Wedeen, R.P., 1989. Were the hatters of New Jersey "mad"? *American Journal of Industrial Medicine*, [e-journal] 16(2), pp. 225–233. DOI: 10.1002/ajim.4700160213.
Weston, P. and Osborne, S. 2019. Climate strike – live: Millions across the world demand urgent action to save planet in largest environmental protest in history. *Independent*. [online] 20 September. Available at: <www.independent.co.uk/environment/global-climate-strike-live-protests-greta-thunberg-speech-demonstrations-a9112986.html> [Accessed 19 September 2019].
Westra, L., 2011. *Human Rights: The Commons and the Collective*. Vancouver: UBC Press.
Whitheridge, 2006. Medieval Farming Year. *The Centuries in Words and Pictures*. [online] 18 September. Available at: <www.witheridge-historical-archive.com/medieval-year.htm> [Accessed 2 October 2017].
Wilde, R., 2018. *British Poor Law Reform in the Industrial Revolution*. [online] 16 July. Available at: <www.thoughtco.com/british-poor-law-reform-industrial-revolution-1221631> [Accessed 14 August 2019].
Wylie, H., 2019. 16 children, including Greta Thunberg, file landmark complaint to the United Nations Committee on the Rights of the Child: Child petitioners protest lack

of government action on climate crisis. *UNICEF Press Release*. [online] 23 September. Available at: <www.unicef.org/press-releases/16-children-including-greta-thunberg-file-landmark-complaint-united-nations> [Accessed 3 October 2019].

Worldometers, 2019. *Current World Population*. [online] 14 August. Available at: <www.worldometers.info/world-population/> [Accessed 14 August 2019].

12
INDIGENOUS PEOPLE'S RIGHTS AND TOURISM

12.1 Introduction

Indigenous peoples around the world have been subject to colonisation and conquest; resulting in displacement, exploitation, discrimination, loss of dignity; and the decline of tradition, language, and way of life. Stephens, et al. (2006) are concerned that the contamination of their ancestral lands and water systems "through mining, oil exploration, or agricultural chemicals (p. 2022)," and lack of access to the proper health care systems has resulted in Indigenous Peoples ranking very low on health indicators. The purpose of the United Nation's Declaration of Rights of Indigenous People (UNDRIP) (2007) is to restore and ensure the basic Human Rights of Indigenous Peoples, including access to health care. The Declaration identifies the multifaceted issues of the human rights of Indigenous Peoples, and is designed to enhance self-determination of Indigenous individuals and their communities; and encourages the State to support its implementation. Yet, the UN Millennium Development Goals – and to an extent the UN Sustainable Development Goals – are criticised for the fact that the loss of Indigenous Populations would not affect achieving these goals (Stephens, et al., 2006).

Globally, Indigenous tourism has been steadily growing, and Indigenous communities are looking to tourism as way to achieve a better economic future (Whitford and Ruhanen, 2010). Indigenous peoples have found many different roles in tourism and hospitality. They may be operating Indigenous tourism companies on their own, or in collaboration with external businesses; or they may be presenting their culture as an attraction or performing for tourists. On the other hand, their land and natural resources have been taken away to make way for tourism development, and they have been exploited by tourism as a new form of colonialism (see Chapter 7 on displacement). This chapter will review Indigenous

Peoples' Rights in the context of tourism, raising the question: to what extent is the United Nation's Declaration of Rights of Indigenous People upheld.

From an etic approach, this chapter examines current issues of Indigenous Peoples' rights in different countries, particularly within the development of Indigenous tourism products. This chapter will begin by examining definitions of Indigenous People, and trace the context of historical conflict between Indigenous peoples and non-Indigenous peoples from the impacts of the Columbian Exchange to present-day examples. The chapter then turns to examine Indigenous People's Rights, and the evolution of the UN Declaration on the Rights of Indigenous Peoples (UNDRIP). In the final section the chapter will explore Indigenous Rights in the context of the challenges and opportunities in Indigenous tourism. The authors are aware of the fact that the ways in which groups of people who are long time Indigenous inhabitants of the land have been referred to has been done so differently by region, by time, and by the political environment. Terms considered to be derogatory and disrespectful today have been used in the past, and may have even been integrated into the title and content of older documents. In this chapter, the terms used will adopt the approach by the United Nations and other supranational organisations and wherever possible, older, disrespectful terms are changed in accordance with these more recent approaches.

12.1.1 Definition of Indigenous people

The definition of 'Indigenous People' is not simple. Different countries have different criteria for their Indigenous Populations and Tribal Populations. For instance, the names to address these groups of people include: Aboriginal Peoples, *Adivasi*, First Nations, Hill Tribes, Hunter-gatherers, *Janajati*, or Native Peoples (ILP, 2018). Most widely understood is that these groups of people have already inhabited the place for a considerable amount of time before outsiders came to conquer, colonise, or set up the current 'national boundaries'. These groups' "heritage, their ways of life, their stewardship of this planet, and their cosmological insights" are distinctly different from those of the current inhabitants in the area, but "not all of these groups are considered indigenous or inherent to their particular geographic area" (Welker, 2016). To illustrate this point, Canada used the distinction between "Status" and "Non-status" Indigenous People based on the Indian Act of 1951. Non-status Indians, i.e. the Inuit and the Métis people, were not registered as Indigenous peoples and thus excluded from rights under the Act (Coates, 2008). Today, Canada recognises three groups of Indigenous Peoples in its geographical boundaries: the First Nations, the Métis and Non-status Indians, and the Inuit (Government of Canada, 2017). As seen in the case of Canada, different countries have different laws, Treaties, Acts, and other legally binding documents to define who is to be recognised as Indigenous Persons, and what rights and privileges are granted or restricted.

Interestingly, the International Labour Organization (ILO) Convention No. 169, Article 1 (Entry into force: 5 Sep 1991) specified the criteria of Indigenous/Tribal designation applied to:

(a) tribal peoples in independent countries whose social, cultural and economic conditions distinguish them from other sections of the national community, and whose status is regulated wholly or partially by their own customs or traditions or by special laws or regulations;
(b) peoples in independent countries who are regarded as indigenous on account of their descent from the populations which inhabited the country, or a geographical region to which the country belongs, at the time of conquest or colonisation or the establishment of present state boundaries and who, irrespective of their legal status, retain some or all of their own social, economic, cultural and political institutions (ILO, 2017).

The ILO's practical approach to define Indigenous and Tribal People in this way is a widely accepted definition today (see Table 12.1). By adopting the inclusive definition, the ILO Convention or UN Declaration on the Rights of Indigenous Peoples (UNDRIP) ensures the ability to ascribe the same set of rights to both groups.

Although the ILO's definitions of Indigenous and Tribal Peoples are broad and inclusive, existing laws and treaties often complicate who should be recognised as Indigenous Persons. For instance, since the late 1990s, discourse and dispute on the pre-Māori civilisation in New Zealand has developed surrounding whether or not the Māori people are the Indigenous Peoples of Aotearoa (see Ansell, 2013;

TABLE 12.1 Summary of ILO's Definition of Indigenous and Tribal Peoples

	Subjective Criteria	*Objective Criteria*
Indigenous Peoples	Self-identification as belonging to an Indigenous People	Descent from populations, who inhabited the country or geographical region at the time of conquest, colonisation or establishment of present state boundaries.
		They retain some or all of their own social, economic, cultural and political institutions, irrespective of their legal status.
Tribal Peoples	Self-identification as belonging to a Tribal People	Their social, cultural and economic conditions distinguish them from other sections of the national community.
		Their status is regulated wholly or partially by their own customs or traditions or by special laws or regulations.

Source: (ILO, 2018).

APNZ, 2012 for example). From the perspective of Humanities Studies, it is an interesting argument worth investigating; however, such arguments can bear political significance. It could lead to a possible change of the Māori People's status as the Indigenous Peoples of New Zealand, and their rights and privileges that are settled and protected by treaties. Even though the ILO definition (2018) specifies that the Indigenous Peoples are "populations, who inhabited the country or geographical region at the time of conquest, colonisation or establishment of present state boundaries," politically inclined parties can, and will, use such arguments to their advantage.

Definitions and the recognition of Indigenous Peoples often happen through legal proceedings and even legal battles. Some legal documents that defined Indigenous Persons use the degree of racial purity as an ethnic group. For example, before the criterion of the Māori People was revised in 1953, the Māori had to be 'half-castes and people who were intermediate in blood between half-castes and of pure descent.' The revised criterion states: 'a person of the Māori race of New Zealand; and includes a descendant of any such person'. Currently Māori people are defined by their lineage in accordance with Māori tradition (Coates, 2008). Similarly, until recently Canada did not recognise the Métis Nation as Indigenous Peoples, who are descendants of mixed marriages of First Nations and Europeans emerging during the 18th–19th century fur trade period in Western and Maritime Canada; hence they distinguish themselves from First Nations for their unique language, culture, and traditions (Gaudry and Welch, 2016; Métis Nation, n.d.). For the reasons of both mixed marriage ancestry, and their emergence after the time European settlement had begun, the Métis Nation was not considered as Aboriginal Peoples of Canada. The Canadian Supreme Court ruled in 2003 R. v. Powley to recognise the Métis Nation as being a separate group from First Nations, and recognised formally as the Métis Nation. They were additionally recognised as Non-status Indians as Aboriginal Peoples under the Canadian Constitution in 2016 Daniels v. Canada SCC 12 case (Government of Canada, 2017; Pape, Salter, Teillet LLP, 2016; Canadian Press, 2016; Métis Nation, n.d.).

As seen in the above examples, even a widely used definition such as that by the ILO of Aboriginal/Indigenous Peoples can only merely be regarded as a guideline, and each government cannot be forced to adopt the same definition. Each country has its own historical accounts, and relationships with Aboriginal/Indigenous peoples, and Treaties and Laws, which were enacted long before UNDRIP or ILO convention were agreed upon. Even if a universal definition is adopted, the legal and social support systems may not be in place to enact it. What is more, the perceptions of the rest of the members of society may not be fully in accordance with the universal definition of Aboriginal Peoples or Indigenous Peoples. The UN has made efforts to promote Indigenous rights, declaring 1993 as the year of the World's Indigenous People, as well as declaring two decades (1995–2004, and 2005–2014) as the decade of the World's Indigenous People. More recently, 2019 was proclaimed the International Year of Indigenous Languages.

12.1.2 Evolution of conflicts between Indigenous peoples and non-Indigenous peoples

Indigenous Peoples around the world had their own civilisation in which they had established their territorial boundaries, laws and governance systems, social structures, economic activities, unique culture, language, and cosmology/religions/ spiritual worlds. However, encounters with non-native newcomers who settled in Indigenous People's lands have brought almost irreversible changes to Indigenous Peoples and their civilisations. Throughout human history, people have migrated – moving into new territories for hunting-and-gathering, seeking a better place to live, trading, wars, etc. (McLaren and Ramer, 2010). Even Indigenous Populations colonised each other (e.g. Hawai'i). History shows that the expansion and military campaigns of the Roman Empire, the Muslim conquests, followed by conquest and colonisation by European imperialists – usually ended with subjugation, and oftentimes the massacre of Indigenous Populations.

In many New World countries, Indigenous Peoples encountered colonists, explorers, and missionaries, (e.g., Marco Polo, Vasco da Gama, and Christopher Columbus); Anthropologists/geographers/scientists seeking new knowledge – such as Charles Darwin, Captain Cook, Francisco Moreno, Margaret Mead, and Alexander von Humboldt, and later artists and writers (e.g., Paul Gauguin, Francisco Petrarch, Bill Bryson, etc.) who romanticised the newly found land and can be seen as outsiders opening up remote communities. In recent years, international aid agencies, industries, and developers have moved into previously uncharted areas; history shows that such encounters were not always amicable.

The phenomenon known as the Colombian Exchange originally described Christopher Columbus' exploration and exchange of disease, ideas, food crops, and population between Old and New Worlds. The term Columbian Exchange can be applied to similar situations anywhere in the world, and to any religious, settlement, or military expansion. The newcomers brought diseases, to which Indigenous Peoples had no immunity. It is estimated that between 1492 and 1642, up to 95% of the Native American population was decimated, and some became extinct (Nunn and Qian, 2010). With emerging demands of the New World, and its failing crops and loss of Native American population as labourers, the Americas could no longer keep up with demands from the Old World. To remedy this, 12 million slaves from African countries were shipped to the Americas between 16th and 19th centuries; and thus, left African Natives and Nations depopulated, weak, and vulnerable (Global Black History, 2016; Nunn and Qian, 2010).

While initial relationships between European settlers and Indigenous Peoples were influenced by mutual interests, in time, the governing bodies of settlers often neglected or misinterpreted their own Treaties and Laws in favour of the mistreatment of Indigenous Peoples – beginning periods of the illegalisation of Indigenous traditions and cultures. The European settlers' misunderstanding of Indigenous culture, land ownership, and agricultural practices led to the imposition of European culture, confiscation of land and resources, the transformation of agricultural practices in line with European agriculture, and other significant changes. The Columbian Exchange can be viewed as an early form of globalisation; spreading the supposed superiority of European cultures in the New World, starting in motion the forces to shape the contemporary world (see Mann, 2011 for more details). This primitive form of globalisation transformed the world's systems, especially in the Americas, Africa, the Middle East, and Asia. The Indigenous inhabitants of these areas were placed under the domination of Europeans and during that time and subsequently, Indigenous People have been deprived of their human rights.

Indigenous People have long been living in geographical areas before settlers arrived, setting up current state boundaries; however, the extent to which this is acknowledged in Treaties varies. The British Crown started relationships with the Indigenous Peoples in Canada and the Māori in New Zealand, along the lines of more equitable partnerships: with Native titles, authorities, and rights being recognised (Coates, 2008; Murphy, Duncan and Piggott, 2008). Nevertheless, the mismanagement, misinterpretation, and disregard of Proclamations, Treaties, and Protection Acts led to conflict and strife between the Indigenous population and new settlers. Legal frameworks, both domestic and international, can pose challenges in the interpretation of Indigenous Rights. Murphy, Duncan and Pigott (2008) examined the case of British Columbia, Canada, and entrenchment clauses in the Canadian Constitution protecting the welfare of Aboriginal Peoples. Aboriginal and Treaty Rights – and their resulting protections – are part of the Canadian Constitution (Section 35(1)); however, they fall outside the *Canadian Charter of Rights and Freedoms*. As they are outside the *Charter of Rights and Freedoms*, the federal government cannot extinguish Aboriginal and Treaty Rights under Section 33 of the Constitution, which is a legislative override, also referred to as the 'notwithstanding clause' (Murphy, Duncan and Pigott, 2008). After multiple court cases, as a general principle, a decision was made to deal with Section 35 in the Constitution Act 1982 (Rights of the Aboriginal Peoples of Canada): "courts must construe it purposively and give it "a generous, liberal interpretation"" and "Any ambiguity in the scope of s. 35(1) is to be resolved in favour of Aboriginals" (Murphy, Duncan and Pigott, 2008, p. 4). This framework has therefore entrenched Indigenous Rights in Canada. Canadian Provincial and Territorial laws do not have jurisdiction to extinguish Indigenous Rights.

In Japan, the Ainu people used to have frequent interactions and trade with the Japanese population, who are ethnically different and in the majority. Since the 10th Century, the Ainu expanded their settlements from southern Sakhalin to Hokkaido, even down to the North Eastern region of mainland Japan, and intermarried with the Okhotsk people in Hokkaido (Ainu Museum, n.d.). The Tokugawa Shogunate assigned oversight of southern Hokkaido and the Ainu to the Feudal Domain Matsumaé in the 16th century (frpac, 2015; Kawakubo, Sawada and Dodo, 2009; Stevens, 2001). During the era of the Meiji Restoration [late 19th century] – the beginning of the modernisation of Japan – an army of pioneers were sent to Hokkaido to cultivate the land. That led to the traditional Ainu practices and rights (access to natural resources such as fishing, hunting, felling trees, etc.)

becoming illegal, and the prime agricultural land was given to the pioneers (Stevens, 2001). The 1899 Hokkaido Former Aboriginal Protection Act was to ensure the Ainu People's welfare by educating Ainu children within the Japanese education system; resulting in devastating cultural destruction by the 1920s. What complicated the situation was the perception of the Japanese judiciary system in regard to the Ainu people and other ethnic minorities; officially, there were none. In 1980, the Japanese Government reported to the UN that no ethnic minority group exists in Japan (McLauchlan, 2001; Stevens, 2001).

As mentioned in the introduction, Stephens, et al. (2006) advocated with strong language: "the Millennium Development Goals as they stand today could be achieved even while whole populations of Indigenous peoples disappear (p. 2026)." Similarly, scientists are concerned that the UN Sustainable Development Goals (UNSDGs) are so focused on large scale – e.g. national and international level indicators – that the dire situation of marginalised populations, particularly Indigenous Populations, do not affect the results of the UNSDGs. In Canada, the document entitled, 'Reclaiming Power and Place: The Final Report of the National Inquiry into Missing and Murdered Indigenous Women and Girls (MMIWG),' claimed the Canadian state committed human rights violations against the Indigenous Peoples of Canada, to the comparable level of 'genocide' (MMIWG, 2019, p. 164). The document summarised that "the combination of systems and actions that has worked to maintain colonial violence for generations" led to the human rights abuse against Indigenous women, girls, and 2SLGBTQQIA People; therefore, there is a need for immediate action to rectify the situation. The UN Declaration of Rights of Indigenous Peoples (UNDRIP – further discussed below) expressed in its Preamble that Indigenous Peoples' sufferance from colonisation, and dispossession of their lands and resources, further prevents them from exercising their rights to development of their own accord. Its recommendation for states is, henceforward, to effectively implement all of their obligations to Indigenous Peoples. The state has obligations to Indigenous Peoples in the areas of "justice, democracy, human rights, non-discrimination and good faith" (UN, 2018). Developed nations were reluctant to ratify and fully adopt the UNDRIP for quite some time. Adoption was slowed, not only because of the reluctance of governments, but also the reluctance of the involved parties, including Indigenous Groups. These Indigenous Groups have fought long and hard to win precious rights enshrined in existing treaties and constitutions; and adopting UNDRIP could mean the possible loss of some of these rights. However, global attention is now on Canada to provide a pioneering example of how governments will respond to the results of reports such as the MMIWG. Movements and campaigns, like those that led to the report on MMIWG in Canada, will unquestionably gather strength around the world in the foreseeable future.

Along with the rise in awareness of Indigenous Rights, is the shift to decolonisation, self-determination, and Indigenisation. Elliott (2016) outlines the process of decolonisation of Indigenous Peoples stating, "Examinations of prevailing norms around matters of political authority and organisation, gender and sexuality, law, health, and relationships to land, ecosystems, among others have sought to shed light on the extent to which Indigenous normatives are excluded, marginalised, or otherwise denigrated in the contemporary public sphere." He argues that much of the critique has been around the politics of recognition and reconciliation that has emerged as the common vernacular of justice. While there have been important local improvements realised, critics argue that this paradigm is based on a profound misrecognition of Indigenous Peoples, and rather than being a reciprocal relationship between partners of equal status, recognition is based upon the settler/state gaze (Elliott, 2016). The language of 'reciprocity' and mutuality veils the clear disparity in the status of the parties. "Indigenous Peoples are present here merely as objects of recognition; their status as sovereign peoples and hence as equal partners is denied" (Elliott, 2016). Participatory parity (Fraser, 2009 in Elliott 2016, p. 423) is put forward as one approach to better understand the deeper processes behind subordination and lead to a more progressive discursive environment in settler-colonial contexts. According to Article 1 of the International Covenant on Civil and Political Rights, "All peoples have the rights of self-determination. By virtue of that right they freely determine their political status and freely pursue their economic, social and cultural development," which has been reinforced in UNDRIP. Indigenisation recognises Indigenous worldviews (which may be unique to each Indigenous community or nation), identifies opportunities for Indigeneity to be expressed, and incorporates Indigenous ways of knowing (ICT, 2020).

Along with efforts on and debates over decolonisation, self-determination, and Indigenisation, protests and calls for action over Indigenous Rights issues have recently come to the forefront. In Canada, there are over 100 First Nations communities that lack access to safe, clean water and sanitation, which has become even more critical during the COVID-19 pandemic (Barlow, 2020). Barlow (2020) states, "all the human rights in the world will not provide clean water where there is none." In February 2020, solidarity protests over Indigenous Rights sprang up across Canada, blocking rail lines in support of the Wet'suwet'en hereditary chiefs, who were opposed to the construction of the Coastal GasLink Pipeline in British Columbia (Laframboise, 2020). The Black Lives Matter protests which emerged out of the USA in the summer of 2020 spread around the globe. In some countries, these protests widened in scope to include the protests over the treatment of Indigenous Peoples. In Australia for example, thousands protested across the country opposing the deaths of Indigenous Peoples in police custody (Fisher, 2020).

12.2 Indigenous people's rights and the evolution of the UN Declaration on the Rights of Indigenous Peoples (UNDRIP)

Following a 1982 UN study on discrimination, and the recognition of problematic economic and social situations that Indigenous Peoples face known as the Cobo study, the need for creating international frameworks/documents to protect Indigenous Peoples' Rights became evident. It was pointed out in Cobo's study that the UDHR and other documents were meant to include all human beings;

yet, there was "no explicit or specific mention of Indigenous Populations" (UN/DESA, 2014).

After the UDHR was adopted, the Economic and Social Council (ECOSOC) authorised the Commission of Human Rights to form a Sub-Committee for the 'prevention of discrimination and protection of minorities' in 1947 (which was renamed as the UN Sub-Commission on the Promotion and Protection of Human Rights in 1999). Based on the findings of the Sub-Committee's report on "Measures taken in connection with protection of Indigenous people" as part of a racial discrimination study in 1971, the ECOSOC endorsed a further comprehensive study on the discrimination against Indigenous Populations. In 1982, ECOSOC established the Working Group on Indigenous Populations, led by Martinez Cobo to study the oppression, marginalisation, and exploitation suffered by Indigenous Peoples. The report was submitted in 1981, 1982, and 1983 in three parts as the Cobo Study, which concerns issues of slavery, servitude, and oppression, in addition to the reality that many UN Member States were not implementing the UDHR mandates to protect human rights of Indigenous Populations (UN/DESA, 2014; Favel and Coats, 2016; UN, 2018).

Based upon the findings and recommendations of the 1982 Cobo Study, a UN Working Group on Indigenous Populations was formed as a Sub-Commission on the Promotion and Protection of Human Rights. This group not only undertook research on issues impacting Indigenous Peoples, but also reviewed "national developments concerning the promotion and protection of Indigenous Peoples' human rights and develops international standards for Indigenous Peoples' human rights and freedoms" (University of Minnesota Human Rights Center, 2003). The working group submitted an initial draft 'Declaration' to the then UN Commission on Human Rights for further discussion in 1994. The process leading to the Declaration on the Rights of Indigenous Peoples was slow, as not only did numerous Indigenous People's groups around the world have to be consulted about the contents of the Declaration – "the right to self-determination of indigenous peoples and the control over natural resources existing on indigenous peoples' traditional lands," but also due to strong concerns expressed by many UN Member States about this Declaration (UN, 2018). Finally, in 2006, the UN Commission on Human Rights was replaced by the UN Human Rights Council, and the Council adopted the Declaration on the Rights of Indigenous Peoples, with a draft resolution to defer considerations and actions. It was only in September 2007 that the Declaration on the Rights of Indigenous Peoples (UNDRIP) was finally adopted. While it was adopted by 144 member states, Flavel and Coats (2016) drew attention to who exactly voted for the UNDRIP (quoting Isaac, 2016). To begin with, 144 member states voted for UNDRIP, yet only 43 of these member states have Indigenous Populations: of the 88 member states who recognise Indigenous Populations, 42 voted for the Declaration, four voted against it, 11 abstained, and 31 nations did not attend the General Assembly vote (p. 7). All of the member states that voted against or abstained from voting have Indigenous Populations. Out of the 31 members that did not show up to vote, 28 members have Indigenous

Populations. The four countries who voted against were Australia, Canada, New Zealand, and the USA. Details on their reasons of voting against or abstention can be viewed on the UN Press Release website (2007). Since the adoption of UNDRIP, the four countries that voted against the UNDRIP have changed their stance (Rodgers, 2009). In April 2009, Australia adopted the UNDRIP, followed by New Zealand in April 2010 (Watkins, 2010); the USA signed in December 2010 (Richardson, 2010); and Canada finally adopted the UNDRIP in May 2016 (Favel and Coates, 2016; Morin, 2017).

The UNDRIP has 46 Articles covering a wide range of human rights topics. Article 3 is on the right to self-determination, while Article 5 (UN 2018) states "Indigenous peoples have the right to maintain and strengthen their distinct political, legal, economic, social and cultural institutions, while retaining their right to participate fully, if they so choose, in the political, economic, social and cultural life of the State." Unfortunately, international laws are still lacking in concepts or theories to help incorporate Indigenous Rights, even after the UNDRIP was finally ratified. Chen (2014) points out that empirical work that offers "explanatory and causal claims of indigenous rights in international law" is in earnest need. Many of the Articles in the UNDRIP have implications for Indigenous tourism, which is explored in the following section.

12.3 The significance of Indigenous people's rights in tourism

Indigenous tourism is an important component of tourism in many destinations, however it has been criticised for the way in which it has evolved – linked to exploitation and human rights violations. Hillmer-Pegram (2016) identified some of the major challenges of Indigenous tourism as follows: colonialism and systematic exploitation in the development of Indigenous tourism; commodification of Indigenous culture; relationships and conflicts between Indigenous peoples and their natural environment on which their subsistence depends; and the challenges of indigenous control over Indigenous tourism product development. In 1997, the World Tourism Organization in association with the WTTC developed guideline principles for sustainable tourism development based on Agenda 21. One of the principles stated: "Tourism development should recognize and support the identity, culture and interests of indigenous peoples" (WTO, 1997). In a review of the literature, Whitford and Ruhanen (2016) found that Indigenous tourism research was initially case study-based, and examined what was compatible with sustainability. After 2000, more complex problems associated with sustainability were investigated, and focused on topics such as barriers and impacts, Aboriginal rights, cultural communication and inclusion, Indigenous heritage, management and capacity, employment opportunities, and policy.

Very early forms of Indigenous tourism have been characterised as outsiders coming to a place occupied by Indigenous people and being led by Indigenous guides. Tahana, et al. (2000), referring to the Rotorua region in the Northern Island of New Zealand, indicated that Māori tourism began with domestic tourism amongst the Indigenous peoples of the islands, and then the same hospitality was extended to Europeans in the 1870s. As Rotorua was not the most desirable location for tourism development, the arrival of tourists gave an opportunity for the local Te Arawa people to establish businesses in the "hospitality industry, focusing mainly in accommodation, guiding and the souvenir trade" (Te Awekotuku, 1986, cited in Tahana, et al., 2000, p. 23). However, in many locations Indigenous tourism seldom started with Indigenous entrepreneurs. Indigenous people were merely a part of the attraction, and often were not aware that they were the attraction, becoming somewhat of a 'human zoo' (e.g. Human Safari tours targeting the Jarawa people of Andaman Island (The Jarawa Foundation, 2019; Survival, 2017; Chamberlain 2012a, 2012b) and Kayan 'Giraffe' Women in Thailand (Theurer, 2014; Harding, 2008; Mirante, 1998) see Chapter 7, Box 7.2). The development of early Indigenous tourism has oftentimes been more exploitative of Indigenous peoples than empowering.

BOX 12.1 THE JARAWA PEOPLE OF ANDAMAN ISLAND – INDIA

The Jarawa people of Andaman Island, India had very little contact with the outside world until 1996, when the construction of the Andaman Trunk Road that went through their territory (The Jarawa Foundation, 2019; Chamberlain, 2014, 2013, 2012). The Jarawa tribe was known to be aggressive – and often attacked wandering strangers – but the road changed the dynamics between the Jarawa tribe and the Andamanese settlers (Halder and Jaishankar, 2014). The road brought local entrepreneurs with truckloads of tourists and poachers. Jarawa women were lured out of the jungle to dance and sing for the promise of food handouts from tour groups.

After the initial encounter in 1996, there were more interactions between the Jarawa people and the local settlers. The locals began to give food and clothes to the seemingly poor, naked Jarawa people. While the State faced the demand to provide for these Indian citizens with modern facilities, medical services, and rehabilitation, there was a debate as to whether or not to assimilate the Jarawa people into mainstream Indian society or to leave them alone and isolated (Abraham, 2018). It seemed that co-existence with the Andamanese settlers was the final choice; however, media reports revealed that local settlers introduced alcohol and marijuana to the Jarawa tribe, and sexual violence against Jarawa women (Abraham, 2018; Halder and Jaishankar, 2014). Such encounters regularly took place along the Andaman Trunk Road, with bus- and truckloads of tourists passing through the reserve everyday (Abraham, 2018; Chamberlain, 2012a). After *The Observer* reported human safari tours, and how mistreated the Jarawa people were, it brought global censure and the

Indian Supreme Court ordered a ban to such tours, and the Indian government introduced a punitive law for interference with the Jarawa tribe (Chamberlain, 2012b, 2013). The NGO *Survival International* Campaign began, yet the Andaman authorities fought against the ban at all cost (Chamberlain, 2013). The Andaman authorities also refused to comply with the 2002 closure-of-the-road order from the Supreme Court, or to create an alternative means to the road (Chamberlain, 2013; Abraham, 2018). A human safari video was released on YouTube, which most likely has contributed to the start of the global campaign on banning human safari tours. Some researchers raised concerns that the video might have been used to spread the image of naked Jarawa women online as 'sexual commodities' (Halder and Jaishankar, 2014). Many years after the ban of human safari tours, hundreds of tourists still come to see the Jarawa people. What is more, additional reports on sexual violence and abuse of the Jarawa people by other Andaman settlers and tribes have been revealed (Chamberlain, 2014).

Being forced to be a tourist attraction does not allow for a dignified lifestyle for Indigenous peoples. Henry and Hood (2015) further describe expropriation of land, appropriation of cultural expressions, and suppression of economic activities as some examples of exploitation (see also Box 12.1). There are clearly two different types of Indigenous tourism products: Indigenous-themed tourism, and Indigenous-controlled tourism (Zeppel, 2006). Hinch and Butler (2007, p. 5) defined Indigenous tourism as a "tourism activity in which Indigenous people are directly involved either through control and/or having their culture serve as the essence of the attraction." Notzke (1999) suggests that Indigenous tourism provides an opportunity to the Indigenous population to strengthen traditional land-based activities. Smith (1996 cited in de Bernardi, Kugapi, and Lüthje, 2017) described Indigenous tourism in terms of the following categories: habitat (geographical setting), heritage (traditions), history (acculturation, assimilation), and handicrafts (tangible marketable products). Components of Indigenous tourism overlap with community-based tourism or village tourism, which stress the importance of empowerment. Zeppel (1998, 2006) emphasises first and foremost 'control' is the key word in developing Indigenous tourism. *Site Traditionnel Huron* is an example of an authentic recreated First Nations village on the Huron-Wendat reserve at Wendake, Quebec, Canada. Visitors learn about the past and present life of the Hurons by touring a long house (Huron traditional housing), smoke house, sweat lodge, tee-pee, and learning about their means of transportation. There is a restaurant serving traditional meals, performance stage, and a gift shop with handicrafts from North American First Nations (Huron Traditional Site Wendake, 2020). The enterprise is controlled by the First Nations community and it has become a major attraction.

In contrast, McLaren and Ramer (1999) developed a list of examples of conflicts between Indigenous peoples and the tourism industry that clearly illustrate violations of human rights:

- Beach resort hotels displacing local fishing communities (e.g. Malaysia and Thailand)
- Mohawk uprising against the extension of golf courses on to Mohawk burial grounds
- Desecration of Indigenous burial sites in Hawai'i and Bali
- Tourists' interruption of religious ceremonies in the Amazon jungle
- Bringing diseases to Indigenous communities
- Native Sioux workers as low-wage labourers
- Thai Hill tribes as Human Zoo exhibits
- Exploitation in sex tourism
- Stereotyping of Native people – romanticising
- Tourism using up resources on Indigenous open land (the commons)
- National parks displacing Native People and threatening their survival

Rather than utilising tourism as a form of empowerment, strengthening pride, providing livelihoods, or improving their quality of life, tourism is often viewed as subjugating Indigenous peoples and violating their rights. An important consideration of Indigenous rights in tourism is land rights. Aboriginal people have lived around Uluru in central Australia for over 30,000 years and for the Anangu people, their culture has always existed there (Parks Australia, 2020). Uluru was named Ayers Rock in 1873 (after the Chief Secretary of South Australia), and the Ayers Rock National Park was declared in 1950. In 1976 the Aboriginal Land Rights (Northern Territory) Act came into effect, recognising Indigenous land rights and established the framework for Indigenous Peoples to win back their land. In October of 1985, the Governor General of Australia returned the title deeds of the Uluru-Kata Tjuta National Park to the Anangu, which was then leased to Parks Australia for 99 years. The Park is jointly managed by the Anangu and Parks Australia. In October of 2019, Uluru was permanently closed to climbers, even though tourists had been asked not to climb the rock since the 1990s. In 2011, the Indigenous Land Corporation purchased the Ayers Rock Resort located in Yulara, also home to the National Indigenous Training Academy, which trains Indigenous People to work in tourism and hospitality (Parks Australia 2020). The return of land to Indigenous Peoples, however, does not necessarily guarantee success in relation to tourism. Although there is joint management of the Park, Judd, et al. (2019) argue that if the aim was to improve the economic and social outcomes for the Anangu, it has been a spectacular failure. While the tourism resources are in Yulara, Mutitjulu (home to the Anangu) is characterised by overcrowding, underemployment, poverty, and high rates of suicide and preventable diseases (Judd, et al., 2019). Judd, et al. (2019) note the structural problems in involving the Anangu in tourism, but note the end of the climb may present opportunities for more Indigenous People to be involved in the benefits from tourism around Uluru.

Another example of conflict over land rights between tourism and Indigenous Peoples was the proposed Jumbo Glacier resort in British Columbia. A proposed 5,500-bed, 110-hectare ski resort was planned for an area that was home to a grizzly bear habitat. The Indigenous Ktunaxa considered this land home to the grizzly bear spirit, part of their spiritual practice. After decades of controversy including the involvement of the Supreme Court, the land is to be given to the Ktunaxa to be managed as an Indigenous Protected Area, along with $21 million to design and plan the conservation area (Weber, 2020). In this case, tourism was forced to give way to Indigenous Land Rights.

12.4 Challenges and opportunities in Indigenous tourism

As with many non-Indigenous cases around the world, Indigenous tourism does not always bring in promised successes. In Australia, for example, Ruhanen, Whitford and McLennan (2015) found that while Indigenous tourism was a central component of the Governments' global marketing activities, participation in Indigenous tourism experiences in both the domestic and international market was on the decline. Indigenous/Aboriginal tourism is seriously challenged for success for various reasons explored below. Contemporary tourism is a social and economic phenomenon, based in part on Euro-American traditions. The development of mass tourism since the 1950s spread around the world, often following postcolonial locations. The practices of colonialism set the framework for human rights violations and abuses of Indigenous peoples and their culture, which have been extended through tourism. This is linked to structural violence by the state, international agencies, and multinational enterprises. The unique cultural manifestations of Indigenous culture have been used as tourist attractions or commodities. Various Acts or Treaties between mainstream governments and Indigenous peoples have not always protected them from human rights abuses in the tourism and hospitality industry.

Despite the negative sides of Indigenous tourism, once the Indigenous communities take control over the development and operation of tourism, it can bring social and economic benefits to the community and individuals. There are a growing number of case studies highlighting the successes of Indigenous tourism entrepreneurs. In October of 2018, Tourism HR (Human Resources) Canada and the Indigenous Tourism Association of Canada held a workshop as part of on-going efforts to develop an Indigenous Tourism Labour Marketing Study. Guest speakers included representatives from Great Spirit Trail (hotel and conference centre in North-eastern Ontario offering nature based and cultural tourism with Aboriginal perspectives), Tundra North Tours (offering authentic Arctic experiences in Inuvik, linking visitors with land, culture and the people of the north) and Metepenagiag Heritage Park (state-of-the-art facility celebrating

Mi'kmaq culture through exhibits, music, oral history, trail tours, and protecting two Indigenous National Historic Sites in New Brunswick). The presentations focused not only on necessary business skills for tourism, but also about maintaining cultural integrity (Tourism HR Canada, 2018).

Studies have examined both the challenges and opportunities of Indigenous Tourism. de Bernardi, Kugapi, and Lüthje (2017) for example investigated tourism by the Sámi, whose territory is referred to as Sápmi, and is located in northern Norway, Sweden, Finland, and Russia. The Sámi have issues of control related to tourism as symbols of their Indigenous culture – the symbols related to Sámi culture have been used by the non-Sámi tourism industry. The community also struggles politically, as Norway is the only country that has signed the ILO-169 Convention for Indigenous Populations. de Bernardi, Kugapi, and Lüthje (2017) examined the challenges and opportunities for the use of labels (certification) in Sámi tourism. While it would, for example, provide tourists with assurances the products they have purchased are made by Sámi, there are concerns the labels may exclude some groups which consider themselves as Sámi but have lost the language. The sections below will further review the challenges and opportunities of Indigenous tourism development, and how they are intertwined with Indigenous rights.

12.4.1 Challenges of Indigenous tourism

Early Indigenous tourism development reveals that Indigenous people were mainly viewed as a passive attraction, rather than an active participant. Governments or developers often appropriated the prime land they lived in – displacing Indigenous peoples and locals. Protected areas and national parks around the world are in many cases created to protect nature and wildlife at the cost of Indigenous People and locals who rely on resources in that area. Yellowstone National Park in the US was opened in 1872 by displacing the Shoshone, Bannock, Blackfoot, and Crow peoples, and depriving them from their livelihood (Neef, 2019). Kruger National Park in South Africa was created with the idea of a 'Third Nature', or re-imaging the landscape for wilderness tourism. In this Third Nature, human presence was excluded, and various strategies were employed to keep human beings out of sight (Brooks, et al., 2011), i.e. forceful eviction. Parks are established for conservation measures, but also for income from tourism. Sometimes forceful evictions are politically and militarily motivated – as in the case of the Karenni tribe in Myanmar (see Box 7.2 for details). Certain ethnic groups or minority groups are physically displaced from an area, so that they will not revolt against a governing body and once evacuated, the area is redeveloped for tourism.

Indigenous populations and locals suffer from not only physical displacement, but also from economic displacement (see Chapter 7). Land grabbing by the state is common, replacing traditional and Indigenous ways of production and consumption, with the patterns of mass consumption of international businesses. For instance, in Goa, India (Centre for Responsible Tourism, Goa, 2015), wealthy Goan landowners forsook their rice fields and switched to lucrative tourism businesses (Wrisley, 2009). The abandoned fields gave the Government the excuse to acquire 'waste land' for public purposes. The Government of Goa passed two new laws in 2017: The Goa Requisition and Acquisition of Property Bill, 2017, and the Goa Compensation to the Project Affected Persons and Vesting of Land in the Government Bill, 2017. These two bills "make compulsory land acquisitions swifter and cheaper" under the name of public purpose, i.e. mass tourism development or airport construction, rather than "safeguarding the rights and interests of vulnerable sections of society" with "adverse impact on the environment and on the rights of the dispossessed" (Nielsen, Bedi and Da Silva, 2017, pp. 14–15).

Although many Indigenous values can be significantly different from the global economic imperative of profit maximisation and growth, offering services to tourists and participating in the world of global capitalism has the danger of drawing Indigenous communities into wage economies, resulting in socio-cultural and environmental commodification. The challenge for many Indigenous communities is how to operate within an exploitative global capitalism and find a way to generate profits and benefits for their communities (see Box 12.2). The Indigenous population may be used as a tourist attraction, however, the revenue from cultural entertainment they perform may mostly end up in the hands of non-Indigenous attraction operators. In small scale, community-based tourism, the number of direct jobs can be very limited (i.e., tour guides, hotel staff, transportation drivers, activity instructors, etc.), even if the community is in charge of tourism development and operation. In Indigenous tourism developed around a community, it is important to consider to what extent the benefits are extended to all members of the community or if it is only a local Indigenous elite that benefit. In an Alaskan study, the Indigenous people felt unfair competition from non-Indigenous tour operators in the same community (Hillmer-Pegram, 2016). Non-Indigenous companies are also mass-producing and selling inauthentic Indigenous souvenirs, violating copyright and limiting the extent Indigenous cultures can economically benefit from their own culture (Guttentag, 2009). This is a violation of UNDRIP, for example Article 31 – Indigenous peoples have the "right to maintain, control, protect and develop their intellectual property." Guttentag (2009) claims that traditional copyright laws offer little protection for Indigenous groups to establish legal rights over the production of their own products, and advocates the development of *sui generis* (unique) laws to achieve this goal. Guttentag (2009, p. 31) further argues that "Indigenous intellectual property rights are often indirectly associated with land rights and autonomy" in that if a government recognises the *sui generis* rights of a group with respect to art, it then serves as a base argument in relation to land rights and autonomy. In a study of souvenirs in Niagara Falls, Canada, Hashimoto and Telfer (2007) explored the concept of displaced authenticity and found Indigenous souvenirs such as totem poles being sold, although these objects were not part of the local Indigenous culture, but rather were from the Haida Nation in British Columbia in western Canada. Other souvenirs were fashioned after a generic stereotypical image of Indigenous Peoples, rather than from a specific Indigenous Nation.

Many studies on Indigenous tourism argue that it should be based in the principles of sustainable development. Whitford and Ruhanen (2016) assert that the main challenge is to obtain a more comprehensive understanding of Indigenous tourism from the perspective of Indigenous stakeholders, which is both an ethical imperative and pragmatic approach to ensure the sustainability of Indigenous tourism. However, in an earlier analysis of Australian governmental policies on Indigenous tourism, Whitford and Ruhanen (2010) found that the majority of the policies demonstrated "sustainability rhetoric" and lacked depth and rigour to realising sustainable tourism development for Indigenous Peoples.

BOX 12.2 INDIGENOUS TOURISM DEVELOPMENT IN NORTHERN CANADA AND ALASKA

In the early 1970s in Northern Canada, it was mainly local, non-Aboriginal interests that developed tourism in the region. However, the development was unplanned and unstructured, without local involvement; as a consequence, there were no benefits to the local Indigenous communities. In response, Aboriginal Tourism Team Canada (ATTC) was established in 1996. ATTC wanted to develop Aboriginal tourism that reflected stronger cultural aspects of Aboriginal life and harmony with nature, such as their traditions – i.e. hunting and fishing for subsistence; and trapping and fishing for material exchange (Hashimoto and Telfer, 2003; Wenzel, 1999; Usher, 1987). As Aboriginal/Indigenous tourism tended to be more "resource-based" tourism (Shultis and Browne, 1999; Ewart, 1997), Weaver (1998) suggested it is more appropriate to talk about "socio-cultural alternative tourism" rather than "ecotourism."

Hillmer-Pegram (2016) worked with the Iñupiat people in Barrow, Alaska. Their Indigenous tourism development is a good example of community-based, Indigenous value-oriented tourism development. First and foremost, the Iñupiat people are aware that the cornerstone values of their culture (i.e. subsistence hunting, fishing, and whaling) may conflict with the non-Indigenous tourism industry. The community has set up the Arctic Slope Regional Corporation (ASRC), a Native corporation, to run the "Top of the World Hotel." As the hotel was owned and operated by the ASRC, the profits from the operation of the hotel are distributed to every individual in the community who is a corporate shareholder. The Iñupiat people can make good use of this income for their cultural activities. One of the conflicting situations is the external entrepreneurs, i.e. "tour companies based outside of Barrow bringing people into town, utilising the community's resources" (Hillmer-Pegram, 2016, p. 1204). Arguing based on Bunten's concept of Indigenous capitalism through tourism (2008, 2010, 2011 cited in Hillmer-Pegram, 2016; see also Bunten and Graburn, 2018) and Zeppel's Indigenous-controlled tourism (2006), Hillmer-Pegram concludes, Indigenous tourism is sustainable only when its political economy supports traditional cultural values, then "tourism can turn people, places and nature into commodities for market-based consumption," but this commodification "is not necessarily a bad thing if the process is Indigenously controlled for Indigenous benefit" (2016, p. 1206).

In the northern territories of Canada, expedition cruise tourism had been gaining popularity prior to COVID-19. Similar to the Alaskan study above, northern Canada is affected by climate change. Global Warming allows for the Northwest Passage in the High Arctic to be open for roughly 125 days a year (Johnston, et al., 2012). Suddenly, the Arctic has become accessible to more tourists and tour companies. Tourists want to see the Arctic before it disappears due to climate change (Johnston, et al., 2012); the media is calling this phenomenon 'extinction tourism' (McKie, 2016; Britten, 2016). Tourism Nunavut's website lists two external tour operators who run expedition cruises, of which capacity ranges from 30 guests (+50 crewmembers) to 198 passengers (Travel Nunavut, n.d.); whereas commercial Arctic cruise ship websites show that international exploration ships (size range 50–240 passengers) utilize operators from the US, the UK, France, and other countries (Polar Cruises, n.d.). Prior to COVID-19, an online search for Arctic expedition cruises produced 70 trips listed for between January and December 2020 (Ocean-wide Expeditions, n.d.). When the luxury cruise ship, the Crystal Serenity - with over 1,700 passengers and crew – sailed through the Northwest Passage and made a stop at an Inuit Community of 400 inhabitants, it did not only overwhelm the Inuit communities, but also raised the concern of it paving the way for mass tourism (McKie, 2016; Britten, 2016). Although the Nunavut government oversees Nunavut tourism, Arctic expedition cruise tourism is not entirely controlled by Indigenous communities. One cruise ship operator, Adventure Canada – albeit an external tour operator – promotes and educates its clients that it is a privilege to visit the Inuit communities (Blades, 2017). Nevertheless, some communities have already expressed the sense of resentment that the community was "'sold' as an attraction and ... being 'used'" (Johnston, et al., 2012, p. 79). The Nunavut government is aware that there is an urgent need to implement policy, planning, and regulations to protect small communities, and infrastructure and environmental management to accommodate cruise tourism (Johnston, et al., 2012, p. 79). In collaboration with the Government of Canada, and Parks Canada, the Nunavut Fisheries and Marine Training Consortium provide training, and on-board internship programs for young Inuit people to benefit the communities directly (Brown, 2017). The cruise industry has been hit hard by COVD-19. The Government of Canada extended the ban on all large cruise ships carrying over 100 people until the end of October of 2020. Similarly, passenger vessels carrying more than 12 people are banned from entering Canadian Arctic coastal waters, although restrictions do not apply to pleasure crafts used by locals or essential vessels for transportation or subsistence fishing, harvesting, as well as hunting (MacGregor, 2020). Those communities that depend on cruise business will face economic decline until the industry reopens.

12.4.2 Opportunities in Indigenous Tourism

When an Indigenous community or entrepreneur decides to develop a tourism product, the motivation may vary. A common motivation is economic benefit. Although economic success from tourism development is not always guaranteed, if the Indigenous community has an extremely high unemployment or social welfare rate, jobs created from tourism can be an attractive alternative. In Canada, the Métis People's unemployment rate is roughly 25 percent, while Inuit and First Nation people's unemployment rate is approximately 39 percent. Among the First Nations peoples, those living off reserve have a lower unemployment rate (33 percent) than those living on reserves (42 percent) (Trovato, et al., 2015). Colton's study on the Woodland Cree First Nation in Alberta, Canada (2005) found that 65 percent of the community were on social assistance. The Indigenous community lives on trapping and hunting, a traditional subsistence economy.

Some communities have considered developing Indigenous tourism for sociocultural motivations. The Canadian Indian Residential School system was set up 1831 and was finally closed in 1996. The Residential Schools were government-sponsored religious schools, created in order to assimilate Indigenous children into the Euro-Canadian culture (Miller and Marshall, 2018). The Residential School system created a rift between generations; the Elders are concerned that the younger people did not have a chance to learn the traditional knowledge and skills of the Indigenous Peoples. Similar cases include the "Stolen Generations" among the Australian Aboriginal peoples (Read, 1981), and the integration of Ainu children into Japanese culture between 1899 and 1937 (Ogawa, 1993). Utilising tourism might help younger Indigenous Peoples to connect themselves with the land and Elders (Colton, 2005). Opportunities for the Aboriginal youth to reconnect with their land are believed to boost their physical and mental health (Davis, 2012). It is thought that the forms of Indigenous tourism that use museums and heritage centres effectively, and subsistence activities to educate tourists, will help community members – especially youth – to appreciate the value of their own culture (Hillmer-Pegram, 2016). As mentioned earlier in this chapter, land was returned to Ktunaxa Nation of Canada. The Ktunaxa Nation Council has also transformed a former residential school into a First Nations-run resort with a golf course, casino, RV park, and resort hotel. The on-site interpretation centre was inspired by the late elder Mary Paul's words: "since it was within the St Eugene's Mission School that the culture of the Kootney Indian was taken away, it should be within the building that it is returned." The website of the resort states:

> To our knowledge, the St. Eugene Mission is the only project in Canada where a First Nation has decided to transform the icon of an often sad period of its history into a powerful economic engine by restoring an old Indian Residential school into an international destination resort for future

generations to enjoy. Elder Mary Paul would indeed be proud of the many successes we have had thus far.

(St Eugene Resort, 2020)

The third possible motivation to establish Indigenous tourism can be political. Weaver (2008) cited examples from the Northwest United States (Pitchford, 2006 cited in Weaver 2008) and South Australia (Higgins-Desbiolles, 2003 cited in Weaver 2008), where Indigenous tourism can politicise past human rights violations – such as the Residential School system, racism, day-to-day prejudices, and exclusions – and emphasise reconciliation. Many indigenous groups fought hard to regain their rights to land, rights to resources, and their ways of life. Researchers in Arctic Canada tend to draw the conclusion that political and economic benefits can be drawn from Indigenous subsistence tourism (Hillmer-Pegram, 2016; Colton, 2005; Notzke, 1999). The Woodland Cree First Nation in Canada attempted to use commercial activities such as tourism to legitimise their claim to traditional proprietorship, and to gain greater control of the land (Colton, 2005). Likewise, the study on the Iñupiat People in Alaska, USA also found that some of the community members believe that Indigenous subsistence tourism – which exposes tourists to traditional activities such as hunting, fishing, and gathering – would support maintaining their subsistence rights (Hillmer-Pegram, 2016).

In many cases, Indigenous populations have been subjected to human rights violations for centuries. Even if initial encounters between the new settlers and the Indigenous populations were mutually agreeable, there was almost always a degree of acculturation amongst Indigenous communities, and tourism products were often developed and operated by local non-Indigenous interests (see Canadian example in Hashimoto and Telfer, 2003). Ecotourism is often considered to be the best example of sustainable tourism; however, its non-consumptive activity principles and external non-Indigenous operators' interests often do not align with the Indigenous rights of land and resources. Moreover, the Indigenous communities' strong relationship to the ecosystem and natural environment forges their unique culture. Subsistence activities, including the consumptive activities of hunting and fishing, are part of their culture and ecosystem. The Territory of Nunavut in northern Canada promotes hunting as part of its tourism activity, and their website (Travel Nunavut) provides information on hunting polar bears, muskox, caribou, walrus, wolf, ground squirrel, hare, and ptarmigan (game bird). Therefore, the Indigenous idea of 'sustainability' does not necessarily align with the outsiders' idea of 'sustainability'.

Indigenous communities need to exercise their spatial, temporal, cultural, and activity limitations (Zeppel, 1998) so that the Indigenous tourism is operated and managed on their own terms. In order to do so, the Indigenous communities often require more financial support for start-up, and the assistance of technical experts, ideally from various levels of governing bodies, than non-Indigenous businesses.

The Indigenous Tourism Association of Canada (ITAC, 2020) assists in the creation of partnerships between associations, organisations, industry leaders, and governments from across Canada to support the growth of Indigenous tourism. The central purpose of ITAC is to improve the social-economic situation of Indigenous Peoples across Canada. They provide the following services to Indigenous tourism operators and communities: economic development advisory services; conferences; professional development training and workshops; and industry statistics and information. Marketing is a key component including 'Nations: Indigenous Lifestyle Magazine' which highlights Indigenous tourism companies across Canada. It is important to highlight successes, and Table 12.2 illustrates ten sample companies and their products in B.C. In June of 2020 the Government of Canada (2020) announced funding to Indigenous businesses ($133 million) as well as an additional $16 million to support the Indigenous tourism industry as a result of COVID-19.

Other opportunities come in the participation in developing Indigenous tourism plans. The Indigenous Tourism Alberta Strategy 2019–2024 was directed by Indigenous People. While the main priorities revolve around developing sustainable market ready and export ready products, the key opportunities in the plan include:

- Strengthen the quantity and quality of Alberta's Indigenous tourism experiences to be competitive with other Canadian travel destinations;
- Increase awareness and demand for Indigenous tourism in Alberta;
- Change the common traveller's perception that all Indigenous tourism experiences are the same;
- Align the efforts and interests of Alberta's tourism industry under a common Indigenous tourism strategy (Indigenous Tourism Alberta, 2019).

Finally, if Indigenous tourism is done in a sustainable manner, there is an opportunity to not only protect culture and generate income, but also protect the natural environment (see Chapter 11). Indigenous nature-based, wildlife or ecotourism tourism such as those in Table 12.2 have the potential to educate tourists about the importance of conservation. Chernela and Zanotti (2014) examined the complexity of the relationships between Indigenous Peoples, NGOs, and ecotourism in the Eastern Amazon of Brazil. While the project offered the opportunity to protect the natural environment, it was important to understand the social and moral economies. The authors argue that "networks of exchange, with far-reaching webs of obligation and expectations, are a principal source of social capital for small-scale societies" (p. 314). They also argue that successful projects need to consider the long term social and economic benefits by looking at market activities and political events from a historical perspective, and not just viewing them in spatial or temporal isolation. It is important that if outside tour companies visit these villages they are remunerated fairly.

12.5 Conclusion

This chapter adopted a broad orientation, including both Indigenous and Aboriginal peoples, and examined how the relationship between these groups and newcomers has evolved. Often this interaction has resulted in the violation of Indigenous People's

Indigenous people's rights and tourism 317

TABLE 12.2 Examples of Indigenous Tourism Companies in British Columbia, Canada

Company Name	Product
Takaya Tours	Canoe tour in 25-foot ocean-going canoes (replicas of those used by Tsleil-Waututh Nation) observing wildlife and hearing about legends, songs, and stories of Coast Salish Nations
Knight Inlet Lodge	Lodge set in one of the largest concentrations of grizzly bears in B.C.; on the territory of the Da'naxda'xw Awaetlala Nations; view wildlife
Moccasin Trails	Canoe down the South Thompson and Adams Rivers following the trails of the Secwepemcuu'l'ecw (Shuswap Nation) narrated by a local Knowledge Keeper; observe Sockeye Salmon
Haida Style	Explore Haida Gwaii village (UNESCO World Heritage Site); Haida feast of salmon; fishing; hear traditional stories from locals of the Tsaahl Eagle Clan
Sidney Whale Watching	Whale watching; wildlife viewing (seals and sea lions)
Homalco Wildlife Tours	From viewing platform, observe grizzly bears feast on spawning salmon; boat tour to observe wildlife (whales, dolphins, eagles) led by a Homalco First Nation guide
Spirit Bear Lodge	4–7 day ecotourism package on the territory of the Kitasoo/Xai'xais First Nation observing grizzlies, sea wolves, white spirit bears, whales, dolphins; listen to stories from the Klemtu locals
Sea Wolf Adventures	Explore wildlife (grizzly bears, whales) in the region, being led by a guide from one of 19 different tribes of the Kwakwaka'wakw Nation
Talaysay Tours	Tours by First Nations guides; eco-adventure discovering uses of plants and trees (medicinal, artistic, culinary, technological) of the Coast Salish First Nation in Stanley Park; canoe on Salish Sea to view wildlife
Xwisten Experience Tours	Guided by the St'at'imc Nation to learn about importance of salmon, visit archaeological village site, Indigenous culture; traditional feast

Source: (Bayley, 2020).

rights. This is an extremely complex and difficult topic, as exploitation has often been at the centre of these contacts and tourism has played a further role in taking advantage of these groups. While a single book chapter cannot comprehensively cover this topic, an attempt has been made to focus on issues relevant to Indigenous tourism.

In addition to other various covenants and charters created to promote and protect human rights, and monitor the implementation of human rights treaties (see Chapter 1 for details), the UNDRIP was finally adopted in 2007. Many UN member countries expressed dissent to this Declaration; however, the four major countries initially opposed (Australia, Canada, New Zealand, and the USA) adopted the Declaration, with Canada being the last signatory as late as 2016. The real challenge for states and lawmakers begins with the acceptance of the Declaration. What is more, states have the responsibility to inform and educate non-Indigenous populations, and to change current general perceptions about the relationship between Indigenous and non-Indigenous peoples. The processes of decolonisation, self-determination, and indigenisation have begun the long road to changing people's perceptions and misconceptions about Indigenous Peoples.

Indigenous people have been an important part in tourism development, though they have not shared many of the benefits from Indigenous-themed tourism so far. The Indigenous peoples' unique culture, worldview, and way of life have fascinated non-Indigenous tourists. Unfortunately, the tourists' view of Indigenous Peoples was not in terms of a reciprocal relationship of equals. Though it is still in its initial stages, Indigenous-controlled tourism created by Indigenous communities is emerging, and more Indigenous entrepreneurs are becoming successful. For example, there are now two Indigenous wineries operating in British Columbia, Canada. Leading researchers in tourism strongly advocate for the importance of Indigenous control in the development of Indigenous tourism; however, Whitford and Ruhanen (2010) caution that there cannot be a 'one-size fits all' framework for Indigenous tourism development and policies need to draw upon Indigenous diversity. Caution is also needed, as Indigenous communities are being drawn into the global capitalist economy to the point that their traditional relationships with nature, and their culture is being compromised (see more discussions in Hillmer-Pegram, 2016). The core value of Indigenous tourism must be a form of tourism with desired outcomes that respect the human rights of Indigenous peoples, their rights to a subsistence economy, their rights to natural resources and their land, and their rights to evolve and change as they see fit.

References

Abraham, I., 2018. The Andamans as a "sea of islands": reconnecting old geographies through poaching. *Inter-Asia Cultural Studies*, 19 (1), pp. 2–20. DOI: https://doi.org/10.1080/14649373.2018.1422344.
Ainu Association of Hokkaido, 2018. Ainu minzoku no rekishi. *AINU Indigenous people*. [online]. Available at: <www.ainu-assn.or.jp/ainupeople/history.html> [Accessed 28 May 2018].
Ainu Museum, n.d. Ainu Bunka Nyūmon: I History. [online]. Available at: <www.ainu-museum.or.jp/nyumon/rekishibunka/> [Accessed 28 May 2018].
Ansell, J., 2013. *Kupe's descendant confirms other races were here first. David Rankin, elocal, National Archives, Waipoua Forest Stone City*. [online] 10 May. Available at: <https://treatygate.wordpress.com/2013/05/10/kupes-descendant-confirms-other-races-were-here-first/> [Accessed 28 May 2017].

APNZ, 2012. Rankin: Maori are not the indigenous people of New Zealand. *New Zealand Herald*. [online] 27 December. Available at: <www.nzherald.co.nz/northern-advocate/news/article.cfm?c_id=1503450&objectid=11086095> [Accessed 28 May 2017].

Barlow, M., 2020. COVID_19 puts the human right to water front in centre. *Canada's National Observer*. [online] 22 April. Available at: <www.nationalobserver.com/2020/04/22/opinion/covid-19-puts-human-right-water-front-and-centre> [Accessed 4 July 2020].

Bayley, N. 2020. 10 Ways to be wowed by a B.C. Wildlife Adventure. Nations. [online] Available at: <https://indigenoustourism.ca/corporate/wp-content/uploads/2019/11/Nations-Magazine-web-EN.pdf> [Accessed 5 July 2020].

Blades, T., 2017. Arctic tourism provides insight into Inuit culture. *CBC News Looking North*. [online] 28 October. Available at: <www.cbc.ca/news/canada/newfoundland-labrador/looking-north-cbc-artic-tourism-1.4370911> [Accessed 27 September 2018].

Britten, L., 2016. Vancouver Maritime Museum joining largest ship to sail Northwest Passage. *CBC News*. [online] 5 August 206. Available at: <www.cbc.ca/news/canada/british-columbia/vancouver-maritime-museum-northwest-passage-1.3709993> [Accessed 28 May 2017].

Brooks, S., Spierenburg, M., Van Brakel, L.O.T., Kolk, A. and Lukhozi, K.B., 2011. Creating a commodified wilderness: Tourism, private game farming, and 'third nature'landscapes in Kwazulu-natal. *Tijdschrift voor economische en sociale geografie*, 102(3), pp. 260-274. https://doi.org/10.1111/j.1467-9663.2011.00662.x

Brown, B., 2017. For young Nunavut Inuit, tourism training's an adventure. *Nunatsiaq News*. [online] 8 November. Available at: <https://nunatsiaq.com/stories/article/65674for_young_nunavut_inuit_tourism_trainings_an_adventure/> [Accessed 14 December 2017].

Bunten, A.C. and Graburn, N.H. eds., 2018. *Indigenous Tourism Movements*. Toronto: University of Toronto Press.

Canadian Press, 2016. What does Metis mean? A look at who qualifies as Metis under the Supreme Court ruling. *Global News*. [online] 15 April. Available at: <https://globalnews.ca/news/2639611/what-does-metis-mean-a-look-at-who-qualifies-as-metis-under-the-supreme-court-ruling/> [Accessed 24 May 2018].

Centre for Responsible Tourism, Goa, 2015. *Corporatization of Tourism Spaces*. [online] 12 February. Available at: <http://responsibletourismgoa.com/corporatization-tourism-spaces/> [Accessed 29 March 2019].

Chamberlain, G., 2012a. Andaman Islands tribe threatened by lure of mass tourism. *The Guardian*. [online] 7 January. Available at: <www.theguardian.com/world/2012/jan/07/andaman-islands-tribe-tourism-threat?> [Accessed 15 February 2012].

Chamberlain, G., 2012b. Human safaris may be banned, but still tourists flock to Andaman Islands. *The Observer*. [online] 1 September. Available at: <www.theguardian.com/world/2012/sep/01/andaman-islands-human-safaris-continue> [Accessed 10 February 2013].

Chamberlain, G., 2013. 'Human safaris' to end for Andaman tribe. *The Observer*. [online] 27 January. Available at: <www.theguardian.com/world/2013/jan/27/jarawa-tribe-andaman-islands-human-safaris-to-end> [Accessed 10 February 2013].

Chamberlain, G., 2014. Jarawa tribe now face sexual abuse by outsiders on Andaman Islands. *The Observer*. [online] 1 February. Available at: <www.theguardian.com/world/2014/feb/01/andaman-islands-jarawa-sex-abuse-outsiders> [Accessed 22 February 2014].

Chernela, J. and Zanotti, L., 2014. Limits to knowledge: Indigenous Peoples, NGOS, and the Moral Economy in the Eastern Amazon of Brazil. *Conservation and Society*, [pdf] 12(3), pp. 306–317. Available at: <www.conservationandsociety.org/temp/ConservatSoc123306-6353732_173857.pdf> [Accessed 6 July 2014].

Coates, N., 2008. Who are the indigenous peoples of Canada and New Zealand? *Journal of South Pacific Law*, [pdf] 12(1), pp. 49–55. Available at: <www.paclii.org/journals/fJSPL/vol12no1/pdf/coates.pdf> [Accessed 24 May 2018].

Colton, J.W., 2005. Indigenous Tourism Development in Northern Canada: beyond economic incentives. *Canadian Journal of Native Studies* XXV(1), pp. 185–206.

Davis, B., 2012. *Cultural Connectedness as Personal Wellness in First Nations Youth*. MEd. Western University Electronic Thesis and Dissertation Repository. 403. Available at: <https://ir.lib.uwo.ca/cgi/viewcontent.cgi?referer=https://www.google.com/&httpsredir=1&article=1615&context=etd> [27 September 2018].

de Bernardi, C., Kugapi, O., and Lüthje, M., 2017. Sámi indigenous tourism empowerment in the Nordic countries through labelling systems: strengthening ethnic enterprises and activities. In: I. de Lima and V. King, (eds.), *Tourism and Ethnodevelopment: Inclusion, Empowerment and Self-determination*. London: Routledge, pp. 200–212.

Elliott, M. 2016. Participatory parity and indigenous decolonization struggles. *Constellations* 23(3), pp. 413–424. doi: 10.1111/1467–8675.12235.

Eriksson, J., Noble, R., Pattullo P. and Barnett, T., 2009. *Putting Tourism to Rights: A challenge to human rights abuses in the tourism industry*. A report by Tourism Concern [pdf]. Available at: <www.tourismconcern.org.uk/wp-content/uploads/2014/10/LowRes_Putting-Tourism-to-Rights_A-report-by-TourismConcern2.pdf> [Accessed 27 July 2016].

Ewart, A., 1997. Resource-Based Tourism: Introduction and Overview. *Journal of Applied Recreation Research* 22(1), pp. 3-7.

Favel, B. and Coats, K., 2016. *Understanding UNDRIP: Choosing action on priorities over sweeping claims about the United Nations Declaration on the Rights of Indigenous Peoples* [e-book]. Aboriginal Canada and Natural Resource Series 10. Saskatchewan: Macdonald-Laurier Institute. Available at: <MLI-10-UNDRIPCoates-Flavel05-16-WebReadyV4 >.

Fisher, J. 2020. Black Loves Matter rallies held across Australia to protest against mistreatment and deaths of Indigenous people. *ABC News*. Available at: <www.abc.net.au/news/2020-06-06/black-lives-matter-rallies-held-across-australia/12325442> [Accessed 4 July 2020].

frpac, 2015. *Ainu minzoku rekishi to genzai – mirai wo tomoni ikiru tameni* – [pdf]. Available at: <www.frpac.or.jp/history/files/cyugakusei2015.pdf> [Accessed 3 June 2018].

Gaudry, A. and Welch, M.A., 2016. Métis. *The Canadian Encyclopedia*. [online] 16 November. Available at: <www.thecanadianencyclopedia.ca/en/article/metis/#top> [Accessed 24 May 2018].

Global Black History, 2016. *Disease and Depopulation of Africans during Colonialism*. Available at: <www.globalblackhistory.com/2016/08/disease-depopulation-africans-colonialism.html> [Accessed 6 June 2018].

Government of Canada, 2017. *About Indigenous peoples and communities*. [online] 10 January. Available at: <www.aadnc-aandc.gc.ca/eng/1461773087873/1461773141110> [Accessed 24 May 2018].

Government of Canada, 2020. *Government of Canada announces additional support for Indigenous businesses and the Indigenous tourism industry*. News Release. [online] 11 June. Available at: <www.canada.ca/en/indigenous-services-canada/news/2020/06/government-of-canada-announces-additional-support-for-indigenous-businesses-and-the-indigenous-tourism-industry.html.> [Accessed 3 July 2020].

Guttentag, D., 2009. The legal protection of Indigenous Souvenir products. *Tourism Recreation Research*, 34(2), pp. 23–34. DOI: https://doi.org/10.1080/02508281.2009.11081572.

Halder, D. and Jaishankar, K., 2014. Online victimization of Andaman Jarawa Tribal Women: An analysis of the 'Human Safari' YouTube Videos (2012) and its Effects. *British Journal of Criminology*, 54(4), pp. 673–688. DOI: https://doi.org/10.1093/bjc/azu026.

Harding, A., 2008. Burmese women in Thai 'human zoo'. *BBC News*. [online] 30 January. Available at: <http://news.bbc.co.uk/2/hi/7215182.stm> [Accessed 30 January 2008].

Hashimoto, A. and Telfer, D., 2003. Canadian Aboriginal Ecotourism in the North. In: D. Diamantis (ed.), *Ecotourism: Management and Assessment*. London: Thomson Learning, pp. 204–225.

Hashimoto, A. and Telfer, D., 2007. Geographical representations embedded within souvenirs in Niagara: The case of geographically authenticity. *Tourism Geographies*, 9(2), pp. 191–217. DOI: https://doi.org/10.1080/14616680701278547.

Henry, K. and Hood, T., 2015. Chapter 12. Aboriginal Tourism. In: M. Westcott, (ed.), *Introduction to Tourism and Hospitality in BC*. Victoria, BC: BC campus. Available at: <https://opentextbc.ca/introtourism/> [Accessed 23 March 2017].

Hillmer-Pegram, K., 2016. Integrating Indigenous values with capitalism through tourism: Alaskan experiences and outstanding issues. *Journal of Sustainable Tourism*. 24(8–9), pp. 1194–1210. DOI: 10.1080/09669582.2016.1182536.

Hinch, T. and Butler, R., 2007. 1. Introduction: revisiting common ground. In: T. Hinch and R. Butler, (eds.), *Tourism and Indigenous Peoples*. Oxford: Elsevier Ltd. Chapter 1.

Human Rights Commission, n.d. UNDRIP and the Treaty. [online] Available at: <www.hrc.co.nz/your-rights/indigenous-rights/our-work/undrip-and-treaty/> [Accessed 5 May 2018].

Huron Traditional Site Wendake, 2020. *Huron Traditional Site Wendake*. [online] Available at: <www.huron-wendat.qc.ca/en/> [Accessed 5 July 2020].

ICT – Indigenous Corporate Training, 2020. *A brief definition of Decolonisation and Indigenization*. [online]. Available at: <www.ictinc.ca/blog/a-brief-definition-of-decolonization-and-indigenization> [Accessed 5 July 2020].

ILO, 2017. *NORMLEX: C169 - Indigenous and Tribal Peoples Convention, 1989 (No. 169)*. [online]. Available at: <www.ilo.org/dyn/normlex/en/f?p=NORMLEXPUB:12100:0::NO::P12100_ILO_CODE:C169> [Accessed 28 May 2018].

ILO, 2018. *Who are the indigenous and tribal peoples?* [online]. Available at: <www.ilo.org/global/topics/indigenous-tribal/WCMS_503321/lang—en/index.htm> [Accessed 24 May 2018].

Indigenous Tourism Alberta, 2019. *Indigenous Tourism Alberta Strategy 2019–2024*. [online]. Available at: <https://indigenoustourism.ca/corporate/wp-content/uploads/2019/04/ITA-Strategy-2019-2024-FINAL-EDIT-1.pdf> [Accessed 5 July 2020].

ITAC, 2020. *Indigenous Tourism Association of Canada*. [online]. Available at: <https://indigenoustourism.ca/corporate/> [Accessed 5 July 2020].

Johnston, A., Johnston, M., Stewart, E., Dawson, J and Lemelin, H., 2012. Perspectives of decision makers and regulators on climate change and adaptation in expedition cruise ship tourism in Nunavut. *Northern Review*. [pdf]. 35(Spring), pp. 69–95. Available at: <https://researcharchive.lincoln.ac.nz/bitstream/handle/10182/7557/Johnston%20et%20al%20FINAL%20Northern%20Review%2035%20Spring%202012-4.pdf?sequence=1&isAllowed=y> [Accessed 4 August 2018].

Judd, B., Kearney, A., Hallinan, C., Schlesinger, C., Cheer, J. and Reeves, K., 2019. After the climb: how new tourism opportunities can empower the traditional owners of

Uluru. *The Conversation*. [online] 30 October. Available at: <https://theconversation.com/after-the-climb-how-new-tourism-opportunities-can-empower-the-traditional-owners-of-uluru-125929> [Accessed 4 July 2020].

Kawakubo, Y., Sawada, J. and Dodo, Y., 2009. In Search for Ainu's Signs in the Tohoku Region, Japan: Cranial Metric and Nonmetric Analyses of Unearthed Human Skeletal Remains. *Anthropological Science (Japanese Series)*, 117(2), pp. 65–87. [online]. Available at: <www.jstage.jst.go.jp/article/asj/117/2/117_2_65/_pdf> [Accessed 3 June 2018].

Laframboise, K. 2020. Kahnawake Mohawks demand Indigenous rights be upheld as rail blockade peacefully ends. *Global News*. [online] 5 March. Available at: <https://globalnews.ca/news/6634544/kahnawake-announcement-rail-blockade-barricade/> [Accessed 4 July 2020].

MacGregor, S. 2020. Canada Extends Controversial Coronavirus Travel Ban on all Large Cruise Ships. *Forbes*. [online] 5 June. Available at: <www.forbes.com/sites/sandramacgregor/2020/06/05/canada-extends-controversial-coronavirus-travel-ban-on-all-large-cruise-ships/#4541cb651a8c> [Accessed 3 July 2020].

Mann, C.C., 2011. *1493: Uncovering the New World Columbus Created*. New York: Alfred Knopf.

McKie, R., 2016. Inuit fear they will be overwhelmed as 'extinction tourism' descends on Arctic. *The Guardian*. [online] 21 August. Available at: <www.theguardian.com/world/2016/aug/20/inuit-arctic-ecosystem-extinction-tourism-crystal-serenity> [Accessed 28 May 2017].

McLaren and Ramer, D., 1999. The History of Indigenous Peoples. *Cultural Survival Quarterly June 1999*. [online] 1 April 2010. Available at: <www.culturalsurvival.org/publications/cultural-survival-quarterly/history-indigenous-peoples-and-tourism> [Accessed 20 February 2018].

McLauchlan, A., 2001. The Japanese Authorities' Attitudes Toward the Burakumin from Meiji to the Present Day. In: R. Starrs, (ed.), *Asian Nationalism in an Age of Globalization*. Reprint 2013. London: Routledge. Chapter 12.

Métis Nation, n.d. *Métis Nation*. [online] Available at: <www.metisnation.ca/index.php/who-are-the-metis> [Accessed 24 May 2018].

Miller, J.R. and Marshall, T., 2018. Residential Schools in Canada. *The Canadian Encyclopaedia*. [online] 24 September. Available at: <www.thecanadianencyclopedia.ca/en/article/residential-schools> [Accessed 24 September 2018].

Mirante, E. T., 1990. Hostage to Tourism. *Cultural Survival Quarterly Magazine*. [online] March. Available at: <www.culturalsurvival.org/publications/cultural-survival-quarterly/hostages-tourism> [Accessed 30 January 2008].

MMIWG, 2019. Reclaiming Power and Place: The Final Report of the National Inquiry into Missing and Murdered Indigenous Women and Girls. [online]. Available at: <www.mmiwg-ffada.ca/final-report/> [Accessed 3 June 2019].

Morin, B., 2017. Where does Canada sit 10 years after the UN Declaration on the Rights of Indigenous Peoples? CBC News. [online] 13 September. Available at: <www.cbc.ca/news/indigenous/where-does-canada-sit-10-years-after-undrip-1.4288480> [Accessed 13 September 2017].

Murphy, A., Duncan, G. and Piggott, G., 2008. *Primer: Canadian Law on Aboriginal and Treaty Rights*. Vancouver, B.C.: University of British Columbia Faculty of Law. [pdf] Available at: <www.allard.ubc.ca/sites/www.allard.ubc.ca/files/uploads/enlaw/pdfs/primer_complete_05_10_09.pdf> [Accessed 25 May 2018].

Neef, A., 2019. *Tourism, Land Grabs and Displacement: A Study with Particular Focus on the Global South* [pdf]. 14 February 2019. Available at: <www.tourism-watch.de/system/files/document/Neef_Tourism_Land_Grab_Study.pdf> [Accessed 29 March 2019].

Nielsen, K.B., Bedi, H.P. and Da Silva, S., 2017. Enabling the Great Goan Land Grab. *Economic & Political Weekly*, 50(41). [online] 14 October. Available at: <www.epw.in/journal/2017/41/commentary/enabling-great-goan-land-grab.html> [Accessed 5 June 2019].

Notzke, C., 1999. Indigenous tourism development in the Arctic. *Annals of Tourism Research*, 26(1), pp. 55–76. DOI: 10.1016/S0160-7383(98)00047-4.

Nunn, N. and Qian, N., 2010. The Columbian exchange: A history of disease, food, and ideas. *Journal of Economic Perspectives* [pdf] 24(2), pp. 163–188. Available at: <www.kellogg.northwestern.edu/faculty/qian/resources/NunnQianJEP.pdf> [Accessed 6 June 2018].

Ocean-wide Expeditions, n.d. *Arctic cruise overview*. [online]. Available at: <https://oceanwide-expeditions.com/the-arctic/cruises?date=20190401-20190630> [Accessed 10 June 2019].

Ogawa, M., 1993. A Historical Study on "Ainu School Hokkaido(3): The actual Conditions of the Education Policy against Ainu 1920–1940's. *Hokkaido University Collection of Scholarly and Academic Papers: HUSCAP*, 61. pp. 37–79. [pdf] Available at: <http://hdl.handle.net/2115/29404> [Accessed 3 June 2018].

Pape, Salter, Teillet LLP, 2016. *A Summary of Daniels v. Canada at the Supreme Court of Canada Publications*. [online]. Available at: <www.pstlaw.ca/publications.html> [Accessed 3 June 2018].

Parks Australia, 2020. *History of Uluṟu-Kata Tjuṯa National Park*. [online]. Available at: <https://parksaustralia.gov.au/uluru/discover/history/> [Accessed 4 July 2020].

Polar Cruises, n.d. Polar Cruises home page. [online]. Available at: <www.polarcruises.com/> [Accessed 10 June 2019].

Read, P. 1981. *The Stolen Generations: The removal of Aboriginal children in New South Wales 1883 to 1969*. [pdf]. Available at: <https://web.archive.org/web/20060820150941/http://www.daa.nsw.gov.au/publications/StolenGenerations.pdf> [Accessed 24 September 2018].

Richardson, V., 2010. Obama adopts U.N. manifesto on rights of indigenous peoples. *The Washington Times*. [online] 16 December. Available at: <www.washingtontimes.com/news/2010/dec/16/obama-adopts-un-manifesto-on-rights-of-indigenous-/> [Accessed 22 August 2017].

Rodgers, E., 2009. Aust adopts UN Indigenous declaration. *ABC News*. [online] 3 April. Available at: <www.abc.net.au/news/2009-04-03/aust-adopts-un-indigenous-declaration/1640444> [Accessed 22 August 2017].

Ruhanen, L., Whitford, M. and McLennan, C., 2015. Indigenous tourism in Australia: Time for a reality check. *Tourism Management*, 48, pp. 73–83. DOI: https://doi.org/10.1016/j.tourman.2014.10.017.

Shultis, J.D. and Browne, A.J., 1999. Aboriginal Collaboration. *Parks & Recreation*, 34(9), pp. 108–116.

Stephens, C., Porter, J., Nettleton, C. and Willis, R., 2006. Indigenous Health 4: Disappearing, displaced, and undervalued: a call to action for Indigenous health worldwide. *The Lancet*, 367(9527), pp. 2019–2028. DOI: https://doi.org/10.1016/S0140-6736(06)68892-2.

Stevens, G., 2001. The Ainu and human rights: Domestic and international legal protections. *Asia-Pacific Journal on Human Rights and the Law*, 2(2), pp. 110–133. DOI: 10.1163/157181501400649044.

St. Eugene Resort, 2020. *About us: St Eugene Resort*. [online]. Available at: <www.steugene.ca/en/about/> [Accessed 6 July 2020].

Survival, 2017. *Outrage as tour operators sell "human safaris" to Andaman Islands.* [online] 17 October. Available at: <www.survivalinternational.org/news/11839> [Accessed 1 November 2017].

Tahana, N., Grant, K.T.O.K., Simmons, D.G. and Fairweather, J.R., 2000. *Tourism and Maori development in Rotorua* [pdf]. Tourism Research and Education Centre (TREC) Report No. 15, Lincoln University. DOI:10.1.1.1011.6404.

The Jarawa Foundtion, 2019. Who are the Jarawa People? [online]. Available at: <https://organicthejarawas.com/pages/who-are-the-jarawa-people> [Accessed 21 May 2019].

Theurer, J., 2014. Trapped in their own rings: Padaung women and their fight for traditional freedom. *International Journal of Gender and Women's Studies* [pdf]. December, 2(4). pp. 51–67. DOI: 10.15640/ijgws.v2n4a3.

Travel Nunavut, n.d. Arctic Cruises and Yachting. [online]. Available at: <www.nunavuttourism.com/things-to-see-do/cruises/> [Accessed 10 June 2019].

Tourism HR Canada, 2018. Aligning Dreams: Insights from Successful Indigenous Tourism Entrepreneurs. [online]. Available at: <http://tourismhr.ca/aligning-dreams-insights-from-successful-indigenous-tourism-entrepreneurs/> [Accessed 15 August 2019].

Trovato, F., Pedersen, A., Price, J.A., Lang, C. and Aylsworth, L., 2015. Economic Conditions of Indigenous Peoples in Canada. *The Canadian Encyclopaedia.* [online]. (Last updated 24 July 2015). Available at: <www.thecanadianencyclopedia.ca/en/article/aboriginal-people-economic-conditions> [Accessed 24 September 2018].

UN, 2007. General Assembly Adopts Declaration on Rights of Indigenous Peoples: 'Major Step Forward' towards Human Rights for All, Says President. *Press Release GA/10612.* [online] 13 September. Available at: <www.un.org/press/en/2007/ga10612.doc.htm> [Accessed 8 May 2017].

UN, 2018. United Nations Declaration on the Rights of Indigenous Peoples. [online]. Available at: <www.un.org/development/desa/indigenouspeoples/declaration-on-the-rights-of-indigenous-peoples.html> [Accessed 20 May 2018].

UN/DESA, 2014. *Martínez Cobo Study: Study of the Problem of Discrimination Against Indigenous Populations: Final report submitted by the Special Rapporteur, Mr. José Martínez Cobo.* [online]. 8 September. Available at: <www.un.org/development/desa/indigenouspeoples/publications/2014/09/martinez-cobo-study/> [Accessed 8 May 2017].

University of Minnesota Human Rights Center, 2003. Study Guide: The Rights of Indigenous Peoples. Available at: <http://hrlibrary.umn.edu/edumat/studyguides/indigenous.html> [Accessed 8 May 2018].

Usher, P.J., 1987. The North: One Land, Two Ways of Life. In: L.D. McCann, (ed.), *Heartland and Hinterland: A Geography of Canada (Second Edition).* Scarborough, Ontario: Prentice-Hall Canada Inc., pp. 483–529.

Watkins, T., 2010. NZ does U-turn on rights charter. *Stuff.* [online] 24 April. Available at: <www.stuff.co.nz/national/politics/3599153/NZ-does-U-turn-on-rights-charter> [Accessed 29 May 2018].

Weaver, D. B., 1998. *Ecotourism in the Less Developed World.* Wallingford, Oxon: CABI Publishing.

Weaver, D., 2008. Indigenous tourism stages and their implications for sustainability. *Journal of Sustainable Tourism,* 18(1), pp. 34–60. DOI: https://doi.org/10.1080/09669580903072001.

Weber, B., 2020. Once proposed as a ski resort, B.C.'s Jumbo Glacier turned over to First Nation. *CTV News.* [online] 18 January. Available at: <https://bc.ctvnews.ca/once-proposed-as-ski-resort-b-c-s-jumbo-glacier-turned-over-to-first-nation-1.4773513> [Accessed 6 July 2020].

Welker, G., 2016. *Indigenous Peoples Literature*. [online]. Available at: <www.indigenouspeople.net> [Accessed 24 May 2018].

Wenzel, G., 1991. *Animal Rights, Human Rights: Ecology, Economy and Ideology in the Canadian Arctic*. Toronto: University of Toronto Press.

Whitford, M. and Ruhanen, L., 2010. Australian indigenous tourism policy: practical and sustainable policies? *Journal of Sustainable Tourism* 18(4), pp. 475–496. DOI: https://doi.org/10.1080/09669581003602325.

Whitford, M. and Ruhanen, L., 2016. Indigenous tourism research, past, and present: where to from here? *Journal of Sustainable Tourism*, 24(8–9), pp. 1080–1099. DOI: 10.1080/09669582.2016.1189925.

Wrisley, J., 2009. Tourism and the Decline of Red Rice. *The Atlantic*. [online] 14 May. Available at: <www.theatlantic.com/health/archive/2009/05/tourism-and-the-decline-of-red-rice/1213/> [Accessed 05 June 2019].

WTO, 1997. *Agenda 21 for the Travel and Tourism Industry. Towards Environmentally Sustainable Development. World Tourism Organization*. [pdf] Madrid: UNWTO. DOI: https://doi/book/10.18111/9789284403714.

Zeppel, H., 1998. Land and culture: sustainable tourism and indigenous peoples. In: C.M. Hall and A. Lew, (eds.), *Sustainable Tourism: A Geographical Perspective*. Harlow: Prentice Hall, pp. 60–74.

Zeppel, H., 2006. *Indigenous Ecotourism: Sustainable Development and Management*. Oxford: CABI. DOI: 10.1079/9781845931247.0000.

13
SEX TOURISM

13.1 Introduction

Sex tourism, where one of the contents of the journey is the exchange of sexual services from another individual, has been growing exponentially during recent years. While sex tourism, in one form or another, has been around for a long time, the phenomenon has received more attention during the past decades. Sex tourism has been denounced at the international level (WTO Statement on the Prevention of Organized Sex Tourism, 1995; Global Code of Ethics for Tourism, 1999; Framework Convention on Tourism Ethics, 2019), as well as at the national level in different countries. Despite the near-universal consensus in the tourism industry that sex tourism is not a desirable part of the sector, recent estimates (ECPAT International, 2016; Fernanda Felix de la Luz, 2018) show that globalisation, development of information communication technologies, increased possibilities of travel, and the expansion of the travel and tourism sector have led to a simultaneous increase in sex tourism as well as an increase in the commercial sexual exploitation of children in tourism.

In this chapter, the development of sex tourism as part of the tourism industry is explored. In particular, the focus is on human rights violations in the sex tourism industry. In Section 13.2, the origins and legal responses to the development of sex tourism are described. In addition, a brief discussion on the causes and effects of prostitution from an economic, social and political economy perspective forms part of Section 13.2. In Section 13.3, the exploitation of children in the commercial sex industry is analysed, while Section 13.4 focuses on human trafficking, modern slavery and forced sexual exploitation of adults in the tourism industry. Section 13.5 contains a discussion on possible corporate measures against commercial sexual exploitation in the tourism industry followed by Section 13.6, which includes some concluding remarks on the topic.

13.2 Sex Tourism: Origins, Legal Responses and Impact on the Economy

In 1995, the United Nations World Tourism Organization (UNWTO) General Assembly published the WTO Statement on the Prevention of Organized Sex Tourism. Sex tourism was in the statement defined as "trips organized from within the tourism sector, or from outside this sector but using its structure and networks, with the primary purpose of effecting a commercial sexual relationship by the tourist with residents at the destination" (WTO Statement on the Prevention of Organized Sex Tourism, 1995). The UNWTO statement has been criticised as too narrow, since it only includes tourists who primarily travel for sex. Many tourists do not travel for the primary purpose of effecting commercial sexual relationships at the tourism destination but are instead classified as situational sex tourists, buying sex when the opportunity arises.

Several tourism researchers have tried to provide a more multifaceted account of sex tourism. Ryan and Hall (2001, p. 10) have for example argued that to understand the nature of sex tourism an examination of the relationship between the body, sex and self-identity, as well as the liminal nature of holiday experiences, places and the tourist role is required. Ryan and Kinder argue that there are many similarities with tourism and prostitution; both offer an escape from daily life and the ability to fulfil a fantasy (1996). Oppermann (1999) has proposed a more holistic definition of sex tourism, looking at six parameters; monetary exchange, purpose of travel, length of time spent together, the relationship between the seeker and the provider of sexual services, the nature of the sexual encounter and who travels, the seeker or the provider of the services. The included parameters do not allow for a simple classification but provide a useful starting point. For example, is an encounter considered sex tourism if no monetary exchange takes place, but the seeker of sexual services provides for clothing or pays for hospital visits? Is it considered sex tourism if no sexual penetration takes place, but the seeker of sexual services travels for the experience of voyeurism, for example to visit topless bars? Oppermann (1999) notes that in many countries a large number of the prostitutes are of foreign origin or from other parts of the country, travelling to a destination to earn money, thus making the prostitute the business tourist, making the traditional definition of sex tourism inadequate. Therefore, in order to fully understand the relationship between sex and tourism, a multidimensional perspective is of importance.

The origins of sex tourism are often linked to war and the deployment of large number of troops to certain destinations. There is ample evidence of the linkages between the sex industry in close proximity to military bases and the development of commercial sex tourism on a larger scale (Hanochi, 1998; Weiss and Enrile, 2020). For example, in the 1960s, a growing number of rural Thai women started working as prostitutes, offering massage services and dancing. The growth of nightclubs, bars, massage parlors and strip clubs in Thailand was directly linked to the U.S. military service personnel spending on recreation and entertainment.

Around 11–16 percent of the total number of visitors to Thailand between 1966–7 were American servicemen stationed in Thailand or visiting Thailand on rest and recreation leaves from the Vietnam war, accounting for around 20 percent of total visitor expenditure (Ouyyanont, 2001, p. 164). When the American troops left the country in 1975, the commercial sex industry geared more towards local and international leisure tourist customers. By that time, the legacy left behind by the U.S. army bases had already changed the international travel image of Thailand (Brodeur, Lekfuangfu and Zylberberg, 2018). Similarly, the demand for commercial sexual services from the servicemen on American military bases in South Korea and the Philippines led to the creation of red-light districts and shanty towns providing sexual services in close proximity to the military bases (Tan et al., 1989; Dery, 1991; Lee, 2007; Weiss and Enrile, 2020).

Countries have adopted different legal strategies in response to sex tourism, sex work and prostitution. Many countries, such as Netherlands, Finland and Spain, have legalised prostitution. Often, sex work is still restricted in different ways. For example, Finland, Netherlands and Spain all distinguish between voluntary and involuntary sex work. Persons who force individuals to prostitute themselves or exploit sex workers are punished severely (Dutch Penal Code/Wetboek van Strafrecht, 1881, art. 273f; Spanish Penal Code/Código Penal, 1995, art. 187–188; Finnish Penal Code/Rikoslaki, 1889, Ch. 20, art. 8–9). In addition, in countries where sex work is legal, it is still often restricted in regulations covering health, sanitation and public order. In the Netherlands, individuals who voluntarily opt to work in the sex industry as entrepreneurs have to be registered with the Netherlands Chamber of Commerce (Kamer van Koophandel, KVK) as sex workers. In addition, municipalities can require sex workers to apply for a license. The Amsterdam Municipal Ordinance requires for example license holders to provide a safe hygienic working environment and ensure that the sex workers are healthy and independent as well as over the age of 21. Furthermore, window sex workers are only allowed in three areas in the city, the Red-Light District (De Wallen), Ruysdaelkade and Singel area. No new permits for window establishments are granted anymore (Amsterdam General Local Ordinance/Algemene Plaatselijke Verordening, 2008, art. 3.27–3.30).

In 2019, the mayor of the city of Amsterdam initiated a public consultation, with the object to open a debate on window prostitution in Amsterdam. According to the initial consultation, the historic city centre was in danger of becoming an area dominated by nuisance and one-sided commercial activities. The public space had become dominated by facilities connected to sex, drugs and drink. Furthermore, the large number of tourists frequenting the area had an adverse impact on sex workers, who were regarded as sightseeing attractions. The report set out four scenarios for the future on window prostitution in Amsterdam (City of Amsterdam, 2019). The two most likely options are to close the Red-Light District and move the prostitution to a room rental complex for prostitutes (a prostitution hotel) or to open an erotic centre with prostitution as well as other sexual services.

FIGURE 13.1 The Red-Light District, Amsterdam, November 2019.
Photo: Alyssa Jalali

In other countries, the selling or buying of commercial sexual services in any form is illegal. Buyers and sellers are punished with fines or jail time. In some countries, those committing the criminal offence of organising or forcing prostitution could in especially serious cases be sentenced to the death penalty (see for example Criminal Law of the People's Republic of China, 1979, art. 358). An alternative approach to the criminalisation of sex work is the Swedish model, which criminalises the buying of sex, but not the selling of sex. The purpose is to shift the responsibility from the victim to the perpetrator of the crime. The Swedish model has been hailed in recent years as an approach where the government signals the moral disapproval towards the practice, without blaming the victim. The model has been adopted in several other countries, such as Norway, Iceland, France, Northern Ireland, Ireland, Israel and Canada. Some countries, such as Norway, have taken additional steps in trying to diminish the demand for sexual services, by criminalising the buying of sexual services abroad. Norwegians who buy commercial sexual services while on vacation in another country can be prosecuted when they return to Norway, regardless of if prostitution is legal or not in the destination country (The Norwegian Penal Code/Straffeloven, 2005,

§5, §309, §316). The extraterritorial application of laws criminalising the purchase of sexual services is seen as an important deterrent, considering that many individuals purchase commercial sexual services while travelling outside their country of origin.

Despite the fact that commercial sexual services are illegal or restricted in different ways in most countries, they contribute substantially to economic activity. In recent years, a growing number of actors have argued that prostitution should be officially recognised as an economic activity. As of 2014, the European Union for example requires that member states incorporate estimates of sales from illegal drugs, prostitution services and the smuggling of alcohol and tobacco into national accounts and balance of payments statistics (Eurostat, 2018, ¶66–67). Exact numbers are difficult to verify, due to the fact that prostitution is often part of the shadow economy, but different studies have estimated that commercial sexual workers contribute to between 2 to 14 percent to the GDP of Indonesia, Thailand, Malaysia and the Philippines (Lim, 1998, p. 7; Chia 2016). The impact of including prostitution in the national accounts in the European Union seems to be smaller, with GDP increases of less than 0.5 percent in most countries (Adair and Nezhyvenko, 2016; ECB, 2019).

Some countries have in the past actively promoted sex as part of the tourism experience (Lee, 1991). At the global level, the message has however been a clear denunciation of sex tourism. The UNWTO has for example stated that it rejects all organised sex tourism activity as subversive to the fundamental goals of tourism. Organised sex tourism is seen as having negative health, social and cultural consequences for both sending and destination countries, especially when it exploits gender, age, social and economic inequalities in destination countries (WTO Statement on the Prevention of Organized Sex Tourism, 1995). Similarly, the Global Code of Ethics for Tourism (1999), adopted by the UNWTO General Assembly in 1999, denounces the exploitation of human beings in sex tourism. The statement from the code was recently included in the UNWTO's Framework Convention on Tourism Ethics (2019, art. 5(3)), creating duties and obligations on the states that ratify the convention to implement the ethics principles in domestic policy (see Box 13.1).

BOX 13.1 GLOBAL CODE OF ETHICS FOR TOURISM, ART 2 (3)/FRAMEWORK CONVENTION ON TOURISM ETHICS, ART. 5(3)

The exploitation of human beings in any form, particularly sexual, especially when applied to children, conflicts with the fundamental aims of tourism and is the negation of tourism; as such, in accordance with international law, it should be energetically combatted with the cooperation of all the States concerned and penalised without concession by the national legislation of both the countries visited and the countries of the perpetrators of these acts, even when they are carried abroad.

Source: (Global Code of Ethics for Tourism, 1999; 2019 World Tourism Organization, 2020).[1]

The exploration of discourse on sex tourism as to why prostitution cannot be controlled or eradicated in spite of regulations and penal codes is beyond this chapter. However, two distinct arguments will be briefly reviewed here (Hashimoto, personal communication, 2020); how social structures and constructs affect the development of the sex industry and how the political economy affects the development of the sex industry. For instance, Buddhism teaches self-negation, and abstinence from worldly wants; Confucius teaches filial piety, a child's obligation to its parents, and women's duty to family. These are just a few religious and spiritual teachings that are woven into the social fabric of many countries. In countries where sex tourism is well-known, often prostitution is illegal or does not even officially exist. To illustrate the point, the sex industry does not officially exist in countries such as Thailand and Cambodia: people working in nightclubs, topless bars or other establishments do not sell sex. What they do during their private time is not the state's concern (Montgomery, 2001).

Social structures promoting short-term marriages can also serve as a front for sexual exploitation. Many world religions hold the belief that sex should not be pursued outside marriage. Temporary marriages that do not come with a long-term commitment can be an alternative to dating in religiously conservative countries, but such marriages can also lead to sexual exploitation of vulnerable girls and women and provide an opportunity to exploitative men to take advantage of their partner (Badran and Turnbull, 2019). Sunnis (around 90 percent of Muslims) have generally rejected short-term marriages and the vast majority of Sunni legal scholars agree that the practice is forbidden. However, short-term marriages remain acceptable among Shia Muslims (around 10 percent of Muslims) and have experienced a recent revival in some communities in the Middle East, North Africa and Europe. Badran and Turnbull note that it is important to distinguish between temporary marriages carried out domestically and transnationally. Transnational, temporary marriages often facilitate sexual exploitation of vulnerable women and children, while domestic marriages are often based on a mutual understanding between the parties. For example, reports show that temporary transnational marriages have more recently started to attract foreign child sex offenders to India. Men, often from the Gulf States, come to India to marry younger girls, sexually exploit them and then return to their home country (ECPAT International, 2016).

In order to prevent suffering of the family, in certain countries where a large proportion of citizens are living below the poverty line, children are sometimes sold into servitude as bonded workers. It is considered an obedient child's duty to sacrifice themselves for the good of the family (Hashimoto, personal communication, 2020). Often families are unaware of where exactly their children are sold. In countries where a social class system or a caste system exists, children from the lowest caste are sometimes dedicated to religious establishments in culturally sanctioned practices involving sexual exploitation. For instance, the devadasi system in India is an ancient social support system, where lower caste girls are dedicated to local gods, and once initiated, they are compelled to partake in sexual activities with community members against their will (Hashimoto, personal communication, 2020). Although the practice is criminalised in several laws in India, it was estimated in 2013 that there were about 450,000 devadasis in the country (ILO, 2018a).

Social norms, particularly related to the discrimination of homosexual and transgender persons in society, also contribute to sex tourism. In Thailand, sex reassignment surgery is world renowned, yet "ladyboys"/"katoeys" – those who cross-dress, adopt female gender roles or are surgically transformed into female bodies – are, when compared to persons whose gender identity corresponds with their biological sex, more often victims of human rights violations (Hashimoto, personal communication, 2020). Although widely tolerated and visible in society, their job prospects are often limited to a few stereotypical jobs due to structural discrimination and hostile work environments (Suriyasarn, 2016). Many "katoeys" end up working in the entertainment and sex industry, due to a lack of prospects in other types of jobs. Similarly, in Latin America, homophobia is widely present, with families rejecting homosexual or transgender children, driving them to the streets where they are vulnerable to sexual exploitation by tourists (ECPAT International, 2016). Last, but not least, national acceptance towards sex and sexuality also plays an important role (Hashimoto, 2000). Tourists from countries where national attitudes towards sex and sexuality are more accepting or tolerating, tend to embrace the use of services provided by the sex industry. Additionally, the "money can buy anything" mantra of consumerism in more economically developed countries sees sexual performance as a commodity in the market.

A related but different discourse is focusing on the political economy of the sex market (Hashimoto, personal communication, 2020). Despite the denunciation of sex tourism by the UNWTO and the fact that many countries criminalise the provision of commercial sexual services, it is not considered a violation of human rights if an adult sex worker freely, without any coercion, decides to work in the sex industry, receives a fair wage, and the business is controlled similarly to other businesses in that society. The Human Rights Watch for example supports the full decriminalisation of consensual adult sex work and considers criminalisation as incompatible with the human rights of sex providers to personal autonomy and privacy (Human Rights Watch, 2019). However, when sex tourism in less economically developed countries caters to clients from more economically developed countries, the concerning issues of the political economy emerge (Chheang, 2008; Jeffreys, 2009; Brooks and Heaslip, 2019). Critics argue that in a typical situation where clients are male, and service providers are women and children, that situation reinforces male dominance and female subservience; or in the situation where clients are tourists from more economically advanced countries and service providers are from less economically advanced countries, it reinforces the North-South power imbalances (Hashimoto, personal communication, 2020). A concern is also that globalisation has led to increased levels of trafficking of women and children from less economically developed regions to more economically developed regions. For example, trafficking flows to Western Europe come mainly from Central and Eastern Europe, as well as Asia, Africa and South America. Imbalances of powers could also be used for the political purpose of subduing minority groups. Indigenous children in Australia, Maori children in New Zealand, Roma children in Europe, as well as Native Americans in Canada and the USA are all, due to their perceived low social status, preferred targets of sexual offenders. For example, in Canada, an estimated 14–60 percent of First Nations youth are involved in the sex trade. In some cities as many as 90 percent of sexually exploited children are of First Nations origin (Government of Canada, 2011; Beyond Borders, 2013; ECPAT International, 2016).

In the following sections, the focus is on commercial sex tourism, where the individuals involved in the provision of sexual services for payment are either underage or where the human rights of individuals are violated in other ways, for example because they are forced or coerced to work in the sex industry. These types of sex tourism are denounced universally as grave violations of the human rights of victims of forced sex work.

13.3 Children in commercial sexual exploitation

The ILO has estimated that on any given day in 2016, approximately 152 million children are in child labour globally. Out of those children, 73 million children were involved in hazardous work that affected their health, safety and moral development (ILO, 2017a). Most work is done in an agricultural setting within the family unit. However, many children are also involved in hazardous labour. In 2016, about 4 million children were in forced labour, with an estimated 1 million children who were victims of commercial sexual exploitation (ILO, 2017b). Most children exploited in the global sex tourism industry are estimated to be in the 15–17 age range (ILO, 2002, p. 26). Child victims in the sex industry come from many different backgrounds (U.S. Department of Justice, 2007; ECPAT International, 2016). Children from dysfunctional families suffering from absent, negligent or abusive parenting, previous victims of sexual abuse, children who are left behind when parents find work away from the home region/country or children who are sent away to work in another region/country, children with a disability, children of sex workers as well as working children, particularly in the travel and tourism industry, are especially vulnerable to sexual exploitation. ECPAT International (2016) notes that "children from minority groups, boys and young children are far more vulnerable than previously understood, along with girls and children living in poverty" (p. 15). Cultural violence, for example in the form of "bacha bazi", where poor families sell their sons to wealthy families for entertainment and sexual purposes, is socially and culturally tolerated in some communities in Afghanistan and parts of Pakistan (Borile, 2019). The children represent a symbol of prosperity and are displayed during private parties. Another often cited problematic belief is that sex with a virgin or a young child has powers of rejuvenation, even the power to heal terminal illness (ECPAT International, 2016).

Sexual abuse and exploitation of children is considered one of the most heinous crimes today. The Stockholm Declaration in 1996 (UNICEF, 1999), and the second and third World Congress Against Sexual Exploitation of Children and Adolescents – taking place in Yokohama, Japan in 2001 and Rio de Janeiro, Brazil in 2008, respectively – identified the state's responsibility in the protection of children (Hashimoto, personal communication 2020). According to article 34 of the United Nations Convention on the Rights of the Child (CRC) (1989) signatory states shall take all appropriate measures to prevent "the exploitative use of children in prostitution or other unlawful sexual practices". In 2000, an optional protocol to the CRC was adopted, in order to better achieve the protection of children from sexual violence (CRC-OP). The CRC-OP has so far been ratified by 176 state parties. State parties who ratify the CRC-OP undertake to prohibit the sale of children, child prostitution and child pornography. Child prostitution is defined as the use of a child in sexual activities for remuneration or any other form of consideration (art. 2) (see Box 13.2).

BOX 13.2 OPTIONAL PROTOCOL TO THE CONVENTION ON THE RIGHTS OF THE CHILD ON THE SALE OF CHILDREN, CHILD PROSTITUTION AND CHILD PORNOGRAPHY

Article 3

1. Each State Party shall ensure that, as a minimum, the following acts and activities are fully covered under its criminal or penal law, whether such offences are committed domestically or transnationally or on an individual or organised basis:
   (a) In the context of sale of children as defined in article 2:
      (i) Offering, delivering or accepting, by whatever means, a child for the purpose of:
         a. Sexual exploitation of the child;
         b. Transfer of organs of the child for profit;
         c. Engagement of the child in forced labour;
      ...
   (b) Offering, obtaining, procuring or providing a child for child prostitution...
   (c) Producing, distributing, disseminating, importing, exporting, offering, selling or possessing for the above purposes child pornography...
2. Subject to the provisions of the national law of a State Party, the same shall apply to an attempt to commit any of the said acts and to complicity or participation in any of the said acts.

> 3. Each State Party shall make such offences punishable by appropriate penalties that take into account their grave nature.
> 4. Subject to the provisions of its national law, each State party shall take measures, where appropriate, to establish the liability of legal persons for offences established in paragraph 1 of the present article. Subject to the legal principles of the State Party, such liability of legal persons may be criminal, civil or administrative...
>
> Source: (Optional Protocol to the Convention on the Rights of the Child on the sale of children, child prostitution and child pornography, 2000).

The Worst Forms of Child Labor Convention (1999, art. 2) as well as the CRC (1989, art. 1) identify anyone younger than the age of 18 as a child; however, international human rights law does not set a minimum age of consent for sexual relations, but refers to national legislation on age of consent. According to the CRC (1989, art. 34) states undertake to protect children from "inducement of coercion of a child to engage in any unlawful sexual activity". The Council of Europe Convention on the Protection of Children against Sexual Exploitation and Sexual Abuse (2007, art. 18) makes it a criminal act to engage "in sexual activities with a child who, according to relevant provisions of national law, has not reached the legal age for sexual activities". National legislation on age of consent and age of marriage varies from one country to another. The low age of consent in some countries leaves many children vulnerable to sexual exploitation. The age of consent is for example 12 in the Philippines (Revised Penal Code, §335(3), 1930) and Uruguay (Penal Code of Uruguay/Código Penal No. 9155, art. 272, 1933), 13 in Argentina and Costa Rica and 14 in most other Latin American countries (UNICEF, 2016, p. 27).

> ECPAT notes that "the age of criminal responsibility and age of sexual consent work together to increase the likelihood that child victims in their teens will be treated as willing sex workers, undocumented migrants or juvenile delinquents and arrested rather than being treated as sexually exploited and trafficked children in need of help."
> *(ECPAT International, 2016, p. 67)*

In addition to the low age of sexual consent in some countries, the loopholes related to the age of marriage are also problematic from a child protection perspective. Although many countries as a general rule allow persons to marry when they attain the age of 18, there are several loopholes in legislation. For example, children are often allowed to marry with the consent of parents at an earlier age than 18 years of age. UNICEF (2016, p. 16) estimates that around 30 percent of girls in Cuba, Nicaragua and the Dominican Republic and around 20–25 percent of girls in Brazil, Mexico, Guatemala, Honduras, Belize, El Salvador and Bolivia were married before they turned 18. Around 5–10 percent of the girls were married before the age of 15. Allowing for several loopholes in age of consent and age of marriage legislation at the national level makes the enforcement of child protection laws difficult.

One of the requirements of the CRC-OP is that signatories adopt territorially applicable legislation covering sex crimes committed within the territorial boundaries of a country. However, part of the reason why sex tourists flock to certain destinations in greater numbers compared to other destinations, is the lax enforcement of existing legislation covering sex crimes as well as the ready availability of numerous vulnerable children, why territorially applicable legislation can only form part of the solution. When laws at home illegalise sex with children, pedophiles and other child sex tourists travel to less economically developed countries, where regulations and/or enforcement measures for protecting children are almost non-existent.

> [t]he demand for CST [child sex tourism] comes mainly from wealthy industrialised countries, such as the Western European countries, North America, Japan and Australia, although many CST destinations also experience tourist inflows from within the country as well as from neighbouring countries. Destination countries are often poverty ridden with a non-existent or developing tourism industry. The geographical proximity to the destination country is of importance in CST travel patterns. Western European child sex tourists travel in large numbers to Eastern Europe and Africa, Australian child sex tourists travel to South-East Asia, while child sex tourists from North America are reported to travel to Central and South America in increasing numbers. In addition, established CST destinations, such as the Philippines, Cambodia and Vietnam, appeal to child sex tourists from all over the world.
>
> (Härkönen, 2015)

ECPAT International notes in its 2016 global study on commercial sexual exploitation of children in tourism that even if there are some established travel patterns, the exploitation has in recent years become far more complex.

> It is "involving not only tourists but business travellers, migrant/transient workers and ´volun-tourists´ intent on exploiting children, as well as large numbers of domestic travellers … [O]ffenders can come from any background and that they do not all fit the stereotypical profile: a white, Western, wealthy, middle-aged male paedophile. Some may be paedophiles, but most are not. Offenders may be foreign or domestic, young or old. Some are women, and a few may be other children…the majority are ´situational´ offenders–who may have never dreamed of sexually exploiting a child until

given the opportunity to do so–rather than preferential offenders. The one thing both types of offenders have in common is ever-greater opportunities to exploit children, especially in environments where corruption is rife and impunity is the rule."

(ECPAT International, 2016, p.15)

It is often overlooked that a large number of child sex tourists are domestic travellers or travel in the region. For example, law enforcement authorities in the Philippines believe that foreign men are responsible for only 10–15% of sex crimes against children. Similarly, in Cambodia, it is estimated that Cambodian nationals commit 75% of all cases of sexual exploitation of children (ECPAT International, 2011; 2016; 2018). Territorially applicable legislation and effective enforcement of such legislation at the place of the crime is therefore a necessity, if the practice is to be quelled.

In addition to territorially applicable legislation, the CRC-OP allows member states to introduce extraterritorial legislation covering child sex tourism crimes. Extraterritorial legislation covers criminalised acts that have been performed outside the territorial boundaries of the home country of the perpetrator, for example during a tourism trip. According to art. 4, extraterritorial jurisdiction may be established if the perpetrator is a national or habitual resident of the state, or if the victim is a national of the state in question. Extraterritorial jurisdiction shall be established, "when the offender is present in its territory and it does not extradite him or her to another State Party on the ground that the offence has been committed by one its nationals".

Although there is no absolute requirement according to CRC-OP that state parties introduce legislation covering sex crimes committed outside the territorial boundaries of the state in question (except for the special circumstances with extradition), many countries have introduced such legislation in order to prosecute persons who travel to another country and commit sex crimes at the destination. Furthermore, according to art. 25 in the Council of Europe Convention on the Protection of Children against Sexual Exploitation and Sexual Abuse (2007), it is mandatory for state parties to the convention to establish jurisdiction over child sex offences both when the offence is committed on its territory and when the offence is committed by a person who is a national or has its habitual residence in the country. The convention thus opens up for the prosecution of tourism sex offenders who travel to other countries where the risk of detection is lower and the enforcement of laws against commercial sexual encounters with children is lax. The convention had in May 2020 entered into force in 45 European countries.

In *R. v. Klassen*, a 59-year old Canadian man (K.K.) was sentenced to 11 years in prison under the Canadian child sex tourism law (Criminal Code of Canada, section 4.11, 271). K.K. was charged with having sex with a number of teenage and prepubescent girls as well as with the making, importation and possession of child pornography with children as young as three to five years to older teens. The crimes had taken place in Cambodia and Colombia. K.K.'s conduct was discovered when a customs official investigated a package K.K. had sent to himself from the Philippines to Canada. The package contained 65 DVDs with different types of pornography. A further search of K.K.'s home and a storage facility disclosed filmed evidence of numerous sex acts between K.K. and teenage and prepubescent girls. K.K.'s defence lawyer argued that he was merely a customer, who participated in the sex acts with willing participants. K.K. stated that he was attracted to extremely thin women, but that he found it impossible to find so thin women over the age of 18 in Canada. He further stated that he went "overboard" on his last trip buying pornography as it was so cheap and "all over the place." "It's just millions and millions, it was like a, like a megastore." K.K. also stated that he was not travelling for the purpose of child sex tourism, "sometimes I have some extra time, it's not like the reason I go some place. I'm not a sex tourist." It was during the trial established that each of the girls on the DVDs were under 14 years of age. Ten of the girls in the DVDs were estimated to be under the age of 11, with three of the girls estimated to be under the age of 9. All of the sexual encounters had been consensual according to K.K. (R. v. Klassen, 2008 BCSC 1762; R. v. Klassen, 2012 BCCA 405).

The Klassen case shows that many tourists who travel to other countries and engage in commercial sexual encounters with children do not self-identify as sex tourists or organise their travel solely with the purpose of engaging in commercial sexual encounters with children. Also, many of the offenders have families and are functional members of the society in every other respect. For example, K.K. was a father of three and had a successful business as an art dealer. K.K. stated in the police interviews that he kept all the child pornography away from his family in his storage facility and never bothered anyone. There is often a clear power discrepancy between the victims of child sex tourism and the perpetrator of the crime, something acknowledged by K.K. during the investigation. According to K.K.: "[y]oung are less complicated because they haven't had it so good [sic!] they don't demand so much. Canadian women want everything." Also, K.K. pointed out that he never engaged in child sex encounters in Canada. "I never hurt anybody here" (R. v. Klassen, 2012 BCCA 405). Destination countries of child sex tourism often struggle with poverty, many destitute children, inefficient judicial systems with few resources to investigate child sex tourism crimes and corrupt officials. As witnessed by the Klassen case, many child sex tourists take advantage of the wealth and power discrepancy between tourists and victims as well as the lax enforcement of existing laws in destination countries. In order to stem the flow of child sex tourists from relatively wealthy countries to economically less developed countries, extraterritorially applicable legislation in sender countries functions as an important deterrent.

13.4 Human trafficking, modern slavery and forced sexual exploitation

Throughout the history, humans have been sold and moved between different countries and continents, in the pursuit of monetary objectives. One of the better-known accounts of humans treated as commodities is the slave trade taking place between Europe, Africa and the United States in the 17th and 18th centuries. Slavery as a state-supported practice has now been abolished. However, there are still a large number of humans who are today treated as commodities and forced into prostitution and other sexual exploitation. The International Labour Organization (ILO) estimated that in 2016 more than 40 million people were victims of modern slavery, defined as individuals "who were being forced to work against their will under threat or who were living in a forced marriage that they had not agreed to". Close to 5 million adults and children out of the victims of modern slavery were involved in forced sexual exploitation (ILO, 2017b, p. 18).

Women and girls are disproportionately represented in modern slavery, accounting for more than 70 percent of the victims. When it comes to forced sexual exploitation, the gender disparity is even more startling, with 99.4 percent of the victims being female (ILO, 2017b, p. 23). A substantial number of the victims of trafficking are young. Child victims account for more than 30% of the total number of trafficking victims detected at the same time as sexual exploitation is the most common form of exploitation among detected trafficking victims. Children involved in the child sex tourism industry are thus often both victims of trafficking as well as victims of commercial sexual exploitation (Capaldi, 2014; UNODC, 2014; Härkönen, 2015).

Modern slavery as a concept is not defined in international conventions denouncing the practice. Instead, the related concept of trafficking in persons is used at the international level. Trafficking in persons (or the interchangeable term human trafficking) has been regulated in the Protocol to Prevent, Suppress and Punish Trafficking in Persons, Especially Women and Children, supplementing the United Nations Convention against Transnational Organized Crime (2000). Trafficking in persons is in the protocol defined as

> the recruitment, transportation, harbouring or receipt of persons, by means of the threat or use of force or other forms of coercion, of abduction, of fraud, of deception, of the abuse of power or of a position of vulnerability or of the giving or receiving of payments or benefits to achieve the consent of a person having control of another person, for the purpose of exploitation.

Exploitation includes the exploitation of the prostitution of others as well as other forms of sexual exploitation (art. 3). State parties to the protocol are required to criminalise trafficking as well as to provide assistance to and protection of victims of trafficking (arts. 5–6). The protocol also regulates the repatriation of victims to their home countries as well as preventive measures the states are required to establish in order to prevent and combat trafficking in persons. The aim of the protocol is to provide a universal instrument which addresses all aspects of trafficking in persons.

The 2018 United Nations Office on Drugs and Crime (UNODC) report shows that most trafficking victims are detected within their own national borders. The crime of human trafficking thus does not always involve the crossing of borders, but often involves victims who are exploited within their countries of origin. Trafficking for sexual exploitation is the most detected form of human trafficking, with victims who are either physically abused or trapped because the perpetrators abuse their vulnerability (UNODC, 2018, p. 13). The ILO's estimate in 2018 shows that US$99 billion per year were illegally generated worldwide; 67% of the profits are believed to be from forced labour. Asia and the Pacific region are accountable for 16.5 million persons in forced labour; this figure is incomparable to the second highest number of 3.4 million persons in the Africa region (ILO, 2018b). Asia and the Pacific coincide with well-known child sex tourism destinations (Hashimoto, personal communication, 2020). With such a large economic contribution, the trafficking of humans for forced labour seems to have no end. In many cases, tourism establishments are either unwittingly or knowingly aiding or abetting offenders either by providing accommodation in a hotel used to sell trafficking victims, or providing transportation, needed to move trafficking victims between different destinations.

13.5 Corporate measures to eliminate forced and underage sex tourism

In addition to criminal liability targeting the offenders of child sex tourism crimes, in recent years the responsibility of the tourism industry has become a topical issue. In countries where the legal framework is strong, corporate liability legislation could function both as a stick and as a carrot for tourism operators who would otherwise be tempted by the economic rewards in child sex tourism, or deterred by the economic costs in making sure that employees in destination countries do not acquiesce in such tourism (Härkönen, 2015). The CRC-OP marked a shift in international human rights regulation, with the introduction of corporate liability for child sex tourism crimes. According to article 3 (4), states shall, where appropriate, establish corporate liability for offences according to article 3(1). Such liability may be criminal, civil or administrative, subject to the legal principles of the state party. State parties do not have any obligation to enact corporate liability provisions according to CRC-OP if such an implementation would be contrary to national law. Similar, but stricter, requirements on states to adopt corporate liability legislation are included in the Council of Europe Convention (see Box 13.3).

BOX 13.3 COUNCIL OF EUROPE CONVENTION ON THE PROTECTION OF CHILDREN AGAINST SEXUAL EXPLOITATION AND SEXUAL ABUSE

Article 26 – Corporate liability

1. Each party shall take the necessary legislative or other measure to ensure that a legal person can be held liable for an offence established in accordance with this Convention, committed for its benefit by a natural person, acting either individually or as part of an organ of the legal person, who has a leading position within the legal person, based on:
   a) a power of representation of the legal person;
   b) and authority to take decisions on behalf of the legal person;
   c) an authority to exercise control within the legal person.
2. Apart from the cases already provided for in paragraph 1, each Party shall take the necessary legislative and other measures to ensure that a legal person can be held liable where the lack of supervision or control by a natural person referred to in paragraph 1 has made possible the commission of an offence established in accordance with this Convention for the benefit of that legal person by a natural person acting under its authority.
3. Subject to the legal principle of the Party, the liability of a legal person may be criminal, civil or administrative.
4. Such liability shall be without prejudice to the criminal liability of the natural persons who have committed the offence.

Source: (Council of Europe Convention on the Protection of Children against Sexual Exploitation and Sexual Abuse, 2007).

Härkönen (2015) gives four examples on how the legal framework covering corporations can be improved in an effort to suppress sexual exploitation of children. First, legislation covering organisational failures in sender countries is necessary. With the ever more complicated organisational structures of legal persons, it is important that legislation not only covers individual acts by employees or agents in the enterprise, but also covers organisational failures, where the commercial sexual exploitation of children is made possible by the acts of many persons in the organisation. Second, sender countries should introduce negligence-based corporate liability provisions instead of strict liability-based provisions. This would give an incentive to corporations to educate and monitor their employees and agents. Third, corporate liability legislation should cover both the active organisation as well as the passive facilitation of commercial sexual exploitation of children. Corporations organising commercial sexual exploitation of children are unlikely to be deterred by corporate liability legislation. However, reputable companies in the tourism and travel sector are likely to adapt their behaviour to liability provisions prohibiting the facilitation of child-sex crimes. Lastly, enforcement efforts targeting non-compliant corporations in sender countries should be increased. Currently, enforcement of corporate liability regulation focused on commercial sexual exploitation of children is non-existent.

In addition to intergovernmental regulation, where state parties undertake to adopt national laws combating child sex tourism and human trafficking, both non-governmental organisations and the tourism industry have been active in trying to stem the flow of sex tourists. One of the most influential non-governmental actors combating child sex tourism is ECPAT International, a global network of organisations, present in over 100 countries. In 1998, ECPAT Sweden, the Swedish tourism industry and the UNWTO together developed a Code of Conduct for the Protection of Children from Sexual Exploitation in Travel and Tourism (The Code, 2020). Tourism operators adhering to The Code commit to six essential steps to protect children from sexual exploitation (see Box 13.4).

BOX 13.4 THE CODE OF CONDUCT FOR THE PROTECTION OF CHILDREN FROM SEXUAL EXPLOITATION IN TRAVEL AND TOURISM

1) *Establish a policy and procedures* against the sexual exploitation of children.
2) *Train employees* in children's rights, the prevention of sexual exploitation and how to report suspected cases.
3) *Include a clause in contracts* throughout the value chain stating a common repudiation and zero tolerance policy of sexual exploitation of children.
4) *Provide information to travellers* on children's rights, the prevention of sexual exploitation of children and how to report suspected cases.
5) *Support, collaborate & engage stakeholders* in the prevention of sexual exploitation of children.
6) *Report annually* on implementation of the six criteria.

Source: (The Code, 2020).[2]

The Code has been adopted by more than 300 providers of tourism and travel services, including major brands, such as Accor Hotels, Wyndham Hotels & Resorts and Marriott International (Accor Hotels, 2015, p. 23; Wyndham Hotels & Resorts, 2018; Marriott International Inc., 2019). The Code is an important self-regulatory initiative, in that it involves stakeholders in the tourism industry more directly in the efforts to suppress child sex tourism.

Härkönen (2015) has noted that "there is no independent agency that is exclusively dedicated to monitoring that there is no sexual exploitation of children at travel destinations; a tourism operator thus needs to monitor employees and agents at destinations internally. Such control measures are made more difficult by the fact that there is often a high level of acceptance of commercial sexual exploitation of children among the tourism industry in destination countries for CST (Sakulpitakphon, 2012) … In some Kenyan coastal areas, more than 75% of respondents, the majority of them employed by the tourism industry, thought that it was acceptable for teenage girls to have sex for money (Jones, 2006)."

Employees who are trained in how to prevent and report child sex tourism can function as frontline defenders of children's rights to live free from sexual exploitation. However, a general disadvantage with self-regulatory initiatives, such as The Code, is the lack of enforcement. It is not difficult to insert clauses in contracts throughout the value chain, as required by The Code, but much harder to monitor who is complying with the requirements (UNICEF, 2012; Sakulpitakphon, 2012).

13.6 Conclusion

The commercial sexual exploitation of another human forms one of the gravest violations of human rights. It is denounced in several international human rights conventions as well as by the UNWTO in its Global Code of Ethics for Tourism and Framework Convention on Tourism Ethics. It is also covered at the national level by criminal law in most countries. Yet, the commercial sexual exploitation of humans, in the form of commercial sexual exploitation of children, trafficking for sexual purposes and forced labour in the sex industry continues. The economic rewards for organisers and facilitators of the crimes are immense. In countries where corruption of law enforcement and politicians is rampant, owners of sex businesses can bribe law enforcement officers and be protected from any repercussions, and corrupt politicians can endorse seedy businesses as legitimate, profiting from exploitation. Victims of exploitation come from various backgrounds. They are escaping from poverty, insecurity, physical and sexual abuse or being deceived as to the kind of work, which is expected from the victims. However, most of them have one thing in common – they are vulnerable, due to social marginalisation, poverty or unstable family relations.

In addition to focusing on decreasing the supply of sex tourism, by introducing social support systems and improved life possibilities for victims and potential future victims of sexual exploitation, it is important to focus on the demand for sex tourism. For example, most child sex tourists are situational offenders, which means that they interact with children when given the possibility, but do not actively seek out children exploited in the commercial sex industry. A multifaceted approach, with education and prevention efforts, combined with introduction of international and national legal measures as well as self-regulatory initiatives can deter such tourists from becoming situational offenders.

Sexual exploitation through tourism is a combination of multiple human rights violations and human security violations. Due to forced labour in the sex industry, sex workers' dignity as a human being, their rights to work, decent wages, and work conditions, rights to a healthy and safe work environment – and in the case of child sex tourism, protection of a child and childhood – are not respected, implemented or enforced. Coerced sex work could traumatise the enslaved victims and could be a matter of life and death – e.g., victims may die from HIV/AIDS or violently at the hands of brothel owners or clients, or they may die from suicide. Such violations of human rights and human security are coming from a violation and neglect of social, cultural and economic rights of individuals (Hashimoto, personal communication, 2020). In many countries, there is no real political will to abolish commercial sexual exploitation of vulnerable persons. Cultural, social and collective beliefs are changing slowly as globalisation spreads different philosophies and ethical codes – but the change is very slow. Moreover, shame, guilt or remorse over exploitation of other human beings through forced sexual services does not seem to be strong enough to cause any social change (Hashimoto, personal communication, 2020).

The legal framework forms an important part in preventing the atrocities of human trafficking and child sex tourism. Most destination countries already have strict laws on child sex tourism and human trafficking, covering the facilitation of child sex crimes and trafficking crimes. However, the enforcement of such laws is often lax. It is therefore important to adopt laws covering perpetrators and corporations, who facilitate the exploitation of victims, in their country of origin. In addition to legal rules, self-regulatory initiatives within the tourism sector are necessary, if abusive forms of sex tourism are to be curtailed. Even though international human rights law provides for an important institutional framework, it is obvious that international human rights law is not alone enough. In order to extinguish commercial sexual exploitation in travel and tourism a multifaceted approach is needed. International human rights legislation has to be supported by a multitude of actors in the international community. In particular, tourism and travel enterprises have to be involved in the implementation and enforcement of laws protecting vulnerable persons at the national level. As the United Nations, including agencies like the UNWTO, denounce the continuation of sex tourism for being antithetical to the Sustainable Development Goals, immediate action to fight against commercial sexual exploitation through more effective education, stronger law enforcement and penal codes, the implementation of a consortium of responsible businesses, and interventions by domestic and international courts will be required. It is important to understand that the tourism industry is on the front lines in the fight to end human trafficking for sexual purposes as well as child sex tourism. Stakeholders from the industry have a unique position to educate, prevent and stop the abuse of victims.

Permissions

1 Box 13.1 is reprinted from World Tourism Organization (2020), *Framework Convention on Tourism Ethics*, UNWTO, Madrid, p. 13, DOI: https://doi.org/10.18111/9789284421671 ©UNWTO 92844/15/20. Reprinted with the permission of the World Tourism Organization, ©UNWTO 92844/15/20.

2 Box 13.4 is reprinted from The Code of conduct for the protection of children from sexual exploitation in travel and tourism. 1998, by The Code, ©2020, The Code. Available at: www.thecode.org/about/. Reprinted with the permission of The Code.

References

Accor Hotels, 2015. *Ethics and corporate social responsibility charter.* [online]. Available at: <https://group.accor.com/en/commitment> [Accessed 6 May 2020].

Adair, P. and Nezhyvenko, O., 2017. Sex work vs. sexual exploitation: Assessing guesstimates for prostitution in the European Union, *Proceedings of the 6th OECD Economics & Finance Conference, OECD.* Paris, France. 6–9 September, Paris: OECD.

Amsterdam General Local Ordinance/Algemene Plaatselijke Verordening 2008 (Neth.).

Badran, Z.S. and Turnbull, B., 2019. Contemporary Temporary Marriage: A Blog-analysis of First-hand Experiences. *Journal of International Women's Studies*, 20(2), pp. 241–256.

Beyond Borders, 2013. *Fact Sheet Commercial Sexual Exploitation of Children (CSEC).* [online] June. Available at: <www.beyondborders.org/wp-content/uploads/CSEC-Fact-Sheet-Revision.pdf> [Accessed 3 July 2020].

Borile, S., 2019. Bacha Bazi: Cultural Norms and Violence Against Poor Children in Afghanistan. *International Review of Sociology* 29(3), pp. 498–507.

Brodeur, A., Lekfuangfu, W. N. and Zylberberg, Y., 2018. War, migration and the origins of the Thai sex industry. *Journal of the European Economic Association*, 16(5), pp. 1540–1576.

Brooks A. and Heaslip, V., 2019. Sex trafficking and sex tourism in a globalised world. *Tourism Review* 74(5), pp. 1104–1115.

Capaldi, M., 2014. Unfinished business: Ending child prostitution, child pornography and child trafficking for sexual purposes. Bangkok: ECPAT International.

Chheang, V., 2008. The political economy of tourism in Cambodia. *Asia Pacific Journal of Tourism Research*, 13(3), pp. 281–297.

Chia, J., 2016. Rethinking Thai Sex Work: The Mistress Culture. *Harvard International Review*, 37(4), pp. 9–10.

City of Amsterdam, 2019. *Letter to the Council from Femke Halsema, "Scenarios for window prostitution in the city centre".* [online] 3 July. Available at: <www.amsterdam.nl/en/news/window-prostitution-debate/> [Accessed 6 May 2020].

Convention on the Rights of the Child, Nov. 20, 1989, 1577 U.N.T.S. 3.

Council of Europe Convention on the protection of children against sexual exploitation and sexual abuse, 2007. CETS No. 201. (Oct. 25, 2007).

Criminal Code of Canada (1985) (Can.).

Criminal Law of the People's Republic of China (1979) (China).

Dery, L. C., 1991. Prostitution in Colonial Manila. *Philippine Studies: Historic and Ethnographic Viewpoints*, 39 (4), pp. 475–489.

Dutch Penal Code/Wetboek van Strafrecht (1881) (Neth.).

ECB, 2019. Estimation of Prostitution Services in Europe in the Context of the External Accounts. *IMF Informal Economy Reports.* [online]. Available at: <www.imf.org/en/Data/Statistics/informal-economy-data/Reports> [Accessed 6 May 2020].

ECPAT International, 2011. *Global Monitoring status of action against commercial sexual exploitation of children–Philippines.* Bangkok: ECPAT International.

ECPAT International, 2016. *Offenders on the Move, Global Study on Sexual Exploitation of Children in Travel and Tourism.* Bangkok: ECPAT International.

ECPAT International, 2018. *Cambodia. Country Overview. A report on the scale, scope and context of the sexual exploitation of children.* Bangkok: ECPAT International.

Eurostat, 2018. *Handbook on the compilation of statistics on illegal economic activities in national accounts and balance of payments.* Luxembourg: Publications Office of the European Union.

Fernanda Felix de la Luz, M., 2018. Child sex tourism and exploitation are on the rise. Companies can help fight it. *World Economic Forum on Latin America.* [online]. Available at: <www.weforum.org/agenda/2018/03/changing-corporate-culture-can-help-fight-child-sex-tourism-heres-how/> [Accessed 30 June 2020].

Finnish Penal Code/Rikoslaki (1889) (Fin.).

Framework Convention on Tourism Ethics, Sep. 9–13, 2019, UNWTO 110th session, resolution 707(XXII).

Global Code of Ethics for Tourism. WTO General Assembly Res. 406 (XIII), U.N. Doc. A/RES/406(XIII) (Sep. 27-Oct. 1, 1999).

Government of Canada, 2011. *The Sexual Exploitation of Children in Canada: the Need for National Action.* s.l.: Government of Canada.

Hanochi, S., 1998. A Historical Perspective on the Japanese Sex Trade. *Refuge: Canada's Journal on Refugees* 17(5), pp. 19–23.

Härkönen E., 2015. Corporate liability and international child sex tourism – with special reference to the regulation in the Nordic countries. *Scandinavian Journal of Hospitality and Tourism,* 16(3), pp. 315–332.

Hashimoto, A., 2000. Young Japanese female tourists: An in-depth understanding of a market segment. *Current Issues in Tourism,* [e-Journal] 3(1), pp. 35–50. DOI: https://doi.org/10.1080/13683500008667865.

Human Rights Watch, 2019. *Why Sex Work Should Be Decriminalized.* [online] 7 August. Available at: <www.hrw.org/news/2019/08/07/why-sex-work-should-be-decriminalized>. [Accessed 6 May 2020].

Jeffreys, S., 2009. *The Industrial Vagina: The Political Economy of the Global Sex Trade.* London: Routledge

ILO, 2002. *Every Child Counts-New Global Estimates on Child Labour.* Geneva: ILO.

ILO, 2017a. *Global Estimates of Child Labour, Results and Trends 2012–2016.* Geneva: International Labour Organization.

ILO, 2017b. *Global Estimates of Modern Slavery, Forced Labour and Forced Marriage.* Geneva: International Labour Organization

ILO, 2018a. *Observation (CEACR)-adopted 2018, published 108th ILC session (2019). Forced Labour Convention, 1930 (No. 29)-India* (2018).

ILO, 2018b. *Ending forced labour by 2030: A review of policies and programmes.* Geneva: International Labour Organization.

Jones, S., 2006. *The extent and effect of sex tourism and sexual exploitation of children on the Kenyan coast.* S.l.: UNICEF & Government of Kenya.

Lee, N., 2007. The Construction of Military Prostitution in South Korea during the U.S. Military Rule, 1945–1948. *Feminist Studies,* 33(3), pp.453–481.

Lee, W., 1991. Prostitution and tourism in South-East Asia. In: N. Redclift and T. Sinclair, (eds.), *Working Women, International Perspectives on Labour and Gender Ideology.* London: Routledge, pp. 79–104.

Lim, L. L., ed., 1998. *The Sex Sector: The Economic and Social Bases of Prostitution in Southeast Asia.* Geneva: International Labour Organization.

Marriott International Inc., 2019. *Annual Report 2019, Implementation of The Code's Six Criteria.* [online]. Available at: <http://thecode.force.com/apex/publicPdf?id=0019000001zXJMmAAO&year=2019> [Accessed 6 May 2020].

Montgomery, H., 2001. Child Sex Tourism in Thailand. In: D. Harrison, (ed.), *Tourism and the Less Developed World: Issues and Case Studies*. Wallingford, Oxon: CAB International. pp, 191–202.
Norwegian Penal Code/Straffeloven (2005), (Norw.).
Oppermann, M., 1999. Sex tourism. *Annals of Tourism Research*, 26(2), pp. 251–266.
Optional Protocol to the Convention on the Rights of the Child on the sale of children, child prostitution and child pornography, May 25, 2000, 2171 U.N.T.S. 227.
Ouyyanont, P., 2001. The Vietnam War and Tourism in Bangkok's Development, 1960–70. *Southeast Asian Studies* 39(2), pp. 157–187.
Penal Code of Uruguay/Código Penal No. 9155, 1933 (Uru.).
Protocol to prevent, suppress and punish trafficking in persons, especially women and children, supplementing the United Nations convention against transnational organized crime, Nov. 15, 2000, 2237 U.N.T.S. 319.
Revised Penal Code, Act. No 3815, 1930 (Phil.).
R. v. Klassen, 2008 BCSC 1762 (Can.).
R. v. Klassen, 2012 BCCA 405 (Can.).
Ryan, C. and Hall, C. M., 2001. *Sex Tourism: Marginal People and Liminalities*. London: Routledge.
Ryan, C. and Kinder, R., 1996. Sex, Tourism and Sex Tourism: fulfilling similar needs? *Tourism Management*, (17)7, pp. 507–518.
Sakulpitakphon, P., 2012. An evaluation of the code of conduct for the protection of children from sexual exploitation in travel and tourism. *ECPAT International Journal* (4), pp. 21–27.
Spanish Penal Code/Código Penal (1995) (Spain).
Suriyasarn, B., 2016. Discrimination and Marginalization of LGBT Workers in Thailand, In: T. Köllen, (ed.), *Sexual Orientation and Transgender Issues in Organizations*, Switzerland: Springer International Publishing, pp. 197–215.
Tan M., De Leon, A., Stoltzfus, B. and O'Donnell, C., 1989. AIDS as a Political Issue: Working with the Sexually Prostituted in the Philippines. *Community Development Journal*, 24(3), pp. 186–193.
The Code, 2020. *Code of conduct for the protection of children from sexual exploitation in travel and tourism. 1998.* [online]. Available at: <www.thecode.org/about> [Accessed 6 May 2020].
Totman, R., 2011. *The Third Sex: Kathoey: Thailand's Ladyboys*. London: Souvenir Press Ltd.
UNICEF, 1999. *Declaration and Agenda for Action 1st World Congress against Commercial Sexual Exploitation of Children Stockholm, Sweden, 27–31 August*. Stockholm: UNICEF.
UNICEF, 2012. *Assessing the code of conduct for the protection of children from sexual exploitation in travel and tourism: Innocenti Discussion Papers, no. 2012-01*. Florence: UNICEF.
UNICEF, 2016. *Las Edades Mínimas Legales y la Realización de los Derechos de Los y las Adolescentes*. Panama: UNICEF.
UNODC, 2014. *Global report on trafficking in persons 2014*. New York, NY: United Nations.
UNODC, 2018. *Global Report on Trafficking in Persons 2018*. New York, NY: United Nations.
U.S. Department of Justice, 2007. Commercial Sexual Exploitation of Children: What do We Know and What Do We Do About It? *Issues in International Crime, National Institute of Justice Special Report*. Washington: U.S. Department of Justice.
Weiss, E. L. and Enrile, A., 2020. The US Military–prostitution complex, patriarchy, and masculinity. In: Zaleski, K., Enrile, A., Weiss, E., and Wang, X., (eds.), *Women's Journey to Empowerment in the 21st Century*. New York, NY: Oxford University Press, pp. 403–420.
World Tourism Organization, 2020. *Framework Convention on Tourism Ethics*, Madrid: UNWTO, DOI: https://doi.org/10.18111/9789284421671.

Worst Forms of Child Labour Convention (No. 182), June 15, 1999, 2133 U.N.T.S. 161.

WTO Statement on the Prevention of Organized Sex Tourism, WTO General Assembly Res. 338 (XI), U.N. Doc. A/RES/338 (XI) (Oct. 17–22, 1995).

Wyndhamn Hotels & Resorts, 2018. *Annual Report 2018, Implementation of The Code's Six Criteria*. [online]. Available at: <http://thecode.force.com/servlet/servlet.FileDownload?file=00P0o00001yjsAz> [Accessed 6 May 2020].

SECTION 3
Conclusion

14
HUMAN RIGHTS IN TOURISM
Concluding remarks

14.1 Introduction

While numerous advances have been made in human rights, implementation is still problematic, and exploitation continues for many – including those reliant on the tourism industry. Much of the tourism industry is focused on lowering costs to attract more visitors and this can come at the cost of human rights. It has been over 70 years since the adoption of the UDHR signifying individuals have natural human rights, yet it is still up to the will of individual states to accept the various human rights articles, ratify, and then implement them into their legal systems at the national and sub-national level. Many nation-states that signed the UN Bill of Human Rights have not necessarily ratified and implemented these documents into their constitutions and laws, leaving a variety of rights unprotected. For example, although Judge Christian Weeramantry of the International Criminal Court argued in 1997 that environmental rights are human rights, human rights to the environment have not been achieved in many states, and are not yet entrenched in law (Westra, 2011, p. 9). Another example is USA and the case of Women's Rights: in 1972 the United States Congress approved an amendment to the United States Constitution guaranteeing equal rights under law for both sexes. Amendments to the U.S. Constitution take effect if three-quarters of the states ratify them. Technically, the amendment has been approved by 38 states since it was approved by Congress in 1972, but some states rescinded their initial approval after concerns that the amendment would threaten traditional conservative values. Furthermore, the initial deadline for approval lapsed before the required number of states had approved the amendment, why it is still uncertain if the Equal Rights Amendment to the U.S. Constitution will be taking effect or not in the future (see also H.J. Res. 79, 2020, proposing an extension of the initial deadline). Similarly, with regards to the abolition of child labour, many countries do not recognise it fully for a variety of reasons despite its appearance in the UN Bill of Human Rights. Even if states have included the abolition of child labour in their laws, exceptions occur such as laws allowing younger children to assume "light work" – for reasons such as permitting children to take up apprenticeships, to supplement their allowance money, to have work experiences in their family business, etc. – the state can use its economic difficulties as a justification to allow child labour without violating the law (ILO, 2000). In Vietnam, steps have been taken to specifically address child labour in tourism, which often includes work in street vending, attendants in hotels, restaurants, *karaoke* bars, and as tourist porters or guides (ILO, 2014). Although there have been programme interventions, there are socio-economic challenges that limit the extent of these programmes. These examples demonstrate that achieving the provision of human rights cannot simply be accomplished through a political agenda; and that there are socio-economic factors in place, which ultimately lead to human rights violations. Despite these challenges, it is important to recognise the advancement in human rights through international organisations, such as the UN, ILO or NGOs/NPOs, as well as national and local governments, and the business community. The links between tourism and the rights-based UN SDGs have put human rights and sustainability at the forefront of the tourism debate with ties to broad programmes such as the UN Guiding Principles on Business and Human Rights and the UN Global Compact, as well as individual corporate responsibility statements.

The purpose of this chapter is to outline the contributions of the various chapters, as well as propose discussion questions so readers can further probe the relationship between tourism and human rights. While the authors were completing this book, the unprecedented COVID-19 pandemic was spreading globally. In order to contain the spread of the disease, non-essential travel was banned, and non-essential or human-to-human contact businesses were shut down. Curfews and lockdown became mandatory in many towns, regions, and countries. This is the first time, on such a wide scale, that human beings have had to give up a variety of freedoms and rights in order to protect the global population. The appearance of the COVID-19 pandemic has brought new perspectives on freedoms, privacy, security, and human rights resulting in a paradigm shift discussed later in this chapter, along with a discussion on the constitutionalisation of international laws. The chapter concludes with some final thoughts and proposes areas for future research.

14.2 Chapter contributions and discussion questions

This book has attempted to bring together chapters that present a fundamental understanding of human rights, and their relationship with tourism and the hospitality industry. It is designed so that the readers may select chapters of interest, rather than starting the book from the beginning. Each chapter begins with a generic understanding of the topic and then moves on to tourism examples including legal cases. Human rights issues are complex, and various subject disciplines may argue about human rights differently, e.g., an anthropological approach emphasises different points than a political science approach would on the topic of rights-based development. As such, it is not possible to include all perspectives and topics on human rights. Readers will find below the key concepts from each chapter, followed by discussion questions the authors hope will generate additional dialogue.

The first section of this book presented a foundation of human rights concepts, which could be used to explore the relationship between tourism,

Concluding remarks **353**

hospitality, and human rights. Chapter 1 introduced the historical evolution of human rights. It examined how the UDHR is derived from Western concepts of human rights, albeit the final draft incorporated input from non-Western scholars. The universalism-relativism discourse was presented, as it is important to acknowledge there are ongoing, disquieting debates that go beyond the scope of this chapter. An increase in hate crimes, state policies enforcing discrimination, and a backing away from multi-lateral collaboration at a global level are just a few of the developments which are a cause for concern for human rights. Anti-racism protests spread globally in June of 2020, highlighting the continued discrimination that many face on a daily basis. Chapter 1 also examined the relationship between human rights and civil rights, and the challenges with incorporating international human rights laws into domestic laws.

The questions for Chapter 1 include: What is the influence of notable human rights documents for the tourism industry? To what extent are human rights and civil rights upheld in, and by, various tourism destinations and enterprises? What are some possible reasons human rights are not always upheld in a country? Take an example of human rights in one country not being protected by national level law and discuss a possible solution (or solutions) to effectively address the issue and make changes.

The following three chapters covered distinct but related areas including human rights and tourism enterprises, sustainable development, and the political dimensions of human rights and tourism. Throughout Chapter 2, the relationship between human rights and the operations of tourism enterprises were explored. International human rights have traditionally been developed and enforced by states. However, globalisation and the growing economic importance of corporations have led to a movement towards involving third parties, such as businesses, in the fight against human rights violations. At the same time, tourism development can also exacerbate poverty, and tourism businesses can contribute to the violation of human rights in the pursuit of profit. This chapter examined various international, transnational and national instruments focusing on the responsibility of tourism enterprises.

What constitutes good evidence that tourism enterprises have contributed to the advancement of human rights? What are the dangers of relying on the tourism industry to self-regulate (soft law) in the protection of human rights? What is the significance of extraterritoriality in terms of meaningfully handling human rights violations by a corporation or a group of individuals abroad?

Although the political dimensions of human rights and the nature of development are intertwined, these aspects are examined over two chapters: Chapter 3 focused on tourism development issues and human rights, and how tourism development plays a role in the implementation of human rights. The main focus of development theory and practice shifted from economic rejuvenation and modernisation after the World Wars, to an approach more environmentally focused on "sustainable" development and, more recently to a human rights-based development paradigm. The human rights-based approach of the UN SDGs is viewed as a platform in which to advance human rights in tourism, as tourism has slowly followed the global shift in development paradigms.

What influence do different development paradigms have on the protection of human rights in tourism? To what degree does sustainable tourism promote human rights? Why is embracing the UN SDGs unpalatable to some tourism corporations; and what do these corporations do to advertise their contributions without genuinely contributing to the SDGs?

Chapter 4 presented an overview of the political dimensions of human rights, and its impacts on tourism development. In order for human rights to be implemented, there needs to be a political environment and political institutions to establish, and implement laws (both international and domestic), policies and programmes. Following a brief examination of the theoretical dimensions of the politics of human rights, a range of political perspectives including how a state functions, a state's record on human rights, and the global political economy, were examined to understand how they influence tourism operations. Political instability impacts tourism investment and visitor numbers, while good governance can support human rights and provide a platform for sustainability.

How significant is the role of government policy on political stability, tourism operations, and human rights? To what extent does globalisation and economic neoliberalism influence the tourism industry, and how does this economic model impact human rights in tourism? What is the significance of the principles of good governance in protecting human rights?

The second section of the book focused on more tourism-specific issues in human rights discourse. Chapter 5 focused on the concept of human security, which emerged from the 1994 UNDP Human Development Report and its relationship to tourism. Human security is viewed as a major shift from the traditional realist/national aspects of security, to a much broader concept focusing on the human dimension and the security of people, instead of nations. Human security issues that affect tourism including personal safety, health, and human needs were explored. Human security places emphasis on real and perceived threats to people, all vital for tourists and locals.

What is the significance of the shift to human security for human rights and for tourism? To what extent does the provision of security for tourists impact the health and safety of local residents? There are many different security issues that impact tourist destinations. Select one tourist destination and argue which security issue is of the utmost importance in that destination; what proposed changes need to be made to this security issue?

Chapter 6 focused on the right of privacy as a human right, and the applicability of this right in the tourism sector. The chapter provided an overview of the relevant regulations of the right to privacy in international and national laws; and different examples including requests for information from state agencies from both tourists and tourist enterprises (e.g. tourism accommodations and airlines). Advances in technology have made the collection and storage of personal data an important security and privacy issue. The chapter also explored the difficult question of the proper balance between individual rights and national security.

How do different privacy laws in different countries impact travel? Examine the types of violations of the right to privacy at each stage of a travel experience and discuss why these violations of privacy are acceptable/unacceptable and on what grounds. How do you determine the adequate balance between individual privacy and national security?

Displacement issues are one of the major sources of contention in tourism development as discussed in Chapter 7. Local people have lost land, resources, and access to economic livelihoods due to tourism. This chapter examined concerns from the perspectives of the physical displacement of peoples, the displacement of businesses, and the displacement of cultures. Different concepts such as political migration, gentrification, creative destruction, land grabbing, disaster capitalism, and acculturation and assimilation were employed to understand the complexity of displacement issues in tourism.

What mechanisms can be used to compensate those who are displaced by tourism development? To what extent has growth in the sharing economy led to gentrification, overtourism, and the displacement of local residents? How has the COVID-19 pandemic caused economic displacement?

Chapter 8 examined an overview of the classical grounds of discrimination of tourism patrons, such as race, national or ethnic origin, disability and religion, to new evolving grounds of discrimination, such as sexual orientation, as well as gender identity. The right to live a life free from discrimination is of particular importance for tourism establishments, and this chapter focuses on the context of their treatment of customers. Cases of discrimination of patrons in tourism were explored along with inherent conflicts in different laws.

To what extent are the different kinds of discrimination examined in this chapter prevalent within the tourism industry? To what degree do different laws in different countries impact the level of discrimination faced by tourists or tourism employees? What reasons other than legal systems play a significant role in the continuation of discrimination in the 21st century?

Chapter 9 investigated the Freedom of Movement and its relationship to human rights and tourism. Although tourism is a social phenomenon concerned with people's movements, there are many violations of mobility that may impinge on tourism development. International tourism is based on people's ability to move across political borders controlled by policies of states, including the issuing of passports and visas. Migrant workers and seasonal workers who contribute to the labour force in tourism and hospitality are impacted by ever-changing border control policies. While the tourism industry takes advantage of cheap labour from migrant workers, foreign policies that exclude migrant workers deprive employment opportunities for such workers.

What determines whether governments place travel restrictions on specific groups of people? To what extent are the conditions placed on migrant tourism workers a violation of human rights? To what extent have tourism enterprises complied with new regulations related to accessibility?

The most frequently discussed Human Rights violations in tourism are related to labour conditions in tourism and hospitality services and these were addressed in Chapter 10. Regardless of the ILO standards, numerous cases of problematic working conditions in tourism have been the subject of criticism. In addition to low wages and job insecurity, concerns have been expressed in terms of child labour, discrimination of employees, rights of migrant labour, and sex tourism. This chapter examined legal frameworks to ensure working conditions, the right to decent work, the freedom of association and collective bargaining, the rights of migrant workers and safeguarding children from child labour are respected.

What regulations are in place to provide tourism workers with just and favourable conditions of work? To what degree are people employed in the formal tourism sector at an advantage over those employed in the informal tourism sector in terms of human rights? What is the difficulty in ensuring fair working conditions for international labourers across borders (e.g. on cruise ships)?

Chapter 11 introduced the concepts of rights to environment. Tourism heavily relies on a healthy natural environment as an attraction; however, tourism has been contributing to climate change, putting that environment at risk. This chapter began with the recognition that a healthy and sustainable environment enables people to enjoy many human rights, while at the same time, the world has been unable to secure "human rights to environment". Influential UN documents which have influenced environmental laws and UNWTO policies were examined, followed by an examination of the relationship between tourism and climate change.

What are the implications for the tourism industry given that many countries have not passed legislation on the right to the environment? To what extent are local residents' human rights violated if their government focuses on the long-haul tourist market, which contributes to climate change? Why is it crucial to consider the right to a healthy environment as an "environmental security" to human beings, and how does this revised view affect the tourism industry?

Indigenous environmental stewardship illustrates the importance of local knowledge in protecting the natural environment. However, Indigenous Peoples have long suffered from a wide range of human rights abuse at the hands of colonialists and immigrants, and tourism has been portrayed as a newer form of colonisation. Chapter 12 discussed Indigenous Peoples' rights, and the importance of the UNDRIP. This chapter introduced how the UNDRIP came into existence, the implications of the recognition of the human rights of Indigenous peoples on states, and how Indigenous populations play significant roles in tourism. Indigenous tourism is not always developed and managed solely for the purpose of economic improvement but can include wider social developments or political purposes. A critical dimension of Indigenous tourism is local control over tourism. There will also be a need for collaboration between Indigenous communities, states, and non-Indigenous communities.

How does a country having a colonial past impact the development of locally controlled Indigenous tourism enterprises? What is the influence of the UN Declaration of Rights on Indigenous Peoples on the development of Indigenous tourism enterprises? What are some of the challenges Indigenous Peoples face in operating Indigenous tourism products for non-Indigenous tourists? How can such challenges be turned into advantages for Indigenous populations?

The overall objective of Chapter 13 was to explore the existing legal and soft law instruments for addressing sex tourism. Special focus in the chapter was on instruments covering vulnerable groups, such as sex trafficking victims, as well as sexual exploitation of children in travel and tourism. A contextual approach was used to explore the issue of sex tourism, where regional/cultural differences occur with respect to age of consent, and power imbalances (female vs. male sex tourism, rich vs. poor countries). As illegal (child) sex tourism often happens extraterritorially, this chapter also examined legal mechanisms and voluntary initiatives to combat this criminal activity across political borders.

What laws need to be passed in order to protect those being exploited through sex tourism? To what extent do power imbalances in sex tourism impact human rights? Why are exiting laws and regulations not effectively used to eradicate coercive and exploitative sex tourism practices?

14.3 The COVID-19 pandemic, tourism, human rights issues, and global governance

Human rights discourse is, at best, open to various interpretations, if not lacking a universal hermeneutic device. However, the recent global COVID-19 pandemic has halted human activities around the world; as well as forced human populations to reconsider their rights and freedom. A respiratory disease of unknown cause was detected at the end of 2019, initiating sweeping lifestyle changes and lockdowns beginning in Wuhan, China, which were quickly adopted around the world in early 2020 as the virus spread globally. The COVID-19 pandemic has severely constrained the movement of people. The World Health Organization (WHO) declared a Public Health Emergency of International Concern on the 30 January 2020; a large number of cruise ship passengers and crews were identified as testing positive with the new coronavirus and quarantined offshore; it was later declared a pandemic by the WHO on 11 March 2020; following this declaration, many countries called upon their citizens abroad to return home immediately, while simultaneously barring inbound foreign travellers. Community, cities, regions, and countries went into various states of lockdown to prevent the spread of disease. The closing of borders had an astounding impact on air, land, and water travel. Many foreigners were stranded in foreign countries where they were enjoying holidays as flights were unexpectedly cancelled. People were confined to certain places and shelters due to curfews and lockdown situations. In many countries, those citizens who returned home in time from abroad had to undergo self-isolation for two weeks or longer. During the first quarter of 2020, pleasure travel admittedly became defunct. This pandemic revealed that travelling for pleasure is not a human right, but a privilege.

As the COVID-19 pandemic is still ongoing at the time of writing, the full extent of the impact on the world economy is yet to be seen. The pandemic has claimed many lives in a short period of time. The seriousness of the pandemic was recognised by some states as early as January 2020, but some did not take drastic enough measures until late March or early April 2020. Economically, the pandemic has crippled the world's economy. The fragility of tourism was revealed as it was one of the first businesses to be hard hit. To prevent the spread of the disease, unnecessary travel including holidaymaking had to be stopped. The outbreak on cruise ships was another wake-up call to the tourism industry. The transportation, accommodation, food and beverage, recreation and attraction, and events industries – all components of tourism industry – were closed or had to reduce services; many employees lost their jobs. Even occupations like travel writers, bloggers and vloggers, and social media influencers lost jobs, as sponsors withdrew money, tickets and vouchers, and contracts that allowed them to travel around the world. Non-essential businesses, which are comprised of many small and medium-size enterprises, had to be shut down indefinitely. Office workers shifted to work remotely from home wherever possible. Online shopping and delivery services began to thrive as people self-isolated, however, delivery services began facing a shortage of drivers. Those governments that were able, launched massive emergency funding relief programs to help their citizens. A prolonged pandemic will ruthlessly affect people's rights to decent wages and dignified life; the less privileged or marginalised groups of people may face even more severe consequences. COVID-19 has been regarded as a threat multiplier. Questions yet to be answered are: can the virus be brought under better control, can states protect citizens' economic rights throughout the pandemic and in the aftermath? What will tourism look like when restrictions begin lifting?

The pandemic's impact on world politics and policies has been unmistakable. Although the WHO has taken a critical role in this time of crisis, it has fallen to individual nation-states to produce emergency guidelines and strategies due to the right of state sovereignty. As soon as the pandemic was announced in March 2020, many countries started to shut down borders, prevented the arrival of incoming foreigners, repatriated nationals from abroad, and cut down scheduled and chartered flights. Additional lockdown orders in communities, towns, regions, and even entire nations followed. However, not all countries used the same approach, with Sweden for example opting for significantly fewer restrictions. In April 2020, international postal services were impacted with reduced or delayed services. In mid-April of 2020, some US citizens began protesting against the lockdown, based on the complaints of interference with the human right to work, income, and freedom of movement; the protest was seen as political amid the crisis was supported by the President, which could be perceived as going against the state lockdown laws (BBC, 2020). Concerns were raised that unpopular anti-immigration laws were being disguised as necessary measures to keep the pandemic under control. Social media became a platform for political propaganda and conspiracies, fuelling people's fear of the pandemic.

There have been significant social impacts. The expression of "war-time" mentality has often been used to describe the austerity and self-restraint required to combat against this invisible foe. Social distancing, prohibitions against gathering, reduction of face-to-face interactions, and indefinitely staying home all go against the social nature of human communities. Many countries shut down schools and institutions. Students are learning remotely on digital platforms or using videoconferencing software to replicate a virtual classroom. Some countries where softer versions of the lockdown were applied earlier – in which citizens were still allowed to visit cafés or bars – gradually shifted to apply more controlled measures, as the number of patients and deaths did not decline. Due to the lockdown or job cuts, a large number of people faced financial difficulties, while the need for an unprecedented scale of unemployment or emergency funds placed a significant drain on national and regional economies. The elementary right of mobility was curtailed; people were confined to a limited space, unable to interact with family and friends, and unable to go outside, causing tremendous stress to individuals. Those who came into contact with an infected person or returned from overseas had to self-quarantine for 14 days. Seeing some success in "contact tracing" systems to prevent the widespread of the virus, some countries attempted to have citizens install a "tracking" app on their mobile/cell phones. Some concerned citizens argued the apps were a violation of privacy, however, states now have a stronger argument that the temporary compromise of privacy is for the greater good to curb the contraction rate of the virus. The restrictions on mobility to prevent the spread of the disease have also caused tremendous impact on food production and access to food. FAO (2020) and WFP (2020) are predicting a food security crisis will follow the pandemic, which links to human security, discussed in Chapter 5. With agriculture and food supply chains being affected, 265 million people in 2020 will face acute food insecurity, of which 100 million are those who lost their regular wages due to COVID-19 pandemic (WFP, 2020). The Horn of Africa also experienced a crop failure due to drought followed by extremely heavy rainfall in 2019, and in 2020 an exceptional desert locust invasion followed (Picheta, 2020). The UN has raised the alarm that the number of people in dire situations may surpass one billion in 2020 (FAO, 2020; WFP, 2020). The New York Times already reported in April 2020 that there were desperately hungry people waiting for humanitarian aid and food around the world (Dahir, 2020). The UN is calling for immediate action to prevent a hunger pandemic, as those affected are among the most vulnerable people in society. Nevertheless, the impacts of mobility restrictions are not all negative. A month or so after the world was locked down, citizens noticed changes, which were supported by satellite images, revealing less air pollution and less noise pollution. Evidence of changes in lifestyle has been covered in online news articles: caring actions and interactions between neighbours and communities have increased and learning to manage without non-essential travel, including holidaymaking, was discussed. With less travel, there is a reduced demand for oil, resulting in a drastic reduction in the price of oil impacting those nations whose economy relies on the oil industry. This may provide the impetus to change economies away from fossil fuels, which would benefit the fight against climate change. The shift to online meetings may further reduce travel to business meetings, conferences, and events after the pandemic. By the end of June 2020, the WHO was recording over 10 million cases and almost 500 000 deaths in 216 countries/areas/territories. Some countries were successfully reducing infection rates and were in the process of reopening their economies, while other nations were dealing with surging infection rates or a second wave. Many companies in tourism, including some airlines, had declared bankruptcy. A staged reopening was being allowed in some destinations, such as restaurants operating outdoor patios before dining was allowed inside. Domestic tourism is being allowed in some areas and seen as a way to get the economy going while countries such as Spain and Greece have begun to attract international visitors. All tourism companies now face the additional expense of extra cleaning, installing protective barriers, and providing Personal Protective Equipment (PPE). As many customers switch to online payments, the use of cash has declined, leaving those who rely on cash tips or payments in tourism further struggling. While the pandemic is still raging, it is impossible to grasp the entire picture of the social, economic, and environmental impacts of the COVID-19 pandemic. However, scholars are already researching possible directions for tourism after the pandemic (e.g., On Tourism & Sustainability, 2020).

The COVID-19 pandemic has revealed a number of things directly relating to human rights protection, however, only two points are discussed here: the weakness of human rights protection being based primarily on a nation state's domestic level laws at the time of crisis; and international and domestic demands to shift from the protection of individual rights to collective rights, which could consequently protect individual rights. The concept of the prisoner's dilemma can be used in this instance. As countries and regions re-evaluate lockdown procedures, two possible scenarios have arisen. The first is to resume economic activities in the hopes of restarting the economy; though this could come at the cost of many more lives, the pandemic is still raging, and there is no vaccine on the immediate horizon. The second scenario is to stay in lockdown to various degrees, in order to save more human lives; however, the state and citizens would continue to suffer economic consequences. Either way, neither collective rights nor individual rights will be fully protected, yet which choice is the lesser evil? The pandemic threatens human lives at a global scale. In order to combat the spread of disease speedy international collaboration is essential. However, beyond the limited ability of the WHO, there is no designated global governance structure for an emergency like this, each nation state takes measures as it deems fit, with limited global coordination. As a result, some nations have experienced harsher lockdown measures than others, whereas others have experienced higher death rates. Meanwhile there are debates over effective leadership styles in crises (Robson, 2020; American Psychological Association, 2020), it has been suggested that countries where there is a culture of high trust in governments who initiated an early response to the outbreak led to quickly flattening the curve of the spread of the virus (Wilson, 2020). Citizens who defied state laws such as an emergency lockdown by claiming individual human rights violations have been perceived to be selfish and irresponsible, and seen to be endangering the lives of others. Societies react differently to tremendously stressful situations, and this pandemic has proven to be a testing ground for a society's willingness to temporarily compromise the assertion of individual rights in favour of collective rights for survival. However, COVID-19 has also demonstrated that a government's response does not always assure the protection of human rights, rights to life, and social-economic welfare such as securing food and shelter. A question raised here is, how valuable is the status of state sovereignty when an effective global governance system is most needed.

The Constitutionalist school of thoughts explores the idea of global governance as necessary, not only in cases of an emergency like this pandemic, but also for human rights provisions to be implemented successfully. There is a proposal for the "constitutionalization of international laws" based on the premise that the "international community is a legal community", where rules and principles govern, not power (Westra, 2011, p. 261). Globalisation has already strained the responsibilities of governments concerning international laws: multinational enterprises and other organisations have already dealt with international laws and foreign domestic laws in regard to their own business operations without the intervention of home governments. As a consequence, globalisation has eroded the power of the state (Peters, 2009). The application of global constitutionalism principles may improve the effectiveness of fairness in the international legal system, however, not without dissent and objections. Peters (2009) identified challenges of the constitutionalisation of international laws, yet advocates that the benefits outweigh the negatives. Every nation state has a constitution or Basic Laws in one form or other, be it coded, un-coded, or through traditions. However, international human rights laws remain ineffective unless they are entrenched in that state's basic laws. The global constitutionalisation of international laws will help prevent uncontrolled "deformalization" of international law; a flexible approach to constitutionalism seems to "correspond better to the current state of global legal integration than the idea of a strict hierarchy," namely, international human rights laws vs. less important norms in domestic laws; and "global constitutionalism deploys ... a constructive, not obstructive, critical potential" for global governance policies (Peters, 2009). When there is a decline in the COVID-19 pandemic there are opportunities to re-evaluate how to better ensure human rights are protected through international treaties and laws, as well as domestic laws. It will also provide the opportunity to re-evaluate how societies operate over a wide range of areas, including what basic livelihood assistance can be provided and how it can be delivered, how developed countries can better support developing countries, how health care systems can be strengthened, and how the economies should be structured and resources used, including a greater shift away from fossil fuels.

14.4 Conclusion and final thoughts

This book has attempted to present an introductory overview of the relationship between tourism and human rights. It is not primarily aimed at students of law, rather it is aimed at those with a broad interest in tourism from a variety of disciplines and practical interests. Court cases and examples from around the world have been used to illustrate points where tourism and human rights meet and sometimes collide. Due to the broad dimensions of human rights, it has not been possible to cover all aspects of the topic. Additional research could be taken within each of the existing chapters, as well as areas not the subject of individual chapters here, i.e. women's rights, rights of the child, economic rights, freedom of speech, rights to natural resources such as the right to water, and human rights violations in the context of hosting mega events. In 2020, the COVID-19 pandemic has had a tremendous impact on all aspects of life, and it is difficult at this point early on in the pandemic to comprehend what the outcomes will be, not only for societies around the world, but also for economies and industries including tourism. Some countries have begun to reopen, and people have begun to travel again, while other countries are facing a surge in cases and destinations are still in lockdown. What tourism will look like in the coming years is unknown, as individual and collective rights collide under the pandemic. Therefore, more research will be required within the context of mobility and human rights as the pandemic declines. The pandemic has had some beneficial environmental impacts with cleaner air, yet the threat of global climate change and the growing water crisis will continue to impact tourism and human rights. As international and domestic laws continue to evolve and more human rights court cases are decided, there is a need for additional research as to how this will impact the operations of the tourism industry so human rights are protected. Democratic governments, which typically have human rights as a central component, have been under threat. Additional research is needed on the evolving political climate across the globe, and how this relates to government policies, e.g., how they interact with industries such as tourism. Will multi-lateral collaboration expand or contract? Multinational tourism operators have long been criticised for exploiting destinations and workers. However, as the body of literature on corporate social responsibility evolves and court decisions are implemented, it will be important to investigate to what extent these business policies and legal decisions are implemented and support human rights in tourism. There are philosophical, legal, moral, and practical dimensions to human rights. Measures have been taken by governments, NGOs/NPOs, courts, the tourism industry, and tourists themselves to better recognise that a human rights approach is needed in tourism in line with sustainability. An inexpensive holiday should not come at the cost of human rights violations at the destination. We hope this book will not only generate further discussion on the relationship between tourism and human rights but that it has also revealed that there is a lot more work to be done in regards to the implementation and protection of human rights.

References

American Psychological Association, 2020. *How leaders can maximize trust and minimize stress during the COVID-19 pandemic.* [online] 20 March. Available at: <www.apa.org/news/apa/2020/03/covid-19-leadership> [Accessed 29 March 2020].

BBC, 2020. Coronavirus: US faced with protests amid pressure to reopen. *BBC.* [online] 19 April. Available at: <www.bbc.com/news/world-us-canada-52348288> [Accessed 19 April 2020].

Dahir, A.L., 2020. 'Instead of Coronavirus, the Hunger Will Kill Us.' A Global Food Crisis Looms. *New York Times.* [online] 22 April. Available at: <www.nytimes.com/2020/04/22/world/africa/coronavirus-hunger-crisis.html> [Accessed 22 April 2020].

FAO, 2020. *Coronavirus disease 2019 (COVID-19): Addressing the impacts of COVID-19 in food crises April–December 2020. FAO's component of the Global COVID-19 Humanitarian Response Plan.* [pdf] Available at: <www.fao.org/3/ca8497en/CA8497EN.pdf> [Accessed 23 April 2020].

H.J. Res. 79, 116th Cong. (2020).

ILO, 2000. *The effective abolition of child labour.* [pdf] Available at: <www.ilo.org/public/english/standards/relm/gb/docs/gb277/pdf/d2-abol.pdf> [Accessed 6 August 2019].

ILO, 2014. *Prevention and Elimination of Child Labour in the Tourism Sector in Mountainous Ethnic Minority Areas Documentation of the Potential Interventions Model in Sa Pa district, Lao Cai province, Viet Nam.* [pdf] Available at: <www.ilo.org/ipec/Informationresources/WCMS_IPEC_PUB_27735/lang—en/index.htm> [Accessed 24 April 2020].

On Tourism and Sustainability, 2020. *OTS Webinar Series: After the Virus.* [video online] Available at: <www.youtube.com/watch?v=xi1DCYKG9Ho> [Accessed 17 April 2020].

Peters, A., 2009. The merits of global constitutionalism. *Indiana Journal of Global Legal Studies,* 16(2), pp. 397–411. DOI: 10.2979/gls.2009.16.2.397.

Picheta, R., 2020. Coronavirus pandemic will cause global famines of 'biblical proportions,' UN warns. *CNN.* [online] 22 April. Available at: <www.cnn.com/2020/04/22/africa/coronavirus-famine-un-warning-intl/index.html> [Accessed 23 April 2020].

Robson, D., 2020. Covid-19: What makes a good leader during a crisis? *BBC.* [online] 27 March. Available at: <www.bbc.com/worklife/article/20200326-covid-19-what-makes-a-good-leader-during-a-crisis> [Accessed 29 March 2020].

UN, 2020. *Deputy Secretary-General Calls for Stronger Food Systems amid Risks Posed by COVID-19 Pandemic. Press release.* [online] 17 April. Available at: <www.un.org/press/en/2020/dsgsm1401.doc.htm> [Accessed 20 April 2020].

Westra, L., 2011. *Human Rights: The Commons and the Collective.* Vancouver: University of British Columbia Press.

WFP, 2020, *2020 Global Report on Food Crises Joint Analysis for Better Decisions. World Food Programme.* [pdf] 20 April. Available at: <https://docs.wfp.org/api/documents/WFP-0000114546/download/?_ga=2.35395425.1599638146.1587691415-1267542731.1587691415> [Accessed 23 April 2020].

Wilson, A., 2020. The countries that are succeeding at flattening the Curve. *Foreign Affairs.* [online] 2 April. Available at: <https://foreignpolicy.com/2020/04/02/countries-succeeding-flattening-curve-coronavirus-testing-quarantine/#> [Accessed 2 April 2020].

Appendices

A UNIVERSAL DECLARATION OF HUMAN RIGHTS (1948)

Preamble

Whereas recognition of the inherent dignity and of the equal and inalienable rights of all members of the human family is the foundation of freedom, justice and peace in the world,

Whereas disregard and contempt for human rights have resulted in barbarous acts which have outraged the conscience of mankind, and the advent of a world in which human beings shall enjoy freedom of speech and belief and freedom from fear and want has been proclaimed as the highest aspiration of the common people,

Whereas it is essential, if man is not to be compelled to have recourse, as a last resort, to rebellion against tyranny and oppression, that human rights should be protected by the rule of law,

Whereas it is essential to promote the development of friendly relations between nations,

Whereas the peoples of the United Nations have in the Charter reaffirmed their faith in fundamental human rights, in the dignity and worth of the human person and in the equal rights of men and women and have determined to promote social progress and better standards of life in larger freedom,

Whereas Member States have pledged themselves to achieve, in cooperation with the United Nations, the promotion of universal respect for and observance of human rights and fundamental freedoms,

Whereas a common understanding of these rights and freedoms is of the greatest importance for the full realization of this pledge,

Now, therefore,

The General Assembly,

Proclaims this Universal Declaration of Human Rights as a common standard of achievement for all peoples and all nations, to the end that every individual and every organ of society, keeping this Declaration constantly in mind, shall strive by teaching and education to promote respect for these rights and freedoms and by progressive measures, national and international, to secure their universal and effective recognition and observance, both among the peoples of Member States themselves and among the peoples of territories under their jurisdiction.

Article 1

All human beings are born free and equal in dignity and rights. They are endowed with reason and conscience and should act towards one another in a spirit of brotherhood.

Article 2

Everyone is entitled to all the rights and freedoms set forth in this Declaration, without distinction of any kind, such as race, colour, sex, language, religion, political or other opinion, national or social origin, property, birth or other status.

Furthermore, no distinction shall be made on the basis of the political, jurisdictional or international status of the country or territory to which a person belongs, whether it be independent, trust, non-self-governing or under any other limitation of sovereignty.

Article 3

Everyone has the right to life, liberty and security of person.

Article 4

No one shall be held in slavery or servitude; slavery and the slave trade shall be prohibited in all their forms.

Article 5

No one shall be subjected to torture or to cruel, inhuman or degrading treatment or punishment.

Article 6

Everyone has the right to recognition everywhere as a person before the law.

Article 7

All are equal before the law and are entitled without any discrimination to equal protection of the law. All are entitled to equal protection against any discrimination in violation of this Declaration and against any incitement to such discrimination.

Article 8

Everyone has the right to an effective remedy by the competent national tribunals for acts violating the fundamental rights granted him by the constitution or by law.

Article 9

No one shall be subjected to arbitrary arrest, detention or exile.

Article 10

Everyone is entitled in full equality to a fair and public hearing by an independent and impartial tribunal, in the determination of his rights and obligations and of any criminal charge against him.

Article 11

1. Everyone charged with a penal offence has the right to be presumed innocent until proved guilty according to law in a public trial at which he has had all the guarantees necessary for his defence.
2. No one shall be held guilty of any penal offence on account of any act or omission which did not constitute a penal offence, under national or international law, at the time when it was committed. Nor shall a heavier penalty be imposed than the one that was applicable at the time the penal offence was committed.

Article 12

No one shall be subjected to arbitrary interference with his privacy, family, home or correspondence, nor to attacks upon his honour and reputation. Everyone has the right to the protection of the law against such interference or attacks.

Article 13

1. Everyone has the right to freedom of movement and residence within the borders of each State.
2. Everyone has the right to leave any country, including his own, and to return to his country.

Article 14

1. Everyone has the right to seek and to enjoy in other countries asylum from persecution.

2. This right may not be invoked in the case of prosecutions genuinely arising from non-political crimes or from acts contrary to the purposes and principles of the United Nations.

Article 15

1. Everyone has the right to a nationality.
2. No one shall be arbitrarily deprived of his nationality nor denied the right to change his nationality.

Article 16

1. Men and women of full age, without any limitation due to race, nationality or religion, have the right to marry and to found a family. They are entitled to equal rights as to marriage, during marriage and at its dissolution.
2. Marriage shall be entered into only with the free and full consent of the intending spouses.
3. The family is the natural and fundamental group unit of society and is entitled to protection by society and the State.

Article 17

1. Everyone has the right to own property alone as well as in association with others.
2. No one shall be arbitrarily deprived of his property.

Article 18

Everyone has the right to freedom of thought, conscience and religion; this right includes freedom to change his religion or belief, and freedom, either alone or in community with others and in public or private, to manifest his religion or belief in teaching, practice, worship and observance.

Article 19

Everyone has the right to freedom of opinion and expression; this right includes freedom to hold opinions without interference and to seek, receive and impart information and ideas through any media and regardless of frontiers.

Article 20

1. Everyone has the right to freedom of peaceful assembly and association.

2. No one may be compelled to belong to an association.

Article 21

1. Everyone has the right to take part in the government of his country, directly or through freely chosen representatives.
2. Everyone has the right to equal access to public service in his country.
3. The will of the people shall be the basis of the authority of government; this will shall be expressed in periodic and genuine elections which shall be by universal and equal suffrage and shall be held by secret vote or by equivalent free voting procedures.

Article 22

Everyone, as a member of society, has the right to social security and is entitled to realization, through national effort and international co-operation and in accordance with the organization and resources of each State, of the economic, social and cultural rights indispensable for his dignity and the free development of his personality.

Article 23

1. Everyone has the right to work, to free choice of employment, to just and favourable conditions of work and to protection against unemployment.
2. Everyone, without any discrimination, has the right to equal pay for equal work.
3. Everyone who works has the right to just and favourable remuneration ensuring for himself and his family an existence worthy of human dignity, and supplemented, if necessary, by other means of social protection.
4. Everyone has the right to form and to join trade unions for the protection of his interests.

Article 24

Everyone has the right to rest and leisure, including reasonable limitation of working hours and periodic holidays with pay.

Article 25

1. Everyone has the right to a standard of living adequate for the health and well-being of himself and of his family, including food, clothing, housing and medical care and necessary social services, and the right to security in the event

of unemployment, sickness, disability, widowhood, old age or other lack of livelihood in circumstances beyond his control.
2. Motherhood and childhood are entitled to special care and assistance. All children, whether born in or out of wedlock, shall enjoy the same social protection.

Article 26

1. Everyone has the right to education. Education shall be free, at least in the elementary and fundamental stages. Elementary education shall be compulsory. Technical and professional education shall be made generally available and higher education shall be equally accessible to all on the basis of merit.
2. Education shall be directed to the full development of the human personality and to the strengthening of respect for human rights and fundamental freedoms. It shall promote understanding, tolerance and friendship among all nations, racial or religious groups, and shall further the activities of the United Nations for the maintenance of peace.
3. Parents have a prior right to choose the kind of education that shall be given to their children.

Article 27

1. Everyone has the right freely to participate in the cultural life of the community, to enjoy the arts and to share in scientific advancement and its benefits.
2. Everyone has the right to the protection of the moral and material interests resulting from any scientific, literary or artistic production of which he is the author.

Article 28

Everyone is entitled to a social and international order in which the rights and freedoms set forth in this Declaration can be fully realized.

Article 29

1. Everyone has duties to the community in which alone the free and full development of his personality is possible.
2. In the exercise of his rights and freedoms, everyone shall be subject only to such limitations as are determined by law solely for the purpose of securing due recognition and respect for the rights and freedoms of others and of meeting the just requirements of morality, public order and the general welfare in a democratic society.
3. These rights and freedoms may in no case be exercised contrary to the purposes and principles of the United Nations.

Article 30

Nothing in this Declaration may be interpreted as implying for any State, group or person any right to engage in any activity or to perform any act aimed at the destruction of any of the rights and freedoms set forth herein.

Acknowledgment

From the International Covenant on Civil and Political Rights, opened for signature in New York on 19 December, 1966, ©(1967) United Nations. Reprinted with the permission of the United Nations.

INTERNATIONAL COVENANT ON CIVIL AND POLITICAL RIGHTS

The States Parties to the present Covenant,

Considering that, in accordance with the principles proclaimed in the Charter of the United Nations, recognition of the inherent dignity and of the equal and inalienable rights of all members of the human family is the foundation of freedom, justice and peace in the world,

Recognizing that these rights derive from the inherent dignity of the human person,

Recognizing that, in accordance with the Universal Declaration of Human Rights, the ideal of free human beings enjoying civil and political freedom and freedom from fear and want can only be achieved if conditions are created whereby everyone may enjoy his civil and political rights, as well as his economic, social and cultural rights,

Considering the obligation of States under the Charter of the United Nations to promote universal respect for, and observance of, human rights and freedoms,

Realizing that the individual, having duties to other individuals and to the community to which he belongs, is under a responsibility to strive for the promotion and observance of the rights recognized in the present Covenant,

Agree upon the following articles:

PART I

Article 1

1. All peoples have the right of self-determination. By virtue of that right they freely determine their political status and freely pursue their economic, social and cultural development.

2. All peoples may, for their own ends, freely dispose of their natural wealth and resources without prejudice to any obligations arising out of international economic co-operation, based upon the principle of mutual benefit, and international law. In no case may a people be deprived of its own means of subsistence.
3. The States Parties to the present Covenant, including those having responsibility for the administration of Non-Self-Governing and Trust Territories, shall promote the realization of the right of self-determination, and shall respect that right, in conformity with the provisions of the Charter of the United Nations.

PART II

Article 2

1. Each State Party to the present Covenant undertakes to respect and to ensure to all individuals within its territory and subject to its jurisdiction the rights recognized in the present Covenant, without distinction of any kind, such as race, colour, sex, language, religion, political or other opinion, national or social origin, property, birth or other status.
2. Where not already provided for by existing legislative or other measures, each State Party to the present Covenant undertakes to take the necessary steps, in accordance with its constitutional processes and with the provisions of the present Covenant, to adopt such laws or other measures as may be necessary to give effect to the rights recognized in the present Covenant.
3. Each State Party to the present Covenant undertakes:
    (a) To ensure that any person whose rights or freedoms as herein recognized are violated shall have an effective remedy, notwithstanding that the violation has been committed by persons acting in an official capacity;
    (b) To ensure that any person claiming such a remedy shall have his right thereto determined by competent judicial, administrative or legislative authorities, or by any other competent authority provided for by the legal system of the State, and to develop the possibilities of judicial remedy;
    (c) To ensure that the competent authorities shall enforce such remedies when granted.

Article 3

The States Parties to the present Covenant undertake to ensure the equal right of men and women to the enjoyment of all civil and political rights set forth in the present Covenant.

Article 4

1. In time of public emergency which threatens the life of the nation and the existence of which is officially proclaimed, the States Parties to the present Covenant may take measures derogating from their obligations under the present Covenant to the extent strictly required by the exigencies of the situation, provided that such measures are not inconsistent with their other obligations under international law and do not involve discrimination solely on the ground of race, colour, sex, language, religion or social origin.
2. No derogation from articles 6, 7, 8 (paragraphs I and 2), 11, 15, 16 and 18 may be made under this provision.
3. Any State Party to the present Covenant availing itself of the right of derogation shall immediately inform the other States Parties to the present Covenant, through the intermediary of the Secretary-General of the United Nations, of the provisions from which it has derogated and of the reasons by which it was actuated. A further communication shall be made, through the same intermediary, on the date on which it terminates such derogation.

Article 5

1. Nothing in the present Covenant may be interpreted as implying for any State, group or person any right to engage in any activity or perform any act aimed at the destruction of any of the rights and freedoms recognized herein or at their limitation to a greater extent than is provided for in the present Covenant.
2. There shall be no restriction upon or derogation from any of the fundamental human rights recognized or existing in any State Party to the present Covenant pursuant to law, conventions, regulations or custom on the pretext that the present Covenant does not recognize such rights or that it recognizes them to a lesser extent.

PART III

Article 6

1. Every human being has the inherent right to life. This right shall be protected by law. No one shall be arbitrarily deprived of his life.
2. In countries which have not abolished the death penalty, sentence of death may be imposed only for the most serious crimes in accordance with the law in force at the time of the commission of the crime and not contrary to the provisions of the present Covenant and to the Convention on the Prevention and Punishment of the Crime of Genocide. This penalty can only be carried out pursuant to a final judgement rendered by a competent court.
3. When deprivation of life constitutes the crime of genocide, it is understood that nothing in this article shall authorize any State Party to the present Covenant

to derogate in any way from any obligation assumed under the provisions of the Convention on the Prevention and Punishment of the Crime of Genocide.
4. Anyone sentenced to death shall have the right to seek pardon or commutation of the sentence. Amnesty, pardon or commutation of the sentence of death may be granted in all cases.
5. Sentence of death shall not be imposed for crimes committed by persons below eighteen years of age and shall not be carried out on pregnant women.
6. Nothing in this article shall be invoked to delay or to prevent the abolition of capital punishment by any State Party to the present Covenant.

Article 7

No one shall be subjected to torture or to cruel, inhuman or degrading treatment or punishment. In particular, no one shall be subjected without his free consent to medical or scientific experimentation.

Article 8

1. No one shall be held in slavery; slavery and the slave-trade in all their forms shall be prohibited.
2. No one shall be held in servitude.
3.
    (a) No one shall be required to perform forced or compulsory labour;
    (b) Paragraph 3 (a) shall not be held to preclude, in countries where imprisonment with hard labour may be imposed as a punishment for a crime, the performance of hard labour in pursuance of a sentence to such punishment by a competent court;
    (c) For the purpose of this paragraph the term "forced or compulsory labour" shall not include:
        (i) Any work or service, not referred to in subparagraph (b), normally required of a person who is under detention in consequence of a lawful order of a court, or of a person during conditional release from such detention;
        (ii) Any service of a military character and, in countries where conscientious objection is recognized, any national service required by law of conscientious objectors;
        (iii) Any service exacted in cases of emergency or calamity threatening the life or well-being of the community;
        (iv) Any work or service which forms part of normal civil obligations.

Article 9

1. Everyone has the right to liberty and security of person. No one shall be subjected to arbitrary arrest or detention. No one shall be deprived of his

liberty except on such grounds and in accordance with such procedure as are established by law.
2. Anyone who is arrested shall be informed, at the time of arrest, of the reasons for his arrest and shall be promptly informed of any charges against him.
3. Anyone arrested or detained on a criminal charge shall be brought promptly before a judge or other officer authorized by law to exercise judicial power and shall be entitled to trial within a reasonable time or to release. It shall not be the general rule that persons awaiting trial shall be detained in custody, but release may be subject to guarantees to appear for trial, at any other stage of the judicial proceedings, and, should occasion arise, for execution of the judgement.
4. Anyone who is deprived of his liberty by arrest or detention shall be entitled to take proceedings before a court, in order that that court may decide without delay on the lawfulness of his detention and order his release if the detention is not lawful.
5. Anyone who has been the victim of unlawful arrest or detention shall have an enforceable right to compensation.

Article 10

1. All persons deprived of their liberty shall be treated with humanity and with respect for the inherent dignity of the human person.
2.
    (a) Accused persons shall, save in exceptional circumstances, be segregated from convicted persons and shall be subject to separate treatment appropriate to their status as unconvicted persons;
    (b) Accused juvenile persons shall be separated from adults and brought as speedily as possible for adjudication.
3. The penitentiary system shall comprise treatment of prisoners the essential aim of which shall be their reformation and social rehabilitation. Juvenile offenders shall be segregated from adults and be accorded treatment appropriate to their age and legal status.

Article 11

No one shall be imprisoned merely on the ground of inability to fulfil a contractual obligation.

Article 12

1. Everyone lawfully within the territory of a State shall, within that territory, have the right to liberty of movement and freedom to choose his residence.
2. Everyone shall be free to leave any country, including his own.
3. The above-mentioned rights shall not be subject to any restrictions except those which are provided by law, are necessary to protect national security,

public order (ordre public), public health or morals or the rights and freedoms of others, and are consistent with the other rights recognized in the present Covenant.
4. No one shall be arbitrarily deprived of the right to enter his own country.

Article 13

An alien lawfully in the territory of a State Party to the present Covenant may be expelled therefrom only in pursuance of a decision reached in accordance with law and shall, except where compelling reasons of national security otherwise require, be allowed to submit the reasons against his expulsion and to have his case reviewed by, and be represented for the purpose before, the competent authority or a person or persons especially designated by the competent authority.

Article 14

1. All persons shall be equal before the courts and tribunals. In the determination of any criminal charge against him, or of his rights and obligations in a suit at law, everyone shall be entitled to a fair and public hearing by a competent, independent and impartial tribunal established by law. The press and the public may be excluded from all or part of a trial for reasons of morals, public order (ordre public) or national security in a democratic society, or when the interest of the private lives of the parties so requires, or to the extent strictly necessary in the opinion of the court in special circumstances where publicity would prejudice the interests of justice; but any judgement rendered in a criminal case or in a suit at law shall be made public except where the interest of juvenile persons otherwise requires or the proceedings concern matrimonial disputes or the guardianship of children.
2. Everyone charged with a criminal offence shall have the right to be presumed innocent until proved guilty according to law.
3. In the determination of any criminal charge against him, everyone shall be entitled to the following minimum guarantees, in full equality:
   (a) To be informed promptly and in detail in a language which he understands of the nature and cause of the charge against him;
   (b) To have adequate time and facilities for the preparation of his defence and to communicate with counsel of his own choosing;
   (c) To be tried without undue delay;
   (d) To be tried in his presence, and to defend himself in person or through legal assistance of his own choosing; to be informed, if he does not have legal assistance, of this right; and to have legal assistance assigned to him, in any case where the interests of justice so require, and without payment by him in any such case if he does not have sufficient means to pay for it;
   (e) To examine, or have examined, the witnesses against him and to obtain the attendance and examination of witnesses on his behalf under the same conditions as witnesses against him;

(f) To have the free assistance of an interpreter if he cannot understand or speak the language used in court;
(g) Not to be compelled to testify against himself or to confess guilt.
4. In the case of juvenile persons, the procedure shall be such as will take account of their age and the desirability of promoting their rehabilitation.
5. Everyone convicted of a crime shall have the right to his conviction and sentence being reviewed by a higher tribunal according to law.
6. When a person has by a final decision been convicted of a criminal offence and when subsequently his conviction has been reversed or he has been pardoned on the ground that a new or newly discovered fact shows conclusively that there has been a miscarriage of justice, the person who has suffered punishment as a result of such conviction shall be compensated according to law, unless it is proved that the non-disclosure of the unknown fact in time is wholly or partly attributable to him.
7. No one shall be liable to be tried or punished again for an offence for which he has already been finally convicted or acquitted in accordance with the law and penal procedure of each country.

Article 15

1. No one shall be held guilty of any criminal offence on account of any act or omission which did not constitute a criminal offence, under national or international law, at the time when it was committed. Nor shall a heavier penalty be imposed than the one that was applicable at the time when the criminal offence was committed. If, subsequent to the commission of the offence, provision is made by law for the imposition of the lighter penalty, the offender shall benefit thereby.
2. Nothing in this article shall prejudice the trial and punishment of any person for any act or omission which, at the time when it was committed, was criminal according to the general principles of law recognized by the community of nations.

Article 16

Everyone shall have the right to recognition everywhere as a person before the law.

Article 17

1. No one shall be subjected to arbitrary or unlawful interference with his privacy, family, home or correspondence, nor to unlawful attacks on his honour and reputation.
2. Everyone has the right to the protection of the law against such interference or attacks.

Article 18

1. Everyone shall have the right to freedom of thought, conscience and religion. This right shall include freedom to have or to adopt a religion or belief of his choice, and freedom, either individually or in community with others and in public or private, to manifest his religion or belief in worship, observance, practice and teaching.
2. No one shall be subject to coercion which would impair his freedom to have or to adopt a religion or belief of his choice.
3. Freedom to manifest one's religion or beliefs may be subject only to such limitations as are prescribed by law and are necessary to protect public safety, order, health, or morals or the fundamental rights and freedoms of others.
4. The States Parties to the present Covenant undertake to have respect for the liberty of parents and, when applicable, legal guardians to ensure the religious and moral education of their children in conformity with their own convictions.

Article 19

1. Everyone shall have the right to hold opinions without interference.
2. Everyone shall have the right to freedom of expression; this right shall include freedom to seek, receive and impart information and ideas of all kinds, regardless of frontiers, either orally, in writing or in print, in the form of art, or through any other media of his choice.
3. The exercise of the rights provided for in paragraph 2 of this article carries with it special duties and responsibilities. It may therefore be subject to certain restrictions, but these shall only be such as are provided by law and are necessary:
   (a) For respect of the rights or reputations of others;
   (b) For the protection of national security or of public order (ordre public), or of public health or morals.

Article 20

1. Any propaganda for war shall be prohibited by law.
2. Any advocacy of national, racial or religious hatred that constitutes incitement to discrimination, hostility or violence shall be prohibited by law.

Article 21

The right of peaceful assembly shall be recognized. No restrictions may be placed on the exercise of this right other than those imposed in conformity with the law and which are necessary in a democratic society in the interests of national security or public safety, public order (ordre public), the protection of public health or morals or the protection of the rights and freedoms of others.

Article 22

1. Everyone shall have the right to freedom of association with others, including the right to form and join trade unions for the protection of his interests.
2. No restrictions may be placed on the exercise of this right other than those which are prescribed by law and which are necessary in a democratic society in the interests of national security or public safety, public order (ordre public), the protection of public health or morals or the protection of the rights and freedoms of others. This article shall not prevent the imposition of lawful restrictions on members of the armed forces and of the police in their exercise of this right.
3. Nothing in this article shall authorize States Parties to the International Labour Organisation Convention of 1948 concerning Freedom of Association and Protection of the Right to Organize to take legislative measures which would prejudice, or to apply the law in such a manner as to prejudice, the guarantees provided for in that Convention.

Article 23

1. The family is the natural and fundamental group unit of society and is entitled to protection by society and the State.
2. The right of men and women of marriageable age to marry and to found a family shall be recognized.
3. No marriage shall be entered into without the free and full consent of the intending spouses.
4. States Parties to the present Covenant shall take appropriate steps to ensure equality of rights and responsibilities of spouses as to marriage, during marriage and at its dissolution. In the case of dissolution, provision shall be made for the necessary protection of any children.

Article 24

1. Every child shall have, without any discrimination as to race, colour, sex, language, religion, national or social origin, property or birth, the right to such measures of protection as are required by his status as a minor, on the part of his family, society and the State.
2. Every child shall be registered immediately after birth and shall have a name.
3. Every child has the right to acquire a nationality.

Article 25

Every citizen shall have the right and the opportunity, without any of the distinctions mentioned in article 2 and without unreasonable restrictions:
(a) To take part in the conduct of public affairs, directly or through freely chosen representatives;

(b) To vote and to be elected at genuine periodic elections which shall be by universal and equal suffrage and shall be held by secret ballot, guaranteeing the free expression of the will of the electors;
(c) To have access, on general terms of equality, to public service in his country.

Article 26

All persons are equal before the law and are entitled without any discrimination to the equal protection of the law. In this respect, the law shall prohibit any discrimination and guarantee to all persons equal and effective protection against discrimination on any ground such as race, colour, sex, language, religion, political or other opinion, national or social origin, property, birth or other status.

Article 27

In those States in which ethnic, religious or linguistic minorities exist, persons belonging to such minorities shall not be denied the right, in community with the other members of their group, to enjoy their own culture, to profess and practise their own religion, or to use their own language.

PART IV

Article 28

1. There shall be established a Human Rights Committee (hereafter referred to in the present Covenant as the Committee). It shall consist of eighteen members and shall carry out the functions hereinafter provided.
2. The Committee shall be composed of nationals of the States Parties to the present Covenant who shall be persons of high moral character and recognized competence in the field of human rights, consideration being given to the usefulness of the participation of some persons having legal experience.
3. The members of the Committee shall be elected and shall serve in their personal capacity.

Article 29

1. The members of the Committee shall be elected by secret ballot from a list of persons possessing the qualifications prescribed in article 28 and nominated for the purpose by the States Parties to the present Covenant.
2. Each State Party to the present Covenant may nominate not more than two persons. These persons shall be nationals of the nominating State.
3. A person shall be eligible for renomination.

Article 30

1. The initial election shall be held no later than six months after the date of the entry into force of the present Covenant.
2. At least four months before the date of each election to the Committee, other than an election to fill a vacancy declared in accordance with article 34, the Secretary-General of the United Nations shall address a written invitation to the States Parties to the present Covenant to submit their nominations for membership of the Committee within three months.
3. The Secretary-General of the United Nations shall prepare a list in alphabetical order of all the persons thus nominated, with an indication of the States Parties which have nominated them, and shall submit it to the States Parties to the present Covenant no later than one month before the date of each election.
4. Elections of the members of the Committee shall be held at a meeting of the States Parties to the present Covenant convened by the Secretary General of the United Nations at the Headquarters of the United Nations. At that meeting, for which two thirds of the States Parties to the present Covenant shall constitute a quorum, the persons elected to the Committee shall be those nominees who obtain the largest number of votes and an absolute majority of the votes of the representatives of States Parties present and voting.

Article 31

1. The Committee may not include more than one national of the same State.
2. In the election of the Committee, consideration shall be given to equitable geographical distribution of membership and to the representation of the different forms of civilization and of the principal legal systems.

Article 32

1. The members of the Committee shall be elected for a term of four years. They shall be eligible for re-election if renominated. However, the terms of nine of the members elected at the first election shall expire at the end of two years; immediately after the first election, the names of these nine members shall be chosen by lot by the Chairman of the meeting referred to in article 30, paragraph 4.
2. Elections at the expiry of office shall be held in accordance with the preceding articles of this part of the present Covenant.

Article 33

1. If, in the unanimous opinion of the other members, a member of the Committee has ceased to carry out his functions for any cause other than absence of a temporary character, the Chairman of the Committee shall notify

the Secretary-General of the United Nations, who shall then declare the seat of that member to be vacant.
2. In the event of the death or the resignation of a member of the Committee, the Chairman shall immediately notify the Secretary-General of the United Nations, who shall declare the seat vacant from the date of death or the date on which the resignation takes effect.

Article 34

1. When a vacancy is declared in accordance with article 33 and if the term of office of the member to be replaced does not expire within six months of the declaration of the vacancy, the Secretary-General of the United Nations shall notify each of the States Parties to the present Covenant, which may within two months submit nominations in accordance with article 29 for the purpose of filling the vacancy.
2. The Secretary-General of the United Nations shall prepare a list in alphabetical order of the persons thus nominated and shall submit it to the States Parties to the present Covenant. The election to fill the vacancy shall then take place in accordance with the relevant provisions of this part of the present Covenant.
3. A member of the Committee elected to fill a vacancy declared in accordance with article 33 shall hold office for the remainder of the term of the member who vacated the seat on the Committee under the provisions of that article.

Article 35

The members of the Committee shall, with the approval of the General Assembly of the United Nations, receive emoluments from United Nations resources on such terms and conditions as the General Assembly may decide, having regard to the importance of the Committee's responsibilities.

Article 36

The Secretary-General of the United Nations shall provide the necessary staff and facilities for the effective performance of the functions of the Committee under the present Covenant.

Article 37

1. The Secretary-General of the United Nations shall convene the initial meeting of the Committee at the Headquarters of the United Nations.
2. After its initial meeting, the Committee shall meet at such times as shall be provided in its rules of procedure.
3. The Committee shall normally meet at the Headquarters of the United Nations or at the United Nations Office at Geneva.

Article 38

Every member of the Committee shall, before taking up his duties, make a solemn declaration in open committee that he will perform his functions impartially and conscientiously.

Article 39

1. The Committee shall elect its officers for a term of two years. They may be re-elected.
2. The Committee shall establish its own rules of procedure, but these rules shall provide, inter alia, that:
   (a) Twelve members shall constitute a quorum;
   (b) Decisions of the Committee shall be made by a majority vote of the members present.

Article 40

1. The States Parties to the present Covenant undertake to submit reports on the measures they have adopted which give effect to the rights recognized herein and on the progress made in the enjoyment of those rights: (a) Within one year of the entry into force of the present Covenant for the States Parties concerned;
   (b) Thereafter whenever the Committee so requests.
2. All reports shall be submitted to the Secretary-General of the United Nations, who shall transmit them to the Committee for consideration. Reports shall indicate the factors and difficulties, if any, affecting the implementation of the present Covenant.
3. The Secretary-General of the United Nations may, after consultation with the Committee, transmit to the specialized agencies concerned copies of such parts of the reports as may fall within their field of competence.
4. The Committee shall study the reports submitted by the States Parties to the present Covenant. It shall transmit its reports, and such general comments as it may consider appropriate, to the States Parties. The Committee may also transmit to the Economic and Social Council these comments along with the copies of the reports it has received from States Parties to the present Covenant.
5. The States Parties to the present Covenant may submit to the Committee observations on any comments that may be made in accordance with paragraph 4 of this article.

Article 41

1. A State Party to the present Covenant may at any time declare under this article that it recognizes the competence of the Committee to receive and consider

communications to the effect that a State Party claims that another State Party is not fulfilling its obligations under the present Covenant. Communications under this article may be received and considered only if submitted by a State Party which has made a declaration recognizing in regard to itself the competence of the Committee. No communication shall be received by the Committee if it concerns a State Party which has not made such a declaration. Communications received under this article shall be dealt with in accordance with the following procedure:

(a) If a State Party to the present Covenant considers that another State Party is not giving effect to the provisions of the present Covenant, it may, by written communication, bring the matter to the attention of that State Party. Within three months after the receipt of the communication the receiving State shall afford the State which sent the communication an explanation, or any other statement in writing clarifying the matter which should include, to the extent possible and pertinent, reference to domestic procedures and remedies taken, pending, or available in the matter;

(b) If the matter is not adjusted to the satisfaction of both States Parties concerned within six months after the receipt by the receiving State of the initial communication, either State shall have the right to refer the matter to the Committee, by notice given to the Committee and to the other State;

(c) The Committee shall deal with a matter referred to it only after it has ascertained that all available domestic remedies have been invoked and exhausted in the matter, in conformity with the generally recognized principles of international law. This shall not be the rule where the application of the remedies is unreasonably prolonged;

(d) The Committee shall hold closed meetings when examining communications under this article;

(e) Subject to the provisions of subparagraph (c), the Committee shall make available its good offices to the States Parties concerned with a view to a friendly solution of the matter on the basis of respect for human rights and fundamental freedoms as recognized in the present Covenant;

(f) In any matter referred to it, the Committee may call upon the States Parties concerned, referred to in subparagraph (b), to supply any relevant information;

(g) The States Parties concerned, referred to in subparagraph (b), shall have the right to be represented when the matter is being considered in the Committee and to make submissions orally and/or in writing;

(h) The Committee shall, within twelve months after the date of receipt of notice under subparagraph (b), submit a report:
- (i) If a solution within the terms of subparagraph (e) is reached, the Committee shall confine its report to a brief statement of the facts and of the solution reached;

(ii) If a solution within the terms of subparagraph (e) is not reached, the Committee shall confine its report to a brief statement of the facts; the written submissions and record of the oral submissions made by the States Parties concerned shall be attached to the report. In every matter, the report shall be communicated to the States Parties concerned.

2. The provisions of this article shall come into force when ten States Parties to the present Covenant have made declarations under paragraph I of this article. Such declarations shall be deposited by the States Parties with the Secretary-General of the United Nations, who shall transmit copies thereof to the other States Parties. A declaration may be withdrawn at any time by notification to the Secretary-General. Such a withdrawal shall not prejudice the consideration of any matter which is the subject of a communication already transmitted under this article; no further communication by any State Party shall be received after the notification of withdrawal of the declaration has been received by the Secretary-General, unless the State Party concerned has made a new declaration.

Article 42

1. (a) If a matter referred to the Committee in accordance with article 41 is not resolved to the satisfaction of the States Parties concerned, the Committee may, with the prior consent of the States Parties concerned, appoint an ad hoc Conciliation Commission (hereinafter referred to as the Commission). The good offices of the Commission shall be made available to the States Parties concerned with a view to an amicable solution of the matter on the basis of respect for the present Covenant;
   (b) The Commission shall consist of five persons acceptable to the States Parties concerned. If the States Parties concerned fail to reach agreement within three months on all or part of the composition of the Commission, the members of the Commission concerning whom no agreement has been reached shall be elected by secret ballot by a two-thirds majority vote of the Committee from among its members.
2. The members of the Commission shall serve in their personal capacity. They shall not be nationals of the States Parties concerned, or of a State not Party to the present Covenant, or of a State Party which has not made a declaration under article 41.
3. The Commission shall elect its own Chairman and adopt its own rules of procedure.
4. The meetings of the Commission shall normally be held at the Headquarters of the United Nations or at the United Nations Office at Geneva. However, they may be held at such other convenient places as the Commission may determine in consultation with the Secretary-General of the United Nations and the States Parties concerned.
5. The secretariat provided in accordance with article 36 shall also service the commissions appointed under this article.

6. The information received and collated by the Committee shall be available to the Commission and the Commission may call upon the States Parties concerned to supply any other relevant information.
7. When the Commission has fully considered the matter, but in any event not later than twelve months after having been seized of the matter, it shall submit to the Chairman of the Committee a report for communication to the States Parties concerned:
    (a) If the Commission is unable to complete its consideration of the matter within twelve months, it shall confine its report to a brief statement of the status of its consideration of the matter;
    (b) If an amicable solution to the matter on tie basis of respect for human rights as recognized in the present Covenant is reached, the Commission shall confine its report to a brief statement of the facts and of the solution reached;
    (c) If a solution within the terms of subparagraph (b) is not reached, the Commission's report shall embody its findings on all questions of fact relevant to the issues between the States Parties concerned, and its views on the possibilities of an amicable solution of the matter. This report shall also contain the written submissions and a record of the oral submissions made by the States Parties concerned;
    (d) If the Commission's report is submitted under subparagraph (c), the States Parties concerned shall, within three months of the receipt of the report, notify the Chairman of the Committee whether or not they accept the contents of the report of the Commission.
8. The provisions of this article are without prejudice to the responsibilities of the Committee under article 41.
9. The States Parties concerned shall share equally all the expenses of the members of the Commission in accordance with estimates to be provided by the Secretary-General of the United Nations.
10. The Secretary-General of the United Nations shall be empowered to pay the expenses of the members of the Commission, if necessary, before reimbursement by the States Parties concerned, in accordance with paragraph 9 of this article.

Article 43

The members of the Committee, and of the ad hoc conciliation commissions which may be appointed under article 42, shall be entitled to the facilities, privileges and immunities of experts on mission for the United Nations as laid down in the relevant sections of the Convention on the Privileges and Immunities of the United Nations.

Article 44

The provisions for the implementation of the present Covenant shall apply without prejudice to the procedures prescribed in the field of human rights by or under the constituent instruments and the conventions of the United Nations and of the specialized agencies and shall not prevent the States Parties to the present Covenant from having recourse to other procedures for settling a dispute in accordance with general or special international agreements in force between them.

Article 45

The Committee shall submit to the General Assembly of the United Nations, through the Economic and Social Council, an annual report on its activities.

PART V

Article 46

Nothing in the present Covenant shall be interpreted as impairing the provisions of the Charter of the United Nations and of the constitutions of the specialized agencies which define the respective responsibilities of the various organs of the United Nations and of the specialized agencies in regard to the matters dealt with in the present Covenant.

Article 47

Nothing in the present Covenant shall be interpreted as impairing the inherent right of all peoples to enjoy and utilize fully and freely their natural wealth and resources.

PART VI

Article 48

1. The present Covenant is open for signature by any State Member of the United Nations or member of any of its specialized agencies, by any State Party to the Statute of the International Court of Justice, and by any other State which has been invited by the General Assembly of the United Nations to become a Party to the present Covenant.
2. The present Covenant is subject to ratification. Instruments of ratification shall be deposited with the Secretary-General of the United Nations.
3. The present Covenant shall be open to accession by any State referred to in paragraph 1 of this article.

4. Accession shall be effected by the deposit of an instrument of accession with the Secretary-General of the United Nations.
5. The Secretary-General of the United Nations shall inform all States which have signed this Covenant or acceded to it of the deposit of each instrument of ratification or accession.

Article 49

1. The present Covenant shall enter into force three months after the date of the deposit with the Secretary-General of the United Nations of the thirty-fifth instrument of ratification or instrument of accession.
2. For each State ratifying the present Covenant or acceding to it after the deposit of the thirty-fifth instrument of ratification or instrument of accession, the present Covenant shall enter into force three months after the date of the deposit of its own instrument of ratification or instrument of accession.

Article 50

The provisions of the present Covenant shall extend to all parts of federal States without any limitations or exceptions.

Article 51

1. Any State Party to the present Covenant may propose an amendment and file it with the Secretary-General of the United Nations. The Secretary-General of the United Nations shall thereupon communicate any proposed amendments to the States Parties to the present Covenant with a request that they notify him whether they favour a conference of States Parties for the purpose of considering and voting upon the proposals. In the event that at least one third of the States Parties favours such a conference, the Secretary-General shall convene the conference under the auspices of the United Nations. Any amendment adopted by a majority of the States Parties present and voting at the conference shall be submitted to the General Assembly of the United Nations for approval.
2. Amendments shall come into force when they have been approved by the General Assembly of the United Nations and accepted by a two-thirds majority of the States Parties to the present Covenant in accordance with their respective constitutional processes. 3. When amendments come into force, they shall be binding on those States Parties which have accepted them, other States Parties still being bound by the provisions of the present Covenant and any earlier amendment which they have accepted.

Article 52

1. Irrespective of the notifications made under article 48, paragraph 5, the Secretary-General of the United Nations shall inform all States referred to in paragraph I of the same article of the following particulars:
   (a) Signatures, ratifications and accessions under article 48;
   (b) The date of the entry into force of the present Covenant under article 49 and the date of the entry into force of any amendments under article 51.

Article 53

1. The present Covenant, of which the Chinese, English, French, Russian and Spanish texts are equally authentic, shall be deposited in the archives of the United Nations.
2. The Secretary-General of the United Nations shall transmit certified copies of the present Covenant to all States referred to in article 48.

Acknowledgment

From the International Covenant on Civil and Political Rights, opened for signature in New York on 19 December, 1966, ©(1967) United Nations. Reprinted with the permission of the United Nations.

INTERNATIONAL COVENANT ON ECONOMIC, SOCIAL AND CULTURAL RIGHTS

The States Parties to the present Covenant,

Considering that, in accordance with the principles proclaimed in the Charter of the United Nations, recognition of the inherent dignity and of the equal and inalienable rights of all members of the human family is the foundation of freedom, justice and peace in the world,

Recognizing that these rights derive from the inherent dignity of the human person,

Recognizing that, in accordance with the Universal Declaration of Human Rights, the ideal of free human beings enjoying freedom from fear and want can only be achieved if conditions are created whereby everyone may enjoy his economic, social and cultural rights, as well as his civil and political rights,

Considering the obligation of States under the Charter of the United Nations to promote universal respect for, and observance of, human rights and freedoms,

Realizing that the individual, having duties to other individuals and to the community to which he belongs, is under a responsibility to strive for the promotion and observance of the rights recognized in the present Covenant,

Agree upon the following articles:

PART I

Article 1

1. All peoples have the right of self-determination. By virtue of that right they freely determine their political status and freely pursue their economic, social and cultural development.

2. All peoples may, for their own ends, freely dispose of their natural wealth and resources without prejudice to any obligations arising out of international economic co-operation, based upon the principle of mutual benefit, and international law. In no case may a people be deprived of its own means of subsistence.
3. The States Parties to the present Covenant, including those having responsibility for the administration of Non-Self-Governing and Trust Territories, shall promote the realization of the right of self-determination, and shall respect that right, in conformity with the provisions of the Charter of the United Nations.

PART II

Article 2

1. Each State Party to the present Covenant undertakes to take steps, individually and through international assistance and co-operation, especially economic and technical, to the maximum of its available resources, with a view to achieving progressively the full realization of the rights recognized in the present Covenant by all appropriate means, including particularly the adoption of legislative measures.
2. The States Parties to the present Covenant undertake to guarantee that the rights enunciated in the present Covenant will be exercised without discrimination of any kind as to race, colour, sex, language, religion, political or other opinion, national or social origin, property, birth or other status.
3. Developing countries, with due regard to human rights and their national economy, may determine to what extent they would guarantee the economic rights recognized in the present Covenant to non-nationals.

Article 3

The States Parties to the present Covenant undertake to ensure the equal right of men and women to the enjoyment of all economic, social and cultural rights set forth in the present Covenant.

Article 4

The States Parties to the present Covenant recognize that, in the enjoyment of those rights provided by the State in conformity with the present Covenant, the State may subject such rights only to such limitations as are determined by law only in so far as this may be compatible with the nature of these rights and solely for the purpose of promoting the general welfare in a democratic society.

Article 5

1. Nothing in the present Covenant may be interpreted as implying for any State, group or person any right to engage in any activity or to perform any act aimed at the destruction of any of the rights or freedoms recognized herein, or at their limitation to a greater extent than is provided for in the present Covenant.
2. No restriction upon or derogation from any of the fundamental human rights recognized or existing in any country in virtue of law, conventions, regulations or custom shall be admitted on the pretext that the present Covenant does not recognize such rights or that it recognizes them to a lesser extent.

PART III

Article 6

1. The States Parties to the present Covenant recognize the right to work, which includes the right of everyone to the opportunity to gain his living by work which he freely chooses or accepts, and will take appropriate steps to safeguard this right.
2. The steps to be taken by a State Party to the present Covenant to achieve the full realization of this right shall include technical and vocational guidance and training programmes, policies and techniques to achieve steady economic, social and cultural development and full and productive employment under conditions safeguarding fundamental political and economic freedoms to the individual.

Article 7

The States Parties to the present Covenant recognize the right of everyone to the enjoyment of just and favourable conditions of work which ensure, in particular:
(a) Remuneration which provides all workers, as a minimum, with:
  (i) Fair wages and equal remuneration for work of equal value without distinction of any kind, in particular women being guaranteed conditions of work not inferior to those enjoyed by men, with equal pay for equal work;
  (ii) A decent living for themselves and their families in accordance with the provisions of the present Covenant;
(b) Safe and healthy working conditions;
(c) Equal opportunity for everyone to be promoted in his employment to an appropriate higher level, subject to no considerations other than those of seniority and competence;
(d) Rest, leisure and reasonable limitation of working hours and periodic holidays with pay, as well as remuneration for public holidays.

Article 8

1. The States Parties to the present Covenant undertake to ensure:
   (a) The right of everyone to form trade unions and join the trade union of his choice, subject only to the rules of the organization concerned, for the promotion and protection of his economic and social interests. No restrictions may be placed on the exercise of this right other than those prescribed by law and which are necessary in a democratic society in the interests of national security or public order or for the protection of the rights and freedoms of others;
   (b) The right of trade unions to establish national federations or confederations and the right of the latter to form or join international trade-union organizations;
   (c) The right of trade unions to function freely subject to no limitations other than those prescribed by law and which are necessary in a democratic society in the interests of national security or public order or for the protection of the rights and freedoms of others;
   (d) The right to strike, provided that it is exercised in conformity with the laws of the particular country.
2. This article shall not prevent the imposition of lawful restrictions on the exercise of these rights by members of the armed forces or of the police or of the administration of the State.
3. Nothing in this article shall authorize States Parties to the International Labour Organisation Convention of 1948 concerning Freedom of Association and Protection of the Right to Organize to take legislative measures which would prejudice, or apply the law in such a manner as would prejudice, the guarantees provided for in that Convention.

Article 9

The States Parties to the present Covenant recognize the right of everyone to social security, including social insurance.

Article 10

The States Parties to the present Covenant recognize that:
1. The widest possible protection and assistance should be accorded to the family, which is the natural and fundamental group unit of society, particularly for its establishment and while it is responsible for the care and education of dependent children. Marriage must be entered into with the free consent of the intending spouses.
2. Special protection should be accorded to mothers during a reasonable period before and after childbirth. During such period working mothers should be accorded paid leave or leave with adequate social security benefits.

3. Special measures of protection and assistance should be taken on behalf of all children and young persons without any discrimination for reasons of parentage or other conditions. Children and young persons should be protected from economic and social exploitation. Their employment in work harmful to their morals or health or dangerous to life or likely to hamper their normal development should be punishable by law. States should also set age limits below which the paid employment of child labour should be prohibited and punishable by law.

Article 11

1. The States Parties to the present Covenant recognize the right of everyone to an adequate standard of living for himself and his family, including adequate food, clothing and housing, and to the continuous improvement of living conditions. The States Parties will take appropriate steps to ensure the realization of this right, recognizing to this effect the essential importance of international co-operation based on free consent.
2. The States Parties to the present Covenant, recognizing the fundamental right of everyone to be free from hunger, shall take, individually and through international co-operation, the measures, including specific programmes, which are needed:
   (a) To improve methods of production, conservation and distribution of food by making full use of technical and scientific knowledge, by disseminating knowledge of the principles of nutrition and by developing or reforming agrarian systems in such a way as to achieve the most efficient development and utilization of natural resources;
   (b) Taking into account the problems of both food-importing and food-exporting countries, to ensure an equitable distribution of world food supplies in relation to need.

Article 12

1. The States Parties to the present Covenant recognize the right of everyone to the enjoyment of the highest attainable standard of physical and mental health.
2. The steps to be taken by the States Parties to the present Covenant to achieve the full realization of this right shall include those necessary for:
   (a) The provision for the reduction of the stillbirth-rate and of infant mortality and for the healthy development of the child;
   (b) The improvement of all aspects of environmental and industrial hygiene;
   (c) The prevention, treatment and control of epidemic, endemic, occupational and other diseases;
   (d) The creation of conditions which would assure to all medical service and medical attention in the event of sickness.

Article 13

1. The States Parties to the present Covenant recognize the right of everyone to education. They agree that education shall be directed to the full development of the human personality and the sense of its dignity, and shall strengthen the respect for human rights and fundamental freedoms. They further agree that education shall enable all persons to participate effectively in a free society, promote understanding, tolerance and friendship among all nations and all racial, ethnic or religious groups, and further the activities of the United Nations for the maintenance of peace.
2. The States Parties to the present Covenant recognize that, with a view to achieving the full realization of this right:
    (a) Primary education shall be compulsory and available free to all;
    (b) Secondary education in its different forms, including technical and vocational secondary education, shall be made generally available and accessible to all by every appropriate means, and in particular by the progressive introduction of free education;
    (c) Higher education shall be made equally accessible to all, on the basis of capacity, by every appropriate means, and in particular by the progressive introduction of free education;
    (d) Fundamental education shall be encouraged or intensified as far as possible for those persons who have not received or completed the whole period of their primary education;
    (e) The development of a system of schools at all levels shall be actively pursued, an adequate fellowship system shall be established, and the material conditions of teaching staff shall be continuously improved.
3. The States Parties to the present Covenant undertake to have respect for the liberty of parents and, when applicable, legal guardians to choose for their children schools, other than those established by the public authorities, which conform to such minimum educational standards as may be laid down or approved by the State and to ensure the religious and moral education of their children in conformity with their own convictions.
4. No part of this article shall be construed so as to interfere with the liberty of individuals and bodies to establish and direct educational institutions, subject always to the observance of the principles set forth in paragraph I of this article and to the requirement that the education given in such institutions shall conform to such minimum standards as may be laid down by the State.

Article 14

Each State Party to the present Covenant which, at the time of becoming a Party, has not been able to secure in its metropolitan territory or other territories under its jurisdiction compulsory primary education, free of charge, undertakes, within two years, to work out and adopt a detailed plan of action for the progressive implementation, within a reasonable number of years, to be fixed in the plan, of the principle of compulsory education free of charge for all.

Article 15

1. The States Parties to the present Covenant recognize the right of everyone:
    (a) To take part in cultural life;
    (b) To enjoy the benefits of scientific progress and its applications;
    (c) To benefit from the protection of the moral and material interests resulting from any scientific, literary or artistic production of which he is the author.
2. The steps to be taken by the States Parties to the present Covenant to achieve the full realization of this right shall include those necessary for the conservation, the development and the diffusion of science and culture.
3. The States Parties to the present Covenant undertake to respect the freedom indispensable for scientific research and creative activity.
4. The States Parties to the present Covenant recognize the benefits to be derived from the encouragement and development of international contacts and co-operation in the scientific and cultural fields.

PART IV

Article 16

1. The States Parties to the present Covenant undertake to submit in conformity with this part of the Covenant reports on the measures which they have adopted and the progress made in achieving the observance of the rights recognized herein.
2.
    (a) All reports shall be submitted to the Secretary-General of the United Nations, who shall transmit copies to the Economic and Social Council for consideration in accordance with the provisions of the present Covenant;
    (b) The Secretary-General of the United Nations shall also transmit to the specialized agencies copies of the reports, or any relevant parts therefrom, from States Parties to the present Covenant which are also members of these specialized agencies in so far as these reports, or parts therefrom, relate to any matters which fall within the responsibilities of the said agencies in accordance with their constitutional instruments.

Article 17

1. The States Parties to the present Covenant shall furnish their reports in stages, in accordance with a programme to be established by the Economic and Social Council within one year of the entry into force of the present

Covenant after consultation with the States Parties and the specialized agencies concerned.
2. Reports may indicate factors and difficulties affecting the degree of fulfilment of obligations under the present Covenant.
3. Where relevant information has previously been furnished to the United Nations or to any specialized agency by any State Party to the present Covenant, it will not be necessary to reproduce that information, but a precise reference to the information so furnished will suffice.

Article 18

Pursuant to its responsibilities under the Charter of the United Nations in the field of human rights and fundamental freedoms, the Economic and Social Council may make arrangements with the specialized agencies in respect of their reporting to it on the progress made in achieving the observance of the provisions of the present Covenant falling within the scope of their activities. These reports may include particulars of decisions and recommendations on such implementation adopted by their competent organs.

Article 19

The Economic and Social Council may transmit to the Commission on Human Rights for study and general recommendation or, as appropriate, for information the reports concerning human rights submitted by States in accordance with articles 16 and 17, and those concerning human rights submitted by the specialized agencies in accordance with article 18.

Article 20

The States Parties to the present Covenant and the specialized agencies concerned may submit comments to the Economic and Social Council on any general recommendation under article 19 or reference to such general recommendation in any report of the Commission on Human Rights or any documentation referred to therein.

Article 21

The Economic and Social Council may submit from time to time to the General Assembly reports with recommendations of a general nature and a summary of the information received from the States Parties to the present Covenant and the specialized agencies on the measures taken and the progress made in achieving general observance of the rights recognized in the present Covenant.

Article 22

The Economic and Social Council may bring to the attention of other organs of the United Nations, their subsidiary organs and specialized agencies concerned with furnishing technical assistance any matters arising out of the reports referred to in this part of the present Covenant which may assist such bodies in deciding, each within its field of competence, on the advisability of international measures likely to contribute to the effective progressive implementation of the present Covenant.

Article 23

The States Parties to the present Covenant agree that international action for the achievement of the rights recognized in the present Covenant includes such methods as the conclusion of conventions, the adoption of recommendations, the furnishing of technical assistance and the holding of regional meetings and technical meetings for the purpose of consultation and study organized in conjunction with the Governments concerned.

Article 24

Nothing in the present Covenant shall be interpreted as impairing the provisions of the Charter of the United Nations and of the constitutions of the specialized agencies which define the respective responsibilities of the various organs of the United Nations and of the specialized agencies in regard to the matters dealt with in the present Covenant.

Article 25

Nothing in the present Covenant shall be interpreted as impairing the inherent right of all peoples to enjoy and utilize fully and freely their natural wealth and resources.

PART V

Article 26

1. The present Covenant is open for signature by any State Member of the United Nations or member of any of its specialized agencies, by any State Party to the Statute of the International Court of Justice, and by any other State which has been invited by the General Assembly of the United Nations to become a party to the present Covenant.
2. The present Covenant is subject to ratification. Instruments of ratification shall be deposited with the Secretary-General of the United Nations.

3. The present Covenant shall be open to accession by any State referred to in paragraph 1 of this article.
4. Accession shall be effected by the deposit of an instrument of accession with the Secretary-General of the United Nations.
5. The Secretary-General of the United Nations shall inform all States which have signed the present Covenant or acceded to it of the deposit of each instrument of ratification or accession.

Article 27

1. The present Covenant shall enter into force three months after the date of the deposit with the Secretary-General of the United Nations of the thirty-fifth instrument of ratification or instrument of accession.
2. For each State ratifying the present Covenant or acceding to it after the deposit of the thirty-fifth instrument of ratification or instrument of accession, the present Covenant shall enter into force three months after the date of the deposit of its own instrument of ratification or instrument of accession.

Article 28

The provisions of the present Covenant shall extend to all parts of federal States without any limitations or exceptions.

Article 29

1. Any State Party to the present Covenant may propose an amendment and file it with the Secretary-General of the United Nations. The Secretary-General shall thereupon communicate any proposed amendments to the States Parties to the present Covenant with a request that they notify him whether they favour a conference of States Parties for the purpose of considering and voting upon the proposals. In the event that at least one third of the States Parties favours such a conference, the Secretary-General shall convene the conference under the auspices of the United Nations. Any amendment adopted by a majority of the States Parties present and voting at the conference shall be submitted to the General Assembly of the United Nations for approval.
2. Amendments shall come into force when they have been approved by the General Assembly of the United Nations and accepted by a two-thirds majority of the States Parties to the present Covenant in accordance with their respective constitutional processes.
3. When amendments come into force they shall be binding on those States Parties which have accepted them, other States Parties still being bound by the provisions of the present Covenant and any earlier amendment which they have accepted.

Article 30

Irrespective of the notifications made under article 26, paragraph 5, the Secretary-General of the United Nations shall inform all States referred to in paragraph I of the same article of the following particulars:
(a) Signatures, ratifications and accessions under article 26;
(b) The date of the entry into force of the present Covenant under article 27 and the date of the entry into force of any amendments under article 29.

Article 31

1. The present Covenant, of which the Chinese, English, French, Russian and Spanish texts are equally authentic, shall be deposited in the archives of the United Nations.
2. The Secretary-General of the United Nations shall transmit certified copies of the present Covenant to all States referred to in article 26.

Acknowledgment

From the International Covenant on Economic, Social and Cultural Rights, opened for signature in New York on 19 December, 1966, ©(1967) United Nations. Reprinted with the permission of the United Nations.

INDEX

Note: Tables are shown in **bold** type and figures in *italics*. Footnotes are indicated by an "n" and the footnote number after the page number e.g., 100n1 refers to footnote 1 on page 100.

9/11 terrorist attacks 92, 117, 149, 225

Abolition of Forced Labour Convention 15, 239, 242
Aboriginal peoples 299, 301, 314, 316
Aboriginal tourism 98–99, 309, 312
absolute rights 21, 204
abuses 4, 5, 11, **165**, 167, 242, 274, 356; and Indigenous people's rights 302, 307, 309; and politics 86, 87, 92, 94, 96, 98, 99; and privacy 115, 117, 119; sexual 333, 334, 335, 337, 339, 340, 341, 343–344; and tourism enterprises 44, 45, 46
access to justice 7, 26–31
accessibility, of persons with special needs 216–220, **220**
accountability 4, 24, 48–49, 73, 75, 86, 91, 165, 271
acculturation 124, 172–173, 177, 307, 315, 355
Accumulation by Dispossession 168, 171
ACI (Airports Council International) 226
Acquired Immunodeficiency Syndrome (AIDS) 30, 65, 120, 344
ADA (Americans with Disabilities Act) 200, 251
additionality 167
advance passenger information programs 152–154

A.F. v. Starwood Hotels and Resorts Worldwide 193
African Convention/Charter on Human and Peoples' Rights (AfCHPR) 269
African Court of Human and Peoples' Rights 27
African Union (AU) 25, 93, 220
age discrimination 252–255
Agenda for Sustainable Development (Agenda 2030) 74, 76, 200, 237, 247
agriculture 122–123, 165, 188, 243, 245, 333, 359; and development 67, 74; and the environment 272, 275–276; and Indigenous people's rights 296, 300–301, 302
AIDS (Acquired Immunodeficiency Syndrome) 30, 65, 120, 344
Ainu people 301–302, 314
air travel 128, 148–152, 153–154
Airbnb 123, 168–169
airports 148–149, 150, 152, 154, 159, 209, 225–226, 281
Alaska 311, 312–313, 315
American Convention on Human Rights (AmCHR) 27, 138, 269
Americans with Disabilities Act (ADA) 200, 251
Amnesty International 5, 87, 91–92, 125
Andaman Island 306–307

anthropogenic climate change 272–273
anti-corruption 46, 47, 50, 91
anti-discrimination legislation 191, 192, 196, 198, 201–202, 202–203
Aotearoa *see* New Zealand
apartheid system 17, 188–189
appropriation 124, 127, 168, 307
APTA (Asia Pacific Trade Agreement) 224
Arab Spring 86, 93, 117–118, 125–126, 128
arbitrary interferences 139
Argentina 143, 335
ASEAN (Association of Southeast Asian Nations) 138, 176, 220
Asia Pacific Trade Agreement (APTA) 224
assimilation 124, 172–173, 177, 307, 355
Association of Southeast Asian Nations (ASEAN) 138, 176, 220
asylum seekers 14, 87, 159, 166–167, 209, 223, 227, 229
AU (African Union) 25, 93, 220
Australia 92, 191, 224, 333; and displacement 166, 169, 173–174; and human security 117, 119, 120–121; and Indigenous people's rights 305, 308, 318; and labour conditions 244, 247–248, 253, 254, 255, 258; and privacy 149, 152, 154
Ayers Rock 308, 309

basic needs 62, 63, 109, 115, 122–123
Beijing Declaration and Platform for Action 63, 72
Berlin Declaration on Transforming Tourism 5, 61, 72–77, 78
biodiversity 67, 127, 278, 282, 285
Black Lives Matter 86, 191, 203, 303
black tourism, in South Africa 189
Bostock v. Clayton County, Georgia 197, 256–257
Brazil 64, 87, 118–119, 162–164, 166, 265, 316, 334, 336
British Airways 142–143
Brundtland Report 64, 71, 267, 268, 269, 282
Burma *see* Myanmar

CACM (Central American Common Market) 224
Cambodia 117, 161, 331, 336, 337, 338
Campbell v. Womack 146
Canada-United States-Mexico Free Trade Agreement 222
Cangiano v. Forte Hotels 146

capitalism 69, 99, 124, 168, 221, 223, 311, 312; disaster 86, 128, 166–167, 168, 177, 355
Caribbean Community (CARICOM) 224
caste system 332
CAT (Committee Against Torture) **12**, 26, 28–29
Cathay Pacific 142, 249
CE (Council of Europe) 25, 223
CED (Committee on Enforced Disappearances) 30
CEDAW *see* Committee on the Elimination of Discrimination Against Women; Convention on the Elimination of All Forms of Discrimination against Women
CEFTA (Central European Free Trade Agreement) 224
Central American Common Market (CACM) 224
Central European Free Trade Agreement (CEFTA) 224
CERD (Committee on the Elimination of Racial Discrimination) 18, 29
CESCR (Committee on Economic, Social and Cultural Rights) 29
CFR (United States Code of Federal Regulations) 200, 251
Charter of Fundamental Rights 141, 191
Charter of the United Nations 10, 29
child, rights of the **12**, 13, 29, 65, 127, 138, 193, 212, 243, 265, 334–335, 362
child labour 13, 47, 96, 126–127, 351–352, 356; and labour conditions 237, 238, 239, 243–245, 259; and sex tourism 333, 335
child pornography **12**, 334–335, 337–338
child prostitution **12**, 71, 244, 334–335
child sex tourism (CST) 53, 336, 337–338, 339, 340, 342–343, 344, 357
children: crimes against 53, 334, 336, 337, 338, 340, 342, 343, 344; exploitation of 96, 117, **165**, 244, 326, 333–338, 341–343, 357; sale of 334–335
China 5–6, 10, 152, 174, 216, 241, 270, 357
Christianity 17, 18, 21, 71, 97, 174, 196
CIS (Commonwealth of Independent States) 224
cities 67, 123, 124, 164, 266, 280, 281, 333
City of Los Angeles v. Patel 147–148
civil liberties 3, 7, 18–21

civil rights 7, 18–21, 31, 48, 62, 89, 196–197, 353; and displacement 159, 166
Civil Rights Act 190–191, 192, 197, 198, 250, 256
climate change 67, 75, 90, 165, 313; and the environment 265, 266, 267, 269, 270–271, 272–273, 274, 275, 278, 280–281, 284, 285, 286; and human rights in tourism 3, 5, 16, 32, 356, 360, 362; and human security 109, 115, 127, 128
CMW (Committee on Migrant Workers) 29
CO_2 emissions 6, 266, 279, 280, 281, 282, 286
Cobo Study 303, 304
Code of Conduct for the Protection of Children from Sexual Exploitation in Travel and Tourism 342
Code of Federal Regulations (CFR) 200, 251
Cold War 20, 25, 111, 112, 116, 173
collective bargaining 13, 47, 238, 239, 240–241, 246, 356
collective rights 19, 31, 274, 276, 360, 361, 362
Colombian Exchange 300
colonialism 91, 168, 172–173, 210, 296, 305, 309, 357
colour 185, 187, 190, 191, 192, 196, 247
commercial sexual exploitation 326, 328, 329, 330, 332, 343–344; children in 326, 333–338, 339, 341–342, 343
Commission on the Status of Women (CSW) 30
Committee Against Torture (CAT) **12**, 26, 28–29
Committee on Economic, Social and Cultural Rights (CESCR) 29
Committee on Enforced Disappearances (CED) 30
Committee on Migrant Workers (CMW) 29
Committee on the Elimination of Discrimination Against Women (CEDAW) **12**, 28, 29, 192–193
Committee on the Elimination of Racial Discrimination (CERD) 18, 29
Committee on the Rights of Persons with Disabilities (CRPD) 30
Committee on the Rights of the Child 29, 265

commodification 121, 124, 305, 311, 313; and displacement 159, 168, 171–172, 173–176
Commonwealth of Independent States (CIS) 224
communicable diseases 120–121
community security 123–125
comparative politics 83, 84, 86–88
complaints 11, 20, 26–27, 29, 145, 147, 255, 271, 358
compulsory labour 47, 239, 241–243
conflict minerals 51
conflicts 3, 92, 175, 225, 330, 355; anti-discrimination law 201–203; and human security 111, 112, 113, 115, 125; involving Indigenous peoples 300–303, 305, 308
constitutionalism 361
control 125, 201, 356, 358, 359; and displacement 161, 171, 177; and freedom of movement 210, 212, 213, 214, 215, 221, 223, 229; and Indigenous people's rights 304, 305, 307, 309, 310, 311, 315, 318; and politics 84, 85, 98–99; and sex tourism 339, 341, 343
Convention (No. 138) Concerning Minimum Age for Admission to Employment 239, 243, 244
Convention (No. 172) Concerning Working Conditions in Hotels, Restaurants and Similar Establishments 240, 246
Convention (No. 182) Concerning the Prohibition and Immediate Action for the Elimination of the Worst Forms of Child Labour 239, 244
Convention on Action against Trafficking in Human Beings 53, 54
Convention on the Elimination of All Forms of Discrimination against Women (CEDAW) 63, 65, 192–193, 248
Convention on the Prevention and Punishment of the Crime of Genocide 13, 25, 26
Convention on the Protection of Children against Sexual Exploitation and Sexual Abuse 335, 337, 341
Convention on the Rights of Persons with Disabilities (CRPD/ICRPD) **12**, 27, 28, 200, 213, 217–219; and labour conditions 250, 251, 252
Convention on the Rights of the Child (CRC) **12**, 65, 127, 138, 193, 212, 243, 334–335

Convention on the Rights of the Child, Optional Protocol (CRC-OP) **12**, 334, 336, 337, 340
corporate human rights obligations 48–52
corporate liability 49, 54, 55, 88, 340–342
corporate responsibility, to respect human rights 4, 45, 352
Corporate Social Responsibility (CSR) 43–44, 50, 52, 55, 278, 282–283, 362; and development 66, 73, 74
corruption 16, 50, 84, 87, 164, 337, 343; anti- 46, 47, 50, 91
Council of Europe (CE) 25, 223
court jurisdiction 20, 27, 88, 100n1
Covenant of the League of Nations 9
COVID-19 40, 41, 142–143, 236; and discrimination of patrons 192, 203; and displacement 159, 167, 169–171; and the environment 266, 279, 280, 281, 282, 286; and freedom of movement 209, 210, 214, 215, 216, 225, 228, 229; and human rights in tourism 4, 5, 6, 21, 32–33, 352, 355, 357–361, 362; and human security 120, 127; and Indigenous people's rights 303, 313, 316; and politics 93, 94; and Sustainable Development Goals 76–77, 78
CRC *see* UNCRC (United Nations Convention on the Rights of the Child)
CRC-OP (Convention on the Rights of the Child, Optional Protocol) **12**, 334, 336, 337, 340
creative destruction 167, 168, 171, 355
crimes 20, 49, 72, 114, 123; of aggression 28; against children 53, 334, 336, 337, 338, 340, 342, 343, 344; of genocide 13, 23, 27, 53, 187; hate 187, 191, 192, 195, 353; human rights 49, 52, 100n1; human trafficking 344; against humanity 13, 27, 53; of piracy 53; terrorism-related 149, 150; of torture 53; violent 92, 93, 118–119; war 3, 13, 27, 53, 61
criminal liability 49, 54, 340, 341
CRPD *see* Committee on the Rights of Persons with Disabilities; Convention on the Rights of Persons with Disabilities
CST (child sex tourism) 53, 336, 337–338, 339, 340, 342–343, 344, 357
CSW (Commission on the Status of Women) 30
Cuba 87, 121, 201–202, 335–336
cultural commodification 173–176
cultural displacement 124, 160, 171–176, 355

cultural relativism 7, 16–18
cultural values 171, 172, 312–313

data privacy 138, 143, 154
decent work, right to 67, 236, 237, 238, 240, 245–247, 259, 356
Declaration on Fundamental Principles and Rights at Work 46, 239
Declaration on Race and Racial Prejudice 14, 187
Declaration on the Elimination of All Forms of Intolerance and of Discrimination Based on Religion or Belief 14, 198
Declaration on the Elimination of Violence Against Women 16
Declaration on the Right to Development 5, 16, 61–65
decolonisation 302–303, 318
democracy 139, 150, 215, 221, 240, 302, 362; and human rights 3, 17, 24, 25, 27; and human security 117–118, 125–126; and politics 85, 89, 91, 95, 99
Department of Economic and Social Affairs (DESA) 30, 76–77, 109, 279, 304
dependency theory 62
descent 187, 188, 190, 247, 298, **298**, 299
desertification 67, 122, 165, 272
development, sustainable *see* sustainable development
development paradigm 60, 61, 62, 73, 286–287, 353-4
direct displacement 160
disabilities, rights of persons with **12**, 13, 30, 200, 213, 217–219, 250
disability discrimination 199–201, 204, 250–251
disaster capitalism 86, 128, 166–167, 168, 177, 355
disasters 110, 165–167, 276; natural *see* natural disasters
disclosure 50, 51, 52, 55, 138, 143, 144, 148
discrimination 4, 19, 20–21, 32, 259, 285, 353; age 252–255; based on belief 14, 92, 225, 230; against children 65; disability 199–201, 204, 250–251; in education 14; in employment 14, 47, 238, 239, 241, 247–257, 356; by ethnic origin 185, 186, 187–192, 247, 248–249; gender 68, 185, 192–194, 203, 230; based on gender identity 194–198; against Indigenous peoples 296, 302, 303–304; against migrants 16, 96, 228,

230, 257; and movement 210, 213; based on national origin 187–192, 222; non- 11, 21, 72, 73, 75, 185, 255–256, 302; racial **12**, 18, 23, 29, 65, 187–192, 230, 247, 248–249; based on religion 14, 198–199, 222, 250; sex 192–194, 203, 248, 249, 255, 256, 257; based on sexual orientation 194–198, 255, 256, 257, 259–260, 332; social 109, 226; in tourism establishments 185–204, 201–203, 355; based on values 92, 225; against vulnerable populations 162, 165; against women **12**, 29, 63, 65, 96, 203, 248
diseases 65, 92, 93, 96, 160, 300, 308; and the environment 266, 276, 279; and human security 109, 114, 115, 119, 120–121, 122; *see also* COVID-19
displacement: cultural 124, 160, 171–176, 355; direct 160; economic 159, 167–171, 173, 177, 310, 355; indirect 160, 161, 167, 176; population 160–167, **165**, 176, 177, 310, 355
Displacement Decathlon 163
Division for the Advancement of Women 30
Dodge v. Ford Motor Co. 42–43
domestic law 21–26
Dominican Republic 121, 335–336
dualism, in human rights 25, 26, 87
Durban Declaration 14, 188
Duty of Vigilance Law 51, 88

E. A. v. West End Hotel Partners et al. 145
Earth Summits 64, 278
ECHR (European Convention for the Protection of Human Rights and Fundamental Freedoms) 20, 27, 138, 139–140, 149–150, 269, 271–272
Economic Community of West African States (ECOWAS) 224
economic displacement 159, 167–171, 173, 177, 310, 355
economic exploitation 243
economic growth 6, 42, 43, 237, 266, 287; and development 60, 66, 67
economic security 120, 126–127
ecotourism 69, 74, 279, 312, 315, 316, **317**
ECOWAS (Economic Community of West African States) 224
ECPAT (End Child Prostitution and Trafficking) 5, 71, 96, 117; and sex tourism 326, 331, 332, 333, 334, 335, 336–337, 342

ECtHR (European Court of Human Rights) 20, 27, 138–139, 149–150, 151
ECtWT (Ecumenical Coalition on Third World Tourism) 71
education 14, 15, 176, 190, 199, 302, 343, 344; and development 62, 63, 65, 67, 71, 72, 74; and freedom of movement 209, 222, 227; and human security 109, 115, 119, 122; and labour conditions 236, 237, 243, 258; and politics 87, 90, 91
EEOC (United States Equal Employment Opportunity Commission) 250, 252, 256
EFTA (European Free Trade Association) 224
Egypt 86, 93, 118, 125, 126, 284
El Niño Southern Oscillation (ENSO) 165, 272
El-Al Israel Airlines Ltd v. Jonathan Danielwitz 255–256
Electronic System for Travel Authorization (ESTA) 152, 224
Electronic Travel Authorizations, Australia (ETA) 224
Electronic Travel Authorizations, Canada (eTA) 224
Employment Division, Department of Human Resources of Oregon v. Smith 195–196
employment insecurity 96, 356
empowerment 4, 32, 63, 88, 100, 125, 165, 200; of Indigenous peoples 306, 307, 308; political 90; of the poor 73, 74; of women and girls 30, 63, 64, 65, 67, 68, 97
End Child Prostitution and Trafficking *see* ECPAT (End Child Prostitution and Trafficking)
energy 67, 125, 170, 284
England 8, 49, 167, 274, 275, 276
ENSO (El Niño Southern Oscillation) 165, 272
environment, rights to 88, 266, 268–272, 277, 285, 286, 351, 356; *see also* Rio Declaration on Environment and Development
environmental changes 266, 275–276
environmental degradation 69, 127, 266, 268, 276
environmental exploitation 69, 70–71
environmental impacts 73, 278, 279, 281, 282, 285, 360, 362
environmental issues, in tourism 127, 266, 269, 278–279, 281–285, 286
environmental justice 269, 271–272, 285

environmental law 267–268, 269, 270, 271, 273, 282, 284–285, 356
environmental movements 276–278
environmental pollution 266, 271, 276, 277
environmental rights 88, 266, 268–272, 277, 285, 286, 351, 356
environmental security 115, 127–128, 278, 356
environmentalism 276–278
equity 69, 75, 90, 91, 251, 270
ESTA (Electronic System for Travel Authorization) 152, 224
ETA (Electronic Travel Authorizations, Australia) 224
eTA (Electronic Travel Authorizations, Canada) 224
ethical values 18
Ethiopia 93–94, 122
ethnic origin, discrimination on basis of 185, 186, 187–192, 198, 203, 247, 248, 355
ETIAS (European Travel Information and Authorisation System) 224
European Convention for the Protection of Human Rights and Fundamental Freedoms (ECHR) 20, 27, 138, 139–140, 149–150, 269, 271–272
European Court of Human Rights (ECtHR) 20, 27, 138–139, 149–150, 151
European Free Trade Association (EFTA) 224
European Travel Information and Authorisation System (ETIAS) 224
eviction 161, 162, 163, 164, 168, 310
exploitation 32, 63, 71–72, 99, 114, 117, 330–331, 351; of children 96, 117, **165**, 244, 326, 333–338, 341–343, 357; economic 243; environmental 69, 70–71; of Indigenous peoples 296, 304, 305, 307, 308, 317; labour 3, 4, 77, 88, 115; of migrants 16, 242, 258; natural resource 268; political 111; sexual *see* sexual exploitation
extraterritorial jurisdiction 52–53, 337

fair conditions of employment, right to 16
FAO (Food and Agriculture Organization) 30, 359
favelas 162, 163
FIFA World Cup 162
First Amendment, of United States Constitution 21, 196

First Nations 7, 297, 299, 303, 307, 314, 333
First World War 31, 68, 201
flags of convenience (FOC) 88, 207
flight shaming 281–282
FOC (flags of convenience) 88, 207
Food and Agriculture Organization (FAO) 30, 359
food insecurity 122, 359
food security 67, 121, 359
Football World Cup 162
forced labour 15, 47, 51; and sex tourism 333, 334, 340, 343–344; in tourism establishments 237, 238, 241–243, 244, 259
Forced Labour Convention 15, 239, 242
forced sex tourism 339–340, 340–343
forests 67, 266, 274, 283
Fourth Amendment, of United States Constitution 140, 148, 225
Framework Convention on Tourism Ethics 48, 326, 330–331, 343
France 7, 49, 52, 118, 198–199, 281, 329
freedom from fear 110, 111, 113
freedom from want 110, 111, 113
freedom of association 13, 47, 214, 238, 239, 240–241, 259, 356
freedom of movement 21, 32, 72, 159, 167, 208–230, **220**, 355, 358
freedom of religion 6, 22, 204
fundamental International Labour Organization conventions 239–240

Gama v. Qantas Airways 248
GATS (General Agreement on Trade in Services) 214
GCC (Gulf Cooperation Council) 224
GCET (Global Code of Ethics for Tourism) 48, 72–73, 326, 330–331, 343
GDP (gross domestic product) 44, 280, 281, 330; global 40, 76, 236
GDPR (General Data Protection Regulation) 141, 142–143
gender discrimination 185, 186, 192–194, 203, 228, 230
gender equality 8, 30, 63, 65, 67, 68, 96, 97, 119, 250
gender identity, discrimination based on 194–198, 255, 332, 355
gender inequality 238, 248
gender orientation 202–203
gender roles 91, 332
gender segregation 215
gender stereotyping 249–250, 256

gender-based violence **165**
General Agreement on Trade in Services (GATS) 214
General Data Protection Regulation (GDPR) 141, 142–143
general principles of law, recognised by community of nations 22, 23, 27
genocide 13, 23, 25, 26, 27, 53, 160, 187, 302
gentrification 96, 116, 124, 355; and displacement 159, 163, 164–165, 167, 169, 171, 177
Germany 7, 216, 277, 282, 285
Gillan and Quinton v. the United Kingdom 149, 151
Global Code of Ethics for Tourism (GCET) 48, 72–73, 326, 330–331, 343
global development 5, 286–287
global governance 89–90, 357–361
global gross domestic product 40, 76, 236
global health 110
global mobility 216
Global Report on Women in Tourism 249–250
Global Reporting Initiative (GRI) 52
global security 92, 110, 154
global warming 165, 272, 279, 280–281, 286, 313
globalisation 62, 97, 98, 159, 177, 301; and human rights in tourism 3–4, 31, 353, 354, 361; and human security 112, 114, 115, 124, 126; and mobility 208, 209, 210, 211, 214–216, 220–222, 226–227, 228, 229, 230; and sex tourism 326, 333–344
Goethe, Johann Wolfgang von 195
good governance 24, 31, 64, 278, 354; and politics 84, 86, 88–91, 99
governance: global 89–90, 357–361; good *see* good governance
government interference 139
Greece 86, 111, 166, 360; see also *Kyrtatos v. Greece*
"green tourism" 69
greenhouse gases 266, 272, 273
GRI (Global Reporting Initiative) 52
grievances 28, 86
gross domestic product (GDP) 44, 280, 281, 330; global 40, 76, 236
Guidelines on Decent Work and Socially Responsible Tourism 240, 246–247
Guiding Principles on Business and Human Rights (UNGP) 4, 45, 46, 52, 55, 76, 240, 352

Guiding Principles Reporting Framework (UNGPRF) 52, 66
Gulf Cooperation Council (GCC) 224

HABITAT (United Nations Human Settlements Programme) 30
hate crimes 187, 191, 192, 195, 353
Hatton and Others v. The United Kingdom 139–140
health care 13, 62, 74, 96, 159, 199, 296, 361; and human security 110, 115, 119–122
healthy environment, right to 6, 18, 65, 114, 128, 265, 356; and human–environment relationship 273, 274; and rights to environment 268, 269, 270, 271; and World Tourism Organization 285–286, 287
Heart of Atlanta Motel Inc. v. United States 190–191
Helen Tsang v. Cathay Pacific Airways 249
heritage 18, 91, 94, 124, 266; cultural 127, 171–172, 274, 284; and displacement 167, 168, 173, 177; of Indigenous people 297, 305, 307, 314, **317**
HIV (Human Immunodeficiency Virus) 30, 65, 120, 344
holidaymaking, right to 213–214, 229, 286
homophobia 332
hospitality industry 41, 76, 137, 195, 203, 226, 306, 309, 352
housing 162–163, 166, 169, 218, 273; and human security 109, 114, 115, 116, 119, 122, 123
HRBA (human rights-based approach) 165, 230, 353–354; to development 60, 61, 64, 68, 76, 77
HRC (Human Rights Committee) 11, 29, 212, 255
human development 5, 50, 64, 65, 73, 110, 111, **116**, 354
Human Development Report 110, 111, **116**, 354
human dignity 69–70, 113, 238, 285
Human Immunodeficiency Virus (HIV) 30, 65, 120, 344
human rights bodies 29–30
Human Rights Committee (HRC) 11, 29, 212, 255
human rights concepts 7–9, 352–353
human rights conventions 27, 28, 48, 203, 343; and labour conditions 238, 241, 243, 247, 259
human rights crimes 49, 52, 100n1

human rights records, of nations 84, 86–88, 94, 99
human rights violations 4, 5, 26–31, 41–44, 50, 52–55, 113
Human Rights Watch 5, 24, 25, 87, 94, 98, 192, 332
human rights-based approach (HRBA) 165, 230, 353–354; to development 60, 61, 64, 68, 76, 77
human security 84, 109–128, **116**, 154, 270, 343–344, 354, 359
human trafficking 50–51, 53, 96, 115, 117, 237; and sex tourism 326, 339–340, 342, 344
Human Zoo 306, 308
human–environment relationship 273–278
humanitarian intervention 61, 125
hunger 15, 65, 67, 109, 359
hygiene 119, 120, 121–122, 198, 274

IASC (Inter-Agency Standing Committee) 30
IATA (International Air Transport Association) 68, 225–226, 282
ICAO (International Civil Aviation Organization) 216
ICC (International Criminal Court) 13, 20, 27–28, 31, 49, 351
ICCPR *see* International Covenant on Civil and Political Rights (ICCPR)
ICESCR *see* International Covenant on Economic, Social and Cultural Rights (ICESCR)
ICF (International Classification of Functioning, Disability and Health) 199
ICO (Information Commissioner's Office) 142
ICRPD *see* Convention on the Rights of Persons with Disabilities
IDD (Inter-Agency Internal Displacement Division) 30
ideology 17, 61, 77, 175, 187; and freedom of movement 215, 220, 226; political 87, 95, 99
ILO *see* International Labour Organization (ILO)
immigration 92, 96, 147, 149, 258; and freedom of movement 218, 222, 223, 227, 228
India 5, 44, 140, 152, 160, 174, 274, 306–307, 331, 332; discrimination of patrons in 195, 198, 203; and the environment 280, 283–284; freedom of movement in 215, 224; human security in 121, 124; labour conditions in 241, 244–245, 248
Indigenisation 302, 303, 318
Indigenous and Tribal peoples, International Labour Organization definition of 298, **298**
Indigenous communities 124, 266, 276, 356
Indigenous peoples and minorities, rights of 14, 161, 269, 296–318, **298**, **317**, 356
Indigenous Populations 71, 165, 166, 274, 356, 357
Indigenous Rights *see* Indigenous peoples and minorities, rights of
indigenous tourism, challenges and opportunities in 309–316
Indigenous Tourism Alberta Strategy 316
Indigenous Tourism Association of Canada (ITAC) 309, 315–316
Indigenous tourism companies in British Columbia, Canada **317**
Indigenous values 311, 312–313
indirect displacement 160, 161, 167, 176
individual rights 8, 16–17, 18, 48, 355, 360, 361; and privacy 149, 150, 151, 153
Indonesia 124, 152, 161, 174, 330
industrialisation 67, 68, 275–276, 277
inequality 17–18, 114, 119, 162, 164, 187, 238, 248; of freedom of movement 209–210, 211, 222–224, 229
Information Commissioner's Office (ICO) 142
infrastructure 40, 94, 98, 115, 122, 209, 242–243, 313; and development 67, 73; and displacement 159, 164
insecurity 343; employment 96, 356; food 122, 359; health 122; human *see* human security; job 96, 356; legal 17; political 84, 86, 92–93, 94, 115, 118
Institute of Governance (IOG) 90
integration principle 282
Inter-Agency Internal Displacement Division (IDD) 30
Inter-Agency Standing Committee (IASC) 30
Inter-American Court of Human Rights 27
internally displaced peoples 159
International Air Transport Association (IATA) 68, 225–226, 282
International Bill of Human Rights 10, 11, 62, 351
International Civil Aviation Organization (ICAO) 216

International Classification of Functioning, Disability and Health (ICF) 199
International Convention on the Elimination of All Forms of Racial Discrimination **12**, 65, 187, 247
International Convention on the Protection of the Rights of All Migrant Workers **12**, 253, 257, 258
International Covenant on Civil and Political Rights (ICCPR) 90, 138, 266, 269, 303; and development 61–62, 65, 68; and discrimination of patrons 185, 187, 192, 198; and freedom of movement 208, 212, 214; and human rights in tourism 11, **12**, 18, 19, 21, 26, 27, 28; and labour conditions 238, 240, 247, 248, 253, 255
International Covenant on Economic, Social and Cultural Rights (ICESCR) 62, 68, 90, 171, 173, 214, 269; and discrimination of patrons 185, 187, 192; and human rights in tourism 11, **12**, 18, 19, 28; and labour conditions 238, 240, 245, 247, 248, 253
International Criminal Court (ICC) 13, 20, 27–28, 31, 49, 351
international customary law 23
international human rights conventions 27, 28, 48, 203, 259, 343
international human rights instruments 7, 9–16, **12**, 46
international human rights law 45, 48, 63, 138–140, 154, 335, 344; and discrimination of patrons 185, 186, 187, 200, 203; and human rights in tourism 19, 20, 21–26, 28; and labour conditions 238, 247–248, 250, 253, 255, 259, 260
International Labour Organization (ILO) 25, 30, 40, 41, 126, 269, 352, 356; conventions of 239–240, 247; and Indigenous people's rights 298, **298**, 299, 310; and sex tourism 332, 333, 339, 340; *see also* labour conditions, in tourism establishments
international law 89, 100n1, 113, 187, 202, 244, 305, 330–331; and the environment 268, 273; and freedom of movement 212, 229; and human rights in tourism 22, 23, 24–25, 26, 27, 44, 45, 52–53, 361
international treaties 23, 26, 361
Inuit people 173, 266, 297, 313, 314
Iñupiat people 312, 315

invasion of privacy, in tourism establishments 143–148
IOG (Institute of Governance) 90
Irish Republican Army (IRA) 149–150, 225
Islam 18, 93, 117, 126, 137, 160, 186, 198, 208, 250, 300, 331
Israel 17–18, 143, 255–256, 329
ITAC (Indigenous Tourism Association of Canada) 309, 315–316

Japan 5, 64, 143, 152, 166, 270, 276; Ainu people of 301–302, 314; and freedom of movement 215, **220**, 226; and sexual exploitation of children 334, 336
Jarawa people 306–307
Jewish nationalism 17–18
job insecurity 96, 356
Joint United Nations Programme on HIV/AIDS (UNAIDS) 30
jurisdiction: court 20, 27, 88, 100n1; extraterritorial 52–53, 337; state 26, 31, 41, 52–55, 201, 212, 285, 301; universal 53
justice 5, 67, 87, 110, **165**, 302; access to 7, 26–31; environmental 269, 271–272, 285; social 114, 209–210

Kayan people 124, 173, 174–176, 306
Kiribati 166, 281
Kyrtatos v. Greece 271

labour conditions, in tourism establishments 32, 46, 117, 126–127, 229–230, 236–260, 356; and politics 85, 88, 96, 98, 100
labour exploitation 3, 4, 77, 88, 115
labour standards 238–240, 247
land grabbing 128, 168, 177, 310, 355
language 10, 74, 89, 172, 185, 191, 270, 285; and freedom of movement 221, 227, 229; gendered 8, 68; and Indigenous people's rights 296, 299, 300
Latif et al. v. Holder et al. 153, 154
law enforcement 147, 148, 149, **165**, 337, 343, 344
LDC (less developed countries) 62, 338
League of Nations 9, 31, 68, 223
LEDS (Less Economically Developed Countries) 114–115, 332, 336
legal insecurity 17
legal rights 9, 19, 21, 311
legitimacy 70, 84, 85, 90, 91, 95, 125

Lesbian, Gay, Bisexual, Transgender, Queer/Questioning *see* LGBTQ+
less developed countries (LDC) 62, 338
Less Economically Developed Countries (LEDS) 114–115, 332, 336
LGBTQ+ 6, 32, 68, 87, 255, 256–257, 259–260; and discrimination of patrons 186, 195, 196, 197–198, 202, 203–204
liberalism 89, 99, 168
Liberia 115, 120, 227
Libya 93, 125, 208
life, right to 8, 21, 167, 271, 273, 284
lifestyle 227, 275, 307, 316, 357, 359; and displacement 161, 172, 173, 176
livelihoods 4, 76, 77, 216, 308, 310, 355, 361; and displacement 159, 160, 161, 162, 165, **165**, 166, 167, 171, 172, 177; and the environment 270, 281, 286; and human security 109, 121, 126, 127–128
lockdowns, due to COVID-19 4, 170, 209, 216, 266, 279, 281; and human rights in tourism 4, 352, 357, 358, 359, 360, 361, 362
low wages 96, 228, 230, 246, 356

Maclean v. the Barking Frog 194
malnutrition 15, 109
Manila Declaration on World Tourism 69–70, 72
Maōri people 298–299, 333
marginalised people 4, 159, 168
marriage 146, 174, 196–197, 255, 299, 331, 335–336, 339
Marriott International 142, 143, 342
mass consumerism 279
mass consumption 68–69, 310
mass tourism 69, 161, 211, 309, 311, 313
Masterpiece Cakeshop Ltd. v. Colorado Civil Rights Commission 196, 197
M.C. Mehta v. Kamal Nath & Ors. 283–284
MDGs (United Nations Millennium Development Goals) 5, 61, 65–68, 74, 77, 270, 296, 302
MEDS (More Economically Developed Countries) 258, 332
mega events 124, 362
MENA (Middle East and North Africa) region 117–118, 125, 126, 128
Mennonite community 168
mental health 13, 96, 159, 167, 314
MERCOSUR (Southern Common Market) 224
Métis Nation 297, 299, 314
Mexico 87, 119, 222, 336

Middle East and North Africa (MENA) region 117–118, 125, 126, 128
migrants, rights of 14, 238, 257–259, 356
migration of labour, in tourism 226–228, 229–230
military 95, 124, 201, 215, 222, 242, 243, 300, 327–328; and displacement 160, 171, 173, 175; and human rights in tourism 5, 24, 30, 31
Millennium Development Goals (MDGs) 5, 61, 65–68, 74, 77, 270, 296, 302
MNE (multi-national enterprise) 88, 100n1
mobility, right to freedom of *see* freedom of movement, rights to
modern slavery 50–51, 117, 237, 242, 244, 304, 339–340
modernisation 62, 301–302, 353
morality 85, 114, 115, 139, 212, 244, 316, 329, 333; and discrimination of patrons 187, 191, 198; and human rights in tourism 9, 11, 17, 19, 20, 21, 31, 41, 49, 362
More Economically Developed Countries (MEDS) 258, 332
Moreno Gómez v. Spain 139
multi-national enterprise (MNE) 88, 100n1
Murray v. United Kingdom 149–150
museumisation 173
Muslims 18, 93, 117, 126, 137, 160, 186, 198, 208, 250, 300, 331
Myanmar 95, 160, 174–176, 215, 242–243, 310

NAACP (National Association for the Advancement of Colored People) 191
NAFTA (North American Free Trade Agreement) 222
National Action Plan on Responsible Business Conduct, The (RBC) 44, 278
National Association for the Advancement of Colored People (NAACP) 191
National League for Democracy (NLD) 95
national origin 14, 247, 257, 355; and discrimination of patrons 186, 187–192, 196, 198, 202
national security 20, 92, 128, 139, 149, 153, 355; and freedom of movement 208, 210, 212, 214, 222, 224–226, 229
national values 77, 210, 220
nationalism 17–18, 30–31, 210, 220–222
nationality 14, 152, 218, 219, 223; principle of 53, 55
Native Americans 172, 196, 300, 333

NATO (North Atlantic Treaty Organization) 220
natural disasters 70, 92, 122, 127–128, 267, 272; displacement due to 159, 160, **165**, 177
natural law 7–8, 8–9
natural resources 4, 15, 127, 128, 161, 162, 168, 362; and development 61, 64, 66–67, 70; and the environment 266, 268, 270, 274, 277, 279, 281, 285, 286; and Indigenous people's rights 296, 301–302, 304, 318
natural rights 8–9, 89, 112, 269
negative rights 18, 62
neoliberalism 62, 110, 168, 354
Netherlands 8, 49, 139, 188, 281, 328
Nevsun vs Araya 88, 100n1
New Zealand 143, 152, 244, 270, 285, 333; and Indigenous people's rights 298, 299, 301, 305–306, 318
9/11 terrorist attacks 92, 117, 149, 225
NLD (National League for Democracy) 95
no-fly lists 92, 152–154
non-governmental organizations (NGOs) 110, 124, 160, 277, 278, 307, 316; and development 71, 73, 75–76; and human rights in tourism 3, 5, 27, 352, 362; and politics 84, 88, 92, 94, 95, 99
North American Free Trade Agreement (NAFTA) 222
North Atlantic Treaty Organization (NATO) 220
Northern Canada 312–313, 315
Norway 49, 227, 285, 310, 329

occupational safety and health 43, 246
oceans 67, 265
OECD (Organisation for Economic Co-operation and Development) 44, 98, 224, 228, 229, 236, 238
Office for the Coordination of Humanitarian Affairs (OCHA) 30
Office of the High Commissioner for Human Rights (OHCHR) 45, 90, 91, 119, 160, 167, 219, 265, 273; and development 61, 62, 63, 64, 65, 68, 73, 75; and human rights in tourism 4, 5, 11, **12**, 16, 21, 22, 24, 29, 30
Office of the Privacy Commissioner of Canada (OPC) 147, 148, 150–151
Office of the Special Adviser on Gender Issues and the Advancement of Women (OSAGI) 30
older persons, rights of 14

Olympic Games 162, 163, 164
Organisation for Economic Co-operation and Development *see* OECD
OSAGI (Office of the Special Adviser on Gender Issues and the Advancement of Women) 30
Our Common Future 64, 71, 267, 268, 269, 282
overtourism 4, 96, 124, 161, 177, 214, 355

Padaung long neck women 124, 173, 174–176, 306
Pan-American games 162
Pan-Arab Free Trade Area (PAFTA) 224
pandemic *see* COVID-19
partnerships 67, 68, 74, 90, 301, 315–316
passive personality principle 53
passports 92, 98, 202, 221, 222–224, 225, 229, 355
PCIJ (Permanent Court of International Justice) 52
peace 67, 69, 70, 110, 111, 177, 187; right to 15, 18
Peace of Westphalia 31, 112, 221
"peeping Tom" cases 145
penal codes 198, 328, 329, 335
Permanent Court of International Justice (PCIJ) 52
personal data 137, 138, 141, 142, 143, 144, 146, 147, 148, 153, 154, 354–355
personal information 140, 142, 143–144, 147, 148, 150–151, 152–154
personal safety 92, 116–119, 354
persons with disabilities, rights of **12**, 13, 30, 200, 213, 217–219, 250
Philippines 64, 94, 95, 161–162; sex tourism in 328, 330, 335, 336, 337, 338
physical displacement, of peoples 160–167, **165**, 176, 177, 310, 355
physical invasion of privacy 138, 143
physical searches, before air travel 148–152
Poland 49, 126, 216
police brutality 191
political development 64, 91, 267
political economy 84, 85, 92, 97–99, 312–313, 326, 331, 332, 354
political empowerment 90
political environment 83, 84, 85–86, 90, 92, 99, 125, 297, 354
political exploitation 111
political insecurity 84, 86, 92–93, 94, 115, 118
political instability 84, 86, 93–94, 119, 354
political migration 176, 355

political security 111–112, 125–126, 220
political stability 91, 92–97, 354
political theory 83, 85, 99
politics: comparative 83, 84, 86–88; of human rights 83, 84, 85–86, 354
"polluters pay" principle 282; and the case of India 283–284
pollution 109, 115, 127, 359; and the environment 265, 266, 267, 269, 270, 271, 274, 276, 277, 279, 281, 282, 283, 284
population displacement 160–167, **165**, 176, 177, 310, 355
positive rights 62
positivism 9, 112
post-colonial nations, low migration potential from 224
post-colonial tourism development 115
potable water 87, 119, 121, 122, 270
poverty 4, 17, 45, 98, 227, 277, 286, 308, 353; and development 60, 62, 63, 64, 65, 67, 71, 73–74, 76, 77; and displacement 159, 173; and human security 109, 111, 114, 115, 117, 122, 123; and sex tourism 331, 333, 336, 338, 343
power 24, 52, 54, 63, 72, 115–116, 168, 240, 357, 361; and discrimination of patrons 188, 191, 201; over freedom of movement 210, 212, 214, 216, 223, 224, 229; political 83, 84, 85, 87, 89, 90, 91, 92, 97, 98, 99; and sex tourism 332, 334, 338, 339, 341
precautionary principle 268, 272, 282, 285
prevention of discrimination 14, 304
prevention principle 282
privacy, right to 92, 137–155, 173, 195, 225, 226, 255, 332; and human rights in tourism 32, 352, 354–355, 359
privatisation 98, 121, 166, 168
pro-democracy uprisings, in Arab countries 86, 93, 117–118, 125–126, 128
progress 43, 74, 76, 87, 195, 210, 239, 245, 277; on human rights in tourism 3, 11, 15–16, 28
property values 116, 123, 164, 169
pro-poor tourism 73–74, 110
prostitution 15, 71, 96, 144, 189; child **12**, 71, 244, 334–335; and sex tourism 327, 328, *329*, 329–330, 331, 339
Protect, Respect and Remedy Famework 4, 45
protective principle 53
public participation, in decision-making 65, 91, 268, 282, 285

public safety 92, 139, 149, 163, 198

qualified rights 21, 204
quality environment, right to a 70, 267, 269
Qantas Airways Ltd v. Christie 254

R. v. Klassen 337–338
race 10, 14, 20, 119, 230, 247–248; and discrimination of patrons 185, 186, 187–192, 196
racial discrimination **12**, 18, 23, 29, 65, 187–192, 230, 247, 248–249
Racial Discrimination Act (RDA) 191, 247–248
RBC (National Action Plan on Responsible Business Conduct, The) 44, 278
RDA (Racial Discrimination Act) 191, 247–248
reasonable accommodations 250–251, 252
red-light districts 328, *329*
refugees 5, 14, 30, 128, 208, 209, 227, 273; and displacement 159, 160, 166–167, 171, 174, 175–176
regionalisation 220, 221
religion 119, 215, 250; and discrimination of patrons 190, 191, 192, 196–197, 198, 204
religious orientation 186, 198–199, 250
religious values 17, 18
relocation 159, 163, 165, 167, 176; *see also* displacement
remedies, for human rights violations 26–31, 242
reporting 46, 50, 52, 66, 248, 260
residence 53, 160, 166, 167, 211, 212, 218, 337
Residential School system 314–315
resilience 75, 77, 110, 166, 278
Responsibility to Protect 125, 267
Responsible Business Conduct (RBC) 44, 278
rest and leisure, right to 213, 214, 229, 238
rights: of the child *see* child, rights of the; civil *see* civil rights; collective 19, 31, 274, 276, 360, 361, 362; to decent work 67, 236, 237, 238, 240, 245–247, 259, 356; to development 61–65, 66, 302; to environment 88, 266, 268–272, 277, 285, 286, 351, 356; to fair conditions of employment 16; to freedom of mobility *see* freedom of movement, rights to; to freedom of movement *see* freedom

of movement, rights to; to healthy environment *see* healthy environment, right to; to holidaymaking 213–214, 229, 286; of Indigenous peoples and minorities 14, 161, 269, 296–318, **298**, **317**, 356; individual *see* individual rights; to land and property 167, 269, 315; legal 9, 19, 21, 311; to life 8, 21, 167, 271, 273, 284; of migrants 14, 238, 257–259, 356; moral 19, 21; natural 8–9, 89, 112, 269; negative 18, 62; of older persons 14; of persons with disabilities **12**, 13, 30, 200, 213, 217–219, 250; positive 62; to privacy *see* privacy, right to; qualified 21; to a quality environment 70, 267, 269; to rest and leisure 213, 214, 229, 238; to sanitation *see* sanitation, right to; of self-determination *see* self-determination, right of; to strike 240–241; to tourism 213–214, 229, 286; to travel 211–214, 286; violations of 4, 5, 26–31, 41–44, 50, 52–55, 113; to water 279, 362; of women 5, 8, 16, 63–64, 85, 192, 351, 362; to work *see* work, right to

Rio Declaration on Environment and Development 46, 267, 268, 269, 274, 282

rights-based approach, to development *see* human rights-based approach (HRBA)

risk analysis 86, 91, 109

Romania 49, 271–272

Sabena discrimination court case 249

SACU (Southern African Customs Union) 224

SADC (South African Development Community) 224

safe drinking water 87, 119, 121, 122, 270

safety: personal 92, 116–119, 354; public 92, 139, 149, 163, 198

SAFTA (South Asian Free Trade Agreement) 224

sanitation, right to 67, 119, 120, 121–122, 303, 328; and the environment 265, 273, 274, 279

SARS (Severe Acute Respiratory Syndrome) 93, 120, 192

Saskatchewan Federation of Labour v. Saskatchewan 240–241

Saudi Arabia 210, 215

SCC (Supreme Court of Canada) 88, 240–241, 299

SDGs (Sustainable Development Goals) 5, 60–78; Agenda 2030 74, 76, 200, 237, 247

seasonal work 228, 355

Second World War 10, 31, 61, 62, 68, 112, 120

security: basic needs 122–123; community 123–125; economic 120, 126–127; environmental 115, 127–128, 278, 356; food 67, 121, 359; global 92, 110, 154; health 119–122; human 84, 109–128, **116**, 154, 270, 343–344, 354, 359; political 111–112, 125–126, 220

security screenings 148–152

security technology 225–226

self-determination, right of 5, 15, 18, 167, 273, 274; and Indigenous people's rights 296, 302, 303, 304, 305, 318

Severe Acute Respiratory Syndrome (SARS) 93, 120, 192

sex discrimination 192–194, 203, 248, 249, 255, 256, 257

sex industry 242, 326, 327, 328, 331, 332, 333, 343–344

sex tourism 53, 117, 120, 308, 326–344, *329*, 356, 357; and development 63, 71, 72

sex work 96, 117, 328, 329, 332, 333, 335, 344

sexual exploitation 15, 71, 115, 117, 308; and sex tourism 326, 330, 331, 332, 339–340, 343–344

sexual orientation 6, 255, 256–257, 355; and discrimination of patrons 185, 186, 191, 192, 194–198, 202

sexual violence 3, 306, 307, 334

sexuality 195, 209, 302–303, 332

shareholders 42–43, 50, 312

sharing economy 4, 96, 116, 355; and displacement 164, 167, 168–169, 177

shelter 110, 122–123, 128, 361

short-term marriages 331

Sierra Leone 115, 120–121

slavery 15, 21, 23, 190; modern 50–51, 117, 237, 242, 244, 304, 339–340

social discrimination 109, 226

social exclusion 226, 229

social justice 114, 209–210

social media 63–64, 95, 125, 151, 173, 215, 358, 359

social responsibility, doctrine of 43, 44; *see also* Corporate Social Responsibility (CSR)

social security 122, 245, 246, 247, 248

social welfare 15–16, 110, 314
societal values 43
Somalia 93–94, 166, 208
South Africa 17, 64, 66, 119, 120–121, 152, 188–189, 310
South African Development Community (SADC) 224
South Asian Free Trade Agreement (SAFTA) 224
Southern African Customs Union (SACU) 224
Southern Common Market (MERCOSUR) 224
sovereignty 15, 28, 91, 149, 285, 358, 361; and freedom of movement 212, 221; and human security 110, 112
Spain 8, 49, 63, 88, 139–140, 216, 328, 360
special needs 216–220, **220**
state jurisdiction 26, 31, 41, 52–55, 201, 212, 285, 301
state policy 92–97, 99
statelessness 14
Statement on the Prevention of Organized Sex Tourism 72, 326, 327, 330
stockholders 42–43, 50, 312
Stockholm Declaration 267–269, 272, 274, 282, 334
Stolen Generations, Australia 314
strike, right to 240–241
strong institutions 67
structural violence 62, 66, 68, 78, 309
subsidiary means for the determination of rules of law 22, 23–24
subsistence 162, 268, 275; and Indigenous people's rights 305, 312, 313, 314, 315, 318
Supreme Court of Canada (SCC) 88, 240–241, 299
sustainability 51, 52, 60, 65, 66, 68–72, 267, 278; and human rights in tourism 32, 352, 354, 362; and human security 123, 125, 128; and Indigenous people's rights 305, 312, 315; and politics 90, 91, 97, 98–99, 100
Sustainable Development Goals (SDGs) 5, 60–78; Agenda 2030 74, 76, 200, 237, 247
Sweden 49, 147, 265, 282, 286, 310, 329, 342, 358
Syria 86, 125, 126, 208

Tatar v. Romania 271–272
Te Arawa people 306

technology 15, 47, 151, 354–355; and the environment 275–276, 277, 279; and freedom of movement 208, 210, 215, 216–217, 218, 224, 229; national security 92, 154, 225–226
TEN (Third World Tourism Ecumenical European Net) 71
terrorism 5, 92, 93, 198, 208–209, 225; and human security 110, 112, 114, 115, 117–118, 119, 126; and privacy 149–150, 151, 153, 154
Terrorist Identities Datamart Environment, The (TIDE) 153
Thailand 71, 121, 166, 174–176, 306, 308; and sex tourism 327–328, 330, 331, 332
Third Nature 310
Third World Tourism Ecumenical European Net (TEN) 71
Thunberg, Greta 265, 286
TIDE (Terrorist Identities Datamart Environment, The) 153
Toonen v. Australia 255
torts 140, 145, 148
torture 53, 87, 89, 195; and human rights in tourism **12**, 21, 24, 28, 29, 30
tourism, right to 213–214, 229, 286
tourism boycotts 95–96
Tourism Concern 4, 5, 71, 76, 88, 95, 100, 117, 160–161
tourism development 41, 45, 84, 94, 96, 115, 124; and displacement 161, 164, 166, 172, 176; and the environment 266, 271, 279, 281, 285, 286; and human rights in tourism 4, 5, 19, 353, 354, 355; and Indigenous people's rights 296, 305, 306, 310, 311, 312–313, 314, 318; sustainable 60, 61, 63, 64, 68, 69, 70, 72, 77–78
tourism employment 96–97, 127, 242, 249, 258, 355
tourism enterprises, and human rights 32, 40–55, 84, 91, 92, 98, 353
tourist arrivals 4, 93, 118, 126, 189, 280
tourist attractions 124, 171, 173, 174, 175, 307, 309, 311
TPP (Trans-Pacific Partnership) 222
Trading with the Enemy Act 201
trafficking, human 50–51, 53, 96, 115, 117, 237; and sex tourism 326, 339–340, 342, 344
"Transforming Tourism" 5, 76, 78
Trans-Pacific Partnership (TPP) 222
transparency 24, 90, 91, 110, 141; of tourism enterprises 49, 50, 51, 52, 55

418 Index

transphobic crimes 195
travel, right to 211–214, 286
travel patterns 4, 32, 186, 204, 282, 336
travel visas 210, 222–224
tribal peoples 14, 161, 269, 298, **298**
Tunisia 86, 93, 118, 125, 126

Uber 142, 168, 169
UDHR 3, 11, 18, 46, 61–65, 77, 89, 113, 138, 185, 213, 214, 238
Uluru 308, 309
UNAIDS (Joint United Nations Programme on HIV/AIDS) 30
UNCED (United Nations Conference on Environment and Development) 65, 267
UNCRC (United Nations Convention on the Rights of the Child) **12**, 65, 127, 138, 193, 212, 243, 334–335
underage sex tourism 340–343
UNDP (United Nations Development Programme) 30, 60, 65, 270, 285, 286, 354; and human security 110, 111–112, **116**, 116, 122, 123, 125, 127
UNDRIP (United Nations Declaration on the Rights of Indigenous Peoples) 14, 161, 171, 266, 296, 297, 298, 299, 302, 303–305, 311, 317–318, 356
UNESCO (United Nations Educational, Scientific and Cultural Organization) 30, 94, 112, 160, 171, **317**
UNESCO heritage designations 171
UNFPA (United Nations Population Fund) 30
UNGP (Guiding Principles on Business and Human Rights) 4, 45, 46, 52, 55, 76, 240, 352
UNGPRF (Guiding Principles Reporting Framework) 52, 66
UNHCR (United Nations High Commissioner for Refugees) 30, 159, 176
UNICEF (United Nations Children's Fund) 30, 121, 334, 335–336, 343
United Kingdom 123, 258; and right to privacy 139, 140, 142, 145, 147, 149–150, 151
United Nations: Assistance Mission in Somalia (UNSOM) 93–94; Children's Fund (UNICEF) 30, 121, 334, 335–336, 343; Conference on Environment and Development (UNCED) 65, 267; Convention on the Rights of the Child (UNCRC) **12**, 65, 127, 138, 193, 212, 243, 334–335; Declaration on the Right to Development 5, 16, 61–65; Declaration on the Rights of Indigenous Peoples (UNDRIP) 14, 161, 171, 266, 296, 297, 298, 299, 302, 303–305, 311, 317–318, 356; Development Programme *see* UNDP (United Nations Development Programme); Educational, Scientific and Cultural Organization (UNESCO) 30, 94, 112, 160, 171, **317**; Entity for Gender Equality and the Empowerment of Women (UN-Women) 30; Global Compact 46–48, 55, 240, 352; High Commissioner for Refugees (UNHCR) 30, 159, 176; Human Development Report 110, 111, **116**, 354; Human Rights Committee 11, 29, 212, 255; Human Settlements Programme (HABITAT) 30; International Bill of Human Rights 10, 11, 62, 351; Millennium Development Goals (MDGs) 5, 61, 65–68, 74, 77, 270, 296, 302; Office on Drugs and Crime (UNODC) 339, 340; Population Fund (UNFPA) 30; Sustainable Development Goals (UNSDGs) 5, 109, 270, 282, 285, 296, 302; Universal Declaration of Human Rights *see* UNUDHR
United States: Code of Federal Regulations (CFR) 200, 251; Constitution 21, 140, 148, 190, 196, 225; Equal Employment Opportunity Commission (EEOC) 250, 252, 256; Supreme Court 49, 140, 144, 147–148, 195, 254, 256; Terrorist Screening Center 153; values of 220–221
Universal Declaration of Human Rights *see* UNUDHR
Universal Islamic Declaration of Human Rights 18
universal jurisdiction 53
universalism 7, 16–18, 85
UNODC (United Nations Office on Drugs and Crime) 339, 340
UNSDGs (United Nations Sustainable Development Goals) 5, 109, 270, 282, 285, 296, 302
UNSOM (United Nations Assistance Mission in Somalia) 93–94
UN-Women (United Nations Entity for Gender Equality and the Empowerment of Women) 30
UNWTO (World Tourism Organization) 4, 48, 60, 70, 71, 93, 305, 327, 331
Uruguay 143, 335

values 84, 90, 92, **116**, 225, 226, 240, 266; cultural 171, 172, 312–313; ethical 18; Indigenous 311, 312–313; moral 49; national 77, 210, 220; property 116, 123, 164, 169; religious 17, 18; societal 43; United States 220–221; Western 16, 18
Vašák, Karel 18–19, 30, 274
violations, of human rights 4, 5, 26–31, 41–44, 50, 52–55, 113
violent crimes 92, 93, 118–119
visa-free freedom of movement 210, 222–224, 229
voluntary human rights guidelines, for corporations 41, 44–48
vulnerability 96, 99, 110, 111, 127, 165, 166, 241, 278, 280–281, 339, 340

war crimes 3, 13, 27, 53, 61
water 67, 87, 303, 362; and displacement 161, 162, 164, 167; and the environment 265, 266, 269, 270, 273, 274, 276, 285; and human security 110, 115, 119, 120, 121, 122, 128; pollution of 277, 279, 283–284, 296; right to 279, 362
Western Air Lines v. Criswell 253–254
Western values 16, 18
WFP (World Food Programme) 359
wheelchairs 219, **220**, 251, 252
WHO (World Health Organization) 4, 30, 116, 199, 357
women: empowerment of 67, 97; rights of 5, 8, 16, 63–64, 85, 192, 351, 362
work, right to 16, 72, 238, 248, 286, 343–344, 358; and displacement 159, 167; and freedom of movement 227, 228

work environment 3, 32, 127, 228, 246, 247, 332, 343–344
working conditions *see* labour conditions
World Charter for Sustainable Tourism +20 75
World Congress Against Sexual Exploitation of Children and Adolescents 334
World Cup, Football 162
World Food Programme (WFP) 359
World Health Organization (WHO) 4, 30, 116, 199, 357
World Tourism Organization (UNWTO) 4, 48, 60, 70, 71, 93, 305, 327, 331
World Trade Organization (WTO) 60, 62, 70, 71, 305
World Travel and Tourism Council (WTTC) 40, 41, 70, 75, 94, 96, 126, 210, 226, 305
World War I 31, 68, 201
World War II 10, 31, 61, 62, 68, 112, 120
Worst Forms of Child Labor Convention 335
WTO (World Trade Organization) 60, 62, 70, 71, 305; Statement on the Prevention of Organized Sex Tourism 72, 326, 327, 330
WTTC (World Travel and Tourism Council) 40, 41, 70, 75, 94, 96, 126, 210, 226, 305

xenophobia 159, 175, 188, 192, 222

Yemen 122, 125, 208
Young v. Australia 255

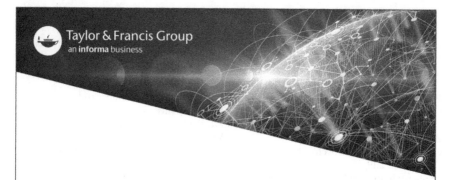